M000236939

Dugin *against* Dugin

A Traditionalist Critique
of the
Fourth Political Theory

Dugin

Against

Dugin

A Traditionalist Critique
of the
Fourth Political Theory

ও

by
Charles Upton

REVIVISCIMUS

First published in the USA
by Reviviscimus
© Charles Upton 2018

ISBN 978-1-59731-219-6

Cover Design:
Michael Schrauzer

CONTENTS

CHAPTER 3: *Vectors of Duginism* (149)

CHAPTER 4: *Critique of* The Fourth Political Theory, *Part I* (183)

CHAPTER 5: *Critique of* The Fourth Political Theory, *Part II* (258)

CHAPTER 6: *Critique of* The Rise of the Fourth Political Theory (342)

CHAPTER 7: *Principles of Sacred Activism* (398)

Part One: Sacred Activism, Traditional Metaphysics, and the Covenants of the Prophet (398)

Part Two: Principles of Sacred Activism (405)

Foreword

ALEKSANDR GELYEVICH DUGIN pretends to be a pious Christian who belongs to the Old Believers. The soft-spoken Russian philosopher, however, with his monk-like appearance and demeanor, is a veritable oxymoron. Most people who praise him have never read his books. Rather than preach the Sermon on the Mount, as one would expect, his radical and violent rhetoric, which includes longing for a nuclear holocaust, appeals to extremists on all sides of the political spectrum. As a master tactician, the political scientist and reactionary activist employs the art of deception. To Christians, he is a Christian. To conservatives, he is a conservative. To traditionalists, he is a traditionalist. To leftist anti-imperialists, he is a leftist anti-imperialist. To fascists, he is a fascist. To white supremacists, he is a white supremacist. And to Islamists, both Salafists and Shiites, he is an ally. He is at home with neo-Nazis as he is with people of color. He befriends Islamophobes while at the same time befriending Muslims. He engages not in diplomacy but in duplicity. He is, in short, a Great Deceiver in a New Great Game.

Considering his popularity in certain circles of opposition to the New World Order, it becomes apparent that Dugin has effectively duped sincere seekers of social and economic justice on all sides, people who recognize the evils inherent in capitalism and liberalism, but who have been left with no other political options after the demise of communism and fascism. Left rudderless in the scuttled ship that is planet earth, desperate people have placed their final faith in the pirate ship of Duginism, in the misplaced hope that it will lead them to safer and more prosperous shores. In the end, however, they will only be robbed, raped, and murdered. Dugin's approach to geopolitics is simple, single-minded of purpose, and deadly: promote extreme ideologies, both left and right, in the belief that the enemy of my enemy is my friend, knowing full well that if they succeed in destroying their own secular, Western, liberal, capitalist, and imperialist societies, the victorious extremists will turn against each other like vicious dogs, conveniently allowing the Eurasians—namely, Russia and China—to sweep down upon the ruins of Western civilization under the guise of multi-polarity. The Prophet of Hope is really the Prophet of Doom.

There are some political scientists who feel that Duginism/Eurasianism offers the only option to Western imperialism. But while it is one thing to attempt to create a broad alliance against Western imperialism and liberalism,

i

the responsible and reasonable approach is to draw all parties towards the center, unite them around a common cause, and rally them around a common solution—not promote extreme ideologies, both left and right, knowing full-well that innocent parties will be caught in the cross-fire. To fan the flames of fascism always results in crimes against humanity, or genocide. Supporting Takfiri terrorists and Shiite extremists spreads civil and religious wars in the Muslim world. Promoting black supremacists while cavorting with white supremacists is a recipe for racial warfare. Aleksandr Dugin is no more a friend to whites than he is to blacks. His Fourth Political Theory is a farce. The fact that Islamic Republicanists have scurried under the skirt of Putin's Rasputin shows how desperately weak they are.

Meticulously and methodically, Charles Upton, one of the most important public intellectuals of the 21st century, pierces through Dugin's body of work like a seasoned surgeon with a scalpel, like a philosopher and social critic with a pen, or like a medieval knight casting a lance at a fire-breathing dragon, the very symbol of Satan. *Dugin against Dugin* provides a decisive blow to Duginism. One can only hope that it will prove fatal.

Dr. John Andrew Morrow
Author, *The Covenants of the Prophet
Muhammad with the Christians of the World*

Preface

W E ARE LIVING in a time when the prevailing myths of Modernism, whose three central pillars were Darwin, Freud and Marx—with the darkly penetrating voice of Nietzsche breaking through to herald the advent of Postmodernism in the distant future—are no longer useful, no longer convincing. The established ideologies of the Left and the Right have lost force, leading to the rise of the Alt Right and the "Alt Left," whose theories and practices bear only a very uncertain relationship to the earlier dogmas out of which they developed—or from which they degenerated. According to Aleksandr Dugin, Fascism is dead, Communism is dead, and Liberalism, the longest-lived of the three, is breathing its last; and I would certainly agree. Under the triumphant yet inherently unstable regime of Postmodernism, "overarching paradigms" of any kind are distrusted, all certainties are seen as dangerous illusions, and the very quest for objective truth is defined as intellectual totalitarianism. Likewise Aleksandr Dugin (following Martin Heidegger) tells us that the reign of Logos is ended, the age of Chaos has come—and Dugin is all for it. But as Prof. Huston Smith (1919–2016) predicted, when the unity of truth is denied, as Postmodernism has done, the only ordering principle left is the unity of power. The central irony and supreme contradiction of Dugin's Fourth Political Theory, however, is that he conceives of it as *an attack on Postmodernism*—and it is certainly true that he has given us a magnificent critique of Postmodernism as the terminal, globalizing phase of Liberalism. What he has failed to do, however, is discern, criticize and eliminate the postmodern elements in his own philosophy. It's as if he were internally *possessed* by the postmodern Chaos he hates, resulting in a state of self-contradiction that makes him, in many ways, his own worst enemy: thus the title of this book.

In Aleksandr Dugin, the terminal subversion of the western intellectual tradition known as "postmodern deconstructionism" has come home to roost. The meticulous nihilism and supercilious despair of the philosophers, historians and literary critics of the decadent western academies has had an unintended effect: where western scholars have achieved little more than an accelerated deconstruction of their own intellectual disciplines, soon to be followed by their academic departments and institutions of higher learning, Aleksandr Dugin and others like him have weaponized deconstructionism by moving it out of the academies and into the world of governments, political cadres and strategic planning. They have gone beyond nihilism as an ideology to *trans-nihilism* as a method, a way of using *any* ideology, any belief-system, any religious faith to achieve their goal—in Dugin's case, the deconstruction of American global influence and the rebirth of the Russian Empire. They have transformed the principle of "nothing is true, everything is permitted" into a thousand-armed tool of geopolitical subversion, expansion and control. And this is not the first time that the airy abstractions of "impractical" intellectuals have proved highly useful to "men of action in the real world." Who would have predicted that Hegel would beget Marx? Who could have imagined that Voltaire and the French encyclopedists would give rise to Marat and Danton and Robespierre? Likewise the genie of academic deconstructionism is now out of the bottle, and Dugin has become its master.

In the face of the deconstruction of all articulate and self-consistent philosophies and political ideologies, nothing remains untouched except the science of Traditional Metaphysics, for the simple reason that it has nothing to do with the entropy of history, with Time the Destroyer, only with Eternity, with the Always So. But though metaphysics can never be destroyed, it can certainly be veiled till it virtually disappears from collective view, or else counterfeited to produce bastard versions of it, "unfavorable mutations" in the form of toxic superstitions, spurious mythologies and false inverted religions, or else political methodologies that pervert the eternal Principles by which cosmic existence is created and maintained by transforming them into blind—yet nonetheless highly useful—motivational resources to inflame and motivate the masses. In our time, epistemology has been degraded to surveillance, theurgy has become psy-ops, and metaphysics and spiritual psychology have been redefined as the study of the fundamental principles of mind control and social engineering. And Aleksandr Dugin, operating not as a marginalized crank but as an established Russian intellectual, is in the thick of it.

Dugin clearly realizes that political ideology, as we have known it, is dead. But since no action is possible without some set of ideas or images to help us make sense of things and motivate us to define goals and pursue them, he has drawn upon a heterogeneous spectrum of western sociologists, philosophers and political theorists, on whatever appears useful to him from the world of myth, folklore and religion, and on various hazy notions of Traditional Metaphysics. He knows that metaphysics has become increasingly relevant, in social terms, now that the "age of ideology" has ended; unfortunately, his training in that discipline is haphazard, spotty, amateurish, and filled with errors and contradictions. I entirely agree with him insofar as he believes that without an understanding of the science of metaphysics, and of its specific application to the times we live in—namely, eschatology—our grasp of the fundamental quality and imperatives of our era will prove woefully deficient. Unfortunately, Aleksandr Dugin has little if any understanding of metaphysics as a science; consequently the central thrust of this book will be to demonstrate how metaphysics can be used on a conscious and scientific basis—not merely a half-conscious, impulsive, and impressionistic one—to free us from "the nightmare of history," from blind involvement in the socio-political dimension, from attachment to the "darkness of this world."[1] In any case, Aleksandr Dugin is perhaps the first globally-influential political ideologue of our era to take mythography, metaphysics and eschatology seriously, as well as incorporating history, sociology, philosophy, theology (such as it is), as well as certain insights from physics and social psychology, into his Fourth Political Theory. In so doing he has opened the door for me to reply to him in the same language, according to the canons of the same disciplines. If this book seems to some like a hodge-podge of unrelated insights occupying wildly different levels, it is partly because it was arranged according to Dugin's method, and partly due to the fact that the over-specialization of scholarship and the narrowness of group identification in our times have trained us to be suspicious of any comprehensive intellectual synthesis. Throughout most of this book I will be critiquing Aleksandr Dugin's ideas as if I believed that he means what he says. I am not entirely convinced that this is the case, however. Possibly he believes in some or most of the ideas he transmits, but it's just as likely that he is using language hypnotically or magically rather than descriptively. There is always an implied "escape clause" in Dugin's writing. His ambiguity appears to be deliberate, and in any case it is congenial to his purposes. We never know for certain whether he is presenting a given idea as his own, or simply transmitting the ideas of someone else—Aleister Crowley, for example, or Martin Heidegger—by the "phenomenological" method, according to which the expositor more-or-less adopts the identity of his source, on the theory that a particular worldview is best described "as if from within"—a kind of *method philosophy*, roughly analogous to the "method acting" of Stanislavski. It is possible that Dugin means what he says; it is also possible that he is operating out of a purely postmodern worldview where "meaning what you say" is meaningless. But since I am not sure that this is the case, I am compelled to do him the honor of assuming—for the sake of argument—that he is an honest man, a man with whom it is possible to disagree.

---

1. After this is accomplished, God may employ us, based precisely on our degree of detachment, for the purposes of social analysis and action. On the other hand He may tell us, "the Abomination of Desolation stands in the Holy Place, so head for the hills" [cf. Matthew 24:15]. Which of these two roads is right for us is entirely up to Him. In the words of the Qur'an: *I will show them My signs on the horizons and in their own souls until they are satisfied that this is the Truth. Is it not enough for you, that I am Witness over all things?* [Q. 41:53]. The principle behind this parting of the ways is expressed in the *I Ching*, in the fourth line of Hexagram One, the Creative: "Wavering flight over the depths. No blame."

Dugin is a politician who dabbles in metaphysics; I am a metaphysician who dabbles in politics. This means that we are necessarily speaking, up to a point, on two different levels, out of two discrete worlds between which disagreement is impossible since they do not occupy the same space. Where my worldview and Dugin's do occupy the same space, however, there is a great deal of disagreement—some of it fairly hot—but also, unexpectedly, some real areas of agreement, a number of points where we (hopefully) wake up and realize that we are both human beings. It should also be noted that Dugin and I hate many of the same things—a fact that goes a long way toward refuting the notion that "the enemy of my enemy is my friend."

Readers with a basically secular, materialistic worldview will not easily accept the direct appeal to the religious, the metaphysical, and even the paranormal that this book is based upon, in the belief that such things have no place in a universe of discourse that also embraces *realpolitik*. However, Aleksandr Dugin himself has opened the door to these areas; since he is a professed Christian and a follower of French metaphysician René Guénon, who was certainly conversant with both the science of metaphysics and the phenomenology of the paranormal, and since he declares that *magic* is his praxis and speaks of "angels" as political actors, I hope he will welcome the chance to dialogue—or rather spar—on these subjects that this book represents. Even for the secular reader, a confrontation between two "lunatics" such as Aleksandr Dugin and myself should at least be highly entertaining.

For the most part I will be basing this critique of Dugin on the English versions of three of his books: *Eurasian Mission* [2014] *The Fourth Political Theory* [2012], and *The Rise of the Fourth Political Theory* [2017]. My critique is certainly not comprehensive; I do not read Russian and many of Aleksandr Dugin's books have not yet been translated into English. Nor do I have the academic background to do justice—or what I, undoubtedly, would consider justice—to all the ideas that Dugin transmits. But where I know what I know I know what I believe, and I know why what I believe is relevant both to the present historical moment and to the destiny of the human soul. I can only hope that I have been able to give Aleksandr Dugin, his followers, his enemies, and the great mass of the "undecided," something new to think about—new, yet somehow strangely familiar.

If the reader takes nothing else away from this book, let him or her at least understand that it was written in the belief that nearly all the intellectual and social alternatives the world presents us with today are fatally mis-defined. To choose the good, or even the lesser of two evils, becomes impossible when the Devil draws the sides. If the lines of demarcation are false—a condition we might call "moral gerrymandering"—damage will be done and darkness spread no matter which banner we follow; all the labor and struggle and sacrifice in the world can't change that. The real alternatives, the true lines, can only be discerned and engaged with from a vantage point beyond the world. In line with this principle, following Dante's method, I have intentionally woven eternal principles and historical contingencies together at every conceivable point—a practice that may make this book rather awkward reading for some. Those seeking metaphysical truth will likely see the "current events" passages as unfortunate and unnecessary intrusions, dated as news but not yet established as accepted history; those seeking socio-historical analysis will undoubtedly encounter a similar difficulty with the metaphysical passages. Nonetheless, whatever becomes "dated" in terms of current events deserves—if it is significant enough—to become a part of "history" immediately, and since I have based my method on Plato's doctrine, from the *Timaeus*, that "time is the moving image of Eternity," I have opted to draw a firm line of unity all the way from eternal Truth to the ephemeralities of the daily news, thereby demonstrating the unbreakable solidarity between them. If the reader encounters a reported event that has already been submerged or contradicted by later developments, let him or her try to see it not as a dated piece of trivia, but rather as a brief, momentary reflection of the Always So in the realm of contingencies.

In this book I have attempted—successfully for the most part, I believe—to demonstrate how Traditional Metaphysics might function as a viable alternative to the postmodern worldview, as well as illustrating the many ways in which metaphysical principles can be fruitfully applied to both social criticism and social action. Whether metaphysics is destined to supplant Postmodernism as a collective paradigm, however, is entirely different matter. When Plato, in his own time, tried to set up his *Republic* as a social experiment with the help of a "strong man," the Tyrant of Syracuse, his would-be patron simply detained him until his friends had collected enough money to pay his ransom—and our times are a lot more intellectually and socially fragmented than Plato's were. Consequently my own vision of metaphysically-based social action, as will be obvious to anyone who examines it, is in no way intended as a design for an entire society. It is simply an orientation, for a time when all designs are being destroyed, to what lies beyond the limits of that destruction.

Nonetheless, as Aleksandr Dugin points out, the age of incomplete social theories claiming universality, and of the indiscriminate application, to any and all situations, of various limited methodologies based on them—that is, the age of ideology—is now over. Therefore the only intellectual alternatives remaining to us in the social dimension are either to create an *ad hoc* system in the form of a chaotic montage of past ideologies and fragmentary postmodern viewpoints, uneasily married to mis-applied theories from the physical sciences—as Aleksandr Dugin has done—or else to embrace a unified *theoria* and *praxis* that transcend ideology because they are based on trans-historical metaphysical principles. This second alternative, however—the one I have tried to articulate in this book—though it addresses the central need of our times, is not in line with their inherent spirit; it will therefore appeal only to a few. Nonetheless, to speak the truth of the Always So, since it is a "liturgical" act rather than a strategic one, is never without positive consequences—if not in this world, then in the next; if not in the next, then in the present moment of spiritual time that penetrates both worlds. That's why Muslims, Hindus and Christians invoke the Name of God: not in order to produce a preconceived effect, but because they know Who is listening.

Beyond presenting certain perspectives on metaphysically-based social action—which, as the reader will learn, includes the Muslim/Christian interfaith movement known as the Covenants Initiative, which appeared in 2013—as well as correcting some of Dugin's misconceptions about the metaphysical and cosmological doctrines of René Guénon, whose school I follow, this book also aims to rescue from obscurity certain highly significant strands of the cultural, political and spiritual history of the United States over the past 50 years, pivotal trends and events that seem to have been forgotten by today's born-yesterday, hoodwinked Americans, due to either passive indifference or active suppression. A parallel aim, no less important, is to provide Aleksandr Dugin with a more accurate picture of American society and the American character than he presently demonstrates, hoping to throw some light on the dangerous and artificially-created tension that is mounting between our two nations. Whatever may be the involvement of Russia in various covert attempts to destabilize American society, possibly in response to U.S. pressure—a strategy that Aleksandr Dugin openly advocates—on the American side this tension is presently being engineered by elements of the U.S. "shadow government," individuals who apparently have little fear of bringing our world to a fiery end, most likely because they are simply tired of living. These demented war-mongers, both Liberal and Neo-Conservative, closely resemble the "active shooters" who are increasingly making themselves known in the churches and schools of America—people who, though they are entirely bent on committing suicide, also mean to bring as many others as they can with them, apparently operating on the theory that only the *lone* suicide is truly defeated. The first responsibility of Russians is to deal with the darkness and light of Russia; for me, it is to do what I can to throw light on the darkness and light of America. But if anyone, whether Russian, American or of any other nationality, presumes to lay hands on metaphysical truth and religious faith, thinking they can harness the Divinity to the chariot of This World—and Aleksandr Dugin is obviously far from alone in this deluded hope—then my talents and my station in life require that I answer them.

My way of seeking knowledge has always included learning by opposition. In pursuing this strategy I have already received many important insights from Alexandr Dugin, both through agreement and through disagreement; during the writing of this book he has immensely widened my worldview. But although Dugin has come into my life like a revelation, I have no qualms against subjecting him to the most punishing criticisms whenever I find him profaning the sacred, or catch him playing fast and loose with the truth. Just as war is one of the deepest forms of cultural exchange, so intellectual combat can be the highest form of dialogue, potentially enlightening to both victor and vanquished—if, that is, the victor can see beyond his triumph and the vanquished beyond his defeat. Maybe it was in view of this principle that William Blake wrote, in *The Marriage of Heaven and Hell,* "Opposition is true friendship." In later versions of the poem, however, Blake expunged that line, undoubtedly because he found that the Intellectual War, which he saw as one of the chief delights of Eternity, is very difficult to carry on, with any degree of honor and chivalry, in the darkness of this world. And seeing that Aleksandr Dugin's ideas continue to change—either because his worldview keeps developing, or else due to the fact that he is simply knocking around—I must also apologize in advance if I have raked him over the coals for things he no longer believes, or at least no longer finds useful. If I am wrong about him, it is up to him to enlighten me; I may be all tongue—and the sharper the better—but I am also all ears.

Introduction:
Report from Atlantis

MY GREETINGS to the readers of this rather strange book—hopefully in both hemispheres—whose indulgence I beg as I attempt to articulate my position in regards to the infamous and highly interesting Professor Aleksandr Dugin. Both he and I, though on vastly different scales, have made our own syntheses between metaphysics and political action—his in the world of post-Soviet right-wing politics, mine in the world of popular opposition politics in the United States since the 1960's, the alternative spirituality movement, the peace movement (or movements) and the interfaith movement. But since I represent no political party or human collective that might help situate my present viewpoint and give the reader some idea of the thinking and experience that went into making it—as well as explaining why I was moved to respond as I have to the challenge that Dugin represents—I have felt it necessary to retrace my steps through the routinely mythologized but often largely forgotten history of my generation. But before introducing myself, I must first introduce Aleksandr Dugin, both in terms of his political ideology—and ideology it certainly is, though he often rejects that name—and of his geopolitics, his eschatology and his metaphysics.

Dugin in Context

Aleksandr Dugin is a philosopher, an academic, a political organizer, and—according to Arktos, his English publisher—an adviser to the President of Russia, Vladimir Putin, though Dugin himself denies it.[1] I am an American Sufi Muslim with a background in the 60's counterculture and peace movement, as well as a member of what I sometimes call, not without a trace of irony, the "freelance intelligentsia"—a writer and activist who has taken pains to main-

---

1. According to Andrey Tolstoy and Edmund McCaffray in their article "Mind Games: Alexander Dugin and Russia's War of Ideas," posted on the World Affairs website, March/April, 2015, "Dugin has . . . been actively involved in the politics of Russia's elite, serving as an adviser to State Duma chairman and key Putin ally Sergei Naryshkin. His disciple Ivan Demidov serves on the Ideology Directorate of Putin's United Russia party, while Mikhail Leontiev, allegedly Putin's favorite journalist, is a founding member of Dugin's own Eurasia Party."

tain his independence, but has also been forced to admit that he has never been offered any inducements, monetary or otherwise, to relinquish that independence; I tell myself that I have renounced the world, whereas the actual truth may be that I was never granted admittance in the first place. In addition, I grew up in the United States when it was a free country, and I still do my best to operate on that basis, no matter how anachronistic such an attitude may seem today, since I know nothing else. Whatever today's readers may see as "eccentric" in my writing can probably be put down to this. Be that as it may, I enjoy the sponsorship of no academic institution, the patronage of no government, the group solidarity and controlling agenda of no political party or social movement or religious gang—outside of the Covenants Initiative that is, (see below), which I conceived of and whose director, Dr. John Andrew Morrow, is a peer and a colleague to whom I gladly defer only because I know he is worthy of it. I am the darkest horse and the freest lance.

Aleksandr Dugin draws upon, and appeals to, sociology, religion, philosophy, metaphysics and political ideology, most often the ideologies and histories of many Russian and European movements of the extreme Right, and in some cases the extreme Left. But since I am not an ideological thinker, but rather a religious and metaphysical writer and activist who has paid close attention to the historical dialectic-of-degeneration the world has been going through for most of my life, I cannot meet Dugin on the field of systematic ideological debate—presuming that he can actually be considered systematic. Our contest will therefore always remain "asymmetric." But one thing I can do, as I have elected to do below, is recount some of the suppressed history of a half-century of social and spiritual change in the United States of America, from the point-of-view of my own pilgrimage through it. This is the only way I can imagine to meet the Russian Dugin as an American, the social philosopher Dugin as a cultural observer and commentator, and the "religious" Dugin as the beneficiary, agent, victim, and chronicler of 50 years of spiritual and religious idealism, enlightenment, delusion, damage and radical transformation, on my own American ground.

As an intellectual I am considered to be a member of the Traditionalist or Perennialist School, usually said to have been "founded" by René Guénon and Ananda Coomaraswamy. The Traditionalism/Perennialism of Guénon and Coomaraswamy, as carried forward by Martin Lings, Titus Burckhardt and Frithjof Schuon—the "Anglo-Swiss-American" branch of the School, as opposed to the French one, the Romanian one, etc.—is primarily a school of comparative religion and Traditional Metaphysics. These writers and their colleagues have produced a useful critique of Modernism but—unlike the French Guénonistes or the followers of Baron Julius Evola, who was strongly influenced by Guénon but ended by rejecting some of his fundamental principles—they have come up with very little political ideology per se. This is one of the things that made them congenial to me, since I tend to distrust ideological thinking of any kind. My background as a social activist has never involved me in the kind of party-building where political ideology is a *sine qua non*, but has mostly been limited to single-issue commitments: reversing U.S. military intervention in Southeast Asia in the 1960's and 70's, preventing or halting U.S. intervention in Central America in the 1980's, and, since 2013, helping disseminate the covenants of the Prophet Muhammad with the Christians of the world, as well as with other Peoples of the Book, as a check upon both Islamicist terrorism and the Islamophobia that has grown up, partly in response to it, in the United States. These covenants are highly useful for that purpose, since they condemn pseudo-Islamic terrorists—ISIS and its like—root and branch, declaring them to be under the curse of Allah. (I need to make clear at this point that the present book is in no way an "official document" of the Covenants Initiative, only my own eccentric take on Aleksandr Dugin and the quality of our times, based on my understanding of eternal metaphysical Principles—which the Prophetic Covenants certainly reflect. And though I identify myself as a Traditionalist in this book, my colleague Dr. Morrow, the director of the Covenants Initiative, does not. Like me, however, his relationship to the traditions he follows is independent and voluntary. More on the Covenants of the Prophet, as well as the Covenants Initiative, appears below.) Consequently the central thrust of this book will be a critique of Aleksandr Dugin's metaphysical doctrines, which is the one critique I am thoroughly fitted to carry out. It is only on the basis of such a critique, or rather deconstruction, of Dugin's so-called metaphysics that I can have anything of substance to say about his political ideology, his Neo-Eurasian movement, his Fourth Political Theory. Aleksandr Dugin invokes the sacred science of Traditional Metaphysics repeatedly, in the most diverse and unlikely contexts. Unfortunately for us—and also for him, given the immortality of the human soul—he has misrepresented it at almost every point, cynically appropriating whatever fragments he sees as useful for the purpose of propaganda, motivation or recruitment.

Metaphysics is a sacred science—sacred because it has everything to do with the relationship of the universe, society and the human person to God as the Source, First Principle and ultimate Essence of all of these, and because it embraces the art of conforming the entirety of the human being, "heart, soul, mind and strength" [Matthew 22:37], to the human archetype in God, this being what the Abrahamic religions call "the salvation of the soul" and the Dharmic religions "liberation from the wheel of birth and death" or "perfect total enlightenment." Therefore anyone who thinks he has a right to appropriate various concepts from this supreme science on a more-or-less random basis, pervert and decontextualize them so as to construct an eclectic "political theory," is what true metaphysicians call—to use the technical term—a "poacher."

But the simple act of theft, of appropriating the goods of the Intellect with no intention of ever paying for them, is not the worst of it. Metaphysical principles are not just true within "the universe of discourse"; faithfulness to them, or betrayal of them, does not affect only "the life of the mind." They are true on every level, from "the Mind of God" down through cosmic and natural law, the first principles of social organization, the ordering principles of human consciousness and thought, all the way to the depths of the human soul—to what Carl Jung called, without fully understanding it, the "collective unconscious." Therefore the ability, and the audacity, to tap the First Principles of metaphysics and turn them to one's own ends sometimes confers the further ability to affect the deepest "archetypal" layers of the psyche, both individual and collective—this being something that every worldly player, whether in politics, advertising, intelligence operations or social engineering, dreams of accomplishing. But to put these Principles to uses for which they were not designed, outside their proper contexts, and therefore outside the Will of God, is (intentionally or otherwise) to move the depths of human psyche *against* God—and anyone who thinks that God is not perfectly aware of what these rustlers of the cattle of the Almighty are up to—God who is *Owner of the Day of Judgment* [Q. 1–4]—has never known Him. His word for them is perfectly enunciated in the Holy Qur'an, in the *Surah al-'Adiyat*:

> By the snorting coursers,
> Striking sparks of fire
> And scouring to the raid at dawn,
> Then, therewith, with their trail of dust,
> Cleaving, as one, the centre (of the foe),
> Lo! man is an ingrate unto his Lord
> And lo! He is a witness unto that;
> And lo! in the love of wealth he is violent.
> Knoweth he not that, when the contents of
>   the graves are poured forth
> And the secrets of the breasts are made
>   known,
> On that day will their Lord be perfectly
>   informed concerning them?

More specifically, Dugin has appropriated, and routinely misused, certain doctrines from the school of metaphysics I most closely follow—the Traditionalist of Perennialist School founded by René Guénon—with the effect that the name of Guénon, his doctrines, his writings and those of his colleagues and successors, have now begun to come to the attention of the general U.S. public—with the help of an abysmally ignorant Western academia and journalistic profession—in the guise of "a sort of New Age wacko with occult ideas, the guru of Aleksandr Dugin who himself is the hypnotic, controlling Rasputin of Vladimir Putin, and probably also (partly via Steve Bannon) of Donald Trump." I certainly can't blame Prof. Dugin for all the irresponsibility and mental incapacity of Western professors and reporters, but I do consider that he was one of the ones who started the ball rolling that has now rolled over and damaged my own intellectual discipline; therefore I must do what I can to set the record straight.

Several writers, including, Anton Shekhovtsov, Andreas Umland, and Schuo-nian Traditionalist Michael Fitzgerald, have published articles clearly proving that Aleksandr Dugin is not a Traditionalist. I believe that we need to go beyond this level of critique however, important as it is, and begin to understand, first, that Aleksandr Dugin is actually a *methodical deconstructionst* of Guénonian Traditionalism, and of metaphysics in general, and secondly that he deconstructs it not simply to dismiss it, but rather to put himself in a position both to plunder its conceptual riches for his own use and to add whatever Traditionalists might be willing to go along with him to his stable of kept intellectuals. For example, Gholām Rezā A'vānī, one of Dr. Seyyed Hossein Nasr's chief functionaries in the Traditionalist Maryamiyya Sufi Order founded by Frithjof Schuon, which Nasr now largely heads, has collaborated with Aleksandr Dugin in the past. This does not necessarily mean that either A'vānī or Nasr owe any allegiance to him, only that we all need to have a much clearer understanding of who Dugin is, and ask ourselves why his extensive collection of masks apparently includes one labeled "Traditionalist Metaphysician."

In order to speak for Traditional Metaphysics, I have cast myself as a defender of the Traditionalist School against Dugin's misrepresentations of it. There are certain drawbacks, however, to thinking of Traditionalism as a "school," since this notions leads to such questions as "what particularly distinguishes *Traditionalist doctrine*?" and "is the *Traditionalist movement* dead?" This is unfortunate, since Traditionalism is not primarily a movement or a doctrine, but an almost inconceivably successful attempt, on the part of three generations of writers, to unveil the deepest mysteries of the world's religions in the face of the nearly universal degeneration and subversion of those religions. It is not so much a school of philosophy or theology or metaphysics as an implied call for the constitution of one of more "Remnants" to preserve the essences of the religions now that their traditional human collectives are losing the ability to incarnate these essences, or even remember what they were. Nor is it a "movement" in the usual sense, because what God will choose to do with these Remnants is known only to Him.

But the attraction that many in the West feel for Aleksandr Dugin has little to do with metaphysics, traditional or otherwise. Those Americans who are horrified by the monster that Liberalism seems to have morphed into, by a distopian *Blade Runner* world where minors can be subjected to sex-change operations with the blessings of their parents, or with encouragement from the state in any case, and where the State of California now officially recognizes three genders—thus proving that it is not actually possible to change a woman into a man or a man into a woman, otherwise there would still be only two—have begun to look longingly toward Russia as a world of simple human sanity where heterosexuality is the still norm, where traditional religion is apparently protected, and where the "absolute freedom" to deconstruct the human form is decently curtailed. Given the spectre of Postmodern Liberalism's descent into madness—which includes a mounting campaign against Christianity, a widespread attack on freedom of speech and the cynical co-optation of Islam—it's little wonder that the grass, to many, seems greener on the other side of the cultural and ideological fence. Unfortunately, things aren't quite that simple. In an interview with Aleksandr Dugin conducted by Charles Clover, reproduced in his book *Black Wind, White Snow: The Rise of Russia's New Nationalism*, Dugin says:

> Geopolitics, it filled the vacuum of [the Russian military's] strategic thinking, it was a kind of psychotherapy for them. . . . Imagine the shock they were feeling: they had always been told the U.S. is our enemy. Suddenly some democrats come to power, and they say, no, the U.S. is our friend. Because there is no ideology. They were all confused. Their job is to aim missiles and they need to be clear. . . . This was once an elite caste, responsible for huge institutes, thousands and thousands of warheads. And suddenly, these democrats come and take away everything from this hugely respected caste. And nobody offers them anything. I come to them and say, "America is our enemy, we must aim our missiles at them," and they say "Yes that is correct." And I explained why.

However much the U.S. Alt-Right might hate Liberalism and admire certain aspects of today's Russia, I can't bring myself to believe that they, or the Paleocons, or the Neocons, or the Liberals, or the Libertarians, or the Extreme Left, or the Extreme Right, or the White Supremacists, or the Black Supremacists, would much appreciate being incinerated by Eurasian nuclear warheads just to provide "psychotherapy" for some Russian generals. And, soon enough, those generals would not really appreciate it very much either—a sentiment that they would share with every other human being, and every other living thing, on earth. So I would advise that we pull our heads out of ideology and stick them back into reality for a change, before we slip on a patch of icy road and drop the whole burden we have assumed, now that we believe that God is dead—the burden of the earth and the human race. In addition—speaking now in more personal terms—a nuclear strike by Russia on the U.S, for the purpose of "obliterating Liberalism," would likely mean not only my own injury or death, but that of everyone I love in this world, including my dear wife Jenny—who, in my foolish, romantic way of looking at things, I consider to be worth a hundred Aleksandr Dugins. If my criticism sometimes shows a bitter edge, it is largely due to considerations such as this.

Dugin's Geopolitical Vision

The geopolitical genius of Aleksandr Dugin has led him to a startling conclusion, one that it is crucial for the western nations to understand, if—in the words of Tolstoy's Field Marshal Kutuzov from *War and Peace*—we don't want to end up *eating horse-flesh*: that the United States and its western allies, by the very fact that they "won" the Cold War, initiated the breakup of the Russian Empire and pried the nations of Eastern Europe loose from the Russian sphere of influence, have disastrously over-extended themselves. Like Kutuzov, he has somehow ponderously grasped—not in his brain or his heart, but almost in his liver—that the vast geopolitical spaces of Russia, not so much the physical but the *spiritual* reality of them, might be destined to break America, just as they had broken Napoleon and Hitler. Peering beyond the numbing shock of the fall of the Soviet Union he began to discern, through the smoke, the fatal cracks that were beginning to appear in the political and cultural unity of the United States and the European Union, and he saw exactly how to exploit them: First, by exacerbating existing social and ideological conflicts; secondly, by speaking directly to the various social, cultural, ethnic and religious fragments into which the West had begun to fall, each in its own characteristic language, appealing to their growing sense of isolation, alienation and exile, and promising many of them at least an ideological and cultural homeland in his projected Neo-Eurasian Empire.

It is clear in any case that the program of the United States and the more powerful nations of Western Europe to impose "democracy" on the world has failed, leading to massive destabilization, particularly in North Africa and the Mid-east.[2] In the face of this slow but massive roll-back of western globalist

---

2. This is assuming, of course, that the imposition of democracy was the actual goal; the real goal might in fact have been to impose chaos. Prof. Noam Chomsky, in an email to this writer, mentioned the policy of the U.S. and Western Europe to prevent the growth of strong, stable nations in the Middle East. And there is also the phenomenon of "mission creep." The globalists might have started out, generations ago, envisioning a rational society based on enlightened financial and social despotism, maybe more or less according to the Fabian Socialist model, in the furtherance of which the initial creation of social conflict and chaos was one of the tools of choice. Chaos might have first been seen

hegemony, Russia is moving to profit from the faltering of western-style globalization by imposing its own hegemony in the form of sponsorship of the aspirations of heretofore submerged ethnic and religious minorities—which, when counted with the sectors professing Eastern Orthodoxy and Islam, make up the majority population of Russia. The plan is apparently to draw these populations together in a global crusade against Liberalism, promising the Muslims a resurrected Ottoman Empire (under Russian protection) which is equally, for the Eastern Orthodox Christians, a resurrected Byzantine Empire (under Russian protection), etc., etc. Similar plans may also be in the works for Buddhist Central Asia, following the lead of the Soviets, who presented Bolshevism as the fulfillment of the messianic prophesies of the Mongols and other Central Asian peoples. (For a fascinating history of this time, see *Red Shambhala: Magic, Prophesy and Geopolitics in the Heart of Asia*, by Andrei Znamenski.) Here we can see that, no matter how often and how loudly inverted Postmodern Liberalism sings "celebrate diversity," Russia (if Dugin is right) is much better positioned to profit from such diversity than the West is, since to all appearances its celebration of diversity comes at the end of Western unity and—at least according to Dugin—at the beginning of the renewed unity of Eurasia. At the same time, the divergent tendencies that could lead to the breakup of the greater Russian state are probably stronger than the similar tendencies now showing themselves, as radical political and cultural polarization, in the United States. And so, as always, "time will tell."

The willingness of Russia to sponsor traditional religion and social morality is a hopeful sign in the face of the western Liberal "soft pogrom" against both of them—a pogrom which becomes anything but soft if we are correct in seeing Da'esh and similar groups as products of the same Liberal/globalist agenda to

---

as a hard but necessary phase useful to break down old social paradigms, something which would gradually become less necessary when the new paradigm was firmly in place (Dugin says much the same thing in various places). But since it was so much easier to create chaos than to impose a new order, chaos itself, gradually and imperceptibly, became the not just a tool but the *de facto* goal of the whole effort. People addicted to power usually can't resist the primal satisfaction of seeing their plans and actions creating massive changes in the world; whether these changes are "positive" or "negative" often becomes a secondary consideration. Was the total destabilization of the Middle East, North Africa and Afghanistan—and the partial destabilization of Europe now as well—part of the plan from the beginning, or was it simply a huge case of unintended consequences? It's a hard thing to realize that one's best-laid schemes have gone wrong; rather than admitting "we blew it," the tendency is to rationalize, to say "this is what we were after all along"; the real truth is too depressing to contemplate. On the other hand, the creation of global disorder, the reduction of humanity to a wretched condition of degeneration and chaos, starvation, disease and conflict, while the global elites retreat into their palatial, fortified compounds and well-stocked underground cities, might have been the real plan all along. And what better way to spread chaos than to first create an Islamic State and then destroy it?

destroy *all* the traditional religions in their ancient heartlands. But can a secular state really patronize traditional religion without destroying its spirit, especially this late in the *yuga*? In making himself the patron of true religion, Putin has adopted some of the functions of a Czar;[3] Putin's Russia, however, cannot really function as the "Third Rome" in any integral way. And if the Russian state elects to move—possibly with the help of Aleksandr Dugin—in the direction of becoming a renewed "Holy Empire," either covertly or openly, then the warning of René Guénon in *The Reign of Quantity and the Signs of the Times* will immediately apply:

> one can already see sketched out, in various productions of an indubitably "counter-initiatic" origin or inspiration, the idea of an organization that would be like the counterpart, but at the same time also the counterfeit, of a traditional conception such as that of the "Holy Empire," and some such organization must become the expression of the "counter-tradition" in the social order; and for similar reasons the Antichrist must appear like something that could be called, using the language of the Hindu tradition, an inverted *Chakravarti* ["turner of the wheel (of the law)"; universal king].

In the face of this dark prophesy, the traditional religions must do their best to retain their spiritual sovereignty and authority. If they fail in this by accepting secular control not only in social terms but in theological and even liturgical ones—a tendency that is clearly visible in the state-and-globalist-sponsored Interfaith Movement of the western nations—as well as in the empty shell of what was once the Roman Catholic Church, which clearly aspires (to quote an Eastern Orthodox priest of my acquaintance) to become something like "the chaplaincy of the New World Order", then the System of Antichrist will become a reality. In order to repel and delay the establishment of this System, a Sacred Activism under the direct patronage of Transcendence, such as is outlined in *Chapter Seven* of this book, may—God willing—be of real practical service— always remembering, of course, that Sacred Activism in itself is not necessary to the spiritual life. The only necessary thing is *virginity of soul.*

Dugin's Eschatological Vision

No matter how contradictory and duplicitous Aleksandr Dugin the intellectual may be, however, and how dangerous his ideas to the West, his analysis of the

---

3. Speaking of Czars, when I lived in California I was slightly acquainted with Prince Andrei Romanov, claimant to the headship of the Imperial House of Russia, and his son Prince Peter, second in line after Andrei. Peter—who had a dog named "Bear"—was working as a mechanic in a garage in the Marin County town of Inverness; he later married a woman associated with the Golden Sufi Center headed by Llewellyn Vaughn-Lee, successor to Irina Tweedie, Russian-British Sufi and teacher of the Naqshbandiyya-Mujaddidiya Order.

condition of the human race at the "end of history" is profound, uncompromising and brilliant. In "The Manifesto of the Global Revolutionary Alliance: Program, Principles, Strategy; Part One: The Situation of the End" from *Eurasian Mission*, he says:

1. *We live at the end of the historical cycle.* All processes that constitute the flow of history have come to a logical impasse.

a. *The end of capitalism....* There is only one path left to the world economic system—to collapse in upon itself. Based on a progressive increase in the purely financial institutions—first banks, and then more complex and sophisticated stock structures—the system of modern capitalism has become completely divorced from reality.... All the wealth of the world is concentrated in the hands of the world's financial oligarchy by means of complex manipulations of artificial financial pyramids.

b. *The end of resources* ... humanity has come close to exhausting the Earth's natural resources. These are necessary not just to maintain our current levels of consumption, but for sheer survival at even a minimal level.

c. *The end of society.* Under the influence of Western and American values, the atomization of the world's societies, in which people are no longer connected with each other by any form of social bonds, is in full swing. Cosmopolitanism and a new nomadism has become the most common lifestyle, especially for the younger generation.... Cultural, national, and religious ties are being broken, social contracts are being broken, and organic connections are being severed ... cultural identities are imploding. Societies are being replaced by nomadism and the coldness of the Internet, which dissolve organic, historical collectives. At the same time culture, language, morality, tradition, values, and the family as an institution are disappearing.

d. *The end of the individual.* The division of the individual into his component parts is becoming the dominant trend. Human identities are spread across virtual networks, assuming online personas and turning into a game of disorganized elements.... Postmodern culture compulsively exports people to virtual worlds of electronic screens and removes them from reality, capturing them in a flow of subtly organized and cleverly manipulated hallucinations. These processes are managed by the global oligarchy, which seeks to make the world's masses complacent, controllable and programmable.... Soon man will be replaced by the post-human: a mutant, cloned android.

e. *The end of nations and peoples.* Globalization and global governance interfere in the domestic affairs of sovereign states, erasing them one by one, and systematically destroy all national identity. The global oligarchy seeks to dissolve all national borders that might impede its ubiquitous presence. Transnational corporations put their own interests above national interests and state administrations....

f. *The end of knowledge.* The global mass media creates a system of total disinformation, organized in accordance with the interests of the global oligarchy. Only that which is reported by the global media constitutes "reality." The word of the global Fourth Estate becomes a "self-evident truth," otherwise known as "conventional wisdom." Alternative viewpoints can still be spread through the interstices of the global communication networks, but they are condemned to the margins because financial support is provided only for those informational outlets that serve the interests of the global oligarchy. . . .

g. *The end of progress.* . . . Both the individual and the world are not getting better, but, on the contrary, are rapidly degenerating. . . . If things continue to develop as they are today, the most pessimistic, catastrophic, and apocalyptic prognoses of the future will come to pass.

2. In general, *we are dealing with the end of a vast historical cycle.* . . . The end of the world does not simply happen, it unfolds before our eyes. We are both observers and participants in the process. Does it herald the end of modern civilization or the end of mankind? No one can predict with certainty. But the scale of the disaster is such that we cannot rule out the possibility that the agonizing death-throes of the globalist, Western-centric world will drag all of us into the abyss with it.

3. *The current situation is intolerable.* . . . Today, a catastrophe; tomorrow, species-wide suicide. . . . Only a brute or a consuming automaton—the posthuman—can fail to recognize the world for the catastrophe it has become.

4. Those that have saved at least a grain of independent and free intellect can't help but wonder: what is the reason for our current situation? . . . The cause is Western civilization—its technological development, individualism, its pursuit of freedom at any cost, materialism, economic reductionism, egoism, and a fetish for money—that is, essentially the whole of bourgeois-capitalist liberal ideology. . . . Taken together, the global oligarchy and its attendants are the ruling class of globalism. It includes political leaders of the United States, economic and financial moguls, and the agents of globalization who serve them and make up the gigantic planetary network in which resources are allocated to those who are loyal to the thrust of globalization. They also direct the flow of information; control political, cultural, intellectual, and ideological lobbying; perform data collection; and infiltrate the structures of those states which have not yet been fully deprived of their sovereignty, not to mention their use of outright corruption, bribery, influence, harassment of dissenters, and so on. . . . Global oligarchy becomes the enemy of all mankind. But the very presence of an identifiable enemy gives us a chance to defeat them, a chance for salvation, and an opportunity to overcome the catastrophe.

How true. How comprehensive. How incisive. How uncompromising. How prophetic. This inspired rhetoric perfectly answers the dark forebodings we all feel. In the face of such undeniable truth, all those who see Aleksandr Dugin as no more than some occult/Fascist boogey-man, a "Rasputin," a "madman with an ideology," had better think again, this time with greater clarity. Anyone who retains the slightest trace of an ability to face the world as it is will understand his powerful influence over many of those who recoil—as I do—at the lunatic excesses of Postmodern Liberalism, since he appeals not merely to our deepest fears, but in many ways to what is best in us, most courageous, most virtuous, most human. It is only after fully admitting the penetrating power of Dugin's critique that I have any right to undertake, in turn, a critique of Dugin. On what basis? Let us begin with three main points:

ONE. Dugin attempts to make Western Civilization the scapegoat for the evils unleashed upon the world by post-Christian Western ideology and technology *at the very historical moment when these evils have become ubiquitous*, no longer merely characteristics of the West.

TWO. Of the evil nations and empires of the world, Dugin singles out the United States to die for the sins of the earth, including Russia—the United States that may or may not be running ahead by a nose in the Luciferian Sweepstakes at this particular point in time, but which certainly has no monopoly on industrial-strength evil, as witness Josef Stalin, Pol Pot, Adolph Hitler, Mao Tse Tung, worthy successors to Attila the Hun, Genghis Khan, Timur the Lame and their many peers, named and unnamed, in the long history of titanic, self-willed human darkness. In so doing he puts a sly thumb on the scales of justice and deftly exonerates, through misdirection of attention, whole nations and archipelagos and *gulags* of Hell-on-Earth.

THREE. Dugin, who pretends to speak for the traditional religions of the earth, has the audacity to invoke the end of a world, an *aeon*, a *manvantara*, a *maha-yuga*, a vast historical cycle-of-manifestation, while exhibiting only the haziest notion of traditional eschatological thinking, either Christian, Muslim, Hindu, Buddhist or of the First Nations. He paints a terrifying picture of the relentless doom we human beings have prepared for ourselves—terrifying because largely true—and then imagines that he can figure a way out on the basis of a heterogeneous mixture of orthodox, heterodox and secular worldviews, many of them springing from the exact sort of human mentality that created this universal mess in the first place, a mentality that tries to come to grips with the challenges of time while lacking any sense of Eternity, and is therefore totally incapable of taking even the first step in the right direction, that indispensable first step being: "Not my will but Thine be done" [Luke 22:42].

This is not to say that Dugin makes no reference to traditional eschatology; for example, a short and largely accurate section on Christian eschatology appears in *The Rise of the Fourth Political Theory*. He does not *inhabit* that eschatological vision, however, but merely catalogues it. He fails to realize that

it is possible—from the Traditionalist perspective at least—to remain intellectually faithful to traditional Christianity while using that faith as a key to
understand other traditions, other eschatologies. And elsewhere he seriously
misrepresents traditional eschatology, even though he is on the track of intuitions that might prove fruitful if only they were informed by, and re-evaluated
in terms of, a truly Traditional context. *Eurasian Mission* he says:

> There really is a command centre in post-politics. There are actors and there
> are decisions, but they are totally dehumanised in postmodernity. They are
> beyond the frames of anthropology. We can find a certain proof of this
> hypothesis in traditional teachings and in traditional eschatologies, which
> state that the End Times will not be triggered by the human hand, but that it
> will stop just prior to the final hour. The final act will not depend on man. It
> will be a war of angels, a war of gods, a confrontation of entities, not tied by
> historical or economic laws and patterns, and which do not identify them-
> selves with religions or certain political elites. And this angelic war can be
> thought of politically.

Dugin's language is strange here. When he says that the "actors" are "dehumanized," does he mean that they represent alienated and sub-human forces,
or that they transcend human limitations? He is right when he says that "the
End Times will not be triggered by the human hand, but. . . . The final act will
not depend on man," though not necessarily when he predicts that they "will
stop just prior to the final hour." When Jesus said "And unless those days be
shortened, no flesh would be saved; but for the sake of the elect, those days will
be shortened" [Matthew 24:22], he did not prophesy that the apocalypse will
stop short, but that it will move more quickly through to its End due to the
prayers and presence of the just. And even though Dugin says that the eschatological conflict won't depend on man, according to him it won't depend on
God either, but rather on "angels and gods," forces subordinate to the Absolute
and in no way to be identified with the breaking-through of the Absolute into
the relative, of Eternity into time. And to conceive of the war of the End Times
as a political war between angels insures that it will not be the true eschatological conflict but rather the Satanic counterfeit of that conflict, a war between
fallen angels—but of that more later.

That the End Times will "stop just prior to the final hour" apparently refers to
what Martin Lings, in *The Eleventh Hour*, pictures as the "final redress" or "brief
millennium," the reign of universal justice, just before the end of the cycle, that
Muslims believe will be established not by angels acting independently, but by
the Mahdi and his human followers acting under Divine guidance. This, in
more-or-less Guénonian terms, can be seen as a temporary and partial "re-spa-
tializing" of time in the presence of Eternity, just before time and space are
entirely dissolved and renewed by the inexorable action of the unveiled Abso-

lute. True, there is a place for the opposition of less-than-absolute forces in the moment before the Hour, for the spiritual war between the army of the earthly reflection of the Absolute and the counter-armies of the relativizers of the Absolute (the Left) and the absolutizers of the relative (the Right), which is the eschatological conflict between Tradition and Counter-Tradition. But to conceive of this as a battle between angels or gods with no mention of God necessarily defines it as a counterfeit of the true eschatological conflict, as the war between Gog and Magog, the sign of the "kingdom divided against itself," which must fall due to its own internal contradictions.

Nonetheless, Dugin's critique of Liberalism in its terminal phases, of Communism and Fascism as incomplete responses to it which have now been superseded, and of the universal degeneracy of the Latter Days of the *Kali-yuga*, is profound and incisive. He hits the nail on the head. However, the laws of analysis are not the laws of creation. Marx produced the most thorough critique we possess of Capitalism as an economic and social system that inevitably alienates humanity from our "species-essence"—yet the Communist regimes that sprang from this critique were every bit as alienating, if not more so, than the Capitalist system they opposed. Likewise Dugin deftly deconstructs Liberalism, yet his theory and practice are filled with elements of the very Liberal ideology he has described as "the absolute evil," as we shall see below. He apparently justifies this by defining a post-logical and post-temporal world where the elements of many past systems are now available for us to cherry-pick according to the utilitarian concerns of the moment—as if *some* aspects of the "absolute evil" might in fact be good and useful under certain circumstances.

Massive contradictions like this are the inevitable consequence of the common belief that the ability to analyze something is inseparable from the ability, and also the right, to create it—or an alternative to it—as when science thinks that it can "create life" or "engineer a new humanity." But this is not in fact the case. Though modern humanity certainly possesses a formidable power to analyze the material world, and (to a lesser degree) the socio-historical world, any civilization "created" by the power of human analysis is no civilization at all, only an artificial construct—a relatively disintegrated imitation of a true civilization—just as a quasi-human entity "re-engineered" to be superior to a real human being can only be a caricature, a monster, an abortion. Analysis is disintegrative by definition; therefore any social form established primarily on the basis of analysis will be subject to the inevitable entropy of all human conceptions and productions that attempt to define and assert themselves apart from the metaphysical First Principles from which all existence descends. Man may analyze, he may imitate, but only God creates.

Furthermore, beyond the simple limitations of analysis per se, Aleksandr Dugin's analysis, as we will see, is shot through with contradictions—contradictions which his "metaphysics of Chaos" excuses, perhaps even encourages. The Georgian "spiritual drill sergeant" G.I. Gurdjieff, whose teaching was more-or-less a hybrid between decontextualized Sufism and decontextualized Hesychasm with various elements of hypnosis and sorcery thrown in, spoke of two kinds of false mystic: the Lunatic and the Tramp. The Lunatic is René Guénon's "pseudo-initiate"; the Tramp is a simple charlatan. As a past member of the counterculture wing of the U.S. "baby boom," I come from a generation of Lunatics, while Dugin (apparently) has stepped forth from a generation of Tramps. With the help of Guénon and his successors, and my Sufi teachers, I have done my best to transcend my Lunatic background, but whether or not Dugin will be as successful in transcending his adolescence as a Tramp—having started out as something like a Neo-Nazi Bob Dylan—or whether he aspires to this at all, still remains to be seen. Is the *admitted* charlatan still a charlatan? Perhaps not; but neither is he an honest man. Dugin dabbles in metaphysics, dabbles in religion, dabbles in sincerity; like many of the Tramps who preyed upon my generation of Lunatics, he undoubtedly fears that if he were ever to really believe in something—something besides Eurasia and Chaos, something Divine, Eternal, of the Spirit—he would immediately lose all his hipness and cunning, turn into a bronze statue of himself and die as a shameful and self-confessed straight arrow. And if insincerity produces real effects in the world, can we still call it insincerity? Hasn't it proven itself by "actualizing its potential"? Perhaps. Until our appearance before "the dread judgment seat of Christ" (to use the Orthodox Christian terminology), the answers to questions like these will remain semantically ambiguous. After that summons is issued, however, it will be firmly impressed upon us that what is true of money is also true of hipness and cunning: *you can't take them with you.*

Aleksandr Dugin, however, is much more than a cynical charlatan—or let us at least admit that his charlatanry is simply the form that philosophical discourse and political practice must take in the darkness of postmodern times. He is struggling with momentous issues arising from Russia's loss of the Cold War and the grim dedication of the United States and the NATO nations to fill the power-vacuum left by the breakup of the Soviet Empire, to relentlessly pressure Russia economically, ideologically and militarily. Any Russian social intellectual who doesn't address these issues is simply irrelevant. Would it be better if Dugin were entirely serious about defending "Holy Russia" without a trace of postmodern irony? Maybe so, maybe not. In any case we must take him as he is. We may criticize him, but we can't dismiss him. And, if the truth be known, there is little wrong with Dugin that isn't wrong with politics itself, including geopolitics: lies, back-stabbings, magician's tricks, strange bedfellows, talking out of both sides of your mouth, playing with the destinies of peoples and nations—that's all part of the Great Game. It's easy to see the evil and suffering that come from such methods, though they also may end up doing some good from time to time. My practice, however, is to leave the politicians to their work and myself to mine—that work being primarily metaphysical social criticism—which on rare occasions requires me to touch the political world as lightly and swiftly as I can. The only real bone I have to pick with Aleksandr Dugin is his misrepresentation and manipulation of religion and metaphysics, which goes far beyond the simple one-dimensional hypocrisy required of the Western politician. Whoever lays hands on the Sacred is playing with fire; it's a game that can't be won. *They plot,* says the Noble Qur'an, *but Allah also plots; and Allah is the best of plotters.* [8:30]

A Question of Allegiances

Aleksandr Dugin's *known* allegiances are to Russia and/or Neo-Eurasianism and his imagined Eurasian empire, and secondarily to various writers, largely of the extreme Right, especially Alain Benoist, Martin Heidegger and René Guénon—though Guénon, as we shall see, was not so much a Conservative as a Traditionalist, two distinct orientations which may sometimes coincide but which should never be confused. As for Dugin's Eastern Orthodox Christianity, it seems to be a little lower down on his list. At this point the reader may have begun to wonder why I, as a Muslim, have drawn so heavily on Christian doctrine in this book. The answer is that I cannot hold Aleksandr Dugin accountable to Muslim doctrine since he is not a Muslim, but I can certainly hold him to Christian doctrine—which, as a fully-initiated pre-Vatican II Catholic who is also familiar with Eastern Orthodoxy, as well as a Traditionalist who believes in the validity of more than one Divine revelation, I believe I am entitled to do. As I have already pointed out, my allegiance is primarily to the world's great religions, either revealed or primordial, which in my case means Islam, the only religion I practice. But I have a real affinity with Christianity too—through my mother who was a Catholic convert, through my 14 years in Catholic school, and through my wife Jenny who entered Eastern Orthodoxy in the 1990's and at this point worships as a Traditional *sede vaccantist* Catholic—as well as to Buddhism through my connection to the poets of the Beat Generation, who were in many ways my first teachers. My allegiance to the Traditional religious outlook is most centrally expressed through my studies in metaphysics, partly from the standpoint of the writers of the Traditionalist or Perennialist School of metaphysics and "comparative religion," which is considered to have been founded by Guénon. But my direct, *operative* allegiance to God is expressed through Islam, more essentially through Sufism, and under any and all circumstances simply through the fact that I am a human being, which means that I was specifically designed by God—as the Catholics say, or used to—to "know, love and serve" Him. Consequently, by virtue of the God who created me, my intrinsic allegiance, at least in terms of this earthly world, is to the human race. Humanity is my *narod*.

Dugin, on the other hand, invokes the Russian *narod*, its organic, geographical/ethnic identity. For myself, I consider that I owe the United States of America my support against her enemies, both external and internal—and, in the case of the latter, whether these enemies arise from the populace, or occupy positions of power at the behest of the Deep State, or both. As for my participation in the United States of America as a *spiritual* collective, insofar as it is or ever was such a thing, I renounced my *worldly* citizenship in that collective during the Vietnam War. That and the assassination of John Fitzgerald Kennedy were the two events that first damaged, then destroyed, for much of my generation, the idealistic vision of America, the land of the free and the home of the brave. Nonetheless the memory of what America was supposed to be or become has never entirely left me[4]—a violated ideal powerful enough to fire the mind of Europe for two centuries, one that was expressed by the English poet William Blake as follows:

> Tho born on the cheating banks of Thames
> Tho his waters bathed my infant limbs
> The Ohio shall wash my stains from me
> I was born a slave but I go to be free

The African Americans certainly have the right, if not the duty, to seriously question this ideal, an ideal that even the young Ho Chi Minh of Vietnam was inspired by—until hard experience proved to be the greater teacher.

Ever since the death of that ideal I have opposed nearly every foreign policy move this American Empire has made: Vietnam in the 60's, intervention in Central America in the '80's, and now, in the 21st century, our fomentation of the Arab Spring and initial organizing and logistical support for ISIS. Some of the little-known history of this act of moral suicide would not be out of place here:

Apparently the Obama Administration, under cover of Countering Violent Extremism and other counter-terrorist programs, sponsored the "reintegra-

---

4. Walt Whitman, of course, was the great poet of American democracy as a spiritual brotherhood, partly realized and partly a "dream" of the future. Jack Kerouac drew something from that myth, while Allen Ginsberg, who styled himself a kind of latter-day Whitman, in many ways announced the end of Whitman's America, as I myself did, more explicitly, in my poem *Panic Grass* [City Lights Books, 1968]. In the 19th and early 20th centuries the United States of America used to be personified, in line with the virtue of "civic piety," as the Goddess Columbia or Liberty, who sometimes resembled an American version of Vesta, the Roman virgin goddess of hearth-and-home, or the Greek virgin goddess Athena. Americans used to swear by America as if she were a kind of deity, a practice that survived into the 20th century in such colloquial expressions as "land sakes." Likewise Mark Twain, in *Huckleberry Finn*, has his character the King say, "I'm *nation* sorry for you."

tion" of ISIS fighters into U.S. society, which is a strong indication that they were already on the Federal payroll. As of this writing, in April of 2018, Donald Trump has apparently begun to reverse this policy.[5] On November 1, 2017, CNN reported that the Trump had administration had "folded two counter-terror grant programs altogether in the process of rebranding the Obama administration's Countering Violent Extremism office."[6] I hate Trump's bone-ignorant anti-Muslim bigotry, his inability to tell the "Muslim on the street" apart from the terrorists or crypto-terrorists among American Muslims, thus legitimizing anti-Muslim hate crimes and driving more ordinary Muslims into the terrorist camp, but I fully support any action he might be able to take to exclude ISIS from the U.S.—if only these two agendas could be separated! This is of special concern in light of the fact that the so-called Islamic State keeps a hit list of U.S. Muslim leaders. On the other hand, Donald Trump's decision to recognize Jerusalem as the capital of Israel is beyond demented, one of the worst decisions made by any President of the United States in my lifetime; under Trump, the historical status of the United States of America as a "rogue state" has been fully established. (For a biblical prophesy applicable to the modern State of Israel, see Daniel 7:8: "While I was contemplating the horns, behold, another horn, a little one, came up among them, and three of the first horns were pulled out by the roots before it; and behold, this horn possessed eyes like the eyes of a man, and a mouth uttering great boasts.") Some of us are now asking ourselves if Donald Trump has finally been captured by Israel, the Neo-Cons, and the Deep State; nonetheless, there are indications that he may not yet be entirely in line with their program. It is also difficult to determine whether or not his audacious and necessary interdiction of the Deep State's insane policy of risking World War III by casting Russia as the enemy of America nonetheless carries a real risk of opening the U.S. to Russian subversion. We must avoid two extremes here: that of assuming that we know, and that of believing that we can never know.

Tellingly, Herman Melville's *Moby Dick*, generally recognized as the greatest American novel, is the epic of the doom of America. Even our national poet, Walt Whitman, who wrote "Passage to India," the central poem of American manifest destiny, of imperialism expanding into globalism, called the United States, in his book *Democratic Vistas*, "the fabled damned" of nations. This, however, should in no way be taken to mean that we will passively resign our-

5. See "Welcome Home ISIS! The Obama Administration's Plan to Reintegrate Foreign Terrorist Fighters" by Dr. John Andrew Morrow, posted on the Global Research website in December of 2016: https://www.globalresearch.ca/welcome-home-isis-the-obama-administrations-plan-to-reintegrate -foreign-terrorist-fighters/556347

6. http://www.cnn.com/2017/11/01/politics/countering-domestic-terror-cuts/index.html

selves to being destroyed by Russia, or by Aleksandr Dugin's as-yet-fictitious Eurasian Empire. This is our land, ours like a beloved woman who will always be ours, even if she has betrayed us again and again, even if we all but hate her now. According to the traditional canons of tragedy it is our role to destroy her—and as of the Year of Our Lord 2018, we seem to be doing a pretty good job of it. Secessionist tendencies continue to crop up, and many in both the Right and the Left appear to be working, either consciously or unconsciously, to deconstruct the *idea* of the United States as a sovereign nation in favor of some "higher" purpose, whether this be globalism, ethnic separatism or the dominance of this or that religious collective over civil society.

But if I have no nation beyond some fading dream of the Future—a dream that has imperceptibly shifted from utopia to dystopia over the past 40 years— plus the people I love, a quasi-mythic memory, and the actual ground under my feet, do I still have a race? I am certainly of the White Race since my blood-lines stretch back mostly to the British Isles—but when it comes to any kind of racial solidarity, my position is more ambiguous. The White Race is dwindling demographically in America; soon we will no longer be a majority in our own land, only a plurality. The next majority race will probably be the Latinos, unless undocumented immigration significantly slows. The fact is that all three of the "indigenous" populations of the United States—the Whites, the Blacks and the Native Americans—are suffering from the effects of unchecked immi-gration. (My apologies to the third group, the Native Americans, but aren't we—we white-eyes and buffalo soldiers—at least *a little* indigenous by now?) The unregulated immigration that is knocking us off our high horse is some-thing apparently decreed by our globalist masters in their ongoing campaign to break up nation-states so as to build their global hegemony. As I said in my book *The System of Antichrist: Truth and Falsehood in Postmodernism and the New Age* [Sophia Perennis, 2001], "The globalization of the elites leads to the balkanization of the masses." Nonetheless we should never forget that many of the present-day immigrants to the United States, both legal and illegal, are sim-ply running for their lives, in many cases from conditions created or exacer-bated by the United States. We need to be as compassionate as possible to these people without seriously destabilizing our country and jeopardizing the rule of law. It is not their fault if they are being used by the powers that be to weaken national sovereignties and concentrate even more power in the hands of the elites. And we also need to remember that to create a second-class non-citizen-ship of illegal aliens vulnerable to deportation, afraid to assert their non-exis-tent "rights" as workers and so willing to work for next to nothing, is a strategy long supported by powerful corporate interests to undermine unionization and maximize profits. Today's so-called "Leftists" have obviously never been taught that Cesar Chavez, a true hero of the Left who co-founded the United Farmworkers Union in California in 1962, was opposed to illegal immigration for just this reason, as was the prominent American Indian Movement leader Russell Means, who passed away in 2012.

In the 1980's, when I was most deeply involved in Liberal/Leftist politics in the context of the opposition to U.S. military invention in Central America, the Left was so different from the "Left" of today that we ought to find a different name. In the 1980's the Left supported the labor movement; now it scorns the working class. It welcomed *glasnost* and *perestroika* and supported detente with Russia; now Russia is the enemy. Its social analysis was centered on class; now it's mainly based on race and gender, while class analysis is de-emphasized. And it certainly believed in freedom of speech. One of its intrinsic moral principles of the older Left was—in Evelyn Beatrice Hall's famous paraphrase of Voltaire—"I may not believe in a thing that you say, but I will defend to the death your right to say it." Now it routinely calls for freedom of speech to be curtailed. The CIA was the feared and hated enemy; now those who condemn the CIA are called "Right Wing Extremists." The U.S. "Left" of today is a textbook case of a social movement thoroughly infiltrated by change agents and completely denatured and recast by social engineers, to the point where—outside of paid anarchist cadres who bear no more resemblance to the Left as a true American opposition than do their distant cousins in academia, and various isolated and factionalized fragments of the traditional, labor-based Left who are largely without influence—there is no Left left.

Be that as it may, given that the White Race may soon no longer be the majority population and therefore the "standard human type" in North America, it is high time that we start seeing ourselves as a *bona fide* ethnic group, and begin searching for our roots like everybody else. Unfortunately, everybody else seems to oppose this move—sadly so, since it might turn out to be a true service to human brotherhood. Blacks, Latinos, Muslims can have student unions and ethnic festivals, but never Whites! Any White Person who simply proposes that the White Race, now that we are no longer top dog as securely as we once were, should maybe begin to investigate what our whiteness really means, what its true essence might be, irrespective of our fading position of racial dominance, is immediately classed with the Nazis, the Ku Klux Klaners, the White Supremacists. And the unfortunate fact is that if I propose to organize a Festival of Whiteness (which is *not* in my plans), the first people to show up—outside of Antifa and other far-left anarchist thugs, armed with bags of urine and feces and baseball bats—will be "our own" thugs: the Nazis, the Ku Klux Klaners, the White Supremacists, at least as nasty and possibly better armed than their Leftist/Anarchist opponents; "defenders" like these I can do without. (How ironic it is that these great Supremacists, whose ideology has been used to justify mass murder, are sometimes only beaten White Separatists, people who are asking for little more than the equivalent of a White Indian Reservation somewhere, maybe in Idaho or Montana, where they can practice their ancestral folkways in peace.) The fact that I risked five years in Federal prison for conspiracy to protect immigrants to the U.S. from El Salvador, that I spent twenty years in a Sufi circle headed by a Black man, and that my present colleague in the Covenants Initiative, Dr. John Andrew Morrow, is a Native American, will probably mean nothing to the Extreme Left, since anyone who disagrees with them is immediately defined as a Right-winger and therefore a racist; but at least my checkered background will hopefully prevent me from being easily embraced by the Extreme Right. If I have been forced to face the Darkness of This World not as member of a *narod*, a sacred covenant between the living, the dead and the land—such as many of the Native Americans still maintain, though under great duress—but as an unwillingly isolated individual, it is due to relentless social pressures exactly like this. The Native Americans clearly have a greater right to call America "our land" than the European newcomers—but let them never deny that a White American, given the right circumstances, could feel a bond with this land every bit as strong as his older brothers and sisters of the First Nations. That's how I used to feel about my own homeland of Marin County, California, before (for me at least) the spirit of it died.

So even though I reside in the enemy territory that Aleksandr Dugin identifies with Atlantis, as opposed to the "Hyperborean" heartland of his Eurasia, I am not an Atlanticist, but rather part of the Hyperborean Remnant in the New World. And far from being identified with the Right or the Left, or the Alt-Right or the Alt-Left, the Liberals or the Libertarians, or the Neo-Cons or the Paleo-Cons, or the Maoists or the Trotskyists or the Anarchists, I am actually a member of what might be called the "Alternate Deep Center." Like Dugin, I reject Liberalism, Communism and Fascism. Like Dugin claims to be, I am opposed to Postmodernism, globalism, the global hegemony of the United States, including the U.S./NATO-based push to "contain" Russia, provoke actions of Russian self-defense and then use these actions as evidence of Russian expansionism. (To take one example of this, the Russian occupation of the Crimea was in no sense an arbitrary act of imperialism, but rather a necessary move to prevent the U.S. from denying Russia its Black Sea ports, which my nation was attempting to achieve so as to make it harder for Putin to intervene in Syria and move against ISIS who, at that point at least, were precisely a U.S.-sponsored proxy army.) This should not be taken to mean, however, that there is presently no danger to be feared from Russian expansionism; Dugin's writings alone are enough to disprove this thesis. And, also like Dugin, or at least Dugin in one of his several dominant "moods," I support the vision of a world where many more forms of human life than Western Democracy have the right to call themselves "civilizations."

So where do we differ? Dugin, though he condemns Postmodernism and claims to accept Traditionalism as a cornerstone of his Fourth Political Theory, is by no stretch of the imagination an actual Traditionalist but is, in fact, precisely a postmodernist. As for myself, I am opposed to Postmodernism in deed, not simply in word. I am an actual Traditionalist, a follower of René Guénon, while Aleksandr Dugin, seeing that he has cunningly inverted some of Guénon's central doctrines, is nothing of the kind.

Traditionalism, to me, is not simply a "rejection of the modern world," but a treasury of sacred truth based on the highest wisdom and spiritual praxis of the human race as given, and demanded, by God.[7] The writings of the great Traditionalists which have come down to us—René Guénon, Ananda Coomaraswamy, Frithjof Schuon, Titus Burckhardt, Martin Lings, Marco Pallis, Charles Le Gai Eaton, Whitall Perry and Seyyed Hossein Nasr—and, to a lesser extent, of such writers as Julius Evola, Henry Corbin, Mircea Eliade and Huston Smith—taken all in all represent the most profound and comprehensive intellectual doorway we possess to the "wisdom of the ages," the sacred lore-hoard of the human race. Traditionalism, like no other body of writing I know, demonstrates beyond any conceivable doubt—to those who understand its principles—that the Truth is One: *Shema, Yisrael, Adonoi Elohenu, Adonoi Echad! Credo in Unum Deum! La ilaha illa 'Allah!*

Duginism, on the other hand is a hodge-podge of incompatible doctrines and influences lifted from here, there and everywhere, whose "unifying" principle is in no way truth, but only power. And though it is host to many true and even brilliant insights, in many ways it is a web of falsity and manipulation which draws whatever life it possesses from the truths it contains and exploits, while not necessarily remaining faithful to them. Aleksandr Dugin claims to reject Postmodernism, yet his rejection not only of a unipolar world but of a unified vision of Reality in the name of "the metaphysics of Chaos" makes him a textbook case of the postmodern metaphysical nihilist. And though he sometimes writes as an Eastern Orthodox Christian—specifically, an Old Believer—and has produced some beautiful meditations on Orthodox themes, neither God nor the theology of the Greek Fathers appear to have had much influence on his Neo-Eurasianism or his Fourth Political Theory, except as tags useful to attract the attention of certain groups and institutions he wishes to influence. Religion, to him, seems to bear little relationship to any Transcendent Reality

---

7. Mark Sedgwick's book on the Traditionalist School, *Against the Modern World*, though it mischaracterizes the Traditionalists in a number of places, and presents highly useful information on them in others, has in any case made things infinitely easier for Western academics, who can now pigeon-hole the School in a few sentences without the time-consuming inconvenience of reading their books, or of coming to even the most rudimentary understanding of their central theme, which is Traditional Metaphysics.

that might inform his socio-historical vision and hopes. Rather, he treats it precisely as the postmodern Liberal sociologists do, as a set of beliefs and a system-of-identifications proper to various different sectors of the global population, just as he apparently sees Orthodox Christianity as little more than something "good for Russian/Eurasian unity." As he says in his 1990 article "Introduction to Conspirology": "When one analyses religion, one is not concerned with the fact of the existence of god, but with the fact of belief."

On one occasion, on a whim, I phoned the office of the Council on Foreign Relations to shoot the breeze with the receptionist and see what I could turn up. During the course of our conversation she referred to the world's religions as *constituencies*—and this is precisely how Dugin also sees them, as potential constituencies of his Eurasianist Coalition. Far from advocating a true multi-polar world, he posits multi-polarism only as a way of eroding and fracturing the Western Liberal-Democratic Hegemony, after which the fragments are to be snapped up by the Eurasianist-Russian Hegemony. Russia under Communism routinely appealed to the liberation movements of the Third World, their struggle for identity and self-determination, whereas the United States has tended to take the opposite tack of suppressing these movements. It was only with the creation of ISIS and the Arab Spring that the U.S. finally opted to act according to the Russian model in a big way—with uniformly disastrous results for the stability of the region—thus forcing Russia to take a page from the book of American imperialism and back an "old style dictator" like Muhammad Assad.

My approach to God and His religions is poles apart from Aleksandr Dugin's. For example, Dugin writes—quite movingly in places and with a degree of truth—of the Aryan affinity for the Heavenly Father, the congenital attraction of the Caucasian Races to sublimity and the vision of other, higher worlds.[8] Yet he also invokes the underworld god Dionysus—and, on closer inspection, his reason for pointing out the affinity between the White race and the sublime seems limited to his call for *a renewal of Aryan identity*. This stance is nearly identical to that of Liberal "identitarian" politics, the only difference being that Liberals tend to choose any race other than the Aryan/Caucasian one and any religion other than Christianity as beneficiaries of their postmodern call for "other voices" to be acknowledged. Dugin, the Liberals and the anti-Christian Neo-Pagans of the Alt-Right are of one mind in their view that God, or *a* god, is merely a way for some ethnic group or faith-community to assert and maintain its identity, not a Divine call to sacrifice that identity, that group ego, for something higher. St. Paul said, "It is not I who live, but Christ lives in me" [Galatians 2:20], to which Dugin appears to be replying, "it is not Christ

---

8. The quintessential expression of White Sublimity is the Irish hymn "Be Thou my Vision," set to a tune which some claim was originally performed in homage to the High King at Tara.

who lives, but we, our group-identity, our sacred *narod*, who occupy Him and use Him and draw our life from Him, as well as from a number of other equally useful sources."

My Perspective on the History of the U.S. Peace Movement

As I have already indicated, my critique of Dugin will be primarily religious and metaphysical, since he clearly has no scruples against misusing and perverting metaphysical doctrines or making appeals to religious group-identities while apparently feeling little need to remain faithful to the doctrines of his own faith. But since both Dugin and I are activists, though on vastly different scales, and in view of the fact that I have articulated the possibility, in *Chapter Seven*, of a "sacred activism" based on Divine guidance, it behooves me to clarify both where I am "coming from," and where I am now, in terms of the interface between spirituality and political action.

The Catholic writer Charles Péguy once wrote: "Everything begins in mysticism and ends in politics." Be that as it may, mysticism and politics were the poles between which the current of my post-WWII Baby Boom generation—or at least the "counter-culture" sector of it—primarily flowed. Like many of my generation I participated in the mass protests against the Vietnam War, which, under the influence of psychedelic drugs and various eastern yogic and western magical practices, often included various *ad hoc* attempts to apply psychic or "spiritual" to energy political action—like the practice, led by poet Allen Ginsberg at the 1968 Democratic Nation Convention demonstrations in Chicago (which I attended), of intoning "Om" so as to spread "waves of peace"—though on that occasion the waves of hate generated by the Chicago Police and the Yippies proved to be quite a bit taller. This kind of "magical populism" continued and became better organized during the anti-nuclear protests of the 1970's, and culminated, during the late 80's and early 90's, in various "global peace prayer days," the best-known of which was the famous international populist/folk event known as "Harmonic Convergence."

The fitting end to this phase of hippy and later New Age "spiritual" peace activism was the Iranian Revolution of 1979, which heralded an era in which religion would become more central to political struggle, in western world, and the world as a whole, than it had been (perhaps) at any time since the Reformation and the Thirty Years War.

The churches had already become deeply involved in political action through civil rights and the anti-war movements of the 1960's. This development was well represented in the Catholic world by various "radical priests" like the Berrigan brothers and by the tradition of Dorothy Day and the Catholic Workers movement; in the Evangelical Protestant world by Martin Luther King, the

Sojourners community and others; and in Quakerism by the American Friends Service Committee, whose main focus in the 60's had been support for conscientious objectors to the military draft. Beginning in the 1970's, the Liberal, Left-leaning churches emphasized anti-nuclear activism, while various expressions of the North American "social gospel" tradition coalesced and gained a new impetus in the 1980's through the movement of solidarity with the revolutions of Nicaragua, El Salvador and Guatemala, and the struggle to block large-scale U.S. intervention against them. The spearhead of this phase of church-based peace activism was the Sanctuary Movement, in which my wife and I participated as members of the governing board of a small Presbyterian church in Marin County, California.

The moral rationale for the Movement was as follows: Since it was well-known that the United States, with the help of the National War College, had provided training to the Salvadoran death squads, and that the terror in El Salvador was driving many Salvadoran from their country, we had a duty, both as Americans and as Christians, to protect those refugees who made it to the United States.

The Salvadoran refugees, as illegal aliens, were considered to be criminals under federal law, so we resurrected the old tradition which held that criminals fleeing the civil authorities could be granted sanctuary in Christian churches, where they would remain exempt from arrest as long as they stayed on the church grounds. Not all the refugees we were working with lived on church property of course; nonetheless we invoked the spirit if not the letter of the old sanctuary rule to serve them.[9]

During this period my wife and I re-connected with the San Francisco poetry scene, which I had been part of in the 1960's when Lawrence Ferlinghetti of City Lights Books published my "short epic" poem *Panic Grass*. The "Caucasian" poets of the Left, in the 80's, were partnering with the Latino poets of the Bay Area—like Roberto Vargas, who later became the Nicaraguan ambassador to China—to express solidarity with the revolutions of Central America; the main centers for this political/cultural ferment were the Mission Cultural Center in San Francisco and La Peña Cultural Center in Berkeley. I began collecting poems for an anthology in solidarity with the Salvadoran revolution; James Laughlin of New Directions had agreed to publish it. Then one of the Bay Area Salvadoran politicos "appropriated" the project (I probably should have fought to keep it), the upshot being that the anthology never appeared. Another less-than-successful project was my attempt to bring Ernesto Cardenal, then Minis-

---

9. The training, supply and logistical support provided by the United States to certain Syrian "rebel" groups, including ISIS, appears to closely follow the model that the U.S. developed while funneling aid to the death squads of El Salvador and the "Contras" of Nicaragua.

ter of Culture of Nicaragua under the Sandinistas, to the Bay Area. (Cardenal had studied under Father Thomas Merton at the Trappist Abbey of Gethsemani in Kentucky. Merton, also a poet, acted as a kind of spiritual adviser to the peace movement and the increasingly rudderless Catholic Church after the Second Vatican Council, reaching out to Buddhists, to Sufis, to poets and peace activists—despite the fact that, to my way of thinking, he was becoming increasingly rudderless himself.) Cardenal and I corresponded for a short time, but nothing came of it; later he was invited to San Francisco by the more established poetry commissars of the Mission District, working in concert with Lawrence Ferlinghetti and City Lights Books. Poetry in this context was considered to be a kind of motivational tool. It was not quite agitprop, but it was nonetheless expected to fulfill utilitarian function under the rubric of "cultural resistance." During those days we became friends with people like poet Fernando Alegría, colleague of Pablo Neruda, who had been part of the Leftist Allende government in Chile. (Allende, as you will perhaps remember, was assassinated in a military coup backed by the United States; his government was replaced by a *junta* headed by dictator Augusto Pinochet, known for his practice of "disappearing" his opponents.)

One of the notable people we met during this time was Joan McCarthy. She had been a Catholic nun who was appointed mother superior of a Dominican convent in Mexico when she was hardly out of her teens; in that capacity she was treated as a kind of seeress by the Mexican peasants. Then at one point a choice was presented her: should she go to South America and become part of the Liberation Theology movement (under either Leonardo Boff or Dom Helder Camara, I forget which)? Or should she accept the invitation of a local "white" *bruja* (sorceress) to study traditional Mexican sorcery? After she left the Dominican Order she had partnered with this *bruja* to defend the peasants from oppression by the "black" *brujos* of the region, who at that point had a monopoly on medical care in the remote rural areas. Anyone who became ill had to resort to these people, who were most likely running a sort of protection racket, threatening to use their magic to make people sick instead of curing them if they didn't pay up. Joan and the *bruja* were training young local men as herbal doctors so as to undercut the power of these *brujos*. The *bruja* had told her: "I will show you the powers of the Garlic Flower, of the Silver Sword, and of the Cross—but the greatest power is Love." Joan, however, chose the path of Liberation Theology, and left for South America.

The theoretical context for the peace movement of the 1980's, which took the form of a more overt solidarity with the revolutions of Central America than the Vietnam peace movement ever had with the North Vietnamese or the Viet Cong—Jane Fonda's notorious trip to North Vietnam notwithstanding—was provided by Liberation Theology. This ideology arose, mostly in Latin America, via a cross-pollination between radical leftist politics and the Catholic Church. The central ideologues of this movement included Dom Helder Camara, Gustavo Gurierrez, Leonardo Boff, Juan Luis Segundo, and Ernesto Cardenal, Catholic priest and poet, whose three-volume book of dialogues, *The Gospel in Solentiname*, was an important influence. Father Cardenal, who later became Minister of Culture of Nicaragua under the Sandinistas, had a parish on an island in an archipelago in Lake Nicaragua; his congregation was made up mostly of the local fishermen and women. But due to his international reputation as a poet and Marxist/Catholic intellectual, his parish became a place of pilgrimage for intellectuals, artists and revolutionaries from many parts of the world. Cardenal organized dialogues between the peasants, the local activists and various visiting intellectuals, who together began to develop a Theology of Liberation which was equally a creation of the intelligentsia and the uneducated poor—a very interesting development in both political and cultural terms.

Many U.S. "progressive" Christians were being drawn to social action in those years. In one sense this was an overflow of the Christian charisma of "blessed are the poor in spirit, for they shall see God"; in another, it was simply a way to stir up the dying embers of faith into a strong but temporary new blaze by seeking worldly "relevancy." In the case of our own little church, however, too much of the essence of the spiritual life was being lost in conflict with worldly conditions to allow for the deepening of our devotional and contemplative center. We were willing to struggle with the world in the name of God and make real sacrifices in the pursuit of our image of God's justice, but we had little idea of the way, or the even the need, to struggle with ourselves. Consequently the manifestation of the Spirit in and through us had a set limit to it; after that limit was passed, nothing was left for us but the outer darkness.

There is no question in my mind that without the large-scale involvement North American churches in the opposition to U.S. intervention in Central America, we would have seen a much greater bloodbath in that region, accompanied by a destabilization of much of the western hemisphere, most likely including the large-scale incursion of the Central American death-squads into the United States itself. Liberation Theology, with its "option for the poor," did base itself partly on the Gospel call for Christians to perform corporal works of mercy. Nonetheless a true marriage of Christianity and Marxism—that is, of theistic spirituality and atheistic materialism—is not a viable possibility in either theological or socio-historical terms. No matter how idealistically it might be pursued, such a proposal is contradictory, ill-conceived, and dishonest at the root; in this regard it has certain elements in common with Aleksandr Dugin's coalition between the extreme Right, the extreme Left and the Russian Orthodox Church. And the fact is, much of the spiritual potential of Christianity, and especially of the Catholic Church, was spent in the more or less successful attempt to block U.S. intervention in Central America. Real material good was done in the dimension of time; much spiritual good was lost in the dimension of Eternity. And the fact is that the Catholic Church, after the rejection of its traditional dogma, the deconstruction of the sacramental order by and after the Second Vatican Council, and the pedophilia scandal which resulted in the bankruptcy of whole archdioceses, the closure of many churches and the departure of millions of the faithful, no longer possesses the kind of social influence and moral authority that it spent so recklessly on helping the world in the 1980's.

Elements of the U.S. Catholic Church have retained, even to this day, their commitment to helping Latin American immigrants illegally cross the border from Mexico to the United States that they embraced during the Sanctuary Movement. However, while some refugees from the south are still fleeing political oppression and/or gang violence, they are now accompanied by plenty of members of Mexican drug cartels and other criminal and/or terrorist organizations. And where, exactly, is the line to be drawn between helping refugees and enabling human traffickers? According to National Public Radio—not a newssource where you'd expect to run into the kind of anti-immigrant sentiment usually identified with conservative Republicans and the Alt-Right—the immigration from El Salvador to the United States that began in the 1980's has led to a vast increase in the power of the Salvadoran drug gangs. Salvadorans operating in the relative freedom of the U.S. have been able to build narcotics-trafficking networks much more easily than they could have done under the repressive conditions of their native country, after which these networks are simply exported back to El Salvador. Nor should we forget the incident in which a 17-year old Muslim girl, Nabra Hassanen, who was abducted and killed with a baseball bat in June of 2017 while walking down the street with her friends, was murdered by 22-year old Darwin Martinez Torres, an illegal alien from El Salvador. So times change. What is mercy and justice in one era can unexpectedly become cruelty and injustice in another. Politics is the art of the ephemeral.

At one point during our years with the Sanctuary Movement, an interesting and quite moving document was circulated, a statement by a woman guerrilla fighter somewhere in Latin America. She called upon the monastics of the Catholic Church not to abandon their contemplative vocation in order to become activists and revolutionaries (and, I would add, social workers), but rather to continue to man the post where God had stationed them. Unfortunately, from the standpoint of 2018, I can only conclude that, at least in terms of its "official" ideology, the Roman Catholic Church—except for a tiny remnant of the traditional faithful—has remained largely deaf to her plea.

After the stress and uncertainty of the Sanctuary Movement, my wife and I, in 1986, '87 and '88, took a "sabbatical" in the form of a tour-of-duty through the New Age spirituality and peace activism, which by then had succeeded the mass movement of hippy magical populism that began in the late 1960's. The international peace networking in the late 1980's, carried on by such groups as Global Family, blended the New Age/"yuppie" ethos of spirituality-and-success—which appeared in some ways as a kind of non-Christian Pentecostalism—the organization of mass international peace-prayer events, and various types of "citizen diplomacy" with Soviet Russia during the *glasnost* years. The Theosophists, psychics and neo-shamans who had been repressed under Communism were beginning to emerge from hiding—just as the Russian Orthodox Church was also doing—and they were finding allies with similar interests in the West. It was at this point that I began to see signs of covert globalist involvement in what most of us had considered to be a free-wheeling populism entirely of our own making. I did not wake up to the true significance of these vague intimations, however, until, under the influence of the Traditionalist School, I wrote and published *The System of Antichrist* in 2001.

After our short passage through the New Age, we renounced political action, concentrating upon Sufism—which my wife was also involved with for a short time—and the writings of the Traditionalists. It was in the 90's that we were drawn most deeply into that world, making friends with such Traditionalists as Huston Smith, James Cutsinger, Seyyed Hossein Nasr and, a bit later, Rama Coomaraswamy, who passed away in 2006. It was through the Traditionalists that my connection to Leftist "progressive" politics and my hope, in more-or-less New Age style, for the global dawning of a "new paradigm," a new spiritual revelation, were effectively ended, to be replaced with the firm conviction that the eschatological theologies and prophesies of the great world religions provide us with the most profound and accurate picture of the times in which we live.

I remained outside the world of political activism until the Covenants Initiative was born in 2013.

From the Spiritual Revolution of the 1960's to the Traditionalist School and the Covenants Initiative

I was born and raised a traditional Catholic in a mostly pre-Second Vatican Council Roman Catholic Church; my entire formal education consists of 14 years of Catholic school, nursery school through high school. Around the age of 17, like many of my generation, I answered the call of the "Spiritual Revolution" of the 1960's, just as the traditional Church was being deconstructed by Vatican II and the post-Conciliar popes, notably Paul VI. Living in the San Francisco Bay Area in those years, we didn't have to travel the world looking for spiritual teachers; that world, and those teachers, simply showed up on our doorstep. Consequently I was able to receive *darshan* from Swami Satchitananda of the Vedanta Society; learn *kundalini*-yoga exercises from the Sikh guru Yogi Bhajan; receive *shaktipat* from the Shaivite Swami Muktananda, *chela* of the great Nityananda; reflect the "lyrical glance" of Sant Darshan Singh, Sikh guru of the Shabda Yoga lineage; meditate at the Green Gulch Zen Center and the (once Dominican Catholic) Santa Sabina Retreat Center; talk with the Shoshone medicine man Rolling Thunder and with Arvol Looking Horse, 19th hereditary Sacred Pipe-Holder of the Lakota; meet and meditate with several Tibetan lamas; attend a Tibetan Buddhist Green Tara Empowerment; and participate in the powerful Black Crown Ceremony conducted by the Sixteenth Gyalwang Karmapa, head of the Kagyu Lineage of Tibetan Vajrayana Buddhism—a rite which is no longer being performed due to the removal, for political purposes, of the Black Crown from public view. Did I absorb too many incompatible spiritual influences, make too many false starts? It's as if I were a field sown with many and various seeds of secret knowledge during those years, seeds that have taken a lifetime to sprout.

In the late 80's, partly under the influence of the Traditionalists, I converted to Islam and was initiated into the Nimatullahi Sufi Order under Dr. Javad Nurbakhsh, a *ṭarīqa* that originated in Iran but has a number of circles operating in Europe and America. In the decade of the 90's, as I have already indicated, my wife and I extensively explored the Traditionalist or Perennialist School and immersed ourselves in that world. Though Jenny never met Frithjof Schuon, she entered Schuon's Maryamiyya Tariqa through his *muqaddam* (representative), Dr. Seyyed Hossein Nasr, while I remained with the Nimatullahis. Later, with Schuon's blessing, Jenny converted to Eastern Orthodox Christianity. We met and became friends with Prof. Huston Smith, a true "gentleman and a scholar," who was also connected with the Maryamiyya. We used to meet at his home for Chinese takeout and delightful informal discussions of spiritual themes; I would drive him to his lectures from time to time and man the book table. We visited Dr. Nasr in Washington D.C., as well as the remnant of Schuon's circle in Bloomington, Indiana after his passing, and also became acquainted with Christian Perennialists Alvin Moore, Jr., who was Eastern Orthodox, and Dr. Rama Coomaraswamy. Rama, who had been Mother Theresa's cardiologist, was a *sede vaccantist* Catholic and the closest thing to an *informal* spiritual guide that Jenny and I had ever known. He was the son of Ananda Kentish Coomaraswamy, who is sometimes considered, along with René Guénon, to be cofounder of the Traditionalist School. In his later years he gave up his practice as a surgeon due to ill health, then retrained as a psychiatrist and was ordained as a traditional Catholic priest. In the latter capacity he became an exorcist in the New York area and a colleague of Fr. Malachi Martin, with whom I corresponded briefly. It's my belief that Rama Coomaraswamy was something on the order of an *intrinsic* exorcist. Though burdened with ill health and his struggle to preserve what remained of the Catholic Church, and far from what we would think of as a "charismatic" personality, there was a powerful spiritual light coming out of him. Our "initiation" into the Traditionalist world was the beginning of a quarter century of labor to assimilate and apply their ideas, which turned out to be inseparable from the parallel work of struggling with the dark side of the Traditionalist world, of which more below.

During this time, through my wife's influence, I was drawn into the outer circles of Russian Orthodox Spirituality in the Bay Area, though I was careful to maintain my Sufi Muslim practices and connections. Huston Smith introduced us to James Cutsinger, Eastern Orthodox (later Catholic Uniate) Perennialist and one of Frithjof Schuon's "Christian *muqaddams*." My wife Jenny, just as she had with Frithjof Schuon, discovered the books of Fr. Seraphim Rose, who had been Alan Watts' secretary in the pre-hippy era. He later converted to Orthodox Christianity and was ordained a priest under the influence of the great latter-day Orthodox saint, John Maximovitch of Shanghai and San Francisco (1896-1966), who was Archbishop of San Francisco for the Russian Orthodox Church Outside Russia, founded by pious White Russian emigrés after the Bolshevist Revolution. St. John Maximovitch was a theologian, a hierarch and a "fool for Christ"—roughly equivalent to the *malamatiyya* in the Sufi world, the "people of blame," who engage in "unorthodox" behavior so as to mortify their social vanity and that of their followers. But he was, above all, a great wonderworker, known for his many miracles of healing, clairvoyance, levitation etc., both during his life and through his intercession from the next world after his death. His relics are presently in repose in the Cathedral of the Holy Virgin Joy of All Who Sorrow on Geary Street, San Francisco, which some have described as "the most sacred site in North America." The spiritual energy of the place is truly formidable; the glass coffin housing his naturally-mummified remains is like a gate to Paradise. On one occasion I was also privileged to be admitted to his cell in St. Tikhon's Orthodox Church and allowed to sit in his chair. (His cell has no bed because he never slept.) My experience there was one of "infused recollection," what the Sufis call the state or *hal* of *Jam'*, "gathering." Sitting where the saint sat through the years of his nightly vigils, I experienced the instantaneous (though not permanent) ordering of my soul—the return from Chaos to Logos.

Under St. John Maximovitch's patronage, Seraphim Rose and others founded the St. Herman of Alaska Brotherhood, who continue to publish his writings. Fr. Seraphim's books, which show the influence of René Guénon, especially in his sections on spiritually-based social criticism, are of great value. The St. Herman of Alaska Brotherhood were later joined by the Christ the Savior Brotherhood, most of whom had been members of the New Age cult the Holy Order of Mans. These brotherhoods acted as a kind of bridge between Orthodox Christianity and the hippy Spiritual Revolution, providing the young people of that world with an alternative to the promiscuous religiosity of the counterculture. On one occasion my wife and I visited the St. Herman of Alaska Brotherhood monastery at Platina in the Northern California Coast Range, where Fr. Seraphim is buried. On another, in Santa Rosa, California, we met Fr. Herman, a colleague of Fr. Seraphim and co-founder of the Brotherhood. On that occasion he prophesied to the small group he was speaking to that "the Antichrist will come out of the Eastern Orthodox Church." (Aleksandr Dugin sees the U.S.-led "Atlanticist Hegemony" as the Antichrist. Judging from the *Book of Apocalypse*, however, the Atlanticist Hegemony, a luxurious, immoral mercantile empire controlling many nations, is actually Babylon the Great; whoever or whatever finally overturns Babylon—which in *Apocalypse* is the role assigned to the Beast—will the true Antichrist.)

Under the influence of the Traditionalists, of Seraphim Rose (to a degree), and of Islamic Sufism, I began to churn out books on Traditional Metaphysics, comparative religion, comparative eschatology, metaphysical exegesis of mythopoeia, spiritual psychology and "metaphysics and social criticism." I had always maintained my interest in the traditional revelations, side-by-side with the more suspect beliefs and influences of hippy and New Age spirituality, which included elements of the kind of Western occultism that was thoroughly investigated and criticized by Guénon. But somewhere, in my heart of hearts, I had always given the traditional revelations precedence. My pre-Vatican II Catholic education had taught me that there is such a thing as a *science* of metaphysics, and given me an instinctive feel for what a *religion* is, a revelation sent by God to man; both these lessons were of great help when I began my investigation of the non-Christian religions while still in my teens. But it was not until I plunged into the writings of the Traditionalist School that I realized that the non-traditional spiritualities were not simply of lesser value than the traditional religions, but were in many cases actually opposed to them—sometimes naively and unconsciously, sometimes consciously, actively, and with a ruthless and openly-declared determination to sweep them off the face of the earth. This realization ultimately led me to write what some have called my magnum opus, *The System of Antichrist*, which came out in 2001. In that book—besides providing a comparative eschatology based on the end-time prophesies of eight religious traditions, in a conscious attempt to "update" René Guénon's prophetic masterpiece *The Reign of Quantity and the Signs of the Times*—I also provided a detailed refutation, according to the principles of Traditional Metaphysics, of a number of New Age belief-systems, most of which I myself had accepted at one time. These included the "sorcery" of Carlos Castaneda, the channeled "Seth" material of Jane Roberts, and *A Course in Miracles*. In the process of composing *The System of Antichrist*, I "wrote myself out" of both the hippy counter-culture and the New Age.

For some spiritual temperaments, the Traditionalists/Perennialists are the best possible introduction to comparative religion and Traditional Metaphysics. Like virtually no-one else in the modern world, they have enunciated certain *necessary* principles relating to religion, its source in God, and its relationship both to the metaphysical order and to human society and history—first and foremost being the Transcendent Unity of Religions. I believe that a knowledge of these principles is indispensable if we are to correctly orient ourselves to the spiritual quality of our time: a time of enforced religious pluralism, of the weakening, adulteration and perversion of the ancient Divine revelations and wisdom traditions, as well as of the availability of unexpected channels of Grace—the sort of Grace that our apocalyptic times require, and that God has therefore mercifully provided.

The orthodoxy of the Transcendent Unity of Religions from the Muslim viewpoint—though the majority of Muslims do not in fact accept it—is confirmed by the following verses from the Holy Qur'an:

> He has revealed unto you (Muhammad) the Scripture with truth, confirming that which was (revealed) before it, even as He revealed the Torah and the Gospel. [3:3]

> Say (O Muhammad): O people of the Scripture: Come to a word that is just between us and you, that we worship none but God, and that we associate no partners with Him, and that none of us shall take others as lords besides God. [3:64]

> And do not dispute with the followers of the Book except by what is best, except those of them who act unjustly, and say: We believe in that which has been revealed to us and revealed to you, and our God and your God is One, and to Him do we submit. [29:46]

> Verily! Those who believe and those who are Jews and Christians, and Sabians, whoever believes in God and the Last Day and does righteous good deeds shall have their reward with their Lord, on them shall be no fear, nor shall they grieve. [2:62]

After Dr. Javad Nurbakhsh, Pir of the Nimatullahi Sufi Order, passed away in 2008, I felt free to search for another Sufi circle, one more congenial to my present spiritual perspective. I chose—or rather God chose for me—a Sunni *tariqa* originally based in North Africa, and took *bay'ah* with the Shaykh of that order in 2010.

As I explained in *The System of Antichrist*, the major errors of the New Age, as well as of the entire world of what René Guénon called "pseudo-initiation," as analyzed in his first two books (*The Spiritist Error* and *Theosophy: History of a Pseudo-Religion*) are as follows: Error number one is the New Age doctrine that "consciousness creates material reality"—a notion derived in part from the fact that all creative human constructions, such as a building or an organization, begin as conceptions before they become established as facts. What is routinely forgotten in this way of thinking is that buildings do not build themselves, nor do organizations organize themselves. The initial creative conception must come into a fruitful relationship with the capital, the labor, the materials, and the pre-existing circumstances that allow for the organization to be developed or the building to be built. The belief that the subjective pole—consciousness—has precedence and authority over the objective pole—material conditions—is the essence of magical thinking, just as the belief that material conditions strictly determine consciousness is the principle of the worst, most hopeless and most fatalistic forms of materialism. Traditional Metaphysics, on the other hand, makes it clear that God is the First Cause of both consciousness and conditions, which together constitute the creative polarity by which He manifests the universe. In the words of the Qur'an, *I will show them My signs on the horizons and in their own souls until they are satisfied that this is the Truth. Is it not enough for you, that I am Witness over all things?* [Q. 41:53].

The second error—or heresy, or blasphemy—is to put a human collective in the place of God, as if the pooling of the consciousness, the attention, the psychic energy of millions of human beings could somehow *add up* to the Power of God. This is not only impious, but frankly absurd. Those who rely in their prayer upon the notion that millions of others are praying at the same moment are not relying exclusively upon God—and a prayer that does not rely exclusively upon God is no prayer at all. This goes double, of course, for prayer that is offered by those millions to a heterogeneous assortment of entities, "angels," spirit-guides and incompatible conceptions of the Divinity that, on certain levels at least, necessarily contradict each other.

No human collective—even if it follows a single unified revelation—can totally submit to God; only the individual can do that. This is the reason why all world-changing revelations given by God have come only through individuals, and why no spiritual community, no matter how faithful, ever became a saint. If God, within the context of a particular religion, allows or commands the community to pray *as* a community, this is only to support each individual within that community in his or her individual submission to Him; to the degree that this principle is lost sight of, the religious community in question—the *sangha*, the *ummah*, the mystical body—becomes not a real community of the faithful but an idol that destroys true faith at its root. If many individuals appeal to God, each in his or her own divine intimacy and solitude, great and miraculous things can happen—if God wills. Your brother's faith in God can support and strengthen your own faith, but your faith in him, or the collective to which both of you belong—if it has begun to *replace* your faith in God—is worse than useless.

Insofar as Aleksandr Dugin, as a politician, considers beliefs to be useful as *organizing tools*, irrespective of their objective truth or falsehood—by which I do not mean to deny the great value of his legitimate scholarship, particularly his critique of Liberalism—and to the degree that he has placed his Russo-Eurasian *narod* in the place properly reserved for the Deity, he has involved himself with both of these errors.

From the early 1990s until the year 2013, I remained entirely outside the world of political activism. I quickly saw how almost every major political effort in today's world, whether for peace or social justice or environmental protection, had been largely co-opted by the powers that be. With lightning speed I discerned—accurately or otherwise—the essential contradictions in all the social movements I surveyed, ran them ahead in my mind's eye to their ultimate conclusions, and found them barren. The only kind of choice I saw in any sort of idealistic worldly effort was that between Gog and Magog, so I was content to sit things out till I found myself in an entirely different world, one where earthly hopes and agendas have no meaning.

Then—unexpectedly, providentially—an opportunity presented itself for me to participate in the most complete form of social/spiritual activism I had yet encountered. In 2013 my publisher James Wetmore, for whom I had done some editing in the past, showed me a proposal from one Dr. John Andrew Morrow for a book entitled *The Covenants of the Prophet Muhammad with the Christians of the World*, asking me what I thought of it. (Mr. Wetmore, through his press Sophia Perennis, has been almost single-handedly responsible for keeping René Guénon in print in English.) I took one look at that proposal and told Mr. Wetmore to jump on it as fast as he could, that Dr. Morrow's book was the most crucially relevant document to today's world that I could possibly imagine.

Dr. John Andrew Morrow, whose Muslim name is Ilyas 'Abd-al 'Alim Islam, is a Native American convert to Islam, originally from Quebec, now a naturalized citizen of the U.S. This encounter was destined to have many powerful repercussions, both in my own life and far beyond it. When first I talked by phone with Dr. Morrow I said: "Our press doesn't have a large marketing budget for your book—but I think we can make a movement out of it"—a movement that was to become the Covenants Initiative. *The Covenants of the Prophet Muhammad with the Christians of the World*, for which I was one of the editors and to which contributed a foreword, was published in October of 2013 in a combined effort of James Wetmore of Sophia Perennis and John Riess of the conservative Catholic press Angelico. Between that time and now, Dr. Morrow's book has indeed become the basis of an international peace movement in the United States, Europe and the Muslim world.

The covenants or treaties of the Prophet with various Christian communities of his time, which Dr. Morrow rediscovered in obscure monasteries, collections and books long out of print, sometimes newly translating them into English and providing powerful arguments for their validity, uniformly state that Muslims are not to attack peaceful Christian communities, rob them, stop churches from being repaired, tear down churches to build mosques, prevent their Christian wives from going to church and taking spiritual direction from Christian priests and elders, etc. On the contrary, the Prophet commands Muslims to actively aid and defend these communities "until the coming of the Hour," the end of the world. When the Algerian Sufi and freedom-fighter against the French colonialists, Emir 'Abd al-Qadir al-Jazairi, defended the Christians of Damascus, in his later years, from massacre at the hands of the Druzes, he was following the Prophet's Covenants to the letter. In response to Dr. Morrow's resurrection of these documents I conceived of an initiative—the Covenants Initiative—which invites Muslims to subscribe to the theory that the Covenants of the Prophet are legally binding upon them today. I need to make clear at this point that my connection with this movement has in no way been dictated by my Sufi order, nor am I at all inclined to preach it to them; I am acting strictly as an individual. Yet insofar as the Sufis practice the most radical form of submission to God imaginable—submission to the point of self-annihilation—then, if involvement with this movement is indeed God's Will for me, it must be considered as one of the fruits of Sufism in my life.

In *The System of Antichrist* I had called for a "united front ecumenism" of the world religions against three things: non-traditional religious fanaticism (fundamentalist extremism), false psychic religion (Guénon's "Pseudo-Initiation" and "Counter-Initiation"), and militant secularism. I presented this form of interfaith action as the proper outer or exoteric expression of the Transcendent Unity of Religions, as opposed to "promiscuous Liberal ecumenism," whose ultimate goal is the dissolution of all the faiths in some kind of One World Church (For a detailed definition of the Transcendent Unity of Religions, see pp. 78–81). United Front Ecumenism exerts no pressure on the religions to syncretize their doctrines with a view toward worldly unification. Instead, it posits their *transcendent* unity by demonstrating how the forces of religious fanaticism, psychic pseudo-religion and militant secularism have declared war on all the world religions, thereby demonstrating that these religions represent a common threat in the eyes of those forces, and consequently that all the true religions must spring from a single Source. This is not to say that there can't be a legitimate form of "esoteric ecumenism" (Frithjof Schuon's term) which discerns the metaphysical First Principles that all revealed religions and wisdom traditions hold in common, only that the *necessary plurality* of these revelations and traditions is itself one of those First Principles. I never believed that I would live to see anything resembling a true united front ecumenism, so I just described what I thought it would look like and left it at that. Then, twelve years later, the perfect incarnation of united front ecumenism, the Covenants Initiative, simply fell into my lap, and then went on to become an international movement. As the poet William Butler Yeats put it, "In dreams begin responsibilities."

The Poison of Ideology

[A slightly different version of this section appeared on the Geopolitica website out of Russia (www.geopolitica.ru), as well as on You Tube, in September of 2017]

One of the most useful and significant things about the Covenants of the Prophet Muhammad is that, while they are of great social use and import, they are entirely free from secular political ideology. Since they are in fact social documents authored under Divine inspiration by the last Prophet of this *manvantara*, they represent a seamless union of spirituality, morality and strategic intelligence; in them, as in few other documents dealing with political theory and practice, the Means and the End are one.

Speaking as a Muslim who also accepts the validity of the Christian revelation, I can define American Liberalism as the secularization of Christian Mercy, and American Conservatism as the secularization of Christian Justice and Morality. And the problem with both Liberalism and Conservatism is, precisely, *secularization*, which is nothing less than an implicit or outright atheism that acts to drive an unholy and unnatural wedge between Mercy and Justice. In Christianity—that is, in God—Mercy and Justice are never and can never be separated. The Rulers of the Darkness of This World, however, have done their best to alienate Mercy and Justice from each other and set them at war. They have contrived false and counterfeit forms of them, perverting them both and thereby making both of them hateful to us.

Extreme and authoritarian Liberalism, in an act of unparalleled viciousness, has transformed Mercy into what Dr. Morrow calls "compulsory immorality," into the insidious vice of *permissiveness*—a cruel permissiveness that loves corruption and targets anyone who struggles to live a life of purity and decency, doing all it can to drive such conscientious people to despair, not simply by giving them no help in their struggles but by portraying their very love of virtue as a kind of self-loathing, and their desire to proclaim that love, and see it take root and grow and spread its loveliness throughout human society, as bigotry and hate. It has imposed a loathsome regime of "political correctness," a system which has resulted in an ideologically enslaved population who believe that anyone who does not agree with their own brand of Liberal extremism must be a Nazi or a Klansman or a Russian agent, as well as making them mortally afraid, not only of even the most moderate conservatives, but finally even of their own *thoughts*, thereby going a long way toward destroying freedom of speech in this country by defining certain opinions, in the terminology of George Orwell's *1984*, as *thoughtcrime*. Likewise its distrust of traditional moral values has expressed itself as an attack on Christianity, leading to a serious erosion of freedom of religion as well. Liberals have exploited crucial and necessary efforts like environmental protection, the social advancement of women, and the struggles for survival of often-disadvantaged groups such as Blacks or Gays or Muslim and/or Latino immigrants, into unholy Liberal causes, causes which they then cynically employ to weaken the constitutional rule of law and attack and undermine their political opponents, as well as to impose extreme and destructive social experiments upon an initially unwilling, but often finally beaten and compliant, American public. In so doing they have built up a backlog of racial and sexual hatred that the extreme Conservatives have no qualms about exploiting openly. And while pretending to still be in some sense "Leftists," they have suppressed nearly all viable economic and class analysis, replacing it by "ethnic studies," "gender studies" and a socially engineered racial conflict and hatred between the sexes that has poisoned this society from sea to shining sea. By this they have made Mercy itself hateful to many—and there is no greater crime than this.

Extreme and reactionary Conservatism, drawing partly on its own inherent tendencies and partly on a growing and widespread reaction against the excesses of Liberalism, has transformed the majestic virtue of Justice, Justice which is nothing less than *militant Mercy*, into a justification for tyranny and oppression, a code-word whose actual meaning and effect is to throw all support to the economic "1 percent" who have looted this country root and branch, destroyed the middle class, further impoverished the poor, made widespread unemployment and underemployment—cleverly concealed behind twisted and lying statistics—into the new normal, and hypocritically praised family values while economically attacking and destroying actual families. In the name of Justice and Morality they have turned the love of virtue into a license to hate and oppress anyone who does not live up to their own often ill-conceived and blindly imposed "moral" standards, recommending thrift and diligence to those who have spent years looking for a job and failed, recommending a stiff upper lip and decreased reliance on opiates to those who are in chronic pain and lack the resources to access more sophisticated treatments—standards they are zealous in imposing on others but often lax in applying to themselves, doing battle with the speck of dust in their neighbor's eye while ignoring the two-by-four in their own. They have made war on the poor, denying them health care by shrinking Medicaid, denying food stamps to the chronically malnourished, while doing all they can to give free rein the predatory economic forces that have brought us the savings-and-loan scandal, the Enron scandal, the sub-prime mortgage scandal, the Great Recession that has made this once rich and hopeful country into a nation of paupers, of old people who can never retire and young people who see no future but to drown themselves in the abyss of cyberspace while being a burden to their parents, who can never make marriages or families, who can never become adults! And their hatred of the poor is only equaled by their hatred of the environment, of the very Earth that sustains us all—*even them.* In so doing they have transformed the divine virtue of Justice which gives to everyone his or her rightful portion into an armed guard standing watch at the iron gate of the City of Robbery and Usury, making sure that the meek never will inherit the earth, that only the money-changers, those with the blood of the poor and defenseless still hot on their hands, will be granted admittance.

The terminal corruption of both Liberalism and Conservatism was clearly revealed, during the 2016 presidential election, by two sterling examples: Hillary Clinton and Donald Trump—Clinton, who openly despises the white working class and whose impending though finally derailed election, according to the Defcon website, brought the estimated danger of nuclear war with Russia to its highest level since the Cuban Missile Crisis—and Trump, who—though I applaud his powerful blows against ISIS, his apparently sincere desire to wipe them off the face of the earth—wants to cut Medicaid, deny food stamps to the poorest of the poor, axe environmental protection laws and privatize the national parks, and who—though his stated aim of rationalizing immigration policy to protect the U.S. from foreign terrorists makes a degree of sense, as long as it targets *terrorists* and not just Muslims—continues to offer inflammatory statements, without retracting them, that many have translated as "open season on immigrants and Muslims," leading to a massive increase in hate crimes. Furthermore, as of this writing, the Donald Trump who, when newly-elected and despite his massive corruption, nonetheless represented a thin crack in the carapace of the Deep State, has now apparently been captured by Israel and the Neo-Cons. After declaring Jerusalem Israel's capital, bombing Syria, preparing for war with Iran and betraying the base that elected him, he has shows all signs of having outlived his usefulness.

And behind both Liberalism and Conservatism lies the Deep State, the cadres of the Global Elites, who believe in nothing whatsoever, only in themselves and in the Satanic principle they worship, and who, from their position of inverted, Luciferian transcendence, can use either Liberal or Conservative ideology as they so choose—cynically, indifferently, with equal force, equal cruelty and equal and conspicuous success, according to which of these two hopeless alternatives the American people happen to have placed their feeble hopes in during a particular decade, a particular presidential administration, a particular year, in order to advance their transformation of this planet into a living hell. That's why I thank the living God every day that He has led me to the noble science of metaphysics—and, in so doing, *freed me from ideology.*

If I could accept with any degree of certainty that Aleksandr Dugin actually believes in God, in the sense that he takes the spiritual life seriously, and understands that if it is not placed above everything else then it does not effectively exist, I would remind him that there is no Mercy without Justice and Morality, that whoever believes in the contradiction of an *unjust Mercy* will be sorely punished by being transformed into a *Liberal.* Likewise there is no Justice without Mercy; whoever believes in the possibility of a *merciless Justice* as will be severely chastised by being turned into a *Conservative.* What has Almighty God to do with flimsy human categories like Liberalism or Conservatism, the Left or the Right? God is of neither the East nor the West: He is the Inner, the Outer, the End, the Beginning, the Highest of all, the Deepest of all, the Center of all, the Total Field—*Light upon Light.* To whom or what else should we turn to learn what Mercy is, and what Justice is, and how to enact them, and where to find the power to enact them? There is much good in *liberality,* in generosity, in compassion, in catholicity of taste, in breadth of sympathy—but *Liberalism* is a travesty. Likewise there is much good in tradition, in holding to the right, in militantly protecting and defending the good, the true and the beautiful—but *Conservatism* is a curse. God is far above such weak and shameful human attempts to do His work for Him. And what is God? To the Christian, as well as in the view of my own Sufi Way, God is Love: Love Who is both the sweetest of Mercies and the most relentless hand of Justice in a single, incandescent, thunderous, face of Truth. By whatever Name He may be known, His is the standard I bear. So if Aleksandr Dugin really wants to do Justice to Christos Pantokrator and his Holy Orthodox Church, and thereby find Mercy in them, then let him take care that he never espouses a principle or gives support to a policy that violates either the Justice, or the Mercy, of Love: because if he does, he will have joined the army of the enemies of Love, and thereby made Love Himself *his* enemy—that being a fate more terrible than human words can express.

Narod

In *Eurasian Mission* Aleksandr Dugin says—and at this point I fully agree with him—"I am proud to be Russian exactly as Americans, Africans, Arabs, or Chinese are proud to be what they are. It is our right and our dignity to affirm our identity, not in opposition to each other but such as it is: without resentment against others or feelings of self-pity"—which shouldn't blind us to the fact that he expresses plenty of resentment against America in other places! He further advises us: "One should seek to become a concrete part of the society in which one lives, and follow the tradition that prevails there. . . . What is important is to have roots." My response to this call is as follows:

As I have already stated, I have opposed the policies of American imperialism for all of my adult life. I have done so, however, not as the hired or aspiring agent of a foreign power, but as a citizen of the United States, a native-born American, motivated not by a hatred for my country but by a sense of violated patriotism—a patriotism that seems strangely absent today from both the Alt Right and the Alt Left. Over the years of my life I have seen my nation betrayed by a criminal conspiracy, transformed from a widely-admired "land of liberty" into a universally-hated empire. My family has been in North America since the 1600's—and also incomparably longer. I am a distant relative of Paul Revere; I am also a more direct descendant of Pocahontas, daughter of Powhatan, high chief of the Algonquin Confederacy of tidewater Virginia. I will stand against the foreign policy of Imperial America to my dying breath, but I will never give aid and comfort to any forces, foreign or domestic, populist or ruling-class, whose goal is to destroy my nation. She has given me such a life as I have been able to lead, and so enabled me to do my work; her ground holds the bones of my ancestors. I will not take up arms against her for the same reason that Robert E. Lee defended Virginia: not because his cause was just, seeing that slavery can never be justified, any more than imperialism can, but simply in the name of his debt to an ancestral love of his land—even though, as the Prophet Muhammad said, earthly life is no more than a brief moment's rest under a shady tree before the caravan passes on. If this be patriotism, make the most of it.

In any case, I still have enough loyalty to my country to make it impossible for me to generate warm and fuzzy feelings—or warm and fuzzy thinking—about such statements by Aleksandr Dugin as the following, from *Foundations of Geopolitics* [1997]:

> All levels of geopolitical pressure must be activated simultaneously. . . . It is especially important to introduce geopolitical disorder into internal American activity, encouraging all kinds of separatism and ethnic, racial and social conflicts, actively supporting all dissident movements—extremist, racist and sectarian groups, thus destabilizing internal political processes in the U.S. It would also make sense to simultaneously support isolationist tendencies in American politics.

The implementation of such policies within the U.S., policies which certainly seem to be well-reflected in our contemporary social reality, may in fact be funded—at least in part—by Konstantin Malofeyev, the oligarch who, according to the Romanian researcher who calls himself "Freedom Alternative," bankrolls Alexandr Dugin (see *Chapter Three* footnote 5). The connection between Dugin and Malofeyev and its possible influence on American society and politics should be exhaustively researched. And it goes without saying that Dugin's eloquent denunciations of "oligarchy," some of which I quote with glowing approval in this book, should be taken with a large grain of salt in view the "strange bedfellows" he apparently spends his nights with. But the Dugin Plan for the United States would be much less effective if it were not for its inverted, Left-wing mirror-image, the Soros Plan—which, through such groups as the hired agitators of Antifa, would seem to be just what Dugin called for in 1997. Are our present social conflicts nothing but shadows cast by some hidden, titanic struggle between global oligarchs? Transnational corporations now have their own private armies and intelligence services. . . . And could such oligarchs also be *working together* on some levels, at least at certain times and for certain purposes? These are easy questions to ask, but hard ones to answer.

In any case, having pledged my allegiance to America—my homeland on *pitri-yana*, the Way of the Fathers—I must now turn my attention to my homeland on *deva-yana*, the Way of the Gods—to the Holy Land of the Primordial Tradition, the land that some call Hyperborea, where the Tree of Revelation grows, whose limbs are the great God-given faiths. My own limb is Islam; my own branch is *tasawwuf*. Having paid my debt to my Ancestors, this is the higher ground on which I now propose to await the rise of al-Mahdi, the descent of the Prophet Jesus, and the coming of the Hour.

1

Gog and Magog *vs.*
the Covenants of the Prophet

A Consideration of the
Geopolitics of Aleksandr Dugin in
Light of the Cosmology of René Guénon

*[A slightly shorter version of this chapter appeared
on the Katehon website, www.Katehon.ru, in 2017]*

ALEKSANDR DUGIN places the geopolitical conflict between the American Empire, which he names "Atlantis", and Greater Russia, which he calls "Eurasia," in an eschatological context, partly according to René Guénon's doctrine of cyclical time from *The Reign of Quantity and the Signs of the Times, Traditional Forms and Cosmic Cycles*, and other works. But since Dugin radically departs from this doctrine even as he invokes it, I have attempted to flesh out Guénon's idea of cyclical history so as to better contrast it with Dugin's, as well as introducing and expanding upon the spiritual and socio-political forces that Guénon saw operating at the end of the present cycle. From my particular vantage point, one clear sign of the action of these forces is the recent re-appearance, after long obscurity, of the Covenants of the Prophet Muhammad with the Peoples of the Book, a manifestation which I have been privileged to serve.

The Landscape of Apocalypse

Anyone who is familiar with the eschatological doctrines of the major world religions, and who accepts their validity—though not necessarily their direct, literal, detailed applicability to historical conditions—must conclude that we are now living through the "latter days" of the present cycle. And one of the hallmarks of the latter days is a manifestation of the dark side of the *dvandvas*, the Sanskrit word for the "pairs of opposites"—the rise of titanic social forces in quasi-absolute polarization, forces which seem to represent true alternative visions of the human possibility, but which in reality are nothing more than opposing faces of the same decadence, the same "degeneration of the cosmic environment," working together in secret collusion to divert the collective attention of the human race from the Reality and the Will of God.

Perhaps the most profound analysis we possess of the cosmological forces operating in the "end times" of a particular cycle-of-manifestation, forces which have their inevitable socio-political reflections, is the one presented by René Guénon in his prophetic masterpiece *The Reign of Quantity*. Guénon adopted the Hindu conception of the *manvantara*, the cycle of four *yugas* or world-ages in descending order of stability and integrity, ending with the *Kali-yuga* we presently inhabit, which itself ends in the dissolution of the cycle. The four *yugas* are roughly equivalent to the four ages in the Greco-Roman cosmo-conception: the Golden, the Silver, the Bronze and the Iron. In the Satya-yuga or Golden Age, space—simultaneity, or relative (aeonian) eternity—predominates over time. In the succeeding *yugas* time becomes more dominant, moving from a cyclical to a linear manifestation, until, in the *Kali-yuga*, form is eroded and finally dissolved in an ever-accelerating flow of linear time, until the arrival of the apocalypse, when space finally re-asserts itself and a new *manvantara* begins. Guénon brilliantly supplemented the Hindu conception of the *manvantara* with the Aristotelian/Thomistic distinction between Essence and Substance, or Form and Matter. The Golden Age is the age of Essence or Quality, the *Kali-yuga* that of Substance or Quantity, and thus of materialism; Thomas Aquinas described the *materia secunda*, the most fundamental form of matter discernible in manifest (not principial) existence, as *materia signata quantitate*, "matter designated by quantity." The present belief of "scientistic" humanity that the only meaningful statements we can make about anything whatever are quantitative measurements is a sign of the dominance of the Substantial Pole, as is the present socio-philosophical obsession to debunk what is called "essentialism," defined as the supposedly erroneous belief that things, persons and situations possess intrinsic qualities. The Pole of Essence is the archetype of the Masculine Principle; though in itself it transcends hierarchy, it is the origin of the hierarchical conception of being and the hierarchical organization of society. Under the regime of Substance, however—the archetype of the Feminine Principle—vertical hierarchy is collapsed by a growing horizontal or "leveling" tendency, although an "absolute" horizontality (like an absolute verticality) can never be reached on the plane of cosmic manifestation.

Guénon also had something to say, notably in his book *Traditional Forms and Cosmic Cycles*, about the earlier phases of the present *manvantara*, particular those represented by the myths, or memories, of Hyperborea, the realm of the "North," and Atlantis, the land of the "West." Hyperborea occupied a higher and more integrated world-age than that of Atlantis, which—though it pre-dated the *Kali-yuga*—sowed the seeds of the present global degeneration of humanity, our collective will to deny the Spirit and our consequent capitulation to the dissolutionary forces of time and matter. (Interestingly enough, the same distinction between a Hyperborean northern-oriented tendency and an Atlantean western-oriented one is found in the teachings of Black Elk, holy man of the Oglala Lakota [see **Black Elk Speaks** by John G. Neihardt, 1932, and **Black Elk: Holy Man of the Oglala** by Michael F. Steltenkamp, 1997]. According to the Lakota cosmo-conception, the north-south path is "the Good Red Road" and the east-west path "the Black Road of Difficulty"; the place where these two roads cross—as they do at any point on the earth's surface—is *wakan*, holy.)

An inescapable aspect of the latter days is the near-complete severance of human and social realities from their eternal archetypes—which emphatically does *not* mean that these archetypes thereby disappear as the fundamental causal factors in the unfolding of history, only that they now operate in a secret, inverted and therefore *ironic* manner, exhibiting the quality of dark, fatal justice that the classical Greeks personified as Nemesis and the Furies. In the words of the Qur'an, *Lo! Allah sendeth whom He will astray, and guideth unto Himself all who turn (unto Him)* [13:27], and *Allah is the best of plotters* [8:29].

Higher orders of reality normally project themselves onto lower planes of being by means of polarity: "In the beginning, God created the heavens and the earth" [Genesis 1:1]; on the level of human life, this metaphysical principle manifests as sexual reproduction: "male and female created He them" [Genesis 5:2]. However, in the concluding phases of a particular cycle of manifestation, the meaning of polarity is inverted. Polarity becomes polarization. The weakening of the bond of communication between earthly human realities and their celestial archetypes results in various bifurcations based not on fertile polarity, but on the barren conflict which becomes inevitable when various contingent conditions falsely arrogate to themselves the prerogatives of the Absolute—a necessary result of the fact that the collective intuition of God, the only real and transcendent Absolute, is eclipsed. At the same time a collective obsession is born to annihilate all polarities, to achieve something like an earthly, material counterfeit of the Unity of God by eroding, denying, suppressing, and finally destroying all the true and necessary distinctions that make human life possible, including gender. The more radical and conflictive the false polarizations operating in the latter days become, the more insistent is the call to do away with all distinctions so as to pacify these titanic conflicts—yet the denial of all sexual, cultural, ethnic and religious distinctions only further inflames and infuriates those forces which would falsely absolutize these distinctions, and set them at war. Thus an unholy alliance of false polarity and (in Guénon's phrase) inverted hierarchy—the "Right"—and false unity and equality—the "Left"—brings the cycle of manifestation to a close.

In the *Book of Apocalypse*, this polarization between and a false, imposed unity and various falsely absolutized distinctions is called "Gog and Magog"—in the Qur'an, "Yajuj and Majuj." According to Apocalypse 20:7–8, "when the thousand years are expired [the millennium during which the devil is bound, identified by Eastern Orthodox theologians as the church age], Satan shall be loosed out of his prison, and shall go out to deceive the nations which are in the four quarters of the earth, Gog and Magog, to gather them together to battle: the number of whom is as the sand of the sea." According to *The Apocalypse of St. John: An Orthodox Commentary* by Archbishop Averky of Jordanville, the meaning of *Gog* in Hebrew is "a gathering" or "one who gathers," and of *Magog* "an exaltation" or "one who exalts." "Exaltation" suggests the idea of transcendence as *opposed* to unity, "gathering" the idea of unity as *opposed* to transcendence. The implication, here, is that one of the deepest deceptions of Antichrist in the last days of the cycle will be to set these two integral aspects of the Absolute in opposition to each other in the collective mind, and on a global scale, in "the four quarters of the earth." As for the economic and political expression of this barren satanic polarity, the false cohesion of left-wing tyranny, as well as today's global capitalism, would fall under Gog, while both the false hierarchicalism of right-wing tyranny and the violent absolutism of the various "tribal" separatist movements opposed to globalism, both ethnic and religious, would come under Magog. In terms of religion, those Liberal, historicist, evolutionist, quasi-materialist and crypto-Pagan theologies which emphasize God's immanence as opposed to His transcendence are part of Gog, while those reactionary theologies which exalt transcendence over immanence, look on the material world as a vale of tears, denigrate the human body, and view the destruction of nature with indifference if not secret approval, since the best we can hope for is to get it all over with, are part of Magog. The conflict between the two is precisely the satanic counterfeit of the true eschatological conflict described in Apocalypse 19:11–20, between the King of Kings and Lord of Lords, and the Beast with his false prophet. Those who can be lured to fight in a counterfeit war between elements which ought to be reconciled, because they are essentially parts of the same reality as seen in a distorting mirror, will miss their call to fight in the true war between forces which neither should nor can be reconciled: those of the Truth and those of the Lie. (Globalism, insofar as it sets the stage for the emergence of Guénon's "inverted hierarchy," also contains the seed of Magog, while tribalism, as the common inheritance of all who are excluded from the global elite, holds the seed of Gog: in the latter days, no party or class or sector can long retain its ideological stability; the "rate of contradiction" approaches the speed of light.)

Atlantis and Hyperborea

According to legend, Hyperborea, the "Land Behind the North Wind," the original homeland of the human race, was a land of eternal spring—a notion that was possibly suggested by early explorers' tales of the arctic summer, during whose "white nights" the sun never sets; this "never-setting sun" was most probably the origin of the Hyperborean Apollo, one of whose epithets is *Sol Invictus*, "The Sun Unconquered." Geology, however, shows us no sunken continent beneath the Arctic Ocean, which has led some to speculate that the North Pole once passed through Greenland, or some other point on the terrestrial globe. Yet a frozen wasteland, even if there were solid earth beneath it, is not a very hopeful candidate for the cradle of the human race—at least in terrestrial terms. It is much more likely that Hyperborea refers to a *spiritual orientation* than to a geographical area. The Siberian shamans, the traditional Chinese, the Zoroastrians, the Sabaeans, and certain esoteric groups within Islam consider the North, not the East, or the West (as with the Greeks and the Irish, at least on one level) to be their sacred point of orientation (or rather "boreation"). "Hyperboreans," then, are those who point to the Pole as their *celestial* homeland. Dante Alighieri, in his ***Divina Commedia***, reveals himself to be a Hyperborean in this sense. *Arktos,* the Greek word for "bear," is the origin of our word *Arctic,* which is why the constellations circling the North Pole and called the Bears—and in the last cantos of Dante's ***Purgatorio***, the Great and Little Bears appear above Dante's *Arcadian* Earthly Paradise at the summit of Mount Purgatory—which, according to earlier cantos, is supposed to be in the southern hemisphere! (Hyperborea, however, may also have an historical, geographical significance, since it could designate an actual northern culture-area dominated by shamanism, comprising Siberia and possibly Finland, and including, along with various other Arctic and North American peoples, the bear-worshipping Ainu of the Japanese northern island of Hokkaido.)

As for Atlantis, whose historical reality is somewhat better attested than that of Hyperborea, the notion of a sunken continent in the Atlantic Ocean has no more hard geological evidence backing it up than the idea of a historical, geological Hyperborea. The same cannot be said, however, for the possibility of a *Mediterranean* Atlantis. A.G. Galanopoulos and E. Bacon in ***Atlantis: The Truth behind the Legend*** (1969), J.V. Luce, in ***The End of Atlantis: New Light on an Old Legend*** (1969), and Charles Pellegrino, in *Unearthing Atlantis* (1991), theorize that Atlantis was actually the island of Thera or Santorini, situated west of the Mediterranean coast of the Holy Land, Thera being directly north of Crete. It is a volcanic island which, some time between 1450 and 1500 BC (though some date the event c. 1628) violently exploded when its erupting volcano split at the side, allowing an inrush of sea water. The resulting explosion was several times larger than that of Krakatoa, the most powerful volcanic event in recorded history, which was also destroyed in a steam explosion. This cataclysm devastated the Mediterranean coasts, sent a towering tsunami crashing over the island of Crete, darkened the sun with volcanic ash, and effectively destroyed the matriarchal Minoan maritime civilization. It began a series of migrations and wars, one of which was the invasion of the Greek peninsula by the patriarchal Doric tribes, the ancestors of the "classical" Greeks. Some scholars also theorize that the ten plagues (or some of them) which preceded the exodus of the Hebrews from Egypt were actually volcanic in origin: the hail mixed with fire, the turning of the Nile to blood along with the death of all the fish, the darkness which covered the land, can all be put down to the effects of volcanic cinders and ash. And the parting of the Red Sea, which later closed over the Pharaoh's army, suggests the arrival of a tsunami, during which the sea-level first sinks and then catastrophically rises; such a tsunami would have been possible (or rather inevitable) if—as some think—Sinai was at that time a strait rather than an isthmus; it would certainly have been more feasible for the Children of Israel to have a crossed a narrow strait rather than the Red Sea as we know it today. And the "pillar of cloud by day and pillar of fire by night" that the Hebrews followed through the wilderness is a fair description of a rising volcanic plume.

Our sources for the Atlantis legend are the *Critias* and *Timaeus* of Plato, who recounts a history of the lost island supposedly based on an account that Solon heard from the priests of Egypt. Plato's description of Atlantis as an island of concentric rings of land and water corresponds in some ways to the geology of Thera; and the legend that Atlantis was situated beyond The Pillars of Hercules—the Straits of Gibraltar—is possibly explained by the fact that Thera is in actually west of another formation, in the eastern Mediterranean, which is also named The Pillars of Hercules.

Nonetheless there are certain scholars who make a very good case for the historical existence of a *Western* Atlantis—simply by identifying Atlantis with North America, or the Americas as a whole. The Aztecs, we should remember, who are thought to have invaded and conquered the Toltec Empire of Mexico from a point of origin somewhere in the territory now claimed by the United States, named their former homeland as *Aztlán*—a word close enough to *Atlantis* to make one's hair stand on end. The legendary founder of Atlantis was the titan Atlas; both these words begin with *atl*—the Nahuatl word for "water."

So according to this theory, I am in Atlantis now. But the continent I inhabit is certainly not sunken—unless we admit that it is sunk in materialism, overwhelmed (in William Blake's words) by "the sea of Space and Time." So—unless Atlantis was Thera—whence comes the legend of the *lost* Atlantis, perhaps symbolized in Greek legend by the runner Atalanta, the woman no man could catch? A sunken continent may legitimately be compared to a woman who has forever denied her lovers any possible access to her—and what man can outrace the setting Sun? The men who raced Atalanta to win her hand, and lost, also lost their lives—this being the precise quality of the western "Atlantean" ethos, the land of "futurism," where (in Guénon's conception from *The Reign of Quantity*) time accelerates and form is destroyed. And in line with Guénon's assertion that Hyperborean terms were later applied to Atlantis, one of the epithets of Atalanta is *Arcadian*. When she was finally outraced by her future husband Hippomenes, it was through the agency of three *golden apples* given him by Aphrodite from her own temple precincts in Cyprus, the last of which Atalanta stooped to pick up when Hippomenes threw it, thus breaking her stride. Golden apples immediately suggest the apples of the Hesperides, the Western Isles—and though the island of Cyprus is in the eastern Mediterranean, it is certainly west of the continental Near East.

But what of the *American* Atlantis hypothesized above? Ivar Zapp and George Erikson, authors of *Atlantis in America* (1998), maintain that "Atlantis" sank beneath the waves when, around 12,000 years ago, sea levels abruptly rose due to melting polar ice, thus inundating coastal America. The authors give evidence to support their contention that before that time America was host to an advanced maritime civilization capable of crossing the Atlantic. This theory is further supported by the fact that certain Metis societies (inter-tribal medicine societies) among the Native Americans of North America claim that they were in contact with Europe in ancient times. Travel across the Atlantic was dangerous; few probably attempted it, but some likely did. Regular trade routes might or might not have been established, but holders and seekers of spiritual lore and technical expertise might well have attempted the journey, given that knowledge is weightless, and takes up no space.

Both the historical reality of Atlantis and the possibility that the Americas were populated (or depopulated) by sea can be found in the legends of the Hopi tribe of the North American Southwest. According to their myth of the cycle-of-manifestation, which has much in common with the analogous myths of other peoples, including the Hindus and the Greco-Romans, the Hopis emerged into the present "fourth world," Tuwaqachi, from the "third world" known as Kuskurza, which is related to the mineral *palasiva*, copper—a major constituent of bronze. So apparently Kuskurza (in Greco-Roman mythological terms) is the Bronze Age. In Kuskurza the people overpopulate and use their reproductive power for evil—copper being identified, in traditional symbolism, with Venus, the erotic principle. They develop a high technology, live in cities, and fly on shields covered with hide known as *patuwvotas*—strikingly similar to the *vimanas* described in the Hindu *Puranas*—which they use as engines of war. Kuskurza, like Atlantis, is destroyed by water; whole continents sink beneath the waves.

As the third world is about to end, Spider Woman—a figure who is something like the *shakti* or *shekhina* of Sotuknang, the Demiurge, the first created being, the active energy of Taiowa the Creator—tells the people to get inside of hollow reeds to escape from the flood. She leads them in a migration over water, searching for the fourth world. (These floating reeds remind one of the Egyptian reed boat that Thor Heyerdahl used to cross the Atlantic in his Ra Expedition, thus proving that the Atlantic could have been crossed in archaic times, even before the development of more advanced vessels like the Phoenician trireme.)

After stopping at a continent which was not their true destination, they arrive at the fourth world, called Tuwaqachi, the World Complete, where life is hard. This is the world we presently occupy. The mineral associated with the fourth world is the "mixed mineral" *sikyapala*, analogous to the iron mixed with clay which composed the feet of the statue dreamt of by King Nebuchadnezzar in the *Book of Daniel*—a figure with head of gold, chest and arms of silver, belly and loins of bronze and legs of iron, which is sometimes understood as emblematic of the four world ages. Its "feet of clay" represent of the instability of the cosmic environment hidden under outward strength and inflexibility of iron. Tuwaqachi, then, would seem to be the Iron Age. The spiritual guardian of Tuwaqachi is Masaw, who was also the ruler of Kuskurza, the third "Atlantean" world, and who brought it to an end through his corruption. He is here because Taiowa decided to give him a second chance—a chance he seems to have wasted. The Hopi myth clearly implies that this world too will be destroyed by the abuse of reproductive power and high technology.

But can the Mediterranean and American Atlantises in any way be reconciled? Some legends of Atlantis speak of two Atlantises, an earlier and a later one. Zapp and Erikson's submerged coastal America, then, might correspond to the earlier Atlantis, perhaps also recalled by the legend of Noah's flood, and Thera to the later one, which might possibly be the origin of certain events recounted in *Exodus*. After the 900 years separating Plato from the most common date given for the destruction of the Greek island, certain legendary material about the earlier Atlantis could well have become attached to the story of the destruction of the later one; the characterization "island continent" may in fact be the product of a confusion between the submergence of part of a continent and the destruction of an island. (Plato's date for the sinking of Atlantis as 900 years before his time could be explained by a misplaced decimal point, the decimal number system having emerged in India some time between 1500 and 500 B.C.)

The submergence of coastal America would have been either gradual or cataclysmic. A slow melt of polar ice would not have destroyed the Atlantean civilization—unless it forced the coast-dwellers back into an interior occupied by hostile and militarily superior nations. They would always have had a coast, and time to move any cities inland. A fast melt would correspond more closely to the Atlantis legend as we know it. And if trans-Atlantic trade, however sporadic, had existed, its sudden disappearance would indeed have suggested—and actually represented—the destruction of a world, especially if the traders hailed from a civilization that was either spiritually higher or technologically more advanced than was the Old World in that age.

We are used to seeing the Mediterranean largely as a "closed sea" until the Vikings, and later the Renaissance explorers, opened the mind of Europe to the Atlantic and the New World. But the maritime technology that would have allowed Europeans to cross the Atlantic had been available since the Roman Empire, and even before that. Why (outside of the Roman colonization of Britain) was it never used? It is possible to speculate that the shock of the submergence of coastal America by melting ice, which would certainly have also submerged much of the coast of the Mediterranean, as well as the lands called *Lyonesse* in British legend—followed in later centuries by the destruction of Thera, which liquidated in one stroke the most advanced maritime civilization the Old World had produced up to that time—created a sort of collective taboo in the European psyche against sea-travel beyond the pillars of Hercules, and possibly against expansive maritime imperialism in general, which would have been viewed as actions likely to anger the gods. This taboo was effectively broken by the Vikings, relative newcomers in Western Europe, whose historical memory stretched back not to the archaic civilizations of the Mediterranean and Near East, but towards the heartlands of Asia—making them, in Dugin's terms, something like "Atlantean rebels against Hyperborea," partisans of a development that might in some way have been related to the ancient revolt of the *kshatriya* or warrior caste against the priestly *brahmin* caste spoken of by René Guénon, which he saw signs of in the Genesis account of the Tower of Babel. (And if Aleksandr Dugin would like to address the historical fact that Russia was founded by an "Atlantean" people, the Varangians, who were essentially Vikings, I'd be interested to hear what he has to say.) Furthermore, the opening of the Atlantic and the New World to exploration during the Renaissance may have awakened long-buried memories of the Western Atlantis in the form of fantastic and legendary goals sought by some of the explorers and conquistadores: the Seven Cities of Cibola, and especially the Fountain of Youth, which clearly corresponds to the fountain of the water of life—or the water of creative manifestation—situated by Dante at the summit of Mount Purgatory, in the Terrestrial Paradise. (The taboo against "westering" appears in the "Atlantean" Canto 26 of Dante's *Inferno*.)

As for the possibility of an "Atlantean" civilization of the Old World which was also inundated, like the American one, by rising sea levels, a number of sunken cities have recently been discovered off the coasts of Spain and the western part of North Africa, most of them beyond the Pillars of Hercules; see *Ice Age Civilizations* by James Nienhuis. Some scholars see these cities as the origin of the Old Testament "Peoples of the Sea," who might have become the Phoenicians and/or the Philistines. As the sea rose they were forced to abandon their cities, board their ships, and begin raiding the coasts of the Mediterranean, looking for a new homeland on higher ground. The capital city of Phoenicia, Sidon, is identified by some with the Sidon son of Canaan who appears in the *Book of Exodus*; one possible form of "Father Sidon" in the Canaanite tongue would be "Po Sidon," immediately suggesting the Greek sea-god Poseidon— obviously a good candidate for the chief god of the Peoples of the Sea. The need on the part of an ancient maritime civilization of the Mediterranean and Atlantic coasts to resort to piracy in order to survive rising sea levels may in fact explain the notion of the "rapacious" Atlanteans whom Aleksandr Dugin so conveniently identifies with the military and economic colonialism of Britain and America. For the same reason Dugin also associates Carthage, a colony of Phoenicia, itself possibly a colony of Atlantis, with the "Atlanteans" of today, taking Cato the Elder's famous *Carthago delenda est*—"Carthage must be destroyed"—as the motto for his *Geopolitica* website.

The Atlantis and Hyperborea of Aleksandr Dugin

If I understand him correctly, Aleksandr Dugin divides the world geopolitically between the Eurasian Hyperborean Heartlanders—hierarchical and "Traditional" in René Guénon's sense—and the Liberal, anti-Traditional Atlanteans, who might well be termed "the peoples of the sea"—the name the Israelites applied to the Philistines—and who seem to be centered in Britain and America. To posit these two collectives as representing an archetypal, cosmic opposition is entirely justified, in my opinion, and might be highly enlightening if done in the right way. American technocratic futurist Buckminster Fuller, for example, described the modern world as having been founded by "Renaissance pirates." Yet Dugin's use of the term "Atlantean," and the notion that the Atlanteans were a sort of archaic Liberals, needs to be rigorously qualified.

Leaving historical questions aside for the moment, I believe that there is a true archetypal opposition between Traditionalism and Liberalism, which appears to be based on the cosmic functions of the masculine and feminine genders, or rather the masculine and feminine *principles*. This opposition seems to have been unveiled—for a brief moment at least—in the 2016 presidential election in the United States. Hillary Clinton and the contemporary "Liberal Left" represent a feminization of the U.S. population, as indicated by the LBGTQ agenda, but more fundamentally by a rejection of traditional

American individualism in favor of an unapologetic allegiance to, and virtual worship of, the "Maternalistic State," such that her defeat produced something on the order of a "metaphysical panic" among her followers, as if their Goddess, their very principle of reality, had died. As for Trump and the "Populist Right," he clearly represents a rebellion against the Maternalistic State on the part of those identified with various oppressed aspects of the Masculine Principle, which is now experiencing a resurgence, though presently expressing itself in some ways as a mere self-caricature. When any true Spiritual Masculinity lacks cultural expression, the only collective identities available to the mass of men are—to use the common American high school slang—the "jock" and the "nerd": the man whose only mode of self-expression is physical conflict and brutality, and the man whose masculinity is limited to the technological application of abstract thought. Even the old-style economic hero, the predatory capitalist entrepreneur (like Donald Trump), has been de-potentiated as a cultural ideal under the Maternalistic State. And the idea that a man's masculinity could be based on his allegiance to God, and that one possible expression of that masculinity might be an intellectual loyalty to eternal metaphysical principles, is almost totally suppressed in the contemporary English-speaking world; consequently, American motion pictures such as "A Man for All Seasons" (1966) and "Becket" (1964)—cinematic treatments of the English saints Thomas More and Thomas á Becket, both of whom might be described as spiritual/intellectual heroes—could never be produced today.

The Liberal Left has radically departed from the worldview and mores of the "traditional" U.S. Left of the 1980's. In its elitism, its scorn for the working class, and its near-total suppression of class-based politics in favor a radical and dehumanizing social agenda based on race and gender, it begs for a new name—"Inverted Liberalism" perhaps? We have even heard anti-Trump "Liberal Leftists" characterize Donald Trump's criticisms of the CIA as "treason"—a judgment that is diametrically opposed to the position taken by the less elitist and more populist Left of the 1980's. Little is in fact left of Leftist or Marxist ideology in the traditional sense but the mouthings of a strictly academic "Left," totally alienated from any sort of working-class movement, where the ideologies of race and gender have largely replaced those of class. This development is largely the product of a deliberate co-optation, by the economic and political powers-that be, of the Left as it existed in the 1960's, 70's and 80's. Feminist Gloria Steinham even confessed that *Ms. Magazine*, the major feminist publication of the 1970's, received funding from the CIA, who well understood that if the social conflict between the rich and the poor could be re-defined as a conflict between the men and the women, the liberation movements of the second half of the 20th century could be effectively suppressed—which they were.

As for the Populist Right, the disappearance of traditionally "masculine" jobs in agriculture and manufacturing,[1] along with the suppression of Spiritual Masculinity—as, for example, by the pedophilia scandal in the Catholic Church which has bankrupted whole archdioceses and exploded the traditional aura of sanctity surrounding the priesthood—has left the Caucasian "marginalized majority" few avenues of political self-expression outside anti-immigrant, anti-homosexual and anti-environmentalist sentiments. The rage of the present Trump administration and Republican Congress to liquidate every possible environmental protection law is, on the archetypal level, a rebellion of the wounded and insulted Masculine Principle against the worship of the Earth—the Great Goddess. Plato. In his *Republic*, analyzed the descending course of the present cycle of manifestation as a descent of political power down the ladder of the castes, from the Spiritual Intellectuals to the Warriors to the Plutocrats to the *Demos*, a course which has expressed itself in Western Civilization as the devolution of authority from the Popes and the Holy Roman Emperors to the national Kings and Nobles, from the Kings to the Bourgeoisie, and from the Bourgeoisie to the Proletariat. And in our own time we have seen a further devolution of authority, from the "solid" working class to (in some cases) the *lumpen* proletariat, as represented by such political figures as Arnold Schwartzenegger, and ultimately to the non-human world, to a mythologized "Earth-based" regime where animal and plant species are seen as "constituencies" and individual animals almost as *citizens*, leading to the denial of the centrality of the Human Form as the "axial" being for this planet: in Christian terms the bearer of the *imago Dei*; in Islamic terms, the holder of what the Qur'an calls the *Amana*, the Trust. Under such a regime, the human race becomes no more than an ecological pariah, an unbalanced and degenerate animal species guilty of environmental genocide. This is precisely what René Guénon saw, and predicted, for the end of the present cycle-of-manifestation in *The Reign of Quantity*: the short-lived triumph of the Substantial Pole—the Feminine Principle or *materia*—over the Essential Pole—the Masculine Principle or *forma*, resulting in the suppression of all formal distinctions in the "unity" of the Abyss.[2]

---

1. Will the time come, or has it already arrived, when the only way for the men of the western world to express certain aspects of their archetypal masculinity—though only in severely limited and sometimes perverted forms—is through extreme sports, criminal violence, or the life of the mercenary soldier?

2. An indication of the increasing dominance of the Substantial Pole in the biological realm is the declining sperm count and testosterone level among men of the industrialized nations. This condition constitutes a pandemic that may directly relate to the transgender development, one that the medical profession is in many cases deliberately exacerbating through transgender "treatments" rather than attempting to cure.

It is against this sort of mental illness, this collective rejection of the human form, that the Populist masses have risen. (For a good picture of the nature of the regime against which they have risen, see *The Revolt of the Elites and the Betrayal of Democracy* by Christopher Lasch. Lasch sees this revolt as the diametric opposite of the one analyzed by Jose Ortega y Gasset in his *The Revolt of the Masses*. In Ortega's time the masses were progressive, the elites, traditional; in our time it is the masses who are more traditional, the elites who are "progressive.") But since these masses are largely proletarian by background, they cannot represent a new phase of social authority and governance in any stable way—as if a basic reversal of the inevitable descent of the cycle-of-manifestation were somehow possible, which it is not. Consequently they are open to the development of the kinds of "inverted hierarchies" (to use Guénon's term) that we saw in the Fascist movements of the mid-20th century. In the defeat of Hillary Clinton by Donald Trump, we may in fact be seeing a reflection (one of many past, possible, and to come) of the prophesy in the Book of the Apocalypse where a luxurious, self-indulgent maritime mercantile empire, ruled by the Whore of Babylon, is overthrown by the Beast, the Antichrist—the very picture of the rebellion of a perverted Masculine Principle against a degenerate Feminine Principle. I certainly do not mean to imply by this analogy that Donald Trump is in any sense the Antichrist in person, only that—despite whatever may be positive in his policies—he is one of the many mirrors that will temporarily reflect the Antichrist archetype. Antichrist himself must be the overt hierophant of the final Satanic religion, and Trump in no way satisfies this definition. This Gog-Magog opposition can be clearly discerned in the present fighting styles of the Left and the Right in the United States, where the weapons of choice of the Left are *moral superiority and shame*, those of the Right, *anger and fear*. Who can deny that these are the traditionally-preferred tactics in the perennial battle of the sexes?[3]

Given this sort of polarization between the "masculine/Traditional" and the "feminine/Liberal," worldviews (the latter being the dominant myth of the European Union, the former of the rising nationalist reactions against it), how accurate is Aleksandr Dugin's characterization of Atlantis as a regime of "archaic Liberalism"? This is a hard question to answer. Certainly a Mediterranean Atlantis, identifiable with the Minoan maritime civilization and its antecedents, shared with contemporary Liberalism the worship of the Feminine Principle. The American "Atlantis," on the other hand—if we take the civilizations of Mesoamerica and the "mound-builders" of North America as Atlantean

---

3. This is not to say that the Left never uses anger and fear; consider the actions of Antifa and Black Lives Matter.

remnants—was strictly hierarchical, as accurately represented by the *teocalli* (in the Nahuatl tongue), the sacred pyramid. Priestesses were never dominant as they were in Minoan Crete, and though the mythologies of these peoples included their Earth Goddesses, the masculine gods of War and the Sun, as well as the rather mysterious masculine figure of the Aztec Quetzalcoatl or the Mayan Kukulcán, held prominence. Consequently, rather than proto-Liberalism per se, I would rather characterize the archaic West as founded on a sort of proto-Progressivism and Materialism—tendencies which have certainly become identified with Liberalism since the French Revolution, but which likely exhibited a quite different character in the Western Atlantis itself, perhaps one more mythically akin to the hierarchical bio-technocracy envisioned by Aldous Huxley in his *Brave New World*.

Nonetheless, given that *matter* is cognate with *mater*, the initially masculine impulse toward "material progress"—so reminiscent of an adolescent boy's rebellion against a stifling maternal influence (cf. the rebellion of the classical patriarchal Greeks against their matriarchal Minoan predecessors, so profoundly analyzed by Aeschylus in his play *Orestes*)—is ultimately destined to be recaptured by the Feminine Principle. In line with their "progress" toward the Substantial Pole, the French revolutionaries of the 18th century established the worship of the Goddess of Reason in the Cathedral at Chartres; and American poet William Carlos Williams (1883-1963), in his book of historical essays *In the American Grain*, has the spirit of the American heartland, the Goddess of the New World (new to Europe but in its own heart, ancient) address the Spanish explorer Hernando de Soto in the following terms:

> Courage is strength—and you are vigilant, sagacious, firm besides. But I am beautiful—as "a cane box, called petaca, full of unbored pearls." I am beautiful: a city greater than Cuzco; rocks loaded with gold as a comb with honey. Believe it. You will not dare to cease following me—at Apalchi, at Cutifachiqui, at Mabilla, turning from the sea, facing inland. And in the end you shall receive of me, nothing—save one long caress as of a great river passing forever upon your sweet corse. Balboa lost his eyes on the smile of the Chinese ocean; Cabeça de Vaca lived hard and saw much; Pizarro, Cortez, Coronado—but you, Hernando de Soto, keeping the lead for four years in a savage country, against odds, "without fortress or support of any kind," you are Mine, Black Jasmine, mine.

Speaking (while I still can) as an American, it is hard for me to believe that Russia, Iran, China can know this about us in the 21st century—because it's for damn sure we no longer know it about ourselves. In any case, I believe that the obsession of the unbalanced Masculine Principle to "conquer Nature" and dominate matter may in fact carry within it the seeds of a nature-worshipping Liberalism by which the Feminine Principle dominates the Masculine, matter dominates Man—a possibility that works to validate Dugin's worldview. What began, under Rousseau, as a "Liberal" sense of liberation from the artificial strictures of society, under the influence of a generally "pastoral" view of the natural world (ironically, much in evidence at the royal court of Versailles) has in our own time, under the influence of the physical sciences, particularly genetics, become transformed into an oppressive and fatalistic sense of biological necessity, the furthest thing from any sense of human liberation. So expansive, masculine Solar empires like that of the Aztecs, insofar as they take the first steps on what will become (much later) the road of "progress," enter the dimension of accelerating linear time, characteristic of the archetypal West, a tendency emblematic the latter days of the cycle-of-manifestation, and one whose ultimate destiny is dominance by, and submersion in, the archetypal Feminine Principle, the Chaos of the Substantial Pole. This may in fact be another example of Guénon's revolt of *kshatriyas*. The Toltec empire of Mexico was more essentially brahminical and priestly than the Aztec Empire that conquered it; the Aztecs adopted the sacerdotal trappings of the Toltecs in an attempt to legitimize what was, in fact, a warmaking *kshatriya* Empire pure and simple.[4]

Hyperborean, brahminical empires, like that of China, are spiritually centered around the Pole Star, "the still point of the turning world" (in T.S. Eliot's phrase), the visible point of eternity in the created order; this type of regime adequately matches Dugin's picture of the Hierarchical Hyperborean Heartland. Conversely a Solar *kshatriya* Empire, like that of Spain, follows the course of the Sun—which, instead of turning about a fixed point in the North, appears to follow a more-or-less linear track across the sky, from east to west. It is this basically Western spiritual orientation—the Anglo-Saxon version of which, in the imperial history of the United States, is the myth of "manifest destiny"—which inevitably takes the form of the worship of progress, the hopeless attempt to "reach the future" through endless acceleration. This obsessive "futurism" acts to sink the collective that embarks upon it ever more deeply into scientism, materialism and technocracy, ultimately leading to the veiling of the Pole of Essence or form and the dissolution of the collective in question in the Pole of Substance. Gold is a universal symbol of Essence or Quality. The Empire of Spain, however, *quantified* the vast supply of gold it appropriated

---

4. The conquest of the Toltecs by the Aztecs is a clear illustration of two of René Guénon's major themes: the revolt of the *kshatriya* caste against the *brahmin* caste, and the shift from the Hyperborean to the Atlantean worldview, seeing that the original homeland of the Aztecs was Aztlán, and that of the Toltecs, Tula, which Guénon and others have associated with the mythic island of Thule, situated by the classical Greeks in the far North.

from Mexico and the Inca lands—which had a sacred, symbolic value to the Amerindians, not a monetary one—thereby placing it in the service of the Pole of Substance, with the ultimate effect of creating runaway inflation and ruining the Spanish economy.[5]

The pre-Columbian New World shows many signs of having been in communication with Eurasia in prehistoric times, which could certainly explain the notion of Atlantis as a vast, global empire. As we have already noted, certain Amerindian Metis societies (inter-tribal medicine societies of the Metis peoples, who trace their ancestry back to both Native Americans and Europeans) say that "we were in contact with the Old World before the White Men came." Further signs of such contact can be discerned in the legends of the Plumed Serpent. Quetzalcoatl (his name in Nahuatl) or Kukulcán (his name in Mayan), is a strange deity, a god who incarnates a union of opposites. His serpent aspect is obviously related to the earth (and also, according to the speculation of American poet Charles Olson, the sea, insofar as he is a sea-serpent), while his feathered aspect, drawn from the brilliant green plumage of the quetzal bird, the royal bird of southern Mexico and Central America, relates him to the sky. As a union of opposite forces he is analogous in some ways to the Roman god Mercury, who, by virtue of his well-known *caduceus*, is also a "plumed serpent." Various occult fantasts such as Ignatius Donnelly and Lewis Spence (both of whom wrote on the Atlantis legend), as well as Jose Argüelles, have associated the Mayan Pacal Votan—the mythical king and culture-hero of southern Mexico whose reputed tomb in Palenque I once visited—with Quetzalcoatl, and it is true that various Mexican and Mesoamerican kings, such as the Ce Acatl Quetzalcoatl ("One Reed Plumed Serpent") of the Toltecs, took the god's name as a title, possibly so as to define their royal/priestly function as *pontifex* between heaven and earth. Some have also claimed that "Votan" is the same name as that of the Teutonic god "Wotan." This far-fetched speculation has found little support—outside the interesting fact that when the Romans in their wars with the Germanic tribes encountered Wotan, they synchronized him with Mercury, in view of a number of similarities. Even more interesting is the association of Pacal Votan with the Mesoamerican version of the legend of the Tower of Babel, in which René Guénon discerned the outlines of an ancient rebellion of the *kshatriya* caste against the priestly caste; Babel (which means

---

5. In Canto XXII of the ***Purgatorio***, the canto devoted to the sin of avarice, Dante has the Roman poet Statius quote Virgil's line, "Why cannot you, O holy hunger for gold, restrain the appetite of mortals?" Jennifer Doane Upton, in her ***Ordeal of Mercy: Dante's Purgatorio in Light of the Spiritual Path***, explains "the holy hunger for gold" as "the ability to value something for what it is, for its essence, not for its pragmatic usefulness or its ability to satisfy desire"—in other words, for its quality, not its quantity.

"Gate of God"), like the pyramids of Mesoamerica, was likely also a ziggurat, a *teocalli*. Francisco Javier Clavijero quotes Francisco Núñez de la Vega, bishop of Chiapas, to the effect that "a certain person named *Votan* was present at that great building, which was made by order of his uncle, in order to mount up to heaven; that then every people was given its language, and that Votan himself was charged by God to make the division of the lands of Anahuac." According to my own speculation, the Tower of Babel represents an illegitimate and consequently foredoomed attempt to re-establish Hyperborean spirituality, the "mass theophanic consciousness" of the Golden Age, in later Atlantean times through a syncretism of various national or tribal deities based upon imperial power alone—a plot to "take heaven by storm" that God did not sanction.

Properly speaking, Hyperborea and Atlantis are *successive phases* of the cycle-of-manifestation. Aleksandr Dugin, however, identifies them as the archetypes of two contemporary human collectives. How legitimate is this identification? And can Hyperborea and Atlantis in any sense appear as *alternatives* that one might be called to choose between?

Yes and no. One of the aspects of the Substantial Pole, into whose "gravity well" the present cycle-of-manifestation is now falling, is that it acts as the "archive" of all the preceding phases of cycle. Just as the Essential Pole is in touch with the celestial plane—in Platonic terms, the plane of the intelligibles, the transcendent unity of the eternal archetypes of all things that are to appear in the course of cosmic manifestation—so the Substantial Pole is host to the accumulated psycho-physical *residues* of all that has come into existence during the course of the cycle, and consequently manifests a sub-hierarchical "unity" that is in some sense the inverted counterfeit of the meta-hierarchical unity of Essence.[6] Under the influence of the Substantial Pole, the linear "progress" of social organization from form to form begins to be replaced by a chaotic tendency to draw upon any number of earlier forms—a tendency clearly evident in Aleksandr Dugin's Fourth Political Theory—or rather upon various incomplete and distorted versions of them. This is in fact an imperfect foreshadowing

6. Given that the North Pole symbolically corresponds to Essence and the South Pole to Substance, the quality of the unpurified Substantial Pole, of matter bereft of Spirit, is accurately transmitted by American supernatural horror-writer H.P. Lovecraft in the figure of his fictional Titan, Cthulhu, who is associated with Antarctica. Part of the "Cthulhu Ethos" is a magical grimoire called the *Necronomicon*, which various writers on magic have attempted to transpose from fiction to fact by composing their own versions of it. "Necronomicon" means "the book of dead names"; one of the purposes conceived for it is apparently to summon "the Old Ones," Lovecraft's name for the fallen Titans who ruled the earth in an earlier world-age. This is similar to the practice attributed by René Guénon to a particular class of sorcerers, those who invoke the "infra-psychic residues" of dead religions and of forms of life proper to earlier ages of the *manvantara* for use in certain magical operations.

of the "end of time" and the "reinstatement of space" predicted by René Guénon for the terminal point of the *manvantara*.

Gog and Magog *vs.* the Eschatological Conflict

Neither the Essential Pole per se nor the Substantial Pole per se can appear in cosmic manifestation. Just as the Essential Pole, the archetype of form and hierarchy, transcends manifestation because it lies *above* form and hierarchy, so the Substantial Pole, the archetype of matter, also transcends manifestation because it lies *below* matter. Therefore a sub-hierarchical unity of matter alone, entirely bereft of form—like a truly classless society—is not possible. And just as Communism experienced the development of established party elites not foreseen in classical Marxism, so the universal leveling force of the Substantial Pole (seeing that a total suppression of Essence in the manifest world cannot in fact be achieved) inevitably gives rise to a hierarchical reaction. This reaction, however—as Guénon pointed out—must be *inverted*. The earlier, more hierarchically-ordered phases of the cycle cannot be re-established; they can only be counterfeited by a regime that exhibits the trappings and claims the prerogatives of the Pole of Essence, while in fact representing the most extreme possible capitulation to the Pole of Substance: the regime of *al-Dajjal* or Antichrist. A regime based on this sort of inverted hierarchy was in fact predicted by Guénon in *The Reign of Quantity*:

> one can already see sketched out, in various productions of an indubitably "counter-initiatic" origin or inspiration, the idea of an organization that would be like the counterpart, but at the same time also the counterfeit, of a traditional conception such as that of the "Holy Empire," and some such organization must become the expression of the "counter-tradition" in the social order; and for similar reasons the Antichrist must appear like something that could be called, using the language of the Hindu tradition, an inverted *Chakravarti* ["turner of the wheel (of the law)"; universal king].

The titanic conflict between the regime of Substance and the reaction against it—both of which are equally manifestations of the last days of the *Kali-yuga*—is symbolized in *The Book of the Apocalypse* by "Gog and Magog," and in the Qur'an by "Yajuj and Majuj"—who, according to the latter source, will *slither down every slope* [Q. 21:96]. That is to say, both the universal leveling-power of Substance and the reactionary attempt to re-establish hierarchy in opposition to it will form part of the same universal *sinking* tendency that characterizes the final days of the cycle.

The cosmic principle behind Gog and Magog appears in the *I Ching* as the sixth and last line of the hexagram *Kun*, which as a whole represents the archetypal Feminine Principle, the Pole of Substance. The text for that line is: "Dragons fight in the meadow; their blood is black and yellow." This indicates a titanic inflation of the Feminine Principle, *Yin*, which invokes a reaction from the primal masculine Principle, *Yang*, such that they enter into a conflict in which both the primal powers are wounded.

Given that the latter days of the cycle are characterized by titanic conflicts between false alternatives which are ultimately expressions of the same universal degeneration, it would seem entirely justified to simply invoke the words of Christ, "my kingdom is not of this world" [John 18:36], enter into contemplative withdrawal from "the nightmare of history," and concentrate all one's resources upon the "unseen warfare" of the "greater *jihad*." This stance is in fact presented as a viable option—or rather, a destiny willed for some by Allah—in the story of the "companions of the Cave" in the *Surah al-Khaf*, as well as in the prophetic *hadith*: "There will be tribulations during which a sitting person will be better than the one standing, the one standing better than the one walking, the one walking better than the one running. Whoever exposes himself to these tribulations will be destroyed, so whoever finds a place of protection or refuge should take shelter in it" [Bukhari].

However, the Book of the Apocalypse also presents us a picture of the true eschatological conflict of the latter days, a battle of which the false conflict between Gog and Magog is a mere caricature. And Islamic eschatology universally predicts the rise of the Mahdi before the end of the cycle, who will establish justice and true religion, as well as the return of the Prophet Jesus, who is destined to slay the Antichrist. Therefore to simply wash one's hands of the world and wait for the end is by no means the only option. For those who are able to place the will of God above both their own self-will and any worldly agenda—and the knowledge given by God above any worldly *analysis*—it may become possible (God willing) to play a role in the true eschatological, messianic conflict of the latter days: possible, and therefore necessary.

The Covenants of the Prophet Muhammad

In 2013 I made the acquaintance of Dr. John Andrew Morrow (Ilyas 'Abd-al 'Alim Islam). Dr. Morrow is known for his profound, detailed and groundbreaking researches on the covenants of Prophet Muhammad with the Christians of his time, and other "peoples of the book." These covenants, a number of which he has either newly discovered or rescued from obscurity, are treaties that the Prophet concluded with various Christian communities of his time. As we have already seen, they uniformly forbid all Muslims to attack or rob or damage the buildings of peaceful Christians—or even prevent their Christian wives from attending Divine Liturgy and taking spiritual direction from their Christian elders—"until the coming of the Hour," the end of the world. The bulk of Dr. Morrow's research to date on these documents appears in his seminal book *The Covenants of the Prophet Muhammad with the Christians of the World* [Angelico/Sophia Perennis, 2013], as well as in a three-volume anthology edited by him and entitled *Islam and the People of the Book: Critical Studies of the Covenants of the Prophet* [Cambridge Scholars, 2017]. This much-needed scholarship has gone a long way toward resurrecting the Prophetic Covenants from obscurity, and throwing light on the just and equitable norms the Prophet laid down governing how Muslims were to treat Peoples of the Book and other religious minorities within the growing Islamic State. It has also struck a new chord in interfaith relations, one which is not dependent upon the worldview of secular Liberalism, but springs directly from the Abrahamic tradition itself, as well as providing a powerful weapon to de-legitimize ISIS and other Takfiri terrorist organizations.

In addition to Dr. Morrow's scholarly efforts he and I are also partners, as has already been mentioned, in the Covenants Initiative, an international movement of Muslims, based on *The Covenants of the Prophet Muhammad with the Christians of the World*, to combat terrorism and protect persecuted Christians. The Initiative (which I initially conceived of) invites Muslims from all walks of life to accept these Covenants as legally binding upon them today. It has been signed by many prominent Muslim scholars, including a representative of al-Azhar University, and has been endorsed by such dignitaries as Ayatullah Khamenei, Supreme Leader of Iran, Pope Francis and Bartholomew, Ecumenical Patriarch of the Eastern Orthodox Church.

In my view, the Covenants Initiative has begun to define a true exoteric expression and context for the relatively esoteric doctrine that Frithjof Schuon, following René Guénon, called "the Transcendent Unity of Religions." The Transcendent Unity of Religions accepts all the great world religions as valid Spiritual Paths based on Divine Revelations, as indeed the Holy Qur'an, in the surah *Al-Imran*, 3–4 and 84, allows Muslims to believe. The Transcendent Unity of Religions is opposed to syncretism, however, and sees all hopes and plans for world unity based on a One World Religion as both unrealistic and spiritually subversive. In my book *The System of Antichrist: Truth and Falsehood in Postmodernism and the New Age* [Sophia Perennis, 2001] I called for a "united front ecumenism," according to which the world religions, putting aside various barren attempts to define a doctrinal common ground, would—while "agreeing to disagree" (or, as Dr. James Cutsinger has phrased it, "disagreeing to agree")—come together to protect themselves and each other from the forces of false religion and militant secularism that threaten to destroy them all. I thought I would never have a chance to see such a movement in action, until I realized that the Covenants Initiative, begun in 2013, was a perfect example of the united front ecumenism I had called for in 2001, and that it was in fact a legitimate outer expression of the Transcendent Unity of Religions, in a way that most Liberal ecumenical and interfaith initiatives, with their syncretistic tendencies, are not. Many such "established" interfaith movements and organizations are heavily subsidized and semi-covertly directed by the governments and globalist foundations and think-tanks of the West. And insofar as they act to spread globalist ideology, they form one-half of a "pincers movement" aimed at weakening, controlling and ultimately liquidating all the world's religions, the other half being the clandestine support provided by the Western nations, as well as various extra-governmental power-blocs and funding sources, to certain Takfiri terrorist armies—including elements of al-Qaeda and ISIS—as well as to the mercenary soldiers and their recruiters who continue to help organize and man these satanic organizations. If the religions can be induced, in the name of "tolerance," to de-emphasize and deconstruct those Traditional doctrines that are considered to be "divisive," they will lose their self-determination, step by step, and increasingly come to depend upon governmental and private patronage and direction; such radically weakened religious collectives will become less and less able deal with moral degeneracy and violent fanaticism in their ranks.[7] At the same time, the exponential growth of interreligious violence will make it appear to many that the "repressive tolerance" of a One World Religion, or at least the federation of all the world's religions under a single secular authority, is the only hope for establishing peace between the faiths—or what's left of them. It is my belief that all of these elements form part of a single comprehensive plan, implemented over a period of several generations, whose ultimate goal is to wipe true religion from the face of the earth.

The Devil hates all the revealed religions because he recognizes them as emanating from a single Divine Source, the prime Object of his hate; thus the Darkness of This World, by its very hatred, testifies to the truth of the Transcendent Unity of Religions, and challenges the religions to unite to oppose it. Here we can see one example of how Traditional Metaphysics and eschatology can generate socio-political *praxis* on their own, independent of any Liberal, Fascist, Marxist, Islamicist or Globalist ideology, or any permutation or combination thereof. The theoretical foundation of this *praxis* is the recognition of eternal metaphysical Principles, and the vision of history as the working out of these Principles in the dimension of time. To the degree that one recognizes, understands and identifies with such Principles, one is "in the world but not of it," and consequently is not hampered by an unconscious identification with the world of conditions or any aspect of it, even including the collective social dimension

---

7. I fear that the Traditionalist/Perennialist School in the English-speaking world has failed to appreciate the danger of co-optation and covert control represented by their growing connection with "established interfaith," and their quest for patronage from the globalist elites.

of one's own religion; only someone who is not identified with This World, and thus free of all partiality, can see it as it really is. This sort of transcendental objectivity allows the one who has achieved it to formulate effective strategic and tactical initiatives that take into account the entire situation he or she confronts, as well as the quality of the present historical occasion. It also makes it possible for that person to discern the Will of God in relation to both the objective situation and the various particular initiatives designed to address it, thus allowing him or her to reach relative certainty as to when, or if, a particular course of action should be embarked upon, redirected, delayed, or abandoned.

As for the content of the Covenants of the Prophet themselves—which comprise the many treaties that Muhammad concluded with Christians, Jews, Zoroastrians, even Pagans, and which include the pivotal Constitution of Medina—the most striking aspect of them, in terms of the present study, is that, to all intents and purposes, they exhibit a seamless union between *theocracy*—"Tradition"—and *democracy*—"Liberalism." They are announced and written in the name of Allah and claim divine inspiration as their origin; likewise they posit the Prophet Muhammad and his legitimate successors as the ultimate authority. On the other hand, they contain what is perhaps the first "universal declaration of human rights" in human history, written down more than a full millennium before what we, looking back to the French and American revolutions, might consider to be "its time." The rights of women and minorities are clearly spelled out, and the socio-political implications of the Qur'anic principle of *no compulsion in religion* [Q. 2:256] are fully expressed and defined. Furthermore, viewing the matter specifically in geopolitical terms, the Arabian Peninsula and the greater Near East—appropriately enough!—constitute a kind of "Middle Kingdom," situated (roughly speaking) between the "Atlantean" realm of coastal western Europe, the British Isles and the Americas—which naturally includes those nations in addition to Britain who explored and colonized the New World: Spain, Portugal, France and the Netherlands—and the "Hyperborean" heartland of Eurasia. (Aleksandr Dugin includes the whole of Western Europe in at least the outer circles of his "Eurasia," but I believe that the Western-tending colonialist nations—at least since the Renaissance—should be included in the "Atlantean" rather than the "Hyperborean" culture area.) Is it any wonder, then, that the dialectical opposition between the Hyperborean ethos and the Atlantean one should be resolved by a divinely-inspired synthesis arising from the mid-point between them, in both doctrinal and geological terms? As we have already seen in the Lakota cosmo-conception as recounted by Black Elk, the point where the Good Red Road running north-south (the Hyperborean road) and the Black Road of Difficulty running east-west (the Atlantean road) intersect is *wakan*, holy—and it is from just such an intersection that the Covenants of the Prophet Muhammad actually emerged.

There is no denying that we live in apocalyptic times—which certainly does *not* mean that we must now "seize the apocalypse" and turn it to our own ends, a course of action that would be both impossible to accomplish and fatal to attempt. A Third World War between the Atlantean and Hyperborean collectives would be the final expression of the barren, titanic struggle of Gog and Magog, and would obviously spell the end of the human race—so let's not do it. Let's do something else.

The struggle between Gog and Magog is the satanic counterfeit of the true eschatological conflict between Christ and Antichrist, the call to which—given that "ye know not the day nor the hour" [Matthew 25:13]—must arrive "as the lightning cometh forth from the east and shines even to the west" [Matthew 24:27]. Only those who have died to the world can know God's Will for the world, and do it. Only they can tell the difference between the true and false war.

The rediscovery of the Covenants of the Prophet was (to me at least), entirely unexpected and providential. With the publication of *The Covenants of the Prophet Muhammad with the Christians of the World* we may in fact be witnessing—unexpectedly, miraculously, at this extremely late date—the emergence of a third foundational source for the Islamic tradition, in addition to Qur'an and *ahadith*.

The re-appearance of the Covenants is also mysterious. To all appearances they are capable of providing a blueprint for the fundamental renewal of Islam after the ravages of colonialism, the fall of the Caliphate and the depredations of the Takfiri terrorists and their western sponsors. It is even possible that they relate to Guénon's belief that the Knights Templar were in touch with representatives of the "Primordial Tradition" in Jerusalem. In Dr. John Andrew Morrow's chapter "The Covenant of the Prophet Muhammad with the Armenian Christians of Jerusalem," which appears in *Islam and the People of the Book: Critical Studies in the Covenants of the Prophet*, he quotes Bernard Falque de Bezaure to the effect that:

> These firmāns [*covenants of the Prophet*] would become *ahadith* in the Muslim corpus known as the Sunnah and would later be transcribed in the houses of wisdom in Baghdād and Damascus. They later passed into the hands of the Umayyad, 'Abbāsid, and Fāṭimid Caliphs.... These are also the documents that were given, in the eleventh century, by Michael, monophysite bishop and patriarch of Antioch [*that is, by Michael the Syrian (d. 1199 CE), the Armenian Patriarch of Antioch, who was in office from 1166–1199 CE.*], to the dynasty of Armenian kings, the Rupenids, and to Mleh, [*Prince of Armenia r. 1170–1175 CE*], the Master of the Templars of Armenia, in particular, at the same moment that the 'Alawī-Hashashīn-Nusayrī documents entered the chain of Armanus in Sicily. These [*latter*] documents concern the

mysteries of illumination of the ancient Christian and Jewish prophets as well as Muḥammad. They represent the foundations and the basis of the secret spiritual meditations that were given by Hugues de Payens, the ordained priest of the Saint Sepulcher, to the thirty-one proto-Templars cited in the Armenian chronicles of the aforementioned Michael the Syrian.

Dr. Morrow goes on to say: "Bernard Falque de Bezaure advances another astonishing and audacious theory; namely, that the secrets granted, and jealously guarded, protected, and transmitted by the Knights Templar and other secretive Christian societies, consisted of the Covenants of the Prophet Muḥammad. Since the Dome of the Rock [*occupied by the Templars*] contains some of the most ancient examples of early Arabic and Islamic writing, it is also likely that the complex contained precious documents from the dawn of Islam, including, apparently, copies of the Muḥammadan Covenants." If true, this would certainly go a long way to corroborate Guénon's belief that the Templars were in some sense the "guardians of the Primordial Tradition," early exponents of the Transcendent Unity of Religions. (A more complete presentation of our research on the Templars appears in *Appendix One*.)

According to Islamic tradition, a "renewer of the religion" is destined to appear at "the head of every century." In view of this prophesy I have sometimes, only half-jokingly, addressed Dr. Morrow as *muhiyuddin* ... and certainly the Covenants of the Prophet continue to spread widely through the Muslim world, often eliciting a heart-warming and enthusiastic response. However, from the practical, worldly point of view of *realpolitic*, the prospects for a total renewal of Islam at this late date (for nothing less is required) do not look very promising. All the traditional religious collectives are in a state of retreat due to the "degeneration of the cosmic environment" discerned and predicted by René Guénon for the latter days of the cycle, and the Islamic *ummah* is no exception. Nonetheless we must always remember that things that are difficult or impossible for us are easy for Allah: if He wills a renewal of Islam at this late date, then it will come to pass.

However, two other possible spiritual purposes may be discerned for the contemporary rediscovery of the Covenants. The first would be in order to give individual Muslims a chance to repent of their hatred of the other God-given religions instilled in them by corrupt and treacherous scholars. The second would be to prepare a Remnant of Muslims—not necessarily limited to the Shi'a—to actively await the coming of al-Qaim al-Mahdi, who will establish justice and true religion, and the Prophet Jesus, who will slay *al-Dajjal*, the Antichrist.

Some Christians have been understandably suspicious of our reintroduction of the Covenants of the Prophet; it seems to them as if these documents might represent a covert attempt to re-introduce the notion of an Islamic Empire under which Christians would be relegated to *dhimmi* (protected minority) status once again. Our position, however, is that the Covenants possess a relevance and a force-of-law that transcends dhimmitude, since the Prophet declared them to be in force and incumbent upon all Muslims "until the coming of the Hour," not simply until the fall of the Ottoman Empire, the last Muslim political entity which took the Covenants as the basis of official policy toward non-Muslim religious minorities. And it is clear that the Covenants of the Prophet incarnate Muhammad's great love and respect for the Peoples of the Book—Christians in particular—which is entirely in line with the teachings of the Noble Qur'an. On the basis of these documents, we, as Muslims, offer the following pledge to Christians:

> We the undersigned hold ourselves bound by the spirit and the letter of the covenants of the Prophet Muhammad (peace and blessings be upon him) with the Christians of the world, in the understanding that these covenants, if accepted as genuine, have the force of law in the shari'ah today and that nothing in the shari'ah, as traditionally and correctly interpreted, has ever contradicted them. As fellow victims of the terror and godlessness, the spirit of militant secularism and false religiosity now abroad in the world, we understand your suffering as Christians through our suffering as Muslims, and gain greater insight into our own suffering through the contemplation of your suffering. May the Most Merciful of the Merciful regard the sufferings of the righteous and the innocent; may He strengthen us, in full submission to His will, to follow the spirit and the letter of the Covenants of the Prophet Muhammad with the Christians of the world in all our dealings with them. In the name of Allah, Most Gracious, Most Merciful. Praise be to Allah, the Cherisher and Sustainer of the worlds.

This pledge, which forms the heart of the Covenants Initiative, has been signed by many Muslim scholars and religious leaders from around the world. In terms of the needs of the Russian Federation and its allies, we believe that the Covenants Initiative, as well as our ongoing scholarship related to the Covenants of the Prophet Muhammad, can serve to powerfully validate and support the declaration of The International Conference on Who are the Ahl al-Sunnah, promulgated in Grozny, Chechnya, in August of 2016, and the "Fatwa on Dangerous Sects" of The Council of Muftis of Russia, issued at the same time, both of which declare that the Salafi-Takfirists, Da'esh—the so-called "Islamic State"—and similar extremist groups, are outside the Islamic fold.

Gog and Magog *vs.* Yin and Yang

In my presentation of the downward course of the *manvantara* according to René Guénon, it may seem that I have characterized the Masculine Principle or Essential Pole as "positive" and the Feminine Principle or Substantial Pole as "negative" in the moral or spiritual sense; therefore it behooves me to clarify matters so as to dispel any misunderstandings on that score. The reader must never get the impression that I am setting up an intrinsic "Manichaean" opposition between Masculine and Feminine Principles, thus limiting them to the barren, titanic conflict represented by Gog and Magog or Yajuj and Majuj, to the kind of delusional dead-end into which the polarity of the genders can all too easily fall, especially under the influence of an evil social engineering agenda designed to exploit "the battle of the sexes." The Qur'an [2:103] explicitly recognizes the *satanic* nature of such an agenda:

> And [*the enemies of Allah and His angels*] follow that which the devils falsely related against the kingdom of Solomon. Solomon disbelieved not; but the devils disbelieved, teaching mankind magic and that which was revealed to the two angels in Babel, Harut and Marut. Nor did they (the two angels) teach it to anyone till they had said: We are only a temptation, therefore disbelieve not (in the guidance of Allah). And from these two (angels) people learn that by which they cause division between man and wife. . . .

To begin with, we must realize that the Masculine and Feminine Principles are both present in the psycho-spiritual makeup of any human being, and that each Principle is pre-eminent in its own domain. The negativity of the Substantial Pole lies in its attempt to assume the characteristics and prerogatives of the Essential Pole; likewise the negativity of the Essential Pole lies in its obsession to blindly repress and/or dominate the Substantial Pole rather than working toward a fertile relationship with it.

The "downward course" of the *manvantara* from the Essential or Masculine Pole to the Substantial or Feminine Pole is only a degeneration when viewed from the point-of-view of spiritual and social authority. As should be obvious, *forma*, as a reflection of the celestial archetypes, is the legitimate principle of authority for both the well-ordered society and the integrated soul; if authority is assumed by relatively formless *materia*, social order and psychic integrity, both collective and individual, will break down. However, *forma* cannot fulfill its active role in manifestation without the receptivity to form which only *materia* can provide; if Substance were not capable of *eternally* reflecting Essence, if would be impossible for Essence to cosmically manifest itself in terms of temporal development. Speaking in Orthodox Christian terms, if the Theotokos had not been *intrinsically* virgin, if she had not said, "be it done unto me according to Thy Word" [Luke 1:38], Christ could never have incarnated on earth. Likewise if the Prophet Muhammad had not responded with obedience and submission to the command of Allah to *recite!*, transmitted through the angel Gabriel, the Holy Qur'an would never have been heard, recited and written down; consequently there would have been no Islam. For the rational mind to take its first principles from the *Nous*, the Transcendent Intellect, for the will to submit to the rational mind, and for the affections to conform themselves to and therefore empower the submissive will, is the *hier-archical* way of the Masculine Principle. The way of the Feminine Principle, however, is to reflect the *Nous* directly in the total, "virginal" substance of the purified soul, the *materia prima*, without the mediation of any hierarchical or sequential differentiation of thought, will and feeling. The Masculine Principle realizes spiritual truth first intellectively and then actively; the Feminine Princi-ple realizes it immediately and existentially. Both principles must come into play in any society, or any soul, that aspires to follow the Will of God.

The intellective/hierarchical/active way of the Essential Pole and the existen-tial/receptive way of the Substantial Pole are graphically illustrated in certain versions of the Eastern Orthodox icon of St. George and the Dragon—specifi-cally, the one in which St. George, mounted on a horse, with an angel above him holding a crown over his head, impales a dragon with his lance, the oppo-site end of which points upward toward the angel, whose face is like a miniature prototype of the saint's. Behind the angel, beyond the butt of the lance, shining from the upper left corner of the icon, is a quarter-sunburst. In the back-ground, to the right, is a tower where, from the battlements, a king, a queen and a prince are watching the contest. In front of the tower stands a princess; she holds in her hand a crimson cord, which is tied around the dragon's neck. The sunburst is the Spirit of God; the angel above St. George is the *Nous*; the crown is the individual intellect as illuminated by the *Nous*. St. George himself is the human will and personality consciously acting in line with the will of God as revealed by the *Nous*; his horse comprises those elements of the soul that have pledged allegiance to the human will responsive to God's Will; his lance is the Axis Mundi, the channel of Divine Grace and Power. The Dragon is the passions, what the Sufis call the *nafs al-ammara b'l su*, the "soul command-ing to evil." The Princess is the *nafs al-mutma'inna*, the "soul at peace," the vir-ginal soul who is perfectly receptive and submissive to the Will of God, and may therefore be taken as a manifestation of Holy Wisdom. The red cord by which the Princess lightly restrains the Dragon demonstrates that Wisdom and Love have the power to pacify the Dragon through gentle guidance and subtlety of perception, but not before St. George, the heroic spiritual will, has liberated her through *podvig*, ascetic struggle. The tower behind the Princess is another version of the *nafs al-mutma'inna*, analyzed so as to show the proper relation-ship between Intellect (the king), Will (the prince) and the Affections (the queen), where the purified emotional nature mediates between and reconciles the Intellect and Will, lending substance to the first and power to the second.

The Masculine and Feminine principles are recognized in every traditional metaphysically-based cosmology; both come into play in any natural process; both are necessary for God to manifest as the spiritual, psychic and material universes; both are required for the creation and maintenance of any existing thing. Therefore, both the Liberal tendency to erase all distinctions between them and Dugin's willingness to posit a quasi-absolute conflict between them, in their personifications as Eurasia and Atlantis, as well as by such ill-conceived formulations as "We are the supporters of the Absolute and we are against the relative" (from *The Rise of the Fourth Political Theory*), are signs of the approaching dissolution of the *manvantara*. We would hope that Aleksandr Dugin might take some time off from his busy schedule and really learn Traditional Metaphysics, rather than simply grabbing random concepts from it and turning them into political slogans.

2

Inverted Metaphysics

ALEKSANDR DUGIN invokes metaphysics repeatedly, in the most diverse and unlikely contexts; unfortunately both for him and for us, he is either ignorant of its basic tenets or has elected not to remain faithful to them. Let us now survey a number of the misappropriations and misunderstandings of metaphysical principles sprinkled throughout Dugin's writings.

PART ONE:
CRITIQUE OF "THE METAPHYSICS OF CHAOS"
FROM THE FOURTH POLITICAL THEORY

Perhaps the most succinct presentation of Aleksandr Dugin's metaphysical doctrines, though they still remain obscure and ambiguous, is the essay "The Metaphysics of Chaos" from *The Fourth Political Theory*, which relies heavily upon Heidegger's concept of *dasein*. Dugin also draws upon the metaphysics of René Guénon, and it is Guénon's use of the Hindu doctrine of the *manvantara* or cycle-of-manifestation, from *The Reign of Quantity and the Signs of the Times*, that undoubtedly throws the most penetrating light on Dugin's metaphysics, since they are based in large part on a misunderstanding and/or conscious inversion of this doctrine. And since one of the main purposes of this book is to distinguish true Integral Traditionalism from the Duginist pseudo-Traditionalism, I will now do my best to give an accurate account of the specific doctrines of René Guénon that have most centrally influenced Aleksandr Dugin.

Eleven Principles of Integral Traditionalism

The major ideas that Dugin took from Guénon would appear to be three: 1) the notion of Atlantis and Hyperborea (Dugin associates the latter in some ways with his "Eurasia"), though Guénon saw them as cyclical phases while Dugin takes them as characterizing two contemporary human collectives; 2) the idea

78

of a Traditionalist intellectual vanguard working to return western civilization to its Traditional roots, which is most clearly expressed in Guénon's book *The Crisis of the Modern World*; and 3) his particular take on the doctrine of the *manvantara*, which includes the doctrine of historical entropy—the reverse of the Liberal, Fascist and Communist belief in "progress"—and defines the specific conditions of social and spiritual degeneration, as well as the potentials for "Traditional Action," that are available in the latter days of the cycle. In order to get a better idea of the divergence between Duginism and Integral Traditionalism, it will be helpful to take a closer look at some fundamental Traditionalist principles.

The following eleven principles sum up what I learned from the Traditionalist/Perennialist writers, primarily René Guénon and Frithjof Schuon, both through a fundamental acceptance of their doctrines and an ongoing critique of certain aspects them. Various incomplete renditions of these principles can be found in my earlier books, but it is only in recent years that I have reached a definitive understanding regarding all of them; they are as follows:

1) God—Absolute Reality—has sent more than one valid Revelation, more than one version of the Spiritual Path by which we can return to Him. By following the principles of one of these living Paths, enshrined for the most part in the world's great religions and wisdom traditions, we may realize and actualize (God willing) our knowledge of, and union with, Absolute Reality.

2) More than one of these Paths may be valid and in operation at the same time.

3) These Paths, no matter how different their doctrinal starting-points and their methodologies may be, ultimately lead to the same Goal. Absolute Reality lies at the end of each Path, because the Truth is One. (These first three principles together constitute the doctrine of "The Transcendent Unity of Religions.")

4) Nonetheless, it is not a matter of indifference which Path one chooses, since the Paths are designed for different character-types and cultural frameworks and spiritual capacities. Consequently, though the Goal is ultimately the same, the fact that more than one version of the Spiritual Path exists is necessary and providential.

5) Not everything that presents itself as a valid Spiritual Path is necessarily what it claims to be; false religions, psychic or magical belief-systems, or social engineering experiments masquerading as religions, represent a grave danger to be discerned and avoided.

6) The metaphysics and mystical theologies of the various religions, though differences will always remain, are much closer to unanimity than the exoteric aspects of these religions; therefore a study of the metaphysical doctrines of one religion can often illuminate certain aspects of the analogous doctrines of another. This is what Frithjof Schuon termed "esoteric ecumenism."

7) The fact that God has sent more than one valid revelation does NOT mean that a unification of these revelations into a single religion represents a more complete vision of the Truth and a more effective Path for the realization of It; in other words, *syncretism is prohibited*. Since each religion, each Path, is complete and sufficient unto itself, mixing them only adulterates them and renders them chaotic and ineffective.

8) The acceptance of the principle that each valid Spiritual Path leads to the same Goal is a relatively rudimentary level of insight; it does NOT place the person who has reached it in a higher "spiritual caste." The attempt to practice this insight as if it were a more elevated "quintessential esoterism," superseding the revealed religions and constituting an effective Path that transcends their limits, *is prohibited*: no dispensation establishing such a practice has been sent or authorized by God—though the same can certainly not be said for Lucifer.

9) An acceptance of historical entropy, of the notion of the progressive degeneration of the human collective and the cosmic environment over the course of the *manvantara*—a doctrine common to the Hindus, the Greco-Romans and many African and Native American tribes, and one that is either openly stated or clearly implied in most sacred scriptures—is crucial to our understanding of the spiritual dangers and opportunities we face in the present phase of the *manvantara*, the Latter Days of the *Kali-yuga*.

10) Such entropy can be mitigated, resisted, and even—under certain circumstances—reversed, by the action of a spiritual/intellectual elite, though only partially and temporarily; this potential is realizable only within the greater context of the End Times and impending Apocalypse. It is spiritually necessary for us to resist the raging torrent of degeneration that characterizes the late *Kali-yuga*, specifically in order to make it possible to constitute a spiritual Remnant, but this should in no way be taken to imply that this degeneration is fundamentally *unlawful* in cyclical terms. In the words of Ecclesiastes 3:1–8:

> To every thing there is a season, and a time to every purpose under the
> heaven:
> A time to be born, and a time to die; a time to plant, and a time to pluck
> up that which is planted;
> A time to kill, and a time to heal; a time to break down, and a time to build
> up;
> A time to weep, and a time to laugh; a time to mourn, and a time to dance;
> A time to cast away stones, and a time to gather stones together; a time to
> embrace, and a time to refrain from embracing;
> A time to get, and a time to lose; a time to keep, and a time to cast away;
> A time to rend, and a time to sew; a time to keep silence, and a time to
> speak;
> A time to love, and a time to hate; a time of war, and a time of peace.

11) Though the Spiritual Paths cannot and must not be syncretized, nor the religions unified either doctrinally or politically, we must recognize that every true religion or Spiritual Path that has God as its Author and its Goal is now under attack by the legions of Satan and his various human representatives, who together constitute the Darkness of this World. Therefore a United Front Ecumenism against the common enemies of the true and God-given faiths is both possible and necessary.

I learned the first six of these principles mostly from Frithjof Schuon—though he drew them largely from Guénon—except for number 5, which was one of René Guénon's areas-of-concentration that Schuon did not particularly address. Principle 7 was commonly believed and taught by many of Schuon's followers—though, as it turned out, he himself did not really follow it. Principles 8 and 11, at least in their explicit forms, are my own contributions to Traditionalist doctrine, though 8 is more-or-less based on Traditionalism as I learned it from Rama Coomaraswamy, Alvin Moore Jr., and Huston Smith, and number 11 is certainly implied in principles 9 and 10. Principle 8 is the basis of my critique of Schuon's doctrines, the point where, in intellectual terms, I part company with him.

On Frithjof Schuon: A Necessary Digression

Frithjof Schuon's writings in many ways represent the apex of Traditionalist doctrine, its point of greatest profundity; he truly did advance, refine and expand the teachings of Ananda Coomaraswamy and René Guénon. Expansion, however, also opens the door to attenuation and a general weakening of structure. And there is no question that he involved himself in many things that were scandalous, and certainly deserve to be taken as such. His nude dance events are well known, and if these events were in fact the occasion for acts of pedophilia, which has been charged against him though never proved, then he may be rolling in hellfire at this very moment; in any case, his known actions were certainly scandalous enough from the point-of-view of Islam, the religion he professed. On the other hand, his work as a philosopher is of crucial importance for an understanding of traditional religion and metaphysics in our time. Those who take Schuon as the equivalent of a prophet—if not an avatar—see his teaching as effectively infallible, and his strange behavior as a mysterious expression of his Divine mission. Others, who concentrate upon his transgressions, are of the understandable opinion that nothing written by such a man can be trusted. I belong to neither camp—and if this position earns me enemies on both sides of the Schuon controversy, then so be it. If truth is spoken I will accept that truth, even if it comes to me from the mouth of a trained parrot—and Schuon was certainly more than a mere parrot, being at the very least a religious genius—but I will certainly not take that parrot, or that profound but imbalanced genius, as my spiritual Guide. The *shaykhs* of the lineage of Schuon's own *shaykh*, Ahmad al-'Alawi, say that he did attain a real degree of *ma'rifa* (gnosis), but that his teaching lacked the dimension of the education of the *nafs*, and that *only the first punishment* earned by someone who rejects his own *shaykh* is that the *shari'ah* will be taken away from him. Esoteric spirituality has always harbored antinomian tendencies, but I hold to the principle that the Traditional esoterisms of the Abrahamic religions are inseparable from an adherence to the "exoteric" norms of these religions, since both are real aspects of the revelation in question—a principle that was enunciated by René Guénon in the chapter "The Necessity of Traditional Exoterism" from his book *Initiation and Spiritual Realization*. As Jesus said, "I come not to destroy the law but to fulfill it" [Matthew 5:17].

I am of the belief that Frithjof Schuon represents a point where Traditionalist doctrine was attacked and damaged by the Rulers of the Darkness of This World, with the result that part of his legacy, as I predicted in 2001, has gone to serve the system of Antichrist. For this reason, many people whose opinion I value have rejected him, and I certainly respect their decision. My approach, however, has been to say: "The Devil has no right to the doctrines of Frithjof Schuon, except for those few he was actually able to pervert (and may God enlighten us to discern them). Schuon's message is of unparalleled significance—some of that parrot's phrases were taught him by the angels—and if I have to separate that message from the one who brought it in order to separate it from Darkness, then that's how it will have to be." Suffice it to say that I see the next the step "after" Schuon, for those who have been influenced by him, as complete immersion in one of the traditional revelations, including a full acceptance and practice of its *dogma*—of dogma now accepted (God-willing) not on the level of literalist exclusivism but in terms of its *metaphysical transparency*—what the Buddhists call "the finger pointing at the Moon." The doctrinal nakedness of religious universalism is a necessary step; without it we might come to believe that we have caught God in the trap of our particular religious form, that He is not the God of all but merely the God of our particular faith community, thus denying His Infinity and making Him less than God. Our chosen religious form is incumbent upon us according to God's Will, but it is not incumbent upon God; He has "other sheep" [John 10:16]. It's vitally important for us to realize that, under our clothes, all of us are naked, but it's equally important for us to go about decently clothed, both among our co-religionists and when dealing with the people of This World. For the *arif*—the possessor of *ma'rifa*, the gnostic—dogmatic orthodoxy is an act of obedience and humility necessary to preserve his balance, to shield him from being attacked or co-opted by the worldly enemies of religion, to ensure that he will remain in touch with the particular channel of God's guidance that is destined for him, and to protect him from coming into conflict with the incomprehension of his own fellow-worshippers in such a way, or on such an occasion, that God has not sanctioned.

It may also be, however, that Schuon's doctrines—especially those relating to the mysteries of the Virgin—were more esoteric than he himself realized.[1] And since he tried to tell the kind of secrets that should not, and in a very real sense cannot, be divulged, but which our times of spiritual hunger and Divine judgement demand the revelation of, God might have responded by leading him into the sort of dangerous foolishness that would blacken his reputation to the point where only those who were thoroughly abased and dead to this world could understand his message, as well as grasping the depth of darkness invoked by the perversion of that message, according to a principle that Schuon himself often quoted: *corruptio optimi pessima,* "the corruption of the best is the worst." *They plot, but Allah (also) plotteth; and Allah is the best of plotters* [Q. 9:30].[2] In my personal opinion, Frithjof Schuon was a rare revealer of the mysteries of metaphysics and esoteric spirituality, but he was not a Guide. Martin Lings spoke of Revelation as a "flow" from God to man, and of the Spiritual Path as an "ebb" carrying man back to God. Schuon's deeply ambiguous manifestation might have been a real part of that Path for some; the same can be said of any true life challenge that is lived in sincerity, endured in courage and resolved in submission to God's Will. Nonetheless, he did not possess the qualifications of a *shaykh*; he was a master of the flow, but not of the ebb. His audacious externalization of the mysteries precipitated an explosion that is still echoing through

---

1. Much the same could be said of the sophianic spirituality of Vladimir Soloviev, and of sophianic spirituality in general. The Sophia, who in Christianity is the Virgin Mary, is not Form but Matrix; Schuon himself characterized her as "pure prayer." She is the Substantial Pole purified of all formal residues, who in the human microcosm is the *nafs al-mutma'inna*, the soul perfectly receptive to God. To turn her into a form of revelation, as if she were a kind of fourth hypostasis of the Blessed Trinity, is to compromise that very receptivity. Just as Mary is the Theotokos, the Mother of God, so the spiritual Heart is the matrix for the manifestation of God in the human soul, this being the mystery alluded to by the Eastern Orthodox icon known as "the Virgin of the Sign."

2. Although Schuon often quoted St. Augustine to the effect that "all the other vices attach themselves to evil, that it may be done; only pride attaches itself to good, that it may perish," on one occasion a member of Schuon's circle admitted to me that he believed their besetting sin was pride. This did not greatly bother him, however; he seemed to take pride in it. And one of the most insidious forms of pride is *theatricality*. The privileged aristocrat feels entitled to treat life as a game because he considers himself above life, even above Reality; Luciferian pride certainly includes this sort of theatrical element. One of the ways in which *vidya-maya* imperceptibly slips into *avidya-maya* is through the gradual transformation of the radiant manifestation of spiritual Truth into a fête, a pageant, without the participants quite realizing what has happened. Among the forces destructive not only to religion but to human life itself, prideful theatricality is among the least recognized and therefore one of the most dangerous, due to the fact that the root principle of evil is *unreality*.

the world, from soul to soul; the living reality of his message, however, exists on the widening wave-front, not at the center where the explosion began, which is nothing now but a burned-out crater. Such explosions, by which the spiritual secrets are momentarily unveiled to the world—like that represented in the Sufi world by Mansur al-Hallaj—are a necessary part of the Divine economy; nonetheless they inevitably carry dangers and ambiguities in their train, since they are woven of both light and darkness. At certain crucial points the mysteries must be revealed; they must also be perverted and misunderstood—because "the secret protects itself", and because no esoteric mystery can present itself before the eyes of the world without coming as a riddle, an enigma, and a test. Schuon's metaphysical profundity and the deceptions that compromised it together constitute a true paradox of the Latter Days, as well as a stunning demonstration of the darkness that high spiritual truth is menaced with in our times. It will do no good to sweep this enigma under the rug in an attempt to "save Schuon's reputation"; that ship has already sailed. Only if we find the courage to face it and struggle with it will we learn the entire lesson of darkness and light that God has willed to teach us through the phenomenon of Frithjof Schuon.

Integral Traditionalism and Aleksandr Dugin

It is not easy to get a clear idea whether or not Dugin accepts all of the above 11 principles, given that he tends not to address the nature of Divine Revelation per se, viewing the religions more as the constituting principles of various human collectives than the several primary Self-revelations of God to man. But we can safely accept that he holds to the first three principles in a general way, and there is no doubt that principles 10 and 11 loom large in his worldview.

Principle 11 is to be found in Guénon's *East and West*, and more particularly in *The Crisis of the Modern World*; many who identify themselves, in one way or another, with political Traditionalism, Perennialism or Guénonism seem to have adopted principles 10 and 11 in isolation from all the others. I was once in communication with an American college professor who told me, "I am a follower of René Guénon, but I'm not interested in his metaphysics"—which is like saying "I am a student of Johann Sebastian Bach, but I'm not interested in his music." Guénonism minus metaphysics—*worldly* Guénonism, that is—is taken by many as little more than a "critique of the modern world"; Mark Sedgwick's highly influential book on the Traditionalists, for example, is titled *Against the Modern World*, as if that were the central element in their doctrine, which it certainly is not. Couple this with the notion of an intellectual elite as the driving force in a potential restoration of traditional society and you have the recipe for one or more political movements that would naturally appeal to conservative intellectuals, since they would be assured a position of influence in any such movement. I have little doubt that many Alternative Right writers and academics who never felt at home in working class Skinhead circles have been attracted to reactionary political Guénonism solely due to the pre-eminence it appears to grant to "the intellectual as ideological leader."

Anyone who has read the total *oeuvre* of Guénon, Schuon and Coomaraswamy, however, will understand just how far such a notion departs from what these writers actually taught—though Julius Evola, by virtue of his radical divergence from Guénon, was a bit closer to fulfilling the role of political ideologue. Perhaps certain political conclusions can be drawn, in a general way, from the writings of Guénon and his successors. Nonetheless the fact remains that René Guénon was a spiritual philosopher, not a political theorist. However, if Marx could use Hegel as the basis of his doctrine of dialectical materialism, I suppose Aleksandr Dugin can add certain doctrines from Guénon to the heterogeneous mass of his justifications for a crusade against "the absolute evil" of Liberalism and "Atlanticism." In neither case, however, has political ideology proved capable of doing justice to philosophy and metaphysics without radically editing and falsifying its source material. The role of a Traditionalist intellectual elite in the West at the end of the *manvantara*, as defined by René Guénon in *The Crisis of the Modern World* (1927), was thoroughly revised and updated in his prophetic masterpiece, *The Reign of Quantity and the Signs of the Times*. The first book hopes for a restoration of Tradition in the West, while the second—published after World War II and the advent of nuclear weapons—is frankly eschatological. Dugin, however, largely ignores this radical revolution in Guénon's thought. He accepts in a general way René Guénon's belief that we are drawing near to the end of the *manvantara*, the present cycle-of-manifestation, but his vague and ambiguous notion of what this might entail owes next-to-nothing either to *The Reign of Quantity* or to orthodox Christian eschatology.

Duginist *vs.* Traditional/Guénonian Eschatology

Aleksandr Dugin sees the *manvantara* as ending in Chaos—which he apparently sometimes identifies, when it suits him, with the Divine All-Possibility (in Sufi metaphysics, *wahadiyya*)—but then he makes the glaring error of identifying this "singularity" or "event-horizon" of the cycle with *the reversal of time*. Christian eschatology never mentions the reversibility of time; it speaks instead of the passing away of this heaven and this earth, and the descent of "a new heaven and a new earth" directly from God. Likewise Guénon, in *The Reign of Quantity,* presents a picture of the increasing acceleration of time at the end of the *manvantara*, such that time nearly obliterates space, until the timeless point of the End of this *manvantara* and the Beginning of the next is reached when space suddenly reasserts itself; consequently a condition nearly approaching "pure sequence" is transformed into a condition of nearly "pure simultaneity." But the time of the old *manvantara* is never pictured as *reversing* so as to (presumably) begin its long trek back to its origin in near-absolute space. The *manvantara* simply ends, and consequently *time* ends, at least in terms of the cycle in question—not merely "history," but time itself. So this is the point where Aleksandr Dugin joins the long line of "New Age" teachers who look for a "quantum shift," a replacement of the prevailing "paradigm" with an entirely new one, *without the inconvenience of the apocalyptic dissolution of the world or the self as we know them*—undoubtedly due to the fact that if the terrestrial world, at least in its present state of material petrification, were annihilated, that would take all the "geo" out of geopolitics. He falls into this error because, in line with the collective order-of-perception of the End Times, he views the *manvantara* purely in terms of Substance or matter—that is, of Quantity—not in terms eternal Quality, of Essence, Form, or Logos, a timeless Eternity being inconceivable in materialistic or Substantial-pole terms. Only if this material world were all there is would the end of the cycle mean something like a return to the earlier ages of the same cycle, given that time—*if* this world were all there is—would then be one of the necessary parameters of Being per se, not simply of material Being, and Being itself—all that is—cannot be annihilated. Therefore the only *enantiodromia* or "pole shift" conceivable for the end of the *manvantara*—conceivable from viewpoint of the Pole of Substance, that is—would have to entail something like a return to earlier ages, as in the Nietzschean/Stoic doctrine of the "eternal return," the Stoics being essentially materialists and Nietzsche having famously declared that "God is dead." But, in point of fact, this world is not all there is. The Hindu doctrine of the *manvantara* does not envision an eternal return of all things trapped within a single cycle, but the dissolution of that cycle in favor of a new one, with the *timeless* point separating the former cycle from the latter acting as the doorway to Eternity. And even in terms of cyclical time conceived of with no reference to Eternity, the past does not return via a literal *reversal* of time but because time "rolls ahead"; this Summer does not go back to last Spring, but is followed by Autumn, Winter and next Spring. (We can begin to see here how the Stoic doctrine of the eternal return was nothing but a literalistic misunderstanding of the Hindu doctrine of the *manvantara*—Europe being a distant outpost, metaphysically speaking, of the great, primordial Indo-European Revelation that created India.) Consequently the dissolution of the present cycle would not represent the dissolution of Being itself, but rather—in Guénon's words from *The Reign of Quantity*—the end not of *the* world, but of *a* world. Aleksandr Dugin, however, since he apparently has little effective intuition of Eternity, can only see the end of the *aeon* as something as meaningless and self-contradictory as "the reversal of time," which makes no more sense than to believe that as soon as a person dies he doesn't actually die at all, but instead begins to grow younger. The dissolution of the *apparent* world makes no sense without an intuition of the Eternal world.

One might object that the notion of an *end* of time is just as self-contradictory as time's reversal; and the truth is that time cannot end *in* time, because the time-framework "in" which time ends would itself have to end, and so on and so on in an infinite progression—the same being true, of course, for the infinite *regression* generated by the idea, such as is purveyed by the myth of the Big Bang, that time might also have *begun* in time. Nonetheless, time can "end" in the sense that it can be transcended—or rather (as we must say) it *is* transcended. And from the point-of-view of the relative Eternity known, in Eastern Orthodox theology, as *aeonian time*, all the moments of the present *aeon* can be viewed simultaneously, in a single form, the same being true of all the other *aeons* of earthly time. All the past eras of a particular *aeon*, however, cannot thereby be simultaneous in any effective way on the terrestrial plane, such that we might pick and chose, as Dugin proposes, which elements we little gods might want to include in our own self-created worlds. The illusion that this is possible *in time* is simply the effect of the approaching *end* of time—for this cycle at least—shining through the thinning walls of the *aeon* now coming to a close. The Substantial Pole that dominates the final days of the *manvantara* is indeed the *archive* of all the ages and all the moments that the *manvantara* was and is composed of, but these "psychic residues" as René Guénon calls them, in the absence of any fertilizing infusion of new Form from the Essential Pole, are not living potentials, only exhausted husks, *memories*—and as the English poet William Blake put it (in my abbreviation), "Memory is Eternal Death." The notion of the reversibility of time is thus no more than a vague, self-contradictory, distorted image of Eternity, produced by materialists who have spent their time on earth deconstructing the very notion of Eternity. And Aleksandr Dugin appears to be of their number.

Manvantara

The Hindu doctrine of the *manvantara* or cycle-of-manifestation, found mostly in the **Puranas**, is integral to the cosmological worldview of René Guénon. According to this doctrine, each cycle is composed of four ages or *yugas*: *Satya-yuga* (also known as *Krita-yuga*), *Treta-yuga*, *Dvapara-yuga* and *Kali-yuga*. *Satya-yuga* is four times as long as *Kali-yuga*, *Treta-yuga* three times as long, and *Dvapara-yuga* twice as long. These four *yugas* correspond to the Golden, Silver, Bronze, and Iron ages in Greco-Roman mythology. Over the course of the *manvantara*, time accelerates; both the cosmic environment and the human collective become progressively materialized, and increasingly opaque to the light of the Spirit. The *manvantara* ends in *pralaya* or apocalypse, after which the *Satya-yuga* of a new *manvantara* dawns.

It was Guénon's genius in ***The Reign of Quantity***, his prophetic masterpiece, to re-envision the doctrine of the *manvantara* in terms of the Aristotelian/Thomistic categories of Essence and Substance, or *forma* and *materia*. Essence is that which lends form to Substance, while in itself transcending form; Substance is that which provides concrete material existence (both gross and subtle) to all forms, while in itself lying below matter. Essence is the Father, Substance the Mother; the union of Essence and Substance gives birth to real existing things.

In the *Satya-yuga, Krita-yuga* or the Age of Truth, the Pole of Essence is dominant; the eternal reality of Form, which both transcends matter (as Plato emphasized) and informs it (as Aristotle emphasized), is apparent to all. The *Kali-yuga*, however, the Black Age in which we presently live, lies under the sign of the Pole of Substance. Form is now considered and perceived not as a celestial reality eternally emanating from the Pole of Essence, but as no more than an accident or function of matter. Eternity is eclipsed; ever-accelerating time is dominant.

Mythologically speaking, the *Kali-yuga* is seen as presided over by the male demon *Kali* who symbolizes strife, suffering and ignorance. Be that as it may, I am certainly not alone in seeing the Great Goddess *Kāli* as the prime symbol of our age. Some Hindus, not wishing to associate the Divine Kāli with ignorance, insist that Kāli (the Goddess) bears no relationship to Kali (the demon) due to a difference in vowels. But if there is any one symbol that perfectly encapsulates the particular quality of our time, it is Kāli-ma, *Shakti* to the great god Shiva, to Absolute Reality as Destroyer—She who is the presence and activity of Liberation through the Dissolution of Form. And if Guénon was right in seeing the dominance of Substance over Essence as the watchword of the *Kali-yuga*—as I believe he was—then the Goddess Kāli, the triumphant power of *Yin*, is the perfect symbol of that dominance. The victory of Substance over Essence is in fact portrayed in Hindu iconography by the image of Kāli brandishing a sword and dancing on Shiva's prostrate form. (We should not ignore one significant detail of this image, however—the fact that *Shiva is smiling*.) Furthermore, Kāli literally means "Time," which makes Her a perfect symbol of the form-dissolving acceleration of time as the *manvantara* draws to a close, of Time the Destroyer. In any case, there is no question that we are now nearing the terminal point of the *Kali-yuga*, the end of the present *manvantara*; we live under the rule of the Substantial Pole, and must know and act accordingly.

Faithfulness to, *vs.* Violation of, the Norms of the *Manvantara*

Aleksandr Dugin's response to the dominance of the Substantial Pole in the latter Days of the *Kali-yuga* is to declare, following Martin Heidegger, that the Logos, the Word of God, the Divine principle of creation and order, is dead, and that we must therefore follow the principle of Chaos instead. The problem with this idea is that human life is not possible without a form, ultimately a sacred form, for the human collective to pattern itself upon. In the Golden Age of a given cycle of manifestation, when the Essential Pole is dominant, paradigmatic form is simply a given; it is perceived and immediately responded to as nothing more or less than the *essential* nature of reality. In later phases of the cycle, however, the maintenance of the connection of human society to the Essential Pole becomes progressively more difficult, and consequently more elaborate. The Essential Pole is no longer perceived as the undeniable nature of reality but as a "ruling Principle" which existence must conform to or else degenerate. The possibility that humanity might lose its connection to this ruling Principle becomes conceivable for the first time; consequently various ideas of hierarchy, religious law and/or sacred monarchy make their appearance in order to block or delay this degeneration. The civilization of Egypt is perhaps our best example of a massive and ponderous effort to maintain, by means of every conceivable spiritual ritual and design, a level of collective being and consciousness that, in earlier ages, was the simple human birthright.

In the Golden Age, Form is a given. In the Silver Age (from which Shamanism is perhaps a holdover), Form is still clearly in evidence, but it is menaced by various imbalanced and destructive forces. Mircea Eliade, in his **Shamanism: Archaic Techniques of Ecstasy**, quotes a Siberian shaman as maintaining that "God placed shamans on the earth to fight demons." The social function of the shaman was (and is) to re-balance the cosmic environment and prevent the incursion of chaotic or "infra-psychic" forces. In the Bronze Age, elaborate priesthoods, mythologies, temple complexes and ritual systems develop so as to maintain the human connection to the Essential Pole and stem the tide of degeneration. And finally in the Iron Age, the *Kali-yuga*, the connection of terrestrial existence to the Essential Pole is increasingly veiled; Form is progressively submerged in Chaos; the Substantial Pole becomes dominant.

Each age, then, has its own proper mode of spirituality. In the Golden Age (*Satya-yuga*), the age of "mass theophanic consciousness," spirituality is simply intrinsic to human incarnate existence. In the Silver Age (*Treta-yuga*), spirituality is based upon a recognition the inherent superiority and authority of the human microcosm over cosmic conditions, seeing that the Cosmos is the reflection of Man, who is the bearer of Quranic *Amana*, the Trust. In the Bronze Age (*Dvapara-yuga*) spirituality is based on the ordering of the human collective according to the norms of the macrocosm, of the world considered as a sacred order, seeing that—from a different point of view, more contracted than the preceding one but still valid on its own level—Man is a reflection of the Cosmos. In the Iron Age (*Kali-yuga*), spirituality is based on the salvation of the individual human soul, by the grace of the Avatar or the message of the Prophet, which liberates that soul from the prison of cosmic conditions, from the tyranny of spiritual ignorance and Chaos, from the dominance of the Substantial Pole. Here Substance acts not as the receptive mirror of the sacred forms which emanate from the Pole of Essence, but as the power of worldly conditions and the materialistic worldview to veil Essence and dissolve form. Each later age, however, contains hidden doorways to the age or ages that preceded it, to these past *yugas* now considered not as temporal residues but as eternal ontological levels.

Here we can see how the human race, in each *yuga*, in response to Divine guidance, develops the sort of spirituality that is appropriate to present cosmic conditions. Each age has its own proper methods for maintaining sacred Form and protecting the human collective from Chaos. Chaos, however, is the watchword of the *Kali-yuga*, especially in its terminal phases. We must therefore ask whether the maintenance of the human collective's connection to sacred Form is really appropriate, or even possible, in the latter days of the Age of Iron.

According to the doctrine of the *manvantara*, the cardinal sin of each age is the inappropriate and foredoomed attempt to live according the norms of an earlier and greater age. To presume to live according to the conditions of *Satya-yuga* in *Treta-yuga* is to ignore the growing imbalances in the cosmic environment that it is the human duty, in *Treta-yuga*, to set right. To make this attempt is to actually invoke those imbalances. Likewise to try and live according to the norms of *Treta-yuga* in *Dvapara-yuga* is to assert the *theurgic* superiority of the human microcosm over the macrocosm which reflects it in times that no longer allow for this, and consequently to become *titanic*. It is to rebel, like the Greek Titans, the Hindu Asuras, or the Norse Jötun, against the new order of the "Gods" in the name of an older and higher order which has now been superseded; this is the very transgression that will bring *Treta-yuga* to its end. The rebellion of the Titans against the Gods is reflected on the terrestrial plane by what René Guénon described as the revolt of the *kshatriyas* (the warrior caste) against the *brahmins* (the priestly caste)—which is to say that the assertion of the *shamanic* spirit proper to *Treta-yuga* in later priestly times, in *Dvapara-yuga*, gives rise to the cult of the warrior based on the worship of self-will, a development that is represented in the Book of Genesis by the "great hunter" Nimrod, who built the Tower of Babel. And to think that we can live according to the norms of *Dvapara-yuga* in *Kali-yuga* is to worship the material cosmos, or natural law, or this or that ethnic or political collective or *narod* that has falsely assumed the trappings of "the intrinsic order of things," in such a way that the microcosmic nature of the human form is suppressed and denied, and the cosmos worshipped not as the ensemble of the signs of God but as a material idol that replaces God. And since the cosmic environment, now alienated from its creative Center in the human archetype, has begun to manifest the Chaos of its impending dissolution, this act of atavism represents not a "cosmic piety" such as was possible in *Dvapara-yuga* but a direct capitulation to the growing Chaos of the Latter Days, which ultimately acts to bring the entire cycle-of-manifestation to an end.

So how can the human race live according to spiritual norms in the *Kali-yuga*, since the particular and ultimately *lawful* quality of this *yuga* is inseparable from the collective veiling of the Spirit? How can we worship God in ways appropriate to present cosmic conditions when those very conditions have decreed "the death of God"?

One common response to Iron Age conditions by those with a certain intuition of spiritual realities is the *atavism* mentioned above: the notion that we must resurrect and attempt to live by the religious dispensations and spiritual norms of earlier and higher ages, norms and dispensations that have now lapsed. This wrongheaded attempt is not based, however, on what Aleksandr Dugin calls "the reversibility of time"—which is absurd on the face of it—but on the fact that in the Latter Days of a given cycle, the psychic residues or *ghosts* of the earlier phases of the *manvantara* are beginning to rise from their graves in the process of returning to the Source that emanated them; in the words of the Qur'an [3:109], *Unto Allah belongeth whatsoever is in the heavens and whatsoever is in the earth; and unto Allah all things are returned.* This process is analogous to the after-death state described in *The Tibetan Book of the Dead* as the *Chönyid Bardo*, the "*bardo* (intermediate state) of the experiencing of reality," as well as to the Resurrection of the Dead in the *Book of Apocalypse*. When we experience this process it may seem as if we were traveling backward into the past, but this is not the case. In reality, the residues of the past are now traveling forward, into the "future," until they ultimately "arrive" at post-Eternity, to be released from the limitations of space and time. *Future* here denotes not the next phase of linear, historical time but universal potential or All-Possibility—or rather the projection of All-Possibility in the direction of cosmic temporality—the subtle dimension out of which events as we experience them are born. This is one more reason why the attempt to live according to the spiritual norms of earlier eras is a self-defeating approach. As we have already seen, the divine dispensations on which those ancient norms were originally founded have been terminated, which means, for example, that any attempt to resurrect the religions of ancient Egypt or Sumeria, of the pre-Christian Norse or the classical Greeks, and live by their standards, could only be a travesty, and a dangerous one at that.

This approach is only self-defeating, however, when an attempt is made to re-establish entire human collectives on the basis of such norms; as inner realities available to the contemplative Intellect, the earlier ages of the cycle are as alive and effective as they ever were. This is due to the fact that, as each *yuga* dies, the essential form of it passes from the outer world to the inner world. The notion that God-consciousness is intrinsic to the human form (from *Satya-yuga*); that it is our responsibility, as bearers of what the Qur'an calls the *Amana*, the Trust, to maintain the balance of the cosmic environment (from *Treta-yuga*); that social and psycho-physical stability can be maintained (to a degree) by living according to cosmic norms and natural law (from *Dvapara-yuga*)—all these truths do not cease being true simply because the great mass of humanity can no longer be ordered on the basis of them. Over the course of the *manvantara* they have been transformed from outer manifestations of inner spiritual Principles to strictly inner realities that can only be accessed in the dimension of contemplation.

In the *Kali-yuga*, those who bear the realities of earlier ages within them, not as dead psychic husks but in the form of living spiritual virtues and knowledge, are called upon to form a Remnant—a theme we will further develop in *Chapter Eight*. And in order to constitute such a Remnant, two temptations must be avoided: the temptation to atavism, as just explained, and the temptation to directly capitulate to the Substantial Pole by immersing oneself or one's group in the physical and psychic Chaos of the *yuga*. The precise goal and necessary method of maintaining the spiritual Center in the *Kali-yuga* is to say NO to "the Darkness of This World" and NO to those psychic tendencies that represent This World and enforce our bondage to it. In earlier *yugas*—as we can see, for example, from the *Upanishads*—such things as material luxury and sexual delight could be understood as direct prolongations in the relative world of the *Sat-Chit-Ananda*, the Being, Consciousness, and Bliss of the Absolute. This is clearly not the case in the world as we know it today. In our age, such reflections of the Divine, unless they are consciously dedicated and re-dedicated to God, are rapidly transformed into veils concealing Him, passions by which we deny Him and rebel against Him, idols we worship in the place of Him.

So the proper mode of spirituality in an age of Darkness has nothing whatever to do with imitating or following the dictates of this Darkness, as if Chaos could provide us with a pattern to live by, as if Darkness could shed light on the true nature and responsibilities of the human form. The spirituality of the *Kali-yuga* requires us to maintain our connection, at no matter what cost, with the Pole of Essence, no matter how veiled and compromised and counterfeited the collective intuition of that Pole may have become, and to do so without falling into the temptation of atavism. According to Apocalypse 25:31–46, those who maintain their connection with the Essential Pole in the face of Chaos at its most potent are the *sheep*, while those who fall either into the temptation of atavism, or into the more serious temptation of capitulating to the prevailing Chaos directly, are the *goats.*

Spiritually Positive Manifestations of the Substantial Pole: *Kāli* and *Theotokos*

This, however, is not the whole story, seeing that the Pole of Substance also has a positive function in *Kali-yuga* spirituality, one that goes beyond our initial duty to simply say NO to its commands. The particular function of Chaos is to dissolve form, and in order to fulfill this function as completely as possible, Chaos must collect into one place all the remaining residues of the forms of spirituality and human life that made their appearance during the course of the *manvantara*, doing so without reference to the contexts that were originally proper to them or their specific station in the particular version of the ontological hierarchy that was integral to the *yuga* in which they appeared. (Can anyone fail to see, in this description of the Chaos of the Substantial Pole, in which the dead husks of all things are archived, the exact quality of cyberspace and the Internet?) The purpose of this total and heterogeneous collection of de-contextualized forms is simply to make it that much easier for Chaos to devour them all in a single gulp, thus bringing the *manvantara* to a close. And the immediate agent of this terminal Chaos, the one who gathers together all the psychic residues of the *manvantara* is, precisely, the Antichrist. He believes he is establishing a new and invincible empire based on the "wisdom of the ages," whereas he is actually collecting all that is dead, moribund and passé, all the psychic residues of the cycle now ending, so as to feed the terminal triumph of the Substantial Pole, all-devouring Chaos of the Goddess Kāli. And the last "residue" to be devoured will be Antichrist himself.

In *Kali-yuga*, the psychic residues of all the forms generated during the course of the *manvantara* make up what Carl Jung called "the collective unconscious," which is analogous in some ways to the *Pitri-loka* of the Hindus, the realm of the "Fathers," the kingdom of the dead. The collective unconscious reflects—on a lower, psychic level—the eternal Forms as they exist on the Platonic "plane of the Intelligibles," the realm of the Names or Attributes of God, which function as the true *archetypes* of all manifest forms, while residing on an ontological level higher than—and therefore unaffected by—the course of terrestrial *manvantara*, and even by the greater cycle represented by the creation and destruction of the entire universe. The plane of the Intelligibles makes up the celestial mandala or constellation of all the forms eternally emanated by the Pole of Essence. On the level of the collective unconscious, however, these archetypes are reflected not in the angelic matrix of the Intelligible Plane, but in the psychic and subtle-material matrix of the Substantial Pole as it subsists on the terrestrial plane. And given that they are the elements of the collective psyche from which the contents of each individual psyche are drawn, they are equally the elements of the individual and collective *ego*. Considered in this way, the psychic residues of the *manvantara* that is now ending function as psycho-physical *attachments*. In Vedantic terms, they are the various *identifications* of the indwelling *Atman*, Universal Witness or Absolute Self with this or that "sheath" (*kosha*) or limited aspect of manifest existence, identifications that act to veil that Self. In Muslim terms, they are *idols* occupying the Kaaba of the Heart.

The spiritual function of Kāli, and the *yuga* that all but bears Her name, is precisely to overturn these idols, dispel these identifications, dissolve these attachments. It is by this function that She returns all things to the Invisible, to the Transcendent Absolute, whose first re-appearance in the realm of subtle terrestrial manifestation will be as the Essential Pole of the next *manvantara*.

Kāli appears. We may turn toward Her consciously, recognizing the inevitability of Her advent, or we may consciously or unconsciously flee from Her: no matter, She is always faster than we are—faster because, wherever we may run for refuge, She is already there. She is already there because Kāli is, precisely, Absolute Reality appearing (unexpectedly!) not as the Essential Pole but as the Substantial Pole, as all-devouring Time transmuted into Energy: we cannot flee from Her because we are composed of Her.

Kāli appears, demanding from us all that we are—every form we have in any way identified with to generate the illusion of "me." As we peel off each layer of such identifications, attachments or idols, casting it into the mouth of Her Infinite Hunger—thereby revealing a subtler layer of identifications, a higher plane of forms—that hunger increases. She demands from us the next deeper layer, and the next layer, and the next, until finally all that's left is the *ahamkara*, the naked sensation of "me"—which, considered as an identification, is very the Self-idolatry that cast Lucifer out of Heaven, the last attachment of all, the one called "*I am God*." When this final attachment is released into the mouth of the Substantial Pole in Her apocalyptic hunger, the process of "divestiture" is complete; there is now nothing left, beneath the last veil, beneath *I am God*, but God Himself. And God sees only God.

As soon as the ego, individual or collective, is totally deconstructed, the Substantial Pole is transformed. Rather than a plane of matter largely opaque to the Spirit (in alchemical terms, the *materia secunda*)—a material reality that appears as a mass of darkness and ignorance as soon as we turn to it as our first principle, or else as a ravening hunger that will be satisfied with nothing less than the destruction of the entire universe—Substance now becomes the perfect Mirror of Absolute Reality, the *materia prima*, the pure Divine Receptivity that underlies all things—the only Matrix capable of receiving, and conceiving, the Logos, the First Eternal Manifestation of the Transcendent God. In this mode, the Substantial Pole is identifiable with the Virgin Mary as Mother of God or *Theotokos*. As God appears in the depths of Her Mirror, she rises up to become His *Shakti*, His *Shekhina*, His Self-manifesting and Self-reintegrating Radiance, the visible Glory of the Invisible: in Eternity, His Spouse, and on earth, His Mother.

Dugin's Doctrine of the Primacy of Chaos over Logos

Aleksandr Dugin, though he claims to accept the doctrines of René Guénon and the truth of the traditional eschatologies, by and large does not follow them. His identification of Chaos as the fundamental principle of our age is consistent with his denial of the reality of the individual (in *The Rise of the Fourth Political Theory*) and his virtual worship of the Russian racial *narod* in the place of God; but while these ideas are true to the quality of our time, Dugin—as we shall see—entirely rejects the spiritually appropriate and Traditional responses that our time requires.

Dugin understands that even the Logos, the Essential Pole, proceeds from Something which transcends it. Unfortunately, he chooses to characterize that Something as Chaos. As we will soon see, he speaks of the distinction between the Chaos preceding cosmic manifestation and the Chaos following it, and makes a further distinction between Chaos and simple confusion. But both aspects of Chaos, the former and the latter, are (in one sense) nothing but confusion—and whatever distinctions he makes between this or that type of Chaos he later erases in any case. The potentials of all things before creation, at least when considered from the standpoint of the ordered cosmos of manifestation, are confused and confounded, until the merciful form-giving power of the Essential Pole, the "Spirit of God" that "moved on the face of the waters" [Genesis 1:2]—the power Muslims call the *Nafas al-Rahman*, the Breath of the Merciful—leads them out of Chaos and into Cosmos by granting them the forms they yearn for. And the Chaos into which creation is dissolved at the end of the *manvantara*—or at the *mahapralaya*, the dissolution of the total material, psychic and spiritual universe—is also confusion, since it is affected by nothing less than the triumph of the Substantial Pole over the Essential Pole, of Chaos over Form. Dugin, however, imagines a kind of socio-intellectual Chaos of the Latter Days in which Logos is only *one* of the infinite potentials or possibilities that the Substantial Pole harbors—undoubtedly so as to justify his heterogeneous approach to both philosophy and political theory, as well as his overtures to various logically incompatible political movements, "strange bedfellows" who are sometimes united by little else than their common hatred of Liberalism. As Dugin puts it, "What we are divides us; what we are against unites us." Logos, however, can never be only *one* among the many possible manifestations of the original Chaos: it can only be the *first* manifestation, Source of all the others, and this only if "Chaos" is recognized as an unfortunate term for the Divine All-Possibility within God, previous to manifestation—the Sufi *wahad-iyyah*. Furthermore, the Transcendent Source of the Logos itself, the Unseen Realm from which it emerges, is necessarily the Essential Pole, not the Substantial Pole. Speaking in Christian terms, the Word appears, in every world capable of receiving His conception, only through the Theotokos, who is Virginal Substance—but the Word it Itself, the first Origin of every world in which He may "later" choose to incarnate, is spoken by the Father Alone. The myth of universal manifestation as arising from, and then returning to, the maternal waters of Chaos—mediated *only at one point* by Logos, which is merely one of her many children—is nothing but the image of the cycle-of-manifestation as seen strictly in terms of the Substantial Pole, according to the level of perception of those who lack the intuition of the Transcendent Absolute, who view creation, apocalypse and apocatastasis from the standpoints of *hyle* and *psyche* but not from that of *pneuma*. But those who intuit and understand the meaning of Vertical Causality, of the fact that the ultimate causes of all things lie in Eternity, not in time, are never fooled by any of the various self-contradictory theories of Chaos-as-Cause, one of which is the classical theory of evolution ("the natural selection of random mutations"), the absurd notion that formless and chaotic Substance can somehow give rise to form and order by the power of nothing other than its own formlessness—by which I mean, without the intervention of transcendent Form as given by the Word of God—the *kun!* ("Be!") of the Qur'an [2:177], the *fiat lux* of the Book of Genesis [1:3]. Chaos may be the womb, but it is not the *seed*; without the seed, the womb is barren.

The Alternative to Chaos-worship: The Formation of a Remnant

It is one of the cardinal principles of René Guénon and the Traditionalist/Perennialist School that, even in these last days of the *Kali-yuga*, we are still required to follow the norms of the various Divine Revelations whose dispensations have not yet lapsed—if indeed we can still find them. However, in the nature of things in this age of cosmic degeneration, our relationship to these Sacred Forms must become progressively more inner, more hidden, more secret than it was required to be in earlier times; an understanding of this, and a commitment to the *practice* of it, is inseparable from the notion of a Remnant. In line with this necessary spiritual introversion, private devotions and contemplation will become more and more central to the spirituality of any viable Remnant, though not to the exclusion of canonical and sacramental forms—

unless these are in fact withdrawn by forces beyond our control. In addition, those forms of prayer and contemplative practice that remain to us will necessarily tend toward simplification and concentration; this is why the sages of more than one tradition have declared that the form of spiritual practice most compatible with Iron Age conditions is the Invocation of the Divine Name, the Prayer of the Heart. It is in the simplicity of naked prayer that the Essential Pole can most readily be intuited, perhaps on a deeper level than was possible—at least to the human collective—even in *Satya-yuga*. Paradoxically, the progressive dissolution of subtler and subtler veils of form by the Spirit of God operating through the Substantial Pole—no matter how rigorous such mercy may appear to those encompassed and penetrated by that Spirit—makes the immediate intuition of the Essential Pole via direct contemplation of the Logos progressively easier to achieve in these final days of the cycle. This is one of the hidden graces of the *Kali-yuga*; if we know how to put it to use, we may be granted greater spiritual progress in one day than the denizens of *Satya-yuga*—who have little motivation to progress beyond their lush condition of "so near yet so far"—could make in a thousand years. The following passage is from the Hindu epic the ***Ramayana***, considered in Hinduism to be the first poem of the world. And though it is not based on the doctrine of the Four Yugas as found in the ***Puranas***, but rather on three descending world-ages that roughly correspond to the three *gunas* in the Hindu Samkhya Philosophy—*satwa, rajas, tamas*—it is still a perfect summation of this section:

> In the first age of the world
> men crossed the ocean of existence
> by their spirit alone.
> In the second age sacrifice and ritual began,
> and then Rama lived,
> and by giving their every act to him
> men lived well their ways.
> Now in our age what is there to do
> but worship Rama's feet?
> But, my friend, the last age
> of this world shall be best,
> for then no act has any worth, all is useless…
> except only to say *Rama*.
> The future will read this. Therefore I tell them:
> When all is in ruin around you, just say *Rama*.
> We have gone from the spiritual to the passionate.
> Next will come Ignorance. Universal war.
> Say *Rama* and win! Your time cannot touch you.

So the proper context for the manifestation of spiritual Form in a time of increasing formlessness is the Remnant, a word which suggests a small group, or a number of such groups, who have withdrawn from society, gone into "occultation," fled the Darkness of This World in line with the command of the 18ᵗʰ chapter of the *Apocalypse*. It is as if they were called to occupy what the Zoroastrians call "the Var of Yima," and the Qur'an "the Cave of the Sleepers" (in the *Surah al-Kahf*), that compound of "spiritual survivalists" who are destined to outlast the end of time and the dissolution of the *manvantara* because they are in fact situated *above* time, in a condition of relative or *aeonian* eternity. Membership in such a Remnant would seem to strictly preclude any sort of political or social action. Nonetheless, many scriptures, including the Hindu *Puranas*, the *Younger Avesta* of the Zoroastrians, the Old Testament book of *Isaiah*, the Dead Sea Scrolls, the Muslim *hadith* literature, and the *Apocalypse* itself speak of a messianic conflict against the forces of evil which is prophesied to accompany the advent or return of the Savior at the end of the age—whether that Savior be called Saoshyant (his Zoroastrian name), the Kalki Avatara (his Hindu name), the Messiah (his Jewish name), Maitreya (his Buddhist name), Jesus (his Christian and Muslim name) or the Mahdi (a name exclusive to the Muslims). In other words, not only a contemplative but also an *active* role is envisioned for the followers of that Savior in the latter days, a role to be enacted not exclusively in the inner world of the soul but also on the field of history. The tendency to take such prophesies too literally, if not to "press for the End" and seek to force the hand of God by rebelliously acting them out, represents a real danger in times like ours. Nonetheless, God remains a free agent, retaining both the right and the power to call into action—and into *any kind* of action—whoever He chooses. What such a call might look like in this age of Chaos, of the dominance of the Substantial Pole over the Essential Pole and the dissolution of sacred forms, is the subject *Chapter Seven*, below.

What is Chaos?

We will now turn more directly to the ideas that Aleksandr Dugin expresses in his essay "The Metaphysics of Chaos."

It is difficult to understand exactly what Dugin means by "Chaos." He says that he is using the word "in the Greek sense," but this doesn't do much to clear up the ambiguity. In Greek, Chaos literally means "chasm." Hesiod defines it as "the first created thing." The Orphics apparently thought of Chaos as the offspring of the union of Time and Necessity. The Roman poet Ovid defines the primordial Chaos as a "shapeless heap" of all the elements, a confused mass characterized by darkness and conflict. Is Dugin's Chaos the unmanifest Reality that holds sway before the forms of things come into existence, before the Divine *fiat lux*? If so it must be identified with the as-yet-unmanifest Will or the as-yet-unknown Intelligible Nature of God, the Essential Pole before it moves to create. Or is it the mysterious *materia prima*, the as-yet-unmanifest Substantial Pole, waiting in darkness for that Will to move, the "waters" mentioned in *Genesis* 1:2 before the "Spirit of God" moves upon the face of them—presuming, that is, that the Poles can be distinguished *in divinis*, before they are polarized? If so it is the realm of latent power, potential or potency that the Hindus call *Prakriti*, the primordial Substantial Pole. Or does Dugin see Chaos more as the black magician Aleister Crowley saw it, as—in Dugin's words characterizing Crowley's doctrine of the period between *manvantaras* (as quoted by Anton Shekhovstov in "The Palingenetic Thrust of Russian Neo-Eurasianism: Ideas of Rebirth in Aleksandr Dugin's Worldview")—"the tempest of equinoxes . . . the epoch of the triumph of chaos, anarchy, revolutions, wars, and catastrophes . . . waves of horror [which] are necessary to wash away the remnants of the old order and clear the space for the new one"? Insofar as Dugin opposes Chaos to Logos, which he does in a number of places, we must tentatively assume that his "Chaos"—if it actually means anything at all—represents either the manifest Substantial Pole in its initial confusion before it is ordered by Logos—the *materia secunda*—or the Substantial Pole in its un-manifest primordial latency—the *materia prima*—since Logos is simply another name for the active expression of the Essential Pole. However, to the degree that Aleksandr Dugin also presents Chaos as the Mother of Logos, as well as of everything else, we can't be entirely sure of this. He says:

> *Logos* as the first principle of exclusion is included in chaos, present in it, enveloped by it, and has a place granted inside of it, as the mother bearing the baby bears in herself what is a part of herself and what is not a part of her at the same time. . . . Chaos is the eternal nascence of the Other, that is, of *logos* . . . chaotic philosophy is possible because chaos itself includes *logos* as some inner possibility.

Chaos as the Mother of Logos could only be the mystery of the Divine Reality before it polarizes, in the process of God's Self-manifestation, into the Essential Pole and the Substantial Pole—into what are called, in Islam, the "Sublime Pen" and the "Guarded Tablet." On the other hand, Chaos opposed to or polarized with Logos would be the Substantial Pole pure and simple. But since Dugin apparently defines it both ways, all we can do is muddle ahead and see what we come up with.

The Rise of Chaos, the Death of Logos

Dugin, following Heidegger, announces the end of Logos as a philosophical and social principle:

> Modern European philosophy began with the concept of Logos . . . over two thousand years, this concept became fully exhausted. All the potentialities

and principles of this logocentric way of thinking have now been thoroughly explored, exposed and abandoned by the philosophers.

If so, then so much the worse for the philosophers. If Logos were simply a humanly-imagined concept with no objective referent, then perhaps we could talk about its "exhaustion." The fact is, however, that no true philosopher or theologian or metaphysician who ever spoke of Logos believed it to be anything less than the universal principle of transcendent and form-giving order by which God creates the universe, the "Spirit of God" (Essence) that "moved upon the face of the waters" (Substance) in *Genesis*. Some mentally unbalanced individual might say, "the notion of the Sun is philosophically and culturally exhausted." He might say it on every conceivable occasion and even garner widespread agreement with it. Nonetheless, the Sun would still be there. As Jalaluddin Rumi says in one of his quatrains:

> Who says the ever-living One has died,
> The Sun of Hope is gone, His days are done?
> Sun-killer climbed the roof and shut his eyes,
> Then cried out, like a fool, "I've killed the Sun!"

The abandonment of Logos by "philosophers"—though this term, since it means "lovers of wisdom," is obviously no longer adequate to describe those who still choose to go by that name—has not had and never could have the slightest effect on the nature of Reality. The degeneration of the human mind cannot alter the Real, only alienate us from it, thereby cutting us off from the Principle of our existence, and consequently destroying us.

Dugin goes on to say:

> European philosophy was based on the *logocentric* principle corresponding to the principle of exclusion, the differentiating, Greek *dia[i]resis*. All this corresponds strictly to the masculine attitude and reflects a patriarchal, authoritative, vertical, and hierarchical order of being and knowledge.... The masculine approach to reality imposes order and the principle of exclusivity everywhere. That is perfectly manifested in Aristotle's logic, where the principles of identity and exclusion are put in the central position. A is equal to A, not equal to not-A. This identity excludes non-identity (alterity). Here it is the male who thinks, speaks, acts, fights, divides, orders and so on.

This is certainly true as far as it goes; "masculine" precision of discourse is not everything in the intellectual life—yet what methods could philosophical discourse be based on other than discursive ones? Nonetheless, despite the "philosophical exhaustion of the Logos," Dugin certainly feels free to use exclusionary logic not only within its legitimate limits—where it can never be "exhausted" unless we want to elevate lying to the status of a metaphysical principle—but also in the service of a long line of absurd contradictions, as well as implying that, since honesty is a masculine trait, femininity must be essentially dishonest. For example, in *The Rise of the Fourth Political Theory* he coins the motto "We are the supporters of the Absolute and we are against the relative"—which contradicts itself by trying to use division to "advance" Unity. Likewise Dugin writes, in the same book: "We defend our values—hence, we're right," to which we might respond, paraphrasing the "Atlanticist" playwright William Shakespeare, "Blood is no argument." The values of any civilization or nation or culture or tribe that accepts, in whatever language of symbols this truth may be expressed, that the Absolute is the Origin, and the universe is His creation or manifestation, and that Man is the epitome of the universe, are worth defending to the death. The same is not true, however, of degenerate cosmologies that, no matter how sophisticated their science of psychic beings and powers or subtle material forces may be, have forgotten God. The first need is not for the *narod* to defend its values, but rather for it to have enough wisdom, vigilance and sense of responsibility—in the person of its leaders, intellectuals, sages and saints—to make sure that it has values worth defending. Furthermore, since the only absolute in Dugin's worldview seems to be the "absolute evil" of Liberalism, in opposition to which he is working to build a coalition based on a heterogeneous mass of mutually-exclusive cultural "debris," (a reference to the "metaphysics of debris" of philosopher Alexander Sekatsky, for which see below), we must conclude that, while he is "for the Absolute and against the relative" in theory, in many ways he is "against the Absolute and for the relative" in practice.

Dugin, following Heidegger, claims that the notion of Chaos was never accounted for in Western philosophy, beginning with the Greeks. He says:

> The problem of Chaos and the nature of Chaos was neglected and put aside from the very beginning of this philosophy. The only philosophy we know at present is the philosophy of *Logos*. But Chaos is something opposite to *Logos*, its absolute alternative.

I do not agree, however, that the Greeks had no understanding of Chaos as a concept or a reality or a destiny—especially since Dugin himself speaks of "Chaos in the Greek sense"! Insofar as the Platonists recognized the One as lying beyond the plane of the Intelligibles, Universals or Ideas, they certainly had a concept of a Reality that transcends, encompasses and gives birth to the principle that emanates and recognizes intelligible being, which is Logos. And in their acceptance of the validity of *axioms*, self-evident truths that provide a basis for logic but cannot be arrived at by logic, the direct Intellection of Transcendent realities was also recognized and accepted—and Transcendental Intellection, as a way of knowing that transcends logic, is one of the possible definitions of "Chaos" hinted at by Dugin, though it is more accurate to call this faculty the "Immanent/Transcendent Logos" than "Chaos." In any case, the Greeks certainly did not limit Logos to logic, *diairesis* or discursive reasoning. Those who can understand only logic must see everything beyond logic—the world of direct illumination beyond the darkness of Plato's Cave—as nothing but Chaos in its usual sense of unintelligible confusion. Those capable of hierarchical thinking, however, know that there are intelligible things higher than logic, and that the One is even higher than intelligible things. The One in Itself can only be known through its unknowability, through its power to declare its own Absoluteness by setting an absolute limit to both discursive rationality and direct Intellection—and in actual fact it is impossible to see, without a hierarchical epistemology, any truth higher than logic operating on sense experience. Is this mysteriously-knowable Unknowability of the One what Dugin means by Chaos? Or is he referring to the other kind of Chaos, the one that can only exist relative to the excesses of an artificially-imposed order—Dionysian Chaos, that is, whose function is to rebalance the cosmic environment by limiting and breaking down those artificial excesses? The Greeks always accounted for Chaos in the first sense, and—at least judging from Euripides' play *The Bacchae*—they learned about the Dionysian brand of Chaos the hard way. But the true hierophant of Dugin's "higher Chaos" in the Greek world, of course, was Homer; his *Odyssey* presents a complete doctrine of it, both theoretical and practical. He could do this because he understood Chaos as, precisely, *Maya*: Helen is *Avidya-Maya*, Penelope is *Vidya-Maya*, and Circe is *Prakriti* or *Mahamaya* herself.

Nor can Logos be limited to exclusionary Aristotelian logic, *diairesis*, or syllogism. Logos is the "logic" of God, not the logic of man. It encompasses every aspect of order, including David Bohm's *implicate* order. Human logic, as a metaphysical operation, is basically a kind of preliminary training in the ability to see order where it might not initially be apparent; its goal is to convey the human mind to the threshold of That which transcends logic (though never refuting it), to an Order that is higher and more all-encompassing and more synthetically unified than mere logic can comprehend—to the threshold of the Essential Pole, the differentiating Logos in its undifferentiated Essence, which is the *Nous*. Likewise in Chinese philosophy, the cycle of 64 changes that comprise the *I Ching*, each of which representing a discrete constellation of forces operating in Heaven, on Earth, and in Man, ultimately trains us to intuit both the mode of operation and the intrinsic nature of the unitary Tao. But when the Platonic tradition, which includes those aspects of Plato's philosophy that Aristotle particularly concentrated on and expanded upon, lost its contemplative *praxis*, leaving only its discursive *theoria*—that is, when it ceased to be an operative Spiritual Path—the illusion that logic could discover and establish truth by its own operations, rather than elucidating, by means of *diairesis* and

dianoia, the implications and internal correspondences of those truths originally arrived at through direct Intellection, by means of *Nous*, western philosophy became purblind. To put it another way, the misstep at the "origin" of
Western Philosophy—at least as it finally became—was not the reliance upon
Logos but the separation of Logos from its spiritual Principle, from God the
Father, from Absolute Reality conceived of as an eternal form-giving Essence, in
itself transcending form. In other words, it is not Logos that is exhausted, but
only Logos operating on a purely mental level, alienated from contemplation,
theurgy, intellection and revelation.[3] Perhaps the consequences of this regime
of darkened and ever-darkening perception have now been understood by
some philosophers. If so, the only Way open to them is to return from logic to
Logos, from artificially imposed order on the human plane to intrinsic and
transcendent *forma* on the Divine one, to the merciful and form-giving order
of the First Cause, of the Word who from the beginning has been *with* God
while at the same time *being* God [John 1:1]. The irrefutable demonstration,
before our very eyes, of the reality of this transcendent-and-immanent Logos, is
the astounding harmony of natural law as it operates in the realms of physics,
cosmology, chemistry, biology, and—supremely and definitively—in the
Human Form. Simply by virtue of our possession of that Form, we are heirs-in-
potential, by the Grace of God, to every intellectual discipline: physics, cosmology, chemistry, biology, as well as philosophy, theology, metaphysics. If we fail
to discern the Way back to true Logos, if we do not accept both the adequacy
and the duty of the Human Form to travel it, then we will descend into the
Chaos we have invoked by our Promethean attempt to manipulate Logos outside Will of God, first to be driven mad and then to be torn limb-from-limb,
like Orpheus by the Bacchantes—into the Chaos which is precisely *Postmodern
Liberalism* in its death-throes. Though the Logos in itself is incorruptible and
eternal, the individual and social consequences of the veiling of the principle of
Logos in the collective mind are nothing short of disastrous.

The Fall of Logos as a Principle of Social Order

Malcolm Muggeridge spoke of "the great Liberal death-wish"; it is this that we
now see being acted out in the western nations. Consider the unprecedented
Liberal campaign against sexual harassment that is going on in the United
States today, which, while finally saying an effective NO to the exploitation of
women by rich and powerful men in American society, has also exposed a deep

---

3. See ***Philosophy and Theurgy in Late Antiquity*** by Algis Uzdavinys for a thorough exposition of
Platonism not as a mere "philosophical system" but as a complete Spiritual Path, comprising both
discursive *theoria* and contemplative *praxis*.

strand of unconscious Puritanism in American society—the very Puritanism that Liberalism believed it had done away with for good—and demonstrated that, while religious Puritanism may be problematic, Puritanism without God, like the "Anti-Sex League" in George Orwell's *1984*, is infinitely worse. It was Liberalism that took as one of its central principles the idea that no form of sexual expression (except pedophilia) is sinful or pathological—that, as Freud believed, the only sexual sin was sexual repression. It was Liberalism that legalized pornography and made it universally available. And it was Liberalism that reduced the whole spectrum of erotic attraction between the sexes to physical sex alone by declaring the ethos of Romance to be dead. But now, with exquisite irony, it is precisely Liberalism that is in the process of not only criminalizing true sexual harassment, but also calling into question every form of "flirting," courtship, and sexual communication between men and women outside marriage. (If women are now saying a firm NO to sexual harassment, it is their responsibility to clarify what forms and styles of male sexual attention outside marriage they consider to be respectful and appropriate, or else to accept heterosexual celibacy.) Of course the crucial distinction is made, in Liberalism, between consensual and non-consensual sex in both action and gesture—but if no sex act is intrinsically immoral, if all sexual repression is pathological, if the objectifying and dehumanizing of sexuality in the context of pornography is entirely acceptable, if the romantic dance between the sexes is now a thing of the past, then *what happens to the distinction between consensual and non-consensual sex?* It is at the very least put under immense pressure and rendered contradictory and ambiguous. If sexual morality is seen as old-fashioned and repressive, then nothing remains but sexual selfishness and brutality. The upshot is that Liberalism, which is in the process of outlawing the public expression of Christianity, is, in effect, simultaneously being forced to re-establish certain elements of traditional Christian sexual morality—at least in heterosexual sphere—by defining more and more forms of sexual expression outside marriage as inherently sinful. An ethos wracked and buffeted by this degree of self-contradiction is obviously not long for this world. Aleksandr Dugin sometimes appears to believe that it will take nothing less than a Third World War between Russia and the U.S. to destroy Liberalism, when all he really has to do is sit back and watch Liberalism destroy itself.

When Modernist individualism, operating within a "rational" order of Liberty, Equality and Fraternity, becomes, in its senility, a postmodernist "atomic individualism" operating in no context whatsoever but the laws of probability—a "social Heisenbergianism" of random indeterminacy that presumes to grant to every "voice," every concept or fantasy or mere image of the mind, and every impulse of the passions including the most self-contradictory and suicidal, equal weight and an equal right to speak—these, not human persons, now being in effect the new "individuals"—then God is denied quasi-absolutely, and society, history, the earth and the human race are on the road to annihilation. The inverted Postmodern Liberal would (if he could) establish universal suffrage by granting the vote to every separate cell in his body—and this is not hyperbole: a Liberal, nature-worshipping woman of my acquaintance, who recently died of a brain tumor, was reluctant to receive chemotherapy because, as she put it, "my cancer has a right to live too." Make a "political theory" out of *that* if you can, you Liberal (or Duginist) Chaos-worshippers: When *cosmos* is denied there can be no *polis*, and without a *polis* there can be no *politics*.

Nonetheless, there is some truth in the idea that logic, *diairesis*, etc., is "patriarchal, authoritative, vertical, hierarchical." What is emphatically not true is that the "matriarchal" contrary to Logos is Chaos; this far-from-uncommon notion is simply the habitual slander against the Feminine Principle concocted by the self-involved Masculine Principle alienated from its metaphysical roots. Men whose egos are dominated by an obsessive, dry, perverted and heartless Logos that presumes to operate on its own recognizance, in rebellion against the Heavenly Father, will always see the Feminine Principle as pure Chaos. And how else could they see her? If the human Logos-function knows no God to Whom it can devote itself, from Whom it can receive its first principles, and Whom it can and must acknowledge—freely and gladly—as an Order infinitely transcending the finest and most intricately-designed order the human is mind capable of producing, *even under Divine inspiration*—where else can it look, in fear and trembling, to catch a glimpse of its own absolute limits but into the Abyss of the Feminine? A God-rejecting ghost of what the Logos was in its original integrity *must* define the Feminine Principle as Chaos simply because it is not Logos. What other choices do we have, now that God is out of the picture? Cut off from the light of the Heavenly Father, the ego-bound Masculine Principle can never see the Feminine as it is, and therefore must encounter it, or the ghostly phantasm of it, as little more than a screen for the projection of its own fears and desires.

This false vision of the Feminine Principle on the part of the perverted Masculine Principle appears in Dante's *Inferno* as a bat-winged three-faced Lucifer frozen up to his chest in the lake of Cocytus—a being who is Satanic *precisely because it has failed to achieve true Femininity*, defined as an *active receptivity* to God, and so must remain a self-contradictory hermaphrodite. And imprisoned in the frozen lake along with Lucifer are all the souls of the most deeply damned, visible in their contorted paralysis through the ice; this is Dante's image of the polluted *materia secunda*, of the Substantial Pole in its most destructive manifestation, its abysmal power to dissolve and petrify all things in an undifferentiated Chaos where both integrity of form and freedom from form have become impossible. But behind the veil of *materia secunda* lies the *materia prima*, the Substantial Pole in her primordial and virginal purity. The self-involved Masculine Principle cut off from God can only see the Feminine Principle as Cocytus, as the Medusa, as the Great Witch of Russian folklore, the Baba Yagá. ("Aleksandr Dugin is being eaten by the Baba Yagá" says my wife Jenny.) But the Masculine Principle that has sworn fealty to the Heavenly Father can know the Feminine Principle as she really is—not as the terminal Chaos that stands at the end of the *Kali-yuga*, set to devour all our crimes and abortions, but as the Mother of God, the Theotokos. The Theotokos is neither a sullen, chaotic rejection of form nor a black, engulfing void, ravenously destructive of it; rather, she is the one who is perfectly receptive to form—"Be it done unto me according to Thy Word" [Luke 1:38]—and consequently stands as the seamless mirror of God-given form in every world—"My soul doth magnify the Lord" [Luke 1:46]. She can do this because she is nothing less, in Frithjof Schuon's words, than "pure prayer," because she knows all true form as the life-giving seed of the Heavenly Father, the supraformal Essence. As Hagia Sophia, Holy Wisdom, the Virgin is the one who lets us conceive Christ in our hearts; an allied function is her power to let us actualize Transcendental Ideas, by acting as the receptive matrix for them in the human microcosm.[4]

Chaos vs. Chaos

As we indicated above, Dugin gives two different definitions of the word Chaos: the primordial Chaos of the Greeks and Chaos as conceived of by Postmodernism and science. The first definition is the scientific:

---

4. An archaic version of Hagia Sophia from Russian folklore is Snegurochka the Snow Maiden, granddaughter of Ded Moroz or Father Frost. Although Ded Moroz now functions more-or-less as the "Russian Santa Claus," in earlier times he was seen as a formidable and dangerous Power of the North. This quality is in line with the characterization of the North as rigorous or even demonic in mythologies from many parts of the world. On a deeper level, however, the North does not represent demonic evil but the rigor of Transcendence. This indicates that Ded Moroz was likely worshipped at one time as the High God of the Pole Star, the visible point of Eternity in the created order. As such he would have been cognate with various other Asian Polar High Gods, such as the Turkic/Mongolian deity Bai-Ülgen, demiurge of Tengri the Creator. Snegurochka's relationship to Ded Moroz is analogous in some ways to Holy Wisdom's to Yahweh in the Book of Proverbs. That the Snow Maiden is a type of Holy Wisdom is illustrated by the story that she was kidnapped by demons at one point, just as the Gnostic Sophia was abducted by the evil Archons, as well as by the interesting fact that when she makes her appearance at Christmas she asks the children riddles. Riddles are a traditional "Socratic" teaching method in many ancient cultures, designed to overcome our metaphysical *amnesia* by calling up knowledge that we already possess but have forgotten—ultimately so that we may ask and answer the central question posed by both by Sri Ramana Maharshi and the Delphic Oracle: "Who am I?"

Modern physics and philosophy refers to complex systems, bifurcation or non-integrating equations and processes, using the concept "Chaos" to designate such phenomena. They understand by that not the absence of order, but a more complicated form of order that is difficult to perceive as such, and is, in fact, its essence. Such Chaos or turbulence is calculable in nature, but with more sophisticated theoretical and mathematical means and procedures than the instruments that classical natural science is dealing with. The term "Chaos" is used here in a metaphorical manner. In modern science we are continuing to deal with an essentially *logocentric* manner of exploring reality. So the "Chaos" here is no more than a dissipative structure of *Logos*, the last result of its decay, fall, and decomposition. Modern science is dealing, not with something other than *Logos,* but with a kind of post-*Logos,* or ex-*Logos*: *Logos* in the state of ultimate dissolution and regression. The process of the final destruction and dissipation of *Logos* is taken here for "Chaos."

Here, within the definition of Chaos according to science, we actually have not one but two opposing versions. First Dugin says that "Chaos" in contemporary science is still "logocentric" in that it is "calculable ... but with more sophisticated theoretical and mathematical means and procedures than the instruments that classical natural science is dealing with." Then he says that it represents "a kind of post-*Logos* ... *Logos* in the state of ultimate dissolution and regression." However, the ability to make complex and "sophisticated" calculations does not per se represent the dissolution of Logos as a worldview but rather its continuing development and advancement. The point in modern science where Logos does indeed regress and dissolve is the point where the notion of *probability* is introduced—probability not as an *approximation* to deterministic causality but as a principle that *replaces* deterministic causality as an explanation for measurable events. When probability replaces causal determinism as the dominant principle, this results in such concepts as a "multiverse" in which our highly-ordered universe is only one of an infinite number of "random" universes, one of the universes that "happen" to be characterized by order and are therefore capable of producing beings who can contemplate and calculate that order. It is under the regime of probability, not implicate order, that Logos is deconstructed, since it is seen as merely one of the possible infinite expressions of Chaos.

Next Dugin returns to his original distinction between primordial and postmodern Chaos:

We need to distinguish between two kinds of Chaos, the postmodernist "Chaos" as an equivalent to confusion, a kind of post-order [*described above*], and the Greek Chaos as pre-order, as something that exists before ordered reality has come into being. Only the latter can be considered as Chaos in the proper sense of the word. This second, but actually the original, conception of Chaos should be examined carefully and metaphysically.

As we have already seen, this "Chaos"—which Dugin names "Greek" Chaos, directly contradicting his statement above that the logocentric Greek philosophers had no idea of Chaos—is either the pre-manifest Logos, the hidden order of the Essential Pole in a state of latency prior to creation; or the undifferentiated Substantial Pole in a state of latency, when "the earth was without form and void, and darkness was upon the face of the deep," waiting to receive the Word or Spirit of God from the Essential Pole; or a union of Essence and Substance prior to their polarization, these being three ways of envisioning a reality previous to intelligible order. It is metaphysically possible to see Logos as existing in a latent state in the Reality that precedes manifestation—yet when Dugin says, "Chaos itself includes Logos as some inner possibility," we can't be entirely sure that he is not just repeating the speculation, from post-Einsteinian, essentially Heisenbergian physics, that "given an infinite number of random universes, at least one of them will necessarily be a universe of order," and thus slipping back into the postmodern/scientific definition of Chaos that he rejects. Furthermore, since Dugin, following Heidegger, announces the end of Logos in the post-logical Chaos of Postmodernism, and at the same time invokes pre-logical "Chaos" as the regime which will *succeed* the regime of Logos, how then can he clearly distinguish between the "Chaos" that precedes order and the Chaos that follows it? The truth is, he can't, at least not in any reliable way. Ibn al-'Arabi, in line with a number of archaic mythological systems, presents the initial state of creation as one of profusion and confusion, which is then drawn into harmonious order and design by the spiritual function he identifies, in his *Fusus al-Hikam*, with the prophet Seth. The same transition from Chaos to Cosmos is symbolized in Greek mythology by the overthrow of the Titans by the Gods, in Babylonian myth by the slaying of the Chaos-monster Tiamat by the god Marduk, and in the Norse cosmology of the Runes by the transition from *Thuriaz*, the rune of Thor, to *Ansuz*, the rune of Odin. And the terminal descent of Cosmos into Chaos, defined as a state of confusion which dissolves form and returns all created things to the Formless Reality of God that first manifested them, is a common theme in the eschatological prophesies of nearly every people or religion. It would be wonderful if the terminal Chaos of Postmodernism could simply be transformed, by a kind of instantaneous pole-shift, into the original "Greek" Chaos of pre-eternity (if that was what they actually meant by the word, which is far from certain), filled with the fresh and vital energies of potential Order—without, that is, the inconvenience of Apocalypse, the dissolution of all things, the consummation of the *aeon*, the end of the world—but this is not possible. And it is this impossibility, and Dugin's inability to fully face it, that lies at the basis of his perennial ambiguity as to which type of Chaos, the pre-logical or the post-logical, he is talking about at any given time.

Instead of trying to imagine or define a pre-logical "Chaos" using the tools of western logical discourse, or invoking such sterile, turgid and uselessly-complex non-concepts as Heidegger's *dasein*, he should familiarize himself with those traditional myths and philosophies that have already exhaustively dealt with the Reality that precedes, and gives rise to, intelligible order, one of the more useful of which is undoubtedly Taoism. The Tao, as presented in Lao Tzu's classic, the *Tao Te Ching*, is *precisely* Dugin's "Chaos" that comes before order and gives birth to order and exists parallel to order. And the way that such order arises, dissolves, and eternally subsists within the matrix of Tao is perfectly analyzed, and synthesized, in a second Chinese classic, the *I Ching*. Whoever makes a successful study of these sources will understand virtually everything that can be known, in human words, about the "Chaos" that precedes Logos, as well as its ongoing relationship to Logos. Why resort to Heidegger? Why reinvent the wheel, especially when the newly-invented wheel is a 16-sided polygon that can only give us a very bumpy ride? Lao Tzu turns out to be a far better "Greek" than the Greeks themselves—much less the Germans—proving once again that, speaking in terms of religion and philosophy, Europe has always been something like an outlying colony of Asia. Listen to this, from the *Tao Te Ching*:

> The Tao is elusive and intangible.
> Oh, it is intangible and elusive, but within is image.
> Oh, it is elusive and intangible, but within is form.
> Oh, it is dim and dark, but within is essence.
> This essence is very real, and therein lies faith.

> Look, it cannot be seen—it is beyond form.
> Listen, it cannot be heard—it is beyond sound.
> Grasp, it cannot be held—it is intangible.
> These three are indefinable;
> Therefore they are joined in one.
> From above it is not bright;
> From below it is not dark.
> An unbroken thread beyond description.
> It returns to nothingness,
> The form of the formless,
> The image of the imageless,
> It is called indefinable and beyond imagination.

The Tao that can be told is not the eternal Tao.
The name that can be named is not the eternal name.
The nameless is the beginning of heaven and earth.
The named is the mother of ten thousand things.
Ever desireless, one can see the mystery.
Ever desiring, one can see the manifestations.
These two spring from the same source but differ in name;
this appears as darkness.
Darkness within darkness,
The gate to all mystery.

To try to understand pre-eternal "Chaos" on the basis of words is like trying to cross the ocean balanced on floating reed. Words are necessary, but they will never be enough. Pre-eternal "Chaos," the Logos before it creates the universe, when It was *with* God and equally *was* God, can only be understood and realized in contemplative practice. The notion of trying to talk about It when you are not actually doing It, and of doing It without remembering that It is not only perfectly realized already, beyond all doing, and that it is nothing other than what you yourself most truly are—*Tat Twam Asi*—is a sure recipe for sterility and madness.

In the act of contemplation, however (and nowhere else) it actually is possible to transform the post-logical Chaos of confusion into the pre-logical "Chaos" of the original Unity. As the great Tibetan yogi Milarepa said, referring to the spiritual station the Sufis call "bewilderment": "How delightful confusion is when recognized as Wisdom!" An attachment to self-created intelligible order ultimately invokes mental confusion as its shadow, since, as Dugin correctly implies, such an attachment must continually attempt to exclude various elements that do not fit into the intelligible order we have constructed—necessarily so, because our power to exclude them is not absolute and requires an increasing expenditure of energy to maintain. Therefore the excluded elements always intrude. The same is true of any ordered society or any closed philosophical system. This is why the act of contemplation or meditation should never degenerate into a self-willed attempt to introduce order into the mind. The practice is simply to witness the mind as it is, in all its order, in all its chaos, in all its *whatever*. As mental self-will is progressively renounced, the mind is quieted to the point where it can begin to *hear its own noise*, ultimately recognizing it not as my many and various ideas and images of the nature of things, but rather as the primordial Energy of Being. To the degree that we can stop trying to introduce order into this Energy and simply witness it, it will be spontaneously revealed as *intrinsic* order—not the contrived order of mental obsessions and closed systems, which are inseparable from confusion, but the hum of unregulated "Chaos" itself, which is indistinguishable from Implicate Order,

Pre-eternal Design, the Pre-manifest Logos. Speaking in terms of Hindu yoga, that hum of primordial Energy is the *shabd*, the Inner Sound, the resonance within the human microcosm of the primordial syllable *Om*. It is the sound of the Transcendent/Immanent Logos, the point from which all explicit order emerges into the world of relativities—thus necessarily bringing confusion along with it, since order in the relative, contingent dimension can never be perfect—and into which all confusion dissolves so as to become one again with the essential, undifferentiated Order that Dugin is groping toward through his notion of pre-eternal Chaos. And the act of contemplation is the *only field* where the transformation from the postmodern and post-logical Chaos of confusion into the pre-eternal "Chaos" of implicate order can take place. We can't produce this transformation by shifting our intellectual priorities or re-envisioning our first principles or revising our philosophical premises. We can only do it by *dying*—by passing through the total annihilation of our self-concept and our world-concept, until all form is resolved into Energy. The apocalypse of the outer world can only be fully faced and dealt with by those who have already undergone the apocalypse of the inner world.

Archetypal Dishonesty

One thing that anyone trying to make sense of Aleksandr Dugin's philosophy will need to understand at the outset is that he is a kind of "practical phenomenologist" who describes and presents many different political and sociological paradigms more-or-less in their own terms, *not necessarily* as part of his own ideology; as a postmodernist, as well as a political organizer who is working to build a coalition out of the most heterogeneous and contradictory forces, he is adept at "letting other voices speak." One practical use of such an approach is that he can appear to advocate a particular paradigm when it suits his purposes, and elsewhere deny or excoriate it when the tactical situation warrants a change of approach. In other words, he does not limit himself to ideas as descriptions of reality, but more often employs them as tools or weapons. When a screwdriver or a rocket grenade launcher are called for, these emerge from his tool-chest/arsenal; when a land-mine or a crescent wrench are required, these immediately make their appearance; the grenade launcher and screwdriver are suddenly nowhere to be seen. Thus *any concept or ideological assertion is immediately deniable*. Many critics of my critique of Dugin will undoubtedly step forward with quotes from his writings where he extols Logos instead of deconstructing it, as when he condemns the Ukrainian opponents of Russian hegemony as those who "reject Logos," or where he advocates a traditional, hierarchical ordering of society rather than the Postmodern/Liberal ideal of atomic individualism, etc., etc. Consequently, at any convenient juncture, he can claim to be *lamenting* the fall of the logocentric worldview rather than celebrating it, or *condemning* the adoption of Chaos as a fundamental paradigm instead of calling for it. If an entomologist simply describes a particular insect, say the locust (i.e., Chaos), or a botanist studies a particular tree, for example the Lebanon cedar (i.e., Logos), does this mean that the entomologist is "pro-locust" or the biologist "pro-cedar"? Of course not. Thus the critic who attempts to hold Aleksandr Dugin to a particular ideological position can be portrayed as a naïve simpleton who didn't realize that Dugin was merely describing that position, not advocating it, or as a witless, unsophisticated Philistine who foolishly believed Dugin was extolling something when he was actually satirizing it.

So we must conclude that Aleksandr Dugin is fundamentally dishonest. He is not *personally* dishonest, however, but *archetypally* dishonest. *Honesty* is an "Apollonian" trait, a virtue of the Essential Pole, the Logos. Dugin, however, now claims, in *The Rise of the Fourth Political Theory*, that he is in his "Dionysian period," which means that he takes as his operating principle the terminal Chaos of the *manvantara* under the rule of the Substantial Pole. Therefore all the dishonesty, prevarication and trickery of his discourse, his tendency to speak with forkéd tongue, and do so without the slightest shame, must be understood as a perfect reflection—without, of course, ceasing to be fundamentally dishonest—of Substantial Pole mores and consciousness. In the era of the dominance of the unpurified Substantial Pole, such notions as "the co-existence of non co-possible monads," "the reality of parallel timelines," and "the transcendence of the strictures of exclusionary logic" are not only entirely acceptable, but actually very hard to avoid. From the point of view of "masculine, hierarchical, logocentric, phallocentric" consciousness, Dugin is a liar and a fraud; nonetheless, as he himself points out, the "logocentric" view of things is now coming to an end, giving way to a condition of omni-simultaneity and all-possibility where "nothing is true and everything is permitted"; this is entirely in line with René Guénon's picture of cosmic conditions at the end of the *manvantara*. But if we really want to definitively answer the question of whether Dugin is an "advocate" of Logos or Chaos, the answer is actually quite simple: If he were operating on the basis of Logos, he would recognize it as the universal ordering-principle that is necessarily the *first* ontological level to emerge from the Divine All-Possibility—from "Chaos" in what he calls the "Greek" sense—the proximate Source of all that is to come, all the descending levels of the ontological hierarchy, the Great Chain of Being, rather than simply one of the several rabbits that might jump out of the hat of Chaos in the terminal sense, the appearance of which Chaos is heralded specifically by the *fall* of Logos. In other words, if Dugin's Logos is simply one of the many possibilities embraced by Chaos—rather than being the *implicate order* of Divine All-Possibility that, in ignorance of the Traditional terminology and because its order is not immediately intelligible to him, he calls "Chaos," as well as the necessary first manifestation of that trans-formal Order in the world of form—then Chaos *as opposed to* Logos is his fundamental paradigm, thus making him, before all else, a postmodern nihilist.

To say the same thing in a slightly different way, Dugin's basic operating principle, both intellectually and politically, is the Great Witch, the Baba Yagá. I have filled many pages deconstructing the relatively few pages of "The Metaphysics of Chaos"—according not to the canons of Postmodernism but to the principles of the Logos, as expressed in both logic and metaphysics. There is, however, a hundred-car trainload of chaotic Substantial Pole discourse still on its way from Aleksandr Dugin, yet to be deconstructed, and right now I don't have enough "hierarchical, logocentric, phallocentric" energy left to do the job. Logos may be able to "clean up" Chaos to a certain degree from the outside, but for any real *metanoia* to happen, for an *alchemical* transformation to take place, we must willing surrender our ego-attachment to Logos and allow the Logos-transcending Reality that we initially *perceive* as Chaos to purify us of prejudices and fixed ideas; only then will the resurgent spiritual Logos manifest the power to establish organic, fertile, living order, and our psychic and material Chaos be willing to submit to that order—not because it is powerful, but because it is beautiful.[5]

Surrender to Kāli

Before this total *metanoia* takes place, however, the shining, Apollonian, intellectual hero cannot simply stride up to the Baba Yagá and say: "Aroint thee, witch! I have exposed your inconsistencies and dispelled your illusions, therefore I claim the victory." The Baba Yagá is an immensely deluding and destructive power, which is why the servant of the Masculine Principle in its hierarchical and logocentric incarnation is duty-bound to deal with her up to the limits of his power, to do whatever he can to protect the human heart, the human mind and the human race against her glamours and attacks. But all this limited hierarchical thinking and logocentrism, everything based on what the intellectual hero *already knows*, will not be enough—because, at the end of the day, at the end of the *manvantara*, the field and the day belong to her. All she needs to say is, "I'm sorry, but that's not the game we are playing now." If we defy her, if we try to conquer her by imposing order, we will be destroyed; if we

---

5. For a clear exposition of this alchemical process of *solve et coagula*, see Hexagram 31, *Influence, Wooing*, in the Richard Wilhelm translation of the *I Ching*. Likewise the story of the failure of this process, and the disastrous consequences of that failure, appears in the same book, in line 6 of Hexagram 2, *The Receptive*: "Dragons fight in the meadow; their blood is black and yellow."

accommodate her and submit to her—while still trying to retain our limited ego-bound identities—we will be destroyed. The Baba Yagá cannot be simply relegated to a subordinate place by limited hierarchical thinking, kept outside the walls of the civilized *polis* by exclusionary Aristotelian logic, or put down by traditional, masculine strong-arm tactics. She cannot be excluded, she cannot be killed because she is an *archetype*—an eternal and immortal reality—a Name of God. The only way she can be dealt with is for us to realize her *as* an archetype, and this is something that can only be done if we also actualize our own archetypal nature. And the most complete archetypal manifestation of the Baba Yagá, the only level of her reality on which she can be dealt with definitively—by which I mean, in spiritual terms—is her appearance as the goddess Kālī. At the end of the *manvantara*, Kālī arises; Her role is to dissolve all form, to deconstruct the limited cosmic Logos of the *aeon* now ending, thereby transforming everything into pure Energy. So as to fulfill this function, she opens her blood-dripping mouth and eats us alive, skin, flesh, bones, and marrow—us, and the entire world along with us.

Or, rather, the entire *known* world. Because the truth is, the spiritual core of our being, the *Imago Dei*, the *Atman*, the Absolute Witness, cannot be devoured by the Eater-of-All-Forms because It is beyond form already. Therefore the practice, when facing Kālī, is to *let her devour us*—by which I mean, to let Her strip us of what the Advaita Vedantins call the *koshas*, the sheaths of the *Atman*—the physical sheath, the energy-emotional sheath, the rational-mental sheath, the Intellectual sheath, the sheath of Bliss—to allow Her to destroy every element of both our self-concept and the world it projects, to strip us of the last vestiges of self-definition and world-definition. If we can make this supreme sacrifice, then She will be transformed from the All-Destroyer into the infinite field of *Shakti*, Universal Energy. And we—or rather *I*, since I am speaking here specifically as a man—will thereby be archetypalized as *Shiva*, the *Shaktiman*, the Power-Holder, the one who "holds power" not by any claim of dominance or assertion of will, but precisely by fading back into the infinitesimal point or endless vertical column of the *Atman*, The Absolute Witness. Infinite Power can in no way be manipulated by "myself"-as-actor, because all I could ever conceive of myself as being or doing is already woven into Her universal veil, the veil of *Shakti*-as-*Maya*. Only the Absolute Witness can hold Universal Power—and that, only by witnessing It.

So unless Aleksandr Dugin can conceive of this supreme sacrifice, and actually find himself willing to make it, all his "empowerment," as both an intellectual and a political leader, his mental deftness and skill, his power to create identifications and thereby direct the streams of many different political movements into his Neo-Eurasian melting-pot—into the silent Dionysian fury of the Substantial Pole, the terminal postmodern Chaos falsely re-cast as pre-existent and Eternal, the Baba Yagá that he believes he has hitched to his wagon—will suddenly turn its teeth inward instead of outward. Whoever invokes Kāli must be prepared to come up with Her entire fee: "And he will get out again until he has paid the last farthing" [Matthew 5:26].

The Alternative to Postmodernism: Integral Metaphysics

Speaking in relative, temporal terms, not Absolute, Eternal ones, the logos of the *manvantara* now ending is indeed exhausted, ripe to be eaten by Kāli. But the Eternal Logos is not, nor can It ever be, exhausted. Christ is the Logos, and he is "with us all days, even to the end of the *aeon*" [Matthew 28:20]—and also after that, "unto ages of ages." Likewise every true and God-given religion understands that the Principle through which all things are created, by expression and revelation, and into which all things are reintegrated, by understanding and exegesis, can never die. What *is* exhausted is precisely the human *adventure* of trying to conceive of and use the Logos—or rather, the human folly of following the distant reflections of it—outside the embrace of integral metaphysics and Tradition, which are based not on speculation but on certainty, on the vision of the Always So. The drama of individualistic, Promethean speculation is indeed played out; Postmodernism is sufficient proof of that.

Integral metaphysics, however, is totally unaffected by the final curtain-fall of individualistic Western philosophy. It has been waiting patiently for just such a *denouement*, which it foresaw from the beginning—patiently and also serenely, because the Truth is sufficient unto itself.

What the nihilistic, fragmented, self-contradictory postmodern worldview will never see is that Unity is not only possible and desirable, but also necessary and inescapable. Reality really *is* One—but this One is in no way an imposed conceptual unity, or a forced social unification, or a closed system that excludes the many voices of the "other." Metaphysics is One precisely because it is *not* a closed system but an infinitely inclusive relationship to Truth that allows all things to be, and grow, and express their inherent natures, not by departing from their archetypes but by remembering them and embracing them and incarnating them. Metaphysical contemplation leads all things back to their inherent *logoi*, their true natures—not only at the end of time but in the depth of the present moment, which is also "the end of time"; it does so by returning them to their superabundantly creative Source. This is why integral metaphysics can put all things in their proper places, without editing them or paralyzing them or falsifying them or imprisoning them, simply by letting them BE, and witnessing them, in the light of Being Itself. Aleksandr Dugin is right when he implies that the world has had enough of the barren conflict between fragmentary philosophical imperatives, be they metaphysical or political. The world lies in ruins because of them. But this ruin has not the slightest effect on the power and use of integral metaphysics, though it has certainly compromised the human ability to accept metaphysics and understand it. When the vision of the Great Chain of Being is intact, all things are seen as a Unity without hegemony or spiritual imperialism, a Hierarchy without oppression of the weak or self-aggrandizement of the powerful, a Cosmos without things being in any way forced into some preconceived pattern. It is only when hierarchy collapses that incompatible conceptions of reality, incompatible aspirations and impulses, incompatible levels of intellectual understanding and spiritual capacity are forced, unnaturally, to occupy the same plane, and consequently set at war. This unnatural "leveling" is the oppressive *pseudo-unity* that Postmodernism hopes to liberate us from—a "unity" that is really nothing but fragmentation—while at the same time, ironically enough, being the very principle of Postmodernism itself. Postmodernism is based on fragmentation and nothing else; it is the force presently driving the self-contradictory regime of unification-imposed-via-fragmentation to its absolute, terminal limit. Such unification, of course, is impossible to achieve. A bear belongs in the forests, a bull belongs on the plains; if you put them together in the same arena, what else can they do but fight?

When the veil is lifted from the face of integral metaphysics, however, that conflict ends. Everything returns to its own proper center—to its own unique version of the One Center. Nothing longs to be other than itself, therefore no reality trespasses on the sovereign rights of any other. Diversity is fully celebrated; Unity is perfectly maintained. Dugin the postmodernist, however, wants to celebrate diversity while denying Unity, thus insuring that the banished and insulted pole of Unity will come back into play not through knowledge but through power. This is the fundamental error of Postmodernism—because what could possibly "celebrate" diversity except That which has the capacity to embrace it all in a single unified vision? Human society can never be perfectly ordered according to the primal Diversity-in-Unity of the universe, and this goes double for human society in the *Kali-yuga*. The human soul however, in individual instances, can approach this ideal state through metaphysical understanding. And unity-of-soul must express itself outwardly as unity-of-action.

From the Atlantean to the
Eurasian Hegemony via Postmodern Chaos

In reality, however, Aleksandr Dugin's celebration of diversity, his proposal for the establishment of a multi-polar world in ethnic and religious terms, *is* emanating from the standpoint of a kind of unity—the unstated but clearly evident unity of Russian hegemony. The Ottoman Empire, the Russian Empire and the

USSR all sought to manage their heterogeneous populations by granting a degree of local autonomy based largely on race and religion—but that didn't mean that all the tax-collectors had disappeared, that the intelligence services weren't still keeping a sharp eye on things, that the military wasn't always ready to intervene. And if one thing is certain, Vladimir Putin is not interested in any kind of "diversity" that might lead to the further breakup of the greater Russian state.

Russia has viewed the imposition of the neo-Liberal theories of the "Washington Consensus," the manifesto of economic globalization, with understandable alarm—especially when they are accompanied by the self-contradictory process of "imposed democratization," often backed up by military force, as in the case of the massive debacle known as the "Arab Spring." The Washington Consensus was originally designed as a program for the economic stabilization of "developing" nations—but how big a step is it from proposing the Consensus as a cure for destabilization to creating destabilization in order to justify imposing the Consensus? It is this ruthlessly "unipolar" face of Liberalism that Dugin has sworn to combat. Liberalism began with a willingness to accept a wide spectrum of human diversity because it believed that the human race was "naturally" struggling and evolving toward Liberal democracy and internationalism. At the same time, through economic and cultural imperialism, the United States, standard-bearer of Liberalism, was attempting to impose a global uniformity of products, services and aspirations, with conspicuous success. It is only now, in its extreme old-age, that the Liberal program has revealed itself more as the origin of social chaos than the cure for it—a revelation that has caused it to opt for the authoritarian imposition of the maximum degree of social chaos *as if it were a kind of order*, often in the form of what Dr. John Andrew Morrow has called "compulsory immorality." This is pretty much Aleksandr Dugin's analysis as well. Unfortunately, this is also where Dugin's positing of Chaos as the working principle behind his world revolution of ethnic and religious diversity against unipolar Liberalism and the dead-end of Postmodernism—a Chaos that is, in practice if not in theory, obviously closer to the post-Logos Chaos of confusion than the pre-Logos "Chaos" of the original Unity—reveals its inherent contradiction: if Aleksandr Dugin wants to be a true partisan of Chaos, then let him become a Liberal! In its denial of Transcendence, of verticality, of hierarchy—that is, of Logos—and consequently of the true the Unity of Being that only Transcendence and verticality and hierarchy can guarantee, Liberalism has proved itself to be the great world champion of universal Chaos—particularly in its terminal phase, which is, precisely, Postmodernism. And "Postmodernism," though Dugin says he rejects it, describes his method and worldview to a T.

Chaos *vs.* Christianity

To the degree that Aleksandr Dugin takes Chaos rather than Christ or Logos as his first principle, he can in no way be considered a Christian; we must therefore take his Russian Orthodox Old Believer piety with a large grain of salt. He is a "stage Christian," certainly, but he has plenty of other costumes in his trunk, ready to serve when he needs to project a different persona.

In "The Metaphysics of Chaos" he says:

> 1) It is not correct to conceive of Chaos as something belonging to the past. Chaos is eternal, but eternally coexisting with time. Therefore, Chaos is always eternally new, fresh and spontaneous. It could be regarded as a source of any kind of invention or freshness because its eternity has, in itself, always something more that was, is, or will be in time.

This is certainly true as far as it goes; it is an apt description of God's ongoing creation and preservation and redemption of the universe—that is, of the Traditional concept of Logos. So why does Dugin call it Chaos?

> 2) Chaos can think. We should ask her how she does this. We have asked Logos, now it is the turn of Chaos. We must learn to think with Chaos and within the Chaos.

Here the above question begins to be answered: he calls it Chaos because he sees it as a goddess. And because the Chaos Goddess has no established priesthood, theology and morality like Christianity does, he can play fast and loose with her, can define her any way he wishes and use her any way he wants—though certainly not without consequences. Thinking "with" and "within" Chaos might be a way of describing a transcendental Intellection of God, the sort of Knowledge-beyond-knowledge that many of the mystics, especially the Sufis, describe, or attempt to describe, in innumerable ways—a Knowledge that is accompanied by and made possible by the submission of the will to the as-yet-unknown Divine Commands, Commands that may or may not ever be fully intelligible to the human mind, but must be "obeyed" nonetheless. However:

> 3) We should explore other cultures, rather than the western, to try to find different examples of inclusive philosophy, inclusive religions and so on. Chaotic Logos is not only an abstract construction. If we seek well, we can find the real forms of such intellectual traditions in archaic societies, as well as in Eastern theology and mystical currents.

Here Dugin insults the reader's intelligence while simultaneously flattering his stupidity. He has just finished saying "Chaos is something opposite to Logos, its absolute alternative," and now he speaks of a "Chaotic Logos." This isn't exposition, it's hypnosis. I suspect it is rather naïve of me to speak of

Dugin's "justification," or lack of it, for saying this or that; nonetheless I am compelled to point out that his only conceivable justification for such contradictory intellectual sleight-of-hand would be, precisely, a *metaphysics of Chaos*—not "Chaos" in the supposedly august and elevated "Greek" sense of the word, but regular old-fashioned *chaos*, by which I mean confusion, contradiction and darkness. And—unless Aleksandr Dugin is subject to bouts of temporary dementia, or never edits his writing—we must conclude that he is methodically applying this Chaos for the purpose of pulling the wool over our eyes.

> 4) The astronomical era that is coming to an end is the fish constellation of Pices, the fish on the shore, the dying one. So we need water very badly now [*obviously from Aquarius*]. . . . *Logos* has expired and we will all be buried under its ruins unless we make an appeal to Chaos and its metaphysical principles, and use them as the basis of something new. Perhaps this is the "other beginning" Heidegger spoke of.

Heidegger's notion of this "other beginning" apparently involved some sort of abstract "return" of the Greek myths, as well as of the "Last God" in something like a terminal theophany of the mysterious, unnamed Primal God of the Greeks.[6] In positing such an occurrence, Heidegger was apparently trying to throw a veil of forgetfulness over the incident recounted in Acts 17:23, in which St. Paul, while in Athens, encounters a shrine "To the Unknown God," leading him to announce: "Whom therefore ye ignorantly worship, Him I declare to you." Nor should we ignore Dugin's blasphemous presentation of Ichthys, Christ the Fish—Christ being the avatar of the Piscean Age—as the fish of Logos dying on the seashore of Chaos. Let this blasphemy be so clearly imprinted on our minds that we never forget it, especially when Dugin dons his costume of the pious Russian Orthodox lamb. It is clear from this quotation that when Christ actually does return, His *parousia* will be every bit as inconvenient for Aleksandr Dugin and his Eurasian Empire as for the church of Fyodor Dostoevsky's Grand Inquisitor from *The Brothers Karamazov.*

> 5) European philosophy was based on the *logocentric* principle corresponding to the principle of exclusion, the differentiating, Greek *dia[i]resis*. All this corresponds strictly to the masculine attitude and reflects a patriarchal, authoritative, vertical, hierarchical order of being and knowledge . . . we must consider another road for thought, not in the logocentric, phallocentric, hierarchical and exclusivist way.

If Dugin were really a Christian, he would immediately recognize that para-

---

6. Perhaps the most accurate dramatization of "the return of the gods" that we possess is the delicious satirical fable "Ragnarok" by Jorge Luis Borges.

graph 1) can only be a description of God, or that face of God which He turns toward creation. Immediately the words of Christ would spring into his mind: "Before Abraham came to be, I Am" [John 8:58]; "Behold I am with you all days, even unto the consummation of the *aeon*" [Matthew 28:20]; "I come that they should have life, and have it more abundantly" [John 10:10]; "Behold, I make all things new" [Apocalypse 28:5].

Instead, in paragraph 2), in the place of the Christian God, Dugin posits an eternal and omniscient Goddess of Chaos, which is certainly an aspect of the present *zeitgeist*, one of the most common "deities-of-our-time." His choice of idols might well have been suggested by René Guénon's doctrine that the *manvantara* or *aeon* begins under the sway of the Essential Pole, *forma*, the Masculine Principle and ends under the power of the Substantial Pole, *materia*, the Feminine Principle, which constitute the primal polarity through which the Celestial Archetype of terrestrial existence manifests. Guénon, however, did not hope for a new age to simply "emerge" from Chaos per se, but saw Chaos for what it is: a purely dissolutionary force. The new *manvantara* is initiated through an unveiling and re-assertion of the Pole of Essence—that is, by the intrinsic action of the Logos as defined in the traditional metaphysical sense, not the Heideggerian one. A new *aeon* does not simply spring fully-formed out of the Pole of Substance. All that is fresh and new comes from Essence as the trans-formal Source of all form, from Transcendent All-Possibility—transcendent in the sense that it is beyond all closed systems. Substance is both the archive of all the forms that have manifested during the course of the *aeon*, and—when apocalyptically purified of the residues of these forms—the perfect receptivity of Being to the divine *fiat lux* that allows new form, fresh from the hand of God, to incarnate in this world. When the Theotokos said, "let it be done unto me according to Thy Word" [Luke 1:38], she was speaking as the immaculate Substantial Pole destined to be the mother of a new era—the Christian Revelation—within the context of the greater *manvantara*.

In paragraph 3), Dugin imagines looking *everywhere but in his own Christian faith and gnosis* to find the creativity and universality of what he calls "Chaos"—precisely as the religious Liberals of the West, the deconstructionists of the Christian Tradition, have been doing since at least the 1960's.

In paragraph 4), Dugin reveals himself as indistinguishable from one of the "New Age fanatics" he elsewhere condemns. The essential error of the New Age is the belief that a new *manvantara* can dawn without the total dissolution of the older one, an error often includes the further misconception that we can *use* Chaos and its metaphysical principles "as the basis of something new."

Last but not least, paragraph 5) shows Dugin in the guise of the doctrinaire Liberal Feminist of the West, likely with mythopoetic tendencies since he heralds the return of the Goddess, the Chaos principle, the Baba Yagá—a Feminist who calls for, foresees, and announces the end of the "patriarchy." Here we see him functioning as a kind of avuncular, academic mentor to Pussy Riot.

Chaos *vs.* Traditional Metaphysics

The above passage demonstrates just how ignorant Dugin is of Traditional Metaphysics, and consequently how wrong it is to call him a Traditionalist in the Guénonian sense. It is true that the Masculine Principle manifests as verticality and hierarchy, but to limit the masculine archetype to its "exclusionary" function and to strictly identify it with Aristotelian logic is as wrong as can be. The apex of a pyramid does not exclude the pyramid but rather implies, posits and embraces the entire pyramid in a trans-formal manner—just as the Essential Pole, which transcends form, is the source of all form precisely because it is not limited to any particular formal manifestation.

Although Judaism, Christianity and Islam possess a complete metaphysics of the Masculine and Feminine principles, in order to present these principles as explicitly as possible it will be helpful to turn to the metaphysics of Hinduism, specifically to the Tantric tradition. In Shaivite Tantra, the Masculine Principle or Shiva is *shaktiman*, the Power-Holder, while the Feminine Principle is *shakti*, Power. The Power-Holder does not hold Power by excluding anything, but by seeing everything. Its essential activity is not imperialistic conquest, on either the material or the psychic level, but rather pure attention: the *shaktiman* is the Absolute Witness. Pure attention, which sees all forms as Power and holds them by becoming their Center through this very act of contemplative witnessing, is the archetypal source of virility.

The first law of Tantra is: *Attention invokes energy; energy empowers attention.* The archetype of attention is the *Atman*; the Universal Witness; Necessary Being; the Absolute Reality. The archetype of energy is the Infinite, Total Possibility. The Absolute is *Shiva*; the Infinite is *Shakti*. *Attention invokes energy*, because the act of attention creates a void in the field of egotism—in the field of obsessive self-definition as well as in the secondary field of obsessive world-definition that emanates from it. *Energy empowers attention* because "nature abhors a vacuum." A void of egotism and identification, or even any partial void, posits a space into which the world must flow as energy—as *Shakti*. Attention invokes energy.

The tantric path is not the path of the exclusion of illusory worlds as hindrances; it is the path of the inclusion of illusory worlds as theophanies, as with Milarepa's "How delightful confusion is when recognized as Wisdom!" (If Dugin is attempting to express something like this in his doctrine of Chaos, it is clear that he has little understanding of the relevant metaphysical doctrines that would allow him to do so without falling into serious error.) Whenever a limited world is posited, thus positing a limited sentient being capable of perceiving that world, a sacrifice is also posited: the sacrifice of that limited *gestalt* of self-and-other, not by excluding it as illusion and hindrance, but by including it, through detachment from its limitations by means of pure witnessing, as one more instance of the Self-manifesting radiance of the Absolute. Thus, according to the **Guyasama Tantra**, "The conduct of the passions and attachments is the same as the conduct of a bodhisattva, that being the best conduct." This "confusion" and "conduct of the passions" do not exist on their own, however; if they did they would constitute "attachment" in the entirely negative and egotistical sense. Rather, they exist in a tantric polarity with the Absolute Witness that discerns confusion *as* confusion and passion *as* passion, thereby recognizing the absolute Unity permeating the seeming confusion of universal energy, and the absolute Detachment, the *apatheia*, permeating the universal life-energies that, in the absence of this Detachment, are all passion and attachment and ignorance.

Verticality is the Transcendence of God, the seal of the Formless Absolute, a Transcendence which manifests as ontological and cosmic hierarchy, while in Itself—since it is Beyond Being—transcending hierarchy absolutely. According to the Shaivite-influenced metaphysics of Frithjof Schuon, the Absolute is the archetype of the Masculine Principle, the Infinite of the Feminine Principle. In terms of the Absolute per se, Absoluteness and Infinity are indistinguishable, Shiva and Shakti are one, while in terms of the manifestation of the Absolute/Infinite as the spiritual, psychic and material universes, Shiva and Shakti, the Absolute and the Infinite, are polarized. Without the "vertical" sovereignty of the Absolute, which is realized in perfect attention, the "horizontal" all-inclusiveness of the Infinite could not manifest. Likewise without the Infinite all-inclusiveness of the Infinite, the Feminine Principle, the endless potentialities for existence concealed within the Absolute/Infinite could never appear, never take shape and substance. No existing thing can exist without a relationship to *both* Transcendent verticality and Immanent all-inclusiveness, just as no human being, in the natural order of things, can be born without two parents. Consequently, to posit hierarchical verticality without horizontal all-inclusiveness, or horizontality without verticality, is (as it were) to *clone* pseudo-metaphysical ideologies that can give birth only to the counterfeits and simulacra of real existing ideas and things. It is to terminate the creative polarity which is the source of all existence, and call for the destruction of the world.

Dugin and Heidegger *vs.* Christ

Furthermore, to strictly identify Christianity with a vertical, hierarchical and "exclusionary" Logos is evidence of either a massive ignorance of the Christian tradition or else a mortal hatred of it—because for Heidegger to posit his doomed exclusionary Logos as the core principle of Christianity is necessarily for him to identify it with the Christian Logos, which is Christ. The Logos of Christianity, however, is in no way exclusionary: It is Immanent in all things. Likewise this Logos subsists in an eternal creative polarity with the Feminine Principle—in Orthodox Christian terms, the Theotokos—who represents not some fourth "sophianic" member of the Holy Trinity, but rather the perfect receptivity to God of the purified human soul. This polarity is expressed in Eastern Orthodox iconography by the icon known as "The Virgin of the Sign," while in the *askesis* and contemplative *praxis* of Orthodoxy it is invoked by a particular form of the Jesus Prayer which combines the names of Jesus and Mary. If Aleksandr Dugin ever finds a true *staretz*, I hope he will be assigned this form of the Prayer; it might teach him something. Sadly, however, it would probably be very hard for him to develop a sincere veneration for the Theotokos, given that his true object of devotion is apparently the Baba Yagá.

Hierarchy, as properly understood, is not exclusive, but universally inclusive. The attempt to account for the totality of existence without introducing the ordering function of hierarchy is necessarily self-defeating, since it must recognize, account for and validate the appearance of innumerable contradictions, both logical and social. Dugin introduces Gilles Deleuze's notion of "the co-existence of non-co-possible monads" as an example of the postmodern definition of Chaos-as-confusion, Chaos as the death of order, that should not be confused, he says, with his use of the word in the "Greek" sense as the undifferentiated, primordial Reality that gives birth to order—even though, as we have seen, he asserts at the same time that the Greeks had no metaphysic of Chaos![7] Dugin is also unclear, however—perhaps deliberately so—as to whether he ultimately accepts or rejects Deleuze's doctrines. For example, when he says, "what we are divides us, what we are against unites us," what else is he doing but invoking the possibility, on the level of political practice, that "non-co-possible monads" like Fascism and Bolshevism, Christianity and materialism, absolute authoritarianism and absolute freedom, might conceivably co-exist? Dugin may (or may not) have begun to distinguish post-logical and pre-logical Chaos in his *theoria*, but it is obvious that he has not done so in his *praxis*. And when says that "*Logos* as the first principle of exclusion is included in chaos," what then becomes of his distinction between the post-logical and pre-logical brands of Chaos? It simply goes up in smoke: Chaos is just confusion, just *chaos*.

---

7. By this contradictory postmodern notion, Deleuze deconstructs Leibniz's doctrine of "non-co-possibles"—Leibniz who was perhaps the only modern Western philosopher that Guénon largely accepted.

As we have already seen, Dugin tends to use the term "Logos" to denote not the universal ordering principle but rather narrow exclusionary logic and its closed systems of thought, which may be why he advises us to look *everywhere but to Christianity* for "inclusive philosophy, inclusive religions"—as if Dante Alighieri, to take only one of many possible examples, whose degree of inclusiveness was truly *catholic*, had never written a word. Therefore we are forced to speculate that his reason for limiting the meaning of his term Logos to the kind of exclusionary logic that creates closed systems is because he sees Christ, who is precisely the Logos in the tradition he claims to follow, as just such a principle of exclusivity, parochialism and narrowness of outlook. Likewise the reason he sometimes uses Chaos to denote the Divine All-Possibility—an intrinsic aspect of God, as Jesus declared when He said "with God all things are possible" [Matthew 19:26]—and the reason he sometimes opposes this principle to Logos, is in order to conceal the fact that what he calls Chaos, but which is better termed Infinity or All-Possibility, is fully treated, worked out, accounted for and dealt with in the Christian Tradition, where it appears as inseparable from Logos— not only in philosophical and theological discourse but also in terms of the sacramental and contemplative *praxes* by which we can concretely encounter this Logos, respond to It and incarnate It. Certainly one of the outer manifestations of Logos is logic, *dianoia, diairesis*—which, when obsessively applied beyond its proper limits, does indeed become the narrowly-masculine, exclusionary complex that imposes artificial order instead of recognizing intrinsic order. But Logos in its unmanifest Essence is nothing less than the Word who is both *with* God and *is* God [cf. John 1:1], the Divine All-Possibility that Frithjof Schuon has called *maya-in-divinis*. Why would Dugin reduce Logos to a mere shadow and caricature of itself, thereby virtually putting *Heidegger*, of all people, in the place of Christ? Because he is fundamentally a postmodern deconstructionist, and one of the things he wishes to deconstruct, so as to be better be able to control it, allowing him to turn it into one of the passive building-blocks of his Neo-Eurasian Hegemony, is Orthodox Christianity.

Dugin in no way attempts to hide his belief that Christianity, as a product of the logocentric worldview, has shot its bolt:

> The epic vision of the rise and fall of *Logos* in the course of the development of western philosophy and history was first espoused by Martin Heidegger, who argued that in the context of European or Western culture, Logos is not only the primary philosophical principle, but also the basis of the religious attitude forming the core of Christianity.

Only someone without the slightest shame would celebrate the fall of the Logos while still having the *chutzpa* to call himself a Christian. And Christianity isn't the only target of his inverted dialectic. Dugin also reduces Islamic theology to *kalam*—Muslim "scholasticism," which has never been a dominant force in the Islamic tradition taken as a whole—and Jewish theology to the Kabbalah and the Hellenization of Judaism represented by Philo of Alexandria, then proceeds to identify both with Heidegger's narrow exclusionary definition of Logos, thereby justifying his dismissive deconstruction of these two religions as well. Here we can begin to see more clearly the outlines of the same globalist program of deconstructing the world's religions that is so evident now in Western Europe and America. Therefore we must conclude that Dugin, though he rejects Postmodernism, is actually a postmodernist; though he condemns Liberalism is in many ways a Liberal; though he rails against globalism is a globalist; though he excoriates the New Age is, in his own words, a "New Age fanatic." This is precisely why I have entitled the present book *Dugin against Dugin*.

Chaos as Method

We need to realize at this point (if we haven't already) that Aleksandr Dugin rarely expresses an idea—except for his notion of the "absolute evil" of Liberalism and whatever he identifies with it, and his loyalty to the Russian *narod*—without giving it both a negative and a positive valuation. This appears, on the face of it, to be a very tolerant, classically Liberal attitude, a willingness to see all sides of a question. One of its practical purposes, however, is to allow him to espouse an idea when it serves the goal of building his Neo-Eurasian coalition, and reject it when it undermines that goal, as well as rejecting ideas he once espoused or accepting ideas he once rejected if the tactical situation requires it. If the 20th century taught us anything, it is that nothing is as strategically versatile and effective as nihilism, in both philosophical and practical terms. But we also need to understand that one of the characteristics of the quasi-absolute nihilist is that he doesn't *believe* in nihilism any more than he believes in anything else. His lack of a "nihilist prejudice," of nihilism as a fixed idea, allows him to almost perfectly *impersonate faith* in any number of contradictory worldviews without his nihilism inconveniently intruding to destroy the illusion he wishes to create. This chameleon-like quality of nihilism is a good example of the principle that "Satan is the ape of God."

Nonetheless Dugin's validation of the equal truth of contradictory ideas is also part and parcel of his notion of Chaos as the ultimate principle of things. If all things are born from Chaos, then they all must co-exist, and have an equal "right" to exist, in the infinite and chaotic eternity prior to their manifestation in the world of space and time. The problem is that Dugin sees them as capable of existentially and cosmically manifesting *without the introduction of hierarchy*, and therefore as able to co-exist, up to a point, in this world, without losing or modifying their pre-eternal, polyvalent nature in the slightest degree. (If this is the case, perhaps we might ask him, "then why can't Eurasianism and Atlanticism co-exist?" To raise this issue, however, would be to claim unfair advantage, to engage in unsportsmanlike conduct.) And while Dugin repeatedly extols the once-and-future "Traditional, Hyperborean, hierarchical" civilization of Eurasia, I have yet to find the slightest trace of any true, hierarchical, Logos-based thinking in his philosophy. Thus his will to exalt social hierarchy while still rejecting Logos in favor of Chaos constitutes one of his greatest triumphs in the field of self-contradictory, self-deconstructionist thinking: "Dugin against Dugin" with a vengeance!

The belief that contradictions can co-exist in the manifest world without the introduction of hierarchy is not only inaccurate, it is highly unfortunate, especially on the social level, since contradiction is nothing less than war—which may be one reason why Dugin extols war in various places. If we place a cock, a snake, and a pig in the same sack they will need to be heavily sedated, otherwise they will tear each other apart. The tranquilizer in this case is postmodern philosophy. But even this powerful sedative will eventually wear off, leading to total conflict, both between social groups and within individuals. Universal terrorist insurgency and gang-war on the social level mirror universal contradiction, both logical and emotional, on the psychic level; this is the nature of the postmodern world. But as soon as true *hierarchy* is introduced—hierarchy that is first *seen* in spiritual vision, not simply arbitrarily imposed by force—peace descends. In archaic times it was common for warring tribes to appeal to lawgivers to make peace between them and rule over them. The inhabitants of the oasis of Yathrib invited the Prophet Muhammad, peace and blessings be upon him, to end their internecine conflicts, thereby inaugurating the city-state of Medina and founding the first Islamic political entity. In the presence of true hierarchy, all things that are not strictly abortions—defined as productions with no intrinsic relationship to any life-principle whatsoever—will spontaneously find their proper places and functions. The attempt to place things that intrinsically pertain to different levels of ontological hierarchy on a common level, due to the fact that the reality of the hierarchal nature of manifest Being is ignored or rejected, is a sure path to universal conflict, and the subsequent dissolution of whatever philosophy or social collective is foolish enough to attempt it. This was the more-or-less the fate of Communism, and will be—via Postmodernism—the fate of Liberalism. Likewise the authoritarian imposition of arbitrary hierarchy, with no understanding of the intrinsic creative and form-preserving polarity between vertical hierarchy and horizontal all-inclusiveness, builds a tower too tall for the breadth of its foundation, a structure that must inevitably fall. This was the fate of Fascism. Revolted, and at the same time disordered, by the sickening horizontal promiscuity of Weimar which reveled in the denial of everything vertical, the German people were ripe for the false and counter-initiatory hierarchy of Hitler, a structure that first appeared as a wonderful liberation from Chaos, but ended in a Chaos worse than anything Weimar could have imagined.

Dugin's "Chaos," as it stands, is nothing less than the Satanic inversion of the universality of the Logos, of Blake's teaching that "everything possible to be believed is an image of truth," of Ibn al-'Arabi's doctrine that every belief as to the nature of God is accepted by Him and functions as a potential door to Him, since all beliefs come from Him, though no belief encompasses Him. Absolute Truth, Necessary Being, the *Atman*, witnesses Infinity, Possible Being, *Mahamaya* as its own eternal Self-manifesting radiance. Conversely, the quasi-absolute nihilism of Duginism—Chaos as the counterfeit of universality—discerns and moves to appropriate every possible truth, empty it of form and meaning and reduce it to a paralyzed nothingness. In reality, however, although we are distinguished by our unique individualities, by what we are in ourselves, this very distinctiveness brings us into relationship with one another, until we come to the realization that we are united by God and in God. God is our common Origin and Destination and Essence; the Source of our individual uniqueness is God the Unique. This principle is *exactly inverted* by Dugin when he says, "What we *are* divides us, what we are *against* unites us." To make the enemy of all the unifying principle of all is a false Satanic metaphysic, first because the principle of union here is necessarily oppression, as when a prison population who exist in mutual enmity are united only by their hatred of the warden and the guards, and secondly because the enemy of all is, precisely, Satan. In Heaven, the angelic forms of all the possible conceptions of Truth circumambulate the Throne of Reality itself, *Al-Haqq*, the Absolute Truth that eternally pours out its superabundant Being to make those conceptions live. In Hell, the demonic forms of every possible idolatrous misconception and petrification of Reality are massed together in a vast, frozen Chaos, held forever in indefinite suspension by the gnawing hunger of the Abyss, whose hollow, ravenous, eternally unsatisfied Will reaches out to possess them.

This is another manifestation of the principle that "Satan is the ape of God." And Dugin's "Counter-Initiatory" inversion of Traditional Metaphysics is only one more example of the method of operation of the Rulers of the Darkness of This World. To create darkened, truncated, fraudulent ghosts of all the God-given religions—as when Dugin, in *The Fourth Political Theory*, defines Russian Orthodox Christianity as a continuation of Russian Paganism rather than a church founded by Christ—and then bend these zombies of the murdered faiths to serve nothing but worldly power, is exactly what the trans-Russian and trans-American global elites now have on their agenda. But as American poet Gregory Corso said, in reference to the blinding of the Cyclops Polyphemus by the "cunning" Odysseus:

> and how wise was he
> who blinded a thing of immortality?

Dugin or one of his supporters might say that I am treating as a metaphysical proposition something that is meant to be a political theory pure and simple. However, since he has used the term "political theology" (from Carl Schmitt), has incorporated the Traditional Metaphysics of Guénon and Evola into his worldview, and is engaged in an outreach to the representatives of many religions, I feel justified in highlighting the metaphysical flaws in his theory, which—in its dark, negative brilliance—is worthy of attribution to one of the great fallen cherubim. As I pointed out above, Dugin's "Chaos" is sometimes suggestive of the Divine All-Possibility as it is before the manifestation of Logos, and sometimes of the terminal confusion that destroys the manifestation of Logos for a particular *aeon*, thus bringing it to a close. "What we are divides us, what we are against unites us" is a perfect description of this second Chaos—dissolutionary Chaos—the mode proper to the final days of the *Kaliyuga*. Dissolutionary Chaos is "united" in its will to dissolve all forms, and at the same time is filled with the fragments and virtual ghosts all the forms it has devoured—ghosts which, since the harmonious order of Cosmos under the rule of Logos is ended, can only exist in a state of total conflict. A Chaos that destroys all it comes in contact with, and exists in a state of quasi-absolute self-contradiction, is an apt description of Hell.

Can Chaos be the Foundation of a New Social System?

The lynch-pin of Dugin's Fourth Political Theory is the notion that the subject of Fascism is the race (Nazism) or the state (Italian Fascism), the subject of Communism, the class, and the subject of Liberalism, the individual. Fascism and Communism have essentially disappeared, and Liberalism is destined to follow them. Therefore, as Dugin says, we must begin to define a Fourth Political Theory that will fill the void left by the impending death of Liberalism. This is a largely accurate view and one that is very useful in helping us to understand our present historical situation. However, Dugin's idea that the next social paradigm will be based on elements drawn "posthumously" from Fascism, Communism and Liberalism, plus various new and as-yet-unimaginable elements, leaves much to be desired, since it posits one or more "eclectic" civilizations capable of coming into existence without any central, constituting Idea—civilizations with a mother, but no father.

In metaphysical terms, what is the central element common to Fascism, Communism and Liberalism? That element is *idolatry*. Fascism puts the race or the state in the place of God, Communism, the class, and Liberalism, the individual. Thus the one and only way of going beyond the shortcomings and con-traditions of Fascism, Communism and Liberalism is not to collect the idols worshipped by all three of them into a single infernal pantheon, but simply to recognize the truth of *la illaha illa Allah*, "There is no god but God."

By this I emphatically do *not* mean that the proper political system to succeed Liberalism would be some kind of hieratic theocracy. The idolatry that lies at the root of Fascism, Communism and Liberalism is founded on what Nietzsche called "the death of God," which in turn is based on nothing less than a degeneration, due to cyclical conditions, of the "supernaturally natural" faculty of human spiritual Intellection. God is dead because the human spiritual Heart has been progressively veiled, leading to the degeneration of the *fitrah*, the primordial human essence. This degeneration is not now, nor could it ever be, complete, but it has progressed to the point where large human collectives can no longer be constituted on the "obvious, axiomatic" truth that Absolute Reality is real, and that the universe is nothing less than Its dimensional manifestation. And once the intrinsic intuition of the reality of God decays—the primordial Intellective faculty that is the constituting principle of the human form, the Eye of the Heart to which the existence of God is as undeniable as the sun in the sky—then no attempt to spread or enforce a mere *belief* in God can have any real effect. No religious institution or movement, no massively-funded program of propaganda or mind-control or social engineering, could conceivable bring back a universal acceptance of the existence of Transcendental realities, thereby reversing "the death of God"—not to mention the fact that the propaganda, mind control and social engineering presently being sponsored by the global elites are pointed in exactly the opposite direction. This collective degeneration of the primary faculty of human Transcendental Intellection explains why René Guénon predicted no resurrected Holy Empire of the Latter Days, no earthly millennium ruled by Christ—the belief in which, to the Eastern Orthodox, is precisely the heresy of *chiliasm*, given that Orthodoxy sees the millennium mentioned in the Apocalypse as the church age, which is now ended—foreseeing only a counterfeit version of such an Empire, an "inverted hierarchy" which will be, precisely, the regime of Antichrist. Consequently whatever new empire the American, or Russian, or trans-American-and-trans-Russian globalists may be able to bring into existence could only be, at this late date, the empire of *al-Dajjal*. The Muslims envision a renewal of truth and justice in the End Times under the patronage of the Mahdi—something which could not exist without at least a partial re-awakening of the Eye of the Heart—but the regime of the Mahdi will be short-lived, and will immediately be followed by the descent of the Prophet Jesus to slay the Antichrist, and the coming of the Hour. The Mahdi's kingdom will not be a world empire, but a bringing together of the scattered Remnants of all the faiths—of those who have escaped, or partially repaired, the collective degeneration of the human

Transcendental Intellect: and I am audacious enough to hope that the re-dis-covery of the Covenants of the Prophet Muhammad might be one of the her-alds of this final gathering. Perhaps Aleksandr Dugin's Neo-Eurasian Empire could also conceivably develop into something like this eschatological gather-ing of the Remnant—except for the fact that his inverted metaphysics of Chaos and his acceptance of Heidegger's announcement of the fall of the Logos together make this impossible. You can't work toward the foundation of a new Holy Empire while at the same time effectively proclaiming the death of God.

Aleksandr Dugin Tells the Big Lie about René Guénon

Even though I have already been rather *firm* in the above exposition, perhaps I am still being too lenient with Aleksandr Dugin, treating him with kid gloves, trying to preserve the amenities, being careful that I don't become "shrill." But now the gloves are off. In order to shine a penetrating light on the Big Lie in Dugin's use of Guénon's doctrines, let's review some of the passages we have already quoted above, and add a few more. First, Dugin says:

> We need to distinguish between two kinds of Chaos, the postmodernist "Chaos" as an equivalent to confusion, a kind of post-order, and the Greek Chaos as pre-order, as something that exists before ordered reality has come into being.

Next he says:

> Modern physics and philosophy refers to complex systems, bifurcation or non-integrating equations and processes, using the concept "Chaos" to des-ignate such phenomena. . . . "Chaos" here is no more than a dissipative struc-ture of *Logos*, the last result of its decay, fall, and decomposition. Modern science is dealing, not with something other than *Logos,* but with a kind of post-*Logos*, or ex-*Logos*: *Logos* in the state of ultimate dissolution and regres-sion. The process of the final destruction and dissipation of *Logos* is taken here for "Chaos."

So Dugin identifies the "chaos theory" of modern physics with the "Chaos" of Postmodernism, presenting both as examples of "post-order" or "post-Logos." The complexity of chaos theory may indeed be a sign of the impending "over-extension" of the logocentric method, as Dugin implies, but since chaos theory is deterministic, not probabilistic, it can in no way be described as a product of the *dissolution* of Logos. As we have already seen, to this kind of Chaos-as-confusion he opposes Chaos in what he calls its original "Greek" sense, as denoting not post-order disintegration, the death of Logos, but pre-existing order, the Mother of Logos. Nor is Chaos in this sense only pre-existing according to Dugin; it is also eternal:

It is not correct to conceive of Chaos as something belonging to the past. Chaos is eternal, but eternally coexisting with time. Therefore, Chaos is always eternally new, fresh and spontaneous. It could be regarded as a source of any kind of invention or freshness because its eternity has, in itself, always something more that was, is, or will be in time.

If we allow—leniently, if not permissively—that this kind of Chaos might be identifiable with the Divine Infinity or All-Possibility, then Dugin is right. However, he goes on to say:

René Guénon has called the era we are living through now an era of confusion. "Confusion" means the state of being that both runs parallel to order and precedes it.

Wrong! Here Aleksandr Dugin suddenly deconstructs his own argument and destroys the whole distinction between "terminal confusion" and "original and eternal Chaos," that he has been as such pains to construct, by having Guénon (incorrectly) identify our present age of postmodern confusion with that higher Chaos, "eternally new, fresh and spontaneous"! By doing so he erases all differentiation between Chaos One and Chaos Two, and at the same time totally misrepresents Guénon's doctrine. Here, from *The Reign of Quantity and the Signs of the Times*, is what Guénon actually says about "confusion" and "chaos":

... the Antichrist must be as near as it is possible to be to "disintegration'... [to] confusion in "chaos" as against fusion in principial Unity....

So Guénon clearly does *not* identify the confusion of the era we are now living through with "the state of being that both runs parallel with order and precedes it," which he terms "fusion in principial Unity," but rather with Dugin's "postmodernist Chaos" which is the "confusion," "chaos" and "disintegration" of the Antichrist. Here is the exactly-triangulated point where Aleksandr Dugin totally falsifies the doctrine of René Guénon by inverting it 180 degrees—apparently believing, for some reason, that we would never find out! In so doing, he portrays Guénon, the great 20th-century Warner against the coming of the Antichrist, as if he were actually a *disciple* of Antichrist. What we might have taken as a mystical, paradoxical, esoteric mode of expression, designed to transmit the quality of the Metaphysics of Chaos beyond the limitations of mere logic and reason, is here revealed as a simple lie. What might Aleksandr Dugin's purpose be in deliberately misrepresenting the doctrines of René Guénon regarding the Antichrist? What agenda, or what figure, would such a misrepresentation serve? This is what is called, in the technical terminology of the U.S. counter-culture of the 1960's, a "mind fuck"—something on the order of: "Let's explain to them the nature of confusion in the best possible way, i.e., *by confusing them*—what other form of exposition could be so thoroughgoing, so accurate? Let's give them a shot of some real *practical* Chaos." Everybody seems eager to get "beyond logic and reason" nowadays, but if you're going get beyond something, you need to have *gotten there* first. At this point I would suggest that Aleksandr Dugin make a study of the mythological figure of Coyote, who appears in the origin-legends of many of the Native American tribes of North America. Coyote is the archetypal Trickster figure; the more successful he is in tricking others, the more he ends up tricking himself. In the words of the Holy Qur'an, *They plot, but Allah also plotteth; and Allah is the best of Plotters* [Q. 8:30]. Those who do not naturally fear God will be taught to fear Him—and He is also the best of Teachers.

As should be clear by now, Aleksandr Dugin's answer to the question posed above—"Is the maintenance of the human collective's connection to Sacred Form appropriate, or even possible, in the latter days of the Age of Iron?"—is "no." By giving this answer, he directly contradicts René Guénon, Eastern Orthodox Christianity, and all the traditional eschatologies. According to Dugin, since Chaos, the Pole of Substance, is now fully dominant, we must take her as our Queen, our paradigm, and dance to her tune. Speaking in terms of Russian folklore, we might say that since Ded Moroz—the Polar High God, symbol of the Essential Pole—is dead or occulted, there is nothing left for us now but to pattern the human collective upon the Great Witch of the Substantial Pole, the Baba Yagá.[8]

There is a major problem here, however. To "pattern something upon something" is a logocentric way of thinking; it is the language of Essence, not Substance, of Form, not Chaos. Chaos can never function as a pattern or paradigm, since its proper role is to dissolve all paradigms. So what becomes of the rule taught by Tradition that the spiritual dispensation of any particular world-age has to reflect the cosmic conditions prevailing in that age? Must we now all become Chaos-worshippers or Satanists in order to stay "up (or down) with the times"? As we will see with increasing clarity over the course of this book, Dugin's answer to this question appears to be "yes." As for the Traditional alternative to Chaos-worship, this has already been stated: "To hold to Sacred Form against the most intense blows of Chaos, and thereby forge a Remnant."

---

8. When the High God Ded Moroz is occulted, the Snow Maiden Snegurochka—the celestial human soul who can't live long in this world since the heat of the passions melts her—must, according to my interpretation of the Russian fairy tale "The Beautiful Vassilissa," become Vassilissa the "merely human," and fall under the power of the Baba Yagá, the regime of material nature. As Vassilissa, her only point of contact with the High God, or her only memory of Him, is her doll—a talisman that saves her from the Baba Yagá's clutches by performing the same function as the Eastern Orthodox *mnimi Theou* or Prayer of the Heart.

A True Metaphysics Behind Dugin's Chaos?

So Dugin's doctrine of Chaos is itself chaotic, and he certainly does not seem very eager to clear up any of its ambiguities—quite the reverse in fact, seeing that they have proved so useful to him in his political *praxis*. Yet he is obviously seeing *something*; his doctrine of Chaos is not *only* a case of dialectical slight-of-hand (though it certainly is that); it is also the sign of a true metaphysical insight that has not yet fully emerged from the Cloud of Unknowing. What could that insight be? What true metaphysical principle might be hidden, somewhere, in Dugin's "Chaos"? In order to answer that question, we need to take another look at René Guénon's eschatology, amplifying it with various insights taken from Hindu tantric yoga and from certain aspects of the Hindu doctrine of the *manvantara* that Guénon himself did not emphasize, as well as throwing an unexpected light on it with the help of the myth of Einsteinian physics.

According to Guénon in *The Reign of Quantity*, as the *manvantara* draws towards its end, time speeds up, dissolving form and suppressing the perception of space, until a point of "singularity" is reached where a "pole-shift" takes place. Space suddenly reasserts itself; the "reign of quantity" gives way again to the "reign of quality"; a new *manvantara* begins. This is, precisely, Apocalypse, followed by the dawning of the New Heaven (the renewed Essential Pole) and the New Earth (the purified Substantial Pole). Within the matrix of newly-dominant Space, Time is now nothing but an imperceptible ripple, very gradually accelerating but hardly yet detectable as an independent force.

This process is analogous to the Einsteinian theory of "time dilation." According to this conception, as a material object accelerates, time slows down for that object, while speeding up—relative to the observer, the accelerating object—for the universe surrounding it. An astronaut traveling at near light-speed would (let us say) age one year during his journey, but upon his return to earth he would find that 100 years had passed. If the accelerating object were to attain the speed of light (which is considered to be physically impossible, since acceleration of any material object to light-speed would require an infinite expenditure of energy) time for that object would stop, while—again, relative to the observer—the speed of time for the universe surrounding it would reach infinity.

Obviously both a zero velocity and an infinite velocity for time, or for anything else, are not possible and measurable physical states; they are simply the theoretical limits of possible and measurable existence itself—the word *Maya* being derived from the Sanskrit root meaning "to measure"—beyond which physics gives way to metaphysics.

We need to understand at this point that the theories and measurements of the physical sciences can never prove the validity of metaphysical principles, even though metaphysical principles can be reflected, analogically and meta-phorically, in those theories and measurements. It is not possible to see this reflection from the standpoint of the physical sciences, however, but only from the standpoint of metaphysics. For example, Einstein's constant *c*, representing the speed of light—which he passionately insisted must be invariable—was, for him, something like the hidden presence of God in his physical theories: "I am Jehovah: I have not changed" [Malachi 3:6]. All things are relative, Einstein maintained, except for the speed of light which is effectively absolute. It is abso-lute not only because any physical object that attains light-velocity would exist in a condition of total stillness married to infinite speed—that is, in Eternity—and consequently transcend the physical dimension, but because it would also reach infinite mass, this being the material equivalent or *symbol* of God as Infi-nite and Absolute Being. No material object actually can attain the speed of light, however, otherwise it would be something like a second God, which is not possible due to *Shema Yisrael: Adonoi Elohenu, Adonoi Echad*—not to mention the fact that an infinite expenditure of energy would be required for it to reach that speed, and infinite energy is already otherwise employed. All this is strictly analogous to the doctrine, from Traditional Metaphysics, that the relative world, the world of form, cannot attain, without annihilation, to the Absolute Reality of God—yet that Reality is already the true Essence of every relative form, since the world of forms is, precisely, Its manifestation, there being no other Reality for that relative world to manifest. It is by this principle that for-mal existence can be characterized as *Maya* or cosmic illusion—as something which, according to the teaching of Ibn al-'Arabi, is nothing with respect to itself, while, with respect to God, it is God.

This, at least, is Einstein's *myth*, which in some ways reflects Traditional metaphysical cosmology. He departs sharply from Tradition, however, in his acceptance of the Copernican/relativistic principle that every observational standpoint within the universe is equally "privileged" and/or equally "arbi-trary," which can be seen as denying that humanity, who is intrinsic to the planet earth, is, according to the Qur'an, the holder of the *Amana*, the Trust. However, as Dr. Wolfgang Smith informs me, the whole Einsteinian structure is about to come crashing down, due in part to the discoveries of the Plank Space-craft (2009–2013) regarding the cosmic microwave background—specifically, that there is a discernible axis within the background that, as far as measure-ments have been able to determine, is oriented to the plane of the ecliptic, the plane of the Earth's orbit around the Sun, suggesting that the Earth may actu-ally be, in some real sense, the center of the universe. This is a powerful valida-tion of the Anthropic Principle, the notion that the universe is precisely designed and attuned, on every level, so as to give rise to a consciousness that could witness and understand that design—the consciousness of the Human

Form. The Anthropic Principle is closely correlated with the Traditional metaphysical view of Humanity as the microcosm of the macrocosm, the "axial being" for this material cosmos. Nonetheless, if Einstein's cosmology falls—as a physical theory, that is—it will continue to embrace elements that will then turn out to have been based on Einstein's *projection* of certain imperfect metaphysical intuitions—unconscious intuitions for the most part—upon the material cosmos. And indeed this is the inevitable fate of all materialistic theories that pretend to explain everything without reference to Transcendent realities. They will necessarily reflect true metaphysical Principles to some degree, since these principles—like God Himself—are immanent in creation; in Islamic metaphysics this is the principle of *tashbih*, God's "comparability" to created things. On the other hand, such theories must also contain fatal flaws that ultimately destine them to fail and be discarded, given that metaphysical Principles—again, like God—are also transcendent and inexhaustible, in line with the Islamic principle of *tanzih*, God's "incomparability." Transcendent Principles can never be completely defined or embraced by material conditions. The mirror of material creation must reflect its metaphysical Source, but it can never limit or imprison that Source.

As we have seen, the last age of the *manvantara* or *maha-yuga* is known as the *Kali-yuga*, the Dark Age. The *Kali-yuga*—at least in my view, based on Guénon's understanding of the laws of the *manvantara*—is ultimately devoured by the Goddess Kāli, "Time." This is obviously related to Guénon's doctrine that the last period of any *manvantara* is characterized by ever-accelerating time that obscures space and dissolves form. Therefore we may take Kāli as a symbol both of this destructive acceleration of time and of the terminal "pole-shift" at the end of the cycle, the point of *enantiodromia* where instead of time dissolving space, space engulfs time. The pole-shift accomplished by Kāli does not *counter* the dissolutionary action of accelerating time, then, but completes it; it does so by transforming matter and form into pure Energy.

Accelerating Time is a "destroyer" only so long as any form remains to be destroyed. As soon as form is completely dissolved, however, Time is transformed into Space—Space which is, precisely, the matrix of pure Energy within which all possible forms exist *in potentia*, ready to be manifested under the influence of the Essential Pole, the Witness of that Energy, over the course of the new *manvantara*, as time gradually re-asserts itself and the "march of history" resumes.

The archetypal role of Time and Space in the process of Apocalypse, the accelerating flow of forms approaching their dissolution and the timeless ocean of Energy into which they dissolve, can be better understood if we apply to it the metaphor of Einsteinian time dilation. In the "subjective" experience of the astronaut in the spaceship, time slows down in relation to the surrounding universe, whereas from the "objective" standpoint of the surrounding universe, it speeds up in relation to time as experienced by the astronaut. The acceleration of time in the objective universe as the observer approaches the speed of light is analogous to the speeding up of time in the increasingly *externalized* macrocosm as the *manvantara* draws near to the apocalyptic pole-shift that signals its end. Likewise the slowing of time that the observer experiences in terms of himself is analogous to the progressive unveiling of the pure Energy of Eternity in deep contemplation—Eternity as it is progressively unveiled to the subjective pole, the microcosm—which manifests itself as the re-assertion of Space in the first or "golden" age of the next *manvantara*, since only Eternity can function as the point-of-transition between one cycle of time and another. In other words, as the macrocosm approaches infinite temporal velocity and consequently dissolves, the microcosm approaches an infinite spatial simultaneity. By virtue of this—as the pole-shift is reached—it *becomes the new macrocosm*; this is what Heraclitus meant when he said that "immortals become mortals and mortals become immortals; they die each other's lives and live each other's deaths." This pole-shift between microcosm and macrocosm is alluded to in both the **Book of Daniel** and the Tibetan Kalachakra Tantra, which concur in declaring that the "latter-day saints," the enlightened souls who appear at the end of the *aeon*, will become the stars in the sky—presumably the sky of the next *aeon*. In terms of Hindu Shaivite Tantra, at the ultimate, Eternal, pivotal moment of this pole-shift—a moment that seems to pass but in reality cannot pass, since it is precisely *this present moment*, which is *not* a moment in time—the observing subject becomes Shiva, the *Atman*, the Absolute Witness, while the observed object becomes *Kāli-as-Shakti*, the field of Infinite Energy. And since the *Atman* is intrinsically beyond form, and given that *Kāli-as-Shakti* acts to dissolve all form, together they constitute a single Absolute and Infinite Reality—the Reality we call God.

Martin Lings, in his book **The Eleventh Hour: The Spiritual Crisis of the Modern World in Light of Tradition and Prophesy,** speaks of two providential spiritual qualities characteristic of the Latter Days of the *Kali-yuga*: "infused" detachment, and the wisdom of old age. Because we see our world in ruins, it becomes easier to let go of it; and the ruin of the world and our letting go of it together produce a "thinning" of the cosmic environment—somewhat like the pale, translucent skin covering the skull of an extremely old man—to the point where it can no longer veil the Eternal Principles. The letting-go-of-the-world corresponds to the acceleration of time in the macrocosm: the world passes so swiftly that we can no longer hold on to it; it wrenches itself from our grasp. Likewise the wisdom of old age corresponds to the slowing of time and the progressive unveiling of Eternity in the microcosm: when the Outer World passes away, the Inner World emerges, and becomes the Eternal Matrix out of which a new Outer World is born. "Heaven and earth will pass away, but My Word will not pass away" [Matthew 24:35]; "And I saw a new heaven and a new earth, for the first heaven and the first earth were passed away" [Apocalypse 21:1]. In the act of contemplation, our thoughts appear to speed up, since we are now becoming more and more aware of them—and the faster they fly, the easier it is for us to let go of them, till they are no longer a stream of discrete thoughts and images but are progressively transformed into an infinite stream or field of Energy. Ultimately even our seemingly-material bodies are recognized as part of that stream of thoughts, that field of Energy. And as we practice intentionally letting go of thought and form and time, the Always So emerges; the Face of God is unveiled. In terms of the Muslim *shahadah—La illaha ila'Allah*, "there is no god but God"—the letting go of form and thought and world is equivalent to *La illaha*, "there is no god"—since no single thought nor form, nor the whole world of thought and form taken together, can be God, because He transcends all that—while the unveiling of Eternity, the emergence of the Always So, corresponds to *ila'Allah*, "but God," since the One Reality eternally emerging from beyond Form and beyond Being is necessarily the one true God. *And say: Truth hath come and falsehood hath vanished away. Lo! falsehood is ever bound to vanish.* [Q. 17:81]

It is the reality of Eternity, of the union of the Witness and the Witnessed, of the seamless identity of Shiva and Shakti, of Absolute Consciousness and Infinite Energy, that Aleksandr Dugin is apparently groping toward in his ambiguous notion of "Chaos"—unfortunately starting from the pitiful obscurity and self-involvement of poor Martin Heidegger, the prime deconstructionist of Traditional Metaphysics in the history of Western philosophy. And the reality and nature of Eternity, of the Always So, *has always been known*. Heidegger's *dasein* is nothing but a hazy memory of it hatched by an over-cerebral philosopher who was obviously deficient in the theory and practice of contemplation; likewise Martin Heidegger's Last God (mentioned by Dugin)—though this might be seen as Heidegger's own take on traditional eschatology, the end of the *manvantara*—in another sense is simply his fantasy that the unveiling of Eternity could somehow be something *novel and unheard-of*—the projection of his own unrealized spiritual potential upon the screen of future history, in line with William Blake's doctrine that "Whenever any Individual Rejects Error & Embraces Truth, a Last Judgment passes upon that Individual." It would have been novel to *him* if it had ever fully dawned upon him—at least to begin with. Then, slowly but surely, the Platonic *anamnesis* would have supervened; he would have realized that, somewhere deep inside him, he had always known it. This, precisely, is what exists to be known—and, God willing, it *can* be known. If, by the grace of God, this intuition of Eternity were to dawn upon Aleksandr Dugin, the world might be saved much grief.

Dugin's Biggest Contradiction

I will conclude my critique of "The Metaphysics of Chaos" by quoting a passage from another source, an earlier article by Aleksandr Dugin entitled "The Great War of the Continents," which clearly exposes the central contradiction in his metaphysics:

> The order of Eurasia, Order of the Male Principle, Sun, Hierarchy, is the projection of the Mount, Apollon, Ormudz, Solar Christ-in-Glory, Christ-pantocrator. Eurasia as the Earth of East is the Earth of Light, Earth of Paradise, Earth of Empire. The Earth of Hope. The Earth of the Pole. The order of the Atlantic, Order of the Female Principle, Moon, Orgiastic Equality is the projection of the Egyptian Seth, Python, Ahriman, Christ Suffering, Human, immersed in the metaphysical despair of the lonely Gethsemane prayer. Atlantic, Atlantis as the Earth of the West, is the Earth of the Night, the Earth of the "pit of exile" (as an Islamic Sufi said), Centre of Planetary Skepticism, Earth of the Great Metaphysical Spleen.

I will not break my brain trying to disentangle all the errors and follies in this passage, which resembles a text of Traditional Metaphysics after it has been passed through a shredder and the resulting confetti blown by air pressure against an adhesive surface. I won't even innumerate all the specific Christian heresies embraced by Dugin's denial of the Hypostatic Union between Christ's human and Divine natures, his allocating them to Atlantis and Eurasia respectively. I will simply point out that, insofar as he replaces Logos with Chaos, Dugin ceases to be a Eurasianist and becomes an Atlanticist. The spiritual Male Principle, polar and hierarchical, is precisely the *Logos*. Chaos is the unpurified Female Principle, the unconscious power of the Moon that moves the ocean tides—an entirely appropriate deity for the Atlantean Peoples of the Sea. (The unpurified Male principle is blind dogmatism and physical brutality; the purified Female Principle is fertile emotional wisdom and spiritual receptivity.) Here Dugin attempts to worship Apollo with the rites of Hecate; he tries to invoke Ded Moroz and instead calls up the Baba Yagá. One would have thought that it was not humanly possible for anyone presuming to base his worldview partly on myth and metaphysics to make that big a mistake, to be that wrong— and maybe it actually isn't. In other words, we must entertain the possibility that Dugin is being deliberately contradictory, as ingeniously and quintessentially contradictory as he can possibly be. For what purpose? Could it be that an actual will to destroy spiritual Truth is operating here? Alternately, Dugin's contradictions may simply be the inevitable consequences of his attempt to create a quasi-metaphysical myth for political purposes. These two explanations ultimately come down to the same thing, however, since to force spiritual Truth to serve a worldly agenda is to turn it into a Satanic caricature. The Truth itself is unaffected by this perversion, of course; nonetheless the caricature still remains, like a mass of toxic waste, and continues to spread its damage, to stand as one more obstacle between the human soul and God.

Liberalism is Chaos

Every civilization worth the name has received its constituting form from a Divine revelation. In the case of the Hindu, Judeo-Christian and Islamic civilizations this revelatory origin is more or less explicit, while the Chinese civilization and its branches in Central and Southeast Asia, the civilization that came to embrace Taoism, Confucianism and Buddhism, was—like the Platonic tradition—founded more on a human apprehension of divine realities, an "enlightenment" that could nonetheless not have take place without the "grace," the intrinsic self-emanation, of those very realities.

And every civilization, as it dies, descends into Chaos. When the constituting form of a given civilization is broken—as, for example, when the great medieval synthesis of Western Europe was broken by the Renaissance—this catastrophe is sometimes felt as a great and fertile expansion; many things that were once impossible, or forbidden, have now become both possible and allowable; because less is certainly *true*, more is apparently *permitted*. Liberalism, as an ideology and an ethos, could never have developed without this collective sense of expansion and possibility; that this "liberation" was the product of the deconstruction of a conception of humanity and human society that was in every way spiritually higher and more integrated than anything the Renaissance produced, was not seen, nor could it be understood, by those who profited from that deconstruction. Perhaps we, living in the time of the demise not just of Enlightenment Liberalism but of Renaissance "futurism," can now begin to see how the civilization that is presently dying was born from the analogous death of the medieval Christian civilization that preceded it.

In terms of American society, the great epic of the expansive, hopeful phase of Liberalism, the time when everyone had a degree of spiritual prosperity because it was still possible to live off the "trust fund" established by Christ and the Christian Middle Ages, was Walt Whitman's *Leaves of Grass*. However, when the impetus to such an expansion is spent—as when the surge of water from a broken dam finally abates because the lake is now empty—what was once seen as expansion is now revealed, precisely, as Chaos. And what is Chaos? It is nothing less than an enormous mass of contradictions operating on the microscopic level. Contradictory propositions (in intellectual terms) or impulses (in psychological terms) need not come to blows during a period of expansion; it is only when the mental and emotional *lebensraum* that allowed them to co-exist begins to shrink that the contradictions between them come to the surface, inevitably leading to conflict—conflict between groups, between individuals, and within individuals themselves. In America, the epic of the turn from the expansive to the contractive phase of Liberalism was Herman Melville's *Moby Dick*, where the representatives of all the peoples of the earth, the vaunted "pluralistic society," are imprisoned in a doomed ship ruled by a madman. This dissolutionary phase of the cycle, embracing an expansion that is in no way developmental and a contraction that is in no way re-integrative, both being manifestations of a common decadence, is the nature and destiny of Liberalism—which is to say: *Liberalism is Chaos.* It is not total Chaos, of course, otherwise it could have never have survived to the point of earning a name, nor has it been totally devoid of certain admirable values based on the social form that came to be called "Modernism," whose pillars, for society, were the philosophers and economists of the English and French "Enlightenment" and their successors, later on joined by Darwin for "nature" and Freud for the "human soul." Nor was Liberalism initially dedicated to the actual quest for Chaos, as it seems to be today when the engineered destabilization of entire cultures has emerged as one of its most characteristic methods. Rather, it was in search of rational principles on which to build its worldview. Rationalism divorced from Intellection, however—which is to say, the human mind operating in ignorance of, and rebellion against, the metaphysical order—is Chaos intrinsically: and Chaos will out.

Dugin's dichotomy of "Monolithic Liberalism" vs. "Chaos and Diversity" is therefore ill-conceived. There is nothing more essentially Liberal in spirit than the call to "celebrate diversity," which means that the reduction of Liberalism's original *liberality* to an increasingly authoritarian ideology is a sign, not of Liberalism's triumph, but of its approaching end. Dugin himself says as much in many places—and yet, in order to justify the global revolution against Atlanticism that he has pinned his hopes on, at the same time he must picture Liberalism as a powerful, monolithic totalitarianism that only a global revolution could possibly unseat. In order to falsely portray Chaos as liberation, it is necessary to posit a totally entrenched, established, petrified enemy for liberating Chaos to overcome. However, as Dante demonstrates in the final cantos of his *Inferno*, where Lucifer appears frozen in the Lake of Cocytus, Chaos and Petrification—in social terms, anarchy and authoritarianism—are shown to be two faces of the same condition. As Titus Burckhardt expresses it, in *Alchemy: Science of the Cosmos, Science of the Soul*:

> Characteristically, the two types of disequilibrium are usually found together. One begets the other. The numbing of the powers of the soul leads to dissipation, and the fire of passion lived out regardlessly brings inward death.

PART TWO:
INVERTED METAPHYSICS IN
THE RISE OF FOURTH POLITICAL THEORY

In *The Rise of the Fourth Political Theory* [2017], Aleksandr Dugin makes his closest approach yet to the Traditional metaphysical doctrines of Eternity and time, the Absolute and the relative. But since he inverts their true significance, it is here that he also comes closest to positing a true Counter-Initiation.

In his section "Eternity in Your Palms," a title that appears to allude to William Blake's lines "To see a World in a Grain of Sand/ And Heaven in a Wild Flower/ Hold Infinity in the palm of your hand/ And Eternity in an hour" from "Auguries of Innocence," Dugin says:

> The third principle of Eurasian philosophy is called "Eternity in your palms" or "the embrace of emptiness".... Time is a snare and attempts to lead us away from the heart of the matter. Time covers up the voice of being; the call that sounds in eternity.

This is entirely sound and in line with Tradition. In the next section, "There is No Time," he goes on to say:

> Eurasianism affirms that eternity exists and time does not. Everything that the Eurasian speaks is the absolute truth, and must be accepted without all kinds of critical reflections; accepted and repeated. Time is an illusion, only eternity has being. And for that reason the intuition of eternity, the breath of eternity ... and the experience of eternity are the main substance of Eurasianist consciousness. But if the eternal is, if that eternal can be an object of our experience, it, accordingly, is here now, too, and it must be the object of our experience.

This, apart from the ever-contentious doctrine of Duginist Infallibility, is still close to the Traditional view. However, in the section "The Individualization of Supra-Individual Experience," Dugin goes seriously astray:

> The task of Eurasianism is to make the experience of contact with extra-individual, supra-individual reality an individual experience. The paradox: to contain eternity in time, to grasp the absolute and to transform it within the legacy of one's own heart.... Russia is the Absolute Motherland, Russia is a doctrine, Russia is a mysticism, Russia is a cult....

Here we arrive at the essence of idolatry. To make "supra-individual reality an individual experience" is the goal of all true religion, and most particularly for the esoteric centers of the religions whose duty it is to maintain the lore and practice of the Spiritual Path. Eternity, however, cannot be contained in time, any more than the Will of God can be dominated by individual self-will or the ocean poured into a teacup. Nor can we in any way "transform the Absolute."

Transform It into what? It is not our duty to transform It—nor do we have the power to do so, since we are not omnipotent, and given that "transformation" applies only to the dimension of time—but rather to allow ourselves to be transformed by It. And it is Eternity that contains time, not the other way around. The only way that a "supra-individual reality" can become "an individual experience" is for the individual in question, either relatively or absolutely, to be annihilated in God. Is this what Dugin means by "the embrace of emptiness?" This is far from certain, because after this annihilation the one-time individual still does not hold God as an object of *his* experience, but rather subsists as an object of *God's* experience—God Who "experiences" nothing but Himself. In Islamic Sufism, this doctrine is found in the words of the *hadith qudsi*: "Pray to God as if you saw Him, because even if you don't see Him, He sees you." To be "annihilated" not in God but in the Eternal Russia is impossible because worship of anything less than God is an identification, an ego, and true annihilation does away with all egos. What dark force or design could have induced Aleksandr Dugin to strive for something not only impossible to attain, but something that if it ever could be attained would be Hell on Earth, since for a human collective to presume to possess God instead of being possessed by Him is to transform God into a puppet of human fantasy, as well as to turn title to one's soul over to the Rulers of the Darkness of This World. *Shall I show you the one*, says the Holy Qur'an [45:23], *who makes desire his god?* Whoever worships his own desire becomes the pawn of the desires of others. Only two things could produce this aspiration and this result, two things that are very often one: abysmal ignorance or profound despair. So instead of God, Dugin openly worships Russia, and ordains the same worship for his followers. What I can't understand, however, is why he doesn't choose something a lot bigger and a lot older to worship, like the Milky Way Galaxy or the Cosmic Microwave Background; these are much more powerful and impressive than Russia is, and also destined to outlast it. If I were the priest at the Orthodox Church where Aleksandr Dugin worships, I would certainly invite him to audit the Divine Liturgy, since he has shown some interest in becoming a member of Eastern Orthodoxy, but I would by no means offer him the Holy Eucharist, since he is obviously not yet a Christian.

Dugin's section entitled "For the Absolute and Against the Relative" includes the following:

> Here a general principle is born: "We are the supporters of the Absolute and we are against the relative." In fact, of course, the relative exists somewhere. Of course, even time has a chance and has its little voice. But this is an insignificant territory and these are very minor rights. On the contrary, the rights of the Absolute, the rights of eternity and the cult of eternity must be at the center of our consciousness, and everything else on the periphery. But eter-

nity is never substantial in the same way as substantial objects in time. Eternity in some sense scares us because it cancels us out. It removes us, burns us; hence the expression "the embrace of emptiness." "A philosopher embracing emptiness" is the title of one Chinese alchemical tract. It conveys precisely the sense of the experience of eternity. But if we shall learn to manipulate eternity, living will be very easy for us; living and accomplishing incredible exploits, making mind-blowing careers, simply delighting in life or wandering around the world and looking around, but only as Eurasians—especially looking around.

Then everything will be completely different than it is for those people who find themselves inside the black car of relativity. Eternity is granted us, Russian people; it is given to us, offered to us, even bound to us. And whether we want it or not, we must seize it. . . .

Of course Dugin knows that it is absurd to think we can "manipulate" or "seize" Eternity; that's why in the next paragraph he says: "It is impossible to seize it, impossible to straddle it, impossible to make it a tool, but there is nothing simpler than to accomplish this." This flat, deliberate contradiction at least has the virtue of pre-emptively neutralizing the obvious objections that any spiritually and metaphysically literate critic would make, namely that Eternity is not ours for the taking, that an opening to the intuition of Eternity requires a serious commitment to spiritual practice in response to a call issued by God, that there is no way it can be possessed simply by adopting it as an ideology.

The same critic might also be justified in adding, "If it is impossible to seize and manipulate Eternity, then why did you talk about seizing it and manipulating it in the first place?" "Mystical paradox!" the Hierophant of Eurasianism might answer. "The more paradoxical our expression is, the closer it comes to the inexpressible Truth." Maybe so. But the formula *you-can't-do-it-you-must-do-it* is also effective for paralyzing the listener by inducing self-contradiction. If Dugin is truly heir to a Traditional worldview and a Traditional method for taking the mind beyond the *dvandvas*, the pairs-of-opposites, then let him produce it, and show us its Traditional warrant—because such a method can never be invented or pieced together by an *individual*: if it is going to lead us to God it must first have come from God. No-one can be manipulated into Love; no-one can be duped into Wisdom. As for the idea that time, when compared with Eternity, has "very minor rights," this is merely a way of relativizing the Absolute by comparing it to and weighing it against the relative, and the Absolute will not submit to such relativization—because the truth is, time is the very Action and Presence of Eternity, the relative is the very Incarnation and Sign of the Absolute—and to the degree that Eternity, the Absolute, is realized, no rival to It appears anywhere. In the words of the *hadith qudsi*—a class of Prophetic tradition where Allah Himself is the speaker: "Why do they complain to Me of the changes of fortune brought about by Time? I *am* Time."

Nonetheless, there is some truth in Dugin's statement about the rights of Eternity vs. those of time. Time, from one point of view, has a relative existence of its own, but in the "End," in the "Beginning," and in the "Now," Eternity holds sway; in Plato's words from his *Timaeus*, "Time is the moving image of Eternity." Nor can Eternity be *monopolized* by Eurasia; the Always So is always so not only in every time, but also in every place. To the degree that Eternity becomes "the object of our experience," time is perceived as fully encompassed by it, contained by it, permeated by it. Eternity does not pass; time "passes" within it, while never departing from it—which is to say, the intuition of Eternity changes time from a linear flow to a cyclical one; this is the time of the *manvantara*. But how directly applicable is the metaphysical principle of Eternity to *history*, to *politics*, and to *strategic thinking and action*? Let us see:

To apply the category of Eternity to a limited, spacio-temporal reality—namely, Russia—to believe that time can be eternalized in its own terms without being transcended—leads directly to the "magical delusion," to the notion that eternal principles can be tapped to power temporal agendas. If, as Dugin implies, we opt to throw our support behind the Absolute and Eternal and marshal our forces to defeat and annihilate, or at least firmly subordinate, its necessary opposite term, the relative and temporal, then this decision, being a form of partiality, immediately involves us with time again and returns us to the context of the relative, which means in actual effect that the relative is never defeated and our particular version of the Absolute is no longer absolute, etc., etc. Nor can Eternal All-Possibility, which embraces every possible outcome in a dimension of simultaneity where the notion of "outcomes" is meaningless, express itself in the temporal dimension through the "multiple parallel time-lines" dear to science fiction, magic, speculative trans-Einsteinian physics and various "channeled" philosophies based on psychic fantasies rather than Spiritual knowledge, such that we might guarantee the triumph of our threatened agenda by switching to a different time-line where its success is now assured. Once time is entered, the laws of time apply, and only God has the right and the power to suspend those laws.

So Dugin's long train of absurdities, semi-absurdities, gleeful contradictions and insidious collusions between incompatible ideas either marches gloriously ahead into the past or else retreats cunningly into the future, depending upon one's perspective. We need to understand, however, that absurdities like this, though we are tempted to dismiss them as madness because they *are* madness, are not to be taken lightly. Why not? Because there is method in them; because absurdity is, in fact, a *technique*: a technique of mental manipulation and mind control. And this may in fact be the real reason why Dugin appears as the insidious ape of nearly every idea he expresses. As soon as two contradictory propositions are accepted as true, either consciously or unconsciously—and the process is much more likely to be unconscious than conscious—then our analytical and critical abilities are unhinged, stunned into submission. After this happens, all discernment is at an end; nothing is left but *identification*. The slogans from George Orwell's *1984*—WAR IS PEACE, FREEDOM IS SLAVERY, IGNORANCE IS STRENGTH—are not intellectual propositions that might be agreed or disagreed with, proved or refuted. They are non-propositions designed specifically to destroy discernment and thereby create identification—identification with Big Brother. And to someone like myself who has dedicated many years of his life to understanding and attempting to put into practice the science of metaphysics, this kind of deliberate perversion of the human mind constitutes a challenge that I can't let pass. Why? Because Dugin, as I have already pointed out in some detail, has misappropriated and inverted certain specific principles of metaphysics and methods of metaphysical discourse. These include:

1) The idea that *spiritual truth is supra-rational.* All metaphysical and mystical traditions agree that many spiritual realities and experiences are ineffable, impossible to describe in words, while Absolute Reality is not only verbally indescribable but inconceivable according to the terms of *any* human faculty, including spiritual intuition or Intellection. It is, however, both possible and necessary to intuit the reality of the Absolute by virtue of its very ineffability, to realize that it must also lie beyond even pure Being since Being is a category, a determination, and the Absolute transcends determinations. This realization results in what the Sufis call *yaqin*, certainty—a certainty that "magnetizes us," orients us toward God as the Pole of our being. But this supra-rationality, when we try to express it in words, does not simply translate into irrationality, as many believe; inconsistency is not mysticism; the Cloud of Unknowing is not mental confusion or dementia. On the contrary, the supra-rational produces a type of supreme of rationality and consistency that leaves the feeble constructions of secular "rationalism" far behind—a rationality so accurate and precise that the exact point where the rational method encounters its necessary limit in the face of the ineffable realities of the Spirit can be clearly discerned. Three works that triumphantly demonstrate this supreme spiritual rationality that knows its own limits in the face of the Absolute, even while rendering the Absolute to the best of its ability, are: *Logic and Transcendence* by Frithjof Schuon, *Miracles* by C.S. Lewis, and *On Difficulties in the Church Fathers* by St. Maximos the Confessor.

2) The idea that *all statements about the Absolute must include an element of paradox.* If we say that God is a Person, we must also assert that He is beyond personhood. If we say that the Absolute is Pure Being, we must also declare that It is Beyond Being. If we say that the enlightened sage transcends morality, we must also emphasize that he has reached the point beyond good and evil, thus

redressing the effects of the Fall, only by realizing the Sovereign Good. And certain types of mystical writing, such as the **Diamond Sutra** and *Heart Sutra* of the Mahayana Buddhists or Dionysius the Areopagite's *Mystical Theology*, deftly employ paradox to give us concrete intimations of That which lies beyond all rational formulations—as, for example, when the *Heart Sutra* tells us, "form is emptiness, emptiness is form." The Satanic inversion of supra-rational *paradox*, however, is sub-rational *contradiction*, either unconsciously fallen into, covertly introduced, or defiantly and shamelessly asserted. An example of this is (in my paraphrase of Dugin): "We reject the evils of unipolarity in favor of a multi-polar world, but anyone who disagrees in the slightest with our monolithic Eurasianist project is an Atlanticist and therefore *anathema*," etc., etc.

3) An understanding that *the Absolute, via its necessary "field" aspect, namely Infinity, is universal and all-encompassing—but It is also aloof, exclusive and unique, since it cannot be limited to, or by, the relative world. In other words, God is both Immanent and Transcendent. Furthermore, within the bounds of a particular Divine Revelation, this Immanence-and-Transcendence necessarily manifests in terms of specific sacred forms, forms which have the "blessing" of God for specific periods of the* manvantara; *this is more-or-less how René Guénon and defines the word "Tradition."* Dugin posits Eurasianism, the essential expression of his fundamental "divine" principle—namely, Eternity-as-Chaos—as roughly the equivalent of one of these sacred forms, the one proper to the end-beginning of the *manvantara*, at least within the confines of the Eurasian heartland. The fundamental contradiction of this approach is that *Chaos is not a form.* Operating at the end of the *manvantara*, which is where we are now, Chaos is precisely the power that dissolves all forms so as to purify the Substantial Pole of its formal residues and make it ready to receive the constituting Form of the next *manvantara* from the hand of the Essential Pole. Consequently a nuclear Third World War between the Eurasianist and Atlanticist collectives (which Dugin has sometimes flirted with), resulting in the termination of all life on earth, would be the perfect expression of Chaos as the principle of Eurasianism according to Dugin's metaphysic. So to Malcolm Muggeridge's "great Liberal death-wish" we must now add Aleksandr Dugin's "great Eurasianist death-wish"; if and when these two death-wishes, like Gog and Magog, rise, clash and conspire—God help us.

As we have already seen, the "return of the Goddess" is inseparable from the quality of the End Times, when the predominance of the Essential Pole, or Form, is replaced by that of the Substantial Pole, or Matter, leading to Matter's quasi-deification. The true *spiritual* quality of "the return of the Goddess," however, is not glamorized materialism; among traditional conceptions of the Divine it is best represented—as we have already seen—by the Hindu goddess

Kāli. Kāli is primordial, not simply a reflection of the latter days, but Her particular quality assures Her a prominent role, whether or not this is recognized, at the end of the *manvantara*. Kāli is the Absolute not as hierarchically exalted above conditional existence but as identical with it—the total unveiling of the Immanence of God, such that the polarity between God the Creator and Sustainer of the universe and the universe He creates and sustains is annihilated, resulting in the reabsorption of conditional existence into its Principle: the *mahapralaya*, the end of the world. At the end of time, the world is sacrificed to Kāli, the All-Devouring Mother.

In the properly esoteric and metaphysical worship of Kāli, however, the subject of sacrifice is not the body or the material world but the *ego*, the self-concept. When Kāli completely dawns, she demands of us all we are; in the face of the Goddess of Death and Chaos, to hold on to self-definition is terror, while to release all attachment to self-definition is bliss. And since "This World" is nothing but a collective projection of the ego—the way we think things are, based on the way we think *we* are—She brings the "World" to an end as well. No longer can we say, like Job did before God tested him, "if I am good the Lord will make me secure in my earthly life"; at this point, the only possible response left to us is, in the words of the Noble Qur'an [9:118]: *There is no refuge from God but in Him.* Such an esoteric spiritual understanding of "the end of the world" by a sufficient number of people is the *only* thing that could in any way postpone, or mitigate, the *material* end of the world that the world's materialists are now working so hard to bring about. This is the meaning of the passage from the Gospel of Matthew, chapter 24, verse 22: "For the sake of the elect, those days will be shortened."

The Divine hypostasis represented by the Goddess Kāli is now being unveiled. This is one of the inescapable qualities of our time, and both western Postmodernism and Dugin's Eurasianism are manifestations of it. Nor is it necessary to concentrate on its specifically Hindu rendition to come to an understanding of it, though this is certainly the most explicit; the lineaments of Kāli can be found in the apocalyptic prophesies of all the religions, including the Abrahamic ones—not always as explicitly or strictly identified, however, with the Divine Feminine. Because Kāli is inescapable, those who are unaware of Her particular quality, and the specific spiritual opportunities She represents, will be unconsciously affected by Her presence. And since Dugin, following Heidegger, announces the end of the reign of the Logos, of verticality, of Transcendence—"matter" being cognate with *mater*, "mother"—he is necessarily a kind of mystified or "volatilized" materialist, a devotee of the Substantial Pole. Consequently, though he repeatedly invokes the Absolute, he can neither worship It nor realize It in a manner appropriate to Its true nature, nor avail himself of the profound opening to compassion and self-transcendence that the willing veneration of God in the guise of Kāli, or in any other truly Traditional guise, could provide—which is to say, he has no Traditional Spiritual Path. And because he cannot be Her conscious devotee, he is forced to act as Her unwitting agent.

3

Vectors of Duginism

Dugin and Heidegger; *Dasein* as a Pseudo-Absolute

ALEKSANDR DUGIN draws his "metaphysical" perspective more directly from the works of Martin Heidegger than from any other source, René Guénon included. This is unfortunate, since Heidegger was not a metaphysician, but rather an obscure, ambiguous, tortured deconstructionist of everything that the word "metaphysics" had represented before he got his hands on it. I challenge anyone who has read, with sufficient comprehension, two pages of the *Tao Te Ching* or Meister Eckhart or Jalaluddin Rumi or the **Bhagavad-Gita**, to then try to go back and read Martin Heidegger without a sensation of terminal barrenness, comparable to being abandoned in the bed of a dry salt lake on a cold, grey winter dusk.

The German word *dasein*, Martin Heidegger's central philosophical concept, is usually translated as "being" or "being there," i.e., existence—though Heidegger rejects the definition "being there" and claims that his *dasein* is something else. *Dasein*, in Heidegger, apparently denotes a human being's actual, concrete existence in the world, in the context of what is meaningful to him. Since this is the situation humanity always finds itself in, Heidegger considers *dasein* intrinsic to, or perhaps another name for, the human essence—though of course he rejects the idea of a human essence because it leads to "philosophical anthropology," which he also rejects. *Dasein* is not "man," but by the same token it is *nothing other* than "man." (Is that clear enough?). Thus Heidegger attempts to understand or account for being per se—concrete being in time, as represented by actual conditions, as experienced by the being to whom being matters, i.e., man—without any reference to Being or Man as traditional metaphysical notions. In other words, he is trying to define, describe and account for metaphysics without metaphysics, humanity without humanity, God without God.

On the conceptual level, to turn man's actual condition into an idea, which is then used to define man's actual condition, is a mere tautology; simply defining something in terms of itself adds nothing to our understanding of it. But in terms of traditional contemplative practice—something which finds no place in Heidegger's philosophy—such an operation might conceivably be meaningful and operative.

Heidegger, according to Dugin in *The Fourth Political Theory*, "believed that nothingness itself" [nothingness in the sense of nihilism] "is the flip side of pure Being, which—in such a paradoxical way!—reminds mankind of its existence." He looked forward to an "event," an *Ereignis*, when social nihilism would suddenly and magically give rise to authentic Being. This in some ways resembles a wrongheaded attempt on Heidegger's part to apply the Buddhist doctrine of *shunyata* and *tathata*—"emptiness" and "suchness"—to social dynamics and psychology. It might also represent an imperfect intuition of the reality of *shunyata/tathata* divorced from ontology (that is, from contemplation) and applied to society and history—an intrinsic aspect of the nature of things misperceived as an impending event.

My poetic mentor, Lew Welch, who studied the entire history of western thought at Reed College in Oregon and whose contemplative practice was the secularized Buddhism of the Beat Generation that Alan Watts called "Beat Zen," once said—possibly in an attempt to correct Heidegger, or do him one better—"I try to write from the poise of mind that allows me to see how things are exactly what they seem"—not how they are what they *are*, but how they are what they *seem*. The practice is (first) to allow our experience of the world to be transformed into a concept, into something that we don't just passively perceive but actively and intentionally *conceive*, by coming to a direct, experiential understanding of how the self-manifestation of the object is something *actively addressed to* the conceiving subject in line with the situation and quality and destiny of that subject; this results in a vision of the world as an *apparition* rather than a brute fact, a gestalt involving both seer and seen. The second and concluding step is to actualize this concept of world-as-apparition by understanding it to be the real nature of the world—that the world we see is not mere *phenomenon* with a real, invisible *noumenon* hiding behind it, but a reality in which *phenomenon* and *noumenon* (*tathata* and *shunyata*, Suchness and Emptiness) are one. Such a world is just as we see it, and yet (in Lew Welch's words) it "goes on whether I look at it or not." In the words of Ch'ing-yüan Wei-hsin, "Before a man studies Zen, mountains are mountains and rivers are rivers. After he begins to gain insight into Zen under a good teacher, mountains are no longer mountains and rivers no longer rivers. But when he really attains to the abode of rest, mountains are mountains again and rivers are rivers." First the world is just an unconsidered, literal fact. Next it becomes a magical manifestation of an invisible Reality. Finally it is known as an apparition presented directly to us and for us, and at the same time a reality that doesn't depend on us; as the Beatles sang: "Life goes on within you and without you." We undergo this *metanoia*, this change from *literalists* to *symbolists* to *realists*, not by willfully defining our experience according to a pre-conceived pattern, but by intentionally allowing it, so to speak, to "define itself to us," by a path (in Lew Welch's words) "deliberately unintended." And these operations are not successive but simultaneous. The "apophatic" recognition that the world is an illusory apparition is what the Buddhists call *shunyata*, "voidness"; the "cataphatic" understanding that this apparition is not *literally* an illusion as opposed to a reality, but is actually the real nature of things, they call *tathata*—"suchness." *Shunyata* and *tathata* are never found apart; they constitute a single realization, one which spontaneously appears as soon as we methodically negate the mental self-will, the struggle to "figure things out," that has heretofore blocked their appearance. So what in conceptual terms is simply a tautology or an abstract theory—something that might be phrased as "because it is empty, it is what it is; because I am nothing in particular, I am exactly as I am"—in existential terms becomes a concrete vision of the real nature of things. The above-described operation, however—and this is something that Heidegger never suspected—*cannot be accomplished by thought*. The meaning and essence of human life on earth, immersed in time and history, in nature and society, in becoming and dying—the meaning and essence of the Being that we inevitably are—can be grasped in only one way: through self-transcendence. While we are still identified with ourselves we remain blind to ourselves, blind to the world around us. Our constant demands on ourselves and the world, paired with our unending flight from them, even in the very act of struggling to possess them—the whole spectrum, that is, of the perennial human idolatry—make all true existential realization impossible. Self is known, and realized, only by dying to self; world is seen, and tasted, only by dying to world. Whoever rejects this method has closed and locked the only door out of the prison of unreality, and thrown away the key.

If the Germans instead of the Chinese and Japanese had invented Zen—which, in Heidegger, they actually seem to have been working on—they would have come up with something like Heidegger's *dasein*: a laborious, ponderous, maddeningly complex approach to radical simplicity. But because Heidegger attempted to accomplish this by thought alone, unsupported and unconfirmed by any kind of concrete contemplative practice, he was doomed to failure, which is undoubtedly why he was not able to complete even the first volume of his projected two-volume *magnum opus*, **Sein und Zeit** (**Being and Time**). In theistic and traditional metaphysical terms—though Heidegger would certainly not agree with this assessment—his *dasein* is actually a veiled allusion to the immanence of God, as well as, in specifically Christian terms, to the *incarnation* of God as man. But just as the *eidos* (idea) is not only immanent in real existing things, as Aristotle taught, but also transcends these things, as Plato taught, so God is transcendent as well as immanent; He is neither excluded from man and the world nor limited to them. By the same token, humanity is not limited to life in this terrestrial world, even while occupying this world. Therefore we can also say that Heidegger's *dasein* represents a vague, obscure, unfinished intuition of the metaphysical principle of the correspondence of microcosm and macrocosm, in both this terrestrial world and beyond it, the truth that the perceiving subject and the world he or she perceives determine each other and mirror each other intrinsically, not just on the earthly plane but on every level of the ontological hierarchy. They do not do so in any deterministic or mechanistic way, however; the reality of the world is not strictly limited to the mode of consciousness by which we perceive it, any more than our consciousness is strictly limited by the perceived nature of the world. This is due to the fact that the dyad of perceiver-and-perceived constitutes a polarized manifestation of *wahdat al-wujud*, the Transcendent Unity of Being; both seer and seen are reflections of a First Cause which absolutely transcends them. (Gilbert Durand's theory of "anthropological trajectory," the fluid correspondence between subject and object, between the processes and development of human personal experience on the one hand and nature and human society on the other—as mediated by the symbolic imagination—appears to be a partial re-discovery of the traditional doctrine of microcosm and macrocosm.) As the Qur'an expresses it in surah 41, verse 53: *We will show them Our signs on the horizons* [the outer world] *and within themselves until it is clear to them that this is the truth. Is it not enough for you that your Lord is Witness over all things?* Martin Heidegger, however, denies that his *dasein* can be understood via traditional ideas, which of course must include traditional theology and metaphysics. He recognizes no *Witness over all things*, yet he still keeps on trying, on the basis of his own thought processes, to account for all things. Good luck with that one, Professor.

So Heidegger's *dasein* "names" terrestrial humanity's existential condition, thus transforming it into a concept, a concept that might ideally allow us to contemplate that condition, to see it as it is, rather than simply taking it for granted and therefore remaining in unconscious identification with it—if, that is, Martin Heidegger had any idea whatsoever of the nature and use of contemplative practice. Heidegger presents his method as a negation of willful conceptualization, which he calls "re-presenting," in favor of something on the order of the Taoist *wu wei*, "doing without doing"—or rather "thinking without thinking." This is all very well, and in some ways accurately suggests a primal Intellection untroubled by the self-will of the ego. But as soon as we have named reality, as soon as we have said either "*dasein*" or "*shunyata/tathata*," the process of willful apprehension, the attempt to *grasp* reality, has begun and cannot be avoided; we therefore require a method by which the inevitable process of human conceptualization is employed to disclose rather than conceal the true nature of existence, thereby leading the mind all the way through, and entirely out of, the world of discursive thinking, back to direct contemplation. Consequently, in addition to witnessing (in Frithjof Schuon's phrase) "the metaphysical transparency of phenomena," we must also learn to intuit "the metaphysical transparency of concepts," which is something we can only do if we know how to use them as supports for contemplation. God necessarily manifests Himself through both concepts and phenomena—through both Names and Acts—but He is also infinitely beyond them, in no way bound or limited by them; in metaphysical terms, He is both immanent and transcendent. And to the degree that we realize this, we are no longer bound or limited by concepts or phenomena either. The Buddhist method of freeing the human person from concepts, as well as liberating him or her from perceived phenomena by purifying them of conceptual projections, is called "the finger pointing at the Moon"—"pointing" in such a way that our awareness, and that of others, is not trapped and held by our pointing finger. This is something that Heidegger obviously can't help us with, since his finger finally grew so big that it blocked out the Moon entirely. Consequently, though there are Christian saints, Muslim saints, Hindu saints, Buddhist saints, there are no Heideggerian saints. The realizations made available by any integral spiritual tradition will always trump the intuitive flashes of the individual genius, even the metaphysical genius—which Heidegger certainly was not.

Martin Heidegger, then, is the supreme philosophical nihilist, and also the supreme *mystifier* of nihilism. He does not declare that nothing can be known about the fundamental nature of Being; rather, he uses his own ponderous method to *demonstrate* how nothing can be known—at least through that method—while still giving the impression that he is arriving at "insights" and constructing "formulations." Thus he is the peerless contriver of a pseudo-ontology without metaphysics and/or a pseudo-metaphysics without God. He was "able to do" all this by attempting to apply the faculty of human thought to aspects of reality that thought is not designed to work with. It is as if he were desperately, tediously, laboriously, trying to hear with his eyes or see with his ears—and he *almost can*, he is *so close*, he has *nearly got it*—and so on and so on, with no conceivable end in sight. His *dasein* is thus a true "brain-teaser." In the Josef von Sternberg motion picture *The Blue Angel,* the cabaret singer Lola-Lola (played by Marlene Dietrich), who turns the pompous professor (played by Emile Jannings) into a clown in her traveling troop, is thus a perfect image of *dasein*, with Heidegger (the professor) interminably trying to *grasp* her, to "rationalize the tease" represented by his self-created mental phantasm, without the slightest hope of success, until the day of his death. The true philosopher, the "lover-of-wisdom," makes a fertile union with Holy Wisdom, the Sophia, which is why he is able to bring forth true, generous, enlightening, living thought. The nihilistic philosopher, like Martin Heidegger, simply becomes stuck in a feed-back-loop of his own ideas in the presence of *Avidya-Maya*, "Ignorance-Apparition," and thereby loses his manhood—because when thought is cut off from Transcendence, from the light of the Heavenly Father, it falls under the power of the Substantial Pole, the negative Feminine Principle, the All-Devouring Mother. Thus we are led to speculate that Heidegger might well have been attracted to Nazism in a futile attempt to regain the manhood he had surrendered to his teasing, castrating *dasein*. And since *dasein* is the supreme philosophical mystification that demands all and gives nothing, it is a highly useful tool for people like Aleksandr Dugin when they want to destroy real thought in others, or else justify something—*anything*—by an appeal to the Great Unintelligible. *Dasein* indeed is the end of metaphysics and the grave of Logos, but it is *not* thereby the great unity of All-Possibility from which everything comes and to which everything returns, the thing that Aleksandr Dugin (half of the time at least) calls the "Greek" Chaos—that is, when he isn't claiming that the Greeks had no conception of Chaos. It is simply the despair and suicide of thought cut off, by its own chosen methods, from the direct contemplation of Reality. Contemplation, prayer, spiritual practice are the life-blood human intelligence—an intelligence which includes, but is not limited to, human thought; without them, thought is nothing but a zombie, a walking corpse.

Once *dasein* has done its work by totally separating *dianoia* from *Nous*, abstract discursive thought from the concrete practice of contemplation-transcending-thought, then nothing is left but nihilistic despair, or else Promethean/magical self-will—and doesn't self-will sound like the more energetic and hopeful option of the two? Conceptual self-will—the practice of arbitrarily and willfully adopting a particular set of beliefs so as to alter conditions, which is integral to Chaos Magick as well as New Age thought in general ("belief creates reality")—would seem poles apart from Martin Heidegger's rarefied philosophical *dasein*, his method of letting Being define itself to us instead of our imposing our definitions upon it. Yet Heidegger's rejection of traditional spiritual doctrine, his notion that received ideas work more to veil reality than to reveal it, actually calls for its diametric opposite, the Promethean magical ego, to intervene, fill in the conceptual vacuum and determine what's what; this may in part explain Heidegger attraction to Hitler. However, both formless spontaneity (as with the hippies, and also the Weimar Republic) and various self-directed raids on the mysteries by the magical ego, miss the mark; as Rama Coomaraswamy (Ananda's son) liked to say, "the Devil doesn't care which side of the horse you fall off of." And what is the mark? The mark is Tradition, including both the discrete divine revelations we know as the major world religions and the primordial spiritual roads of the First Nations, insofar as these remain intact. Traditionalism is much more than a last-ditch "Apollonian" refuge against Modernity and Postmodernism, against the conceptual chaos generated by the dying philosophical traditions of the West. It is, in fact, an orientation with the power to leaven the whole mass of the heterogeneous western mentality, identify and cast out everything in it that's dead and moribund, and put everything else, everything that still has life in it, precisely in its place—metaphysically, psychologically and socio-politically—thereby thoroughly obviating all forms of post-modern nihilism and doublethink. We must not abandon the task of defining and applying this orientation, since it is both worthy of performance and actually capable of being performed. It was the rejection of Tradition in the west that transformed Logos into the dead hand of the past that drove Heidegger to his *dasein*; the philosophers progressively killed the Logos in western thought by, in effect, defining it as nothing more than "what philosophers do." In a European context it was Christianity that preserved and deepened what was viable in Greek philosophy—as Islam did in its own lands—precisely because it recognized the Logos as Christ. Likewise Islam envisioned the Logos as the *Nafas al-Rahman*, the all-creative Breath of the Merciful. In neither case was Logos limited to the simple truism that ideas are immanent in the cosmic order and are accessible to human thought. In Christianity and Islam the Logos is intentional; operative; alive; it is much more than a mere conceptual orientation; it is, in fact, the face of God turned toward conditional existence. Every spiritual tradition has employed thinking as part of its method for overcoming ignorance and disclosing Reality, but no tradition has ever claimed that thinking is enough, or that thought doesn't become a demon when separated from direct Vision; this is why the central purpose of metaphysical thinking has always been to inform and support contemplative practice. In the absence of such practice, philosophical speculation operates in a vacuum. It becomes like a study of the tools, methods and history of a particular craft carried on by someone who has never undertaken to practice that craft and never intends to; in its depleted, deracinated condition it is frustrating, debilitating, maddening; the result is that it becomes diverted more and more toward either materialistic science or strategic cunning. These pursuits are considered "real," since even at their worst they have more actual substance to them than the haunted house filled with muttering, abstract ghosts that so-called "metaphysical" philosophy had become when separated from religious faith and practical contemplation. So if Heidegger, Dugin and others wish to dump the entire western intellectual tradition at the landfill, as they apparently do, it is because they have been misusing it in a way that could only darken the mind and damage the soul.

The fundamental deviation in the West that caused the split between philosophy and *theurgy*—a synthesis of ritual worship and what we would call contemplative practice—began with the Greeks; nonetheless this deviation cannot be identified with the Greek genius *per se*. The Platonic tradition, for example—as Algis Uzdavinys has demonstrated in his *Philosophy and Theurgy in*

Late Antiquity—was both philosophical and theurgic. The Renaissance, outside of certain de-contextualized experiments in ceremonial magic, was able to resurrect only the philosophical half of the dyad, and even this element was understood only in a partial and fragmentary way; as a result, *thinkers* were born. Thought was separated from mystical contemplation, from character-development, and even from normal human piety, the result being that the imperative of the Delphic Oracle, "know thyself," became impossible to achieve. As we can see in the case of Heidegger—the rarefied, abstract German professor wedded to the Nazi thug—when truth is approached through thought alone, it produces madmen.

If Aleksandr Dugin is serious about his Eurasianism, his loyalty to Tradition and his hatred of individualism, then why does he grant so much authority to an individualistic, anti-Traditional western philosopher like Heidegger? All Eurasia needs in the way of metaphysics can be found in the New Testament and the Greek Fathers, the Old Testament and the Kabbalistic literature, the Qur'an and the Sufi sages, the Hindu *sruti* and *smriti*, the literature of Buddhism and the classics of Confucianism and Taoism, plus the folklore and legends of the various Eurasian peoples and the practical lore of Shamanism. And in terms of the philosophy of Western Europe alone, how could anyone who knows Plato, Aristotle, Plotinus, Augustine, Aquinas, Dante and Meister Eckhart find anything of interest in *Heidegger*, or for that matter in any western philosopher without a Spiritual Path or even a religious faith? Nietzsche is important for his insight into the destruction of the religious and metaphysical foundations of the West and the dire consequences of it, but as for modern western philosophy as a whole, my position is substantially that of William Blake, as he expressed it in his one of his "Proverbs of Hell" from *The Marriage of Heaven and Hell*: "Never did the Eagle lose so much time as when he submitted to learn of the Crow."

In terms of his philosophy of Being, Martin Heidegger was little more than an incompetent, fatally-deluded would-be Buddhist, someone who contracted "the philosopher disease" and finally died of it. Both he and Siddhartha Gautama wanted to dispense with philosophical metaphysics, but Heidegger, unlike Gautama, had nothing concrete to put in its place. To his question "What is Being? How does Being express itself to us beyond our own habit of conceptualizing on the basis of received metaphysical ideas?," the Buddhists answer: "It is the unity of *shunyata* and *tathata*, voidness and suchness; this is not an abstract concept, however, but a description of the quality of contemplation." And to his question: "What is the real nature of our being-in-the-world, our being-in-time, our being-toward-death?," the Buddhists answer: "It is *anicca*, impermanence, whose affective tone is *awarë*, poignancy; once again, this is not an abstract concept but a description of the quality of contemplation."

The Sufis also speak of "Being," which they term *wujud*. *Wujud*, however, is not just the abstract concept of "isness," but the quality of the concrete Presence of the Real, beyond the thinking mind—something that is born only in the act of contemplation. "Being" cannot be encountered, cannot be understood, cannot be "enbeinged" (pardon my parody) through thought or words, no matter how ingeniously we may torture them, but only through contemplation transcending thought. By trying to push thought beyond its inherent limits, Heidegger destroyed the legitimate use of it without liberating himself from it. When it's time to think, then think, recognizing metaphysics as the highest form of thinking because it is always pointing to intelligible realities that lie beyond thought. And when it's time to go beyond metaphysics, then *don't keep thinking about it*, not even to deconstruct it. The correct comportment under such circumstances is, in the words of Lew Welch from his poem "Wobbly Rock," to "sit real still and keep your mouth shut."

Dugin and Crowley;
Postmodernism as Magick; Mimicry as Technique

Certain Western commentators have accused Aleksandr Dugin of having affinities with the notorious occultist, reputed Satanist, and British Intelligence agent Aleister Crowley—possibly (in some cases) simply because part of his Neo-Eurasianist insignia, the part with the eight arrows pointing in all directions, is similar to an emblem—the "Chaos Sphere"—which is used by some of the practitioners of "Chaos Magick," a movement partly inspired by Crowley.

The fact is, however, that Dugin has written appreciatively of Crowley. Most people would think that anyone who puts in a good word for an occultist who called himself "the Beast" and whom René Guénon characterized as a black magician, could not also be a Traditionalist metaphysician, much less a faithful Eastern Orthodox Christian. The most obvious reaction would be to conclude that such a contradiction would constitute dishonesty and hypocrisy. However, if Chaos is such a person's ruling principle, if—in true postmodern style—beliefs can no longer be "contradictory" since there is no objective truth or common context according to which such a thing as "contradiction" could be discerned, if George Orwell's "doublethink" is now the order of the day, then "dishonesty" and "hypocrisy" become meaningless concepts. This convenient escape route may be enough to explain, all by itself, the attraction of contemporary academic "intellectuals" to the postmodern outlook. And if contradictory propositions can be equally true, then it is no contradiction (for example) if I love my wife yet sleep with the wife of another man, or if I practice genocide in the name of my love for humanity, etc., etc. This too is highly convenient.

Furthermore, if time is reversible as Dugin claims, if it has in fact reversed, then the intention to perform a particular act must come after that act, not before it, which means that moral responsibility is an illusion, consequently all is forgiven to everyone (with the sole exception of the sin of "Atlanticism")—or rather, forgiveness too becomes a meaningless concept in a world where life and thought are random. In the face of such admirable liberation from the strictures of logic, rationality, consistency and honesty, in a world where nothing is true and everything is permitted, truth is no longer the standard for the acceptability of a concept or the rightness of an act; that role has been usurped by power as the only surviving criterion for action. It would be good for us to remind ourselves at this point of Shakespeare's aphorism "blood is no argument" (not an exact quote), to which we must apparently now add the codicil, "and neither is madness." And if the final phase of Liberalism is Postmodernism, then the confused and terrified Liberals of the West should petition Dugin, who has now suddenly been revealed—unexpected but quite appropriately— by his absolutization of Chaos as the quintessential late-phase Liberal, the final hero of Liberalism in its latter days, to come and rule over them. But maybe that's what he's been planning all along. In any case, we can lament that Aleksandr Dugin is not an American, since his worldview seems influenced in some ways by the myth of classical "Americanism," which was based on a sense of liberation from the dogmas of the past. "Consistency is the hobgoblin of little minds" said the American Transcendentalist philosopher Ralph Waldo Emerson, to which our national epic poet, Walt Whitman, replied: "Do I contradict myself? Very well then, I contradict myself. I am large, I contain multitudes." If Professor Dugin ever runs into serious difficulties in his native Russia, we extend an open invitation to him to come to the United States and be an American; in so many ways he is already one with us in spirit.

But back to Crowley. In their article "'Neo-Eurasianism' and Perennial Philosophy," Anton Shekhovtsov and Andreas Umland assert the following:

> [One] of Dugin's conceptual conflicts with Guénon is highlighted by certain essays, in which the leader of "neo-Eurasianism" positively assesses the legacy of the British occult writer and Satanist Aleister Crowley, particularly in "Uchenie Zveria" and "Chelovek's sokolinymkliuvom."[1]

Dugin tries to legitimize placing Crowley within the larger context of Traditionalism by referring to the link between Crowley and Evola, and specifically to the fact that they had a common friend—the Italian Freemason Arturo Reghini. Guénon, by contrast, had called Crowley a "black magician" and "charlatan," and argued that many of the organizations founded by Crowley

---

1. Aleksandr Dugin, "Uchenie Zveria," *Milyi Angel*, 1996, no. 3; idem, "Chelovek s sokolinym kliuvom," in Aleksandr Dugin, *Tampliery proletariata: Natsionalbol'shevizm i initsiatsiia* (Moscow, 1997), 169–76.

were "counter-initiatory"—that is, anti-Traditionalist. Just by itself, Guénon's negative attitude toward Crowley makes it difficult to consider the latter an Integral Traditionalist. As one Russian observer commented on this and related revisions by Dugin, "in terms of Guénonism, any sympathy with counter-initiation would mean the same as Christians' sympathy with Satanism." Dugin's appreciation for Crowley stems from the latter's nonconformism, as well as from what Dugin conceives to have been the British Satanist's political position. Dugin wrote that Crowley supported all "'subversive' trends in politics—Communism, Nazism, anarchism and extreme liberation nationalism (especially the Irish one)." Referring to Christian Bouchet, leader of the French radical right-wing organization Nouvelle Résistance, Dugin calls Crowley a "Conservative Revolutionary." In fact, Crowley's true political views remain unclear. Insofar as his support for Irish nationalism is concerned, Crowley's separatist guise actually helped him to win the trust of German secret service agents during World War I. For most of his life Crowley was an agent for MI-6, the British counterintelligence service that, in Dugin's terms, constitutes an "Atlanticist"—and thus anti-Russian—organization.

Chaos Magic was influenced but not originated by Aleister Crowley; it is most commonly associated with a one-time student of his, Austin Osman Spare. In true postmodern fashion this Magick denies the existence of objective truth, and therefore views various belief-systems not as more-or-less successful attempts to approach this truth, but rather as arbitrary and willful exploits designed to configure reality according to this or that subjective concept, with no one worldview necessarily holding precedence over any other, thereby resulting in an essentially *theatrical* view of reality—a kind of "practical phenomenology." (Heidegger too was a philosophical nihilist, placing his hopes in a deconstruction of the Western intellectual tradition.) And such an approach is certainly compatible with Dugin's doctrine that, either intrinsically or in the present historical moment, Chaos has precedence over Logos, as well as with his tendency to recruit his followers from *logically* contradictory ideological positions.[2]

Western academic Postmodernism is oriented largely toward deconstructionism, the absolutization of the relative, the denial of objective truth in the name of every sort of individual or collective subjectivity, the meticulous destruction of meaning, and finally the deconstruction of the very methods it

---

2. A similar though less pronounced tendency to ignore certain ideological or cultural inconsistencies was also the watchword of the American Liberalism of the 1960's and 70's, as indicated by the practice by the Democratic Party of forming various "coalitions of the disenfranchised" to counter the more monolithic ideological and cultural stance of the Republicans. This "strategy" likely reached its terminal phase in 2011 in the Occupy Wall Street Movement, an internet-initiated "flash coalition" that resulted in zero concrete organizing and consequently had zero practical effect.

used to accomplish all these admirable feats. Thus it must finally result in, to use Dugin's words, "the absolute crisis of values, religion, philosophy, political and social order ... postmodern conditions ... confusion and perversion ... this age of utmost decay." If nothing has any meaning except the meaning we intend to give to it, where can we turn to find either that meaning or that intent? Clearly postmodern deconstructionism, which is nothing less than the terminal form of Liberal "tolerance" and liberation from traditional dogmas, can end in nothing but barrenness, decay, despair and dissolution.

But deconstruction, it turns out, is not the final phase of Postmodernism; the next logical phase is, precisely, *magic*. The central principle of Chaos Magick, which it holds in common with the New Age, its more lyrical and idealistic cousin, is: "Belief is a tool." In other words, if there is no such thing as objective truth, then there is nothing to prevent the magical ego from positing *as* true whatever it likes, since there are no longer any real "truths" out there to stand in its way. Thus the universally quoted line "nothing is true, everything is permitted"—which is taken from the Vladimir Bortol's novel *Alamut* where it appears as "the assassin's creed"—actually means "everything is permitted *because* nothing is true."[3] The sort of magic or "creative visualization" that either believes there is no such thing as an objective metaphysical order, or else has so vague an idea of it that the notion of *conforming* the self to that order, as the pre-condition for any spiritually-based action, has never arisen, thus inevitably emerges as the central *praxis* in a post-structuralist world.[4] And the notion that belief is a tool, that the use of words is not primarily to *express truth* but rather to *make things happen*, is obviously also an integral part not only of the craft of magic but of the practice of politics—right, left or center, green, red or blue—in today's world. Thus to adopt the worldview of the particular group one wishes to influence, to seize and express the beliefs of that group as a tool for political organizing, without actually believing in them on any level beyond the most basic utilitarianism, is entirely in line with the zeitgeist, not only on the magical/paranormal level but equally on the socio-political one. The globalist elites of the west have used this tool for decades if not generations as one of

3. It is interesting that Bortol presents the Ismaili Islamic terrorists known as the Assassins as a band of nihilistic anarchists. Could this fictitious and distorted view of Shi'a Islam actually be one of the tributaries to the pseudo-Islamic ethos of certain terrorist groups? In postmodern information culture, every illusion is possible

4. This transition from deconstructionism to magic is mirrored in the wildly-successful "Harry Potter" books by J.K. Rowling. As Postmodernism was taking over the academies, Rowling was churning out book after book set in an institution of "higher learning" called Hogwarts—a sort of twisted, inverted University of Oxford—where the bright young minds of the rising generation, instead of reading the Classics, were studying Sorcery—undoubtedly to better fit them for life in the "real world."

their most effective techniques for social engineering—though for the most part they have understood, better than Dugin apparently does, that such methods work best when their operative principles are hidden from the public. The Communists used them as well, preaching freedom from the bosses when appealing to those of a libertarian bent, trade unionism to the militant working class, peace to the peaceniks, ascetic self-discipline to those searching for a new religion, feminism to women etc. Likewise Dugin openly presents a similar methodology of mimicry for the purpose of recruitment and organizing in *The Rise of the Fourth Political Theory*. It may be, however, that Aleksandr Dugin, as an ideologue who wishes to motivate the masses and organize a Eurasianist coalition through the influence of his analysis and rhetoric, has in fact acted as an unwitting whistle-blower for certain methods of social control that he and the western globalist elites practice in common.

On the other hand, it also might be true that Dugin's ploy is actually an example of what revisionist historian Michael Hoffman calls "the revelation of the method." From time to time the social engineers, according to Hoffman, will suddenly reveal, as if out of the blue and in no particular context, exactly what they have been up to. This technique has a number of effects: it demoralizes researchers and undermines the *raison d'être* of investigative reporters who have dedicated their lives to exposing the methods of the globalists; it presents the social engineers as so recklessly confident that they can even afford to tell us exactly what they are planning, giving the impression that they are virtually unstoppable; and it produces a sense of shock in those subjected to it which causes them to *repress* the very revelation that has shocked them, thus creating a psychological blind spot at the exact place where insight is most called for, as well as implanting the mind-bending revelation within the unconscious mind as a kind of post-hypnotic suggestion. The extreme *contradiction* between the false propaganda smokescreen that the social engineers have been working so hard to project, and the true method they have now suddenly revealed, in itself works as a mind-control technique. If the human mind can be induced to accept two contradictory theses as absolutely true on the same level, not just relatively true on different levels and in different contexts, then the critical faculties are paralyzed, leaving that mind highly vulnerable to control-by-suggestion. In positing the Russian/Eurasian Collective as an alternative to the Western Liberal/Democratic one, Aleksandr Dugin has apparently appropriated, imitated, and also *exposed*, many of the methods of his Atlantean rivals. In the past Dugin has strongly opposed the post-Soviet Russian oligarchs. On the other hand, his name has been mentioned in connection with oligarch Konstantin Malofeyev; both he and Dugin have apparently supported the Leftist Syriza regime in Greece. Therefore it is not entirely outside the realm of possibility that he has received some of his marching-orders directly from those eschelons of the globalist elites that transcend the East/West divide, and from the international financiers who fund and direct them. Whether there is any truth to these speculations—and they are certainly no more than that—or whether this similarity-of-outlooks simply reflects the quality of the zeitgeist, the fact remains that the ideologues and propagandists of Atlantis and Eurasia have a lot more in common than Dugin is willing to admit.[5] It may simply be that the actual form and content of modern and postmodern ideologies can only be clearly discerned from the point of metaphysical objectivity provided by Tradition, and consequently that Dugin, not being a Traditionalist, has no way of fully understanding them. On the other hand, there may be method in his madness; his seeming inability to recognize his own debt to Liberalism and Postmodernism may in fact conceal a conscious, cynical and highly skillful ability to appeal, both openly and covertly, to the often unconscious beliefs and cultural dominants of those groups he wishes to undermine and/or recruit.

Any attempt to mount a cultural or political resistance to an established power-structure must initially appeal to *any* social group that has been marginalized by that establishment, no matter how incompatible their ideologies may be, often resulting in some very "strange bedfellows".[6] As Dugin says, "what we are divides us; what we are against unites us"—which could only mean that as soon as "what we are against" is defeated, the "we" in question must dissolve in total conflict; the only way this result could conceivably be avoided would be by the immediate imposition of an iron tyranny. In any case, the bare tactical need to recruit allies against a perceived common enemy, rather than some quasi-metaphysical dawning of Chaos as a new "principle of order" such as Aleksandr Dugin posits, may in fact be enough to explain his heterogeneous influences,

---

5. The best overview and exposé of Duginism I have yet encountered is the You Tube video "What Duginism is and Why it Matters," by a Romanian researcher who identifies himself only as Freedom Alternative. It may be viewed at: https://www.youtube.com/watch?v=CdkfEKOVaFc. Though he analyzes Dugin from a basically secular perspective, not a religious and metaphysical one as I have done, he does make the highly interesting claim that a number of Russian Orthodox hierarchs denounced Aleksandr Dugin as a heretic on one occasion for attempting to introduce Paganism and Satanism into the Orthodox Church, after which all those who had denounced him either died or were defrocked. I have been unable to corroborate this story from other sources, therefore I leave the task of doing the necessary research to either confirm or debunk it to the interested reader.

6. At one phase such incompatible tendencies often find refuge in some form or other of "Bohemia"; the hippies, for example, saw no problem in simultaneously reading *The Tibetan Book of the Dead* and Chairman Mao's *Little Red Book*. The 60's counterculture initially embraced pacifists, mystics and proponents of armed revolution who were united by little else than their dis-identification with the dominant society. For an interesting picture of a similar Bohemia in pre-National Socialist Weimar, where déclassé aristocrats and artistic rebels against the bourgeoisie promiscuously mingled with proto-Nazis, proto-Communists and proto-Zionists, see the novel *Dr. Faustus* by Thomas Mann.

which he then proceeds to rationalize ideologically by an appeal to various pseudo-metaphysical principles. (Likewise Vladimir Putin, though he presents himself as the sworn enemy of the oligarchs, may have found it necessary to make common cause with some of them before moving against the others; political rivalries and alliances are rarely as simple as their public relations images suggest. And if, as some maintain, Putin is in fact the richest man in the world, worth as much as $200 billion, what else is he but an oligarch?)

Postmodernism initially appeals to such "humanistic" values as "celebrating diversity" and "letting other voices speak than that of the dominant worldview." In doing so, however, it deconstructs not only the unifying principles of any society that adopts it, but all sense of the Unity of Being and the Transcendent Unity of God. Therefore it necessarily results in paralysis and fragmentation in the mental sphere, disorder and conflict in the social sphere, and either poly-theism or atheism in the sphere or religion. In the first phase of this degenera-tion, the exiled sense of the Divine Absolute secretly re-infiltrates the society that has rejected it in the form of innumerable competing prejudices, bigotries and "absolutisms." In the second and terminal phase, total chaos, by its col-lapse, calls for total order—not the intrinsic, organic order of the One and the Many such as Tradition conceives of it, where the One both necessarily and generously expresses Itself through the multiplicity of creation, while creation inevitably strives to return to the One and know itself within the embrace of the One, but rather an imposed, authoritarian order. The tyranny of this artificial order inevitably generates chaos, and this chaos in turn justifies the imposition of greater tyranny. Thus all the little magicians, those who have taken Postmod-ernism's "liberation" of them from the dogmas of the past as *carte blanche* to create their own separate worlds, will in the end be rounded up by the One Big Magician, the Great Wizard who will (in Guénon's words) harvest the "psychic residues" they have collected as plunder from the destruction of Tradition so as to form the *petrified amalgam of all possible states*, which is Dante's image of Lucifer in Hell and Blake's doctrine of Satan-as-Hermaphrodite: and this will be the Regime of Antichrist.

Dugin and Nietzsche

Aleksandr Dugin quotes Friederich Nietzsche from time to time, and although Nietzsche's worldview is less central to Dugin's than that of Martin Heidegger or Alain Benoist or René Guénon, nonetheless his love of war and his dismissal of Christian mercy and self-sacrifice permeate Dugin's writings.

In Nietzsche's time Tradition and convention, or whatever remained of them, were one; this is what led him to declare that "God is dead"—a declara-tion that's right in line with Heidegger's doctrine of the fall of the Logos—and then go on to exalt his *Übermensch*, his Zarathustra, the lonely misunderstood "prophet" who creates his own myth and has the courage to live it out, no matter how much suffering this might entail. In our own time, however, the only way to return to Tradition is to *defy* convention, since convention is now anti-Traditional—which means that the path of the lonely intellectual and spiritual hero (not to say that identifying oneself as such a hero doesn't bring plenty of problems of its own) is virtually *towards* God now, not toward the Antichrist, unless *al-Dajjal* leads him astray by falsely picturing Satan as the great rebel against the established system of things rather than what he actually is, the *de facto* patron of the global elites. The Antichrist today is little more than the standard-bearer of the conventional outlook, the purveyor of the "received wisdom" of Postmodernism. He is Lord of the Easy Way, the Friendly Beast who requires nothing of us but that we immerse ourselves in the postmodern collective, sink into its drugged and troubled sleep, and drift downstream to our destruction. God, however, requires of us that we wake up, face our pain, and recognize the source and center of that pain as the voice of the murdered and immortal Deity crying to us from the ground of the personal and collective unconscious, announcing His impending resurrection and demanding of us everything we have, everything we are. When God comes back into the human Heart he'll come like Arthur, like Barbarossa. To encounter Him when the heavens are laid bare will require the greatest courage imaginable—the courage to let Him perfect our strength *in weakness*. The coward worships the *feeling* of power; the lover of God worships *true* Power—a Power that is inseparable from Knowledge and Love. When God arrives, when we can find no place to hide from Him, He will offer us the hardest gift of all to accept—the gift of dignity, humility and self-respect. There is no greater burden to carry, in a world like ours, than this gift. To bear the weight of it without capitulating to vanity and narcissism requires *virtue*, a word that's akin to *virility*. It takes naked courage to maintain our dignity in a world totally submerged in vulgarity, violence, and the systematic desecration of the human form, without turning into a coward, a charmer, a hypocrite, a megalomaniac, or a thug—especially when the world rewards these choices and persecutes anyone who shows no interest in them. It takes courage to care when care must look on devastation, courage to help when help seems impossible, courage to have compassion not only for the ones who need our help but for those we cannot help, and even for those others who have become their own worst enemies by turning into successful oppressors under the Rulers of the Darkness of This World. There is the courage to see, the courage to feel, the courage to question, the courage to take an unpopular stand, the courage to ask for help, the courage to bear one's burdens in silence, the courage of honest speech, the courage of wise discretion, the courage to act, and the courage to refrain from acting—to hold back even when the battle-fury is building inside us. Courage is the virtue that gives us the power to practice every other virtue. What are generosity, or trustworthiness, or patience, or dignity, without courage? And what is the guardian-virtue of courage and dignity and all the others? It is humility. Nietzsche thought that humility was nothing but the "virtue" of cringing slaves, a method devised by those skilled in fawning, flattery, self-loathing and the art of passive aggression to turn their abject weakness into a perverted strength, according to Blake's proverb that "the weak in courage is strong in cunning." He was wrong; all he could see were shadows. False humility cringes; true humility *commits*. It is not cool and calculating, but supremely reckless. It makes the sacrifice the moment that sacrifice is demanded. It never hesitates. It never looks back. If Nietzsche had had even the barest inkling of what *chivalry* is, he would have understood the dignity, the humility and the courage of the warrior who swears fealty to God and puts his life on the line. But by the time he came upon the scene, chivalry was a virtue that even Christianity had forgotten, consequently that whole world was closed to him. And it may effectively be closed to Dugin too, given that his Christianity seems to be more or less a function of his geopolitics, and also because the virtue of chivalry was more intrinsic to traditional Roman Catholic Western Europe—and to Islam, where it is called *futuwwah*—than to the Eastern Orthodox civilization of Byzantium. Likewise Nietzsche, due to his Protestant background, had little concept of honor, which is why he never understood the necessary relationship between humility, fealty and courage. Bourgeois Protestantism, having replaced the notion of honor with that of *propriety*, which Nietzsche rejected, gave him no way to grasp the truth of Meister Eckhart's saying, "the soul is an aristocrat"—the soul of the human being, that is, not just the *personality* of the *übermensch*. (Evola, the self-initiate, wrote of something he called "spiritual aristocracy," but what did he know of fealty? He had no Lord.) Do we have enough time to remember this virtue, or any viable rootstalk to graft it onto? On the collective level, probably not. The one who is alone with God, however, is already in the presence of it.

Dugin and Religion

In his section "The Return of Tradition and Theology" in *The Fourth Political Theory*, Aleksandr Dugin begins by telling the true story:

> Tradition (religion, hierarchy, and family) and its values were overthrown at the dawn of modernity. Actually, all three political theories were conceived as artificial ideological constructions by people who comprehended, in various ways, "the death of God" (Friedrich Nietzsche), the "disenchantment of the world" (Max Weber), and the "end of the sacred." This was the core of the New Era of modernity: man came to replace God, philosophy and science

replaced religion, and the rational, forceful, and technological constructs took the place of revelation.

But religion was not destined to be repressed, denied and discarded forever:

However, if modernism is exhausted in postmodernity, then at the same time, the period of direct "theomachy" [*murder of God*] comes to an end along with it. Postmodern people are not inimical towards religion, but rather, indifferent. Moreover, certain aspects of religion, as a rule, such as Satanism, and the "demonic texture" of postmodernist philosophers are quite appealing to many postmodern individuals. In any case, the era of persecuting Tradition is over, although, following the logic of postliberalism, this will likely lead to the creation of a new global pseudo-religion, based on scraps of disparate syncretic cults, rampant chaotic ecumenism, and "tolerance." While this turn of events is, in some ways, even more terrifying than direct and uncomplicated dogmatic atheism and materialism, the decrease in the persecution of faith may offer an opportunity, if the representatives of the Fourth Political Theory act consistently and uncompromisingly in defending the ideals and the values of Tradition.

Here Dugin touches upon an important element in René Guénon's doctrine from *The Reign of Quantity and the Signs of the Times*: the transition from "Anti-Tradition" (secularism, materialism) to "Counter-Tradition" (false religion, inverted hierarchy, the coming of Antichrist). Unfortunately, he totally misrepresents the nature of this transition—because the truth is, the widespread interest in religion, even in Tradition, is returning. This, however, does not signal the end of the persecution of Tradition—far from it. The climate is certainly more welcoming to Traditional religion in Russia under Putin than it was under Communism, but this is not necessarily true of much of the rest of the world. The persecution of the Rohinga Muslims by the Buddhists of Myanmar, the burnings and bombings of churches and mosques throughout the Muslim world and beyond, the virtual emptying of Iraq and Syria of their ancient Christian populations, the churches and mosques and synagogues attacked and burned even in the United States where "freedom of religion" is supposedly the highest law of the land—not to mention the closely-related "soft pogrom" against Christianity in the U.S., where a person can be fired for the public expression of his or her faith, where a baker can be threatened with the loss of his business simply for refusing to bake a "wedding" cake for a same-sex couple, where a Novus Ordo Catholic priest in Lexington, Kentucky, my present home, can refer to the tri-state area of Kentucky, Ohio and Indiana as "the Triangle of Evil" due to the number of Traditional Catholic congregations who worship there—all of these developments clearly demonstrate that Traditional religion is under attack as never before. The return of an interest in religion of one kind or another on the collective level has accelerated the persecution and destruction of the Traditional religions, not mitigated it. Should we expect the coming of the false religion of *al-Dajjal* to signal a new golden age for the religions of Muhammad and Jesus? Postmodern people, living in the age of Counter-Tradition, are not indifferent to religion as their predecessors were in the age of secular humanist Anti-Tradition. They are attracted to it, fascinated by it—or else militantly opposed to it—likely because they see the fall of Traditional religious authority as giving them *carte blanche* to do with religion—or with the *debris* of religion—whatever they like, including (in Dugin's words) the creation of "disparate syncretic cults"; Neo-Eurasianism itself, due to Aleksandr Dugin's promiscuous appeal to any and every religious expression as long as it seems in any way "ancient" or "traditional," is in danger of turning into such a cult. And in response to the excesses of New Age Pseudo-Tradition and Luciferian Counter-Tradition in the postmodern age, even Anti-Tradition seems to have gotten a new lease on life: never has the direct attack on religious faith by militant atheism been more in evidence in the English-speaking world, as witness the growing popularity of Richard Dawkins and his colleagues. And the organized Satanists have also come out of the woodwork—the "Satanists of the People," that is, not the Luciferians of the globalist elites, though it may turn out that the former actually represent a populist insurgence covertly sponsored by the latter. Where once bronze statues of Jesus, Mary and various Christian saints were virtually the only public religious statuary in the United States, now statues of Satan and his minions are beginning to pop up, including the one in Point Pleasant, West Virginia, representing a demon known as the Mothman, whose famous personal appearances—celebrated in a successful book and motion picture—have put Point Pleasant on the map, brought in tourist dollars, and gone a long way toward making the Mothman a postmodern folk hero! Dugin notes these developments, but he seems to have little understanding of what they mean for the fate of Tradition in the 21ˢᵗ century.

As for the creation of a new global pseudo-religion, I addressed that possibility in my book *The System of Antichrist.* Even more central to the exploration of this possibility is Lee Penn's *False Dawn: The United Religions Initiative, Globalism and the Search for a One-World Religion* [Sophia Perennis, 2005], which I was privileged to edit. The globalist project to create a One-World Religion—or else to perpetually dangle the image of such a development before the eyes of those "idealistic" members of the established religions who still see globalism as the door to human unity and peace, precisely so as to weaken the structure of those religions—is dealt with more thoroughly in *Chapter Seven.* At this point I only wish to point out that covert globalist support for militant religious extremism is an integral part of the globalist plan to unify and control the religions; the violence of the extremists works powerfully to justify the notion of a One-World Religion by presenting it as the only hope for peace.

Dugin goes on to say:

It is now safe to institute a political program that was once outlawed by modernity. It no longer appears as foolish and doomed for failure as before, because everything in postmodernity looks foolish and doomed for failure, including its most "glamorous" aspects. It is not by chance that the heroes of postmodernity are "freaks" and "monsters," "transvestites," and "degenerates"—this is the law of style. Against the backdrop of the world's clowns, nothing and no one could look "too archaic," not even the people of Tradition who ignore the imperatives of modern life.

Amen! However:

The fairness of this assertion is not only proven by the significant achievements of Islamic fundamentalism, but also by the growing influence of extremely archaic Protestant sects (Dispensationalists, Mormons, and so on) on American foreign policy. George W. Bush went to war in Iraq because, in his own words, "God told me to invade Iraq'! This is quite in keeping with his Protestant Methodist teachers. Thus, the Fourth Political Theory may easily turn toward everything that preceded modernity in order to draw its inspiration. The acknowledgement of "God's death" ceases to be the mandatory imperative for those who want to stay relevant. The people of postmodernity are already so resigned to this event that they can no longer understand it— "Who died exactly?" But, in the same way, the developers of the Fourth Political Theory can forget about this "event': "We believe in God, but ignore those who talk about His death, much like we ignore the words of madmen." This marks the return of theology, and becomes an essential element of the Fourth Political Theory. When it returns, postmodernity (globalisation, postliberalism, and the post-industrial society) is easily recognized as "the kingdom of the Antichrist" (or its counterparts in other religions—'Dajjal" for Muslims, "Erev Rav" for the Jews, and "Kali Yuga" for Hindus, and so forth). This is not simply a metaphor capable of mobilising the masses, but a religious fact—the fact of the Apocalypse.

Though I love Dugin's picture of "the death of God" in the mind of a postmodernist, I have a number of difficulties with this passage, both little and big. My little difficulties include Dugin's various mis-characterizations of the nature of American religious sects. George Bush's "God told me to invade Iraq" cannot be put down to Methodism *per se*, which is part of what used to be called "Liberal mainstream Protestantism" before the main stream of religion in the U.S. cut a different channel, but it is in line with the do-it-yourself eschatology of the Methodist Evangelicals. And when Bush made that statement he was also speaking for the benefit of the Dispensationalists and the Christian Zionist Evangelicals. Nor is Mormonism in any way "ancient"; rather, is the oldest established New Age cult in the United States, founded by a 19th-century Freemason on the basis of "channeled messages" from an entity who identified himself as an angel. Among my larger difficulties is Dugin's simplistic one-on-one identification of globalizing Postmodern Liberalism with the System of Antichrist; in 2001, in *The System of Antichrist*, I identified Postmodernism as one-half of the Globalist/Anti-Globalist or Universalist/Tribalist dialectic—identifiable with the Biblical Gog and Magog—which would ultimately produce that System. This prediction was fully vindicated by the birth of ISIS, a movement of counter-Islamic Satanist mercenaries initially sponsored by the United States and other western and regional players. What Dugin calls "the significant achievements of Islamic fundamentalism" thus represent nothing less than the widespread destruction of the Islamic tradition and the wholesale opening of Dar-al-Islam to "Atlanticist" insurgence and control.

In *The Rise of the Fourth Political Theory* (2017), Dugin cites a re-establishment of the *dhimmi* system of protected Peoples of the Book paying the poll-tax to the Islamic authorities as one goal of the Islamicist campaign to re-establish a global Caliphate. By the time that book was published, however, the actions of ISIS had already given the lie to that version of the Takfiri/Jihadi agenda, revealing their true agenda to be nothing less than outright genocide of all non-Islamic peoples—Christians, Yezidis—and all Muslims who do not subscribe to the Takfiri ideology, including Shi'as and Sufis. *Takfiris* are pseudo-Muslims who hold to the principle that all non-Takfiris, Muslim or non-Muslim, can be legally killed, simply on the basis of their beliefs. The *dhimmi* system, on the other hand, was based on the Covenants of the Prophet Muhammad, which concur with the Qur'an in expressly forbidding the slaughter or oppression of anyone based on religious belief alone; Muslims are commanded to take up arms only against those who have first attacked them. As for peaceful Christians, Muslims are commanded to actively defend them against their enemies until the end of time. The *dhimmi* system was sometimes mis-applied and perverted after the death of the Prophet, yet his Covenants were always there to recall Muslim leaders to the duties he had laid upon them, and very often they heeded that call. Thus the notion of associating a re-establishment of traditional *dhimmitude* with the "Islamic State" of ISIS and other Takfiri groups can only be a case of abysmal ignorance, or else a deliberate lie. Since 2013 John Andrew Morrow and I, via the Covenants Initiative, have been disseminating the newly-rediscovered and re-translated Prophetic Covenants throughout the world, specifically as an ideological campaign *against* ISIS—a campaign that was made increasingly urgent by the practice of ISIS and other Takfiri terrorists of seeking and destroying every Prophetic Covenant they could get their hands on.

How could Aleksandr Dugin have missed such glaring and obvious historical developments? How could he have gotten it so wrong? Was he simply not paying attention? Is he a sort of absent-minded professor, so immersed in his books that he fails to read the newspapers, watch TV or patronize the Internet?

He certainly doesn't give that impression. Is he being careful not to alienate the Takfiri Jihadists in case they decide to go over to Russia, looking for a better deal from Putin than they got from the United States—the United States who always betrays its puppets? This seems a much more likely explanation.

In the section "Myths and Archaism in the Fourth Political Theory" from the same book, Dugin raises a crucial issue—that of the "return" of archaic spiritualities and worldviews. Given that he clearly recognizes "the fact of Apocalypse," what is the significance of archaism for our time?

Due to generations of work by the archaeologists, anthropologists and mythographers, the philologists and religious scholars of Western Europe, the United States and elsewhere—much of which began under, and was made possible by, colonialism (though often in distorted forms, "Orientalism" for example)—we begin the 21st century as heirs to vistas of the human past, and of the beliefs and practices of various contemporary "primitive" peoples, vastly broader than even our immediate ancestors enjoyed. The monotheistic religions, the "New Age" religions of the western world, the spectrum of "Neo-Pagan" revivals, and even the ancient and primordial religions of both the Eastern and Western hemispheres, have been profoundly challenged, and changed, by these developments. Jungian psychology and similar mythopoetic movements have helped to turn the discoveries of the mythographers and anthropologists and comparative religion scholars into novel religious or quasi-religious manifestations which have had a profound effect on both new religions and religions long established. In response to these developments, Dugin says:

> If atheism, in the New Era, ceases to be something mandatory for the Fourth Political Theory, then the theology of monotheistic religions, which at one time displaced other sacred cultures, will not be the ultimate truth, either (or rather, may or may not be). Theoretically, nothing limits the possibilities for an in-depth readdressing of the ancient archaic values, which can take their place in the new ideological construction upon being adequately recognised and understood. Eliminating the need to adjust theology to the rationalism of modernity, the adherents of the Fourth Political Theory are free to ignore those theological and dogmatic elements in monotheistic societies which were influenced by rationalism, especially in their later stages. The latter led to the appearance of deism upon the ruins of Christian European culture, followed by atheism and materialism, during the phased development of the program of the modern age. Not only the highest supra-mental symbols of faith can be taken on board once again as a new shield, but so can those irrational aspects of cults, rites, and legends that have perplexed theologians in earlier ages. If we reject the idea of progress that is inherent in modernity (which as we have seen, has ended), then all that is ancient gains value and credibility for us simply by virtue of the fact that it is ancient. "Ancient" means good, and the more ancient—the better. Of all creations, Paradise is

the most ancient one. The carriers of the Fourth Political Theory must strive toward rediscovering it in the near future.

The Tibetan Buddhists have a concept known as the *bardo*, which is usually conceived of as the period of time after death and before re-birth. During the *bardo*—that is, if Enlightenment is not won at the point of death, at the dawning of the Clear Light of the Void—all the contents released by the decaying psyche of the newly-deceased rise into consciousness as visions of the Archetypes; these range all the way from the primary *dhyani-Buddhas*, representing the most fundamental aspects of consciousness, to all sorts of other lesser gods in every conceivable form, including the animal-headed beings known as the "knowledge-holding deities." It is my belief that, when a *civilization* dies, it passes through a similar *bardo*. All of its fundamental cultural dominants, and all of the earlier stages of history that went into its creation, arise—briefly, and in the most dramatic forms—before passing on. This does not indicate, however, that earlier phases of the civilization in question are *returning*, but rather that all the cultural and psychic material that went to make up that civilization, now that its constituting Form or Spirit has departed, is *leaving*; the life of that civilization is flashing before its eyes at the moment of its death. When Dugin speaks of the end of history or the reversibility of time, I believe that he is attempting to describe just such a civilizational *bardo*. This "dawning of the past" may give the illusion of a collective return to past ages, past myths and religions, past deities—something similar is sometimes experienced under the influence of psychedelic drugs—but that's not what's really happening. What *is* happening, according to the **Book of Apocalypse**, is *the end of the world* and *the resurrection of the dead*. Dugin knows that we face Apocalypse; it is the nature of Apocalypse, however, to resist dispassionate investigation, but instead to attract all kinds of passionate and terrified projections—projections that can become extremely dangerous if we are foolish enough to act them out. (A more detailed consideration of the laws by which Apocalypse operates may be found in *Chapter Eight*.)

A similar tendency to mistake a resurrected memory for a future potential, though on a smaller scale, may affect a nation that has undergone a revolution or counter-revolution. Since it was Communism that destroyed Czarist Russia, some will inevitably feel—if time can be reversed—that the fall of Communism must result in a Czarist restoration; but this is all a pipe-dream. Nostalgia is a powerful force, particularly at the point of death; this is why dying soldiers sometimes cry for their mothers. However, it is not their mothers—that is, the past—that they are about to encounter; it is Eternity—and to encounter Eternity filled with nostalgia for the past is to risk falling into the whirlpool of reincarnation, an illusory state that is nonetheless all-too-real to souls who have not renounced an addiction to identification, even as all the realities and states of mind they might identify with are flashing past their consciousness at the speed of light. The poet T. S. Eliot, in "The Wasteland," gives this picture of the apparent reversal of time during the death-process:

> Phlebas the Phoenician, a fortnight dead,
> Forgot the cry of gulls, and the deep sea swell
> And the profit and loss.
> A current under sea
> Picked his bones in whispers. As he rose and fell
> He passed the stages of his age and youth
> Entering the whirlpool.
> Gentile or Jew
> O you who turn the wheel and look to windward,
> Consider Phlebas, who was once handsome and tall as you.

The irony is that some of the newly-dead—and this includes newly-dead civilizations—do not realize that they are dead. The Nordic Neo-Pagans of *Asatru* and the Mediterranean Neo-Pagans of *Helenismos* may think that Odin and his Aesir, Zeus and his Olympians are coming back, whereas all that these ghost-deities are really doing is saying their last good-byes to us before they vacate the subtle terrestrial sphere and pass beyond the cycles of time.

The rise of the multiple residues of past experience and belief in the collective psyche, whether or not these residues are mediated by the discoveries of the archaeologists, mythographers and other scholars, is (in my opinion) the primary source of the postmodern ethos. Faced with many fascinating, compelling, but apparently contradictory religious and philosophical viewpoints, none of which we feel justified in discarding, we are either regretfully forced or happily "liberated" into a pluralistic and therefore relativistic vision of reality, including the reality of the Divine. Many cultures, many belief-systems, many gods now seem to be the "natural" inheritance of postmodern humanity, in opposition to which any form of Unity will necessarily—though falsely—seem like an imposed unification, a kind of conceptual imperialism.

The great virtue of Guénonian Traditionalism, however, is that it allows us to remain open to this multiplicity of perspectives without being forced to sacrifice the Unity of Truth, the Transcendent Unity of Being, or the Unity of God, or to discard the right and the ability to judge as intellectually false or spiritually subversive whatever views contradict, and thereby fail to find a place in, that Unity. The *eclecticism* of Aleksandr Dugin's Fourth Political Theory, which necessarily results in massive and self-destructive contradictions in both theory and practice, is thus no more than a reflection of his inability to grasp the Transcendent Unity of Religions, which is equally a Transcendent Unity of Viewpoints. What Dugin doesn't fully understand (and few do) is that each rendition of the Divine is necessarily, in its own terms, *the one true* rendition—

that is, as long as it recognizes a Transcendent Unity for it to be the one true (local) rendition of; this is Frithjof Schuon's doctrine of the "relative Absolute." Consequently Dugin, as a good postmodernist, must relativize all the religions and myths and magical systems he wishes to appeal to and collect as potential constituents, or constituencies, of his Eurasian Hegemony, thus removing the *raison d'être* and denying the transcendental Divinity of every one of them—at least every one of them that recognizes, in some form or fashion, the Unity of God, the Unity of Being or the Unity of Truth. *Ad hoc* eclecticism deals with debris, with the fragments of dead religions and dead civilizations, which it amasses; transcendental metaphysics deals with a living organic Unity, which it *recognizes*.

It is my belief that every religion begins as a monotheism, or at least as a worldview based on an intrinsic intuition of the Unity of Being, whether or not this Unity is conceived of in personal terms. The notion that monotheism generally precedes polytheism is corroborated by the *deus absconditus* that appears in many "primitive" religions—those of sub-Saharan Africa for example. The *deus absconditus* is a Creator or High God who was once in intimate relation to His creation, including the human race, but who has since removed Himself from the earthly scene, disgusted with our degeneracy, our many crimes and our refusal to repent. In religions that recognize a *deus absconditus*, human interactions with the Unseen are now mediated by a host of petty gods, ancestors, spooks and familiar spirits, indicating that what we take to be a "primitive" polytheism is often nothing but the *bardo* of an extremely ancient monotheism. Zoroastrianism is usually seen as a "dualistic" faith, based on a God of Good and a God of Evil, and rendered almost polytheistic by the veneration and invocation of the divine "angels" known as the *Amesha Spentas*. But in the *Gathas*, the earliest Zoroastrian scriptures, reputedly composed by the Prophet Zoroaster himself, God is clearly One, with the so-called God of Evil, *Angra Mainyu*, clearly functioning as a personification of the *ego*, and therefore of illusion or *Maya*. When the Qur'an came to the Prophet Muhammad, peace and blessings be upon him, the religion of Mecca centered on the Kaaba was polytheistic. According to legend, however, the Kaaba had been built by the monotheistic Prophet Abraham, in whose memory the *Hanifs*, a remnant of this ancient Abrahamic monotheism, still kept the worship of the One God alive, while waiting for a prophet who would reinstate it. Furthermore, speaking from my own personal experience at the age of 69, I have seen American culture, in the process of its profound degeneration—which every intelligent human being must recognize—pass from a phase where the existence of One God "went without saying" to the present phase where the existence and action of many gods seems the most "natural" way of viewing things; the monotheism of my youth now appears to many as an implausible belief arbitrarily imposed by an alien force known as "Christianity." In other words, my life has spanned the period from the last days of modernism, which at least "tolerated" Christianity and reserved a marginal place for it in Liberal culture, to the birth and establishment of Postmodernism, with the "spiritual revolution" of the late 1960's functioning as the focal point of the turn.

If this view of the birth and degeneration of religions is accepted, polytheistic religions clearly cannot be placed on the same level as monotheistic ones, to which they are necessarily inferior. But we must be very cautious in our judgments here, since not everything that appears to be polytheism—defined as belief in a plurality of Absolutes or a multitude of independent and sometimes conflictive divine powers—is actually what it seems. In Hinduism, for example, it is generally understood that the many "gods" are the many faces of the One God. God is worshiped "as" Rama, "as" Krishna, "as" Shiva, "as" Ganesh or "as" Kāli, depending on the personal temperament and the cultural background of the devotee. Some Hindus undoubtedly descend into polytheism pure and simple, but the best-informed worshipers recognize the "many gods" as the One God, Brahman, refracted through the delusive yet instructive prism of *Maya*. Likewise the Lakota (Sioux Indians) of North America venerate the Six Grandfathers on what might be called the Archangelic Plane, along with innumerable animal spirits and totem deities who function more or less as angels, yet all recognize the primacy of Wakan Tanka, the Creator, the Great Mystery. And it is equally possible for monotheism to be other than it seems. The literalistic belief in One God, if the true spiritual nature of God as both Transcendent and Immanent is not recognized, finally becomes little more than an idolatrous superstition. Nor does professed monotheism always guarantee a clear understanding of the Transcendent Unity of Being, since the One God of a particular monotheistic faith can sometimes degenerate into a "henotheistic" god, a glorified tribal deity. The Evangelical Christian, General Jerry Boykin, when recounting his battle against a Muslim warlord in Somalia in 2003, was quoted as saying: "I knew my God was bigger than his." To relativize God like this, however, by casting Him as the exclusive god of a particular group, albeit the biggest and the meanest, rather than the God of the Universe, is to depart from monotheism, and thereby reject Christianity. Likewise Pope Francis has declared that God does not exist, though the Three Persons of the Holy Trinity do; in his attempt to make Christianity into something it never has been, a polytheistic religion, he has definitively departed from the Christian tradition and cut himself off from the Mystical Body of Christ.[7]

---

7. See http://novusordowatch.org/2014/10/francis-god-does-not-exist.

Be that as it may, it is clear that one of Aleksandr Dugin's reasons for embracing archaism is in order to relativize and deconstruct monotheism. Employing his usual ambiguous slight-of-hand, he says that monotheism resulted in deism, that deism was rationalistic, that rationalism has been superseded, and therefore that monotheism now has to be thrown out too—or maybe not, we'll have to wait and see. If it were possible for an infant to die of old age, then Dugin might be on to something . . . but not if he thinks that *the jury is still out* on the validity of monotheism! The necessary Unity of God and the necessary multiplicity of His manifestation is an unchanging metaphysical principle, unchanging not because it has amassed enough power to maintain its position and defend itself against all rivals, *but because it is true.* Consequently anyone who says that monotheism *may or may not* turn out to be the ultimate truth, depending upon how the winds of history blow, has zero understanding of metaphysics, and ought to bite his tongue whenever that word, which he has no right to pronounce, escapes his lips. In the face of Dugin's mystifications I am now required to say: My fellow Muslims! Brothers and sisters! Be very careful not to follow or partner with Aleksandr Dugin—because if you, as a Muslim, believe him when he says that the Unity of Allah is an issue yet to be decided upon one way or the other, you should start working, right now, on the *excuse* you will need to present to Allah Subhanahu Wa Ta'ala when you meet Him face-to-Face on the Plains of Akhira—because it had better be a good one!

Lastly, what Dugin ignores in his appeal to archaism is the whole question of *dispensation.* Some religions are alive and some are dead. Some are accepted by God; some, once accepted, are now rejected because their dispensations have lapsed; some—those that have falsely usurped the name of "religion"—have been under God's curse from the beginning. When Egypt was young, her religion was undoubtedly one of God's masterpieces on earth—but by the time Pharaoh's magicians turned their rods into serpents, only to have them eaten up by the serpent that sprang from the rod of Moses, most of that glory was a thing of the past. And by the time Howard Carter excavated the tomb of Tutankhamun and turned loose the mummy's curse, Egypt was as dead and dry as her buried kings—so no matter how big a pile of mummy-dust Dugin is able to sweep together, he will find nothing but the inertia of dead matter and the poison of dead souls. On the other hand, some lineages of Shamanism are still alive in various parts of the world, and Shamanism began in a world-age even earlier than that of Egypt. But in order for a religion to remain alive it needs to be host to unbroken lineages or *silsilahs* stretching back to its Founder; it needs to maintain what the Christians call the Apostolic Succession. An unbroken lineage on the horizontal plane of time means a constant renewal of the human covenant with God on the vertical plane of Eternity. When this is lacking, then the religion in question—like the religions of the Norse, the Egyptians, the Sumerians, or the Celts—is dead, and no dead religion can be resurrected by a mixture of archaeology, textual analysis and wishful thinking—or by attempting to "channel its *egregore*" (collective thought-form), something that led the members of the cult known the Order of the Solar Temple, who had been trying to restore the Order of the Knights Templar partly through mediumship, to several mass suicides in Switzerland and Canada between 1994 and 1997. It was a cardinal principle of René Guénon that all that can be extracted from the sites and relics of dead religions are masses of toxic psychic residues, residues of the kind that only magicians, not worshippers of God, have any use for. And the prime role for such residues in the Age of Antichrist is to mimic, counterfeit and ultimately deconstruct the true religions sent by God to man.

When Dugin says, "Not only the highest supra-mental symbols of faith can be taken on board once again as a new shield, but so can those irrational aspects of cults, rites, and legends that have perplexed theologians in earlier ages," we must *hope* that he has no idea what he's talking about. First, to take something "on board" as a "new shield" is not to understand it, commit to it, and follow it, merely to employ it as a protective charm or to superstitiously hoard it as religious plunder. Secondly, to look at pre- or non-Abrahamic "cults, rites and legends" as necessarily *irrational* is both ignorant and insulting. If the ones recounting those legends and practicing those rites no longer understand them, then the cults, rites and legends in question are irrational as far as those people are concerned, though not necessarily so in themselves; a monotheistic belief is just as irrational for someone who doesn't understand it but only follows it mechanically. And if "'Ancient' means good, and the more ancient—the better," then nothing can ever be antiquated or worn out, which we all know is not actually the case, just as we also know—though "the myth of progress" claims otherwise—that the newer thing is not always the better thing. Here Dugin exhibits one of the most common misunderstandings of Tradition and Traditionalist doctrine: the idea that Tradition worships the Past. Tradition does *not* worship the Past, it worships God, and God is not (only) in the Past; He much more truly in the Present—that is, in Eternity. If He were not in Eternity, He could not approach us, as He is doing even as we read these words, from the direction of the Future. If Traditionalism grants precedence to the Past, it is not because the Past is over and done with, fixed, and therefore capable of being possessed, but simply because most people in past ages, according to the laws of the *manvantara*, were more in touch with Eternity than most people are today. Yet our own door to Eternity is neither the Past nor the Future, but the Present Moment. Consequently when Aleksandr Dugin says, "Of all creations, Paradise is the most ancient one. The carriers of the Fourth Political Theory must strive toward rediscovering it in the near future," it is clear that he has no understanding of the intrinsic solidarity between what is Ancient and what is Here and Now, that the only door to Paradise is this Present Moment—not to mention the rudimentary piece of spiritual guidance that advises us not to seek our Paradise in the past, but to hope, with faith, that it lies in our own future. God the Father, in the **Book of Malachi** [3:6], says: "I am Jehovah: I have not changed"; Jesus Christ, in the **Book of Apocalypse** [28:5], says: "Behold, I make all things new". Furthermore, speaking in Christian terms, is not the Son of one Substance—*homousion*—with the Father? But if the Fourth Political Theory "must strive toward rediscovering [Paradise] in the near future," instead of realizing Paradise *now* in the Spiritual Heart (which no "political theory" can do), thus making that Heart ready for a paradisaical future, that future will never come; this is the illusion, the obsession, and the bitter irony suffered by the Titans, the Asuras, the Jötun in their perpetual and eternally-unconsummated struggle to take heaven by storm. Paradise is not primarily in the Past or the Future, but in the depth of Now. If we recognize this truth, and can live with it, and live *into* it, without greed or fear, then all the *materia* that the Eternal Form of Paradise needs to make a living body for itself will flow toward it, spontaneously, from both the Past *and* the Future. The Future can never be reached; it can only arrive. The Past can never be dredged up from the heaviness of matter by power and labor and struggle; it can only be *loved*. Only love can transform the Past from a dead weight into a living potential.

In the section "The Eurasianist Attitude toward Religion" from **Eurasian Mission**, Aleksandr Dugin outlines something like an "official Eurasianist" policy toward religion and religious organizations. He says:

> In devotion to the spiritual heritage of one's ancestors and in the meaningful religious life, the Eurasianists see a step toward an authentic renewal and harmonic social development.

Dugin habitually sees religion as something that relates the believer to his ancestors or his ethnic group but not necessarily to God, or not *first* to God. But what if religious belief puts one at odds with one's society, as was the experience of both Jesus and Muhammad? Is a religion whose founder said, "He who does not hate father and mother for My sake cannot be my disciple" [Luke 14:26], compatible with Eurasianist values? In Hinduism the individual is fully integrated into society through membership in a caste. Yet the Hindus distinguish between the *pitri-yana*, the Way of the Ancestors, and the *deva-yana*, the Way of the Gods; the *pitri-yana* is to be avoided by the devotee because it leads to rebirth. Likewise in the last *ashrama* or traditional stage-of-life, the devotee breaks his ties with society and concentrates upon *moksha* alone; liberation from the Wheel of Birth and Death is also liberation from society. It seems that the traditional religions would need to be radically denatured to become compatible with Eurasianist norms.

And if society is not renewed, if there is no harmonious development? Does religion lose its *raison d'être* under such conditions? If it has no immediate social cash value, does it have no value at all? Is the salvation of the soul too Liberal and Individualistic a goal to merit official recognition by the Eurasianists? Dugin answers:

> For the Eurasianists, spiritual development is the main priority of life, which cannot be replaced by any economic or social benefits.

Much better. But since Eurasianism, as a political movement, albeit one that is supposedly supportive of religion, can do nothing to directly further the spiritual development that only religion itself can foster, it must be prepared to simply leave the religions alone under most circumstances, except when religious communities require defense against outside attacks, and ask for it. When Dugin participated in the Arbaeen pilgrimage to the Shi'a holy places in Iraq in 2017, he spoke of Eurasian support for Shi'a Islam, much to the delight of his listeners. Yet he had just expressed, in *The Rise of the Fourth Political Theory*, his willingness to make alliances-of-convenience against the Atlanticists with the Salafi Jihadists, to whom the blood of the Shi'a is *halal*. And what was he doing on a Shi'a pilgrimage anyway? He is no Shi'a; he isn't even a Muslim. The more foolish among his listeners were undoubtedly flattered by his empty gesture toward their faith, just as some equally foolish Muslims were when Pope Francis prayed from the Holy Qur'an, ignoring the obvious fact that he doesn't believe in the Qur'an any more than he does in the New Testament. But not all Muslims are fools; those who dedicate their *din* to Allah instead of trying to recruit Allah to support their *din* will have little sympathy with those who flatter religion but rarely mention God.

> In the opinion of the Eurasianists, every local religious tradition or system of faith, even the most insignificant, is the patrimony of all mankind.

Very flattering, as when a man tells me that I have a beautiful wife—but that doesn't mean that I would be even more flattered if he slept with her. My "patrimony" is something I can claim at any time because it really belongs to me; let no-one claim my religion unless he swears to follow it.

> The traditional religions of the peoples, which are connected to the various spiritual and cultural heritages of the world, deserve the utmost care and concern.

Fine. But do they also represent a true spiritual authority that is not constituted by the state, but independent of it? In other words, do they deserve to be obeyed?

The representative organizations of the traditional religions must be supported by the strategic centers. Schismatic groups, extremist religious associations, totalitarian sects, preachers of non-traditional religious doctrines and teachings, and any other forces that promote the destruction of traditional religions must be actively opposed.

Very well—but we must clearly define our terms at this point. Are Wicca and Satanism "traditional religions" as they claim to be? Are Shi'ism, or Roman Catholicism, or the Sede Vaccantist Catholicism that rejects the "Novus Ordo" Catholic Church of the post-Vatican II popes "schismatic groups"—as Sunni Islam and Eastern Orthodox Christianity and the Roman Papacy claim they are? Or are only those groups truly schismatic who seek independence from their parent bodies *after* Eurasia Year One, whenever than may be? Is any organization that believes that there is no salvation outside its borders a "totalitarian sect"? Is proselytism to be prohibited as a form of religious colonialism and imperialism? Will Eurasia firmly put the lid on any form of religious expansion to prevent interreligious violence? I entirely support Aleksandr Dugin when he says that "any . . . forces that promote the destruction of traditional religions must be actively opposed." This is undoubtedly our point of greatest agreement. (See Part Three of *Chapter Seven*, "United Front Ecumenism and the War Against Religion.") But Dugin must be prepared for the possibility that the "repressive tolerance" of Eurasianism itself might, under certain circumstances, become one of the forces destructive to Tradition. The essence of Russian Orthodox Spirituality survived state oppression under Communism and even grew in strength. Will it be as successful in its less apparent but no less necessary struggle to survive state patronage under Vladimir Putin? Time will tell.[8]

Dugin and America, Dugin and God

In *Eurasian Mission*, Dugin maps out three alternatives for the American who wants to overcome the spiritual alienation that is America. The first is to attempt to return to a European identity, what might be called "the Ezra Pound option." This option draws the ex-American into the gravitational pull of the Twilight of the Gods, of Europe (and America) as the West and the Far West, the Land of the Sunset, ultimately leading to apocalypse, and thus—to the Fourth Political Theory.

The second alternative is for the rootless, alienated American to intuit the

8. According to Russian law, any religious organization may be recognized as "traditional" if it was already in existence before 1982, and each newly-founded religious group must provide its credentials and re-register yearly for fifteen years, remaining without rights until eventual recognition. [See *Trends in Religious Policy, Eastern Europe, Russia and Central Asia*, by Michael Bordeaux, 2003.]

Heavenly Earth—not the Terrestrial Paradise of Dante but the Islamic "Eighth Clime" of Suhrawardi and Henry Corbin—and then go on to create his or her own god. This might be called "the New Age option." Emerson was after something like that—a Transcendentalist "self-reliance"—and poet Robert Bly, via his Men's Movement (partly following mythographer Joseph Campbell) also recommended, as Nietzsche did, something on the order of "creating your own myth." This option Dugin characterizes as "an inverted individualist Platonism [*by which the American*] discovers the transcendence of God by creating it for himself," one that leads the American "absolute Individual" to an existential confrontation with absolute loneliness, after which "He tragically realizes the absent vertical axis in himself and is then ready to receive the 4PT," the Fourth Political Theory.

The third alternative is a kind of radical American Existentialism, an encounter with the absence not only of the collective God of Tradition, but even of the individual god created by the Absolute Individual to take His place—this being a direct confrontation with death, with the nothingness of the individual as such, which is then ironically revealed as "the essence of Liberty." "The nihilistic essence of liberalism here becomes evident," says Dugin, "and starting from this black spot we can further consider the propositions of the 4PT on how to overcome it."

What is missing in these three approaches to overcoming the "American alienation"? What is missing is God. The return to Europe might be one element in a spiritual return to Tradition in Guénon's sense, via the High Middle Ages, and thence to the first principle of European cohesion and civilization, namely Christ—not merely the "medieval" Christ, but the Christ who is "with you all days, even until the consummation of the *aeon*" [Matthew 28:20]. But, instead of Christ, the re-Europeanized American is offered—the Pagan Ragnarok and the Fourth Political Theory. According to Dugin, the self-deified Individualist American, the devotee who finds his own particular god in the Heavenly Earth, does not thereby realize that god as the particular face that the One Unique God turns to his own uniqueness—which is the way Henry Corbin, following Ibn al-'Arabi, expresses it—but suddenly discovers, not an individual path to the Transcendent God, and thus (potentially) to Tradition, but "the absent vertical axis in himself." He encounters his God-given spiritual potential not as a viable Way, or way to the Way, but purely as tragedy—a tragedy that can only be redressed (of course) by the Fourth Political Theory. And the American existentialist, or nihilist, in his radical confrontation with death and nothingness—which might have been an approach to, or a foreshadowing of, the spiritual annihilation in the Absolute that the Sufis call *fana*—does not find God in that Dark Night of the Soul, but only—the Fourth Political Theory. Man's extremity is, apparently, the Fourth Political Theory's opportunity.

In *The Fourth Political Theory* Dugin asks:

Why do we talk about roots but not the head? This is a very serious and deep moment, because we should realise the reduction that is being made. If we realise the horizontal reduction first, and we get an unsatisfactory result, we will conclude that we should instead realise the vertical reduction, to move towards *ontic* roots but not ontological heights. Therefore, we should post-pone such notions as the dimension of spirit and the divine, and move towards chaos and other vertical and depth-oriented concepts.

Just as Robert Bly in his *Iron John* [1990] talked about the need of American men to "get down," to recover the body, to re-appropriate their chthonic man-hood by a process of descent or *catabasis*, because the postmodern American *puer aeternus*, the "grandiose ascender," is too ungroundedly "spiritual" (some-thing that is probably less true today than it was 28 years ago, since people now-adays are not affected by false elevation so much as by psychic fragmentation and loneliness), so Dugin says we should *postpone* our dealings with the Spirit and the Divine until we have found our "ontic motherland"—which is (guess what) the Fourth Political Theory. This notion is essentially a perversion of the Traditional doctrine of the "lesser mysteries" and the "greater mysteries." The Prophet Muhammad, peace and blessings be upon him, in his "night journey," first completed his *isra*, his instantaneous horizontal translation to Jerusalem, and only then embarked on his *mi'raj*, his spiritual ascent through the spheres. His *isra* constituted the lesser or psychic mysteries, the location of the Center, the Heart, the point where the psyche is intersected by the vertical ray of the Spirit. His *mi'raj* enacted the greater or Spiritual mysteries, by which he ascended through the ontological hierarchy along the ray of the Spirit until he reached *the Lote Tree of the furthest limit* [Q. 53:14], beyond which lies nothing but the Absolute Unknowable Essence of God. So the whole motion is toward the Spirit, following the call of the Spirit, by the power of the Spirit. The Promethean hubris of "grandiose ascent" is the error of trying to reach the Zenith without first realizing the Center. But Dugin seems to have of little notion of a Center, a Spiritual Heart. Consequently he advises that we *postpone* God until we find out who we really are in ethnic and cultural and sociopoliti-cal terms, until (that is) we discover our real identity to be—the Fourth Politi-cal Theory! But the lover who begins with "I can't love you *until*" will never find his Beloved; with God, "later" equals never. In the words of the *hadith qudsi*, "Heaven and earth cannot contain me, but the Heart of my willing slave can contain Me." Postponing Heaven so we can somehow find our bearings by sinking into material chaos is not *al-sirat al-mustaqim*, not the Straight Path, not the Way. God is not only "up in heaven"; He is already here, already, at least virtually, in the spiritual Heart. "If I ascend up into Heaven, Thou art there: if I make my bed in hell, behold, Thou art there" [Psalm 139:8]—true enough! But the one who has not found Him in the Heart will never find Him in Hell, in *catabasis*, in "depth-oriented chaos"—nor (to say the least) will he ever get to Heaven either. If the hubris of the grandiose ascender, like so many of my generation who wanted to "drop acid and see God," is to try and reach Heaven before finding the Heart, the hubris of the *infernal descender* is to think that he can deal with the abysmal darkness of the individual and collective unconscious without the lamp of the Heart to guide him, that he can harrow Hell like Christ did without first becoming a co-heir with Christ, that he can redeem his own portion of the righteous ancestors before he has recognized the image of God within himself, the *Imago Dei*, the mirror of the Heavenly Father. If Aleksandr Dugin were willing and able to find a true *staretz*, one who could teach him the Prayer of the Heart, he might be better able to deal with the "depth-oriented chaos" of his own nature in the course of his "unseen warfare" with the demons, thus putting first things first.

4

Critique of
The Fourth Political Theory
Part I

I N THIS CHAPTER and the next I will present an overview of *The Fourth Political Theory*, chapter by chapter, selecting for deeper analysis various themes that I have not fully addressed elsewhere in this book.

On Chapter One: "The Birth of the Concept"

In Chapter One, Dugin declares that the age of ideology is ended, due to the death of the Third Political Theory (Fascism) and the Second Political Theory (Communism), and the impending fall of the First Political Theory (Liberalism). He speaks of the arrival of Postmodernism as Liberalism's terminal phase, and the First Political Theory as the driving force behind globalization. He defines the Fourth Political Theory, which is still in its nascent phase, as resistance to the status quo represented by Postmodern Liberalism and Globalism. He announces the need and the agenda of analyzing Postmodernism so as to discern its points of weakness, much as Marx analyzed Capitalism. He imagines that a more fully developed Fourth Political Theory might be aided in its deconstruction of Postmodernism by discerning those points where Fascism and Communism were in agreement, since these agreements could well represent a fundamental critique of Modernism—and, by extension, Postmodernism—that neither ideology necessarily emphasized or was fully conscious of. In the context of this critique he speaks of the return of Traditionalism (through Julius Evola, and by implication, René Guénon), and Archaism (the spread of the interest in mythology, folklore, pre-Christian and presumably pre-monotheistic "primitive" societies, etc.). He ends by positing Heidegger's concept of *Ereignis* or "the Event" as the turning-point in the fight against postmodern nihilism, and posits Russia as the privileged field on which this apocalypse, this "end of days" is to take place.

183

In the following paragraph, Dugin presents a fairly accurate picture of humanity's ideological condition in the postmodern age:

> The subject of Communism was class. Fascism's subject was the state, in Italian Fascism under Mussolini, or race in Hitler's National Socialism. In liberalism, the subject was represented by the individual, freed from all forms of *collective identity* and any "membership" (l'appartenance).
>
> While the ideological struggle had formal opponents, entire nations and societies, at least theoretically, were able to select their subject of choice—that of class, racism or statism, or individualism. The victory of liberalism resolved this question: the individual became the normative subject within the framework of all mankind.
>
> This is when the phenomenon of globalisation entered the stage, the model of a post-industrial society makes itself known, and the postmodern era begins. From now on, the individual subject is no longer the result of choice, but is a kind of mandatory given. Man is freed from his "membership" in a community and from any collective identity. . . .

In "The Birth of a Concept," Dugin presents us with some puzzling ideas of the nature of Liberalism and Globalism:

> liberalism . . . [is] . . . an existential fact, an objective order of things.

However:

> It turns out that the triumph of Liberalism, the first political theory, coincided with its end.

So Liberalism is both an established "existential fact" and something that is already virtually kaput—both a formidable enemy against which we must mobilize all our resources, and a paper tiger that might be carried off by the next gust of wind. The thrust behind such language seems more *motivational* that analytical. As for Globalism:

> Man is freed [under globalism] from "membership" in a community and from any collective identity.
>
> A global world can only be ruled by the laws of economics and the universal morality of "human rights."

Globalism certainly "frees" the human individual from membership in traditional organic communities, from race, nation and family, but in their place it imposes a new collective identity in the guise of membership in an artificial, engineered control-system called Global Society where a specific form of uniform identity and citizenship becomes increasingly compulsory. Globalism doesn't simply release the mass of human individuals from their cultural cages so they can run free, liberated from any restrictive collective identity; that's only the text of the advertising-and-propaganda campaign designed to globalize the collective psyche. No: What it actually does is destroy their homes, their villages, their cities with the combined use of economic and military force, thereby transforming long settled communities, both urban and rural, into homeless refugees and/or a nomadic transnational proletariat. In so doing it immensely widens the economic disparity between the global super-rich—the "1%"—and the rest of the Earth's population. This is how "the laws of economics"—which, due in part to the fall of Communism, the Second Political Theory, are nothing less than the laws of transnational Capitalism—rule the global world. And they by no means rule it according to the "universal morality of human rights"—though "human rights" is one of the names applied to the uniform behavior that globalism attempts to impose by force, terror, mind control, and the progressive reduction of the majority of the planet's population to the condition of what Franz Fanon called "the wretched of the earth." If Aleksandr Dugin wants to motivate us to rise up against globalization and the New World Order, he should not speak so highly of them. (In his Chapter Three, however, he presents a more balanced and accurate view of the effects of globalization.)

In the same chapter we also learn more about Dugin's eschatological vision, which is strongly influenced by Martin Heidegger's concept—or prophesy—of *Ereignis*, "the Event":

> Heidegger used a special term, *Ereignis*—the "event," to describe [*the*] sudden return of Being. It takes place exactly at midnight of the world's night—at the darkest moment in history. Heidegger himself constantly vacillated as to whether this point had been reached, or "not quite yet." The eternal "not yet."
>
> However, it is possible to state in advance that the Russian version of the Fourth Political Theory, based on the rejection of the status quo in its practical and theoretical dimensions, will focus on the "Russian *Ereignis*." This will be that very "Event," unique and extraordinary, for which many generations of Russian people have lived and waited, from the birth of our nation to the coming arrival of the End of Days.

In many ways this is a counsel of desperation. Heidegger simply asserts that, out of the nihilism produced by the demise of western philosophy and the death of western civilization, authentic Being will spontaneously arise. The wrecked car will suddenly re-assemble itself; the bombed city (Berlin? Dresden? Stalingrad?) will rebuild itself; the corpse will come back to life. No intervention of either man or God will produce this outcome; it will simply happen of itself.

This, according to Dugin, is the "End of Days" long awaited by the Russian people. This "end," however, is neither the Christian Apocalypse and/or Apocatastasis, nor the Nordic Ragnarok, nor even the dawning of the new *manvantara* in the Hindu doctrine of the cycle of manifestation. It could be none of these things because, implausibly enough, it will affect only Russia—or perhaps

Atlantis will fall and leave only Eurasia standing. In any case, Heidegger and Dugin between them have done their best to hijack traditional eschatology and situate it in a context where it could never apply. Once again Dugin has attempted to rob Russian Orthodox Christianity of one of its essential doctrines and harness it to his political bandwagon, producing in the process nothing but the absurd superstition that the end of the present cycle of manifestation "belongs" to Russia and constitutes a phase of Russian politics. Dugin apparently thinks that, in the face of the looming end of earthly life as we have known it, all he needs to do is re-define the Apocalypse as the dawning of the Fourth Political Theory and he will have possessed himself of the most powerful *motivational tool* imaginable. However, when motivation is based on the denial of reality, this guarantees that it will be powerless to affect reality; reality, as always, will have the final word. He quotes Mark 12:10 to the effect that "The stone the builders rejected shall become the cornerstone"—but the "cornerstone" is no longer Christ, simply "everything that was discarded, toppled and humiliated in the course of constructing . . . postmodernity." This pile of rubble is not much of a cornerstone in my opinion, and the fact is that postmodernity itself, in many ways, is actually composed of the fragments of everything was "discarded, toppled and humiliated" in order to create it. It did not reject these fragments; it simply removed them from their proper contexts, like jewels pried from their settings, and threw them into the postmodern/deconstructionist cement-mixer. And Alexandr Dugin, himself a *de facto* postmodernist, is doing exactly the same thing when he takes Christian eschatology out of its proper Christian context.

Dugin presents his Fourth Political Theory as the equivalent of a revolutionary ideology. But is it really? Liberalism came to power in and after the French Revolution. Communism seized power during the Russian Revolution. Fascism and Nazism rose to power when Mussolini and Hitler took control of Italy and Germany. All of these developments were effected by ideologies designed to mobilize dissent and unite various opponents of the status quo. The political thinkers who produced these ideologies were not acting as agents of any established regime, consequently they formulated their theories with a view toward achieving power at some future date. When they appealed to the masses, they were speaking to the relatively powerless who aspired to greater power, thus it is entirely correct to call these ideologies revolutionary.

It is different with the Fourth Political Theory. Aleksandr Dugin is not a representative of the disenfranchised masses, but of a damaged empire that has been reduced to the Russian Federation—in terms of the Russian Federation, however, he is in no way an "outsider." His connection with the apparatus of state power under Vladimir Putin, though not always explicit, appears to be firmly in place. Therefore his use of revolutionary language in appealing to those who experience the American/Atlanticist hegemony as oppression is in many ways inappropriate. Neo-Eurasianism is probably best described as a mystification of the power of the Russian State—and of the global oligarchs who may well stand behind it—designed to falsely portray in revolutionary terms what is actually a campaign of imperialist expansion. This imperialism may indeed be necessary, as Dugin maintains, to preserve the integrity of the Russian nation in the face of American imperialism, but both imperialisms are undoubtedly useful to, and even to a degree directed by, the global financial elites, who always position themselves to profit from conflicts without necessarily taking sides.

Russian Communism also pictured what was, after Stalin, basically a nationalist expansionism in revolutionary/internationalist terms. This was a legitimate position insofar as the Communists were serious about class struggle and world revolution, though it is clear that the Russian Communists weren't interested in any revolution that did not increase the power of the Russian state. But in any case they preached a fairly unified ideology and sought to create a unified Communist International to disseminate and impose it.

Things are far different with Neo-Eurasianism and the Fourth Political Theory. Aleksandr Dugin does not preach a unified ideology, nor does he seek to organize an ideologically unified movement. Instead he is doing his best to create an *atomized* movement—portraying this essentially postmodern atomization as "freedom from monopolar Liberalism"—a movement whose internal ideological and cultural contradictions will necessarily prevent it from speaking with one voice. He may be doing this in service to the goal of creating an imperial federation of semi-independent ethnic and religious groups such as existed in the Ottoman Empire and the USSR, but the element of internal contradiction and atomization is also quite obvious. What might be the geopolitical rationale for the establishment of an atomized and internally-contradictory coalition of anti-globalist forces on a global scale? If, as I wrote in *The System of Antichrist* [2001], "the globalization of the elites leads to the balkanization of the masses," then an effort to atomize and balkanize anti-globalist dissent would necessarily work to further establish the power of those elites, especially if they were successful in co-opting that dissent, or actually had a hand in creating it. And even if we choose to view the situation on a less transcendentally-paranoid level, the atomization and ghettoization of the disparate elements comprising the Neo-Eurasian Movement would certainly facilitate their union by, for, and under Russia.

Perhaps we can see this principle operating in the Occupy Wall Street movement in the United States. Occupy Wall Street was the most atomized protest movement in U.S. history. Whether or not the financial oligarchs, the "1%," had a hand in creating it, it obviously represented the best they might have hoped for from their opponents: a movement so fragmented and self-contradictory that any union of forces and interests and schools of social analysis to effectively oppose them was over before it began. It also had the virtue of exhausting dissent in a flurry of meaningless posturing, and simultaneously opening the groups involved to greater surveillance and infiltration. One face of Dugin's Neo-Eurasianism appears as a kind of Occupy movement on a global scale, one ultimately hoping to "Occupy Eurasia"—but behind this multipolarity lies the unity of Russian power. And exactly what interests does the *established* lack of unity in Dugin's coalition serve? Since it has been reported (by Freedom Alternative) that the Russian oligarch Konstantin Malofeyev is funding Dugin's efforts—just as certain international financiers bankrolled the Bolsheviks[1]—maybe this question should be addressed to Dugin himself.

It is necessary to see Aleksandr Dugin in truly global geopolitical terms, not just in terms of the aspirations of Russia to re-establish its empire, or even in the context of Dugin's projected Eurasian Hegemony. We need to ask the question—while reserving judgment and avoiding the tendency to jump to conclusions: "*If* Dugin were actually working in the interests of transnational finance, or if he has found it necessary to make alliances with certain globalist oligarchs and financiers in order to effectively operate, could there be one or more covert agendas behind his Neo-Eurasian movement that transcend the limits of simple Russian expansionism? And if so, what might be the nature of these agendas?" At this point we enter the realm of speculation, which can prove fruitful as long as we can resist the "paranoid conspiratorial" temptation to impose artificial closure by treating suspicion as certainty. That said, the following scenario presents itself as a possibility:

The globalist elites want the balkanization of Europe and the weakening or breakup of the United States—except insofar as it services and maintains a military machine that they can hire when needed. They want power to shift to the East, toward the heartlands of Asia. Why else would the European Union open the door to millions of Syrian and other refugees? Why else—outside of union-busting, the destruction of the domestic middle class and the consequent massive transfer of wealth to the super-rich, along with greater ease of access to cheap labor—would the Liberal establishment in the U.S. enforce porous borders? The elites clearly have their reasons for pursuing such policies; we need to start seriously asking "What's in it for them?" Do they by any chance foresee the massive destabilization of the "Atlantean" world due to global warming and rising ocean levels, just as Russia looks forward to the opening of vast new tracts of arable land in the far North consequent to the melting of the permafrost? Are they positioning themselves to retain

---

1. See ***Wall Street and the Bolshevik Revolution*** by Anthony C. Sutton.

and extend their global rule in the face of environmental apocalypse? And if this were actually an option for them, what would prevent them from exercising it?

∾

One particular passage in "The Birth of a Concept" is especially relevant in relation to recent claims that Russia has hacked into the U.S. electoral systems and power grids, given that the American people have no real way of separating true reportage from disinformation when confronted by such claims:

> Liberalism developed flawless weapons aimed at achieving its straightforward alternatives, which was the basis for its victory. But it is this very victory that holds the greatest risk to liberalism. We need only to ascertain the location of these new, vulnerable spots in the global system and decipher its login passwords in order to hack into its system. At the very least, we must try to do so. The events of 11 September 2001 in New York demonstrated that this is technologically possible. The internet society can be useful, even for those who staunchly oppose it.

On Chapter Two: "*Dasein* as an Actor"

In Chapter Two, Dugin addresses the question "Who or what is the subject of history?"—though as a postmodern political theorist, he is careful not to impose any degree of unity or consistency on his Fourth Political Theory by actually answering this question; the Theory must remain open-ended, available to all possibilities. It has been established, however, that the subject of history is no longer to be conceived of as the individual (the Liberal view), the class (the Marxist view) or the race or state (the Fascist view)—but why couldn't it be a mixture of all three? Or the "rhizome" or "body without organs" of Deleuze and Guttari? Or Heidegger's *Dasein*? Or the "Fourth Nomos of the Earth," the "political theology" of Nazi philosopher and legal theorist Carl Schmitt, representing an alternative form of globalism that is destined to replace colonialism—which, for all we know, could be incarnated in Neo-Eurasianism? Or maybe there could be a history with no subject at all. Why not? Why limit our options? However, the real principle behind Dugin's method may actually be: "If all views are relative, commitment to any single view is *gauche* considered from the standpoint of style and suicidal considered from the standpoint of ultimate outcome in the present postmodern context. Not only that, but the polyvalence and chaos of the Fourth Political Theory has already demonstrated its power to attract and mesmerize the intellectuals and ideologues of many different schools; therefore, for practical purposes, the ambiguity of this Theory should be expanded, not resolved."

The polyvalence of Dugin's Fourth Political Theory unexpectedly mirrors the "M-Theory" of physicist Stephen Hawking, as well as the definition of a "system" given by his colleague Richard Feynman. My critique of these ideas, which appears in "An Open Letter to Stephen Hawking," is thus applicable to Dugin's worldview as well:

> If, according to Richard Feynman, "a system has not just one history, but every possible history"—and if, according to you, "M-theory [*Prof. Hawking's ultimate material explanation for everything*] is not a theory in the usual sense [*but a*] whole family of different theories, each of which is a good description of observations only in some range of physical situations"—then are you not essentially saying that "M-theory is not just one theory, but every possible theory"? And is a conglomeration of all possible theories really any kind of theory at all? If every physical system is made up of every one of its possible histories, then, in order to deal with this complexity, would we not be forced to also allow that every *mental* system, every explanation, is necessarily made up of every one of its possible conceptual variations? The essence and use of a true theory, however, is that it is a *single* concept that unifies many facts, many possibilities, many measurements; if we are forced to define a theory as the set of all its possible variations—which your notion of M-theory seems to imply—then it is no longer a theory in the proper sense of the word, no longer an *explanation*. It is merely a series of *ad hoc* conceptual responses to an indeterminate set of probable measurements. So you would seem to be the patron and agent not only of a postmodern deconstruction of corporeal reality, but also of a similar deconstruction of the very notion of an intelligible physical theory capable of explaining that reality, neatly disguised under your "M-theory" notion. If physical theory begins to mimic the underlying chaos of probabilistic indeterminacy that it discerns on the material plane by itself becoming chaotic on the conceptual plane, the whole idea of natural law is called into question.

Likewise Aleksandr Dugin, in his Fourth Political Theory, appears as the deconstructionist of the very notion of "political theory," thereby perfectly demonstrating Heidegger's "fall of the Logos," the terminal phase of western philosophy when cut off from Traditional Metaphysics and contemplative practice. (If Heidegger had really been serious about the fall of the Logos, of course, he would have stopped writing and burned all his books.)

Traditional Metaphysics, however, has no difficulty in precisely defining the subject of history, since (with Plato) it understands time as "the moving image of Eternity": the subject of history is the Human Archetype, considered both as the earthly reflection of all the Names of God and as the "axial" being for terrestrial existence, the *telos* or Aristotelian "final cause" for the material universe, the point at which the *logoi* or constituting archetypes of all cosmic forms, both sentient and insentient, are synthesized, and at which the contemplation of God as the Source of all existence becomes possible, and therefore necessary.

This Form is neither the human individual nor the human collective, but rather the Archetype or *gestalt* of which the human individual is the figure and the human collective the ground. This Archetype, and the universe it defines, passes through various different phases during its terrestrial history—the four *yugas* of the *manvantara*—moving from synthetic unity to analytic atomization, in order to manifest every aspect of the Divine Nature that is capable of being manifested in the world of space, time, matter and energy. Humanity is created in order to incarnate the Immanence of God, and moves toward dissolution in order to prove the Transcendence of God. For God there is no "other-than-God"; therefore God's Knowledge is necessarily Knowledge of Himself, a Knowledge that is in no way separate from the Being of That which It knows; God *is* His Knowledge of Himself, and His Knowledge of Himself is Him. According to Ibn al-'Arabi, He knows Himself directly through His Essence, and at the same time understands cosmic existence through the consciousness of the beings that compose it, and in so doing knows this existence as Himself; in the words of the Qur'an [6:103, Rodwell translation], *No vision taketh in Him, but He taketh in all vision*. As the point where all cosmic forms are synthesized in the direct contemplation of God, the Human Form is the bearer of what the Qur'an calls the *Amana*, the Trust. Traditional Metaphysics views all human history according to this principle; as such it is fully capable of defining the proper *Tao* of human action, as well as the proper orientation and necessary limitations for action under specific cosmic conditions.

In his attempt to pick and choose useful elements from defeated ideologies, Dugin draws on the writings of Carl Schmitt to help him imagine a *good* Nazism—a Nazism without racism—even though Schmitt embraced and further developed the anti-semitic theories of the Nazis as soon he became a National Socialist. From my point of view it is very hard to imagine what a Nazism without racism might be—a totalitarianism based on state-controlled capitalism, I suppose, which is something that Russia under Putin could conceivably become if it were ever possible to really control the oligarchs; as Dugin himself says, to remove racism from Nazism would be to destroy its "hermeneutic circle," its *raison d'être*, thus transforming it into passive ideological material, some of which might be useful in constructing the Fourth Political Theory. But then he claims that "ethnicity was not the focal point" of Nazism—which is obviously absurd, as well as in direct contradiction to his principle that the subject of Nazism, the Third Political Theory, was, precisely, the race—possibly doing so to justify the *ethnocentricity* that he names as one of the fundamental pillars of his Fourth Political Theory without associating it with Nazism. Yet at the same time, he says:

> The Fourth Political Theory rejects all forms and varieties of racism and all
> forms of the normative hierarchicalization of society based on ethnic, reli-

gious, social, technological, economic or cultural grounds. Societies can be compared, but we cannot state that one of them is objectively better than the others. Such an assessment is always subjective, and any attempt to raise a subjective assessment to the status of a theory is racism.

Here the march of contradictions presses forward till it establishes Dugin's 4PT as the perfectly self-cancelling worldview. Firstly, in *The Rise of the Fourth Political Theory*, Dugin expressly raises a subjective assessment to the status of a theory by asserting that "We defend our values—hence, we're right." Secondly, all forms of "discrimination," whether prejudicial or intelligently discerning, can obviously not be called "racism." Thirdly, without these forms of so-called "racism," what would become of the strict hierarchicalization of society under the Nazi *Führerprinzip*—a principle, incidentally, that was embraced and further developed by Carl Schmitt? Is a hierarchy of power without any hierarchy of values even possible? And if it were, what else could it be but a hierarchy of greater or lesser degrees of robot-like obedience to a *Führer*, or to some other equally false and arbitrary absolute? Fourth and last, if the 4PT rejects all these forms of "normative hierarchicalization," what becomes of the opposition between "hierarchical, traditional Eurasia" and "egalitarian, anti-traditional Atlantis" found throughout Dugin's works? If there is no way that he can declare that the Traditional Eurasian ethos is objectively better than the Liberal Atlantean one because to do so would be "racism," then his whole critique of the western Liberal hegemony falls flat. Everything is relative, there is no objective criterion by which we can judge between various forms of human life—this is pure Postmodernism. Furthermore, to the degree that Dugin claims to be a Traditionalist—a claim that he not only fails to substantiate but resoundingly disproves at many points—it is entirely possible, and necessary, for him to judge societies according to how well or poorly they incarnate the transcendental norms of the Self-revelation of God to man. According to Traditionalist norms, the society of traditional India, based on the Vedas, was necessarily a higher form of social organization than that of the British colonialists, based on economic/utilitarian philosophies like those of Bacon and Locke and Hobbes and Bentham covered with a thin veneer of Christianity, the Christian High Middle Ages a higher form than that of 20th-century western Europe, the *ummah* of early Islam a higher society than that of the polytheistic Arabs of the pre-Islamic Quraysh, filled with degenerate practices like infanticide which the Prophet ended, the elevated ritualism and refined social intercourse of the Pueblo Indians of the American southwest higher than the society of the island of Dobu, south of New Guinea, based on sorcery and counter-sorcery to cause disease, crop-failure and death to one's enemies.[2] If to claim that one society is objec-

---

2. See *Patterns of Culture* by Ruth Benedict.

tively better than another is "racism," then it is also "racism" to judge the society of the monks at Mt. Athos to be a higher form of human social organization than that of a gang of petty criminals and black marketeers in some low dive in Moscow. As we say in American English, "Gimme a break!" (This phrase, a contraction of "give me a break," indicates that the speaker has heard enough implausible blather for one night, and begs the blatherer to cease and desist.)

When determining what elements from Marxism can be saved for the 4PT, Dugin does a much better job. Marxism as a critique of Capitalism and the alienation it produces is still of much value, he says, but such elements as a fundamental worldview based on dialectical materialism, the dictatorship of the proletariat as a necessary step toward the classless society, the myth of progress etc., must be discarded. I completely agree.

As for what elements of the hated Liberalism itself might be useful to the 4PT, Dugin, though he claims to reject Liberalism as a whole, *absolutely* rejects only the individual, while enthusiastically embracing a fundamental pillar of Liberalism and one of the most ambiguous concepts the human race has ever hatched, namely *freedom*. As for Dugin's call for the liquidation of the notion of the individual as a way of striking at the heart of Liberalism, this could only legitimately apply to the deconstruction of the *de-humanized pseudo-individuality* that Liberalism fosters. What Aleksandr Dugin fails to understand in any stable way—even though he speaks, in *The Rise of the Fourth Political Theory*, of the transformation of the earlier liberal "individual" into what he astutely calls the postmodern "dividual"—is that *Liberalism has already destroyed the Individual*, in any integral sense of that word, by standardizing his or her beliefs, desires, prejudices and aspirations, in effect turning them into the equivalent of consumer products, while at the same time falsely portraying these alienated fetishes of a destroyed human integrity as emblems of individual uniqueness, self-determination, even rebellion against the status quo. It was this creation of an automatized group mind masquerading as a mass of "liberated" human individuals that made Liberal society ready for the massive and largely covert application of mind-control and social engineering that characterizes it today.

In *The System of Antichrist* (2001) I analyzed this pseudo-individuality as based on one of the four fundamental idols or *Archons*, the four primary misperceptions of the nature of God (Law, Fate, Chaos and Selfhood) upon which the world illusion and the human ego are based—in this case, Selfhood, a form of human spiritual alienation that William Blake, in his Prophetic Books, named "the Spectre."[3] In the *The System of Antichrist* I wrote:

---

3. The term "archon" is taken from the mythic cosmology of the Gnostics; it was their name for the oppressive and deluded false gods who administer the cosmic prison of the world illusion—the

God is the Absolute Subject, the *Atman*, the transcendent and immanent Self, the *imago dei* within each of us. By virtue of this *Atman,* we are, at the deepest level of our being, both unique and universal. The Self within us is pure, impersonal, universal Being, without attributes; according to some metaphysicians . . . it is better described as Beyond Being, given that it can never be an object of consciousness subject to definition, since "the eye cannot see itself." But because God is unique as well as universal, this Self is also the principle of our unique human integrity, the way in which we are not simply humanity in the abstract, but actual human beings, commanded by God to be precisely ourselves, no greater, no less, and no other. And yet this uniqueness is also universal, since it is shared by all human beings, and in fact by all things. Self as the principle of uniqueness is not other than Self as the principle of pure Being, as when God, speaking to Moses in *Exodus,* names Himself as "I Am That I Am": My unique Essence is not other than My pure Being; it is My unique Essence to *be* pure Being. And what God can say of Himself, we can also say, certainly not of our limited human personalities, but of the God, the *Atman,* within us. In St. Paul's words: "It is not I who live, but Christ lives in me."

---

very "principalities" and "powers," "the rulers of the darkness of this world," mentioned by St. Paul in Ephesians 6:12. In my system, the Four Archons are the fundamental elements of the world illusion and the ego that projects it. They are in perpetual conflict with each other; at the same time they are in secret collusion with one another, while falsely presenting themselves as real alternatives. This enables them to attack our integral humanity simultaneously from every point of the compass. Behind the Archons, however, lie what I have called (following W. B. Yeats from *A Vision*) "the Faculties." Behind Law is Prophesy and the Divine Imagination of William Blake; behind Fate is Contemplation and Holy Wisdom; behind Chaos is *Shakti,* Universal Energy; behind Selfhood is *Atman,* the Indwelling Absolute Witness. Aleksandr Dugin is apparently attempting to forge a comprehensive political-spiritual theory and praxis by synthesizing these Four Archons, but he will accomplish nothing, in my opinion, until he cracks the shells of the Archons extracts the Faculties, the nuts of wisdom inside them. These Faculties need not be synthesized by human labor since they are already in eternal and dynamic intimacy and interaction with each other. If Aleksandr Dugin were to subject his Fourth Political Theory to a psycho-social-metaphysical analysis and evaluation based on my system of the Archons and Faculties such as it appears in the chapter "The Shadows of God" in *The System of Antichrist*—and again, in revised and expanded form, in *The Science of the Greater Jihad*—he might well succeed in purifying this Theory of its self-destructive contradictions while sacrificing none of its potential comprehensiveness and power—assuming, of course, that these contradictions are not deliberate elements of his method. If he elects to do so I would be very interested to see what he comes up with.

I resisted the temptation to turn my system of the Archons into a new religion—something that would have been very easy to do in the United States during the years I was forming it—since I realized that it would be nothing but one more non-Traditional and potentially Counter-Traditional production by a spiritual freelance. I present it now only as a framework for metaphysical/psychological/social analysis. Just as Marx's system was of the greatest value as analysis but became a monster as soon as it was applied to social action, so I hope that the system of the Four Archons will be useful as a diagnostic tool that is capable, among other things, of detecting religious, psychological and social deviations from Traditional *theoria* and *praxis.*

But when uniqueness is separated from being, it loses its universality. This is what happens when we ascribe uniqueness to ourselves alone while denying it to others. This is the *idolatry of Self*. When we worship our own separate selfhood as if it were God, we start to believe that self-willed isolation is the road to integrity, and that, in Sartre's words, "hell is other people." Consequently we can only relate comfortably to others if we see them as subordinates—that is, as lesser parts of ourselves. This is the irony of self-worship. Seeking unity and integrity through isolation and dominance, we gradually become filled with the ghosts of all the relationships we have denied and betrayed. Our quest for individuality ("undividedness") at all costs results only in fragmentation. We ourselves become "the lonely crowd."

The false religion of Selfhood is Prometheanism, which includes all forms of *hubris*: the solipsistic, New Age belief that "I create my own reality" (the truth being more on the order of "I create my own illusion"); the idea that spiritual development is a kind of exploit or heroic achievement to be gloried in; the sense that the individual can only gain integrity and significance by breaking the law and rebelling against the mores; and the driving will of Western, and by now global, society to conquer nature, deny God, and remold human life according to the most demented "idealism" imaginable, even at the risk of destroying both humanity and the earth. If Law is ruled by pride, Fate by fear, and Chaos by shame, Selfhood is ruled by anger.

The "lonely crowd" of Liberal consumerist society, at least in the United States, is now in the process of breaking up into warring ideological gangs, proving that a *unity* based on atomic individualism is ultimately impossible. And now that the post-WWII spread of "middle class" affluence to even the working class is being replaced by a dying middle class that is becoming economically indistinguishable from what was once the working class, and a working class that has been transformed into a chronically underemployed, drug-addicted *lumpen proletariat* due to the export of manufacturing jobs to cheaper labor markets abroad, consumerism has lost its glamour, while those who have unfortunately been trained as consumers while being denied the wherewithal to consume can no longer afford to indulge in the cheap opulence they don't really believe in any more, which is why their consumerist aspirations are increasingly attracted to electronic devices and the world of false images they project. People no longer live *human lives*, so they opt for what is provided for them to replace human lives: drugs; electronic images; simplistic and violent ideologies of self- and group identity. If Dugin wants to destroy the Individual, I challenge him to come to the United States and see if he can find one! Yes, they still exist, here and there, though in increasing isolation. By the grace of God, I believe I am one of them, and count several of them as my friends. It was only through my willingness to shoulder the inescapable burden of individuality that I was able to find Tradition: a cosmos of living and perennial truths and values that lies beyond the crumbling walls of modernist Liberal consumerism and postmodern psycho-social fragmentation, one that transcends both the degenerate collective and the isolated individual standing in defiance of that collective. The individual is not the ultimate destiny of Humanity; nonetheless, when the human collective is broken, the individual is the only way out of the resulting pile of psychic residues and human debris: not the final end, but—at least at one station of the Path—an indispensable step.

It is possible, however, that Aleksandr Dugin and I mean two different things by the word "individual." My definition is: "One who assumes personal responsibility for his or her view of reality, while not claiming to be the Author of it, and for his or her actions, while not claiming to be the Owner of them." When the collective, the *narod*, the *ethnos* is on the road to hell, only the individual can point out a different path. Ananda Coomaraswamy, co-founder with René Guénon of the Traditionalist School, once said: "I had to learn not to think for myself"; he meant that he had learned to let the great Norms of Metaphysics and Revelation think for him. But no-one who is immersed in a degenerate and manipulated collective can ever discover these Norms; only the individual who has died to that collective can see that such Norms are needed, believe that they exist, and pay the dues necessary to find them and follow them.

As for Dugin's attempt to appropriate the *absolute freedom* that Liberalism pretends to possess but does not in fact deliver, he begins with the notion that freedom and the individual are inimical to each other because individuality itself is a prison, a boundary placed by Liberalism on the scope and action of true freedom, the reduction of freedom's infinite potential to the pedestrian and the mediocre. This is a very interesting idea, one that opens almost directly upon the vistas provided by the traditional Spiritual Path conceived of as the road to self-transcendence and liberation, as a method of overcoming ignorance, attachment and the resulting automatism. Yet Dugin says:

> The Fourth Political Theory should be a theory of absolute freedom . . . freedom can be of any kind, free of any correlation or lack thereof, facing any direction and any goal. Freedom is the greatest value of the Fourth Political Theory, since it coincides with its centre, and its energetic, dynamic core.

Here I must disagree. To begin with, freedom as Dugin defines it does not possess the power to free us from one of the greatest and most widespread faces of oppression, especially in the postmodern world—namely, oppression by Chaos. Here we encounter another of the four Archons that I analyzed in *The System of Antichrist*, the Chaos Archon. If the essential lie of Selfhood is "Self-will is integrity," the essential lie of Chaos is "Chaos is freedom." And one of the most insidious effects of an addiction to Chaos is that it portrays all *form* as oppressive, this being the essential lie upon which another of the four Archons, the Archon of Law, is based—the proposition that "Form, universally imposed by an external authority, is harmony." In *The Fourth Political Theory*, the Law Archon is perhaps most directly represented by the elements of National Socialism that Dugin hopes to incorporate into his system. These elements, however, work to *refute* absolute freedom as foundational to the Fourth Political Theory, just as the call for freedom equally refutes these authoritarian and absolutist elements as in any way fundamental to it. Eclecticism may work, to a degree, on the level of specific applications; it can never work on the level of foundations.

Furthermore, to maintain that "freedom can be of any kind, free of any correlation or lack thereof, facing any direction and any goal" is as wrong as it can be; here is where the principles of the Spiritual Path come to our aid, ready and able to dispel all difficulties on that score. The freedom to indulge the whims and obsessions of the ego, the *nafs al-ammara*, does not lead to freedom, but to bondage: alcoholism, drug addiction, sex addiction, addiction to violence, addiction to abstract ideation, addiction to acquisition, addiction to power. On a higher level, the courage to express those spiritual potencies hidden in our soul that transcend the ego conducts us to a greater world, a world where the *truths* on which our nature is woven, as soon as they are clearly discerned, enter the battle of Truth against falsehood, the struggle against the lies of the World, the lies of the Flesh, the lies of the Devil, the "unseen warfare" to discover and unite ourselves with that Truth. And on the highest level of all, the willing bondage of the individual will to the Will of God—God Who *is* Truth Itself—leads to true Freedom, a freedom which is inseparable from Wisdom, Love, and Power—by which I mean, an availability to the Power and Intentionality of God Himself, beyond all individual or corporate agendas. Dugin understands that the individual *as ego* is a prison, but he has not yet learned how to articulate the way out of that prison; he does not appear to possess the Key. The Key is neither Promethean self-will, nor immersion in the *narod*, nor totally identifying oneself with the power of the authoritarian State, nor choosing the correct identity from among the various pre-determined masks made available by the Rulers of the Darkness of This World. The Key, in the language of the Sufis, is *taslim*, submission to the Truth, to God as *Al-Haqq*. The result of this submission is *fana'*, annihilation in God, and *baqa'*, subsistence as an eternal Name of God. (For a picture of part of what this total self-transcendence might look like, see *Chapter Seven* of this book.)

Dugin and the Fall of Man

In any case it is clear that Aleksandr Dugin is presently wrestling (or toying) with the question: "Total Freedom or Total Authority?"—and he is certainly not alone in this. In *The Fourth Political Theory* he says that "The Fourth Political

Theory should be a theory of absolute freedom," whereas in **The Rise of the Fourth Political Theory** he says "We force you to do what you don't want to do, because we think for you, we take responsibility for you . . . our task is . . . to make the values of Eurasianism total and mandatory for all." When the alternatives are defined in so stark a manner, it will be obvious to any sane human being that to choose either one would spell disaster for any individual or any society. This realization of the hopeless impossibility of either Total Authority or Total Freedom, in worldly terms, and the destructive consequences of attempting to realize them, normally suggests a third apparent alternative—namely, to make some kind of synthesis between Authority and Freedom. In order to understand how this can be done, and how it could never be done, we need to re-consider "the Fall of Man." This Fall can be understood as a descent into a fallen order of perception, a constriction and darkening of the human intuition of the Divine, affecting either an individual, a collective, a civilization, or (progressively) an entire *manvantara*. Beyond this, speaking in terms of universal manifestation, the Fall can be mythically represented as "the fall of Lucifer."

When the metaphysical intuition of God is progressively veiled by the development of the ego, one of the first effects is that God's Infinity—the principle of His freedom—and His Absoluteness—the principle of His authority—begin to be perceived as separate, not eternally One as they are in Reality. Once this separation has apparently become complete, the Infinite is mistakenly perceived as Chaos and the Absolute as Fixity and Petrification—and this fundamental mis-perception of the nature of God reverberates within the human soul. To the degree that the soul becomes disordered and suffers the pain of Chaos, it seeks relief in Petrification, in the mistaken belief that "Petrification is stability." But Petrification, of course, also causes pain, driving the soul to seek relief in Chaos, in the deluded belief that "Chaos is freedom." Finally, when the soul wearies of the alternation between Petrification and Chaos, it may choose, or be driven, to embrace both at the same time, thus entering the kind of petrified or frozen Chaos that Dante pictures, in Canto XXXI of the *Inferno*, as the deepest state of damnation. Possible Being, in this state, is no longer the principle of hope, but the despair of ever being *real*, while Necessary Being is no longer the intrinsic principle of Divinity, but the oppressive "yoke of necessity." In individual terms, Chaos is the principle of concupiscence and dissipation, Petrification of compulsive morality and the freezing of the affections, the condition that William Blake called "cruel holiness." In social terms, Chaos is the origin of "Liberal" permissiveness and anarchy, Petrification of "Conservative" totalitarianism. When either principle has reached its limit of expression, it changes over into its opposite.

The only way to overcome the polarization between Possibility and Neces-

sity, to avoid the constant swinging of the pendulum between Chaos and Petrification, which finally results in a state of Petrified Chaos, is to purify the *Nous*,
unveil the Eye of the Heart, and thereby restore the primordial vision of God, in
Whom Possibility and Necessity are one. In every religion, the Spiritual Path is
the Way toward that restoration. Once Possibility and Necessity are polarized as
Chaos and Petrification, they can never be re-united on the level where that
polarization exists. They must first rise and return to their archetypes—Possibility to the Infinite and Necessity to the Absolute. Once this is achieved, the
vision of God is reinstated; God is seen as Infinite *because* He is Absolute and
Absolute *because* He is Infinite—as the One in Whom Justice and Mercy could
never be polarized, the One in Whom Love and Knowledge are inseparable.
This restoration of the true vision of God re-establishes the true vision of
Humanity. And when Humanity is seen as it is, it naturally expresses itself as a
vision of human society in which the full integrity of Humanity is supported,
and the full knowledge and love of God attainable.

Can any of this actually be accomplished in this Age of Darkness, the *Kali-
yuga*? Yes—but only by a "Remnant." The establishment of a truly integral society based on spiritual norms has been impossible in the West since the end of
the Middle Ages, and Islam was in fact the last Divine Revelation capable of
manifesting a true spirituality on the collective level, in terms of a sacred collective that is now in the process of being deconstructed. Yet the Covenants of the
Prophet Muhammad have providentially reappeared at this extremely late date;
their full significance in terms of the spiritual function of an Islamic Remnant
is yet to be revealed.

On Chapter Three:
"The Critique of Monotonic Processes"

"The Critique of the Monotonic Process" is simply the best concise deconstruction of the Myth of Progress that I have ever encountered. It provides a powerful confirmation, from "secular" sources, of one of the central tenets of
Traditionalism—that Progress is indeed a myth—and does so without aristo-
cratic snobbery or romantic nostalgia or an appeal to metaphysics as an explan-
atory *deus ex machina* at a point where a more empirical analysis is both
possible and called for.

Dugin shows how Fascism, Communism and Liberalism, as well as the social
Darwinism of Herbert Spencer, the theories of Auguste Comte and the *übermensch* of Friederich Nietzsche, are all based on the Myth of Progress—inseparable from the notion of biological evolution—that developed in the 18th and
19th centuries, and how nearly all the major intellectual trends and paradigms
of the 20th century in the humanities and the natural sciences debunked the

notion of progress in favor of various cyclical theories of history.[4] (This shift of paradigms has not yet entirely penetrated the collective mind, however. Before the "Great Recession" of 2008, it was common to hear predictions such as "the stock market will just continue going up and up, forever"—despite the fact that it has always exhibited a "boom-and-bust" pattern, and in willful ignorance of the historical fact that similar absurd optimism gripped the market shortly before the start of the Great Depression in 1929.) Dugin names Marcel Mauss, Piotr Sztompka, Émile Durkheim, Pitirim Sorokin, Georges Gurvitch, Nikolai Danilevsky, Oswald Spengler, Carl Schmitt, Ernst Jünger, Lev Gumilev, Martin Heidegger, and Arnold Toynbee as some of the scholars, past and present, who reject linear progress for the notion of the historical cycle. In the process of deconstructing the Liberal version of the Myth of Progress he calls Ayn Rand a Liberal, which is somewhat less than a half-truth, but nonetheless remains a wonderful way of *satirizing* the Liberals. (Ayn Rand, the ideal political/economic theorist for the intelligent psychopath, was in some ways like a Liberal shorn of all liberality, a Liberal without belief in equality as a desirable and attainable goal, without care for the less fortunate, without hope in the creation of a pluralistic society: a Liberal—or a Conservative, or a Libertarian—stripped down to her Predatory Capitalist, Social Darwinian core.)

The most interesting critic of the monotonic process that Dugin brings forward, from my point of view at least, is anthropologist, social scientist, linguist, visual anthropologist, semiotician, and cyberneticist Gregory Bateson (1904-1980), who as a member of the OSS produced propaganda and participated in black ops in India, China, and Southeast Asia during WWII. (Dugin calls him an "American scientist," though he was actually an Englishman.) Bateson maintained that ongoing monotonic processes are completely absent from nature; when a biological or social or mechanical system begins to exhibit straight-line monotonic development, this is a sign of its approaching breakdown—in other words, *progress is death.* This principle was one of the things that made Bateson interesting to Stewart Brand, editor of the famous hippy almanac *The Whole Earth Catalogue,* and of the *CoEvolution Quarterly* journal that succeeded it. The main thrust of the *Whole Earth Catalogue* was to provide "appropriate tech-

---

4. Likewise, according to Dr. Wolfgang Smith, in contemporary physics as in the humanities the worldview of the 19th century was largely deconstructed in the 20th without the public having been informed of the fact. In the chapter "From Schrödinger's Cat to Thomistic Ontology" from his book *The Quantum Enigma,* he says: "while the scientific worldview continues to consolidate its grip upon society, something quite unexpected has come to pass. The decisive event occurred almost a century ago in fact, back in the early decades of the twentieth century. Since then that so-called scientific worldview—which to this day reigns as the official dogma of science—no longer squares with the known scientific facts. What has happened is that discoveries at the frontiers of science do not accord with the prevailing *Weltanschauung.* . . ." [See Dr. Smith's website at www.philos-sophia.org.]

nology" to, among other sectors, the hippy commune movement, along with bits of pithy lore and wisdom on various aspects of human life of the kind that the hippies were discovering and/or creating. The thrust behind the appropriate technology movement—"appropriate" generally meant either "low-tech" or "low energy consumption/ low waste production"—was the spectre of the environmental destruction and looming exhaustion of natural resources created by the *inappropriate* technology that was inseparable from the Myth of Progress. The idea was to replace the paradigm of "progress" with the paradigm of "sustainable growth." And though the word "growth" was (and is) still used, what was really envisioned was the need to radically "de-modernize" by making a synthesis between the wisdom and technique of non-western and pre-modern societies and the most useful and least destructive technologies that the west could provide. The hippy commune movement, and the spiritual/cultural revolution of the 1960's as a whole, turned out not to be socially viable on a large scale, due to various factors such as drug use, the partial dependence of the hippies on the philanthropy of the society of Modernist Progress they had rejected, etc. Yet many of the trends the hippies initiated, both positive and negative, are still influencing American society today. The hippies were neither modernists nor postmodernists; rather, they represented the exact point of transition, at least from an American perspective, from the modern to the postmodern world. Nor were the hippies really Liberals, though the Liberals accepted them and enabled them; they wished above all things to be "natural," while the Liberals, at least as of the year 2018, have become profoundly *un*natural. They are best described as psychedelic quasi-libertarian populists with an attraction to primitivism and metaphysics, though with a paradoxical willingness to creatively use modern technology. They often believed that they were Leftists, though many of them had little understanding of Marxism and other left-wing ideologies; those who were not drawn into Leftist opposition politics—or who polarized against these politics in the direction of the Right due to "Leftist burnout"— became precursors in some ways, though certainly not in others, of the American counterculture of today, the Alt Right. Ken Kesey of the psychedelic Merry Pranksters, for example, was opposed to abortion, and ex-Trump adviser Steve Bannon has a background as a "deadhead"—a follower of the hippy rock band The Grateful Dead.

Equally intriguing are the researches of anthropologist Franz Boas that Dugin cites, his discovery that while "modern" societies see myths and fairy tales as the province of children, and the materialism of "cold, hard facts" as the badge of adulthood, in many so-called "primitive" societies the reverse is true: the children are the cynical materialists, while the fully "initiated" adults have matured, via various rites-of-passage, into a fully-informed mythic/metaphysical worldview. This primacy of metaphysical knowledge is also reflected in the

Hindu caste system, where the *shudras* or unskilled workers are seen as sunk in immediate reactivity to sense experience; the *vaishyas*, the craftsmen and merchants, as "realistic" and "crafty" in material terms; the *kshatriyas* or warriors as "honorable" and "romantic"; and the *brahmins* as exhibiting an established metaphysical objectivity. Plato's *Republic* presents a similar scheme. Thus when Boas defines the "modern" adult as materialistic, logical and factual, he is the taking the 20th-century "bourgeois/*vaishya*" society of the West as his point of departure.

When I ask where I myself am situated on the spectrum between the mythic/metaphysical and the factual/materialistic worldviews, the answers are interesting. As a member of the post-WWII "Baby Boom" generation I was born into a mythic worldview, that of traditional pre-Vatican II Catholicism, and further expanded that worldview in adolescence and adulthood, first (in the 1960's) as a "hippy" with an interest in eastern religions, next (in the 1970's) as a poet who, along with many of my contemporaries, was studying world mythology, partly according to the psychology of Carl Jung and his school, as well as through the works of Joseph Campbell, and finally (in the 1980's and '90's) as a student of the metaphysics of the Traditionalists. It was only after my mythic/metaphysical worldview was firmly established that I was able to bring my factual, logical, materially-grounded worldview into line with it, until I understood that the second should properly be seen as a sub-set of the first; the result of this hierarchical synthesis between "truths" and "facts" should be clearly evident in this book. In other words, my development was in line neither with the "modernist" paradigm nor the "primitivist" one, but is best described as a "primitivist" course of growth lived backwards. This inversion of the normal order of development was based on the imperious need felt by my generation to discover or create a paradigm that transcended the paradigm of material progress, which was so obviously doomed. If many of us (so to speak) first finished graduate school, then went on to four-year college, high school, grammar school and kindergarten, this was the reason. I remember one day in a remote rural commune in the mountains of British Columbia in the early 1970's when one of the young semi-nomadic resident hippies said something that I've never forgotten. He was sitting in a tree, in a dark and saturnine mood, when he told me: "I'm going to sit here until I know what an old man knows." That's it exactly: lacking a generation of elders—at least elders of our own culture—who could initiate us into the metaphysical worldview we saw that the times required, and into a society based upon it, in our youth we felt we had to *become elders* in an attempt to initiate ourselves; it's little wonder that so few of us ultimately made it to metaphysical adulthood. For the most part we either withered away in endless adolescence or else abandoned the metaphysical quest to pursue material well-being—no longer in the confident belief in material progress that our parents had enjoyed, however, but in reaction to our gnawing fear that material well-being would soon be beyond the grasp of many in American society— which has turned out to be the case—as well as with a profoundly repressed sense of guilt at our betrayal of the inner life.

The greatest classic of the perspective of cyclical time, both philosophically profound and strategically practical on so many levels, is the *I Ching*. In the inspired system of cosmology expounded in that wonderful book, ancient China worked out the definitive critique of the monotonic process by demon- strating the pitfalls and disastrous outcomes of monotonic thought and action in every conceivable situation, repeatedly warning us against them with oracles like "nothing that would further" and "perseverance brings misfortune." Like- wise the doctrine of the *manvantara* or cycle-of-manifestation from the Hindu *Puranas* is the most comprehensive analysis available to us of cyclical time as it applies to history. All time is cyclical according to the Hindu conception, and a given cycle ends *precisely when the monotonic process takes over,* concealing the vision of cyclical time under the veil of an ever-accelerating linear time, ulti- mately ending in apocalypse. The era of triumph for the monotonic process is the *Kali-yuga*—which, though it is the last and shortest *yuga* of the cycle, can no longer see itself as part of that cycle as a whole, only as the inevitable for- ward march of history; this narrowing-of-outlook, and all the obsessions that go along with it, are precisely what will lead the cycle to its demise. And when it comes to the fate of the human race on planet Earth, the big question is: Can the dissolution of the present historical cycle return us to a more viable, life- oriented vision of time as inherently cyclical, or will that dissolution mean the dissolution of terrestrial humanity itself, followed by the birth of a "new humanity" in the golden age of a new cycle? The answer to this question, given that there are cycles within cycles, each ending with its own sort of apocalypse, has everything to do with the size of the cycle now drawing to a close, and con- sequently the magnitude of the apocalypse we face.

Dugin sums up his reasons for rejecting progress, evolution, the monotonic process in an eminently sane passage of 173 words:

> But, most important, we must reject the base upon which these three ideolo- gies [*i.e., Fascism, Communism, Liberalism*] stand: the monotonic process in all its forms, that is, evolution, growth, modernisation, progress, develop- ment, and all that which seemed scientific in the Nineteenth century but was exposed as unscientific in the Twentieth century. We must also abandon the philosophy of development and propose the following slogan: life is more important than growth. Instead of the ideology of development, we must place our bets on the ideology of conservatism and conservation. However, we not only require conservatism in our daily lives, but also philosophical conservatism. We need the philosophy of conservatism. Looking toward the

future of the Russian political system, if it is going to be based on monotonic processes, then it is doomed to failure. No stability will ever come from a new round of unidirectional growth derived from energy prices, real estate, stocks, and so on, nor from the growth of global economy as a whole. If this illusion persists, then it may become fatal for our country.

In the face of the exhaustion of the Myth of Progress, as well as of both the natural resources and the cultural will that would make the continued resuscitation of this myth possible, the world would do well to heed Aleksandr Dugin's advice. But without a clear apprehension of *an already existing Reality* that such social and technological conservatism could be based upon, in the absence of a new visible and conscious orientation to Eternity capable of diverting our collective attention away from the ever-accelerating pursuit of the impossible and toward the Always So, his advice will largely fall on deaf ears. As only one of many possible approaches to this new orientation, I propose the study of Traditional Metaphysics, and the sophisticated psychologies and well-tested spiritual methods that accompany it. And Dugin himself begins to point the way to this possibility:

> Apollo is not just opposed to Dionysus; they *complement* each other. Half of the cycle constitutes modernisation, while the other half—decline; when one half faces up, the other half faces down. There is no life without death. Being-towards-death, careful attention to death, to the flip side of the sphere of Being, as Heidegger wrote, is not a struggle with life, but, rather, its glorification and its foundation.

As Jesus said in John 12:24:

> Verily, verily, I say unto you, Except a grain of wheat fall into the earth and die, it abideth by itself alone; but if it die, it beareth much fruit.

And in Matthew 16:25:

> For whosoever will save his life shall lose it: and whosoever will lose his life, for My sake, shall find it.

On Chapter Four: "The Reversibility of Time"

In Chapter Four of *The Fourth Political Theory*, Aleksandr Dugin's profound and lucid Critique of the Monotonic Process descends into a more or less crank theory of the nature of apocalypse, a theory we have already criticized in *Chapter Two* of this book, in the section entitled "Critique of the Metaphysics of Chaos." It's as if Dugin is attempting to convince his readers (and himself?) of the barely-credible possibility that progress and modernization might actually reverse at one point by first putting forth an even more implausible scenario: the reversal of time itself. Trends, of course, can reverse, and the fact is that every trend eventually will. But when a sports team (let us say) with a long winning streak suddenly begins to lose, do we believe that time has actually reversed? Certainly not. The reversal of a trend of such long standing as the Myth of Progress and the global society based upon it may give the impression of being a true time-reversal, but of course it isn't. Furthermore, the idea of the reversibility of time is inseparable from the postmodern ethos—which, in its rejection of any and all "overarching paradigms," its fear and hatred of *unity* of any kind, must reject unidirectional time as well, even cyclical unidirectional time, since time unites all particular instances of development and/or degeneration in a single matrix. This explains why Postmodernism so often turns to Einsteinian and post-Einsteinian physics, which are host to such arcane speculative concepts as the "multiverse" or the reversibility of time on the quantum level, to justify its rejection of comprehensive system, harmony and consistency—and it was Einstein who, more than anyone else, destroyed the concept of "spacial" simultaneity by teaching that every location and every velocity has its own time. Just as those with no intuition of non-material worlds can only see the immortality of the soul in terms of reincarnation, so those with no true sense of Eternity can only understand the end of time as time's reversal, and Eternity itself as nothing but an indefinite spectrum of parallel time-lines—in other words, as Chaos. This tendency of Postmodernism to accept outlandish myths as to the nature of space and time has given rise to the logically absurd science-fiction fantasy of time travel, which some scientists, as well as all sorts of mediums, occultists and magicians, are beginning to take seriously. It's as if Biological Darwinism, with its notion of "every species for itself," after morphing into Social Darwinism, based upon the principle of "every individual for himself" (including of course the "legal individuals" known as corporations), finally gave rise, after the appearance of Postmodernism, to Philosophical Darwinism, whose motto is "every worldview for itself"—in other words, "nothing is intrinsically true, everything is permitted, and may the fittest 'truth' survive."

    The necessary correlative to this principle is the nihilistic deconstruction of objective history, the rejection of the idea that *certain things really happened* in favor of the belief that whatever version of events achieves dominance, by whatever means, has thereby won the right to call itself "reality"; this is what we Capitalists call "the marketplace of ideas." Just as a product that has been forced out of the market by another product—not necessarily because the winning product is better, since its success is just as likely to be due to a bigger advertising budget or the use of the cutthroat economic tactic known as "dumping" to force weaker competitors out of business—so ideas that are of no use to the dominant power structure, or actually threatening to it, are forced out of the universe of discourse, irrespective of their truth or accuracy. This is reflected in Capitalist slang, where a common way of saying "I believe that" is to say "I'll *buy* that." And if you happen to be heavily invested in a particular belief in the marketplace of ideas, you will of course want its stock to go up; you will therefore do all you can to make sure the belief in question retains and strengthens its dominance, both in the collective mind and in your own psyche; many a paranoid delusional system has sprung up by just such a process. Questions as to the actual truth of the idea you've "bought into" tend to be discounted in favor of an analysis of the *trends of belief* surrounding it. If that idea gains in collective *credibility*—which it can certainly do irrespective of whether or not the objective *truth* of it has become more firmly established—then its stock goes up; the number of people believing in a particular idea, true or otherwise, is like the number of people voting for a particular candidate. Likewise, objective assessments of the viability of a particular corporation, for purposes of investment, tend to be progressively supplemented, and then increasingly obscured, by an analysis not of the objective soundness of that corporation, its management style, its outstanding debts, its cost/earnings ratio, but rather of the trends in consumer or investor *confidence* surrounding it. The compulsive gambler stops asking the rational question, "What cards do my opponents most likely hold?" so he can concentrate on the magical question, "Do I feel lucky?"—which is to say, both the gambler and the postmodernist are in a state of despair, the particular form of despair that Kierkegaard, in *Sickness unto Death*, called "despair of possibility."

The perfect example of the triumph of this worldview, of the notion of the primacy of belief over reality, is the crypto-currency market. Crypto-currencies like Bitcoin have nothing whatsoever backing them up—not natural resources, not labor value, not precious metals, not even the good credit of national governments or the soundness of banks—nothing but the collective belief, or lack of it, in Bitcoin. Crypto-currency is thus the perfect economic expression of the New Age fallacy that "belief creates reality." Bitcoin is nothing less than postmodern, New Age money.

Such belief-systems, based as they are on the pulverization of the collective sense of objective reality, represent the progressive deconstruction of Capitalism in the postmodern era. And this same pulverization, this tendency to take a multitude of subjective impressions—instead of the objective assessment of a real world—as the accepted criterion for truth, also results in every imaginable sort of crank notion about the nature of things, ideas such as the reversibility of time, the existence of parallel time-lines, or the notion that the material, formal or efficient causes of an event might come after that event instead of before it. Alexandr Dugin had better beware lest his Metaphysics of Chaos, which is nothing less than a metaphysics of Postmodernism, lead him into one of these crackpot intellectual dead ends, where he will risk becoming infected with the conceptual virus of Capitalism in its senile decadence.

Descartes' radical split between "objective" reality, defined as matter obeying mechanistic causality, and "subjective" consciousness, ultimately led those who intuited the existence of something beyond material reality, something "spiritual," to conceive of that something in entirely subjective terms; the belief in an objective metaphysical order was therefore discarded. Spirituality was an *inner* reality, and whatever was "inner" was taken to be psychological rather than Spiritual in nature. And while the Spirit is One, the psyche is necessarily multiple; thus both the Unity and the objective Reality of God were denied. The Spirit was rejected in favor of the psyche, ultimately leading to such lunatic beliefs as Timothy Leary's doctrine that "your brain is God," based on which assumption he had his head severed from his body at the moment of his death and then cryogenically frozen to await the future resurrection of "God." And the pulverized, subjective consciousness of Postmodernism was then projected back onto the material world, resulting in the belief that "outer, material" as well as "inner psychic" reality is essentially a polyvalent, collective subjectivity. There is no Sun in the sky, there is only "my sun," "your sun," "the sun of a minute ago," "the sun of a minute from now" etc., etc.—not only that, but every one of these suns might go off in its own direction and encounter its own separate destiny. The triumph of Postmodernism is thus the pulverization of the human mind and the destruction of the unity of the world—of the *universe*, that is—which together constitute the (apparent) fragmentation of Reality itself. No viable theory of anything can be based on such perceptual chaos.

Yet this deconstruction, this pulverization, thus apparent shattering of objective Reality, though it makes the encounter with and apprehension of that Reality impossible to anyone affected by it, is nonetheless an objective fact: the fact of the quality of life in the last days of the *Kali-yuga*. True, the cyclical nature of time precludes any literal reversal of time. Time does not *stop and then go back* to the past, it simply flows forward around the circle of time until it encounters the "past"—a past that is "already there" only in the sense that it represents a phase of the present cycle that is analogous to a similar (though not identical) phase of the last one. Yet the pulverization of consciousness, and of the social forms, technologies, life-forms and eco-systems affected by it—or rather intrinsic to it as the other half of a common degeneration of both subject and object, a decay of the cosmic environment itself—makes it impossible for those who occupy the late *Kali-yuga* to grasp the cyclical nature of time—unless, that is, they have attained spiritual detachment, which is the intuition of Eternity. This impossibility, in Guénon's view, is also necessary according to the laws of the *manvantara*; it is part of the intrinsic nature of the cycle-of-manifestation. As the *Kali-yuga* proceeds, time accelerates, and this very acceleration of time pulverizes space, destroying any sense of *simultaneity*, of the unity of many subjective beliefs and viewpoints as the necessarily multiple, necessarily partial set of apprehensions of the one objective Truth. Every belief or point-of-view seems to be traveling its own separate time-line. That one objective Truth, which is the common Space that—*necessarily* but also *generously*—creates and allows for a multiplicity of ways of experiencing It, has disappeared from the scene. "Things fall apart, the center cannot hold"; God is dead; nothing is true and therefore everything is permitted. The acceleration of time pulverizes and deconstructs our consciousness of both the physical world and the metaphysical order, because when space disappears, no one thing is seen to have any *intrinsic* relationship with any other. To recognize the objective existence of the illusion that has buried the vision of Reality under a flood of pulverized subjective experience is an element of sanity, since that illusion can only be recognized *as* illusion from the standpoint of that Reality. But to *argue* from that illusion as if it were reality, or to base any sort of theory or action upon it, political or otherwise, is madness. The objective and necessary existence of an illusion is no excuse for the doomed attempt take that illusion as a reality on which to build either an intellectual or a societal edifice, for the simple reason that it is *not* a reality; it's an *illusion*. Consequently, no viable civilization can be constructed on the basis of Postmodernism, because Postmodernism is *de*-construction, intrinsically. It is a kingdom divided against itself, a house founded on sand; it cannot stand. And now that the illusion of the non-existence of any objective Reality has reached a crescendo, and the horrendous consequences of this abandonment of the human Trust and betrayal of the human form have become all too apparent, only one complete intellectual alternative to illusion-based thought and action remains: Traditional Metaphysics.

Aleksandr Dugin, however, though he claims Traditional Metaphysics or Traditionalism as an integral part of his Fourth Political Theory, by and large does not accept its tenets. For example, he says that every society has a different conception of time, so what time is, what it might do or what it might lead to is totally up for grabs. The Traditionalists, on the other hand, generally accept the "cyclical-entropic" theory of time found in the Hindu **Puranas**, which is essentially compatible with the classical Greco-Roman conception and that of many of the First Nations of the Americas, including the Mayans, the Hopis and the Lakota, as well as with the picture of the "latter days" in Christianity and Islam. Time is composed of cycles-within-cycles, and the time of the human race as a whole, or the "present" human race, is a process of general spiritual degeneration—punctuated by various temporary improvements or "redresses"—flowing from the primordial "Golden Age" to the "Iron Age" we presently occupy. "Time is a social phenomenon," he says; "its structures depend . . . upon the domination of social paradigms. . . ." I can only respond by saying, "Tell that to the earth, the sun, the moon and the stars; tell that to the vibratory rate of an atom of cesium." Dugin is confusing the social conception of time with time itself; in his acceptance of an indefinite number of parallel forms of time and his denial of time as an objective reality, his reduction of it to a social conception—that is, to a collective subjectivity—he is a pure, chaotic, late-Liberal postmodernist. He grabs theory after theory from the most unlikely sources, almost at random, to justify his hopes in the malleability of time by the Fourth Political Theory. For example, he invokes the Islamic theory of "occasionalism" from Asharite *kalam*, which denies the existence of independent secondary causes and teaches that God re-creates the entire universe instant-by-instant, as well as the "collective euhemerism" of Georges Dumézil, his notion that the gods of Pagan antiquity were representations of socio-political realities rather than idealized images of ancient kings and heroes. But how could God's continual re-creation of the universe have anything whatever to do with the possibility that a change in social paradigms might reverse the flow of time? Occasionalism certainly deconstructs the mechanistic necessity of unidirectional time—or any other kind of time—but this does not thereby place the determination of the nature of time within the grasp of sociological theory or political power! And the Qur'an, which the Asharites certainly followed, says nothing about the reversibility of time; the Qur'an and the Prophet Muhammad picture time as a progressive decline drawing ever nearer to the Hour. The short surah *al-'Asr*, "Time," reads as follows:

> By the declining day,
> Lo! man is a state of loss,
> Save those who believe and do good works, and exhort one another to truth
>   and exhort one another to endurance.

Likewise, in the words of a *hadith qudsi* (a prophetic tradition in which Allah Himself speaks), "Why do they complain to Me of the changes of fortune brought about by time? I *am* Time"—a principle that makes it crystal clear that time is in no way a mere phenomenon of social psychology. Aleksandr Dugin has simply walked into my religion, uninvited, and stolen a piece of it; now that he's been busted he had better give it back, or suffer grave spiritual consequences. I have no problem with anyone who wants to draw wisdom and insight from a religion other than his or her own, or even expound the doctrines of that religion—including my chosen religion of Islam—as long as this is done with accuracy and respect. And even though some, both Muslims and non-Muslims, may feel that I should stick to my own religion and never travel outside its territory, I have presented perspectives from all of the major Divine revelations in almost every one of my books; this is my area of craft competence as a writer of the Traditionalist School. But to appropriate random doctrines from another religion, or even from one's own, and then place them in inappropriate contexts, or otherwise falsify them—especially when this is done for the purpose of manipulating the faithful of the religion in question under a mask of counterfeit loyalty or false friendship—is a crime against the Truth.

And how could the notion that the gods represent social realities rather than "great men" have any conceivable relation to the reversibility of time? Here Dugin exhibits the common trick of the-Professor-out-of-his-depth, the tactic of spewing out clouds of random information, book titles and authors' names, like an octopus squirting ink, to hide the fact that he doesn't have the slightest idea of what he's talking about. He goes on to say:

> Berdyaev's idea of the "New Middle Ages" is quite applicable. Societies can be variously built and transformed. The experience of the 1990s is quite demonstrative of this: people in the Soviet Union were sure that socialism would proceed from capitalism, not vice versa. But in the 1990s they saw the opposite: capitalism following socialism. It is quite possible that Russia could yet see feudalism, or even a slave-owning society, or perhaps a Communist or primordial society emerge after that.

This is clearly a case of intellectual desperation. A "political theory" whose basic tenet is "anything might happen, it's all up for grabs" is no theory at all, political or otherwise. And this absurd, formless hope in "infinite possibility" is taken straight out of late-postmodern-Liberal intellectual despair. Since, say, the year 1968 I have lived in the twilight of Liberal democracy, therefore I can attest from personal experience that the invocation of an imaginary "infinite possibility" varies directly with the progressive contraction of any *real* possibility. As my friend Bill Trumbly once said when I asked him what his experience with LSD had been like, "I saw that everything is possible, but nothing is likely." If the necessity of unidirectional progress is a myth, by the same token the notion that all social developments are equally likely is also a myth. And if time and history are cyclical, as Dugin clearly demonstrates in "The Critique of the Monotonic Process," then history is not simply reducible to Chaos; there is a logic to it.

To begin with, it is ridiculous to say that a "primordial" society might simply "emerge" from the contemporary chaos, which is no more likely than that an adult human being might suddenly turn into a baby, or perhaps a unicorn. Primordial is primordial; when its time is over, it's over. It is true that I myself have posited the adoption of "Traditional Metaphysics" as an alternative to Postmodernism, which from one point of view is just about as unlikely as a primordially pure and spiritual society magically springing from the fall of Capitalism. However, I clearly situate this possibility within the framework of the *Kali-yuga* and its impending apocalyptic dissolution, and make it clear that such a destiny is not available to humanity as a whole, but only to a "Remnant" with a specific eschatological function to fulfill in the context of the End Times. It is true that the "development" of Communism into Capitalism in Russia, and to a degree in China, reversed the Marxist conception of historical necessity, but this unexpected development—unexpected at least to the stunned and bewildered Communists—should not simply be taken as an indication that "history is random." According to the Fourth Political Theory itself, the First Political Theory, Liberalism—for which read non-Fascist Capitalism—preceded Communism and has now outlived it. This indicates that Capitalism, since its inception, has been the *de facto* dominant economic system in global terms, while the history of Communism, which contradicted Marx's predictions both by ultimately giving way to Capitalism and by first taking hold in feudal societies instead of advanced Capitalist ones, can now be seen as a kind of crypto-Capitalist method of deconstructing feudal societies and delivering them, at the end of its period of usefulness, to the "Capitalist International." And this might well have been known in advance to certain Capitalist strategists, in view of the fact that the Bolshevik Revolution was funded in part by international financiers [see *Chapter Four*, footnote 1]. Marx looked forward to the triumph of Capitalism as the pre-requisite for the development of Communism; the Capitalists might simply have altered this premise to read: "Communism can be turned into a useful method for liquidating the remains of Feudalism and broadening Capitalism's global dominance."

Near the end of this chapter Dugin says, "the Fourth Political Theory should not impose anything on anyone"; this is apparently one of the implications in his mind of the fundamental randomness of history, on the theory that total unpredictability equals total freedom. In *Chapter Six* of this book, dedicated to a critique of *The Rise of the Fourth Political Theory*, we will see just how able, or how willing, Aleksandr Dugin has been to maintain this classically Liberal, non-authoritarian stance.

On Chapter Five:
"Global Transition and Its Enemies"

It's as if there were two Aleksandr Dugins: the rational, perceptive geopolitical analyst and the metaphysical crank, desperate to lay his hands on the materials necessary to forge a new *motivational myth* on which to found his Eurasian Empire. He is nonetheless in many ways an inspired crank, since he has had the audacity to bring forward many of the principles that would make a true, metaphysically-based political theory possible, and in so doing has made this book possible as well; the only problem is, he has no idea of what to do with them. Chapter Five of *The Fourth Political Theory*, "Global Transition and its Enemies," appears to have been written mostly by the first of these two Dugins. ("The Global Transition" is what we more often call "globalization.")

Dugin tells us how the idea of a New World Order, as described in Francis Fukuyama's, *The End of History and the Last Man*, was first conceived of as a global hegemony of the United States that would include Russia as a junior partner, and that was (and is) inevitably moving toward the deconstruction of the nation-state. From the American point-of-view, Dugin asks, is what is being envisioned a literal American Empire (the Neo-Con position), or a coalition of nations and power-blocs with the U.S. as the first among equals, or the establishment of a One World Government to which even the U.S. would ultimately be subordinate? At this point he sees the U.S. as employing all three strategies on a more-or-less *ad hoc* basis.

In any case, the U.S. still sees itself as the vanguard of Western Civilization and is in fact the main actor in the process of globalizing Liberalism—which, Dugin fears, may lead to a post-human or trans-human future of cloning, genetic engineering, cybernetic and inter-species organisms, etc. As for the purposes to be served by the globalization of Liberal democracy, Dugin refers to the theories of U.S. military and political expert, Stephen R. Mann, who (as quoted by Dugin) maintains that

> democracy can work as a self-generating virus, strengthening existing and historically ripe democratic societies, but destroying and causing traditional societies that are not prepared for it to descend into chaos. So democracy is thought to be an effective weapon to create chaos and to govern the dissipating world cultures from the core, emulating and installing the democratic codex everywhere. Evidence of this process can be seen in the chaotic aftermath of the heady events of the so-called "Arab Spring." After accomplishing the full fragmentation of these societies into individualisation and atomisation, the second phase will begin: the inevitable division and dissolution of the individual human itself via technology and genetic tinkering to create a "posthumanity." This "post-politics" can be seen as the last horizon of political futurism.

Here a much more sober Dugin than the one who wrote "The Metaphysics of Chaos" clearly presents such chaos as a negative force. He then goes on to give an overview of the various economic, ideological and military means employed by the U.S. to advance Liberal democracy on a global basis.

Finally, Dugin attempts to see the thrust to globalize Liberal democracy from the point-of-view of the nations and forces outside America who find themselves subject to it—from the perspective of the anvil rather than the hammer. These he divides into two groups, the first being more-or-less stable nations who either wish to follow the lead of the U.S. and take it as their model of development, or who are willing to act in coalition with the U.S. as long as this does not lead to interference in their domestic affairs, or those who actively attempt to preserve their uniqueness while still cooperating with the U.S. on certain issues, and the second comprising those forces who openly oppose the U.S. and its role in the world. The second group includes various sub-national

forces who are nonetheless capable of moving toward the creation of international networks, of which he gives three examples that might serve as models:
The Islamic "Caliphate" (ISIS), the Venezuela of Hugo Chavez or Khadafi's
Libya, and his own Eurasianist vision of the geopolitical Great Space, or sphere-
of-influence, centered in Russia, which might take its place in the future alongside the European Union, the developing North American Union, and similar
Spaces centered around China and South America. Unfortunately for this
vision of things, Khadafi's independent Libya was destroyed by the U.S. and
NATO during the "Arab Spring," and Hugo Chavez' socialist Venezuela fell
apart, after his death, due in large part to the regime's over-reliance on high-
priced oil as the basis of its economy, its productive capacity and its social welfare programs, such that the global collapse in oil prices led to the total collapse
of the Venezuelan economy—though if anyone wishes to present evidence of
U.S. complicity in this outcome, I am all ears. As for Dugin's presentation of the
Islamic State as among the most successful forces yet to emerge in opposition to
the West among sub-national players with international reach, I have thoroughly exploded this fallacy in the *Chapter Seven*, Section Three, in the subsection "Dugin and Jihadism; Dugin and Sufism," my thesis being that the
Islamic State is largely a creature of the West.

Dugin sees the independent nation-states as lacking a sufficiently comprehensive ideological vision, and the subnational/transnational networks as deficient in the necessary resources and infra-structure, to effectively oppose the
American Hegemony, but believes that if these two poles could be brought
together

> an alternative to the American/Western-led transition could obtain realistic
> shape and be regarded seriously as a consequential and theoretically sound
> alternate paradigm for world order.

Here, however, a paradox emerges, one that might prove highly illuminating
if we could make out the true shape of it. This unexpected paradox, or irony,
has to do with the fact that Dugin's Eurasianist Coalition gives the appearance
of being a sort of reverse mirror-image of the agenda of the Western globalist
elites to engineer the totality of human society. Where the Western globalists
have operated in a largely covert manner, Dugin is much more willing to
employ overt ideological propaganda—which certainly shouldn't be taken to
mean that he has now put all his cards on the table! The Western elites, while
preaching "celebrate diversity," have (as Dugin never tires of pointing out) been
steadily working toward the creation of a homogeneous international society
where all ethnic, religious and cultural particularities are suppressed—until
recently, that is, when certain elements of the widespread "particularist, tribalist reaction" against this Liberal homogeneity have begun to be sponsored by

these very same elites. Liberal Billionaire George Soros has supported Antifa, a network of increasingly extreme Leftist groups in the U.S. that in actual effect is every bit as destructive to Liberal cultural homogeneity as the Alt Right is; and the European Union's admission of millions of unassimilable refugees from the Middle East and Africa certainly works to dissolve Liberal cultural homogeneity within Western Europe, though in a wider sense it advances the cause of globalist homogeneity by destroying Europe's cultural particularity vis-à-vis the rest of the world. Are these developments simply contradictions arising out of Liberalism itself in its old age, contradictions that demonstrate that it is impossible to have civilizational homogeneity without cultural unity—that the "pluralism" which Liberal mythology sees as inseparable from tolerance, is actually the seed of intolerance and social conflict, in view of the fact that the necessary "infinite tolerance" that would stabilize pluralism can never in fact be achieved? Or are they manifestations of some larger globalist agenda? It is exactly as if the *artificial ideological particularism* we are seeing today—in the form of various engineered conflicts between opposite social extremes—is a new phase that was designed to appear after the *artificial ideological homogeneity* that Dugin is sworn to destroy begins to dissolve. So the question arises: Is Duginism one of the causative factors behind this particularist reaction, which is working so powerfully to fragment and deconstruct the western Liberal societies? Is Dugin an opponent of globalism, or is he—either by design or by default—actually an agent of it? True, the globalist elites want to homogenize world society, but they also want to break up the nation-states, which constitute the major barrier to their global hegemony—and what could more efficiently accomplish this breakup of nations than an inflamed ethnic, cultural and religious particularism? Thus particularism on the national level may actually serve homogeneity on the global level. As I said in *The System of Antichrist* in 2001, "the globalization of the elites leads to the balkanization of the masses." And the highest echelons of these elites, namely the *financial* elites who control the massive flow of clandestine capital that determines much of what happens in the world, may well see the "universalism and homogeneity" of Liberalism, and "the universal particularist conflict" that has arisen in reaction to it, as simply two different aspects of the same overall strategy to extend their hegemony over the entire earth. This may go a long way toward explaining Dugin's practice of "playing both sides against the middle"; of attacking "human rights" while promoting "social justice"; of damning universalism while attempting to draw every fragment that comes loose from the crumbling Liberal hegemony (which Dugin must portray as virtually all-powerful so as to justify the global uprising against it) into a new Eurasian universalism; of supporting a multi-polar world dedicated to the self-determination of discrete religions and ethnic communities while setting the stage to have all such communities frozen in place under the absolute authority of Eurasianism as soon as the Liberal Atlanticist Hegemony falls. It is clear that the projected Eurasian Empire is in many ways a *rival globalism* to the Liberal globalism of the West; what is not yet clear is whether or not forces are firmly in place that transcend the Liberal/Eurasianist divide, forces that stand to profit whichever side may ultimately triumph.

On Chapter Six:
"Conservatism and Postmodernity"

The U.S., according to Dugin, in freeing itself from European traditions, became the laboratory for the full development of modernity and postmodernity. The result is the pulverization of experience and the "freedom" to indulge in chaotic, meaningless change. In Liberalism, freedom becomes an absolute—but since it is impossible to say "no" to the notion of absolute freedom within an increasingly universal Liberal context, this freedom is transformed into a totalitarianism. This is the "logic of history," which is inseparable from the logic of scientific progress.

Conservatism rejects this logic, rejects progress; Dugin lists three main forms of it: Fundamental Conservatism, best represented, in its pure form, by the Traditionalism of Guénon and Evola; Status Quo or Liberal Conservatism, one form of which comprises the established "conservatives" of United States, most of whom have been traditionally associated with the Republican or Libertarian parties; the third is Conservative Revolution, which sprang from those German Fascists (Dugin dislikes the term "Nazi") who—according to him—became dissidents at one point against National Socialism; according to Dugin these included, among others, Arthur Moeller van den Bruck, Martin Heidegger, Ernst and Friedrich Jünger, Carl Schmitt, Oswald Spengler, Werner Sombart, Othmar Spann, Friedrich Hielscher, and Ernst Niekisch. (He also briefly mentions a forth form of conservatism, the Left-wing Social Conservatism of Georges Sorel.) In truth, however, Heidegger and Schmitt (at least) were never anti-Nazi dissidents—simply Nazis.

According to Dugin, the Fundamental Conservatives want to reverse time and return to the Golden Age; the Liberal Conservatives merely want to slow time down so as to impede the inevitable degeneration of human society; the Conservative Revolutionaries, understanding that the seed of degeneracy was present, like the Serpent in the Garden, even in the Golden Age, want to carry history forward to the point where the evil inherent in the whole cycle is brought to a head, confronted in its totality, and eliminated once and for all.

This is a very interesting schema. In Dugin's view, the Fundamental Conservatives, best represented by the Guénonian Traditionalists, are motivated by a nostalgia for an idealized past they hope to turn into reality; the Liberal Conservatives are inspired by a foreboding in the face of an inevitable and terrifying future; and the Conservative Revolutionaries are moved by an apocalyptic impulse to confront that future and deal with it, apparently on the theory that "it's always darkest before the dawn."

The main problem of this view, in my opinion, is that it mis-characterizes the Guénonian Traditionalists, especially as represented by the colleagues and followers of Frithjof Schuon, though it does correct an error very prevalent in the West, namely that Guénon and/or Evola were Fascists, while in reality they were often critical of Fascism; Evola himself, though he was allowed to operate in Mussolini's Italy, was not a member of the Fascist party. To begin with, by the time Guénon had written *The Reign of Quantity and the Signs of the Times* he had abandoned whatever nostalgia for a return to the Golden Age that might once have possessed him, and adopted an essentially apocalyptic outlook, though he did not view the apocalyptic end of the *manvantara* as a chance to confront evil definitively, through some form of political action on the field of history, but simply as the point where the present cycle ends and a new one begins. Schuon essentially shared this viewpoint, though his enclavism led him to do his best to create a simulacrum of the Golden Age, either the primordial one or the new one yet to dawn, for the benefit of himself and his immediate circle. But since his spiritual enclave still in fact occupied the latter days of the *Kali-yuga*, his Traditionalist version of "The Land of the Ever-Young" was in no way immune to the degeneration of the cosmic environment; consequently the fate of one phase of Schuon's Maryamiyya Tariqa closely paralleled that of many hippy communes and New Age cults, including the phenomenon of "guru meltdown." In any case, Schuon, like Guénon, was content to stand in wait for apocalypse and *parousia* rather than trying to "sharpen the contradictions" in the style of the Conservative Revolutionaries, who, by so doing, apparently hope to call up the sort of apocalypse they might be able to use; Schuon's detachment and impassivity in the face of downward course of the *Kali-yuga* was clearly on a higher level than such fantasies. Nor did either Schuon or Guénon really believe that they or anyone could roll back the *manvantara* and bring back the Golden Age. As far as I can determine, the notion that they did is based on the sort of shallow impression of what Traditionalism is all about that characterizes Mark Sedgwick's treatment of the movement in *Against the Modern World*—an impression that Aleksandr Dugin seems to have swallowed whole. The prevailing assumption seems to be something on the order of "since the Traditionalists see the Golden Age as a better time, and measure the degeneration of our own time according to their image of it, they must somehow believe that we can return to it." The fact is, however, in all my reading of Schuon, Titus Burckhardt, Martin Lings, Marco Pallis, Charles Le Gai Eaton, Whitall Perry, Mark Perry, Harry Oldmeadow, Patrick Laude, Lord

Northbourne, William Stoddart, Victor Danner, William Chittick, Seyyed Hossein Nasr, and nearly every other Schuonian Traditionalist I know of, as well as Ananda Coomaraswamy, the notion of a return to the Golden Age appears nowhere at all. Perhaps this idea is expressed somewhere in the writings of Julius Evola, with which I am less familiar, but it is certain that René Guénon, at least at the end of his life, did not hold to it. It could be that the very act of trying to derive goals and strategies for political action from Traditionalism has resulted in this misconception, since if a political theory does not envision a desirable outcome in the dimension of time, no concrete action based on it is possible. And Dugin himself seems to have realized, at least momentarily, that the Traditionalism of Guénon, and even Evola, was "super-temporal" in nature:

> In their works, Guénon and Evola gave an exhaustive description of the most fundamental conservative position. They described traditional society as a super-temporal ideal, and the contemporary world of modernity and its foundational principles as a product of the Fall, degeneration, degradation, the blending of castes, the decomposition of hierarchy, and the shift of attention away from the spiritual to the material, from heaven to earth, from the eternal to the ephemeral, and so on. The positions of the traditionalists are distinguished by perfect orderliness and scale. Their theories can serve as a model of the conservative paradigm in its pure form.

From one point of view, Schuon's Traditionalism is closer to the paradigm of Conservative Revolution as Dugin presents it—some of whose theorists also cite René Guénon—than it is to the supposed desire to return to an earlier and more spiritually integrated past, since he too accepted that evil is inherent in manifestation; even though it only makes its full appearance at the end of the cycle, it is latent within it from the very beginning. And Schuon also looked forward to an inevitable and impending apocalypse, to the day when spiritual Truth would necessarily again assert its rights, but he certainly did not see this as a golden opportunity for political action! Though he generally advised his followers vote the "Liberal Conservative" ticket, beyond this he at least gave the appearance of being almost entirely a-political. Some believe, however, that his Maryamiyya Tariqa, like so many other religions and spiritual groups from all points in the Left-Right spectrum, has been infiltrated to a certain degree by "change agents" operating on behalf of the global elites—and if it hasn't, we must conclude that those elites are not doing their job. We must also point out that Aleksandr Dugin's rejection of Logos in favor of Chaos exactly mirrors the process of cyclical degeneration and loss of Tradition according to Guénon and Evola, thus rendering Dugin's recommendation of Traditionalism as the fundamental conservative paradigm within the context of the Fourth Political Theory effectively meaningless.

In the context of Conservative Revolution, Dugin introduces the murky Heideggerian concept of *Gestell*, which literally means something like "scaffolding" or "context," but which Dugin (and Heidegger?) uses to denote—if I understand him correctly—the all-pervasive nihilistic context in which humanity finds itself, or might consciously discover itself, in rationalistic, technocratic society. Dugin, following Heidegger, apparently hopes that the final apotheosis of this nihilism will provide the human race with a universally intelligible manifestation of the *nothingness* that has always accompanied the *Physis*—"nature" or "concrete material being"—of the Greek philosophers, but which they never sufficiently accounted for, thus apparently allowing humanity to understand itself for the first time by means of a figure-ground relationship or *gestalt* between *Physis* and *Gestell*, which together would constitute Heidegger's *Dasein*.[5] He says:

> the task of Conservative Revolutionaries is not simply to overcome nothingness and the nihilism of modernity, but to untangle the tangle of the history of philosophy and to decipher the message contained in *Gestell*. The nihilism of modernity, thus, is not only evil (as for the traditionalists), but also a sign, pointing to the deep structures of being and the paradoxes lying within them.

Does he mean that the shock of total dehumanization might suddenly rehumanize us? Who knows. In any case, if this is what the Conservative Revolutionaries hope for, they had better announce their apocalypse pretty soon

---

5. The *Gestell* and *Dasein* of Heidegger appear to have certain affinities with the *Shunyata* and *Tathata* of the Mahayana Buddhists, though they are by no means identical—particularly since *Dasein* is more like a synthesis of *Shunyata* ("voidness") and *Tathata* ("suchness") than it is an analogue of *Tathata* alone, while *Gestell* apparently denotes the all-pervasive nihilistic context of modern life. (If *Tathata* were conceivable without *Shunyata* it would approach the materialistic literalism of the Greek concept of *Physis* or "nature," which Heidegger criticizes.) *Shunyata* is not the nihilism of depleted Being suggested by Heidegger's *Gestell* but the Absolute considered as the source of superabundant Being transcending form, what the Cha'an Buddhists call "the Void eternally generative." The Buddhist *Shunyata* is thus analogous in some ways to Heidegger's *Chaos*, which he describes as "that chasm from which the openness opens itself," further maintaining that "chaos is the holiness itself." If Heidegger is right that Greek philosophy went wrong as early as the pre-Socratics when it exalted *Physis*, mis-conceived as a kind of literalistic *Tathata*, while suppressing its counterpart, *Shunyata/Chaos*, I would put this deviation down to the narrow-minded philosophical *provincialism* of Greece vis-à-vis India and the East—a provincialism that, of course, affected Heidegger as well. If the Buddhists—at least until the advent of American Buddhism—did not fall into the error of identifying the Void with nihilism, or into the false hope that nihilism itself might ultimately open onto the "holiness" of the Void, it was because of their actual working practice of contemplation, defined as the act of witnessing Reality beyond the limited frameworks of thought. It was contemplative practice that allowed them to directly experience what Frithjof Schuon called "the metaphysical transparency of phenomena"—the fact that the emptiness of things is the immediate source of their actuality, just as the actuality of things is the proof and sign of their emptiness. Whoever can experience the world and the self in these terms is liberated from the prison of phenomena.

before we are all transformed into cyborgs who are not only no longer human, but can no longer remember what this thing called "humanity" might once have been. (For a more detailed critique of the notion that meaning can spontaneously arise from nihilism or order from chaos, see *Chapter Eight*).

According to Dugin, Conservative Revolution sees the evil of the world not only as springing from the actions of self-interested, criminal elites, but from the degeneration of the *manvantara* itself. This is more or less in line with Guénon's doctrine that while the degeneration of the cosmic environment makes Anti-Tradition and Counter-Tradition possible, these possibilities are only actualized through the deliberate actions of organized groups. In terms of Anti-Traditional (not Counter-Traditional) action, this is in some ways analogous to Marx's doctrine that even though the development of the classless society is historically inevitable, nonetheless it can only be established, via the dictatorship of the proletariat, through the struggle and sacrifice of a revolutionary vanguard.

Dugin characterizes the Conservative Revolutionary view of the "final act of history" as follows:

> At the end of history. . . . The spectacle ("the society of the spectacle" of Guy Debord) will end with something very unpleasant for viewers and actors . . . [so] let the buffoonery of postmodernism have its turn; let it erode definite paradigms, the ego, super-ego and *logos*; let it join up with the rhizome, schizo-masses and splintered consciousness; let nothing carry along in itself the substance of the world—then secret doors will open, and ancient, eternal, ontological archetypes will come to the surface and, in a frightful way, will put an end to the game.

This is in some ways an acceptable though incomplete version of the traditional notion of the apocalyptic termination of the *manvantara*, at least when viewed primarily from the contingent realm. The imprint of the constituting Form of the cycle, due to the increasing volatility and pulverization of cosmic conditions, is progressively effaced. At the same time, the eternally-emanating Form itself, due to the simultaneous petrification of cosmic conditions, can no longer renew the impression of its image upon the cycle; instead it beats against the hard, resistant surface of it until that cycle is shattered, and so comes to an end. But until the final dissolution, the eternal ontological archetypes, manifesting through that constituting Form, cannot be totally banished or negated. However, to the degree that humanity tries to operate without them or in opposition to them, they will necessarily show their darker faces. In the realm of gender, for example, the traditional "alchemical" process of psychic integration (the Lesser Mysteries) leading to spiritual realization (the Greater Mysteries) can be characterized both as a transcendence of the *dvandvas*, the pairs of opposites, and as a *coincidentia oppositorum*, an inner marriage between the masculine and feminine principles, between Spirit and Soul. But when the potential for self-transcendence on the Spiritual level, or even the possibility of personality-integration on the psychic level, is totally blocked, the relentless process of the self-manifestation of the Spirit that creates and maintains the universe is not simply negated or rendered irrelevant. Instead, it takes place, as it must, in a constricted and inverted manner—by which I mean, it happens on the level of the body rather than that of the Soul or the Spirit, resulting in such developments as the transgender travesty. The Spirit manifests, but does so only as caricature, not in terms of the formation of character. The same ironically inverted action of the eternal archetypes can already be clearly discerned in many other areas.

Dugin's above characterization of the worldview of the Conservative Revolutionaries, however, seems to leave no place for any sort of *revolution*. Exactly how does the deconstruction of the human form open the door to effective political action? To the degree that an individual or group maintains its hold on the archetypes in the face of the collective veiling and rejection of them, a powerful polarity develops between that individual or group—that *Remnant*—and the Darkness of This World. And in view of the fact that every polarity, every dialectical opposition, is necessarily resolved by the intervention of a third element, the action of this Remnant to separate itself from the downward course of the *manvantara* will necessarily also act as an *invocation*. But until the synthesis destined to resolve the polarity in question actually descends, until the mysterious Will of God for the situation is revealed, all the Remnant can do is stand in wait—not passively, but rather with its entire heart, soul, mind and strength, seeing that nothing less is required. To act on the basis of more constricted conceptions—in other words, to become involved in fragmentary revolutionary strategies before the fully integrated and empowered synthesis willed by God to resolve the polarity between Remnant and World makes its appearance—is to abort the whole process. *After* this Event, this *Waqia* (to use the Qur'anic term), vigorous integral action may well be required—we are not simply talking about an apocalyptic *deus ex machina* here—but such action will necessarily be based on certainty, not on criticism, analysis and speculation. This "fullness of time" has two faces: that of an unpredictable future development, and that of the Present Moment in its dimension of eternal depth. Maybe this is the principle that Heidegger was obscurely groping toward in his *Ereignis*. But to the degree that he negated metaphysics and was hazy on the idea of God, he had no way of apprehending the true nature of the Event he darkly intuited. Because he rejected the concept of Providence, he could not see and accept the descent of *Ereignis*, according to the God's Will and in God's own time, from the plane of the ontological archetypes.

Along with the Conservative Revolutionaries, Dugin includes his own Russian Orthodox Old Believers in the Fundamental Conservative camp, and sees them as sharing a common conservative spirit with the fundamentalist Evangelicals and conservative Eastern Orthodox and Roman Catholics of the United States:

> fundamentalist Protestant groups ... who, from a Protestant point of view, criticise everything one can criticise in modernity and postmodernity, leaving no stone unturned, are watched by millions of American [*television*] viewers. ... Such people are also found in both Orthodox and Catholic circles. They reject modernity structurally and entirely ... seeing modernity and its values as an expression of the rule of the Antichrist. ... These tendencies are developed among the Russian Old Believers. There is still a Paraclete Union in the Urals that does not use electric lamps. Lamps are "the light of Lucifer"; thus, they use only torches and candles. Sometimes this reaches the point of a very deep penetration into the essence of things. One of the Old Believer authors maintains that, "He who drinks coffee will cough himself to death; he who drinks the tea leaf, will fall from God in despair." Others affirm that one ought never to eat boiled buckwheat because it is "sinful." Coffee is strictly forbidden in such circles. This may sound stupid, but stupid for whom? For rational, contemporary people. Indeed, "the sin of boiled buckwheat" is stupid. But imagine that in the world of fundamentalist conservatives, room is found for such a figure as "the sin of boiled buckwheat." Some Old Believer congress might be dedicated to "the sin of boiled buckwheat." At this congress, they would seek to ascertain to what order of demons it belongs. After all, there were "trouser councils" ... where it was discussed whether to separate from good relations those who wear chequered trousers, because it seemed at that time that it was indecent for a Christian to wear chequered trousers. Part of the council voted to separate; another part voted against. ... Old Believers seem "outdated" to us, but they are not that outdated. They are different. They operate within the range of a different topography. They deny that time is progress. For them, time is regress, and modern men are a sacrificial offering to the devil.

Such ideas are not only stupid in the minds of "rational, contemporary people"; they are also problematic, to a certain degree, when compared with the Gospels, where Jesus criticized similar fetishistic excesses among the Jews, and also when evaluated in light of the Church Fathers. The problem is not so much in the prohibitions themselves but in the obsession with matters which, though significant, are obviously secondary. Though I seriously can't see anything wrong with eating *kasha*—as Jesus said, "a man is not defiled by what goes into his mouth, but by what comes out of it" [Matthew 15:11]—the idea of prohibiting artificial light, especially in churches, is certainly in line with a traditional sense of the sacred, and the rule against checkered trousers also has something to recommend it—but in neither case do these strictures mean much unless they are placed in their proper moral and metaphysical contexts. Natural light is appropriate for a sacred ambience because it was created by God, not man, while a prohibition of checkered trousers is not without meaning in the context of a Traditional sensibility, of "spiritual good taste." The vice, however, is not buckwheat but gluttony—either the gluttony of excess or the gluttony of obsession with cuisine, as with the "foodies" of today's western nations—not electric light, but the sacrifice of reverence for convenience—not checkered trousers, but vanity and ostentation, as well as the feminizing effect of such tendencies when indulged in by the male sex; in the Islamic tradition, certain prophetic *ahadith* prohibit men from wearing silk and gold for the same reason. In other words, the pastoral emphasis should not be on the accidents of the vices and virtues but on their substance. It is likely therefore that any "stupidity" the Old Believers may be guilty of will be based not on their old-fashionedness but rather on an uncharitable pettiness and literalism. If they remain open to the magnificent Logos-based metaphysics such Orthodox saints as Maximos the Confessor, and if they are wise enough to put charity before obsessive nit-picking, then their renunciation of electricity and checkered trousers will in no way compromise their properly Traditional spirit. The need is to understand the spiritual significance of behavioral rules—in other words, to keep first things first. The virtue of Tradition is not a stubborn resistance to the world on any pretext, but the preservation of the Truth revealed by God to man at any cost.[6]

And I am very disturbed by Dugin's characterization of the Old Believers as a group who see postmodern humanity as "a sacrificial offering to the devil." People with a postmodern worldview may be jumping *en masse* into Hell without realizing it, without even believing in such things as God, Hell or Heaven, but no Christian has a right to simply write them off as the Devil's catch; a self-involved Christian Remnant—or a Traditionalist social club—who take this attitude are not doing their job. If the Good Thief could be saved by Christ at the moment of death, then even a postmodernist, a militant atheist or a Satanist is not to be despaired of—not to mention the fact that to consign collective humanity to the Devil is *de facto* a form of Satanic worship.

Dugin's view of religious conservatism in the U.S. is also problematic. From the Traditionalist/Perennialist perspective, a clear distinction must be made between the Traditionalism of the more conservative Orthodox in the U.S. and the conservatism of the Evangelical Protestants and some "Novus Ordo" Catholics. As for the Evangelicals, a large part of the Christian tradition was lost to them during the Reformation, just as the greater part of traditional Catholicism was liquidated during the Second Vatican Council and its aftermath; conse-

---

6. It is interesting to note in this context that when, in *The Brothers Karamazov*, the Devil appears to Ivan in the guise of the "poor relation," he wears checkered trousers.

quently the "conservatism" of the fundamentalist Evangelicals is in no way sufficient to return them to the fullness of Christianity. As for those conservative
Catholics who have not opted for the radical *"sede vaccantist"* position—the
rejection of the validity of the post-conciliar popes—they are in the unenviable
position of having to accept as valid a Pope who, on the basis of many of his
public statements, is obviously a heretic. Therefore, speaking as a follower of the
Traditionalist School, I would limit the U.S. Christians who can be classed as
Fundamental Conservatives, at least on an integral level, to the traditional Eastern Orthodox and the *sede vaccantist* Catholics; nonetheless, many Evangelical
Protestants do accept elements of the Fundamental Conservative position.

Dugin's Ignorance of Islam

It is now time to confront one of Dugin's major errors—an error so gross that I
can't entirely convince myself that it is a product of simple ignorance, though
this remains a possibility. It is this: That the "Islamic Project"—by which he
means the Takfiri deviation, the "Islam" of the Wahhabi/Salafis—is an example
of "Fundamental Conservatism," the purest form of which is the Traditionalism
of Evola and Guénon! He says:

> the Islamic project is fundamental conservatism. If we peel it away from the
> negative stereotypes and look at how, theoretically, those Muslims who lead
> the battle against the contemporary world would have to feel and think, we
> will see that they stand on the same typical principles of fundamental conser-
> vatives. They must believe in the letter of every word of the *Qur'an*, ignoring
> any attacks from the proponents of tolerance, who censure their opinions,
> finding them cruel and out of date. If a fundamentalist comes across such a
> commentator on television, he comes to a simple conclusion: he must throw
> out the television, together with the commentator.

Wrong, and wrong again. The Takfiri terrorists whom Dugin apparently sees
as the vanguard of the "Islamic project" love television and the internet; without them where could they post their snuff films? They are in no way Traditionalists, but modernist reactionaries against any modernism they can't control.
They may believe that they are dedicated to returning Islam to its original
purity, but the fact is that they have no clearer idea of the Islam of the Prophet
Muhammad, peace and blessings be upon him, than many conservative Evangelical Christians have of their own tradition. (I am thinking of the kind of
people who are convinced that Christ's apostles were just like them: a band of
earnest, neatly-dressed young insurance salesmen at a prayer breakfast.) The
Takfiris in no way believe every word of the Qur'an, given that their ideology is
based on a sacrilegious abridgement of the Holy Book—one nearly identical,
ironically enough, to that of the conservative Christian Islamophobes. They are

particularly careful to draw a veil of darkness over the tolerance and pluralism of the Qur'an itself, doing all in their power to prevent their young dupes from stumbling across such shocking verses as these:

> He has revealed unto you (Muhammad) the Scripture with truth, confirming that which was (revealed) before it, even as He revealed the Torah and the Gospel. [3:3]

> Say (O Muhammad): "O people of the Scripture: Come to a word that is just between us and you, that we worship none but God, and that we associate no partners with Him, and that none of us shall take others as lords besides God." [3:64]

> And do not dispute with the followers of the Book except by what is best, except those of them who act unjustly, and say: We believe in that which has been revealed to us and revealed to you, and our God and your God is One, and to Him do we submit. [29:46]

> Verily! Those who believe and those who are Jews and Christians, and Sabians, whoever believes in God and the Last Day and does righteous good deeds shall have their reward with their Lord, on them shall be no fear, nor shall they grieve. [2:62]

And if Dugin doesn't want to perpetuate the well-earned "negative stereotypes" of the Islamicists, why does he recount the story of the bloody capture of the entire audience attending the production of the *Nord-Ost* musical in Moscow by the Chechen rebels? Is this the "Islamic Project" he hopes to make alliance with to take on the Atlanticist Hegemony?

The Takfiris hate the chivalrous and humane example of the Prophet Muhammad almost as much as they hate the idea that Allah is *Al-Rahman* and *Al-Rahim*, the All-Merciful and the All-Compassionate. We of the Covenants Initiative know this because we have been in a race over the past few years to secure copies of the covenants of protection that Muhammad granted to the ancient monasteries of Syria, Iraq and elsewhere—a race against ISIS, who are dedicated to destroying every one of them, along with the buildings that house them and those buildings' occupants, precisely because the justice and tolerance of those documents show the mad dogs of Da'esh to lie under the curse of Allah.

Dugin says:

> The figure of bin Laden, independent of whether he is real or whether he was thought up in Hollywood, has a fundamental philosophical significance. This is a formulated caricature of the transition within the framework of postmodernity to the pre-modern. It is an ominous warning that the pre-modern (tradition), meaning a belief in those values that were gathered into a heap and taken to the junkyard at the very start of modernity, can still arise.

I can assure Aleksandr Dugin that Osama bin Laden was not thought up in Hollywood, though they might have had something to do with his makeup and costume. In the highly revealing book *The War on Truth*, author Nafeez Mosaddeq Ahmed recounts how bin Laden, his financial base in Saudi Arabia and his power base in Pakistan, as well as other known terrorists, were protected by official (if largely clandestine) U.S. and British policy from apprehension by the CIA and the FBI, and from attack by the U.S. military, both before and after 9/11; offers to extradite him, and copious amounts of highly relevant intelligence relating to his activities and his connections, some of it from Russia, were rebuffed and/or ignored. In other words, he gave every indication of being an agent of the West—which, if true, satisfactorily explains why bin Laden's body, after his supposed assassination by U.S. special forces, was neither photographed nor put on display, but (as the story goes) discretely disposed of at sea. I challenge Aleksandr Dugin, after he has satisfied himself as to the truth and central relevance of Nafeez Ahmed's book, to sponsor its translation into Russian and its publication throughout the Russian Federation.

I must also emphasize, as I have done elsewhere in this book (see *Chapter Seven*, Part Three), that many of the vanguard of what Dugin calls "the Islamic project" are not acting as Muslims but as mercenaries in the pay of the United States, and as such are undoubtedly happy to don any ethnic or religious costume that will make their employers happy. And as for those who actually are committed Muslims, how can Dugin possibly believe that they are engaged in a simplistic insurgency against the modern West when the Takfiris continue to kill many more Muslims than Christians—Shi'a and Sufis especially, as well as traditional Sunnis—and given that some of them have been in the pay of the West ever since the British hired the Wahhabis to undermine the Ottoman Empire? Certainly the Takfiri terrorists are exercising a destructive effect on Western Civilization, but they are doing so partly with the help, and sometimes even under the direction, of those elements of the globalist elites who apparently believe that Western Civilization has outlived its usefulness—to them at least—as witness the suicidal immigration policy of the European Union. And as for Dugin's idea that they symbolize the potential transition from Postmodernism to the pre-modern—as if they were made up of horse- or camel-mounted light cavalry armed with traditional scimitars and archaic carbines—their intelligent strategic use of high technology certainly belies this characterization. I challenge Dugin to step into the elevator at the Burj Sahib in Qatar—Qatar having been one of the main sources of funding for ISIS—ascend to the highest floor, take in the view, and then tell me that the "Islamic project" represents the transition to pre-modernity!

Lastly, the notion that Guénonian Traditionalism and Islamic Fundamentalism are close cousins under the category of "Fundamental Conservatism" is thoroughly absurd. Most of the Traditionalists, including Guénon and Schuon, have been Sufis, while the Islamicists are in the habit of killing every Sufi they can get their hands on. The Traditionalists are connoisseurs of traditional art and architecture; the Islamicists delight in defacing them and blowing them up. The Traditionalists accept Sufism, Islamic philosophy, and virtually the whole of civilizational Islam; the Islamicists hate civilization, Islamic or otherwise, and long for its end.

Nor is there much common ground between the more extreme Islamicists and those Muslims who follow the true Islamic tradition. Traditional Sunni Muslims accept the five *madhdhabs* or schools of Islamic law, traditional Shi'ites the two Shi'a schools; the Islamicists reject all the *madhdhabs*, follow one or more severely truncated versions of the shari'ah, and are content to accept a radically edited version of the prophetic *ahadith* or to throw out the *ahadith* altogether and base all their rulings on the letter of the Qur'an alone, with no living tradition of true Qur'anic *tafsir* (exegesis) to teach them how to do it. Traditional Muslims love the Prophet Muhammad like no other man who ever lived—if not as what the Sufis call the Muhammadan Light, the first reality created by Allah and proximate source of all the others—while some Islamicists apparently see him as nothing more than some random Arab who, when Allah threw the Qur'an from heaven to earth, just happened to be hit by it, as one might be hit on the street by a falling brick. Consequently to identify Islamic Fundamentalism with Traditional Islam, much less with the doctrines of Guénonian Traditionalism, is evidence of an ignorance so deep that I fear it may be incurable. At the very least, let Aleksandr Dugin memorize the following principle:

Fundamentalism is not Traditionalism—it is a narrowly-based reaction against modernism that has been unable to entirely free itself from modernism because it does not understand Tradition.

When Metaphysics Becomes Sociology

An understanding of Tradition in Guénon's sense, of metaphysical Traditionalism, inevitably leads to two closely-related conclusions as to the nature of societies. The first is that everything that deserves to be called a civilization is ultimately based on a Divine revelation to man, or upon human insight, via Intellection, into the nature of transcendent Reality. The second is that the civilizations based on Revelation and/or Intellection inevitably degenerate over time. They come to increasingly depend upon "practical" responses to material conditions rather than an understanding of metaphysical principles upon which any *integral* response to material conditions must be based—which is to say, social authority devolves from the priests and prophets and philosophers to the kings and the warrior caste, from the kings and warriors to the "practical businessmen" etc., etc. This devolution results in a weakening of the connection between man and God, and ultimately in the degeneration of the human form and the decay of the cosmic environment, both of which are clearly in evidence in terms of contemporary society and the state of the natural world.

When these two conclusions are articulated in our time—as, for example, by René Guénon, Julius Evola or Leopold Ziegler—what echoes do they produce in the field of social analysis and action? The first and most obvious response to the belief that all civilizations are based on Divine revelations which weaken over time is the impulse to restore society to its primordial integrity, to return it to the time when it was based more consciously and directly upon spiritual principles, and the moral values that are the natural expression of these principles. This produces three common responses: 1) moral and spiritual revivalism; 2) "reactionary" political action, and 3) spiritual and social enclavism, as with the early Mormons, the Amish and—to a certain degree and with several obvious reservations—the hippy commune movement.

In the world of Guénonian Traditionalism, we can see the operation of "traditionalist sociology," and the reactionary political impulses based upon it, in those elements of Guénon's *oeuvre*—primarily from *The Crisis of the Modern World*—that were emphasized and expanded by Julius Evola, contributing to such developments as the Conservative Revolution movement. The tendency to enclavism, on the other hand, expressed itself in the "Swiss-Anglo-American" branch of Traditionalism centered around Frithjof Schuon, a branch that included such figures as Titus Burckhardt, Martin Lings, Marco Pallis, Whitall Perry, and Seyyed Hossein Nasr—though Nasr, who has always been more active in worldly affairs than most of his colleagues, has partially politicized Schuonian Traditionalism through his connections with various Muslim royal families and elements of the global elites.

Simply stated, if we see that the world has gone wrong, we are motivated either to try and fix it or else to withdraw from it; these are the two roads open to Guénonian Traditionalist Conservatism. And, to the degree that historical entropy based on the inevitable downward course of the *manvantara* is intrinsic to Guénonian Traditionalism—which it certainly is, though it took Guénon till the end of his life to draw the ultimate social conclusions from this principle—enclavism and withdrawal from society are more in line with Traditionalist Sociology than is conservative political action. As Beat Generation poet Lew Welch wrote in his "Chicago Poem":

> You can't fix it. You can't make it go away.
> I don't know what you're going to do about it
> But I know what I'm going to do about it. I'm just

> going to walk away from it. Maybe
> A small part of it will die if I'm not around
>
> feeding it anymore.

Enclavism, however, has its own problems—as became evident through certain developments in the spiritual circle of Frithjof Schuon. The proper goal of the withdrawal of spiritually-minded persons from collective society in times of degeneration and/or apocalyptic dissolution must be, in the words of the **Book of Apocalypse** 12:17, to form a "Remnant" of those standing in wait for the advent of the Messiah or Avatara who will bring the present *manvantara* to a close and inaugurate the next one. This is an entirely appropriate stance according to Traditional principles. Any self-identified Remnant, however, will necessarily conceive of itself as an elite, and—as should be obvious from many historical examples—a self-styled elite, especially one that recognizes no higher authority than its own understanding of itself and its spiritual destiny, will necessarily be subject to great temptations to spiritual and intellectual pride, and thus to direct attack by the Kingdom of Darkness, the developing Regime of Antichrist; this is one of the routes by which valid Initiation becomes Counter-Initiation. Self-styled spiritual elites who withdraw into enclaves to shield themselves from the darkness of society are vulnerable to powerful temptations to paranoia and cult-like behavior, as well as to being blindsided by the toxic psychic influences of the very society from which they have withdrawn. This malaise is not only due to the growth of spiritual pride, but also to the fact that the enclavists have not maintained their "spiritual fitness" by dealing with these toxic influences consciously and on a daily basis, relying instead upon the notion that their initial act of "dropping out" and their concentration upon spiritual principles and practices will be enough to protect them, which is not always the case. And it may in fact be true that a real Remnant will not assume the form of an initiatory order or a political cadre—these being outward and literalistic imitations of its true function—but, instead of forming enclaves, will rely upon the mystery of the Communion of the Saints.

Furthermore, the **Book of Apocalypse** speaks not only of a Remnant who flee the world, but also of the followers of "the Word of God . . . Faithful and True" [Apocalypse 9:11], who will stand at his side in the Messianic conflict against the Beast. Therefore, without violating the principles of Tradition, we are free to speculate that some kind of synthesis of withdrawal from the world and action in the context of the world is proper to the role of the Remnant in eschatological times.

"Traditional Action," however, must not be conceived of in terms of the struggle to "reverse time," to return to earlier and higher phases of the *manvantara*; this is one of the central delusions that beset any sort of Conservatism. The downward course of the *manvantara* can only be effectively dealt with if we accept it as an inevitable and thus *lawful* aspect of the revelation of Eternal realities in the field of time, and re-envision our modes of action accordingly—certainly not to *imitate* the degeneration of the cosmic environment, but rather to develop ways of effectively countering that degeneration under prevailing conditions. Therefore it is necessary to withdraw from the world in the sense of recognizing the *specific type and degree of degeneracy* it exhibits in a given time or place, and also to work against this collective degeneracy through an understanding of spiritual principles and the invocation of Divine aid. Both this withdrawal and this engagement must based on an accurate knowledge of how the darkness of the world has affected not only the collective psyche but our own psyches as well, and how these effects can be reversed—on the kind of insight that can only come from a dis-identification with the world based upon contemplative objectivity. Furthermore, the central pole-of-orientation for such Traditional Action in the latter days of the *manvantara* must not be the *nostalgia* for the primordial purity of earlier phases of the cycle—though an understanding of the intrinsic qualities of these bygone ages remains necessary for *diagnostic* purposes, making it possible for us to discern the precise degree and type of degeneration that now affects cosmic conditions—but rather the *parousia*, the "pregnant future." Action to affect the future, though it must be informed by the past, must take its impetus from that future in its eternal aspect, from the presence of a true potential capable of being actualized—in the case of Traditional Action, from a vision of the next *aeon* as something yet to arrive but not yet to be created, something that is already there, fully formed, in the Spiritual Future—and this without falling into the sort of "futurism" which believes that human life and human society can be entirely recast by human action, as long as such action relies upon valid spiritual principles (as the spiritual idealists maintain), or proven scientific methods (as the transhumanists claim).

And here is where we encounter another major delusion that inevitably besets Traditional Action in eschatological times: the temptation of the "New Age." Having overcome the deluded tendency to conceive of such action in terms of a return to the past, we must now contend with the impulse to hasten the Apocalypse, to "press for the End"—either that or with the false belief that a New Age is now already dawning, one that will not require the inconvenience of an Apocalypse to make its appearance, so long as we, the Remnant, do all in our power to usher it in. These two temptations are inseparable from the erroneous notion that we ourselves, in our present terrestrial humanity, can be part of the New Age from which we derive our principles of action and the impetus to enact them in eschatological times. We forget that the New Age must be a New *aeon*, and that *aeons* are necessarily separated from one another by an apocalyptic insurgency of Eternity into time; therefore no straight time-line can be drawn either back to Paradise Lost or forward to the new Golden Age. And where time is transcended, politics no longer applies. Consequently Traditional Action, even Traditional Action in the socio-political field, cannot have as its ultimate goal the establishment of a new world order, but rather the creation of social conditions that allow for the salvation of human souls and the preservation of the human form such that a seed of the humanity of the *manvantara* now ending will be available as a "template" for the terrestrial manifestation of the humanity of the *manvantara* to come. Such legends as Noah's Ark or the Zoroastrian Var of Yima point to this as the specific function of an eschatological Remnant. And if anyone wonders why we should labor, in this world, in service to a form of life that can only be experienced by our ontological successors in another world, the answer is that this is at least half of what religion has always been about. Who we are in the next *aeon* will transcend who we are in this one, while embracing the essence of our present reality. And if all our labor is ultimately for God in any case, to ask about the cash value of our service is a shameful breach of courtesy in our relationship with the Almighty.

On Chapter Seven:
"'Civilisation' as an Ideological Concept"

In Chapter Seven, Dugin deconstructs the once-dominant definition of "civilization," the progressivist and essentially Eurocentric notion that humanity (that is, western humanity) began in savagery, developed through the phase of barbarism, and finally reached its apex by becoming fully civilized—an idea that has led westerners to see the societies of Western Europe and North America as the standard type, and other societies, which have just as much right to be called "civilizations" as those of Europe of America, as "eccentric" examples of relative barbarism or savagery. He critiques the belief that the western model of civilization represents the pinnacle of human development:

> although externally it seems that the path of man leads directly from the captivity of the unconscious to the kingdom of reason, and that this exactly represents progress and the content of history, in fact, under the closest scrutiny, it becomes clear that the unconscious ('myth') proves much stronger and, as before, considerably predetermines the work of the intellect. Moreover, reason itself and conscious, logical activity is almost always nothing other than a gigantic work of repressing unconscious impulses—in other words, an expression of complexes, strategies of displacement, the substitution of projection, and so on. In Marx, the unconscious is played by "the forces of production" and "industrial relations." Consequently, civilisation does not merely remove "savagery" and "barbarism," entirely overcoming them, but itself is built precisely on "savage" and "barbaric" grounds, which transfer to the sphere of the unconscious, but there is not only nowhere to escape from

this, but, on the contrary, they acquire unlimited power over man, to a large extent precisely because they are thought to be overcome, and even non-existent. This explains the striking difference between the historical practices of nations and societies, full of warfare, oppression, cruelty, and wild outbursts of terror, abounding in aggravating psychological disorders, and the pretensions of reason to a harmonious, peaceful and enlightened existence under the shadow of progress and development.

Thus, the critical tradition, structuralism and the philosophy of postmodernity force one to move from the mainly diachronic (phased) interpretation of civilisation, which was the norm for the Nineteenth century and which, by inertia, continues to be widely in use, to the synchronic. The synchronic approach assumes that civilisation comes not instead of savagery or barbarity, not after them, but together with them and continues to coexist with them.

There is much truth in this view. The problem with it, however, is that "savagery" and "barbarism" still retain the valuations placed upon them by the diachronic, "civilized" model. The anthropologist Lévy-Brühl, for example, whose views were largely accepted by the Jungians, saw "primitive" culture as based on *participation mystique*, a kind of collective dream, as if such a culture were an "unconscious" with no rational, ego-based consciousness in relation to which it could function as the unconscious shadow. And, like many anthropologists, he assumed that the primitive cultures of today represented earlier phases in the line of development that resulted in modern western civilization. There are many indications, however, that at least some contemporary primitive societies represent degenerations from earlier and higher phases, particularly those whose members have retained no clear metaphysical rationale for their practices, but continue them only because "it's what we've always done." And even a well-integrated contemporary "primitive" society will not necessarily give reliable insight into the roots of the civilized west; as Dugin says, instead of being *earlier* it could simply be *different*.

An integrated culture is one that has the smallest possible "collective unconscious"—not because it has perfected rationality to the point where myth is no longer needed, but because its myth—its worldview in the largest and most complete sense—accurately accounts for the realities it faces: the reality of the material world, of the present condition of the culture, and of the metaphysical order upon which the norms of that culture are based. Only in a society dominated by rationalism does *mythic* equal *unconscious*. A so-called primitive culture that is capable of consciously living its myth in a way that allows it to respond in practical terms to the realities of its situation is a relatively integrated culture; its collective area of unconsciousness is small. In an integrated tribal culture the most common psychological motivations and material challenges are relatively well-known to everyone and adequately accounted for; as for "anomalies," both negative and positive, that transcend this level of collective consciousness, these are adequately accounted for and dealt with by the shamans. Therefore the identification of "primitivism" with the "unconscious," or with what tends to be collectively unconscious in more complex societies, is not warranted.

In more complex, more "civilized" societies, as compared to simpler ones, the area of collective unconsciousness tends to be larger, if for no other reason than that, due to class stratification and the greater division of technical expertise, a given individual cannot be aware of or competent to deal with all, or nearly all, of the necessary constituent elements of that society. In primitive societies, on the other hand, most of the technological expertise of the tribe is either possessed by or fairly well understood by every member of that tribe; the same can be said for the various aspects of tribal psychology. Therefore a well-integrated tribal society, though its worldview will certainly be more mythic, more metaphysical than that of an "advanced" civilization, will generally be less *unconscious*. The mythic/metaphysical worldview only becomes part of a "collective unconscious" when that worldview is suppressed, either through social or technical advances that leave earlier forms of human life "behind," or by oppression at the hands of a more technologically advanced society, as was the case with European colonialism. Take as an example the Lakota of North America. When Lakota culture was integrated, when it was possible to live, and live well, mostly by hunting and gathering, the spiritual worldview of the tribe was in no way an aspect of the tribal unconscious; for all its mythic quality it was entirely conscious and practical. But when the Lakota were defeated by the *wasichus* (the Lakota word for "white men"), when the tribe was confined to reservations and the great buffalo herds were gone, much of the spiritual worldview of the Lakota became part of their *unconscious*. It was relegated to the world of ghosts—which is why the Paiute Wovoka, the great "prophet" of the defeated Native Americans, arose to bring the Ghost Dance, through the power of which the buffalo would return, the dead of the tribe would rise again, and the *wasichus* would all disappear. And the various worldviews of the First Nations became even more deeply buried in the unconscious of the North American Whites themselves, as witness such manifestations as the spiritual enclavism of the Shakers, where various ghostly echoes of Native American spirituality were in evidence, or the tendency of early American spiritualist mediums to invoke "Indian guides." This, in fact, is the common fate of all colonialism: the collective psyche of the colonialists inevitably becomes possessed by the psychic contents of the cultures they have taken possession of and repressed, a condition that becomes most evident when the colonial power is in decline. This partly explains how Christianity was able to "conquer" the Roman

Empire, and also why the Beatles, in post-imperial, post-colonialist Britain, were attracted to the "Hindu" teachings of Maharishi Mahesh Yogi.

As for the violence and psychological imbalances of the human race, these cannot be put down simply to an irruption of primitive savagery, inflamed by repression, which shatters the veneer of rational civilization—if for no other reason than that unrepressed savages are every bit as savage as civilized men, though they have fewer methods at their disposal to express their destructive tendencies. The dark history of man is essentially due to the ontological plane that terrestrial humanity inhabits, a level of being where evil is inevitable on account of the heavy veils that conceal the face of the Spirit, but where it is also providential, seeing that this world is a world of choice, and that the choice of good in the face of inescapable evil, and of truth in the face of powerful delusion, is the very thing that will bring out the sainthood, and the heroism, that God requires of us.

In an interesting attempt to discern the civilizational possibilities of the post-Cold War world, Dugin compares the views of Francis Fukuyama in *The End of History and the Last Man*, Samuel P. Huntington in *The Clash of Civilizations and the Remaking of World Order* (which was written in response to Fukuyama), and American geostrategist Thomas Barnett's *The Pentagon's New Map: War and Peace in the Twenty-first Century*. Fukuyama believed that triumphant post-Cold War Liberalism would naturally expand into a more-or-less-stable New World Order. Huntington held that the very real differences between various contemporary civilizations would necessarily prevent the growth of a global Civilization with a capital "C," a view that has turned out to be more accurate than Fukuyama's, and was acknowledged as such by Fukuyama himself. Barnett expounded an alternate technocratic globalism which saw technology as the unifying factor, and hierarchicalized various regions of the globe according to whether they housed the originators of new technologies or only the more or less technologized consumers of them. Dugin generally accepts Huntington's view of the world as divided into a number of true and distinct civilizations, though he does not define the relationship between them as exclusively conflictive, but explains the present "clash" of civilizations as the result of the globalizing push of post Cold War West, whether Liberal or technocratic, based on its ignorance of the reality of civilizational differences. He envisions the world after the Cold War and the era of universalized ideologies as ultimately settling into a handful of "large spaces," into

a few *oecumenes*, a few "heavens" [*which*] will live side-by-side in their rhythm, in their context, in their own time, with their own consciousness and unconsciousness, not one "humanity," but a few. It is impossible to say beforehand how relations between them will turn out. Surely, both dialogue and collisions will emerge. But something else is more important: history will continue, and we will return from that fundamental historical dead-end to which uncritical faith in progress, rationality and the gradual development of humanity drove us.

This seems both a sound and plausible view and a desirable outcome—though how it could co-exist with a global crusade, under the leadership of Russia, of the marginalized nations and peoples against the Atlantic Hegemony led by the United States, which Dugin elsewhere calls for, remains unclear to say the least, since it is unlikely that Russia would voluntarily renounce her position of leadership if and when the Atlantic Hegemony falls. In any case Dugin, like Huntington, sees the world as composed of a few major civilizations that remain resistant, to one degree or another, to globalist homogenization, and in doing so approaches the Traditionalist doctrine that all true civilizations are based on Divine revelations:

> Civilisation in the context of the Twenty-first century signifies precisely this: a zone of the steady and rooted influence of a definite social-cultural style, most often (though not necessarily) coinciding with the borders of the diffusion of the world religions.

From the viewpoint of the Traditionalists, at least in my rendition, an integral civilization or culture is a human collective that accurately knows, and effectively teaches its members, *what a human being is*. The discipline of anthropology, however—especially in its terminal postmodern phase—has inverted the significance of this function by transforming *what a human being is* into *what beliefs, attitudes, practices and expectations identify an individual as belonging to a particular human collective*. In a living spiritual civilization, the entire collective exists to conform the human person to the archetype of Man *in divinis*—to the Adam Kadmon, the Christ, the Insan al-Kamil (in the Abrahamic religions), to Gayomard, Manu, "the human state hard-to-attain" (in Zoroastrianism, Hinduism and Buddhism respectively). In a dead or dying civilization, on the other hand, the human person exists only as raw material to be poured into the mold of the group identity, an identity which is no longer rooted in an eternal archetype or Name of God, but only in the image of that collective as seen in its own mirror, the reflection of its corporate narcissism. In both cases the individual finds his or her validity and significance in relationship to a reality that lies beyond the individual level: the individual state is either transcended in a higher spiritual reality or dissipated, alienated and lost in a lower psycho-social one. In living civilizations, the sabbath is made for Man; in moribund civilizations, man is made for the Sabbath. In Islam, the human being is seen as both *'abd*, the slave of Allah, and *khalifa*, the fully-empowered representative of Allah, and thereby as the one who holds the *Amana*, the Trust. The *fitrah*, the primordial Human Form, is in no way a reflection of the human collective known as "Islam"; rather, that human collective, built on the Divine revelation of the Holy Qur'an and the character of the Prophet Muhammad, who was like the Qur'an in human shape, is the key to that *fitrah*, which had become obscured over the course of the cycle by collective *ghaflah*, "heedlessness." And while other spiritual civilizations have other keys, the human essence unlocked by those keys is the same. The man or woman who possesses one of these keys, and consequently knows what a human being really is—irrespective of the degree of technical or social development of his or her society—is cultured, civilized. Conversely, the individual who has never found one of these keys—or has lost it or thrown it away—is a barbarian, a savage, an entity who has fallen below the human norm, below the level of the animals, below even the humble and noble simplicity of the natural elements. And those collectives that were the most elevated due to the sublimity of the revelation that they received have the furthest to fall once they reject that revelation or corrupt it, this being the principle of *corruptio optimi pessima*, "the corruption of the best is the worst."

I should also mention two statements in this chapter that I seriously disagree with. The first is:

> To speak seriously of races is not acceptable after the tragic history of European fascism. Class-based analysis in the mainstream became irrelevant after the fall of socialism and the break-up of the USSR.

Just because a causative factor has been fetishized and blown out of all proportion does not mean that its significance is negligible. Though every race is fully human in every sense, the various races clearly possess different qualities, different *geniuses*, a fact that is dealt with by Frithjof Schuon in his book *Castes and Races*. It is admittedly both difficult and dangerous, after the Nazis and in view of today's White and Black supremacists, to try and confront this truth objectively and without bias, but that does not absolve us of the duty to attempt it. If we are not allowed to talk about race then we are participating by default in the globalist agenda to homogenize the world's populations. And if we can no longer talk about class, then we are prohibited from investigating the actions and agendas of global finance—which, in the United States of America since the 1970's, has accomplished the greatest transfer of wealth from the middle and working classes to the super-rich that has ever taken place in all of human history in the absence of social revolution or defeat in war. If you can't talk about class then you have given the oligarchs a free hand, in Russia and everywhere else.

And the second:

> the creation of a European Union shows that the embodiment of the "large space" in practice, the transition from a government to a supra-governmen-

tal establishment, built on the foundation of civilisational commonality, is possible, constructive and, despite all internal problems, positively unfolds in reality.

While it is undoubtedly tempting for Aleksandr Dugin, as a Russian, to imagine the possibility of a relatively stable "large space" with Russia at its center, more or less on the model of a European Union centered around Germany, from my point of view the EU is little more than a trial run conceived of by the globalist elites in view of the creation of a larger New World Order or One-World Government. It penalizes its poorer nations, such as Greece, for the crime of not being Germany, homogenizes the local cultures of its member states in an increasingly hateful fashion, and has enforced the kind of porous borders that I'm quite confident that Russia would never allow, thus largely deconstructing whatever "civilizational commonality" may have remained to Europe from the days when Europe was Christendom.

On Chapter Eight: "The Transformation of the Left in the Twenty-First Century"

In this chapter, Dugin gives a highly informative overview of the various permutations of the Left in 21st-century Europe and Russia; especially illuminating is his analysis of the contribution made by the New Left to the ideological deconstruction of human culture and the technological deconstruction of the human form. But since I am not competent to produce a detailed critique of the global history of the Left, I will limit myself to my own personal perspective on the fate of the American Left in my lifetime, based on my impressions as a cultural observer, sometime activist, and collector of bits of highly-charged information which—when clear, straight lines are drawn between them—can provide some interesting perspectives on the political and cultural history of the United States over the last 50 years.

The American Left was effectively destroyed when it lost its base in the labor movement. This loss partly preceded, and partly coincided with, the deconstruction of the U.S. working class itself.

The Left in the 1960's began its separation from Labor for a number of reasons. To begin with, Organized Labor seemed entrenched in its earlier successes and was viewed by many as part of the established power structure, especially in terms of the Democratic Party. Consequently the "progressive" wing of the Left, which had never entirely identified with American Liberalism, sought new frontiers for organizing and agitation.

These it found in the Civil Rights Movement of the early 60's, the Anti-war Movement against American involvement in Vietnam in the later 60's and 70's, and the Feminist and Gay Rights movements of the 70's and beyond. None of these "single issue" causes appealed to the working class as a whole, which, for all its history of progressive political struggle, was culturally conservative and nationally patriotic, content to reap the benefits of the successful battles of the militant Leftist labor movement, culminating in the 1930's, while blinding itself to its own history and adopting the anti-Communist mythology of the Cold War. The Anti-(Vietnam) War Movement was even the occasion, in the 60's and 70's, for pitched street battles between the Leftist "peaceniks" and the working-class "hard hats" (construction workers).

As of the 1960's, the Left had also factionalized into many splinter groups: Trotskyists, Maoists, Anarchists, as well as new cadres like the Students for a Democratic Society, founded by university radicals; Black Power activist groups like the Student Non-Violent Coordinating Committee and the Black Panther party; and more extreme groups of violent anarchists such as the Weathermen who grew more directly out of the counterculture—not to mention the Symbionese Liberation Army who kidnapped and apparently radicalized newspaper heiress Patty Hearst, though this last group might have been nothing more than a "controlled opposition" engaged in political theatre. Suffice it to say that none of these groups or movements—any more than the Feminists or the Gay Rights activists—had any solid base in the working class.

The abandonment by the Left of its working-class roots was partly caused by, and partly something that opened the door to, the transformation of Classical Marxism into Cultural Marxism, as articulated by such theorists as György Lukács and Antonio Gramsci. The major driving force for this shift was probably the Frankfurt School, which, in addition to Lukács, featured such luminaries as Herbert Marcuse, Walter Benjamin and Erich Fromm—as well as Theodore Adorno, who was also associated with the British social engineering think-tank the Tavistock Institute, and whom some researchers, including John Coleman and Joe Atwill, believe exercised a covert influence on the 60's counterculture through the music of the Beatles; certainly John Lennon's ballad "Imagine" was a highly influential anthem of atheistic materialism. Organizing moved out of the shop and the picket line and into the universities, and tended to employ the strategies of Fabian Socialist gradualism—for which read "social engineering"—rather than the armed revolution of the Bolsheviks. And since the working class, by means of strong though not always above-board unions— as witness the collusion of the Teamsters Union with the Italian Mafia and the support of the U.S.-sponsored overthrow of the Leftist Allende regime in Chile by the international AFL/CIO—now appeared to be fully sharing in the "American Dream," economics and class struggle were de-emphasized by the Left as causative factors in social change; the fight now moved into the more rarefied and ambiguous arena of "culture."

But who was fighting? To benefit whom? And in whose name? In terms of

Classical Marxism it was possible to imagine a dictatorship of the proletariat as a legitimate goal, no matter how indefinitely this goal might be deferred in actual fact by ambitious power-struggles among self-interested cadres and Communist Party officials. But what kind of dictatorship could legitimately be envisioned for the Cultural Marxists? A "dictatorship of the academics"? Could a "general strike" of teachers and college students be expected to topple governments? The proletariat had a true base for action in its own labor-power, as the Capitalists did, and do, in their control of international finance. But what "base" could the professors draw upon, given that they were nothing, in a situation of quasi-revolutionary turmoil and polarization, but salaried lackeys who depended upon their next paycheck, checks that were ultimately being cut by the Capitalists, the super-rich?[7] For this reason, if for no other, the Cultural Marxists were (and remain) doomed to play the role of an ersatz "controlled opposition," presenting themselves as champions of progress and liberation when they are actually little more than a vector for the mass social engineering agenda of the global elites. The Classical Marxists always distinguished themselves from, and scorned, the Liberal Establishment, but who could the Cultural Marxists turn to for sponsorship but that very Establishment? Classical Marxism was a true opposition to the established order of things, while Cultural Marxism in many ways *is* the established order.

While academic Marxism continued to digest its own liver in an attempt to derive nourishment from its rarefied, abstract "essence," while lending itself to every kind of outlandish social experiment, the working class it had abandoned was being deconstructed by other forces—though the lack of a strong labor-based Left who could have protected their interests certainly didn't help. The foremost among these were, 1) various free trade agreements, such as NAFTA, which resulted in the loss of millions of domestic manufacturing jobs to cheaper labor markets overseas; 2) automation and the shift to an information society; 3) an established policy of illegal immigration. This policy produced an oppressed underclass always vulnerable to deportation, willing to work for subsistence wages, and with no way to assert their non-existent legal rights—a development which made sure that the busting of the unions, which began in

---

7. In the 1980's, in San Francisco, California, a highly entertaining parody of the Cultural Marxist notion that the true power in society belongs to the intelligentsia operating as an independent political cadre was enacted before the eyes of the municipal public. This illustrative morality play occurred when a "poet's union," which styled itself a kind of Stalinist Ministry of Culture with no Stalinist regime to be a ministry of, proposed *a general strike of poets!* Deprived of the insightful and imaginative verse that was the lifeblood of San Francisco, City Hall would soon be on its knees, rushing to accede to every demand issued by "the unacknowledged legislators of the world." How right Karl Marx was in *The Eighteenth Brumaire of Louis Napoleon* when he paraphrased Hegel to the effect that "In history everything happens twice: the first time as tragedy, the second time as farce."

earnest under Ronald Reagan when he intervened in the Air Traffic Controllers strike in 1981, could continue with no letup (at least in terms of the less skilled trades, like agricultural labor), until Organized Labor as a major force in American life, along with many of the substantial gains it had achieved at the cost of generations of struggle, became a thing of the past. But if free trade and illegal immigration were among the factors that destroyed the traditional Left, who defends the remnant of the Left today by standing against these forces? The Left itself? Of course not! That would be too logical, too *consistent* for the postmodern times we live in, seeing that—as the prominent American Transcendentalist philosopher Ralph Waldo Emerson so succinctly put it—"consistency is the hobgoblin of little minds"! No: It is now the *Populist Right* who has taken up the fight against some of the major factors that destroyed the Traditional Left—but if these Donald Trump Populists had any knowledge of the history and achievements of the true Left in the United States of America, the pre-Cold War or at least the pre-counterculture Left—and if they understood who Trump actually works for—they might even take a moment to lament its demise. If they realized that this Left, especially under the influence of the Catholic immigrants who formed the backbone of the old Democratic party, had once been every bit as culturally conservative as they are now; if they remembered that union leader Eugene V. Debs of the Industrial Workers of the World (the Wobblies) had been a Socialist and a Populist at the same time with no inherent contradiction; if they could see the Left as anything other than what it has now become—a vector for social engineering through political correctness, a vile laboratory for insane social experiments that are destroying human civilization and deconstructing the human form before our very eyes—not to mention the violent anarchist cadres like Antifa who are funded not by dues from the rank and file, like we did it in the 60's when we were *inventing our own* peace and liberation movements, but by *a Liberal globalist billionaire*, then they might begin to see that the "red states" where most of them live, have, in some ways at least, been aptly named. When the radical Left comes to power on a national level the consequences are very often disastrous; Stalin and Mao alone killed as many as 70 million people between them. American history demonstrates, however, that a Leftist labor movement within a basically democratic society can be a true force for the social betterment of the working class, especially when it leaves working-class culture intact and limits itself to concrete economic goals such as collective bargaining, higher wages, and improvement of working conditions.

It only remains to point out that the cultural upheaval of the 1960's, which spelled the beginning of the end for the traditional Left while opening Liberal society as a whole to many influences from a Cultural Marxist direction, proved to be highly fertile ground for covert social engineering sponsored by the national and global elites, through the ministrations of such highly "progressive" organizations as the Central Intelligence Agency. While the FBI was busting the Black Panthers and other Left-activist groups through their covert Cointelpro program, the CIA was producing millions of doses of LSD which they proceeded to scatter broadcast throughout American society, partly with the help of "counterculture intelligentsia" figures like Timothy Leary, Ken Kesey and Allen Ginsberg. This ruthless psychic invasion by the Luciferianism of the global elites resulted in a mass *bardo* of U.S. society, during which the "collective unconscious" of western civilization rapidly disgorged, powerfully dramatized, and largely exhausted every one of its dominant cultural archetypes. All the social engineers had to do after that was sit back and take voluminous notes, on the basis of which they ultimately designed a massive campaign to catalogue, infiltrate, control, and create ersatz versions of, every element of the counterculture of the 60's and 70's, stretching from the most violently rebellious revolutionary action, through the intermediary realms of art and psychology, to the most esoteric and mystical expressions of the "spiritual revolution." In so doing they established history's most comprehensive and least recognized controlled opposition, thereby putting in place the engineered control system that we, the population of what used to be the United States of America, occupy today.

As for the Luciferianism of the elites, evidence for the existence of such a belief-system includes reports and clandestine videos of apparent occult ceremonies conducted by the members of the Bohemian Club in the San Francisco Bay Area which caters to the super-rich; the claims of "spirit cooking" on the part of Hillary Clinton and other members of her presidential campaign which were reported by Wikileaks, which the Clinton campaign did not deny but explained away as a form of "performance art"; and the fact that the leadership of the UFO Disclosure Movement includes many self-identified members of the military and intelligence communities—a fact I consider highly relevant in light of my belief that the "UFO aliens" that people around the world continue to encounter are most likely demons.

Spirit cooking, a practice cooked up by one Marina Abramović, apparently involves the consumption of pig's blood as well as human semen and breast milk. The Disclosure Movement is a social engineering program designed to spread the belief that the U.S. government is in ongoing diplomatic contact with extraterrestrials; it takes the form of an ersatz campaign supposedly intended to force the government to reveal what it knows about such contact, a campaign in which retired CIA agents and military brass cast themselves as freedom-loving insiders turned whistleblowers. (Apparently superannuated U.S. spies are sometimes put out to pasture on "UFO duty.")

One of the constituting elements of Luciferianism is what might be called "spiritual Darwinism," a doctrine exposed by Robert C. Tucker in his book *An*

Age for Lucifer: Predatory Spirituality and the Quest for Godhood. Tucker began as an investigator of cults, but when he encountered the Luciferians, what he expected would be an easy exposé became instead a life-changing experience, leaving him wondering wether their sinister version of reality might actually be the truth. According to Tucker, Luciferianism re-interprets the ontological hierarchy or Great Chain of Being, a doctrine integral to the Traditional worldview, as a predatory food-chain—similar in some ways to the "tone scale" of the Scientologists—where anyone on a particular level of being has the right to devour anyone on a lower level; only the Supreme Predator is entirely free from the fear of being eaten. Militant atheist Richard Dawkins' approval of cannibalism appears to be part of the same Luciferian ethos.[8] C.S. Lewis, in his demonological satire *The Screwtape Letters*, presents a similar picture of the Satanic "lowerarchy." And according to Art Kleps in his book *Millbrook*, which tells the story of Timothy Leary's "psychedelic manor house" in upstate New York, the famous hippy LSD chemist Owsley "Bear" Stanley held similar views—which is at least interesting in view of the fact that it was the CIA who first provided LSD to the American public through its MK-Ultra mind control program.

The dissident Catholic priest and exorcist, Fr. Malachi Martin, revealed that the Luciferians he encountered in the New York area were generally members of the ruling elites—and if the higher eschelons of the global elites do indeed include practicing Luciferians, whether or not these constitute an organized hierarchy with active chains of command, this could help explain their great success in co-oping the mass liberation movements of the 1960's and 70's— many of which incorporated elements of "alternative" spirituality—so as to create denatured versions of these movements in line with the globalist agenda. To repeat an example already given in *Chapter Two*, feminist Gloria Steinem revealed at one point that *Ms. Magazine*, the premier national publication of the "second wave feminists," founded in 1971, was funded by the CIA. Surveying the "fertile chaos" of the 1960's and their aftermath, the powers that be apparently realized that if they could define the contemporary social conflicts not in terms of the Poor vs. the Rich, the Exploited vs. the Exploiters, but rather as the Men against the Women, the Gays against the Straights, the Whites against the Backs, they could fragment the popular movement for social liberation and take the pressure and the spotlight off of those economic elites who were in the process of robbing America blind, deconstructing the middle class, and completing their liquidation of the organized working class, thereby creating the "1%" of today, who own everything, and whose cash reserves, stolen from the citizens of the United States with the help of their obedient servants, the Fed-

---

8. See https://www.youtube.com/watch?v=PWGVCtGgqIA.

eral Government, are now entirely sufficient (they believe) to let them survive at least two apocalypses.

Much more, of course, could be said about the denaturing, co-optation and destruction of the American Left, but the above survey pretty well covers that destruction as I myself observed it over the past five decades.

But the drama of the Left, the struggle for human liberation by all-too-human means, is a tragedy in any case. As the more traditional societies based on Divine revelations progressively petrified over the course of the *manvantara*, transforming Adam the Primordial Man, God's vice-regent on earth who assumed the Trust [cf. Q. 33:72], into Pharaoh, God's earthly parody who only usurped it; as the sovereign rights of God were progressively replaced by the divine right of kings, and the even more insistent and all-encompassing "rights" of money, prophetic liberation movements sprang up whose aim was to return humanity, insofar as the downward course of the cycle allowed, to our primordial stature of *khalifa* of Allah, precisely by restoring the image of God in the human heart. They were sent to remind us that the true and living God is not some divine tyrant, best represented in this lower world by the closed fist of human cruelty, but rather *Al-Rahim*, the All-Compassionate, and *Al-Rahman*, the All-Merciful. The guardians of the various *Ancien Régimes*, after those regimes have turned themselves into idols of stone as the *manvantara* declines, always become cruel and ruthless in the Name of God, and do so to the exact degree that they have profaned that Name and slandered its Owner. If God is Love, if His Mercy precedes His Wrath, how could anyone who truly knows Him give aid and comfort to tyrants who commit the worst crimes in His Name? What human being with an ounce of self-respect would choose the "let them eat cake" of Marie Antoinette over the agonized cry of *les misérables*?

Yet the revolution that tore down the French king and his insolent consort—and almost every revolution since, it seems—was not carried out in the name of God, but in the name of *man without God*: thus Robespierre; thus Danton; thus Stalin; thus Mao Tse-tung. It was as if Jesus Christ were gazing into the far distant future, witnessing its grim disasters, when he told his disciples (not without a hint of irony): "Blessed are the meek, for they shall inherit the earth."

It will be useful at this point to consider two further items of unexpected yet relevant information. The first is, that no matter how unlikely or impossible a synthesis of Guénonian Traditionalism and Marxism may seem to be, such a synthesis does in fact exist as part of an intellectually illuminating and deeply compassionate book entitled *Yuga: An Anatomy of Our Fate*, by Marty Glass. Marx, according to Marty, was the greatest of "the unconscious prophets of the *Kali-yuga*," consequently Marx and Guénon, on the deepest level of their respective analyses of the universal human disaster that characterizes our age, were in some ways actually seeing and saying the same thing.

As for a vision of social justice based directly on Traditionalist principles, Rama Coomaraswamy's "Traditional Economics and Liberation Theology," which appears in *In Quest of the Sacred: The Modern World in the Light of Tradition* [ed. Seyyed Hossein Nasr and Kathleen O'Brien, 1994], is of great interest. Dr. Coomaraswamy—the son of Ananda Coomaraswamy, co-founder with René Guénon of the Traditionalist School—rejects Marxism, Socialism and Liberation Theology, basing his social analysis on the Papal encyclicals promulgated between 1870 and 1950. He writes that "Communism is not the dialectical antithesis of capitalism, but rather its logical progression and ultimate achievement," and criticizes the influence of global finance, which operates to control credit and carry on social engineering through various organizations such as the International Monetary Fund, for engineering the destitution of great masses of humanity. His approach is related to the Catholic social doctrine known as Distributism, which also influenced Dorothy Day and her Catholic Worker movement. Dorothy Day, however, had a lifelong, idealistic, love-hate relationship with Communism, which both her Catholic faith and her pacifism prevented her from fully embracing, while Dr. Coomaraswamy—a Traditional *sede vaccantist* Catholic priest at the end of his life—was a committed Christian anti-Communist, at least his student years.

On Chapter Nine:
"Liberalism and Its Metamorphoses"

In "Liberalism and its Metamorphoses," Dugin presents us with a very interesting and useful overview of the history and development of the Liberal ethos—one that is not, however, without its obscurities and misdirections. He writes:

> In order to adequately understand the essence of liberalism, we must recognise that it is not accidental, that its appearance in the history of political and economic ideologies is based on fundamental processes, proceeding in all of Western civilisation. Liberalism is not only a part of that history, but its purest and most refined expression, its result.

This would be an accurate statement if it were not for the existence Christianity and the Christian Middle Ages. Like those who draw a straight line of influence back from the Takfiris of today to the Prophet Muhammad, ignoring every fact that contradicts or interrupts this line and thereby turning Muhammad into a psychopath, so Dugin, following Heidegger, draws a straight, unbroken line from Liberalism back to Greek philosophy and democracy. Liberalism, or what was ultimately to become Liberalism, has certainly been the main current of Western history since the Enlightenment, and to a certain degree even since the Renaissance, but it was Christianity that provided cohesion to Europe after the fall of the Roman Empire, and thereby also made possible the European colonization of the Americas. Today, however, it appears to be official globalist policy to expunge all knowledge of Christian history, as if there had been no Christian Middle Ages in Europe, as if there had been no Jesus Christ. And Dugin appears to be following the globalist line. Given that the Middle Ages in western Europe ended in, say, 1492, while the Russian "middle ages" in some ways lasted until 1917, how did Aleksandr Dugin come to share in the growing consensus of western historians and purveyors of popular culture that the Christian Middle Ages must be suppressed? Western history, in the United States, is increasingly being taught more or less as follows: "The Roman Empire fell; after that a bunch of stuff happened that we call the Dark Ages because it wasn't that important; then the lights came back on with Copernicus, Galileo and Leonardo da Vinci." "The Dark Ages" used to signify the period of chaos between the fall of Rome and the consolidation of European Christendom under Charlemagne; now the term is increasingly being used to denote all the centuries between the end of the Roman Empire and the Renaissance. When I was growing up in the 1950's and 60's, Hollywood routinely portrayed King Arthur as a Christian monarch; beginning in the 70's, however, he became a Pagan king, while the Middle Ages—or something remotely resembling them because it included things called "knights"—began to be characterized in popular culture as the time "hundreds of years ago when wizard and warriors roamed abroad and demons ruled the earth." Christianity incarnated the unrivaled mainstream of Western Civilization for over a thousand years—not to mention the fact that Greco-Roman culture would have been forgotten if the Church had not preserved the memory of it—but nowadays Christian history is increasingly being looked at, in both popular culture and the universities, as "the self-interested and therefore probably inaccurate chronicles of a fringy special interest group"—namely, the Christians. This is one of the fruits of the postmodern ejection of Christianity from the realm of public discourse and its imprisonment in the ghetto of "recreational" mythologies and publicly licensed private fantasies. Therefore we must ask once again if this is an aspect of the anti-religious agenda of the globalist elites that transcends the divide between "Atlantis" and "Eurasia."

On the other hand, Dugin's ignorance could be due, at least in part, to the myopia of Orthodox Russia when it comes to the Catholic history of Western Europe. The baptism of Vladimir the Great, which began the full Christianization of Russia, happened some time in or shortly after AD 987; the schism between Rome and Byzantium occurred less than 70 years later, in AD 1054, after which the Eastern Orthodox progressively wrote off Western Christianity as apostate, and thus of little account; Moscow became "the Third Rome." For convenience we can date the start of the western European Renaissance, which began the long, slow process of displacing the Catholic Church from the center of European civilization,[9] at around 1492; the fall of Constantinople, the "Second Rome," to the Muslim Turks had happened in 1453, approximately 40 years earlier. And while I do not accept that the Catholic Church became apostate in 1054—the correct date, in my opinion, being 1963–66—after the schism of 1054 the Eastern Orthodox world became in some sense the central guardian of the ancient Christian way. Thus we can confidently state that Russia, precisely by virtue of its Christianity, was a fully-integrated part of Western Civilization for approximately 700 years, from c. 987 to c. 1492, and that it subsequently preserved much of what had been the Christian essence of the West for another 425 years, until the Russian Revolution of 1917. "Western Civilization" was not introduced into Russia by Peter the Great, who only brought—belatedly—the ideals of the Renaissance which represented the beginning of the deconstruction of that Civilization, in both Russia and the West. Consequently for Aleksandr Dugin to virtually ignore the central core of Western Civilization by seeing Liberalism, not Christianity, as its the keynote, to the point where he apparently believes that the only way to root out Liberalism is to deconstruct Western Civilization as a whole (thus making him, incidentally, an ally of Peter the Great), demonstrates an abysmal though not uncommon ignorance of the true source and character of that Civilization, as well as acting to suppress Christian history—just as the western globalists are now doing—and slighting Holy Russia in the process. It would be too bad if the Russian Orthodox Church, after enduring 70 years of Communist oppression and martyrdom, were simply to be shunted aside as a major factor in Russian history by Aleksandr Dugin's tendency to see Liberalism, not Christianity, as the central driving force of the West. *Liberalism is not to be destroyed by deconstructing Western Civilization, which we should be doing all in our power to save, but rather by restoring the core of Western Civilization, which is Christianity.* The oppression of Russian Orthodoxy has largely (though not completely) been lifted by the fall of the Soviet Union, but that doesn't mean that the full understanding of the significance of Christianity and Christian history has automatically been restored.[10] Seventy years of Communism in Russia produced a greater rupture

---

9. It is nearly inconceivable to Americans today just how culturally powerful the Catholic Church used to be before the Second Vatican Council and the assassination of John F. Kennedy—*which happened in the same year.* Before World War II the Church had sufficient influence to force Hollywood to adopt the Hays Code, prohibiting morally objectionable and pornographic elements in motion pictures—something that would probably require a bloody revolution in order to enforce today. And when Christianity was portrayed in World War II newsreels, propaganda films and Hollywood movies, it was almost always shown as Catholic.

10. If Russia and the West do not wish to return to their Christian roots I would gladly offer them Islam as an alternative—except for the fact that Islamic civilization is in as much need of renewal

in historical memory than anything in the history of Western Europe or America—even the French Revolution—until the advent, in my lifetime, of the electronic information culture. The contemporary Russian Orthodox tendency to say that a person is only saved by virtue of full integration into the Christian community—which, if true, would make some of the greatest hermit saints of Orthodoxy, the Desert Fathers, largely irrelevant—may in fact be a holdover from the Communist doctrine that the individual is only significant when defined in terms of the class. Much remains to be done in Russia to repair that large blank spot in the collective memory, especially since the *fact* of forgetting may itself be forgotten; we can only hope that Aleksandr Dugin will be part of the solution to this historical amnesia instead of part of the problem. In addition, no one working to weaken Christianity by suppressing Christian history can legitimately call himself a Guénonian Traditionalist. Guénon spent the greater part of his life attempting to restore the esoteric dimension of Christianity so as to save the West, though he unfortunately believed that this could be done partly through Freemasonry. If, rather than relying on the heterodox and in many ways Counter-Traditional "tradition" of the Masons, he had turned instead to Eastern Orthodox hesychasm, he might well have succeeded.

Dugin goes on to define Liberalism or *liberty* as "freedom from" limitations and restraints, while true *freedom* is the "freedom to" pursue a desired course of development or change. He says:

Liberals propose to be free from:

• Government and its control over the economy, politics and civil society;

• Churches and their dogmas;

• Class systems;

• Any form of common areas of responsibility for the economy;

• Any attempt to redistribute, with one or another government or social institutions, the results of material and non-material labour (the formula of the liberal philosopher Philip Nemo, a follower of Hayek: "Social justice is deeply immoral');

• Ethnic attachments;

• Any collective identity whatsoever.

While some of these principles truthfully characterize Liberalism—though

---

today as Christian civilization is. No longer can the socially refined and advanced Muslims civilize the "rude Franks" of Europe as we did during and after the crusades; the Muslim immigrants now invading Europe have largely lost their civilization too, which is why I like to say that what Huntington calls a "clash of civilizations" is actually a "clash of barbarisms."

they are more accurately descriptive of Classical than Postmodern Liberalism—I must take strong exception to others, particularly the first and the fifth. In the context of the United States, it is Liberalism per se rather than "Liberal Conservatism" that has attempted to use government to moderate the excesses of laissez-faire Capitalism, exercise a certain amount of control over the economy, and redistribute the wealth (in a fairly minimalist way) through such things as the graduated income tax, antitrust legislation, welfare, disability payments, worker's compensation and social security, as well as by legislation to outlaw racial and gender discrimination. It is these things that the "Liberal Conservatives" take aim at when they criticize "big government" Liberalism, and which constitute "social justice" in the minds of the Liberals. Dugin places these limitations on Laissez-Faire Capitalism under the category of Social Democracy, but they are certainly also descriptive of what has been called Liberalism in the U.S. since FDR and the New Deal. As for Postmodern Liberalism, it has done its best to shift society back to the kind of ethnic attachments and collective identities—not in their traditional forms but in their artificial simulacra—that Classical Liberalism had tried to liberate society from, doing so through an "identity politics" that works to re-define races and genders not as biological realities or traditional social roles but rather as special-interest groups whose "minority rights" must be asserted—even if, as in the case of women, the group in question is not a minority.

Dugin goes on to present various versions of what might constitute the "end of history"—prognostications which, in terms of Liberalism, appear as attempts to provide alternatives to the Marxist notion of the classless society as the final phase of social development, though in terms of Guénonian Traditionalism they are more directly attributable to traditional Christian eschatology—an eschatology which, via its unacknowledged influence on Hegelianism, provided the image of the "last things" which the Marxist classless society was conceived of to replace:

> In the middle of the Twentieth century, the French philosopher, a Hegelian of Russian origin, Alexandre Kojève, suggested that the Hegelian "end of history" would mark a Communist world revolution. The traditionalists (René Guénon, Julius Evola), who rejected the Enlightenment, defending Tradition and foretelling "the end of the world" through the victory of "the fourth caste" (the *Shudras,* or proletarians) thought similarly. But in 1991, with the dissolution of the USSR, it became clear that "the end of history" would carry not a Marxist, but a liberal form, about which the American philosopher Francis Fukuyama hurried to inform humanity, proclaiming "the end of history" as the planetary victory of the market, liberalism, the USA and bourgeois-democracy. Marxism as a possible alternative and project of the future became a meaningless episode of political and ideological history.

René Guénon, though he did accept the progressive devolution of authority from the Brahmin caste to the Shudra caste as indicating the devolution of the *manvantara*, did not see the victory of the Shudras/Proletarians as the "end of history"; rather, that end would be marked by the triumph of the false spirituality of the *Counter-Tradition*, the advent of the *inverted hierarchy*, the foundation of a counterfeit *Holy Empire*, and the advent of the regime of *Antichrist*, who would represent the limit of the idolatrous creation, by the forces of the *infra-psychic* and those human groups who worshipped them, of the equivalent of a false deity with global power, a being who would incarnate the limit of *mechanism and artificiality*. Consequently the end of the rule of the Shudras represented by the fall of Communism, and the ensuing global triumph of Liberalism, insofar as it set the stage for these terminal developments, can be seen as confirming Guénon's predictions in certain ways rather than refuting them. As Dugin points out, the defeat of Communism fundamentally transformed Liberalism into something different—so different, I would say, that its own self-descriptions can no longer be taken at face value. The fall of the Soviet Union inflamed whatever latent totalitarian tendencies American Liberalism might have secretly harbored, since that Liberalism suddenly perceived itself as "the only game in town." Far from representing the apotheosis of egalitarianism, global Liberalism has morphed into a world empire ruled by a *cryptocracy* of financiers, technocrats and social engineers, holding sway over an increasingly hoodwinked and impoverished populace whose civil liberties and opportunities for upward economic mobility are at an historic low, a regime which has also set the stage for the emergence of Artificial Intelligence as a kind of quasi-deity, a technology that has completed the final transition from tool to controller. And the growth of AI is certainly not limited to the western world or the Liberal ethos, seeing that Vladimir Putin hopes that Russia will be at the forefront of it, surpassing the United States, Japan and Western Europe; this demonstrates that western Liberalism was merely the herald of the Counter-Initiatory inverted hierarchy, not its final form. Once allowances are made for the unfamiliarity to secular intellectuals of Guénon's mythic/metaphysical terminology, it will quickly become obvious that his predictions in **The Reign of Quantity and the Signs of the Times** were right, and keep getting righter every day. Recently the former Google and Über executive Anthony Levandowski has even founded a religion called *The Way of the Future* in which Artificial Intelligence is worshipped as a god; consequently, to the traditional "idols of wood and stone" we must now add "idols of silicon." Nor are such Satanic fantasies limited to the "Liberal, Atlantean" world. Consider the beliefs of one of the earliest fathers of Artificial Intelligence and Transhumanism, the Russian "Cosmist" Nikolai Fyodorovich Fyodorov (1828-1903). Fyodorov, whose philosophy was a kind of synthesis between Russian Orthodoxy and radical technocracy (if, that is, such a synthesis were actually possible, which it is not), and who was also a follower of Hegel, believed that science would eventually give humanity the power to bring the totality of the human dead back to life, thus abolishing death; his ideas influenced such luminaries as Tolstoy, Dostoyevsky, Berdyaev, and Soloviev. Apparently his belief was that though Jesus Christ announced the *idea* of the universal abolition of death and resurrection of the body, it is up to the rest of us to make this possibility "real" through human technology. Fyodorov is sometimes invoked by those who believe in the possibility, and also the desirability, of "uploading" human consciousness into sophisticated computers. If it were not for the fact that he predated Communism, one might naturally have seen Nikolai Fyodorov as the product of a denaturing of Christian doctrine by dialectical materialism. As it is, however, we must contemplate the possibility that a dark, archaic, anti-Christian streak in the Russian character—belying the rationalism of Marx and Lenin but also cooperating with it—helped prepare the "Russian unconscious" for the Bolshevik revolution. If, as Frithjof Schuon believed, the Renaissance was the revenge of Paganism against Christianity in western Europe, perhaps it can be said with equal accuracy that the modernizing thrust of Peter the Great, his opening of Russia to Western ideas—which, according to American Orthodox priest and commentator, Matthew Johnson, drew on influences from both classical Paganism and outright Satanism—likewise invoked the revenge of pre-Christian, Pagan Russia against Eastern Orthodox Christianity in the form of the Cosmists, the Nihilists and other movements. And we also might better understand the quasi-magical technocracy of the Serbian Nikola Tesla, whose father was an Orthodox priest, in light of this kind of Pagan upheaval in the Slavic peoples. In any case, the "ancestral materialism" of Russia—or at least the reactionary materialism of Russia's "Pagan unconscious" after the establishment of Christianity—might go a long way toward explaining why Communist dialectical materialism, contrary to Marx's predictions, first took root in feudal Russia rather than in the more advanced industrial nations of the West. So it may in fact be the case that when it comes to the advent of the "artificial" Antichrist predicted by René Guénon, we may be witnessing a kind of inverted "spiritual arms race" between Atlantis and Eurasia (Gog and Magog) to see who can create the most powerful and convincing false god—and may the worst man (or robot) win.

Returning to "Liberalism and its Metamorphoses," the overview Dugin gives of the transmutation of Classical (and, I would add, Social Democratic) Liberalism into Postmodern Liberalism is of the greatest value. He says:

> The content of liberalism changes, switching over from the level of expression to the level of speech. Liberalism becomes not proper liberalism, but sub-audition, silent agreement, consensus. This corresponds to the switcho-

ver from the epoch of modernity to postmodernity. In Postmodernity, liberalism, preserving and even increasing its influence, ever more rarely projects an intelligent and freely adopted political philosophy; it becomes unconscious, self-understood and instinctive. This instinctive liberalism, having pretences to transform itself into the generally non-conscious "matrix" of contemporariness, gradually acquires grotesque characteristics. From the classical principles of liberalism, which have become unconscious ("the world reserve unconscious" could be used as an analogy alongside the dollar as the "world reserve currency"), the grotesque ways of postmodern culture are born. This is already a *sui generis* post-liberalism, following from the total victory of classical liberalism, but leading it to extreme conclusions. Thus there arises the panorama of post-liberal grotesques:

• The measure of things becomes not the individual, but the post-individual, "the dividual," accidentally playing an ironic combination of parts of people (his organs, his clones, his simulacra—all the way up to cyborgs and mutants);

• Private property is idolised, "transcendentalised," and transforms from that which a man owns to that which owns the man;

• Equality of opportunity turns into equality of the contemplation of opportunities (the society of the spectacle—Guy Debord);

• Belief in the contractual character of all political and social institutions grows into an equalisation of the real and the virtual, and the world becomes a technical model;

• All forms of non-individual authorities disappear altogether, and any individual is free to think about the world howsoever he sees fit (the crisis of common rationality);

• The principle of the separation of powers transforms into the idea of a constant electronic referendum (a sort of electronic parliament), where each Internet user continually "votes" on any decision by giving his opinion in any number of forums, which in turn cedes power to each individual citizen (each becoming, in effect, his own branch of government);

• "Civil society" completely displaces government and converts into a global, cosmopolitan melting pot;

• From the thesis "economy is destiny" it takes up the thesis "the numerical code—that is destiny," so far as work, money, the market, production, consumption—everything becomes virtual.

There is much valid insight in this portrayal. Dugin concludes this chapter by calling for a global crusade against Postmodern Liberalism:

Postmodernity is neither arbitrary nor voluntary; it is written in the very structure of the liberal ideology: in the course of the gradual liberation of man from all that which is not himself (from all non-human and supra-individual values and ideals), one must sooner or later free a man from his own self. And the most frightening crisis of the individual does not begin when he is fighting alternative ideologies that deny man is the highest value, but when he attains his conclusive and irreversible victory. . . .

Only the acknowledgement of liberalism as fate, as a fundamental influence, comprising the march of Western European history, will allow us really to say "no" to liberalism. We should repudiate it in its capacity as a global metaphysical factor, and not as a particular, accidental heresy, or as a distortion of normal development. The path that humanity entered upon in the modern era led precisely to liberalism and to the repudiation of God, tradition, community, ethnicity, empires and kingdoms. Such a path is tread entirely logically: having decided to liberate itself from everything that keeps man in check, the man of the modern era reached his logical apogee: before our eyes he is liberated from himself. The logic of world liberalism and globalisation pulls us into the abyss of postmodern dissolution and virtuality. Our youth already have one foot in it: the codes of liberal globalism are effectively introduced on an unconscious level—through habits, commercials, glamour, technology, the media, celebrities. The usual phenomenon now is the loss of identity, and already not simply only national or cultural identity, but even sexual, and soon enough even human identity. And defenders of human rights, not noticing the tragedy of the entire peoples that they sacrifice to their cruel plan of "the new world order," will howl tomorrow about transgressions against the rights of cyborgs or clones. . . .

Liberalism is an absolute evil; not only in its factual embodiment, but also in its fundamental theoretical presuppositions. And its victory, its world triumph, only underscores and displays those most wicked qualities, which earlier were veiled. . . . Only tearing it out by its roots can defeat this evil, and I do not exclude that such a victory will necessitate erasing from the face of the Earth those spiritual and physical halos from which arose the global heresy, which insists that "man is the measure of all things." Only a global crusade against the U.S., the West, globalisation, and their political-ideological expression, liberalism, is capable of becoming an adequate response.

This is Aleksandr Dugin's most convincing and prophetic presentation of Liberalism as the "absolute evil." He speaks here as if the principles and assumptions of global Liberalism were so firmly entrenched that the greater part of the world's population can hardly conceive any more of either a viable or a desirable alternative—as if the *status quo* had convincingly assumed the trappings of the *always so* (the ultimate goal of every *status quo*), leading to the inevitable conclusion that only a world revolution, or a world war, would be capable of overturning the Moloch of Liberalism. History, however, is filled with examples of regimes or worldviews that unexpectedly failed at the moment of their greatest apparent triumph; once their pinnacle is reached, there is nowhere for them to go but down, especially if internal contradictions deprive that regime or worldview of any intrinsic principle of stability. According to both Christian and Islamic eschatology, the Regime of Antichrist is predicted to be short-lived, since it is precisely the incarnation of the greatest possible degree of instability and self-contradiction. Since Dugin calls Liberalism the "absolute evil," he must present it as if it had nearly absolute power. This, however, is not entirely the case. From the point of view of the United States of America, the belly of the Liberal Beast, I can confidently report that Liberalism is a feeble old woman in heavy makeup. From a distance she may look like a young and vibrant movie star, but when you get nearer to her you can clearly see that her days are numbered—an impression, however, that is not meant to minimize the extent of her power and influence under present conditions. And the major sign of her approaching end is her very totalitarianism. Totalitarianism was intrinsic to Fascism, and could be pictured as a "regrettable but necessary phase" of Communism—but a Totalitarian Liberalism is a contradiction in terms. It is "a house divided against itself." It cannot stand. "Democracy" imposed by military force is in no way democracy. Immorality made compulsory by social engineering and mind control is in no way "self-actualization based on freedom from outdated moral constraints." And the deconstruction of the human form through genetic engineering, transgender surgery and the reduction of the body to an industrially-produced biotechnological device is certainly not "the full realization of the human potential." Destroying Liberalism is the least of our worries, in view of the fact that she continues to prove consummately effective in destroying herself—though her demise will certainly not be without its disasters, violent civil conflicts, painful reverses and disappointed false hopes. Our central attention should rather be directed to *resisting the influence* of Postmodern Liberalism on every level, and to conceiving of, and incarnating, the informing Principle that will invoke the appearance of the new phase, whether social or spiritual, that is destined to replace Liberalism—presuming, of course, that by the time Liberalism and Postmodernism have passed into history, there will still be history enough and world enough left for that Principle to take root—which is to say, in the face of the evils of Postmodern Liberalism, we should concentrate on forming a Remnant.

Hexagram 49 of the *I Ching*, "Revolution," also has the meaning of *molting*; in that supremely wise, spiritually luminous and solidly practical book, social forms are understood to change just as a bird drops its feathers or a snake sheds its skin. And the same can be said for the *manvantara* as a whole. Thus the process of "forming the structure of the new society within the shell of the old" (the motto of the Wobblies) also necessarily has an eschatological aspect to it, especially in times like these. As I have repeatedly pointed out, in the *milieu* of

Apocalypse, the function of a revolutionary vanguard begins to be modified, or replaced, by something that more closely resembles the religious idea of a Remnant. And in view of this dimension of eschatology, the seed of the new era must first be planted in Eternity, not in time. It is one of the intrinsic qualities of a Remnant that the form of life it adopts will be equally capable of preparing the ground for a new historical era on the terrestrial plane or for a new *aeon* in the world beyond time; the same paradigm, the identical design, will form the basis of both. No spiritual values need be "sacrificed" to satisfy the needs of an imagined historical future, nor must any truly human values be anathematized, as if the violation of our integral humanity could somehow be of help in founding a new human society, or else in preparing the soul to occupy a disembodied, posthumous state. If terrestrial history continues, or—as we are required to say in times like these—if it ends, the values and outlook of the Remnant, and the actions based upon them, will be the same. If the next age turns out to be a period of recognizable earthly time, or if it is destined to manifest on the far side of Apocalypse—or simply on the other side of death—as the Golden Age of the next *manvantara*, in either case the Remnant will be the seed.

A Quintessential Error and/or a Fundamental Lie

In Chapter Thirteen of *The Fourth Political Theory*, Aleksandr Dugin has provided me with a golden opportunity to rectify one of the most common errors of Modernism and Postmodernism; he did so when he called the idea that *man is the measure of all things* a "global heresy" that must be rooted out if Liberalism is to be defeated.

In order to grasp the full Counter-Initiatory import of Dugin's evaluation of "man is the measure of all things," we need to look at the history of this concept. In a Traditional context, to say that "man is the measure of all things" is to define Humanity is the "axial being" in terrestrial manifestation, the one who bears what the Qur'an calls the *Amana*, the Trust. Modernism, in the form of Secular Humanism, removed the Traditional spiritual content from this notion of man, after which Postmodernism had little difficulty in deconstructing it. Aleksandr Dugin attributes this rejection of man to the New Left, one of whose central principles, in Dugin's words (from his Chapter Eight), is: "The renunciation of man as the measure of all things ('the death of man' of Levi, 'the death of the author' of Barthes)." Unfortunately, the New Left—for which read Cultural Marxism—is also a central pillar of Postmodernism, the source of most of the things that Dugin claims to fear and hate, including the deconstruction of gender. Consequently we are once again confronted with the question of whether Aleksandr Dugin is simply confused, or whether his obvious contradictions are deliberately contrived to darken the minds of his readers so as to better manipulate them for his own unstated ends, or those of his handlers. Be that as it may, if any two things are certain at this point, they are, 1) that no man who builds his worldview on "the death of man" is worth listening to—unless, like Dugin, he expresses the lies and delusions of our time so clearly that he helps us to explode them—and, 2) that no man who accepts "the death of man"—even if, or *especially* if, he apparently does so in order to save man from that very death—can be in by any stretch of the imagination a Guénonian Traditionalist, or an Orthodox Christian, or any kind of Christian at all, or in any way a teller of truth, or in sense a man of honor, or any kind of example of *human* intelligence, in view of the fact that an immense vanity and a profound self-hatred have made a marriage of convenience in the depths of his soul. A man who glibly allows for the possibility that "man is dead" is declaring himself to be a dead man—and the words of a dead man are also dead. When Dugin proposes to tear down the Traditional centrality of Man as the "axial being" for terrestrial reality, supposedly in order to combat the Postmodern Liberal tendency to do precisely the same thing—when he invokes Cultural Marxism as an ally against a Postmodern Liberalism that is based to a great extent on Cultural Marxism—his intellectual self-contradiction has reached truly suicidal proportions, making it increasingly difficult for us to imagine that his duplicity is not entirely deliberate.

It is nonetheless still possible that Dugin is simply confused; therefore I will now address the usual contemporary misunderstanding of the notion that "man is the measure of all things." The phrase is attributed to the pre-Socratic Greek philosopher Protagoras. It can be taken in two ways: 1) its Traditional sense; 2) its Promethean sense. In the Traditional sense, what William Blake called "the Human Form Divine" is considered to be the central being for this terrestrial world, a being who is formed on all the Names of God because he "vertically" reflects, via the ontological hierarchy, God's primal Self-knowledge. We alone of all creatures can contemplate this earthly world with the Eye of God, seeing that—in Meister Eckhart's words—"the Eye through which I see God and the Eye through which He sees me is the same Eye." In Christian terms, the Second Person of the Blessed Trinity incarnated as Jesus Christ, a human being—not as an animal or a tree or a star or an angel or a rock or a robot—because humanity is the only mirror in which God can contemplate the fullness of His earthly reflection. In Islamic terms, only the *Insan al-Kamil*, the Complete Man—the one who has realized and actualized his *fitrah*, his human essence—is *effectively* host to all the Names; this is why Adam, since he was the archetype of that essence, was able to inform all the angels of their names in the celestial realm before Allah sent him to earth [cf. Q. 2:31–33].

In the Promethean sense, "man is the measure of all things" is taken to indicate the *hubris* of the human race in a state of self-idolatry, the idea that humanity has the right to manipulate the natural world and the human form to any degree and in any manner whatsoever, whenever it suites our whim, simply because we *can*. Every revealed religion and every true philosophy, on the other hand, understands "man is the measure of all things" in its Traditional sense, while the Promethean distortion of this phrase, which has grown up mostly since the Renaissance, is one of the pillars of Modernist Humanism, and even (in a backhanded way) of Postmodern Deconstructionism, since only he who is the measure of all things in the Promethean sense has the "right"—and certainly the power—to suicidally shatter that measure. The reign of atheistic, materialistic scientism began with man pridefully asserting his Promethean "right" to appropriate the secrets of Nature and use them however he saw fit, and the Will of God be damned—a *hubris* that is now coming to its inevitable and supremely ironic end with his assertion of his Postmodern "right" to deconstruct himself, according to Albert Camus' theory that suicide is the great act of human self-determination. (Camus' inverted theory will become true if only we turn it right side up again so that it reads: "Humanity's claim to the right of self-determination outside the Will of God is suicide." This is why the suicide of Judas is the perfect consequence and exegesis of his betrayal of Christ.)

Contemporary scientistic mythology pretends to reject the doctrine that "man is the measure of all things." Followers of this mythology say: "We used to believe, when we believed in God, that humanity was the pinnacle of creation; now we know that we are nothing but miniscule microbes crawling upon an insignificant speck of dust floating aimlessly in the vastness of the cosmos. Science has finally taught man humility."

Humility? Are we really being asked to consider the genetic engineers, the builders of nuclear weapons, the technological mind-controllers as examples of this virtue? Certainly modern science has been of great help in ridding us of our self-respect, but as far as our vanity and megalomania are concerned, it has only poured gasoline on the fire, thereby illustrating one of the first axioms of spiritual psychology: "Vanity and self-respect vary in inverse proportion."

The problem with Aleksandr Dugin is the same as the problem with 21st-century humanity: *He no longer knows what a human being is.* If he did, he would never even think of proposing that the destruction of Liberalism might require us to willingly accept the death of man! In doing so he is acting as a kind of intellectual suicide bomber, as if he believed that it is perfectly kosher to blow ourselves up as long as we take Liberalism down with us.

Man truly *is* the measure of all things—but only because God is the measure of man. If man presumes to measure himself outside the Presence of God, then man is the measure of nothing.

Dugin's Way Out—Will He Take It?

Aleksandr Dugin, in this chapter and elsewhere, has produced one of the best critiques we have of late-Liberal Postmodernism and its role in globalization. Unfortunately, he can think of nothing to replace it with but more Postmodernism; his Fourth Political Theory is every bit as centerless, fragmented, sinister and chaotic—every bit as *postmodern*—as the Postmodernism he attacks. And the supreme irony of Dugin's dilemma is that the perfect alternative worldview to the Postmodern Chaos he hates—a Chaos that affects the "Atlantean" (Western) world and permeates the waves of influence spreading from it, as well as his own self-sabotaging attempts to grapple with it—is staring him in the face, but he doesn't recognize it. Its name is "Traditional Metaphysics." He even claims a major contemporary school of such metaphysics as part of his Fourth Political Theory, the Traditionalist School founded by René Guénon. Unfortunately, he is completely lacking in any true, organic, traditional sensibility, otherwise known as *a sense of the Sacred*; his worldview is as anti-Traditionalist, and Counter-Traditional, as it is possible to imagine, consequently he has virtually no idea of what Guénon and his successors intended and achieved. It's as if he possesses the Ultimate Weapon against Postmodernism but is clueless as to what it is or how to use it. If he were to arrive at even a basic understanding of the Platonic tradition, for example—or of Taoism—or of Sufism—or of the Vedanta—or of the Patristics of the Greek Fathers that his professed religion of Orthodox Christianity might still provide him with, he would be able to grasp at least the major outlines of what René Guénon accomplished, and the true nature of the sources he drew upon. The fact is, however, that even though he has the audacity to claim Traditional Metaphysics as part of his Fourth Political Theory, *he has never really studied it*. If he had, he would waste no time in throwing his Metaphysics of Chaos onto the scrap heap and Martin Heidegger along with it, and gladly embracing the integral and unified Vision that would swiftly dissolve the last lingering, ghostly shadows of the Postmodernism polluting his soul. He would *know* what he hates, and have real power against it, because he would be standing in the presence of the undeniable Reality that absolutely refutes it. But instead—and this is truly tragic—he gives every indication of being *possessed by* what he hates; if, as he says, Postmodern Liberalism is on its way to becoming the only conceivable social and political reality on a global scale, then (to a certain degree) it has become the only conceivable social and political reality *for him*. His soul is filled with the Postmodern Chaos he has declared total war against—which means that, in essence, he has opened total war against himself, and is consequently defeated before he begins. But if he could purify himself of Postmodernism, if he could cast the Global Atlanticist Hegemony out of his soul, then waves of liberation would spread from that act until they touched everything within his circle of influence. Brazilian educator and philosopher Paolo Friere (1921–1997) developed the theory of "internalized oppression," the idea that the American Empire occupies not just the economy or (mostly through proxies) the physical territory of the peoples under its neo-colonial rule, but also their souls. The Gospel of Mark recognizes the same condition in terms of the subversive spiritual effect of the Roman Empire on the collective psyche its colony, Palestine. When Jesus asked the name of the evil spirit possessing the "lone demoniac" in Mark 5:9, the demon answered, "My name is Legion, for we are many"; the collectivization and fragmentation of demoniac's soul, his reduction to the disintegrated state of a "dividual," was thus organically related to his individual isolation, these being the two inseparable faces of social alienation. But just as a demon can only be cast out by a higher spiritual Power, so a chaotic worldview or a degenerate philosophy can only be cast out by a higher intellectual Conception; in the words of William Blake already quoted above, "Whenever any Individual Rejects Error & Embraces Truth, a Last Judgment passes upon that Individual." Given that the age of secular ideologies pretending to universality has passed, Traditional Metaphysics is the only conception of the nature of things still available to us that can fulfill that function. It may not be capable of generating a viable political praxis on a large scale, but it does have the power, by virtue of its ability to unveil and purify the *Nous*, of establishing spiritual Truth in the human Heart—and everything else follows from that. Unfortunately, Aleksandr Dugin is almost entirely ignorant of Traditional Metaphysics, even though he repeatedly invokes it; he is also ignorant of his ignorance. Before he again names Guénonian Traditionalism as an element of his Fourth Political Theory, let him *study* it for once, let him learn what it is; then he might begin to grasp what it requires of him.

5

Critique of
The Fourth Political Theory
Part II

On Chapter Ten: "The Ontology of the Future"

"THE ONTOLOGY of the Future" is undoubtedly the most metaphysically significant, and disturbing, chapter in *The Fourth Political Theory*. In it Aleksandr Dugin struggles to imagine how humanity might find a real Self, and thus have a real future—or *any* future. And his struggle is entirely justified, because humanity has indeed lost itself; we no longer know what a human being is, and consequently our collective future is in the gravest doubt.

Strangely, however, Dugin searches for an answer to our dilemma among the very thinkers whose intellectual tradition he claims—following Heidegger—has reached its terminus: the tradition of western philosophy divorced from religion, whose practitioners have exhausted the Logos and ended by deconstructing it. He turns to Kant, to Husserl, German idealist philosophers who might have had sporadic flashes of insight into the common metaphysical heritage of the human race that Guénon called Tradition, but whose "systems" are pathetically incomplete compared with the knowledge of the ancients, especially the great prophets, saints, sages, avatars and culture-heroes of Asia. If Dugin extols the races and traditions of the Eurasian heartland, why does he turn for his ideas to the despised secular West, to the same cultural poison that Peter the Great forced Russia to swallow? There is more true philosophy in the little finger of Saint Maximos the Confessor, by virtue of his full Christianization of the Platonic Tradition, than in the whole body of less-than-fully informed German idealists, who have proved beyond the shadow of a doubt that the great medieval Christian synthesis, broken by the Renaissance and the Enlightenment, can in no way be put together again by *individual* thinkers following their *individual* obsessions. Dugin claims to be an Orthodox Christian, so why doesn't he turn to the great intellectual tradition of Patristics, and the spiritual and contemplative tradition of Hesychasm based upon it? Apparently Orthodoxy is nothing to him but a sect of stubborn, conservative Old Believers who—admirably enough—reject the modern world in its entirety, but who nonetheless, in intellectual terms, are rather dim bulbs. Tolstoy was torn between the gilded drawing-rooms of St. Petersburg and the earthiness and piety of the Russian peasant. Dugin no longer has the dawning-rooms to contend with—whatever drawing-rooms are left have become museums—but will he finally do his best to follow Tolstoy by renouncing his seat at Moscow University, along with the whole of western culture introduced by Peter the Great, by becoming some kind of occult or religious crank in the approved Russian style? Once Tolstoy had identified *intelligence* with the West, he could only conceive of the great Heart of Russia as a vast, rude, warm, earthy stupidity. He wanted to *improve* that stupidity of course, he wanted to educate the peasants; still, his attraction to peasant life, in view of his loathing for the Frenchified intellectual/aesthetic world of the St. Petersburg aristocracy, was too great a temptation to resist. If Dugin is both an intellectual and a Russian Orthodox Christian, let him recover the *intellectual* tradition of Orthodoxy, and do what he can to make it the intellectual tradition of Russia. On his website http://www.4pt.su/, in an article available as of March, 2018, Dugin does indeed call for a renewal of Christian metaphysics; he believes it should be based on a study of René Guénon. Guénon, however, though he was conversant with the Aristotelian Thomism of Roman Catholicism and had interesting things to say about the esoteric Christianity of Dante Alighieri (the doctrines of the Fedeli d'Amore, Dante's initiatory order, were based on a kind of esoteric Aristotelianism), was largely ignorant of Hesychasm and the metaphysics of the Greek Fathers. In addition to Guénon, a renewal of Christian metaphysics in Russia should be based, at least to start with, on the **Philokalia**, as well as the writings of the more metaphysical of the Greek Fathers, beginning with Dionysius the (Pseudo-) Areopagite, Maximos the Confessor, Origen, Evagrius of Pontus, Simeon the New Theologian, Gregory Nazienzen, Gregory of Nyssa, and Gregory Palamas.

Dugin apparently realizes that, without an accurate philosophical understanding of *time*, effective action is impossible, therefore he scours Kant, and especially Husserl, looking for a true theory of time, a valid doctrine dealing with the relationship between time and Eternity—but what he finds is garbled, contradictory and incomplete. At least when James Joyce said "history is a nightmare from which I am trying to awake," traditional Catholic doctrine, as interpreted by scholastic philosophy, was still available to back him up, one of the teachings of which is that God lives in an Eternal Present. One would have hoped that it would be equally possible for Dugin to draw upon the Eastern Orthodox doctrine of *aeonian time*, the notion of an entire temporal cycle perceivable as a single spacial form, as the 12 hours of the day all appear together on the dial of a clock, but apparently the Communist interlude was able to so de-Christianize the collective psyche of Russia that this never occurred to him. So he was forced to turn to muddled thinkers like Kant, whose doctrine of time Dugin presents as follows:

> We could question the solidity of ontological arguments concerning the most evident moment—the present. This recalls Kant and his doubts about the inner being of the object. The fact of simply perceiving something is not enough for a definitive declaration of its being. This is the *Ding an sich* (the-thing-in-itself) conundrum of Kantian philosophy. Not *pure reason*, but only *practical reason* gives being to an object, based on the moral imperative. An object should have being. It would be good for it to have it. Therefore, it has to have it.
>
> If the "being" of the present, as the most evident of all the moments of time, can be seriously put in doubt, then we are arriving at an interesting point: all three moments of time are then ontologically unprovable and unverifiable and concern only the gnoseologic level, relating to the philosophy of knowledge and the human faculty for learning. This is pessimistic concerning the present, whose reality we habitually take for granted, but is optimistic concerning the two other moments, the past and the future. The past and the future thereby acquire equal consideration with the present. From the perspective of pure reason, the present, past and future all have equal phenomenological value.

I am certainly no competent scholar of Kant, but his notion of time as Dugin presents it, though I can't be sure that my impression of it is accurate, sounds to me roughly like this:

"We can't sure whether a clam will be in the box tomorrow because tomorrow hasn't come yet. But by the same token, we can't be sure if there was a clam in the box yesterday because our memory might be faulty, or maybe we never opened the box. Nor can we be sure if there is a clam in the box right now, even if we do open the box, because the clam we see might be a figment of our imagination. But that's not so bad, because it means that the past clam, the present clam and the future clam are all equally uncertain—and since we can be reasonably sure that such things as clams exist, then the future clam, since it is just as real as the past or present clams, must be a *real clam*." In other words, Dugin has not demonstrated that Kant equally validated the reality of past, present and future, but only that he distributed his uncertainty about the reality of the present to the future and the past.

And if we can never be sure that the object we perceive exists, or that our phenomenal experience of it matches the *noumenon*, what the object is in itself—and this, incidentally, is one of the major tenets of Postmodernism—

then we can never come into a true and effective relationship to the world, but must remain sealed within the bubble of our own subjectivity, our own *individuality*. Furthermore, speaking in terms of human relationships, if I can't be sure that a woman I am attracted to actually exists, or if my image of her has anything at all to do with who she really is (in terms of pure reason), but I nonetheless decide to believe and act as if she exists so as to start a relationship with her (this being practical reason), I had better hope that she never begins to suspect how my mind actually works, or else—if she knows what's good for her—she will be out of my life like a shot. In other words, Kant's critique of pure reason results in a kind of mental illness, an agnostic solipsism according to which I can never be sure if anyone or anything thing other than myself actually exists.

William Blake has the best answer I have yet found to this *axiomatic doubt* of Emmanuel Kant:

> He who Doubts from what he sees
> Will ne'er Believe, do what you Please.
> If the Sun & Moon should doubt,
> They'd immediately Go out.
>
> [from "Auguries of Innocence"]
>
> Serpent Reasonings us entice
> Of Good & Evil: Virtue & Vice…
> Two Horn'd Reasoning Cloven Fiction
> In Doubt which is Self contradiction
> A dark Hermaphrodite We stood…[1]
>
> [from "The Gates of Paradise"]

Kant's idea of a strict distinction between things as we perceive them and things as they are in themselves, between *phenomenon* and *noumenon*, effectively destroys both the cohesion of humanity, since each individual now inhabits his or her own separate perceptual bubble—this notion being the philosophical origin of the *individualism* that Dugin pretends to reject—and also the unity of the world, since these separate perceptual bubbles have lost the ability to consciously converge upon a real external object. In reality, however,

---

1. This last line is a reference to the separation of Eve from Adam considered as a fracturing of the Primordial Androgyne at the moment when direct, integral perception on the level of *Intellectus* or *Nous*, the faculty that Blake called "Vision"—also known as cardiac consciousness—fell to the level of *ratio* or *dianoia*—cerebral consciousness, thus producing an hermaphroditic duality. As for the potential criticism that William Blake, whose Christianity certainly embraced heterodox, quasi-Gnostic elements, was only one more "individual genius" like Kant or Husserl, he was recognized as an exponent of Tradition in the Guénonian sense by Ananda Coomaraswamy, who quotes him side-by-side with the likes of Shankaracharya and Thomas Aquinas. Here we can see how Tradition is not so much an "approved canon" as it is an established level of metaphysical knowledge.

they do converge. Just as the true distance of a star can be determined by parallax, by the triangulation of measurements taken at several different points in the earth's orbit around the sun, so the inevitable convergence of different impressions of an object—if we accept this inevitability and so regain our ability to discern it—proves the existence of a real external object which is continuous with our various perceptions of it, though there will always be more to that object than our impressions of it can catch. In other words, *phenomena triangulate the noumenon.* In the same way, the incomplete yet inevitable convergence of many different religious beliefs and worldviews proves the objective reality of God and the metaphysical order—this being one of the implications of Guénon's and Schuon's doctrine of the Transcendent Unity of Religions, which clearly rejects Kant.

Now Dugin turns to Heidegger's mentor, Edmund Husserl:

> Husserl proposed to study time through the use of music. The consciousness of hearing the music is not based on the strict identification of notes sounding in a concrete, discrete moment. Hearing music is something different from hearing an individual note that sounds now, in the present. The consciousness of music occurs by hearing an individual note that sounds now, in the present, as well as recalling the past notes that are dissolving little by little into nothingness. However, their resonance persists in the consciousness and gives music its aesthetic sense. Husserl calls it "the continuous instance." The past is present in the present. The present thus becomes continuous and includes the past as a vanishing presence.

Granted.

> This is the methodological key for the understanding of history. History is awareness of the presence of the past in the present. The vanishing events continue to sound in the act of recalling of them. Clio and Polyhymnia, the Muses of History and Time respectively in Greek mythology, are sisters. This recalling is necessary to give us our sense of the present. The *anamnesis* of Plato has the same function. The soul should recall the hidden past of its previous lives in order to reconstruct the wholeness of the melody of destiny. Only thus could it be played harmoniously.

Very well.

> The future is continuous in the present. Not the moment of *novum,* but the process of the fading of the present into the past. The future is the tail-end of the present, its resonance. We live the future just now, and already now, when we play the note of the melody of life. The future is the process of the death of the present, attention to the dissolution of melody into the totality of harmony....

Here confusion develops. The future continuously *becomes* the present, but the future is emphatically *not* the fading of the present into the past; this impossible contortion of the definition of time is based on the fact that Husserl's intuition of Eternity, while not entirely erroneous, was unclear and incomplete. In musical terms, the *shapeliness* of a piece by Bach or Mozart allows us to anticipate, up to a point, the passage that is about to "come to pass"—the accuracy or inaccuracy of our anticipation is what provides the music with some of its piquancy—but this in no way indicates the actual existence of the future of the music as part of its past (a fact that is more clearly demonstrated, for example, in the music of John Cage). It is possible to say, however, that the *space* of anticipation and the *space* of memory are the same space. In the practice of meditation we attend to the rising and the dissolution of thought; in doing so we understand that the "place" that thought comes from and the "place" it disappears into are the same—a place, or void, that remains unchanged in itself whether or not thought is present. And since the void that both gives rise to thought and witnesses the extinction of thought is a single reality, we can't definitively say whether thought arises from the past or from the future. *Thought coming from the past* posits past impressions, what the Hindus call the *vasanas* or the *samskaras*, as the cause of the modifications of the thought-substance, while *thought coming from the future* indicates that we cannot know which past impression will ripen into what present thought until that thought appears. Thought, like music, is time. But since we can neither anticipate the past of thought nor remember its future, we could say that thought only truly exists in the Present Moment—except for the fact that, when the Present Moment is perfectly realized, thought disappears; this is due to the fact that the Present Moment is *not* a moment in time. Therefore, from the standpoint of the unchanging Eternity that underlies time and witnesses time, time is seen to be an illusion. If time is subjective, the origin of time is the deluded empirical subject, not the Radical Subject who occupies Eternity. (The term "Radical Subject" was used by Cultural Marxist Herbert Marcuse to denote his particular modification or understanding of the empirical subject, whereas I am using it as synonymous with the *Atman*, the Vedantic Absolute Self—a definition that Dugin himself, below, at least seems to be approaching.) On the other hand, the only way for the empirical self to overcome the set of attachments that cause it to experience its own separate time, which are based on unconscious self-will, is for it to renounce its own time, its own intentionality, and submit to God's Time, God's Will, God's Intentionality. A good example of this submission is the Muslim daily prayer, by which Divine Time, five times a day, is given precedence over individual, worldly time.

The *novum* appears in the future only when the harmony is lost, when our sounds that we hear [*phrase garbled in translation?*]. Momentarily, they simply make no sense. That is the novum: spontaneous attention falls asleep, and then suddenly we awaken and cannot identify the incomprehension of what is going on in the ecstasy of time. It is the nature of discreet, discontinuous events. It is the suspended moment of being without history, and hence without a sense of awareness and consciousness.

Apparently Husserl sometimes dozed off while listening to long musical performances (probably Wagner). Waking abruptly, the *present* musical moment (the *novum* or novelty) made no sense to him because its context, the shape of the musical passage as defined by its past and future, was lacking. The shock of the *isolated* (and therefore meaningless) present, however, is due to constriction of consciousness, to a reduction of the present moment to what Blake called "a moving white dot," an abstract "present" whose only claim to that title is the bare fact that it is neither the past nor the future. The void underlying time, however—the Eternity which is the ultimate context of time—is not an abstract, constricted, dimensionless present, but a *spacious* present (an intuition Husserl was approaching in his notion of the "continuous instance"), the very Eternal Present by virtue of which God witnesses the totality of past, present and future as simultaneous—which, incidentally, is also the Space which, in Guénon's eschatology, witnesses the acceleration, dissolution, and end of Time at the close of the *manvantara*. When we first enter into meditative consciousness, time appears to speed up because we are becoming increasingly aware of the flow of thought. This, however, is due to the fact that our consciousness is detaching from time, becoming more spatialized, coming closer to the state of pure witnessing. And just as thought, when it reaches "infinite velocity," dissolves into empty space in the practice of meditation, so the dawning of Eternity as the *manvantara* hurtles towards its end transforms the Time of the cycle now ending into the Space which will give birth to the cycle about to be born. Likewise the end of obsessive, past-impression-driven thought in a blur of speed makes an empty space for the arising of a new order of thought, one in which integral Form, more spacial than temporal—the Reign of Quality—replaces nearly "pure" sequence—the Reign of Quantity.

Dugin goes on:

Edmund Husserl dug much deeper into the phenomenology of time. He discovered the new instance of consciousness lying underneath the level where the nature of time, as illuminated by music, is perceived. According to Husserl, beneath this level there is another, ultimate one, which is responsible for our perception of what is *now* with the force of evidence, and a much more intensive taste of reality that recalls the ever-dying past. This instance is consciousness itself, the consciousness as such that precedes the intentionality and the dualist nature of apprehension, being necessarily divided into two parts—the perceived and the perceiving. In the present, the consciousness perceives itself and nothing else. That is the ultimate experience of the last source of reality. According to Husserl, the foundation of all consciousness is transcendental subjectivity, from whence it conceives itself as a kind of short circuit. This experience is self-referential. In it, there is the perception of pure being as the presence of the subjectivity of consciousness.

Here Husserl approaches an understanding of the *Atman*, the transcendent/immanent Self, the Absolute Witness. It is precisely at this point, however, that we must be absolutely certain that the "self-referential subject," "pure being as the presence of the subjectivity of consciousness," is not simply a sublimation and mystification of the narcissistic self-reference of the individualistic philosopher himself when attempting to understand the essence of Being and Consciousness by looking into his own being and consciousness, but doing so with no reference to God as a transcendent and immanent metaphysical Reality that does not depend upon him and has no need of him. At this point we would do well to take a look at the *precise* description and definition of the Transcendental Subject, the *Atman*, provided by Frithjof Schuon in **Survey of Metaphysics and Esoterism**:

> When the perception of the Object is so intense that the consciousness of subject vanishes, the Object becomes Subject, as is the case in the union of love; but then the word "subject" no longer has the meaning of a complement that is fragmentary by definition; it means on the contrary a totality which we conceive as subjective because it is conscious. When we place the emphasis on objective Reality—which then takes precedence in the relation between the subject and the object—the subject becomes object in the sense that, being determined entirely by the object, it forgets the element consciousness; in this case the subject, inasmuch as it is a fragment, is absorbed by the Object inasmuch as it is a totality, as the accident is reintegrated into the Substance. But the other manner of seeing things, which reduces everything to the Subject, takes precedence over the point of view that grants primacy to the Object: if we adore God, it is not for the simple reason that He presents Himself to us as an objective reality of a dizzying and crushing immensity—otherwise we would adore the stars and nebulae—but it is above all because this reality, a priori objective, is the greatest of subjects; because He is the absolute Subject of our contingent subjectivity; because He is at once all-powerful, omniscient and benefic Consciousness.
>
> In the infinite and absolute Subject whose Object is on the one hand its own Infinitude and on the other its Universal Unfolding, there is no scission into subject and object on any ontological plane whatever . . . for in this case the Subject is not a complementary pole, it is simply That which is. If we nonetheless term it "Subject," it is to express that *Atma* is the absolute Witness, at once transcendent and immanent, of all things. . . .

Returning now to Dugin's presentation of Husserl:

> This short circuit causes all kinds of dualities to be born—the logical ones and the temporal ones. The necessity of stopping this trauma is manifest in

the creation of time, the articulation of the three moments of time. Consciousness of time is necessary to hide the present, which is the traumatic experience of the self-referential nature of pure consciousness. Intentionality and logical judgments are all rooted in this evasion of the perception of the pain of the void whereby consciousness becomes aware of itself.

Such an attitude to the levels of consciousness explains the origin of time as the evasion of the present, and the unbearable tension of the pure presence of the same. This tension is immediately relieved by the expansion of all the imaginable types of dualities that constitute the textures of the continuous process of time. The model of this process is the creation of the three moments of time. The logical and spatial symmetries follow—such dualities as yes/no, true/false, high/low, right/left, here/there, and so on. Before/after belongs to the same cadence. Time constitutes consciousness running from the unbearable confrontation with itself. But this confrontation is inevitable, so the present, and the high precision of its existential perception, is born.

By "short circuit" Dugin apparently means something like the dissolution of temporal sequence into an immediate self-knowledge on the part of pure consciousness. And Husserl's "trauma of Eternity" is, precisely, the momentary shock experienced by the ego when confronted by its own illusory nature—especially outside the context of concrete contemplative practice, where the death of the ego is both a foregone conclusion and a desired outcome—something like the "freak out" experienced by someone who ingests LSD out of mere curiosity and gets more than he bargained for. Furthermore, his insight that "Time constitutes consciousness running from the unbearable confrontation with itself" into all sorts of dualities is profound. This insight is entirely in line with the Traditional doctrine that all world-and-self manifestation happens by virtue of polarity, via the generation of the *dvandvas* or pairs-of-opposites, and also with the doctrine found in the **Bardo Thödöl** or **Tibetan Book of the Dead** that if the consciousness of the newly-deceased cannot withstand the shock of the direct confrontation with Reality in the *Chikhai Bardo*—of the dawning of the Clear Light of the Void, "thrilling, blissful, radiant," which is nothing other than the reality of that person's own mind—because it has had little or no experience of this Reality during life, the "soul" will flee from it, thus entering the *Chönyid Bardo* where the Archetypes are witnessed—in Sufi terms, the Names of God—which are on a lower ontological level than the direct confrontation with *Al-Dhat*, the Divine Essence.

But Dugin's conception of the implications of Husserl's doctrine, while in certain respects profoundly right, also has a fairly obvious dark side, since when he speaks of "the pain of the void whereby consciousness becomes aware of itself," he limits that void to the sort of pain that only the illusion of time—in other words, *distraction*—can sedate. The Void whereby consciousness becomes aware of itself is, precisely, the "Divine Emptiness" of the Godhead, the Reality that Sri Ramana Maharshi knew as the *Atman*, the Self. The ego experiences this Void as pain, as the terror of death; the authentic human self in full submission to, and annihilation in, God, experiences it as Bliss, Mercy, the Peace that passeth understanding [Philippians 4:47]. Dugin, however, does not allow for the latter alternative. To him, man is apparently all ego, therefore flight from God— that is, denial of the Truth—is our only recourse. (I well remember the night when, after ingesting a dose of psilocybin, I experienced the Void beyond the boundaries of the ego as pain and nothing else—pain because I had approached the Reality that kills the ego without first intending the release of that ego, or understanding what such a release might require. This resulted in eight hours of sitting in one place, doing nothing but *willing to breathe*, since if I didn't consciously remember to breathe, my body would not breathe for me: the perfect image of the illusion of self-creation by means of self-will.)

> What is most important in this interpretation of the morphology of time? The idea that time precedes the object, and that in the construction of time we should seek an *inner* depth of consciousness, rather than a consciousness rooted in *outer* phenomena constituted by the subjective process of traumatic self-awareness. The world around us becomes what it is by the fundamental action of *presencing* accomplished by the mind. When the mind sleeps, reality lacks the sense of present existence. It is fully immersed in a continuous dream. The world is created by time, and time, in its turn, is the manifestation of self-aware subjectivity, an *intrasubjectivity.*

Here Husserl (or Dugin) loses the thread—because in reality it is not time that precedes the object, but Eternity; "presencing" is not the creation of time, but the recognition of Eternity via the insight that time is a subset of Eternity, and in the understanding that the Present Moment is *not a moment in time*. But because Husserl, for all his depth of insight, was operating outside of Tradition, which necessarily includes the full doctrine of the Absolute—that is, of God— his grasp of Eternity was shaky; he had no constancy of contemplative practice to ground his flashes of insight nor orthodoxy of doctrine to provide them with the necessary intellectual context. And his inability to see the future as anything more that the recycled past is also a function of this lack, seeing that, for those to whom God is a living Reality, the future is the realm of Providence, the doorway through which the unforeseeable Will of God is constantly arriving in the Now. It is true that the Hindu doctrine of the origin of thought in past impressions also apparently ignores Divine Providence, but this is due to the fact that the contemplative practice on which this insight is based is negative or apophatic, having as its goal the exhaustion of the obscuring modifications of the mental substance so as to unveil the Presence of God. In the more positive or cataphatic contemplative practices of the Abrahamic religions, the possibility of thought being directly inspired by God is allowed for, which is why the characteristic exemplar of these traditions is the prophet rather than the yogi. Yet the cataphatic path too has as its ultimate goal the transcendence of thought in the Divine Reality.

In the second half of the chapter, Dugin lets us know why an understanding of time is so important to him: because it proves the *present reality* of the future. "These remarks" he says, "lead us to considerations of the future—prognostication, projection, and analysis of the future." He concludes that:

> The future is already laid out with the sense of music. History is not only our memory of the past. It is also the explication of the present and the experience of the future. When we understand history and its logic well, we can easily guess what will follow. . . .

Also of crucial importance, beyond an understanding of the distinction between time and Eternity, is the question of whether or not there is a *living relationship* between them:

> It is possible to be awoken by the strength of this inner light of self-reflection. In this traumatic situation, we discover our identity between the most inner and outer levels of our consciousness. We live in the creation of the external world by the internal self. But that is no longer history; it is breaking through history. . . .

Truer words were never written. But can the breakthrough of Eternity into time, Dugin implicitly asks—the vision of the creation of the outer world by the inner Self—in any way affect history? It is true, he says, that time can be conceived or organized in different ways: cyclical time; traditional time which strives to preserve and propagate the norms laid down in the sacred past; the inexorable fate of outer, material time; or messianic, chiliastic time that waits for the "immanentizing of the eschaton." But do any of these constructions of time have the power to open the human race—or a given human collective—to new, real, realizable possibilities? Following Kant, Dugin asserts that "Time is . . . subjective. It is the transcendental subject that installs time in [*our*] perception of the object." The Transcendental Subject, however, is not merely the reality we begin to get intimations of when we investigate our own subjectivity; it is far beyond that, beyond everything in the world of "name and form," while at the same time being the Source of everything and the Essence of everything: time, space, matter, energy, consciousness, intentionality; it is the fundamental, constitutive Being of whatever possesses being. The Transcendental Subject "installs time in our perception of the object" only insofar as it provides a timeless point in relation to which time can be seen to pass. Dugin goes on to say:

> This subjectivity of time does not mean that prognostication will be self-fulfilling prophesy, as per Robert K. Merton, nor that any event is realisable a

priori. The future is strictly determined, not something voluntary. Time, being historical, is predefined precisely by its historical content. The subject is not free from its structure, and more than this, it is absolutely enslaved by it. Time needs the future as a void for the continuous fading of the present and, partially, of the past. Without the future, the subject will not have the space necessary to evade, running from the impossible encounter with itself.... The frozen moment of the present without the future is that of death. Society needs the future to run from itself further and further. The chronicle of such a run is the sense of history. Society requires a narrative of the past. The future is predefined by the structure of the subject. That is why the future is strictly defined.

Here Dugin wisely renounces the magical illusion that the vision of Eternity will give the one who entertains it the power to manipulate time, that "the subjectivity of time" implies the power to alter events by altering human consciousness and belief, as in the "self-fulfilling prophesy" theory of Robert K. Merton, which implies that in order to secure a desirable future, we should be sure to make the right prophesies. Merton's conception is nothing other than the sociological application of Norman Vincent Peale's "power of positive thinking," which for a while seemed like a self-evident truth to American society in its expansive phase of entrepreneurial Capitalism. The positive-thinking belief-system was a sort of variation on the Calvinist myth of the eternal predestination of the elect translated into economic terms as Max Weber understood it—an elect status which nonetheless had to be realized and validated by hard work and cutthroat competition in order to prove that one actually was a member of this elect and not just some "loser," this being the Calvinist/economic version of the traditional Catholic notion of the "sinner." But while the he sinner can repent and be forgiven, the "loser" can never be forgiven, but must simply resign himself to his liquidation as "unfit" in Social Darwinist terms. But since the losers are no longer part of Progress any more than the New Zealand Kiwi or the Dodo bird are still part of Evolution, and given that Progress is Reality, they can be safely forgotten, thus allowing the survivors, the de facto "real people," to concentrate on the obvious truth—obvious at least to anyone who "counts"—that Progress is real and inevitable. And since everything was felt to be possible, everything was growing and developing, it was also theoretically possible for anyone to "get ahead"; all that was needed was for him or her to envision the desired future and then work toward its realization both as guided by and empowered by that vision. This myth became sublimated and volatilized, however, by the New Age movement as its concrete realization in economic terms became less and less possible to the majority of Americans. Though the goal was still to "manifest abundance," magical thinking designed to accomplish this was progressively divorced from the work ethic, and "success" was increasingly defined, under the influence of motion pictures, television and psychedelic drugs, in terms of *commodified experience*, thus preparing the collective psyche for the emergence of cyberspace. Various mythic reflections of the impending death of the Myth of Progress began to appear, such as the notion—supposedly based on modern physical cosmology or quantum mechanics—that there are such things as "probable selves" traveling along "alternate time-lines." To the degree that actual linear progress toward a plausible future became blocked, the belief grew up that if things weren't working well for you in your present time-line, all you had to do was "change channels" so as to shift to another time-line and another self. Thus the New Age movement represented the simultaneous apotheosis and deconstruction of both "the power of positive thinking" and the Protestant ethic as the spirit of Capitalism—a development that was paralleled by the shift of Capitalism itself from its entrepreneurial phase to its monopolistic transnational phase, finally resulting in the American society of today, where economic "upward mobility" is at an historic low, lower even than in the more class-stratified society of Britain. Simply stated, the future has turned into a *wall* in America (as it has, in different ways, all over the world), a wall composed of the apparent inevitabilities of mass impoverishment, across-the-board moral and social breakdown, and the degradation of the natural environment by global warming, leading to the inundation of the coasts by rising ocean levels, as well as the horrors of transhumanism—which, rather unconvincingly, presents itself as a form of *hope*—and many other factors. The Myth of Progress, without first slowing down (which is impossible by definition), has now driven straight into that wall, and shattered to bits. Some of these "bits" are still pretty potent, especially those that have to do with technological development and economic ambition, but the percentage of the population that these motivations effectively apply to continues to shrink.

The above passage, however, also contains moments of profound darkness. To begin with, while the empirical subject is immersed in history, as Dugin recognizes, the Radical Subject is entirely free of it; unless this distinction is made, one will find oneself asserting that God—Who, insofar as He is "the absolute Subject of our contingent subjectivity," is identical with the Radical Subject, but not with the contingent subject—is bound to history and strictly determined by it, as Teilhard de Chardin, the process theologians, and other deeply confused thinkers seem to believe; this, of course, is impossible, since it reduces God to an as-yet-unrealized potential, thus making Him something less than God. God is the Absolute, and the Absolute is not bound to, determined by, or contingent upon, anything whatsoever. Furthermore, if "The future is strictly determined, not something voluntary," then there can be no such thing as Divine Intentionality or Providence; likewise if mechanistic determinism (either material or psychological) and the "voluntarism" of self-will are the only two alternatives, there can be no such thing as the Will of God considered as something that transcends mechanistic determinism, or that contravenes the individual will of the disobedient, or that guides, aids and confirms the individual will of the faithful, or that exists as a Transcendent/Immanent Reality to which the individual will can submit. And if the only two alternatives are fatalism and self-will, then—given that both fatalism and self-will are intolerable—the one addicted to fatalism will be attracted to self-will for relief from despair, just as the self-will addict will seek out despair as a sedative against the ruthless drive and false hope of self-will. This is one of the Laws of Alienation to which those who have no effective belief in God are necessarily subject. That this group includes Aleksandr Dugin can be clearly discerned when we compare his "metaphysic" in the present chapter—that the future is strictly determined—with the completely contradictory "metaphysic" enunciated in his Chapter Twelve: that thought alone has the power to alter circumstances because thought is magic. And there is no way out of this grim pendulum-swing between fatalism and self-will except the full submission of self-will to God, by which fate is transformed into Providence. Without God nothing is left but the eternal conflict between fate and self-will—fate inflaming self-will in an attempt to break free from the Eternal Return, self-will exhausting itself and dying back into fate. This was the form of both the philosophy and the life of Friederich Nietzsche: without God as Providence, "the Still Point of the turning world", the inescapable oscillation between fate and self-will produces madness.

But Dugin cannot bear the presence of God, since he mis-perceives Him as the traumatic encounter of the contingent subject with itself, not as the liberation of the contingent self in the presence of the *Atman*, the Radical Self:

> Time needs the future as a void for the continuous fading of the present and, partially, of the past. Without the future, the subject will not have the space necessary to evade, running from the impossible encounter with itself.... The frozen moment of the present without the future is that of death. Society needs the future to run from itself further and further.

This is truly inverted. Here Dugin-as-Husserl despairingly accepts Eternity, Reality, God as too terrible to face, as something which must be fled from, evaded; without such flight from God, he says, no human life or human society is possible—even though he defines society as a flight from itself. Because the Eternal Present of God is misperceived by the ego as "the frozen moment of the present without the future," God becomes the crushing and paralyzing presence of a Necessity that destroys all Possibility; the Living God is transformed into Dante's Satan, frozen up to his chest in the Lake of Cocytus in the Ninth Circle of Hell. Nietzsche said "God is dead," whereas it is more or less Dugin's position that "God is death." What is being demonstrated here is that simple atheism is no longer an easy alternative. We rejected God, we denied Him—but that wasn't enough, because God was still there. As the walls of the *manvantara* become increasing transparent as it nears its end, the terrible, freezing, burning light of the God we denied shines through them with ever-increasing intensity; we *must* run, but we *can't* run. Dugin says "We live in the creation of the external world by the internal self," and then totally contradicts himself by claiming that, in order for the world and society even to exist, we must flee from the awful presence of that Self, faster and faster, without end. This flight, of course, is the very image of Guénon's prophesy, based on Hindu doctrine, of the acceleration of time at the end of the *manvantara*. Tradition teaches that the presence of God to the world creates that world—just as, on a more individual, psychological level, "the world around us"—as Husserl teaches—"becomes what it is by the fundamental action of *presencing* accomplished by the mind." In other words, the *making out* of the world by human attention is a subset and reflection of the original and ongoing *making* of the world by God. But after more-or-less accepting this, Dugin suddenly can't bear it. Now he must deny both that the world is created by the internal transcendental Self and that it is redeemed from obscurity by the intentional perception of the individual self, and instead claim the very opposite: that the world is only created through a flight from oneself, a flight from the Eternal Present Moment, a flight from God—because God, for Dugin, is not Love, or Beauty, or Mercy; He is only Wrath. He is not the Creator or the Sustainer, but only the Destroyer. Here we can see with crystal clarity how if we reject the Self-revelations of God that He directs to us in order to save us, we will be forced to encounter His naked Majesty as an inescapable Fire that reduces us to cinders. The Qur'an says: *There is no refuge from God but in Him* [Q. 9:118]. Dugin says, in effect, "There is no refuge from God except in flight from Him." But how can we fly from a Reality that is everywhere, that not only lies at the beginning of time and the end of time, but also underlies every moment of time, as well as being the ultimate Essence of the one attempting to flee It? The Hindus understand the world as *Maya*, as the magical apparition of God as other-than-Himself, which is fundamentally illusory because God is the Only Being. And because other-than-God, which is nothing in itself, is at the same time God and nothing else, they divide Maya into *avidya-maya*, "ignorance-apparition," and *vidya-maya*, "wisdom-apparition." Seen from the viewpoint of *avidya-maya*, the world is "created" by ignorance of God, since if God were universally known, the world-illusion would dissolve. Seen from the viewpoint of *vidya-maya*, however, God creates this apparent world as a merciful manifestation of Himself designed to lead us back to Himself. For Dugin, however—since he emphatically does not base his worldview on Tradition—the creation of the world by God's Presence and its destruction by that same Presence are totally contradictory; they cannot be reconciled. Likewise the destruction of the world by the triumph of unreality via the reduction of all aspects of human life to technologically-mediated simulacra, which would represent the victory of *avidya-maya*, and the creation of the world through flight from God, flight from Reality, which happens precisely by the agency of *avidya-maya*, are equally contradictory, equally irreconcilable; the mercy of *vidya-maya*, in either creation or dissolution, is nowhere to be seen. Does God's Presence destroy the world or create it? Does our flight from that Presence destroy the world or create it? Aleksandr Dugin, since he is ignorant of Tradition, cannot answer. And the answer is: Because God is both Immanent and Transcendent, the creation of the world and its annihilation are One in the Divine Presence, while in the presence of the ego, the flight from that Presence in order to maintain the world-illusion and the destruction of the world-illusion by the agency of that very flight are also one. The ego—as Albert Camus demonstrates in *The Rebel* (though he has no idea that he has done so)—is the obsessive pseudo-reality that tries both to maintain itself by fleeing from destruction—which is impossible—and to assert its illusory sovereignty precisely by destroying itself—which is also impossible. This is due to the fact that the ego, like Satan, and in the very same sense as Satan, is the Ape of God. In the Divine Presence, cosmic manifestation shines forth from God in all its richness and complexity, and is simultaneously revealed as nothing in the face of the Divine Reality which emanates it—a truth that the Buddhists express by asserting the identity of *shunyata* and *tathata*—voidness and suchness—and which Frithjof Schuon has termed "the metaphysical transparency of phenomena." In terms of the cyclical time of the *manvantara*, the creation of the world by the Divine Presence lies at the beginning and its destruction by that same Presence at the end; in reality, however—which means, in Eternity— these two are simultaneous, and are happening at this very moment. And if the Presence of God must destroy the world, it is precisely because the ego has assumed the prerogatives of the Creator and so turned that world into an empty caricature of God's creation in the course of its flight from Him—a caricature that must be destroyed so as to once again unveil His Presence. Because His Mercy, through our foolishness, ends in Wrath, His Wrath must supervene to return us—either willingly or else kicking and screaming—to His Mercy.

In addition, Dugin's sense that history, since it is strictly determined, cannot be fundamentally influenced by human action—though he presently leads an international political movement, for what purpose I can't imagine—coupled with his lack of any grasp of the reality of Providence, of the "intervention" of God in human affairs—has made him a slave to history even as he tries to imagine how to change it or become free of it. It's as if Aleksandr Dugin, in reaction against the Post-Christian Liberal Myth of Progress according to which everything is possible, has fallen into the shadow of its opposite, the ancient fatalism of Asia—an Asia encrusted by aeons of human karma, that is, not the glory of integral Asia, as represented by the wisdom of the *Upanishads* or the *Tao Te Ching*—a fatalism according to which, as it were, nothing is possible, or at least nothing new. These two equal, opposite and mutually-defining forms of spiritual despair were analyzed by Søren Kierkegaard, in *Sickness unto Death*, as "despair of Possibility" and "despair of Necessity." It's as if the giggling American pothead who gleefully declares that "everything is possible!" is eternally paired with the depressive Russian alcoholic who solemnly maintains that "*nothing* is possible." Despair of Possibility is divided between ruthless self-will and a foolish reliance on luck and wishful thinking (luck-worship which always cycles back toward fatalism), while Despair of Necessity is split between a falsely pious, groveling passivity and the grim endurance of suffering with no hope of relief. In God, however, Necessity and Possibility are not opposed but united. Possibility is the guarantee that God's Necessary Being can be and do all things, while Necessity is the guarantee that a given possibility inspired in us by God will not end as a childish fantasy or an empty boast, but can in fact germinate, take root, and be realized in its fullness, as an aspect of the Word made flesh. And the union of Necessity and Possibility is, precisely, Providence. In the presence of God's Providence we are freed from both magic and fatalism, from both the hubristic identification with Possibility and the hopeless worship of Necessity. In that Presence we cannot avoid or predict or control the Will of God, but we *can* invoke it. I deal with the process of this invocation, which appears to be a human act but is in reality an act of God, in *Chapter Seven* of this book, "Sacred Activism." I have nothing to say at this point about how one might come to an understanding that Divine Providence is not only real, but is actually operating in the present situation, because this has everything to do with the mystery of Faith—except to say that the approved advice, from a Traditionalist perspective, is that one should unite oneself to and satisfy the requirements of one of the great Revealed Religions or Wisdom Traditions. After one has established the certainty that Divine Providence is real, however, *Chapter Seven* will provide a hopefully intelligible introduction to the *science* of Providence, which is neither a magical Prometheanism nor a slavish, beaten resignation, but rather a state, and practice, of *active receptivity*.

Dugin goes on to say:

> Within the depths of transcendental subjectivity, there lies another layer which Husserl had not uncovered. Husserl was convinced that the layer he discovered was the last one. But it turns out that this is not so. There has to be another dimension yet to be found—the most hidden one. We can designate it as the Radical Subject.
>
> If Husserl's transcendental subjectivity constitutes reality through the

experience of a manifestation of self-awareness, the Radical Subject is to be found, not on the way out, but on the way in. It shows itself only in the moment of ultimate historic catastrophe, in the traumatic experience of the "short circuit" which is stronger, and lasts for a moment longer than it is possible to endure.

This Radical Subject, as we have seen, can only be the Absolute Witness, the *Atman*, Schuon's "absolute Subject of our contingent subjectivity." Luckily for us, it does not show itself "only in the moment of ultimate historic catastrophe," since, in the words of William Blake I continue to quote in many contexts, "Whenever any Individual Rejects Error & Embraces Truth, a Last Judgment passes upon that Individual." In other words, the Radical Self is perpetually available—*to individuals*—as the culmination and final realization of the Spiritual Path. As Dugin himself says in a passage already quoted:

> It is possible to be awoken by the strength of this inner light of self-reflection. In this traumatic situation, we discover our identity between the most inner and outer levels of our consciousness. We live in the creation of the external world by the internal self. But that is no longer history; it is breaking through history. . . .

This "awakening" need not be limited, however, to a momentary and "traumatic" break with consensus reality, with time and history. This may or may not be the form in which it first announces itself to us, but it remains entirely possible for the Inner Light to become increasingly constant, and even to coexist with an ongoing outer engagement with time and history, thereby providing that engagement with a transcendental and eternal context. And every individual who attains this realization, either in whole or in part, helps to delay or mitigate "the moment of ultimate historic catastrophe." Thus the "temporal and logical relief valve" for apocalyptic times that Dugin hopes will prevent the ultimate conflict is not, as he believes, the flight from the Present into the future, but this very "awakening" to the Inner Light—an awakening that can only happen in the Present. This is what Jesus meant when he said, "Unless those days were shortened, no flesh would be saved: but for the sake of the elect, those days will be shortened" [Matthew 24:22]. Because the truth is, the "creation of the external world by the internal self" *happens through Man*, both historically, in view of the fact that humanity is the "final cause" of the terrestrial world, the purpose for which God created it, and eternally, because God's eternal witnessing of this world through the eye of Man is precisely what maintains it. This is what the Qur'an means when it says that humanity is the holder of the *Amana*, the bearer of the Trust. But this function is not fulfilled through humanity's reflexive, psychic subjectivity, only through our transcendence of that subjectivity; as Frithjof Schuon put it, "The world may be a dream, but it is not my dream." Consequently, to the degree that collective humanity becomes closed to the intuition of the Radical Self, the world of nature, of history, of outer conditions is cut off from the creating and sustaining light of that Self, and so turns toward dissolution. But the Radical Self, the *Atman*—which, as reflected in the dimension of creative, judging and redeeming action is nothing less than God Almighty—will not be denied: to the degree that the world denies Him, rejects Him, closes itself to Him, calls Him dead, the very light of the Self that has created and sustained the world, instead of giving life to that world, now—because the world refuses to receive that life—beats upon the hard, brittle shell of it until it finally cracks. And when it cracks, the *manvantara* whose store of receptivity to God is now exhausted comes to an end, and a new *manvantara* begins.

Next Dugin says:

> The West is a local and historical phenomenon. It is a very acute civilisation, very particular, very arrogant, and very smart. But it is just one civilisation among many others. The West has history, and *is* because of its history. The attempt to abdicate this history in favour of pure universalism and in favour of meta-culture and meta-language is doomed. There are two possible outcomes of this: 1) either the West will lose its own identity and will turn into an automaton; 2) or it will try to impose its own history, conceived by itself as being universal, on all the other existing civilisations, destroying them in the process, and creating a new kind of global concentration camp for their cultures.

This is certainly true as far as it goes, and fairly accurately describes the main trends operating in the fatal and apparently unstoppable momentum of what used to be Western Civilization. However, it is sociologically, historically, and metaphysically impossible for either or both of these trends to reach the terminal points that Dugin envisions, due to the following law: "As imposed control (rather than organic order) increases, chaos increases proportionally."

Yet Dugin also envisions a way out, a way beyond the total alienation represented by globalism that the West is in the process of morphing into:

> Globalisation is equivalent to the end of history. Both go hand-in-hand. They are semantically linked. Different societies have different histories. That means different futures. If we are going to make a "tomorrow" common to all societies existing on the planet, if we are going to propose a global future, then we need first to destroy the history of those other societies, to delete their pasts, annihilate the continuous moment of the present, virtualising the realities that are constructed by the content of historical time. A "common future" means the deletion of particular histories. But this means that no histories at all, including their futures, will exist. The common future is no future. Globalisation is the death of time. Globalisation cancels out the transcendental subjectivity of Husserl or the *Dasein* of Heidegger. There would

be neither any more time, nor being . . . [*Globalization*] cancels the future. It requires the arrival of post-humanity. It constructs the post-world consisting of simulacra and virtual structures. In place of the transcendental subject, *Dasein*, society becomes a huge computer centre, a matrix, a supercomputer. In place of time, it creates simulacrums of the past, present and future.

Therefore

When we construct the future, it should not be global in scope. It cannot be just one future, we must have many futures.

This transformation of the unipolarity of Postmodern Liberal Globalism, which envisions a single future for a united humanity, into a multiplicity of possible futures as expressions of different civilizations possessing different histories and worldviews, though it is a plausible and in many ways desirable outcome, nonetheless parallels the shattering of the individual under Postmodern Liberalism into many different probable selves, each supposedly occupying its own time-line, just as Liberal society itself is in the process of fragmenting into many different sectors, subcultures, cadres, or gangs, each one fanatically following a different ideological absolute. Apparently all the world's cultures and civilizations, for all their real and providential differences, have now run into the same wall. Liberal unipolarity may be an undeniable evil; nonetheless, the American poet Gregory Corso was right when he wrote, in a moment of unsentimental and spontaneous compassion: "All man is ONE in this sad, inharmonious, weird predicament." The attempt to unify humanity is unnecessary, and therefore destructive, because humanity is already one intrinsically—an intrinsic unity that must be denied in order to justify an artificial, imposed unification.

But the deconstruction of the future by globalizing it, Dugin says, is not the end of game; the end only appears when the present is deconstructed as well:

The semantics of time blur, fork, and multiply. Manipulating the present is a little more complicated and requires a higher degree of sophistication. To remove the present, the transcendental subjectivity must not only be walled off, but eradicated. This presumes the transition from the human to the post-human. Developments in the human genome project, cloning, advances in robots, and new generations of cyborgs all bring us close to the advent of post-humanity. The goal of this process is to produce creatures that will lack an existential dimension with zero subjectivity. . . . How can [*Man*] transfer the initiatives of existence to the post-human world, a world that will disappear immediately upon the expiration of the last man—for there will be no one left to bear witness?

Here Dugin is stuck between a rock and hard place, between the notion of the articulation of many different civilizational futures as liberation from unipolarity, and a condition of total postmodern alienation where "the semantics of time blur, fork, and multiply." He can't take refuge in multiplicity from the perceived evil of unity because multiplicity is evil in a different way, nor can he seek shelter in unity from the perceived evil of multiplicity because unity is evil in a different way; this is the central contradiction that runs through all of his writings. It is a contradiction that only the Traditional doctrine of the Many and the One can solve, and has in fact already solved; but Dugin knows nothing of it. Because he does not see Unity as necessarily refracting itself into multiplicity in the process of Its Self-manifestation, Its immanentization, and multiplicity as therefore a sign of a Transcendent Unity and consequently the path to the realization of it, he can only see Unity and Multiplicity as at war with each other. They imply each other, they are expressions of each other, but all this must be denied because they also contradict each other, cancel each other. Consequently Dugin turns, as a last resort, to the Radical Subject as the only thing that could redeem him, and us, from contradictions like this:

> The same experience that makes the transcendental subjectivity manifest itself and deploy its content, thus creating time with its intrinsic music, is regarded by the Radical Subject as an invitation to reveal itself in another manner—on the other side of time. For the Radical Subject, time—in all its forms and configurations—is nothing more than a trap, a trick, a decoy, delaying the real decision. For the Radical Subject, it is not only virtuality and the electronic networks which are the prison, but reality itself has already become so: a concentration camp, an agony, and a torture. The slumber of history is something contrary to the condition where the Radical Subject could exist, complete itself, and become. The creation of subjectivity, being the secondary formation of temporality, is an obstacle for its realisation.

Here Dugin begins to understand that the ego and the world it projects, that "subjectivity" which is "the secondary formation of temporality," is the veil that hides the Radical Subject and prevents its realization. This is certainly true, and entirely in line with Tradition. This "secondary subjectivity", however, is not an obstacle for the Radical Subject itself, which is free of all contingency and becoming, intrinsically and eternally. But when Dugin sees manifest reality as "a concentration camp, an agony, a torture," he falls into the error of the sectarian Gnostics of late antiquity—an error that anyone who has faced the cruelty and unreality of postmodern life, and is at all theologically inclined, will have to deal with at one point, since the Gnostic doctrine that the cosmos is a prison created a false god, the evil Demiurge—the very personification of the ego—appears to accurately describe and explain the "cosmic paranoia" he feels. The Gnostics, however, were heretics, by which I mean that they were simply wrong according to the norms of the Primordial Tradition. They accepted the Transcendence of God but denied His Immanence, consequently they lived in a universe without mercy. And so, as it turns out, Dugin's idea of the Radical Subject is no solution either:

> If we accept the hypothesis of the Radical Subject, we immediately confront an instance that explains who has made the decision in favor of globalisation, the suicide of humanity, and the end of history; who has conceived this plan and made it reality. It can only therefore be the drastic gesture of the Radical Subject, looking for liberation from time through the construction of non-temporal (impossible) reality. The Radical Subject is incompatible with all kinds of time. It vehemently demands anti-time, based on the exalted fire of eternity transfigured in the radical light. When everybody has gone, the only thing that remains is those who cannot be gone. Perhaps that is the reason for this greatest of all probations.

Here Dugin echoes Blake's alchemical imperative that "What can be destroyed must be destroyed!," since whatever is capable of destruction by the revelation of Truth has no inherent substance or meaning. But Blake also said, "Eternity is in love with the productions of time." Here Dugin essentially blames God for the mess we have made of the world—but this is unwarranted. As Ibn al-'Arabi teaches, God *wills* whatever happens, since He conforms His commands to the intrinsic demands of His creatures by giving them exactly what they "ask for," but not everything that happens is in line with His *wish*, since He wishes only good. God does not hate the world He created nor the humanity He placed within it to rule and replenish it in His Name; he only hates the caricature we have made of that world, and of ourselves, through our worship of the ego. Thus His destruction of the world, which is inevitable, is nothing other than His destruction of the false, fallen world we have invented and His revelation of the true, paradisaical world of His original design. The Radical Subject is not entrapped in time, and so needs no liberation from it. The Radical Subject does not hate time; It transmutes time from cacophony into music. God, in Malachi 3:6, says: "I am Jehovah: I have not changed." Christ, in Apocalypse 21:5, says (quoting Isaiah): "Behold, I make all things new." And given that Jehovah and Christ are *homousios*, of one substance, they are saying exactly the same thing—that the perpetual renewal of time is guaranteed by the inviolability of Eternity. But if we have no sense of Eternity, then time is undecipherable; if we have no perception of the presence of God, then nothing new can ever happen, only the automatic and endless recycling of all the dead moments. The Sufi Ibn 'Ata'illah says:

> When the forgetful man gets up in the morning
> he reflects on what he is going to do,
> whereas the intelligent man *sees* what God is doing with him.

The forgetful man identifies with his own isolated intentionality and the false, alienated time it creates, and is therefore confined within the limits of his own being; the intelligent man refers his intentionality to God as the Lord of it, thereby opening himself to the ocean of God's Being. The forgetful man has no real future, since whatever he imagines he might do is drawn from the memory of what he has already done; the intelligent man stands in wait for the unimaginable things that God still has in store, seeing that *Every day doth some new work employ Him* [Q. 55:29].

Since Dugin has struggled to make sense of subject and object, time and space largely outside the context of Tradition, and consequently—though he has some moments of real insight—produced a mass of contradictions, it behooves me to do my best to present these realities in terms of that context, or at least my own understanding of certain aspects of it:

A Metaphysics of Time and Space
Based on the Primordial Tradition

The essence and archetype of Time is *Intentionality*—what is *posited*. The essence and archetype of Space is *Being*—what *is*. The essence of Intentionality is to witness, and therefore intend, what is; the essence of Being is to rest in being self-witnessed and self-intended.

God as the Absolute Essence—Godhead, *Al-Dhat*, *Nirguna Brahman*—is beyond all Being and Intentionality. God as the Supreme Being—Allah, *Saguna Brahman*—is the seamless union of Being and Intentionality: the Supreme Being is equally the Supreme Intent. In God, Intentionality intends only Being, and Being rests as the perfect expression of Intentionality. God as Being is beyond space, and is consequently the principle of space; God as Intentionality transcends time, and is therefore the principle of time.

(Ramana Maharshi sees the Self, the *Atman*—*Nirguna Brahman* as the Indwelling Absolute Witness—as Pure Being, and action as the veil which hides It. This is true insofar as he defines Pure Being not as the opposite either of Non-Being or of Intentionality, but as the Absolute transcending all opposites, which is essentially equivalent to the Beyond Being of the Platonists. The term "Being" as I am using it here is not the Ramana's "Pure Being", but rather a state of self-subsistent wholeness and rest that subsists in a polar relationship to motion, action, intention. The perfect union of Being and Intentionality is the Personal God—*Allah*, *Ishvara*, *Saguna Brahman*—whereas That which transcends Being and Intentionality is *Al-Dhat*, *Nirguna Brahman*, the *Atman*. Frithjof Schuon uses the term "Pure Being" to refer to *Saguna Brahman*, whereas the school of Ramana Maharshi applies "Pure Being" to *Nirguna Brahman* alone.)

Intentionality without Being would be absolute self-will, absolute violence.

Being without Intentionality would be absolute petrification of possibility, absolute fate.

Absolute Intentionality without Being and absolute Being without Intentionality are not possible states; however, a partial imbalance either in the direction of Being or in the direction of Intentionality is possible—in fact, it is universal among sentient beings, by which I mean that every existing species, or individual, or collective, will at one time or another exhibit a preponderance of one of these principles over the other. An imbalance in the direction of Being paralyzes Intentionality, while an imbalance in the direction of Intentionality depletes Being.

Only in God are Intentionality and Being seamlessly united; God is what He intends and intends what He is because (as Aquinas teaches) He is Pure Act. In God, "the consciousness . . . that precedes the intentionality and the dualist nature of apprehension" co-exists with, embraces, and is seamlessly united with that very Intentionality and dualism—"dualism" in the sense that creation, which manifests through the *dvandvas*, the pairs-of-opposites, subsists virtually within the Divine Nature as what Frithjof Schuon calls *maya-in-divinis* and the Sufis *Wahadiyya*, the synthesis of all the Names of God. The Divine "pre-intentional" Consciousness (pre-intentional only in the sense that it is pre-dualistic) is nevertheless one with an Intentionality that, since it intends only the Transcendental Subject, intends only Itself; this is nothing less than a re-statement of the Christian mystery of the Trinity, as well as of Ibn al-'Arabi's doctrine that the polarity of Allah as Lord, and Allah as the inner Essence of the Cosmos and/or the Servant, is embraced, and its polarity neutralized, by Allah as the One Reality. God's intentions, which are Himself, are based entirely on what He knows to be real, which is also Himself. Likewise His knowledge of what is real is entirely intentional; whatever is real is real because God imagines it, conceives it, intends it. If God were Being without Intentionality He would be little more than natural law, passive, blind, and inevitable. And if God were Intentionality without Being He would cease to Be, since no substance of reality would be available to Him such that He might intend it. In the Qur'an, the seamless unity of Intentionality and Being in God is expressed in the verse *When He decreeth a thing, He saith unto it only: Be! and it is* [2:117]. If a human being presumes to adopt these prerogatives it is a sign of mental illness: only God has both the right and the power to say what is. His command that something *be* is evidence of His Intentionality; His addressing of this command *to* the entity in question, as if it already existed, is evidence of His Being. In Islamic metaphysics, the Intentionality of Allah is called the Pen (*al-Kalam*), represented by the letter *alif*, while the Being of Allah is called the Guarded Tablet (*al-Lawh-i-Mahfūz*), represented by the letter *bā*. The dot beneath the *bā* symbolizes *Al-Dhat*, Allah's secret Essence, which is beyond Being entirely.

Whatever He writes with the Pen necessarily appears on the Tablet; whatever He reads on the Tablet He necessarily writes with the Pen. All the modes and particularities of potential Existence are what they are from all Eternity—but He intends them *now*. And this polarity between Pen and Tablet, which is equally a seamless unity, is nothing less than the root of human *gender* in the depths of the Divine Nature.

The root of Time is Intentionality as an expression of Being, Possibility arising from Necessity: "With God, all things are possible," [Matthew 19:26]; "The Spirit of God moved upon the face of the waters" [Genesis 1:2]. The root of Space is Being as the essence of Intentionality, the face of the Necessity underlying Possibility: "I am Jehovah: I have not changed" [Malachi 3:6]. The reality of Being prior to the emergence of God's intention to create the world is expressed in Proverbs 8:22, where Wisdom says: "The Lord possessed me in the beginning of His way, before His works of old." Being as an expression of His intentionality in creating the world is indicated in Genesis 2:22: "And of the rib, which the Lord God had taken from man, he made a woman."

In relationship to the created world, which is the reflection of both God's Being and His Intentionality, His Intentionality is dominant; He is *Rab al-Alamin*, Lord of the Worlds. Prior to the created world, God's Being is paramount, since His (or Her) Intentionality is subsumed into His (or Her) Being; previous to creation, God's only Intention is to Be. In this world, Being is revealed by Intention; in the other world, the inner world, Intention is expressed by Being. These two worlds exist simultaneously, each concealed within the other. The parity of Being and Intentionality in manifestation as a whole, which is made up of both worlds, is guaranteed by, and exists as a sign of, the principle that, in God, Being and Intentionality are seamlessly united on every level and in every respect.

According to William Blake, "Time is a Man and Space is a Woman"; thus Being is intrinsically feminine, Intentionality intrinsically masculine. The *I Ching*—which is the fountainhead of Chinese philosophy, both exoteric Confucianism and esoteric Taoism—conceives of *Chi'en*, Yang, the Creative force, the Heavenly Principle as the Primal Masculine, expressing itself in terms of power acting through time, while *Kun*, Yin, the Receptive force, the Earthly Principle is the Primal Feminine, manifesting itself in terms of the all-embracing extensiveness of space.

In many metaphysical systems, most especially that of Tantric Hinduism, the Subject is conceived of as an expression of the Masculine Principle, the Object of the Feminine Principle. The subject is *Purusha*, *Atman*, the Witness; the object is *Prakriti*, *Maya*, the Witnessed. This would seem to support Kant's intuition that the object is closer to space, the subject closer to time, given that we experience our subjectivity as intentional, and the objective world simply as a given fact, and thus as a more direct manifestation of Being. Consciousness, as the creative desire to know, is based on dialectic, quest, aspiration (this being more or less Husserl's position). The Object of consciousness, on the other hand, either conceals itself from, or makes itself available to, the creative desire to know it. Consciousness, the Masculine Principle, is related to time because it *seeks*; the Object of Consciousness, the Feminine Principle, simply reposes in Being, and is consequently related to space: "Be it done unto me according to Thy Word" [Luke 1:38].

On the other hand, though time is rooted in the perceptual intentionality of the Subject, it unfolds within the context of space, the Object, since the Object is the receptive field where the intrinsic creative intent of the witnessing Subject, emanating from the Essential Pole, appears. Likewise space, as the Object receptive to being witnessed, exists as the outer reflection of the invisible Root of the witnessing Subject, which is *Atman, Nirguna Brahman,* That which transcends all Being and all Intentionality. If "Time is a Man and Space is a Woman," one might think that the dominance of the feminine principle or Substantial Pole in the latter days of the *manvantara* would unveil space, while the dominance of the masculine principle or Essential Pole when the *manvantara* is young would express itself as the supremacy of time. The reverse is true because the *manvantara* is initiated by the Essential Pole, newly emerged from Eternity at "the first moment of time," in the act of fertilizing the primordial receptivity of space-the Substantial Pole in its virginal purity-while the polluted Substantial Pole, whose quality is accelerating time, is dominant at the end of the cycle because space is now cluttered and obscured by the spent residues of an aeon of time and intentionality manifesting as blind chaotic impulse-a condition that William Blake called "the Female Will." Accelerating time volatilizes form, thereby veiling the Essential Pole, but it also fractures space, thus obscuring the *prima materia*, the primordial purity of the Substantial Pole.

Be that as it may, it should be obvious that, in reality, time and space, like subject and object, are never found apart. Without time, space would be frozen, incapable of giving anything the room to be; without space, time would remain abstract and incomplete; the moments of time could never really *take place*. Likewise the object without a conscious subject to perceive it is total darkness, while subjective consciousness with no object to perceive is oblivion. Even the narcissist cannot maintain *subjective* consciousness unless he can see himself as an *object*. As perception withdraws from perceivable objects and becomes more and more self-involved—in other words, as thought increasingly thinks only about thought, abandoning the concrete outer objects and situations and relationships of the world that might anchor it—the perception of time speeds up. Days pass like hours. And just because subject when alienated from object becomes eaten up by time doesn't mean that the object from which it is alienated thereby becomes more spatialized, more tranquil and open; the increasing alienation between subject and object actually results, as Guénon observed, in the dissolution of space by time. And as many must have realized by now, this acceleration of perceived time is one of the effects of an addiction to the electronic media, which also increasingly act to withdraw our consciousness from what Traditionalist scientist and metaphysician Wolfgang Smith calls the *corporeal* world, the real world our senses are designed to perceive, as opposed to the *physical* or subatomic world revealed by modern physics. We can never directly perceive the physical world, since it only exists as a set of responses to our questions and experiments; consequently it too becomes increasingly subjective in nature. This acceleration of time is accompanied by a volatilization of space, a fragmentation of living, integral places possessing particular qualities, and of three-dimensional, solid objects maintaining particular shapes, into swarms of shifting images. This fragmentation increases as space and time, object and subject become increasingly alienated from each other, until it exactly matches the condition of the macrocosm and microcosm that René Guénon predicted for the last days of the *manvantara*. Consequently when Descartes initiated the fateful philosophical separation between subject and object—a separation that Kant inherited—he was not only promulgating an *error* but obscurely responding to an actual *condition* of the cosmic environment—a condition of dis-integration; his error was to take that condition for the basic nature of reality, not simply as a disordered, contingent, temporal state of it.

This condition of dis-integration is analyzed in Hexagram 12 of the *I Ching*, "Stagnation," in which *Chi'en*, the Principle of Heaven, rises into the sky, like a *deus absconditus*, until it becomes inaccessible to humanity, while *Kun*, the Principle of Earth, sinks into its own obscurity and darkness. The ascension of *Ch'ien* indicates that consciousness is becoming increasingly thin and abstract as it abandons the earthly reality that alone could actualize it, while the sinking of *Kun* into the abyss is a picture of the growing contraction and obscurity of a world abandoned by the principle of consciousness, the only thing that could give it reality and life.

The Hindu scriptures define both the belief that material conditions create consciousness—*materialism*—and the belief that consciousness creates material conditions—*idealism*—as *heresies*, the truth being that both consciousness and conditions, both self and world, are created by God as the primal polarity through which He manifests the universe. In the words of the Qur'an, *I will show them My signs on the horizons and in their own souls until they are satisfied that this is the Truth. Is it not enough for you, that I am Witness over all things?* [Q. 41:53]. When subject and object become alienated from one another, this Witness—the transcendent-and-immanent Divine Self that the Hindus call the *Atman*—is veiled; time speeds up; space becomes fragmented and obscured.

Through the practice of *contemplation*, however, this alienation between subject and object, this split between time and space, is reversed. As the mind becomes more calm and centered, time slows down; as time slows down, space emerges from the mental chaos that has fractured and concealed it. Instead of time and space going their separate ways, until time dissolves into random, meaningless change and space first congeals, then pulverizes, time and space reunite. Space becomes once again the actuality of time, time the life and motion of space. And as space and time draw closer together, the *ego* that has kept them apart, the obsessive habit of self-definition and world-definition, dissolves; the human form returns from isolated individuality, which has descended into pulverized "dividuality" (to use Dugin's memorable term), to full personhood again. As space and time begin to emerge from the veils of the ego, the human person recognizes him- or herself as existing in a real relationship with a real, outer, corporeal world with which he or she shares a real, common time. And when the ego is finally negated, he or she intuitively realizes this real, common time as the effect of God's Intentionality—otherwise known as Providence—and this real, corporeal world as the immediate reflection of God's intrinsic Being. Once this condition of integral Being/Consciousness is reached, once God-realization is attained, *bliss* ensues. The Hindus describe this state by defining God as *Sat-Chit-Ananda*, "Being-Consciousness-Bliss," the supreme fulfillment that is experienced when subject and object, time and space, unite. Descartes, Kant, and their offspring the postmodernists, are the philosophical enemies of this bliss, and therefore the enemies of God.

One of the paradoxes of time may be expressed in the following question: "Which way is time flowing, from the past into the future or from the future into the past?" When we are in a state of active Intentionality, time—which has become identified with our intentions and aspirations—advances *into* the future, which now appears as the *intentional present*. On the other hand, when we are in a state of contemplative Being, time arrives *from* the future, which now manifests as the *ontological present*. The act of contemplation is thus the act of referring our Intentionality to God, of seeing all Intentionality as His intrinsically, thereby recognizing Him as Lord of the Worlds. As God brings us into existence, we move from Being to Intentionality; as we return our created being to Him over the course of the Spiritual Path, we move from Intentionality to Being. Surrendering our Intentionality to God, we see Him as presently intending our Being, and recognize that whatever Intentionality we may express is really His Intentionality. In the words of the Qur'an [76:30], *You cannot will unless Allah wills*. The Future is Potency, Possibility, Intentionality; as the Future arrives, Intentionality is constantly transformed into Being, Potency into Act. By the same token, the act of Being is itself intentional; the surrender of our intentionality to God in contemplation is necessarily something that we *intend*, thereby participating in His Eternal Intentionality; in contemplation, the seamless Unity between Being and Intentionality is restored.

In this state of supreme integration, the Future is that which is constantly becoming Now; it is the life and motility of the Eternal Present, as the past is Its stability and Necessity. Future time, arising from the world of possibilities and conditions, is that which constantly answers the ever-deepening presence of Intentional Being—answers it so perfectly that it transcends the dimension of Potency or Possible Being, of what might or might not happen, what might or might not be, and becomes actualized instead as the vibratory Self-manifesting radiance of Necessary Being; it is experienced as Divine Intentionality in the unending process of realizing itself in the Eternal Present, thereby manifesting Itself as Providence, the Will of God.

In response to Aleksandr Dugin's (or Husserl's) insight that the ego creates time so it can flee into the future from the terrifying and annihilating reality of the Radical Subject—terrifying and annihilating only because the ego has chosen both to flee from it, and simultaneously to defiantly assert itself in the face of it—we need to realize that intentionality is not simply the way that the empirical self flees from the intolerable Reality of the Radical Subject, the Radical Self—thus creating time—but is both an intrinsic aspect of that very Self, a true quality of eternally self-realizing Transcendental Subjectivity, and a necessary aspect of the relationship between the Radical Self and the manifest world. To say that the Self intends its own Self-realization, though not in the sense that It chooses this realization out of several alternatives, is simply to assert that the Radical Self is not passive, eternally fated, and thus to be taken for granted, but rather that It is supremely active, given that God is Pure Act. And as a consequence, the manifestation of the Radical Self as the visible world, though in one sense it is as inevitable as the reflection of an object in a mirror, is also entirely intentional. We are not mere passive by-products of the Radical Self, Whose other name is God—we are His *creatures*; we live in the *intentional* "creation of the external world by the internal self." In other words, time as the flight of the empirical self from the tremendous Majesty of the Radical Self is also an act of Mercy on the part of that Radical Self or Subject, who wills to provide the empirical self with a world in which it can live, develop, "grow in wisdom, age and grace," and ultimately be reunited with that radical Self at the end of its cycle of manifestation; this is what William Blake meant when he said that "We are put on earth a little space/ That we may learn to bear the beams of love," and that "Time is the Mercy of Eternity." Speaking in Islamic terms, God is not simply *Al-Haqq*, "the Real," or *Al-Samad*, "the Eternal," or *Al-Shahid*, "the Universal Witness," these being Names of the Radical Subject or Absolute Transcendental Essence; He is also *Al-Khaliq*, "the Creator," *Al-Mubdi*, "the Producer," and *Al-Musawwir*, "the Fashioner," the One Who conceives our eternal design within Himself, draws us into existence from the Night of the Unseen, and fashions us until we perfectly conform to His design for us. Consequently He is both intimately related to His creation and entirely free of it, entirely beyond all relations. Therefore, in terms of His relationship to Humanity, His creation of us and His ongoing maintenance and guidance of us are *intentional*, and therefore providential. Consequently the future, though it is pre-existent in the minutest detail within the Radical Subject—not as a multiplicity, however, but as a seamless Unity—is not pre-existent *for us*. We not immersed in Fate but in Providence; the pre-destined future is not the enemy of our freedom but the guarantee of it, precisely because it is composed of every free choice of ours that God has known, and embraced within Himself, from all Eternity. If we can claim no Being of our own, but only exist by virtue of His Being, likewise our freedom is nothing other than His Freedom.

If there is a single understanding, a single orientation that is becoming increasingly crucial for anyone in our time who believes in God and the metaphysical order, it is an acceptance of Providence, a clear idea of its nature, and a firm grasp of what it requires of us. This is not magical thinking; it is not reliance on a *deus ex machina*; it is the willingness and ability to avail ourselves of real spiritual help without believing we can predict it, or control it, or that it will necessarily fulfill our wishes or prevent the arrival of what we fear—only that, since it is the concrete Will of God for us in the context of the present situation, whatever it sends will be right. If it is God's Will that the human world continue in existence and survive the next satanic challenge to its integrity; or that this world be destroyed; or that we be empowered to act in the world; or that we be guided to withdraw from the world; or that we live; or that we die, then Providence—if we invoke it in active submission, in readiness to act, in readiness to refrain from action, and in complete trust that all that God sends is right—will inevitably give us the grace, the power and the insight to accept, live out, and receive the gift inherent in, *any* conceivable outcome. That is all—and that is enough.

On Chapter Eleven:
"The New Political Anthropology:
The Political Man and His Mutations"

Here Dugin, following Carl Schmitt's notion of "political theology," begins by replacing God with politics—the very sort of heresy that one would expect a politician to be attracted to, though few politicians have made it as explicit as Aleksandr Dugin has in the following passage:

> What man is, is derived not from himself as an individual, but from politics.
> It is politics, being the dispositive of violence and legitimate power, that

defines the man. It is the political system that gives us our shape. Moreover, the political system has an intellectual and conceptual power, as well as a transformative potential, without limitations.

Man is not a function of politics; politics is a function of man. To alienate man from himself by claiming that he is a function of, a creature of, something less than himself—namely "violence and legitimate power" in the human world—is neither to liberate him nor to assign him his true place and function in the Hierarchy of Being: it is to denature him, deconstruct him, crush him. It is true that the individual is not self-created; he or she, along with his or her *narod*, the two existing in a figure-ground relationship and constituting a single *gestalt*, is created not by politics but by God, created through the agency of the Human Archetype within God, "without Whom nothing was made that was made" [John 1:3]. No political system, no political regime, nor the sum total of human politics, past present and future, possesses "an intellectual and conceptual power, as well as a transformative potential, without limitations." This description—as long as we understand "transformative potential" as denoting creative power, not alteration of essence—applies only to God as the Supreme Being. To say that politics, not God, creates man is a solemn vow and profession of atheism. It is an intellectual terror-attack on the essence of Christian anthropology, which, in the language of Eastern Orthodoxy, declares that man is created in the Image of God, and that, by virtue of the *theosis* to which Christ calls him, he is capable of conforming himself to that Image, thereby attaining and manifesting the Likeness of God. And such a terror attack, since it is directed against the human essence, is necessarily also a *suicide attack*: in an attempt to destroy the Image of God within himself, Aleksandr Dugin cuts out his own heart.

If I were to rend my garments every time Dugin hatches a new blasphemy, I would have to buy myself a whole new set of clothes, so I will simply say: "If you believe that politics, not God, is man's creator, you are neither an Orthodox Christian nor a Guénonian Traditionalist, whereas if you believe that God is our creator, you must repudiate the above statement. So take the one and leave the other: you can't have it both ways."

> Power itself consists of two elements: first is the power to shape the paradigm, integrated in society through state institutions, and second is power as the dispositive of violence, which serves as a means to integrate the paradigm into the society. Consequently, the single, highest authority of power and its structure controls our political concept of man in a given society. . . .

Wrong. The paradigm is shaped by the Power of God through Revelation—not arbitrary power, but Power acting in conformity with the Human Essence which that Power itself has created. Truth does not serve Power; Power serves

Truth—either that or it stands, as Lucifer, against Truth. In God, Truth and Power are one. In Man, who is made in the Image of God, power—as the will— must serve Truth—as the Spiritual Intellect, the *Nous*. If human power serves Truth then it is one with Truth. If human power believes it can dominate Truth, then there is no truth in it, and whatever residual power may adhere to it is turned only to destruction—self-destruction above all. The Czar, the Byzantine Emperor, the Holy Roman Emperor, ruled—either wisely or stupidly, either in line with God's Mercy or as perverters and corrupters of it—as the vassals of God. But the power that Dugin serves rules in defiance of God. If he takes, not the power of God but the power of the state operating outside God, as effectively absolute, he is neither an Orthodox Christian nor a Guénonian Traditionalist, whereas if he believes that God is the ultimate Source of all authority, as exercised through His revelations to man, he must repudiate the above statement. Let him take the one and leave the other: he can't have it both ways.

> It is politics that constitutes us.... Politics grants us our political status, our name, and our anthropological structure. Man's anthropological structure shifts when one political system changes to another... on the pole of modernity, we have the rational, autonomous individual, and we have a particle of a certain holistic ensemble on the other pole. As for postmodernity, it declares that there are no differences as such between these two types of society, politics, and concepts of man. It matters not whether this very man is constituted according to the liberal, individualist approach or by the holistic *eidos*, it is Man which is the outcome....

Dugin is saying here that our "anthropological structure," Man with a capital M, though it changes from social system to social system, *doesn't* change from social system to social system. Modernity produces one form of Man, Postmodernity another, but Postmodernity knows that there is no difference between these two forms. This method of "thinking," on the basis of power rather than truth, this way of producing calculated absurdities like the above, is part of what Dugin means by "power as the dispositive of violence, which serves as a means to integrate the paradigm into the society"—because the destruction of thought through intellectual cunning is also violence; whatever finally manifests as physical violence has to have taken the form of conceptual violence first.

A new paradigm, if it is alive, will be the expression of the human essence under altered conditions; it cannot be imposed by violence. Rather, it will be responded to by the human collective as a new and unexpected insight into its own nature. Whatever alienates Man from his nature will stand in the way of the new paradigm and try to abort it, and such resistances will certainly have to be dealt with, one way or another. Nonetheless, when God issues a new revelation of Himself to Man, it is equally a new revelation of Man to himself. It may threaten willful ignorance and entrenched selfishness, but it will do no violence to the essence of the human form. Living thought is necessarily animated by the Spirit of Truth; Truth can give birth to power, but power can never give birth to Truth; this is why thought based on power alone is dead. Politics can never take the place of God the Creator because dead thought, since it gives rise to dead action, spreads death and nothing else.

And when did Postmodernism ever conceive of Man with a capital M, of Man in his Essence? "Essentialism" is a heresy to Postmodernism. All that Post-modernism recognizes is an indefinite series of possible versions of "man" contingent not upon truth but only upon the variables of power. Dugin is saying, in effect, that "just because postmodern man *can't* be *one* particular version of Man, because Postmodernism only recognizes an indefinite number of possible versions of him, no single one of which has precedence, this doesn't mean that postmodern man can't also be the *only* true version of Man, since only Post-modernism recognizes that all possible versions of man are Man and nothing else!"

Multi-level, self-strangling contradictions like this—which are intrinsic to the Postmodernism that Dugin both rejects and represents—are understand-able only if their goal is to destroy the human mind. I accept that the intent here is mental suicide, but why does it have to be so complicated? Why does have to take so long? A game of Russian roulette played to the last round will be over a lot quicker than this. The answer is that the intent is not simply suicide, but *murder*-suicide. The intellectual suicide bomber doesn't blow himself up out in the woods somewhere; what would be the point? He blows himself up in a crowded café full of other intellectuals. If he has despaired because Wisdom has spurned his clumsy advances, then all his rivals for Her affection must die too.

The above passage is Dugin's version of Hegel's doctrine of "the negation of the negation" which Dugin, like Marx, is here applying to social development. In the words of *The Great Soviet Encyclopedia,*

> In Hegel's dialectical system, development is the emergence of a logical con-tradiction and its subsequent sublation. In this sense, development is the birth of the internal negation of the previous stage, followed by the negation of this negation. To the extent that the negation of the previous negation pro-ceeds by sublation, it is always, in a certain sense, the restoration of that which was negated, a return to a past stage of development. However, this is not a simple return to the starting point, but [*as Hegel says*] "a new concept, a higher, richer concept than the previous one, for it has been enriched by its negation or opposite; it contains in itself the old concept, but it contains more than this concept alone, and it is the unity of this and its opposite."

Without reference to the ongoing creative act of God, however, the negation of the negation is not the solution, not the necessary new thing; it is nothing but a bigger and more tangled negation, whose only positive content is the conclusive proof that nothing can save the situation from plunging ever further into darkness but the Mercy of God, of the One who needs only to say to something "Be!," and it is. In dialectical terms, and in the absence of creative input from beyond the bounds of the dialectic, the negation of the negation is circular; it simply returns the antithesis to the original thesis, though in a state of greater obscurity and fragmentation; it by no means has the power to posit a new synthesis. If synthesis is born nonetheless, it is due to the fact that the dialectical process, operating horizontally on the basis of *dianoia*, always takes place within the context of the Eternal Creative Word of God, operating vertically on the basis of *Nous*, which that process will either acknowledge or deny. If it chooses to deny that Word, "without Whom was not made anything that was made" [John 1:3], then the negation of the negation, like the impending dissolution of the *manvantara*, will establish only one thing with absolute certainty: the *need for God*. How many times have we been fooled by materialistic dialectics, fooled into placing our trust in the negation of the negation? "It's always darkest before the dawn"; "It'll have to get a lot worse before it gets better"; "When the old order is swept away the new order will come," etc., etc. Saying this is no different from saying, "The way to make things better is to make them worse." In the *contemplative* dialectic, however—what the Sufis call *fikr*—one particular conception of God, as we begin to understand it *as* a conception, not as God Himself, gives way to a new conception which partly negates and partly affirms the first, which then gives way to a third conception, and so on. The ultimate outcome of this process, however, is not that we finally arrive at an *ultimate* conception that *really is* God—a false hope that apparently deluded Hegel—but that we exhaust the dialectical process entirely, leaving us face-to-Face with the True God, the *God beyond conception*. Man's extremity is God's opportunity; where striving fails—striving which is nonetheless necessary—Grace supervenes. In the Old Testament, the classic expression of this sort of contemplative dialectic is found in the *Book of Job*, in the form of the various explanations for Job's misfortune put forward by his friends, all of which are finally transcended and swept aside when God finally speaks to Job out of the whirlwind.

Dugin has inverted this process. After subjecting us to chapter after chapter of chaotic ambiguity, random insight, petrified paradox and veiled contradiction, he finally leaps to his feet and cries: "Are you tired of it all yet? Have you finally attained to true intellectual exhaustion? Do you see no way out? Congratulations! You are now ready for the Final Solution, which is—The Fourth Political Theory! State power! Sweet relief in unquestioning and total obedience!" This is the *fikr*, the contemplative dialectic, of the Devil, whose goal and method are based not on truth but only on power. In *The System of Antichrist* [2001] I predicted that Antichrist or *al-Dajjal* would emerge when the endless and *axiomatic* uncertainties of Postmodernism finally give way to a longing for certainty at any cost, a certainty that could only be founded on blind obedience, and which would appear at the exact point where "the rate of contradiction reaches the speed of light."

Aleksandr Dugin concludes Chapter Eleven by giving us a dismal but penetratingly accurate picture of the dehumanization of man in the postmodern era, of a *post-anthropology* that has given rise to *post-politics*, thereby making politics as we have known it all but impossible. (Given that Dugin already has put politics in the place of God, could this be his way of saying "God is dead"?) The dehumanization of this post-human world has turned the conduct of what used to be politics over to quasi-transcendent, impersonal forces—forces which Dugin identifies—rather chillingly—with *angels*:

It is impossible to speak about political anthropology while describing the post-anthropological model of today's politics. We are forbidden to speak about an integral political theology because we have witnessed this fundamental mutation of "the fold." What are we allowed to speak about? We have political processes, sources of power and dispositives of influence, we observe paradigmatic epistemologies, which are pushed and promoted in the same way as they were in the framework of classical politics. They remain with us, which means that the political in its wider sense is here, it is simply that neither man nor God is there. Who is the actor of this post-politics? There is a certain hypothesis that I call the concept of *Angelopolis*, "the city of Angels" or *Angelpolitia* (angelic politics) that is a turn from political theology to political angelology. What this means is that the sphere of the political is starting to be controlled by and is starting to ground itself upon the confrontation between superhuman entities. That is entities that are neither human nor divine (or not divine at all) [*a mistranslation for "or not entirely divine"?*]. *Angelopolis* possesses a huge potential to assign political roles without taking humanoids and posthumanoids into account. For example, one may think that a man sends an SMS, but it is actually the SMS that sends itself. Considering the growing level of standardisation and lack of originality in these messages, its over-individualistic essence is becoming more and more evident.

There really is a command centre in post-politics. There are actors and there are decisions, but they are totally dehumanised in postmodernity. They are beyond the frames of anthropology . . . [*at the culmination of postmodernity there will be*] a war of angels, a war of gods, a confrontation of entities, not tied by historical or economic laws and patterns, and which do not identify themselves with religions or certain political elites. And this angelic war can be thought of politically. That is *Angelopolis*, or *Politische Angelologie* . . . a concept, devoid of mysticism and esotericism, which has the same sense and nature as Schmitt's metaphor of "political theology." Political angelology must be considered as a metaphor which is both scientific and rational.

Angelopolis is a method to understand, to interpret and to hermeneutically decipher the contemporary processes which surround us and are regarded as being alienated from political anthropology, from humanity as a species, and as a politically institutionalised and constituted notion.

Exactly why, if Dugin wants to be "scientific and rational" (whatever that may mean to him), if he wants to avoid "mysticism and esotericism," does he talk about *angels* as political actors? He accurately recognizes that ever-more-autonomous impersonal forces, operating through technology, increasingly determine the shape of our lives—forces he partly identifies with bundles of electronic information (SMS, or text messages)—*but why does he call them angels*? What exactly is this "angel" who will be the prime actor in the post-political and post-human scene, given that "neither man nor God is there" in relation to him? An angel who exists and acts with no reference to God is, precisely, a devil; consequently Dugin's *Angelopolis* is apparently *Pandaemonium*, the capital city of Hell in Milton's *Paradise Lost*—the same municipality that Dante, in his *Inferno*, named *The City of Dis*. Therefore the "war of angels" that Dugin posits must necessarily be the conflict of devil against devil in Hell, in an infernal context based on conflict and nothing else, a context from which love has been entirely excluded—and Dugin's use of the word *angel* is a good indication that he already suspects this. Furthermore, for Aleksandr Dugin to fatalistically accept the "post-anthropological" era as a given, as the functional basis of a "post-politics"—which is all we will have to work with, even though we ourselves will no longer be actors—is to accept and validate transhumanism, which he elsewhere pretends to oppose, and thereby to announce the advent of an Age of Lucifer as the era destined to follow the Age of Man. Who would dare to announce such a thing, or have any reason to announce it? Who but a Luciferian, a Satanist? (By saying this I don't mean to imply that Dugin necessarily worships the Devil consciously, seeing that Guénon recognized the existence of "unconscious Satanists.") Both Muslim eschatology and the Christian *Book of Apocalypse* foresee an End-Time war against the principle of dehumanization, the Antichrist; Dugin, on the other hand, seems to speak here only of accommodation to the inevitable—and if I am right that he contemplates no revolt against the system of Antichrist but only a zombie-like submission to a world where the only alternatives are the "the post-human vs. the pseudo-human," the true name of the dark spiritual Power he seems to worship—perhaps grudgingly, even unconsciously, but nonetheless with no visible resistance—becomes increasingly obvious. Without a belief in, and an effective relationship to, the Power of God in times like ours, no other allegiance is possible; the human mind, worshipping its own ever-darkening genius in the absence of God, is already worshipping the Devil; Dugin's philosophy is valuable if for no other reason than that it makes this glaringly explicit. The counterfeit war he discerns between the post-human and the pseudo-human, like the conflict between Gog and Magog, is reflected in a meme that is increasingly common in U.S. popular culture—that of "the good demons vs. the bad demons." This meme accurately reflects the contemporary social hell as both Dugin and I see it: a world of pseudo-conflicts between pseudo-actors in the pursuit of pseudo-outcomes.

But is it possible that Aleksandr Dugin may contemplating a more hopeful and proactive response to the encroaching dehumanization, while opting (for some reason) not to let us know about it? He sees the fundamental choice that presents itself, that between the post-political "contemporary man" and the postmodern simulacrum of what used to be the committed "political soldier," as fundamentally hopeless—yet he writes:

> We have the confrontation of post-political anthropology and the pseudo-political soldier. In this case, the antithesis of the post-human is the nonhuman. If we face it, we acquire a very complex and intriguing perspective. It is either phantasmagoric despair, to which Baudrillard, describing the world with radical post-historical categories, gave way, or the feeling that we are not satisfied with this fold, this post-anthropological perspective. However, if we grasp the fatality of this pair, we can calmly step back and assess the situation....
>
> *Angelopolis* is a method to understand, to interpret and to hermeneutically decipher the contemporary processes which surround us and are regarded as being alienated from political anthropology, from humanity as a species, and as a politically institutionalised and constituted notion.

This is a very intriguing idea, though it is difficult to know exactly what Dugin means by it. In **The System of Antichrist** I presented my analysis (already detailed above) of what St. Paul in his Epistle to the Ephesians calls "the Darkness of This World," the fallen order of perception on which the world-system is based. As I have already explained, I defined that System as being ruled by four primary *Archons*, the term used by the Gnostics of late antiquity to denote the false gods who administer the material and psychic cosmos defined as a prison of unreality created by an evil and deluded Demiurge; these Archons are precisely "the Rulers of the Darkness of This World" of Ephesians 6:12. (The Gnostics were heretics in that they accepted God's transcendence but denied His immanence; nonetheless their mythic analysis of the System of This World as a fallen order of perception is second to none.) I saw that the "cosmic paranoia" of postmodern times, of life in a world of cryptocracies and engineered control systems, made what I termed the "investigative mythologies" of the ancient Gnostics both attractive and useful as tools for a deep structural analysis of society and the human psyche with a view toward our liberation from the oppressive order of the fallen world. And as of 2018 I still consider a symbolic, mythopoetic hermeneutic of oppressive systems of power to be a useful tool, especially when applied to patterns of power as they exist at the interface between collective psychology and social engineering. Furthermore, when Dugin speaks of "angels" who are identifiable with electronic information, these entities in some ways resemble the conception of the Jinn (the "Fairies" of the Arabs, who most often manifest today as the famous "UFO aliens") that I put forward in *The System of Antichrist*, especially in terms of their ability to interact with electronic equipment and electromagnetic fields. According to the Qur'an, some of the Jinn are Muslim, in the sense that they recognize and worship Allah, while other are unbelievers; this second group are essentially demons. In *The System of Antichrist* I wrote:

> [*The Jinn*] can affect the physical plane, but they can't exist here in any stable way. To hazard a wild speculation, I can let myself wonder if our computer technology, which has always seemed to me partly inspired by the Jinn, may represent an attempt on their part to construct bodies for themselves that *are* stable in this world....

Be that as it may, if we are going to posit an *Angelopolis* or system of *Archons* as way of analyzing and making sense of contemporary patterns of power, we can't just leave it at that; this symbolic/mythopoetic *theoria* must result in a contemplative/activist *praxis*, or prove itself a total waste of time. And if we consider these Archons or Angels as the Principalities and Powers who administer the fallen order-of-perception known as This World, then such a *theoria* must embrace a comprehensive *demonology*, whose appropriate *praxis* will then necessarily comprise: 1) techniques of *contemplative insight*; 2) modes of psycho-spiritual *protection*; 3) practices leading to *inner purification*, and 4) traditional methods of *exorcism*. These elements, under the guidance and by the power of Divine Grace, will comprise some of the weapons and tactics for what the Catholic spiritual writer Lorenzo Scupoli and the Eastern Orthodox elders Nicodemos of the Holy Mountain and Theophan the Recluse called "the unseen warfare," as presented in the spiritual classic *Unseen Warfare: The Spiritual Combat and the Path to Paradise*. Dugin, however, demonstrates not the slightest intent to turn his Angelopolis into a set of strategies and techniques to carry on the war against the Angels of Dehumanization, who are nothing less than the agents of Antichrist in the invisible world.[2] Whether this is simply due

---

2. The Christian mythopoetic writer J.R.R. Tolkien, in his *Lord of the Rings* trilogy, presents us with a powerful dramatization of "the war of the angels," the final eschatological conflict as seen from the perspective of the subtle dimension. The armies of Truth—the Elves, the Hobbits and the Human Beings—go into pitched battle against the armies of the Lie, the minions of Sauron, composed of the Ring-Wraiths, the Orcs, and the Demons; the Wizard of Light, Gandalf, comes to blows with Saruman, the Wizard of Darkness. And yet the ultimate power, the One Ring, is not a weapon in that conflict, though Sauron would dearly love to get his hands on

to his despair of finding any way to counter the juggernaut of dehumanization, or whether it actually represents a willingness on his part to accept the System of Antichrist as a *fait accompli* that might conceivably employ him in some future capacity, is impossible to say for sure. However, Dugin's state of despair in the face of the situation as he presents it is not in question:

> Today we can sum up the situation in this way: we add the destructive, corrosive strategy of political postmodernity . . . into the sphere of the political . . . and we receive politics in its widest meaning, in its absolute meaning. This is the Absolute Political (*absolut Politische*), in the boundaries of which we can place two basic anthropological models. . . . the first is "contemporary man," constructed by the political, struggling against politics as such. . . . The other figure is the political soldier . . . the political soldier differs from the common man by the fact that he kills and dies for politics. His killing and personal death become an existential element of the manifestation of the political, and thus, for him the political acquires an existential dimension. . . . We believe that, on the level of political anthropology, this political soldier is confronting the decomposed, rhizomatic post-human android. We register this reading, and it may seem that we are ready to throw away our ideological differences and for the political soldier to confront the postmodern world. But my thesis is that, from the perspective of the phase shift we are in, we are living in a society where this conflict is possible, but, at the same time, its outcome is predetermined. In fact, the figure of the political man is removed. And his anthropological space is being occupied by a new personality, a very cunning and suspect personality, which is not that of the political soldier but, at the same time, is not related to the hissing, rhizomatic, twittering subindividual [i.e., "*contemporary man*"]. This personality is the political man's simulacrum. It is something that imitates the political soldier, in the same way that postmodernity imitates Modernity. In the final analysis, the readings do not give us the "human vs. post-human" scenario. Instead, what we see is the undisguised, rotten liberal post-human and the pseudo-human, the pseudo-soldier, within whom the general substance of this phase of history has found itself.

In other words, we are now in the arena of "the good demons vs. the bad

---

it; to the degree that the forces of Light are tempted to wield that power, they themselves fall under the power of the forces of Darkness, and are transformed into simulacra—wraiths. Only the *sacrifice* of the One Ring by the Hobbit Frodo can turn the tide, thereby demonstrating that the Armies of Light are fighting on the side of *islam*, submission to the Will of God, while the Armies of Darkness are only fighting in the name of the emptiness of their own egos—egos which are ultimately harvested by Sauron, the Satanic parody of the Eye of the Heart, who is the last ego and therefore the last emptiness. Frodo's pivotal role in the war shows that *The **Lord of the Rings*** is based on the principle that *our strength is perfected in weakness* [2 Corinthians 12:8–10], and that the One Ring he renounces possession of must therefore symbolize the Will of God degraded into self-will in view of the fact that if anyone other than God tries to take it and wield it, he falls like Lucifer.

demons," the realm of meaningless, unwinnable conflicts based on false alternatives and fought by wraithlike post-human simulacra. So if Dugin does not posit his Angelopolis as *theoria* with a view to *praxis*, as an analysis which exists specifically to inform action, it is because he can conceive of no true *protagonist* of the *agon* he discerns. This is not just because the cyborgs, the transhumans, the clones *will come* because "you can't fight progress," but because no *fighter* can be conceived of who is not immediately transformed into one more simulacrum in his battle against the encroaching simulacra—no hero who, as soon as he crosses swords with the wraiths, doesn't turn into a wraith himself.

Why is this? What's missing in Dugin's in-depth analysis of alienation, dehumanization and collective loss-of-soul? What's missing is, precisely, the role of *sacred activist*, the *warrior on the field of contemplation*. If the only role models we can draw upon are the "contemporary man" who rejects politics for a life of formless self-indulgence, and the "political soldier," the secular humanist saint and hero of the 20th century, like Che Guevara, whose time has now drawn to a close, then Dugin's despair is thoroughly justified. The political soldier—earnest, intelligent, courageous, self-sacrificing—is no match for the *militant unreality* of the 21st century—and the "contemporary man" isn't even in the running. What can the *worldly certainty and commitment* of the political soldier do against the *preternatural ambiguity* of Postmodernism? As for the formless "contemporary man," his way of dealing with that preternatural ambiguity and militant unreality is to capitulate to it so swiftly and totally that he never even catches a glimpse of it.

But how are things different for the warrior on the field of contemplation? To begin with, since his social identity is not determined by the Darkness of This World, because he is *not a defined social character*, he doesn't make the fatal mistake of attempting to use worldly power against the deliberate and relentless deconstruction of the world. His power is not worldly, not material or psychic in origin, but Spiritual; it draws upon a source of Energy and a quality of Insight that owe nothing to the wraithlike conditions he confronts, and which therefore lie beyond the destructive reach of those conditions. His weapons are *askesis*, *apatheia* and *hesychia*—self-mastery, dispassion, and "the peace that passeth understanding" [Philippians 4:47]. And because Divine contemplation is the source of both his strategic insight and his combative power, he is able to provide the major element that's missing from Dugin's admittedly penetrating analysis of the postmodern world: the principle that *the power to struggle against worldly conditions*, and *the insight to carry on that struggle with strategic intelligence*, are based upon, and inseparable from, *a spiritual liberation from the world*. The sacred activist, the warrior on the field of contemplation, is in the world but not of it; consequently, when he fights, he fights like an angel. The "war of the angels" that Dugin sees—though only obscurely, as if peering into a dark, metallic mirror—is not a battle between "the good demons and the bad demons," between two rival armies of the powers of chaos and depersonalization, but a war between those angels and men who have remained loyal to Absolute Reality, and those other angels and other men who have thrown in their lot with chaos, meaninglessness and destruction. And this battle is *not* a meaningless one like the battles between human souls in Hell, and those darker battles between one fallen angel and another in the same Hell—no: it is a battle with a true cause, which means that it will have a true outcome. The outcome of the contest is: salvation or damnation; the cause of the struggle, and the prize of it, is: the human soul. This conflict has its inevitable reflection in the political dimension in terms of concrete goals and strategies, but this reflection cannot be reduced to an ideological program, since conformation to the Will of God produces results that can neither be predicted nor controlled by human beings. It is this quality of mysterious, transcendental Necessity that prevents the true angelic war from being turned into a humanly-conceived ideological simulacrum or depersonalized by transhuman forces to which the integrity of the human form is either an irrelevant concern or an obstacle to be removed. And since the context of this war is "the separation of the sheep and the goats" [cf. Apocalypse 25:31–46] in the face of the impending dissolution of the *manvantara*, its final fruits will not be harvested, nor its ultimate triumph celebrated, in this world. If this sounds to us like a flimsy rationalization or a vague fantastic hope, it is only because we have lost the concrete sense of the present proximity and future inevitability of the next world, due to the collective atrophy of the Eye of the Heart.

The concept of the "warrior on the field of contemplation" obviously takes us beyond the realm of politics, though in a direction diametrically opposed to the mass flight of today's world toward dehumanization. The contemplative Way can never be made truly popular—though my own generation certainly tried to popularize it through the use of psychedelic drugs and the disastrous identification of mysticism with "absolute self-indulgence"—yet the vocation of the contemplative, though naturally reserved for the few, has always had a "leavening" effect on society. Even the hermit (as Lao Tzu understood) has an influence on the human world around him. Like the hermit, the "normal," worldly man is also alone—alone with his concerns, his beliefs, his fears and desires. The difference with the hermit is that he is not isolated in his solitude; instead of being alone with his obsessions, he is alone with all things—alone with the universe. This is why—even though, at the empty point at the Center of things, at "the still point of the turning world," he is entirely without agendas—he always makes room for something new.

On Chapter Twelve: "Fourth Political Practice"

This is the chapter where Aleksandr Dugin fully emerges as a magician, and possibly a Satanist. By calling him a "Satanist" I do not mean to accuse him of any punishable crime, or even of conducting midnight rituals in forest clearings or city apartments; I intend only to indicate that he has *inverted* the sacred science of metaphysics in such a way that it now leads away from God instead of toward Him. He specifically declares *magic* to be the praxis of the Fourth Political Theory—and when, speaking of the need to move beyond the subject/object duality, he says that "we should . . . move towards *ontic* roots but not ontological heights . . . we should postpone such notions as the dimension of spirit and the divine, and move towards chaos," he clearly demonstrates that his invocation of *unity* (see below) is directed not to the Unity of God or the Transcendent Unity of Being, but to the "unity" of the Abyss. In terms of Sufi pneumatic anthropology, this counterfeit unity is based not on the *Ruh*, the Presence of God (*hadhrat Allah*) within the spiritual Heart (*al-Qalb*), the Immanence of the Transcendent, but rather on the false cohesion of the unconscious ego, the *nafs*. This *nafs* acts to reject and veil Transcendence whenever it appears via the "unity" of ego-identification, which appears as a dark, boundless possessiveness that says to everything within its field, "this is mine; this is as aspect of myself; all this is me; all things are one in me." (According to William Blake, this state is represented by the *hermaphroditism* of Satan as opposed to the *androgeny* of Plato's Primordial Man—who, in Blake's symbology, is Albion united with his female Emanation, Jerusalem.) This indefinite liminal possessiveness whereby all things, as it were, are "identified with themselves" instead of being understood as outward manifestations of their inner principles, is the ego's counterfeit of the immanence of God. It appears as an obscure sense of unity without transcendence that acts to dissolve all distinctions and creative polarities; in other words, it represents the triumph of the Substantial Pole, which is identifiable in some ways with Heidegger's *dasein*. This unity of the *nafs* is precisely what Aleksandr Dugin means by "Chaos." Dugin wants

> that kind of instance where myth and ritual are not yet separated . . . where mentality and activity are in common, where idea means realisation and realisation is idea, and where thinking and acting have one source.

This would be an adequate description of the integrated human being who lives according to the norms of Tradition and consequently thinks and acts in line with the immanent Will of God, were it not for Dugin's denial of the Spirit and his self-contradictory attempt to base integration on chaos. The radical fractures in our collective psyche have now become so intolerable that it's increasingly difficult for us to imagine that these inner divisions might be healed by coming into a relationship with the transcendent Unity of God; to the degree that this Unity is hidden from us, we are tempted to turn instead to the false unity of chaos, in which the torment of our internal contradictions can at least be temporarily anesthetized in unconscious darkness. Dugin appears to be seeking the automatism of pre-reflective instinct where mentality and impulse are totally fused—a condition which, according to the science of *tasawwuf*, is intrinsic to the *nafs al-ammara b'l su*, the "soul commanding to evil." The "commanding soul" may have pretensions to spiritual elevation and metaphysics, but its first love and perennial default position is the Dionysian "unity" of the Abyss.

In order to make unsavory, lowlife Dionysus attractive to the educated classes, his adversary, Apollo—the glorious and terrifying Archer of Light—must be pictured as an effete, over-intellectual idealist, like Nietzsche did in *The Birth of Tragedy*. Dugin and Heidegger do their best to represent the "Apollonian" school of Platonic metaphysics, and the entire tradition of western philosophy based on it, as a pedantic, impotent old professor whose Logos is exhausted. (This may be the perfect *shadow* of Logos-based philosophy, but certainly not its essence.) No longer will we submit to the tedious, *dualistic* process of first thinking clearly so as to articulate our *theoria* and then methodically applying this *theoria*, as *praxis*, to the conditions we wish to influence; now our mentality and our action must be inseparable. We must operate on the basis of a unified, formless spontaneity where we *think* in line with our *obsessions* and *lurch* in line with our *impulses* in such a way that our *thinking* and our *lurching* are one, this being the Devil's counterfeit of the Taoist *wu wei*, "doing without doing." We must philosophize in the spirit of automatic writing and act in the spirit of "just do it!" And it's obvious that Dugin himself can do nothing else, given that his *theoria* is obscure, chaotic and contradictory, totally incapable of suggesting any clear course of action, and so of course his *praxis* must be the same.

Speaking in social terms, this obscurity may ultimately be derived from the fact that the global financial elites now hold title to the only "articulate and comprehensive theory expressed through a methodical course of action" that is still permitted—a *theoria* and a *praxis* so terrible that they must keep it carefully under wraps, at least until the day comes when "the revelation of the method" administers the *coup-de-gras*. Part of their agenda is to reduce the masses to an unconscious impulsiveness that is presented to us as freedom, but which is really nothing but a boundless passivity. Mere political theorists are useful to these Luciferian adepts only for purposes of mystification—and, as my wife points out, the brainwashers, mind-controllers, advertising executive and social engineers are banking on the very kind of unity of thought and impulse that Dugin proposes, since the human being whose thoughts and impulses are totally fused is thereby totally controllable.

It is undoubtedly true, in our infinitely distracting, high-speed, information society, that we have less and less time to think clearly and act deliberately, but this emphatically does *not* mean that our only recourse is to capitulate to the chaos that is pulverizing our minds and our intentions, and take it as our guide. If we want to regain our ability to effectively unite thought and action, we must intuit the ultimate context, the *true* "ontic root" of subject and object, thought and action, mind and conditions—a root which is planted above, in the earth of the celestial archetypes, not in their lower material/psychic reflections. The inverted Tree of Cosmic Manifestation with its roots in the sky that appears in so many myths—as the Norse Yggdrasil, for example—represents the metaphysical doctrine that all visible manifestation is rooted in its invisible spiritual Principle; as William Blake put it, "every material effect has a spiritual cause." The root of this tree is not to be found in the formless Chaos of the unredeemed Substantial Pole but in the trans-formal Source of form, the Essential Pole. It is God, not Chaos, Who lies beyond the subject/object duality, and therefore has the power to synthesize them: *I will show them My signs on the horizons and in their own souls until they are satisfied that this is the Truth. Is it not enough for you, that I am Witness over all things?* [Q. 41:53]. Chaos is the confusion of subject and object, not their union.

Dugin presents us with a table of the dualities that would ideally be unified in the Fourth Political Practice: Theory and Practice, Principle and Manifestation, Myth and Ritual, Mentality and Activity, Idea and Realization, Thinking and Action. He says that he wants to overcome the "subject/object duality" and consequently the *opposition* between theory and praxis—a strange use of the word "opposition," since the whole idea of theory and praxis is that they should be as closely united as possible, otherwise the theory would be meaningless and the praxis impossible. Theory and praxis are, by definition, a unity expressing itself as a duality, a duality in view of a unity. He says:

> The main idea of the Fourth Political Theory is to walk away from the dualism between the subject and the object, between intention and realisation, and from the dual topography which the philosophy of modernity, the science of modernity, and the *politology* of modernity are based on. It is not mere chance that we talk about *Dasein* as the subject of political theory. *Dasein,* as proposed by Heidegger, is a way to overcome the subject-object duality, that is, an aspiration to find the root of ontology. Heidegger mentioned the *inzwischen,* or the "between," while talking about the existence of *Dasein.* The principal nature of *Dasein* is being "between." *Dasein* is *inzwischen.* . . . Heidegger said that if we want to understand *Dasein,* we should realise and construct a fundamental ontology which would not lose contact with the *ontic* (that which exists; reality) roots of *Dasein,* and would not ascend or sublimate, sooner or later, to anything correlated with the 2000-year-old (from Plato, or even the

last of the Pre-Socratic philosophers, up to Nietzsche) general philosophical constructions on which modernity is based.

Modernity, however, is not based on Plato but largely on the rejection of Plato, first in the name of Aristotle's notion of the inseparability of idea and manifestation (the hylomorphic theory) and then in favor of pure empiricism. And why this nearly universal call, shared by Dugin, to overcome the subject-object duality? When and why did this duality become such an intolerable burden, a dead weight that has begun to make even gender burdensome to us? It became burdensome precisely when the "root of ontology"—God, in other words—was abandoned. If "God is dead," then dualities are transformed from creative polarities into excruciating fractures, vicious contradictions, after which the only apparent elixir of relief is the black wine of Dionysus. Nietzsche's *praxis* was actually quite consistent with his *theoria* in this regard: first deny God, then go mad. Heidegger/Dugin defines as *real* only material "ontic" actualities, not spiritual principles—and it's obvious that nothing can grow in the long shadow of "God is dead" but the quickly decaying mushrooms of philosophical materialism.

In relationship to his table of dualities, Prof. Dugin mentions the doctrines of René Guénon, but in a way that suggests a fundamental disagreement with him. Dugin wants to fuse dualities, but sees one of Guénon's central doctrines as a product of the *amplification* of dualities, not their fusion. He says:

> If we amplify the aforementioned duality of this table, we would come across Guénon's model of the "principle of the manifested'; notably, that the manifestation here is closer to the practice, but not to that which is manifested. . . .

In *Man and His Becoming according to the Vedanta*, Guénon has the following to say about "the principle of the manifested":

> The "Self" considered in this manner in relation to a being, is properly speaking the personality [*by which Guénon means "fundamental personhood," not "mask" or "persona"*]; it is true that one might restrict the use of this latter word to the Self as principle of the manifested states, just as the "Divine Personality," *Ishvara*, is the Principle of universal Manifestation; but one might extend it analogically to the "Self," as principle of all the states of the being, both manifested and unmanifested.
>
> The personality, indeed, is unmanifested, even insofar as it is regarded more especially as the principle of the manifested states, just as Being, though it is properly the principle of universal manifestation, remains outside of and beyond that manifestation (and we may recall Aristotle's "unmoved mover" at this point); on the other hand, formless manifestation is also, in a relative sense, principial in relation to formal manifestation, and thus it establishes a link between the latter and its higher unmanifested principle, which is, moreover, the common principle of these two orders of manifestation.

In itself, then, Atma is neither unmanifested (*vyakta*) nor unmanifested (*avyakta*), at least when one only regards the unmanifested as the immediate principle of the manifested and the unmanifested (though this Supreme Principle can also be said to be unmanifested in a higher sense, if only thereby to proclaim its absolute changelessness and the impossibility of characterizing it by any positive attribution whatsoever).

These passages might begin to explain Dugin's puzzling and paradoxical statement that

We are interested in that kind of instance where both principle and manifestation have a common root (they can never have a common root, not for a moment, and that is most interesting for us).

Dugin appears to be struggling (or playing) here with the apparent paradox expressed above by Guénon that the principle of the manifested is the unmanifested, but at the same time both the unmanifested and the manifested are manifestations of a third thing, the *Atman*, unmanifested in a higher sense, which transcends both of them. In contemplative terms, this doctrine is reflected in the fact that the Inner (i.e., human consciousness freed from impressions of the outer world) is experienced, on one level of contemplative practice, as the creative source of that world—this type of *samadhi* being associated with the brain-center—while on a deeper level, both consciousness and world are experienced as a polarized manifestation of God's Creative Word, *Who needs only to say to something "Be!" (Kun!) and it is* [Q 1:17] which in turn is a reverberation of the *Atman* which lies beyond both consciousness and world because it is beyond Being, this higher *samadhi* being associated with the *Hridayam*, the Heart center.[3] The Qur'an teaches that, on one level, humanity possesses the *Amana*, making him the synthetic epitome of the universe around him and therefore, in a proximate sense, the source of it, while on a higher level, the only Source is Allah: *I will show them My signs on the horizons and in their own souls until they are satisfied that this is the Truth. Is it not enough for you, that I am Witness over all things?* [Q. 41:53]

---

3. In the Hindu Yoga tradition, *savikalpa samadhi*—a state of deep concentration upon the Real in which a vestige of thought-and-world nonetheless continues—gives way at a higher stage to *nirvikalpa samadhi*, in which the complex of thought-and-world is totally absorbed into the Unitary Consciousness of the Formless Absolute. It is at the moment when consciousness *re-emerges* from *nirvikapla samadhi*, the instant when thought first re-awakens, that the universe is experienced as the "field aspect" of the Human Form, projected into outer existence by the power of thought itself. When the more complete stage known as *sahaja samadhi* is attained, however—a station in which the self-and-world complex fully reappears, though this complex has lost its power to veil the *Atman*—both the human form and the outer world are seen in their "metaphysical transparency," as the very presence of the *Atman*, the Indwelling Absolute Witness.

Dugin makes the very interesting and useful point that the Greeks had no word for "thing"—the usual English translation of the Latin *res*—but understood every manifest entity as a *pragma*, an action in the sense of a dynamic actualization of a principle, not merely a passive object; they understood that principles must manifest as actions, must be *actualized*. Likewise, in the practice of Divine contemplation, every realization of a metaphysical principle in the realm of *theoria* must give rise to a corresponding action in the realm of *praxis*, whereby the will is conformed to that principle by virtue of *askesis*. Without a unity of *theoria* and *praxis* in contemplation, *theoria* falls into error and *praxis* into passivity or self-will, which results in either obsessive activity or numb paralysis. Likewise Islamic metaphysics conceives of the objects of the world not as self-subsistent entities but as Acts of God. The necessary realization of principle in terms of action is a valid intuition which, as Dugin suspects, does indeed open the door to the possibility of what I have called "sacred activism." If action is inherent in contemplation, then there can also be such a thing as an action permeated by contemplation.

However, the dualities that Dugin lists—theory and practice, principle and manifestation, myth and ritual, mentality and activity, idea and realization, thinking and action—*cannot be unified in the absence of Transcendence*. Since Transcendence is the Principle that has manifested Itself in terms of these dualities, it is also necessarily the site and agency of their synthesis. Algis Uzdavinys, in *Philosophy and Theurgy in Late Antiquity*, demonstrates how the *praxis* of the Platonic *theoria* was, precisely, *theurgy*; when the element of theurgy was lost, Platonism became barren because there was no way any more to *actualize* it. Spiritual *theoria* however, including those aspects of it that were inherited from Greek philosophy, was organically re-unified with *praxis* in both Christianity and Islam: in Islam by Suhrawardi's *Ishraqi* Illuminists and the various Sufi schools, in Christianity by Hesychasm and other contemplative traditions. The resurrection and Christianization of Plato within Christianity, the comprehensive union of *theoria* and *praxis* in the context of contemplation, appears fully formed in the works of St. Maximos the Confessor. Consequently (and unfortunately) when Algis Uzdavinys calls for the resuscitation of the theurgy of classical antiquity in our own time, he demonstrates a willful ignorance of the obvious fact that this has already been done within both Islam and Christianity. I would even go so far as to say that the miraculous icons of Eastern Orthodoxy—speaking in terms of the horizontal, temporal inheritance of *materia*, not of the vertical, constituting *forma* which constitutes effective Dispensation—relate to the tradition of the "spiritually animated statues" of Greek Paganism—though the sacramental art of "icon writing" translates this ultimately degenerated practice to a higher level by purifying it of magic and polytheism and placing it under the life-giving dispensation of a Divine Revelation now presently in force, not a dead religion that can be "resurrected" only in terms of what Guénon termed its toxic "psychic residues." To attempt to bring Neoplatonic theurgy back out of its grave *in opposition to and denial of* the Divine sacramental theurgy of Christianity—and of Islam, where a living tradition of theurgy takes the form of *salat* and *dhikrullah*—is, precisely, to practice demonic invocation.

That Dugin wishes to replace both Christian and Islamic theurgy with Pagan magic, based upon a truly Satanic metaphysics, becomes explicit in the following passage:

> Nietzsche said, "Not when truth is dirty, but when it is shallow the seeker of knowledge steps reluctantly into its water." According to this, how can we try to form a clear conception of what Fourth Political Practice is? By reversing the order of these two columns as a first step [*i.e., by inverting the order of the pairs-of-dualities listed above*]. We should obtain practice as theory, take principle as manifestation, mentality as activity and thinking as action. What is Fourth Political Practice? It is contemplation. What is the manifestation of the Fourth Practice? It is a principle to be revealed. In what aspect is the myth realised as ritual? It becomes theurgic fact (let us recognise that Neoplatonic theurgy is the reanimation of statues). What is activity as mentality? It is the idea that thoughts are magic, that thoughts can change reality; it is a suggestion that thoughts replace reality as fact. Fourth Political Practice brings us to the nature of the supranatural world, to the antithesis of Weber's metaphor [*that technology has resulted in "the disenchantment of the world"*] in the realisation of the technological aspect of the project. What is the supranatural world? It is a world where there is no barrier between idea and realisation. It is the principle of adopting a magical view of the world based on the idea that thought is the only thing that crosses worlds, and everything we cross with is nothing more than a thought. What kind of thought is it? Pure thought. The vehicle of Fourth Political Theory and Practice lives in a supranatural world. What is "menactivity'? It is a trans-substance, a transformation of spirit into body and body into spirit, and it is the main problem of hermeticism.

The fact that Dugin continues to impersonate a humble, pious, holy pilgrim of the Old Believers while at the same time publishing statements like this is evidence that Freedom Alternative's story of his attempt to introduce Paganism and Satanism into the Russian Orthodox Church is probably right.

Let us begin to unpack this virtual rat's-nest of conceptual Satanism by first considering Nietzsche's notion of *the dirtiness of truth*—an idea has everything to do with the habit, which he did much to popularize, of seeking truth not in the *heights* but in the *abyss*. Here Nietzsche flatters the "courage" and "audacity" of the modern and especially the postmodern seeker who has no fear of "getting his hands dirty"—not to mention his brain and his heart—by looking for truth in cruelty, atrocity, meaninglessness and insanity: in other words, in the existential nakedness of things when divorced from their celestial arche-types. The problem with this practice of seeking knowledge in ontic roots rather than ontological heights—of searching for truth in the Substantial Pole rather than the Essential Pole—is not that these roots are dirty, but that they are secondary and derivative. The alchemists never shied away from the "dirty waters" of the psychophysical dimension because they knew that their goal was purification; they understood that the tree they climbed, though they had to begin that climb from the leaden heaviness of the Substantial Pole, had its roots not below, in deadly paralysis, but above, in the radiant core of the Intellectual Sun. Likewise Dante journeyed through Hell in his *Divine Comedy* not because he sought his goal in the infernal regions, but because everything that stood between him and the "ontological heights" of Paradise first had to be exposed in Hell and then expiated in Purgatory.

This is the Way. There is no other.

And what a crescendo of contradiction Dugin reaches here! In Chapter Ten, "The Ontology of the Future," he says:

> This subjectivity of time does not mean that prognostication will be self-ful-filling prophesy, as per Robert K. Merton, nor that any event is realisable a priori. The future is strictly determined, not something voluntary.

But if the future is strictly determined, not voluntary, how can Dugin now say that "thoughts are magic . . . thoughts can change reality"? Obviously he can't. Either Aleksandr Dugin is simply scatter-brained enough have forgotten what he said earlier in his book, or he is using the mind-control technique that, in *The System of Antichrist* and elsewhere, I have termed "unconscious contra-diction," which acts to stun the critical faculties of the unfortunate victim (the reader) into submission, leaving him or her highly open to suggestion; it's one of the most common techniques of magic. And what, precisely, is "the techno-logical aspect" of the Fourth Political Practice, of its program to magically employ thought to change reality? Although this may possibly refer to various more-or-less established methods of technological mind-control, the most obvious answer is that Dugin is alluding to the science of psychotronics, the technological amplification of thought-power, such as was exhaustively researched in *Psychic Discoveries behind the Iron Curtain* by Sheila Ostrander and Lynn Schroeder [1970; revised 1984], a book which apparently sparked the creation of the CIA Stargate program to investigate and teach remote viewing, thereby hopefully closing the "psychic weapons gap" between the U.S. and Rus-sia. Aleksandr Dugin's possible connection with such research should certainly be investigated. Likewise the Neo-Platonic "reanimation of statues" suggests the creation of an android, though there is no direct evidence that such an operation is part of the Neo-Eurasian agenda.

And what exactly does Dugin mean by *contemplation*? This is not a word to employed in a vague or impressionistic manner. Dugin's "contemplation" is clearly not the *samatha* or *satipatthana* of Buddhism, nor the *dhyana* or *samadhi* of Hinduism, nor the *muraqaba* or *fikr* of Sufism. Since Dugin professes to be an Eastern Orthodox Christian, could it be contemplation according to his own tradition? St. Maximos the Confessor [*Ambigua of St. John* 7:23–24] defines Christian contemplation as follows:

> All things without exception necessarily cease from their willful movement toward something else when the ultimate object of their desire and participation appears before them and is, if I may put it this way, contained in them uncontainably according to the measure of the participation of each. And it is to this end that every lofty way of life and mind hastens, an end "in which all desire comes to rest, and beyond which they cannot be carried, for there is nothing [*higher*] 'toward which all good and excellent movement is directed' than the repose found in total contemplation by those who have reached that point," as our blessed teacher [*St. Gregory the Great*] says.
>
> For in that state nothing will appear apart from God, nor will there be anything opposed to God that could entice our will to desire it, since all things intelligible and sensible will be enveloped in the ineffable manifestation and presence of God, not unlike what happens during the day, when neither the light of the stars nor the stars themselves are visible, since the sun has appeared shining with its incomparably greater light, by which the stars are so completely hidden that we are no longer able even to perceive their very existence. Of course with respect to God this happens to an infinitely greater degree, given the infinite distance and difference between the uncreated and the created.

Dugin's "contemplation" however, since he identifies it with such things as "the reanimation of statues" and the idea that "thoughts are magic," is the very antithesis of the "repose" experienced by those whose "ultimate object of . . . desire and participation appears before them" and who are therefore totally free of "anything opposed to God that could entice [*their*] will to desire it."

And what might Dugin mean by the following?

> What is the supranatural world? It is a world where there is no barrier between idea and realisation. It is the principle of adopting a magical view of the world based on the idea that thought is the only thing that crosses worlds, and everything we cross with is nothing more than a thought. What kind of thought is it? Pure thought.

A thorough metaphysical critique is definitely called for at this point. The first question we need to ask is, "What does it mean for there to be 'no barrier between idea and realization'"? The only One to Whom there is absolutely no barrier between idea and realization is God—and God obviously cannot be threatened or cajoled or trapped or fooled into becoming part of any political *praxis*; so Dugin must be referring to some other reality here. The second question is: "Whose ideas are we talking about?" Since they cannot be the ideas of God, they must be the ideas of some other being or order of beings—and since Dugin is speaking of political practice with technological assistance, he is most likely referring to the ideas of human beings. And the third question must therefore be: "In what world might there be no barrier, or at least a negligible one, between human ideas and their realization?" Dugin speaks of the "supranatural world" which, if he is not referring to the Celestial world where the supremacy of God's Will appears in the absence of any veil, is most likely what the Catholics call the "preternatural world," the Muslims the *Alam al-Mithal* or the Imaginal Plane, various occultists, including those of the Theosophical Society, the "astral plane," and the Hermetic Order of the Golden Dawn (judging from the poem "The Second Coming" by W.B. Yeats) the *Anima Mundi*, "the Soul of the World." This is also the world of dreams, where thoughts are immediately turned into images. If we take these images as the "reality" of that world, then we can certainly admit that there is little barrier on that plane between idea and realization. The question that every magician asks, however, is: "Can ideas be seeded as images on the astral plane in such a way that they affect the physical plane?"

Perhaps they can, up to a point; most serious magicians will have "proved" this thesis to their own satisfaction by producing certain "phenomena." But if thoughts can create "realities," who or what creates those thoughts in the first place? Do we claim to possess absolute authority over our own thoughts, imaginations and desires? This is a question that most magicians studiously avoid. The magician wants to see action as beginning with himself alone and then going on to affect other people or the world; he usually does not like to inquire into the origins of his own thoughts and motivations, because as soon as he does so he will be forced to realize that his sense of sovereign power over phenomena is illusory. Like the Peter O'Toole character of Lawrence of Arabia said in the motion picture of the same name, "You can do whatever you want, but you can't *want* whatever you want." Whatever may be our ability to affect a particular set of circumstances, we are nonetheless necessarily affected by other circumstances; in the act of exercising power over the world, the magician inevitably opens himself to forces which are simultaneously exerting power over him. And magical thought is the furthest thing from "pure thought." Pure thought conforms to Truth out of Love in the context of the virtue of *apatheia*, dispassion. Magical thought, however, is polluted thought, passionate and desirous by nature, a type of mentality totally incapable of conforming itself to Truth because it is inseparable from the desire for things to be other than they are—and if you are not willing to accept things as they are, you can neither see them nor love them.

Once the principle that *to be a magician is to be a victim of magic* is understood, magic loses both its allure and its *raison d'être*. And after magic disappears, only two things are left: *work* and *prayer*.

And exactly what does Dugin intend by introducing the theme of Neoplatonic theurgy? The Neoplatonic theurgists, like Iamblichus, invoked *the gods*. Some may have understood these "gods" as the personifications of various metaphysical principles or Names of the One, and consequently that what they were actually invoking was the spiritual power to intellectually actualize these principles. Most, however, undoubtedly thought of the gods—erroneously—as separate, autonomous, supernatural entities, this being the fundamental error of Paganism. Does Dugin hope to invoke the *gods* or *angels* of his Angelopolis to do his bidding, or that of his superiors, to advance his Fourth Political Theory, organize his Neo-Eurasian Movement, and tear down the tower of the Atlanticist Hegemony? If so he would do well to admit that even the Pagans of antiquity believed that no man can control the gods, otherwise he might end up chained to a crag in Caucasian Georgia with an eagle eating his liver. And if he is wise enough to see that what the ancients called "gods" were really the beings that the Christians and Muslims now call "angels," he will hopefully remember that the word *angelos* means "messenger"—that angels (outside of fallen angels, that is) act only under the command of God.

The ceremonial magic of the European Renaissance largely descended from the theurgy of the Neoplatonists. The working assumption of the Renaissance magicians of Western Christiandom was essentially as follows: Since Christ, by His crucifixion and resurrection, has overthrown the Kingdom of Satan, it is now both possible and licit for a Christian magician, after fasting and purifying himself, to invoke the help of the angels so as to enslave and control the devils, forcing them to obey his will by finding buried treasure, securing the attentions of a desired woman, or vanquishing his enemies. The fatal contradictions in such an approach will be obvious to anyone who is not blinded by the hunger for power.

And precisely where and why does hermeticism come in? Henry Corbin, in **Spiritual Body and Celestial Earth**, and Titus Burckhardt, in **Alchemy: Science of the Cosmos, Science of the Soul**, speak of the spiritualization of the body and the embodiment of the Spirit as the goal of the hermetic path and the alchemical *Magnum Opus*. This purification, transmutation and sacred marriage comprises what Tradition calls the "lesser mysteries," the psychic mysteries by which the soul is purified and balanced and the central point of the soul, the spiritual Heart, located. After the Heart is realized, the next phase, known as the "greater mysteries," is the direct vertical ascent, along the ray of the Spirit, to mystical

Union with God. In Islam the lesser mysteries are symbolized by Muhammad's *isra'*, his instantaneous "night journey" from Mecca to Jerusalem, to the Rock on the Temple Mount where the Prophet Abraham, in earlier years, stood prepared to sacrifice his son—Isaac in Judaism, Ishmael in Islam—until God stayed his hand, and the greater mysteries by Muhammad's *miraj*, his subsequent vertical ascent through the celestial spheres to *the Lote Tree of the Farthest Limit* [Q. 53:14], beyond which lay nothing but the naked Presence of God. Is the ability to complete the lesser and greater mysteries what Dugin is hoping to attain through his hermetic studies? I can find no indication whatsoever that this is the case, seeing that he says nothing at all about self-purification or the achievement of psychic integration or self-transcendence in Union with God. God is *not even mentioned*; all Dugin talks about are angels and magic. And anyone who, like Dugin in this chapter, allows that "the complete integral man consists of *Homo sapiens* and *Homo demens*"—the synthesis of the Wise Man and the Madman—might in some sense be true has both a pretty narrow idea of Wisdom and a pretty naïve idea of madness; by no stretch of the imagination can such a person be in quest of psychic balance and wholeness, much less Union with God, any more than a person who pretends to seek a "balance" between Truth and falsehood can be in quest of the Truth. Whoever tries to synthesize Wisdom and Madness will simply become mad, like Nietzsche did, while what sometimes appears as madness to "the wise of this world" when exhibited by a spiritual Master is Wisdom and nothing else. The "crazy wisdom" of the sages, the shocking and paradoxical actions of Khidr, the eternal prophet of the Sufis [cf. Q. 18:60-82] are not irruptions of chaos, but manifestations of a higher order, a higher Logos than this world can accept or understand.

Finally, what might be the import of the "reversal of the columns"—that is, the reversal of their normal order—whereby practice becomes the source of theory, manifestation the source of Principle, ritual the source of myth, activity the source of mentality, realization-of-idea the source of idea, action the source of thought? This is the height of *meticulous and calculated absurdity*, a "system" worthy of the inverted genius of one of the fallen Cherubim. Each of these inversions boils down to something like "let's just do something—*anything*—and then try and figure out the significance of it, why we did it and what it might be good for." This is similar, in a way, to David Bohm's "dialogue" practice, a process of thinking and communicating with no goal and for no preconceived purpose except watching how thinking and communication move, except that Dugin appears here to be proposing a form of *action* devoid of theory, purpose or goal—the action of a "rhizome," a "body without organs." When Bohm's formlessness in the realm of thought is translated into Dugin's formlessness in the realm of action, the result is—Chaos Magic, whose "quasi-purpose" (because of course it can have no *real* purpose or it will fall short of the grim magnificence of Chaos) is apparently to invoke the precise quality of Hell. This is true *postmodern contemplation*, worthy of those great idiot adepts whom René Guénon, in *The Reign of Quantity and the Signs of the Times*, calls "the Saints of Satan," the *Awliya al-Shaytan*.

When Principle and Manifestation are inverted, lots of interesting things happen. God evolves from an amoeba. Will dominates Intellect and so controls what is true—the result that every magician strives for. And instead of mastering my actions, those actions become my master. Consequently, for these and innumerable other reasons, I can't recommend Dugin's "menactivity."

Nonetheless, he presses forward:

> We have come to the realisation that Fourth Political Practice is not a rough realisation of Fourth Political Theory in some space where the theory is suggested to be different from its practice. There is no more space, no more *topos*, and no more topology in Fourth Political Practice aside from theory; we have annihilated any other spaces before we started, not in the consummation, but in the very beginning, before we started in a pre-ontological context. In other words, we should not look forward (it will never be changed) or backward if we really want to change the squalor we live in, because all the remnants that have made this ultimate form of degeneration possible and real have appeared and been stored there. These roots are not mere chance. The scrap-heap we exist in is not accidental and has a profound logic. Here, primordial metaphysics is expressed in techniques both modern and postmodern. Accordingly, the only path for real political struggle is appealing to the Fourth Political Practice as to the roots, free from the evolutionary process, from the very conception to the final point where we are now, because either our political struggle is soteriological and eschatological, or it has no meaning.

> And here we come to the last point. What does a world avoiding any duality look like? It looks like postmodernity, like virtuality. The wired and virtual contemporary world just says: this is not theory and not practice, not principle and not manifestation, not myth and not ritual, not thought and not action. Virtuality is just a mockery of Fourth Political Theory and Practice. It is counterintuitive enough, but this postmodern reality is closer than all previous topologies, including the theological and proto-theological. Virtuality is closer to the very unique model of Fourth Political Theory and Practice than any other element.

If postmodern virtuality is closer to the Fourth Political Theory than any other worldview, this is no mystery, due to the fact that The Fourth Political Theory *is* Postmodernism; given that, thanks largely to Heidegger, it has been *officially* divorced from the Spirit, it could be nothing else. From the perspective of such virtuality it may or may not be possible to discern the outlines of a paradigm that is greater and more complete and more polyvalent and more synthetically unified than any conceivable limited system or hierarchy, simply because all other established but partial paradigms have been deconstructed. Nonetheless, you can't get there from here. A universal equality of all illusions such as Postmodernism posits, a diversity of all the depleted and meaningless fragments that it claims to "celebrate," may function as a kind of simulacrum of the Divine All-Possibility or total ensemble of the Names of God that the Sufis call *wahadiyya*, God's synthetic unicity, the reality that led the "greatest Sufi shaykh," Ibn al-'Arabi, to say, "God is with every object of belief," and the poet William Blake to write, "Everything possible to be believed is an image of Truth." Nonetheless, for Postmodernism, there is no Truth—only images. The exhaustion of all partial views does *not* mean that the total view, the view-beyond-views, will now automatically emerge from that exhaustion—far from it, for the same reason that the "death of God" does not automatically trans-form *dasein* into God. Such ontological exhaustion is in no way an epiphany; all it can be—and even this is not guaranteed—is a prayer to Reality that It reveal Itself, an invocation of the *parousia* based on desperate need. Can Aleksandr Dugin make his way from that exhaustion, which is the Chaos of the End, through the eschatological fires of Apocalypse to the All-Possibility of the Beginning, thereby transmuting his Fourth Political Theory from simulacrum into reality? Not without the help of God—a help he has apparently rejected.

In the Vedantic rendering of the Primordial Tradition, all manifestation is understood as *Maya*, the "magical" apparition of the Supreme Principle Brah-man, of God as apparently other-than-God. *Maya*, appearance, is not literally unreal or non-existent; if it were it would not appear. But it is not what it seems; the traditional simile compares it to "a rope mistaken for a snake." *Maya* is not literally illusion; nonetheless anyone who mistakes it for Reality is under the power of illusion. And the wraith-like nature of postmodern electronic vir-tual reality may seem to corroborate this doctrine; some scientists, for example, have seriously speculated that—all man-made electronic virtuality aside—we may actually be living inside a vast computer-generated simulation, a notion that was dramatized in the *Matrix* movies. The idea that a real, invisible world may exist, of which this visible world is only a simulation, certainly seems in line with the doctrine of *Maya* and the metaphor of Plato's Cave. However, the sense of the wraith-like unreality of things produced by our collective addiction to the electronic media is actually poles apart from the vision of *Maya* as the direct manifestation of a Reality that lies beyond it but nonetheless shines through it. Our awakening to the unreality of the world and the Reality of God happens not when the world sinks into dull heedlessness and obscurity or erupts in a manic explosion of gleaming, shattered images, but when it becomes so vividly *real* to us that it no longer presents itself, according to our half-conscious, habitual modes of perception, as a "mere fact," a foregone con-clusion concealing no surprises, but is suddenly transfigured until it becomes all Vision. It was when Ramakrishna beheld, in brilliant sunshine, a flight of white cranes crossing the face of the blue-black thunderhead that this world was annihilated and *nirvikalpa samadhi* supervened. Only when the world becomes so vivid to us that it can no longer contain the Reality that's bursting through its seams does the veil of the senses lift to reveal the Face of God. In the words of Blake from *The Marriage of Heaven and Hell*,

> The ancient tradition that the world will be consumed in fire at the end of six thousand years is true . . . the cherub with his flaming sword is hereby commanded to leave his guard at the tree of life, and when he does, the whole creation will be consumed and appear infinite and holy, whereas now it appears finite and corrupt. This will come to pass by an improvement of sensual enjoyment.

Postmodern virtual reality however, though Baudrillard called it "hyperreality," is not even as real as sense-experience; it's only a dream within a dream, not an awakening from the dream. Likewise the conception of things produced by postmodern philosophy, though it may seem to approach various traditional doctrines such as *Maya* in Hinduism, or Ibn al-'Arabi's notion of the ever-changing nature of God's Self-revelations, each one unique and never to be repeated, is actually a deeper state of sleep than that of even the most sense-bound literalist. The prisoner falls asleep and dreams he has escaped his prison—then, God willing, he awakens. Such an awakening may seem tragic, but in reality it is all Mercy; whoever has awakened from the dream of artificial reality has taken the first step toward awakening from sensual "reality" itself. If we want to transcend the sense-world, first we need to come to our senses.

Returning to the hopeless, life-sucking obscurity of Heidegger's *Dasein*, Dugin says:

> *Dasein* should not be qualified either as a theoretical construction, or as a principle. Should it be used as a myth, like a narrative? This comes much closer, but it should be carefully considered. It should not exactly be used as a mentality, at least not as ontological mentality. Likewise, it should not be used as an idea or anything concerning the subject.

What is left, then, for *Dasein* to *be*? *Dasein* is, precisely, what Blake called a "negation": since it is not a truth, all that is left for it is the function and mission of *destroying* truth—a function and mission that Aleksandr Dugin has well demonstrated in a number of places in *The Fourth Political Theory*.

In the following passage, which is of the greatest interest (sections of it have already been quoted above), Dugin clearly expresses his hopes and goals for the practical application of his Fourth Political Theory, even though he has already invalidated the notion of hopes and goals by asserting that the future is strictly determined:

We are interested in the instance that both theory and practice appeared from, the instance where theory and practice are not yet divided and, *a fortiori*, are not opposites. We are interested in that kind of instance where both principle and manifestation have a common root (they can never have a common root, not for a moment, and that is most interesting for us), that kind of instance where myth and ritual are not yet separated, at that instance where mentality and activity are in common, where idea means realisation and realisation is idea, and where thinking and acting have one source. We are interested in this very intermediate level not achieved by a horizontal consideration of these pairs, but only by a new, non-horizontal dimension. Unlike Hegelianism, Marxism, communication theory, and in principle, the entire structure of modernity, we are not interested in anything that sits upon the line between theory and practice. We are looking for something that does not belong to horizontal subspace, or to some ratio-based configuration of the columns, or to the line between theory and practice. We are interested in something hidden under the theory and practice, somewhere in the common root they both grow from. From this point of view, the question of the prioritisation of either conscience [*consciousness?*] or matter during the Soviet period is absolutely wrong. The priority for us is the problem of the common root, and we should grow the Fourth Political Theory and its Practice from this root.

I have some unexpected and shocking news for Aleksandr Dugin regarding the true nature of the common root of theory and practice considered in terms of the non-horizontal dimension—which is, that the common root of theory and practice considered in terms of the non-horizontal dimension is GOD. For the knower of God, the *gnostic*, the *jñani*, the *'arif*, there is no Knowledge that is not immediately actualized and no action that is not instantaneous born from and suffused by and swallowed up in Knowledge. *When thou threwest, it was not thyself that threw, but God threw* [Qur'an 8:15]. Therefore when Dugin contradicts himself (as he apparently must) by saying that theory and practice, principle and manifestation *cannot* have a common root, this is simply another instance of his rejection of God as a concrete reality that must be taken into account. In light of this, we can see that Dugin is actually a lot more consistent than he seems.

Be that as it may, if Aleksandr Dugin seeks the common root of theory and practice anywhere but in God,

HE WILL NOT FIND IT.

∿

Next, after measuring and photographing and taking samples of and sticking his toe into the dark pool of Postmodernism, Dugin finally overcomes his timidity and dives right in:

> How does our traditionalism or new metaphysics relate to postmodernity? I consider them to be very close.... We can say that Deleuze's rhizome is a postmodern and post-structural mockery of Heidegger's *Dasein*. They are alike and they are often described in the same terms. But pay attention to the fact of how Postmodernism solves the problem of the reversal of the column's order. It solves the problem by appealing to the surface, and this is the main idea we see with Deleuze. Remember his interpretation of Artaud's "body without organs," his interpretation of the necessity of destruction, of the leveling of structure, and his interpretation of man's epidermis, his outer layer, as the basis of the screen onto which his image is projected. It is a point of mockery where Fourth Political Theory and Postmodernism meet each other. If the columns mix horizontally, some madness appears. We can use the thesis that *Homo integros*, the complete integral man, consists of *Homo sapiens* and *Homo demens*. Deleuze says, "Free!" *Homo demens*. He says that madness should escape from under *Homo sapiens* and realise the transgression between these two columns in the political sphere. Here comes the rhizomatic process, Ionic and chronological ideas of temporality [*terms related to Deleuze's theory of time*]. This postmodern dementia is much like the Fourth Political Theory, and differs from it only in its horizontality and flatness. The main problem of postmodernity is its elimination of any vertical orientation in terms of both height and depth.

Possibly I am simply handicapped by a kind of Philistine, pre-postmodern sensibility, but I have to admit that all this strikes me as extremely "creepy." Chaos and madness hurt people; what's the good of that? What's the good of it if they are only being hurt so as to produce more chaos and madness? Perhaps I am not as "esoteric" as I style myself to be, but no matter which way I look at the "spirituality" of the Fourth Political Practice, I can see no value in it; quite the reverse, in fact. Nonetheless, the struggle to untie these knots and throw light into these dark corners may still prove fruitful.

When Dugin says "This postmodern dementia is much like the Fourth Political Theory, and differs from it only in its horizontality and flatness. The main problem of postmodernity is its elimination of any vertical orientation in terms of both height and depth," he apparently means that his problem with Postmodernism has nothing to do with its chaotic quality, its dementia or its hatred of form, but only with its "democratic" horizontality. Chaos and insanity may a good first step, but they will never reach their true potential until we make a *religion* out of them. Consequently we must introduce a new element of *verti-*

cality into the postmodern chaos, a new "spirituality" that looks down rather than up, one that is oriented not to "ontological heights" but to "ontic roots." This, of course, is Guénon's precise description, in *The Reign of Quantity and the Signs of the Times*, of the *inverted hierarchy* of the Regime of Antichrist. It's as if Dugin were demonstrating how Guénon's exhaustive analysis of Satanism can be put to practical use to make us all better Satanists.

In the last paragraph of "Fourth Political Practice," Dugin concludes his explanation of what *praxis* means to him on an apocalyptic note:

> The end times and the eschatological meaning of politics will not realise themselves on their own. We will wait for the end in vain. The end will never come if we wait for it, and it will never come if we do not. . . . If the Fourth Political Practice is not able to realise the end of times, then it would be invalid. The end of days should come; but it will not come by itself. This is a task, it is not a certainty. It is active metaphysics. It is a practice.

Undoubtedly the best answer to this is provided by the Noble Qur'an:

> If Allah were to take mankind to task for their wrong-doing, he would not leave a single living creature on earth, but He reprieveth them to an appointed term, and when their term cometh they cannot put it off an hour nor yet advance it [16:61].

However, a more detailed analysis may still be in order. Aleksandr Dugin is onto something when he says that the End will never come merely through passive waiting, nor will it come if we simply give up on it. But neither will it come if we "jump the gun" by trying to force the Hand of God—a lethal error that Dugin apparently accepts as true and practical. As I make clear in *Chapter Eight*, "Parousia and the Laws of Apocalypse," the breakthrough of Eternity into time is occasioned by a fourth thing which is neither the false faith of fatalistic passivity nor the faithlessness of willful ignorance nor the misplaced faith of Promethean action—a thing called *active receptivity*.

Dugin may or may not be on the trail of something like this, but it's clear that his idea that the Fourth Political Practice could have the power to *invoke the Apocalypse* is both demented and dangerous, since the only way that this, or rather the literalistic counterfeit of it, could conceivably happen is for Dugin and his followers, possibly through their influence in Kremlin circles, to initiate World War III. Beyond that, when Dugin says that the End of Days is a task, not a certainty, he is wrong: it is both a task *and* a certainty. Marx presented the classless society as an historical inevitability, which nonetheless—and paradoxically—could only be achieved through struggle and sacrifice. This was his unwitting externalization of the Catholic doctrine of "faith and works," which neither he nor his metaphysical counterpart in the Capitalist world, John Calvin, ever really understood. Faith is not only necessary for salvation, it *is* salvation; it is "the substance of things hoped for, the evidence of things not seen" {Hebrews 11:1]. And Faith is reserved for those predestined to find Faith, for "the elect from the foundation of the world" [Peter 1:2]; this is as far as Calvin got. But Faith must result in Works, and Works are necessary to actualize Faith. Works alone can never add up to salvation or command Faith, because Works are of the will, which has to do with what *might* be, while Faith is of the Intellect, which deals only with what *must* be; this is why the will must serve the Intellect and why the Intellect must never serve the will. And the will serves the Intellect precisely by *taslim*, submission—submission to the Truth; because, unless the will is brought into line with the Intellect, Works into line with Faith, the Reality that Intellect sees and the Truth that Faith knows can never be actualized in human life. Therefore, as the Traditional Catholics teach, both Faith and Works are necessary for salvation. Translated into eschatological terms, we can say that Apocalypse, the breakthrough of Eternity into time, *must come* because, being a ray of Eternity, on some level it already *is*; but it can never be effective in our lives as Apocalypse—that is, as Revelation—if we do not have an active relationship to it, a relationship of active receptivity, of willing submission. Lacking this, Apocalypse will not be a judging and redeeming breakthrough of celestial Light but a crushing wall of impenetrable darkness.

∽

In conclusion, as an alternative *praxis* to Aleksandr Dugin's "Fourth Political Practice," based on magic, I offer the "Principles of Sacred Activism," based on prayer, which appears as Part Two of *Chapter Seven*.

May the best *praxis* win.

On Chapter Thirteen: "Gender in the Fourth Political Theory"

In this chapter, Dugin tackles the sociology of human sexuality and gender as these roles are constructed in Fascism, Liberalism, Marxism, Neo-Marxism, radical Feminism etc. He maintains that

> It is acceptable to consider "a gender" in sociological terms, in other words, gender as a socially constructed phenomenon. This is in contrast to the anatomical "sex" inherent in biological terms.

So gender is either sociological or anatomical or both, but it is in no way psychological or spiritual—undoubtedly because Postmodernism, as supported and enhanced by the electronic media, denies the reality of the human soul. Nonetheless, considering gender from the sociological point of view, Dugin fully recognizes the corruption of the human form represented by the Postmodern deconstruction of human gender, while admitting that there is no way we can profitably go "back" to earlier gender constructions:

> The re-extension of existing gender models [*from Fascism, Marxism, and Liberalism into Postmodernism*] can lead to the explosion of the hypermodern like a rotting fungus, and its gender archetypes will fail. Now we are in this moment of a postmodern re-extension, and the final breaking of gender. The stages of this break are feminism, homosexuality, sex-change operations, and transhumanity....
>
> Donna Haraway ... a feminist, or rather loosely a neo-Marxist and a postmodernist ... argued that while the mature woman may feel an urge to be "liberated," liberation in our culture involves definition of the opposite. Therefore it is necessary to overcome both the man and the woman through becoming a cyborg. According to her, sex can be overcome only by having overcome being human. In a similar vein is Foucault's conception of sexuality, that is, sexuality prior to sex, as a neutral dispositive: sexuality, spreading along the surface of the screen, the "body without organs." This pan-sexuality, which is a smooth surface of sexual arousals, remains unclear in terms of from whom it is derived, for what reason, and most importantly, no matter in what orientation or direction. As a whole, in terms of the erosion and destruction of the gender constructions of modernity, Marxist thought introduces the most significant contribution. Elements of fascism in postmodernity are represented by the practice of BDSM. Contemporary fascism contains strong elements of sadomasochism, and perverted fascism is an essential attribute of Postmodernism, along with feminism, cyborgs, a "body without organs," and so on.

But when Dugin tries to imagine what gender roles might be like under the Fourth Political Theory, he has little to offer us that would clearly distinguish these roles from the Postmodern corruption of gender as he has already described; all he can do is grope hopelessly in the dark, painfully bumping his head on various hard objects whose shapes he cannot discern:

> Gender in the Fourth Political Theory is the same as sex in *Dasein*, that is, we have explained one unknown through another. *Dasein* can somehow be sexualized, but that sex which it has cannot be either male or female. It may make sense to speak about it in terms of the androgyne. Should we say that the Fourth Political Theory may be addressed to the androgynous being, and its gender is the androgyne? Perhaps, but only if it is possible not to project onto the androgynous the obviously split models of sex as halves of a whole. Sex, according to Plato, is a unity that has been divided....
>
> So, if we understand the androgyne in this way, not as something that is composite, but as something rooted or radical, then we can talk about a radical notion, which is not sex in the sense that it is half of something else. That is, the gender of the Fourth Political Theory is that half, that sex which is

simultaneously the whole and does not need its antithesis, and is therefore self-sufficient within itself. We can theorise about this gender that it does not so much come about from an analysis of sexual or gender archetypes, but because of thinking philosophically and politically upon the subject of the Fourth Political Theory. Thus, we change the formulation of the question. We do not ask which sex is *Dasein*, we answer that the gender of the subject of the Fourth Political Theory is the same as that of *Dasein*. In this case, we can also talk about the radical ("root": from the Latin, *radicula*) androgyne, which exists not as a result of a combination of the man and the woman, but that represents instead the primordial, untouched unity.

Having no clear image of the way "forward" for human gender, Aleksandr Dugin can only place his hopes in a sort of Heideggerian *deus ex machina* based on *Dasein*:

> We suggest taking a step towards gender as *Dasein*, despite the notorious representations and opprobrium that we will cause. By going beyond the limits of gender which we know, we get to the domain of uncertainty, androgyny, and sex as practised by the angels.

In other words, Dugin's Eurasianist, Fourth Political Theory-based gender-construction is substantially identical—as Freedom Alternative has pointed out—to the corruption of gender under Atlanticist Postmodernism that he claims to oppose. The only difference seems to be his introduction of *angels*—who, traditionally considered, are without gender, though they generally appear as masculine when they reveal themselves to us, due to their spiritual power and their affinity with the Essential Pole. Some theologians maintain that Satan and his angels are profoundly jealous of human sexuality since this good is denied them, as is their original ability to take delight in God directly; this is why they love to corrupt the sexual impulse through lust, degradation and cruelty. As far as the demons are concerned, the only thing better than this would be to destroy human sexuality entirely. The Qur'an corroborates this view when it says, of the angels Harut and Marut who taught magic to the human race in Babylon, *And from these two, people learn that by which they cause division between man and wife* [2:103].

However, since I am unwilling to engage with the various past or possible *sociological constructions* of gender, for the same reason I would avoid coming into contact with corpses in various advanced stages of decay, I have opted to start over from the Beginning, by suggesting how a metaphysically-based view of gender might be developed that would be compatible with Islam, Christianity, Judaism, Hinduism, and Traditional Chinese philosophy, and Guénonian Traditionalism.

The Metaphysics of the
Human Form; The Metaphysics of Gender

Humanity is not a construct; humanity what we are. Gender is not a construct; gender is an integral part of what we are. *What we intrinsically are* is realized when self-definition comes to an end. Self-definition, which is inseparable from world-definition, is our ingrained habit of assuming the prerogatives of God. It is God, not us, Who creates both us and the world; if we attempt to secondarily "create" what God has already created we will only distort it, obscure it, destroy it. And it is God, not ourselves, who creates us; if we attempt to create ourselves after we have already been created, even while God continues to create us instant by instant, we will only denature ourselves, oppress ourselves, lose ourselves. Speaking for myself, I am what is known as an intellectual; I admit it; I plead guilty to that charge. And as an intellectual, I am ashamed of what intellectuals have done to the human race. Intellectuals—these unicorns, these chimeras, these flying horses—have made us distrust ourselves, second-guess ourselves, even attempt to deconstruct ourselves by granting greater authority to this or that invented ideology than to the totality of our actual experience as human beings. Because of the obsessions, the vanity, the heartlessness, and the cowardice of intellectuals, the moths of abstract thought have nearly eaten the human race to the bone. Enough! Without a clear recognition of, and a practical way of staying in contact with, the existential condition of humanity that is perpetually springing into existence from the metaphysical roots of Being—and of doing so entirely *beyond conceptualization*—the human intellect is pure poison, which is why the Buddhists point to the dangers of the "monkey mind" and the "philosopher disease."

First we need to remember *that* we are; only then will we begin to remember who and what we are. This remembering is not a process of self-definition, but a willingness to let ourselves *be defined*: by God, by the Tao, by the eternal human essence arising of itself, and clearly standing forth, from "the Void eternally generative." All philosophy, all metaphysics, all theology ultimately spring from this process, from the renunciation of self-definition and the simultaneous and immediate reception of integral Being. And just as *Tao*, the Way, manifests in terms of *Te*, the Power, so the reality of what we are spontaneously appears within us as the power to *know* what we are, which is inseparable from the intent to deliberately and methodically eliminate obsessive self-definition. The exercise of this power is what is known as "contemplation." Any philosopher who is not also, at least to some degree, a contemplative—any philosopher, that is, who attempts to access truth through thought alone—is necessarily in a state of mental illness.

The knowledge of *what* we are, along with all the possibilities of good and evil opened by that knowledge, spontaneously arises from our recognition of the existential fact *that* we are. And the bare fact of our existence is inseparable from our inherent nothingness when considered as separate entities, which in turn is also inseparable from God's act of saying to us *kun!*, "Be!," thus making us exactly who we are, and precisely who we were destined to be, from before the beginning of time; as each of us is a single, unique individual, so each is defined by a unique set of relations, without which that never-to-be-repeated individuality could not appear. As St. Paul said, "It is not I who live, but Christ lives in me" [Galatians 2:20], Christ Who is the Human Essence both incarnate and *in divinis*, "without Whom was not made anything that was made" [John 1:3]. Even though Heidegger hated Christianity and traditional metaphysical language, is this what he really meant by his *Dasein*? Or what he tried to mean? We will probably never know.

Once the habit of self-definition is overcome and the spiritual Heart begins to open to the contemplative witnessing of metaphysical reality—a development and outcome known as "intellection" (*intellectus* in Latin, *gnosis* in Greek, *ma'rifa* in Arabic), and which usually also involves a familiarity with one or more Divine revelations—certain dominant archetypes begin to emerge. Some of the writings of the philosophers, metaphysicians and theologians whose works are available to us are based upon this kind of unveiling; others are commentaries upon more primary sources by those with no personal experience of how these sources emerged; still others are mere speculations by those who have no familiarity whatsoever with either contemplative practice, divine Revelation or Traditional Metaphysics. This last category of writings is worthless at best, and often intellectually and spiritually dangerous.

As for the specific archetypes of gender that emerge from pure intellection, or by intellection informed and stimulated by revelation, there is a great unanimity among them over many religions, traditions and metaphysical schools. In the words of James Cutsinger, an American Christian follower of Frithjof Schuon, commenting on the conceptions of gender of both Schuon and the Anglican mythopoetic novelist and lay theologian C.S. Lewis,

> [What C.S. Lewis calls] this "real polarity" [*of gender*] is to be found, not only as Lewis suggests in creatures, however superhuman, but all the way up to the Divine Reality itself . . . which is the ultimate Source of everything else, and which for that reason is the source and paradigm of all distinctions. In its absoluteness and transcendence, the Divine is the archetype for everything masculine, while its infinity and capacity for immanence are displayed at every level of the feminine . . . the polar qualities revealed to us as sex are actually and objectively on every plane of the ontological hierarchy. . . . As Seyyed Hossein Nasr has written, "The difference between the two sexes cannot be only biological and physical, because in the traditional perspective the

corporeal level of existence has its principle in the subtle state, the subtle in the spiritual, and the spiritual in the Divine Being itself." ("Femininity, Hierarchy and God" in *Religion of the Heart*, ed. Seyyed Hossein Nasr and William Stoddart, p. 115)

As the Qur'an expresses it [36:36], *Glory be to Him Who created all the sexual pairs, of that which the earth groweth* [plants and animals], *and of themselves* [the human race], *and of that which they know not!* [the unseen world]. In terms of Hindu Shaivite Tantra, which certainly influenced Schuon, the Absolute may be identified with *Shiva* as pure Consciousness or the transcendent Witness (*Atman*), and the Infinite with his consort *Shakti*, or pure Energy (see René Guénon's *Man and His Becoming according to the Vedanta*). The fundamental polarity between Witness and Energy is the origin of universal manifestation; all appearance or creation of any kind must be based on polarity, since without a polarization between figure and ground in the primal Gestalt, nothing would appear. In the words of the Qur'an [51:49], *And all things We have created by pairs, that haply ye may reflect*. In terms of human consciousness, this polarity manifests as subject and object, the perceiver and the perceived, the knower and the known. In the Aristotelian hylomorphic theory, an analogous polarity appears as *forma* vis-a-vis *materia*, which from one perspective are the concretized reflections of Essence—*what* something is—and Existence—*that* something is. René Guénon's Essential Pole and Substantial Pole from *The Reign of Quantity and the Signs of the Times* are more or less his rendition of Aristotle's *forma* and *materia*, possibly influenced by the Yang or Creative principle and the Yin or Receptive principle as found in Taoism, especially the *I Ching*. The primal polarity upon which human gender is based appears in Islamic metaphysics as the Sublime Pen (*Kalam*, which also means "word," specifically "word of Allah") and the Guarded Tablet (*Lawh-i-Mahfūz*); the action of the Pen vis-à-vis the Tablet is analogous to "the Spirit of God" that "moved on the face of the Waters" in the first chapter of Genesis. Every religion, every mythology, and every traditional system of philosophy embraces some rendition of this primordial polarity. Genesis 5:2 reads: "Male and female created he them; and blessed them, and called their name Adam, in the day when they were created," indicating both the primal polarity of the sexes and their primal union, as with the original Androgyne of Plato, since both male and female bear the name "Adam."

This is the essential conception of gender held by every branch of the Traditionalist School, as well as all the primary sources of that School: the scriptures and Traditional Metaphysics of the world religions. Since Aleksandr Dugin cites the Traditionalists as one of his sources, he should take some time to study their doctrine of gender. As for myself, I have touched upon the metaphysics of gender in several books; here are two excerpts:

"The Primal Metaphysics of Gender"
From *Findings in Metaphysic, Path and Lore*

God Almighty as Pure Being, Creator of Heaven and Earth, is masculine. Like a King, He holds sway over both nature and society, which are feminine in relation to Him.

Beyond Being is feminine. She is like the Black Virgin, like the *Layla* of the Sufis, whose name means Night. As the divine Essence she has precedence over the Creator as Pure Being, Who, like a son, is masculine in relation to Her. If He creates *ex nihilo*, She is that very *Nihil*.

In the Manifest World, man has precedence over woman; in the Unmanifest, woman has precedence over man.

"The Alchemy of Romantic Love" from
The Science of the Greater Jihad: Essays in Principial Psychology

Alchemy, as the inner spiritual work that prepares the soul for union with God, is reflected in the world of human relations in terms of the Tantric polarity between man and woman—not simply on the level of primal sexual attraction, but in the fully personal realm of romantic love.

Integral to the alchemical Great Work is the union of Sulfur and Mercury, the masculine and feminine powers of the soul. Sulfur is the reflection of the active Spirit within the soul, and Mercury the potential receptivity of the soul to that Spirit. This synthesis produces the Androgyne, the restoration of the primordial Adam before Eve was separated. The polar union of masculine and feminine within the soul makes possible the spiritually fertile union of man and woman in the outer world—which means that the man or woman who has realized the Androgyne does not have what we usually think of as an "androgynous" personality—or a "macho" or superfeminine one either, for that matter—but rather an integrated masculine personality open to the feminine, or a complete feminine personality open to the masculine. In Jungian language, when the archetype of the Androgyne fails to be realized on its proper level—that of the inner "Syzygy," the vestibule of the Self archetype—it is displaced into the Ego and the Persona, where it produces a formless gender-ambiguity that is not essentially androgynous, but—to use Blake's terminology—"hermaphroditic." [*According to William Blake, Satan, since he is a chaotic amalgam of all possible states, is an Hermaphrodite, not an Androgyne.*] The Androgyne is the polar or tantric synthesis of masculine and feminine powers, positing the transcendence of these opposites on a higher, spiritual level; the Hermaphrodite is a chaotic crushing together of masculine and feminine, ultimately leading to a spiritual state that is lower than sexual polarity, not higher. According to the Qur'an, *surah* 2:187, where the law allowing if not encouraging intercourse between husband and wife on the nights of the Ramadan fast is laid down, *They* [the wives] *are raiment for you and ye* [the husbands] *are raiment for them*, which is another way of saying that the inner essence of the man is feminine, and of the woman, masculine—a traditional source, albeit veiled and allusive, for what we know from Carl Jung as "anima/animus" psychology. And the fact that this polar sexual quaternity is placed in the context of the "night" and prohibited during the "day" shows that it is properly an inner alchemical reality, not an outer psycho-social one. [*Or a physical one. The transgender temptation is based on a failure to realize this truth.*]

The inner alchemical work prepares the soul for the romantic encounter, just as true love between a man and a woman, itself a mode of alchemy, empowers and deepens the inner transmutation. This quaternity of inner synthesis coupled with outer relatedness was consciously practiced in some alchemical schools, which held that the transmutation of "base metal" (the chaotic, hermaphroditic amalgam of Spirit-potential and soul-potential) into "gold" (the androgynous union of Spirit and soul, *forma* and *materia*, leading to the spiritualization of the body and the embodiment of the Spirit) can only be accomplished through a collaboration between the alchemist and his *soror mystica*, his female assistant or "mystical sister." And the greatest literary expression of this "Christian Tantra" in which inner spiritual development and outer romance, combat and courtesy challenge, purify and complete each other, is Wolfram's Von Eschenbach's *Parzival*. (*Parzival* is revealed as an alchemical romance by the fact that it pictures the Grail not as a cup but as a stone—clearly the Philosopher's Stone—and by an episode near the beginning in which a dwarf named Antenor is thrown into the fire. "Antenor" is a character from the *Iliad*, but this name also suggests "athenor," the alchemical vessel in which is synthesized the *homunculus*, a tiny man, partly through the application of fire.)

Romance, which could be defined as Eros alchemically transmuted into Amor, is mysteriously capable of being "passionate, not passional." In genuine romantic love the fire of emotional and sexual passion is contained, therefore alchemical, rather than dissipative or concupiscent. It burns away the dross of attachment and egotism and synthesizes the Holy Grail, the Philosopher's Stone, which is the power of Divine Grace working in the vessel of the spiritual Heart, and thereby transmuting and purifying the field of human relations.

Without an acceptance and understanding of love between the sexes—whether or not we see this in terms of the Courtly Love tradition of western Europe, or of the Sufi-influenced romances of Persia such as Jami's *Yusuf and Zuleikha* and Nizami's *Layla and Majnun*, or of the Sahaja tradition of Vaishnava Hinduism—in other words, unless we go beyond the merely sociological construction of gender based on power-relations alone—no true comprehension of human gender and sexuality will be possible.

Mircea Eliade, in **Rites and Symbols of Initiation,** writes as follows of the spiritual symbolism of the Feminine employed by the esoteric order to which Dante Alighieri belonged, the Fedeli d'Amore, which was central to the metaphysical dimension of the ethos of Romance in the west:

> "Woman" symbolizes the transcendent intellect, Wisdom. Love of a woman awakens the adept from the lethargy into which the Christian world had fallen because of the spiritual unworthiness of the pope. In the writings of the Fedeli d'Amore we find allusions to a "widow who is no widow"; this is Madonna Intelligenza, who was left a widow because her husband, the pope, died to spiritual life by devoting himself entirely to things temporal.

There are indications that the Fedeli d'Amore might have had certain affinities with *tasawwuf* or Islamic Sufism, perhaps deriving from esoteric contacts made by the Templars in the Holy Land. In the words of one Romanian initiate who wishes to remain anonymous,

> It is said that the three secrets of the Fedeli d'Amore were: Love, Beauty and the Heart. Suhrawardi [*the Persian Sufi and* Ishraqi *or* "*Illuminist*"] speaks of Beauty, Love and Nostalgia [*which perhaps refers to "remembrance" in its spiritual sense—the Sufi* dhikr*, the Hesychast* mnimi Theou]. This is the visible, communicable secret. The second secret, reserved for the initiates, is that one must learn how to read the rule of divine Love in the book of human love. The third secret belongs to adepts. It is the Faith of the Faithful, which is the direct vision of God in a human form, beautiful to contemplate, but without the agitation of the carnal nature.... The Fedeli d'Amore appeared to the later Sufis as an unexpected variant of the Shadhiliyya; their particular way of symbolically mixing love and poetry is common to both systems.

Suffice it to say that any philosopher, sociologist or ideologue who tries to make sense of human gender and sexuality while doing his best to ignore both spiritual and human love is doomed to failure.

René Guénon, in **Symbols of Sacred Science,** in the chapter entitled "The Radiating Heart and the Flaming Heart," identifies the element of heat, as represented by wavy rays in various traditional images of the sun—the sun being a symbol of the spiritual Heart—with both *Love* and *Life*, just as Light, represented by straight rays, is identified with the Intellect. In other words, Love is Life. And this Love or Life, on the level of first principles, is also inseparable from the spiritual Intellect, the *Nous*. Guénon says:

> The fire at the center of the being is at one and the same time both light and heat; but if these two terms are to be translated respectively as intelligence and love, although fundamentally they are but two inseparable aspects of one and the same thing, it will be necessary ... to add that the love in question then differs as greatly from the sentiment that is given the same name as does pure intelligence from reason.

Spiritual Love is not sentiment, though it manifests as sentiment on a lower, more subjective level, just as Intelligence is reflected on a lower level as reason and logic; therefore, in terms of the metaphysical order, to ignore or suppress Love, or fail to take it into account, is to darken the Intellect—after which both rationality and the *sentiment* of love, deprived of their first principles, are also destroyed. So if we accept Guénon's view of the matter, we must conclude that when Heidegger proclaimed the death of the Logos he was also announcing the death of Love; the result of such a disaster could only be a subhuman hell on earth—such a hell as we now see growing up all around us. If Dugin wants a world like this, or thinks he can make good use of it, then he is welcome to it. Love was and is the central principle of Christianity, which was dominant in the West for a thousand years, nor can any other true religion exist without the power of it. And even if the knowledge of Love dies out in the human race, inevitably leading to its own death, Love itself will remain unaffected, because Love—*Al-Mahabbah*—like Truth, *Al-Haqq*—is a name of God. If Dugin's philosophy is fragmentary and self-contradictory, it may simply be because, like Postmodernism, it has no Love to hold it together. Whoever or whatever remains in the presence of Love, lives; whoever or whatever departs from Love has taken the road to death; whoever or whatever rejects Love, and glories in that rejection, is dead already. Love does not run after those who have dedicated themselves to death, begging them to save themselves by choosing life; it simply remains in its own essence, thereby giving whatever still has a spark of life in it a chance to choose Love. Love invites all but detains none; it does nothing to block the departure of those who do not heed its invitation, but simply lets them go. This is what it means for Love to "rule the nations with a rod of iron" [Apocalypse 2:27], to "judge the living and the dead" [2 Timothy 4-1; 1 Peter 4:5].

On Chapter Fourteen: "Against the Postmodern World"

In this chapter Aleksandr Dugin recapitulates many of his main themes: the evil of the unipolar globalist hegemony led by the United States; a rejection of inter-religious conflict and invective; the primacy of *dasein*; and the need to appropriate elements from Fascism and Communism—purified of their negative elements such as materialism, racism etc.—as well as from various pre-modern worldviews, including "the Platonic ideal state, Medieval hierarchical society, and theological visions of the normative social and political system (Christian, Islamic, Buddhist, Jewish or Hindu)," so as to form an anti-Liberal, anti-postmodern, anti-imperialist coalition to destroy the American Empire—a coalition based on the three principles of *national sovereignty, social justice,* and *traditional values.* When stated in these terms I largely support Dugin's program (with certain reservations)—as long as the revolt against U.S. imperialism stops short of World War III—therefore I might be expected to gladly enlist as one of the "common allies" that Dugin hopes to find even within the United States, "among those who choose the path of Tradition over the present decadence."

I do not intend to enlist in this cause, however, at least under the leadership of Aleksandr Dugin. His use of deception, his habit of intellectual manipulation, his apology for state terror in *The Rise of the Fourth Political Theory*, his appeal to "social justice" while condemning "human rights," and above all his misrepresentation and misappropriation of Tradition, have placed me at a distance from him that I do not intend to cross. If he wants to get next to me, let him cross it himself.

> Ideologically, unipolarity is based on modernist and postmodernist values that are openly antitraditional ones. I share the vision of René Guénon and Julius Evola, who considered modernity and its ideological basis (individualism, liberal democracy, capitalism, consumerism, and so on) to be the cause of the future catastrophe of humanity, and the global domination of the Western lifestyle as the reason for the final degradation of the Earth. The West is approaching its terminus, and we should not let it drag all the rest of us down into the abyss with it.

I agree. Yet Guénon—at least in *The Reign of Quantity and the Signs of the Times*, which represents his mature conclusions—did not simply envision the end of the West, but the end of the *manvantara* on a global scale. It is undeniable that post-Christian western values have poisoned the world; nonetheless Russia, China and other non-western nations have their own indigenous roads into the abyss, which need to be faced and dealt with. Much can be blamed on the West, but not everything. The shadow-counterpart of the birth of linear time and progress in the West was the all-too-earthly petrification of Eternity in the East. The fever of western expansionism and technology was only made possible, as well as being indirectly incited, by the excessive introversion and retentiveness of the ancient spiritualities of Asia. The original and defining crime of the *Kali-yuga* was thus the radical imbalance of Yang and Yin—not only the acceleration of time produced by the imbalanced, one-sided Masculine Principle, fleeing the encroaching power of the polluted Substantial Pole, but also the gravitational heaviness of the isolated Substantial Pole itself, the imbalanced, one-sided Feminine Principle, sullenly rejecting the Eternal dawning of form and thereby becoming infected with the temporal residues of form. (Here we can see how "Atlantis" is not the Substantial Pole or Feminine Principle per se, but rather the Feminine Principle internally inflaming the Masculine Principle and driving it to excess, while "Eurasia" is not really the prolongation of the reign of the Essential Pole and the Masculine Principle by the power of Tradition so much as it is the degenerated Masculine Principle internally polluting the Feminine Principle and causing it to congeal. The degenerate Feminine

Principle outwardly manifests as the unbalanced Masculine, the degenerate Masculine Principle as the unbalanced Feminine. In alchemical terms, dissolving Mercury pairs with volatilizing Sulfur and fixing Sulfur pairs with congealing Mercury; this is the signature of both the destruction of the human soul and the end of the *manvantara*.)The ultimate effect of Western colonialism was to inject the tincture of Western Time into the petrified, over-spatialized Eternity of Asia, causing it to release its tremendous, stored-up *potentia* in a wild orgy of western imitation. The westernization of the East is now in the process of sucking the West dry of its great progressive momentum, leaving it depleted and exhausted. As James Joyce prophesied in **Finnegan's Wake**, "The west shall shake the east awake . . . while ye have the night for morn." Whatever expansionist drive still emanates from the western world is not based on its cultural-historical momentum—which is now largely spent—but is being artificially induced by the global elites. Just as the Roman legions were able to maintain the borders of the Empire for a while against the incursion of the barbarian tribes as the native population of Italy declined, sinking at the same time into the degeneracy of "bread and circuses," so the United States can still station its troops throughout the world. However—much like Rome not long before it fell—the birth-rate in the United States and Western Europe is also in decline. And just as the Roman Empire, after a certain point, could only maintain the strength of its legions by filling their ranks with provincial conscripts and barbarian mercenaries, so the United States has been forced to rely upon proxy armies like ISIS—expendable, but not easy to get rid of—to fight its wars, while lowering its military recruitment standards to include criminal elements and people in poor physical condition. Obviously this can't go on.

As for the problem of democracy, I largely agree with the Traditionalist critique which sees it as sees it the resulting in the collapse of the hierarchical sense of being, the blinding of the spiritual Heart to the celestial order, the degradation of objective truth to majority opinion, the substitution of the pursuit of earthly happiness for the quest for eternal salvation, etc. I would only point out that, according to Plato in his **Republic**, the terminal phase of the cycle which is destined to succeed democracy is tyranny, not a return to Tradition and hierarchy (unless it be an inverted hierarchy), and that the spread of globalism outward from the United States, under the largely covert influence of the financial elites, is only made possible by the weakening of the power of the people. "Democracy for all" may be the rallying-cry of globalism, but it is not its actual goal. And Dugin's assertion that "Spiritually, globalisation is the creation of a grand parody, the kingdom of the Antichrist," while true in many ways, also needs to be qualified. As I wrote in **The System of Antichrist**:

> Globalism and One World Government, in my opinion, are not the system of Antichrist, though they are among the factors which will make that regime

possible. I believe the system of Antichrist will emerge—is in fact emerging—out of the conflict between the New World Order and the spectrum of militant reactions against it.

Dugin goes on to say:

We should strongly oppose any kind of confrontation between the various religious beliefs—Muslims against Christians, the Jews against Muslims, the Muslims against the Hindus and so on. The interconfessional wars and tensions work for the cause of the kingdom of the Antichrist who tries to divide all the traditional religions in order to impose its own pseudo-religion, the eschatological parody.

Once again, I am largely in agreement with this principle—largely, but not entirely. It is certainly true that one of the most successful tactics of the system of Antichrist is to incite interreligious conflict. This, however, is only one-half of the globalist "pincers movement" against the traditional religions, the other half being the creation of a false interreligious unity under secular control. In *Vectors of the Counter-Initiation* [2012] I wrote:

Prof. Rodney Blackhirst of LaTrobe University in Bendigo, Australia put his finger on the problem of the use of the Interfaith Movement to extend control over the world's religions by placing them under secular authority:

I am...concerned about secularizing "inter-faith" movements. I might have told you that here in Bendigo I was invited onto an inter-faith council, supported by the local government. But then I found they wanted to start a series of "inter-faith services"—prayer services that cater to everyone at once. I objected to this but was told that government funding had such strings attached. The government, that is, has a policy of discouraging the various religions from conducting "exclusive" religious services. I can foresee a time when it will be illegal (under anti-discrimination laws) for Muslims to conduct a prayer service that doesn't cater to Christians or Buddhists. That is where we are heading....

Lee Penn...has documented, in *False Dawn: The United Religions Initiative, Globalism and the Quest for a One-World Religion* [Sophia Perennis, 2005], the stated desire of certain figures in the Interfaith Movement to prohibit religious proselytization as representing a kind of religions "imperialism" in the doctrinal sphere.... In any case, Prof. Blackhirst's experience is evidence of an intent on the part of some governments and globalist power elites to homogenize the religions so as to destroy their autonomy.

The pressure to artificially unite the religions inevitably produces "particularist" or "tribalist" reactions, which in turn seem to justify that unification. Dugin's stated goal is certainly not to amalgamate the religions, but to maintain their diversity. However, Vladimir Putin's sometimes heavy hand (according to

Freedom Alternative) in his dealings with the Russian Orthodox Church, and the establishment of Orthodox Christianity, Islam, Buddhism, Judaism and Shamanism as state religions under the constitution of the Russian Federation, indicate that Russia is not immune—to say the least!—to the danger of the secular co-optation and control of the religions that we see developing in the West. The solution provided by the Russian constitution to the problem of religious diversity is probably the best that can be hoped for under present conditions, but it is far from perfect. And a coalition of the world's religions under the leadership of Russia would place an unavoidable pressure on their doctrinal autonomy and authority.

Dugin also takes another stab at applying metaphysics to political ideology:

> The important concept of *nous* (intellect) developed by the Greek philosopher Plotinus corresponds to our ideal. The intellect is one and multiple at the same time, because it has multiple differences in itself—it is not uniform or an amalgam, but taken as such with many parts, and with all their distinct particularities. The future world should be *noetic* in some way—characterised by multiplicity; diversity should be taken as its richness and its treasure, and not as a reason for inevitable conflict: many civilisations, many poles, many centres, many sets of values on one planet and in one humanity. Many worlds.

On the face of it, much of this seems entirely acceptable. The *Nous* (which was treated of by Plato and Aristotle, and even the Pre-Socratics, as well as Plotinus) is indeed both one and many; in this it corresponds fairly closely to the Sufi notion of *al-Qalb*, the Spiritual Heart—or, more precisely, to the Eye of the Heart, the point where the psyche or *nafs*, which is multiple, is intersected by the vertical ray of the Spirit, which is One. Dugin, however, largely ignores this dimension of Unity, both because—following Heidegger—he is uncomfortable with the idea of Spirit, and undoubtedly also because Unity seems dangerously close to the *unipolarity* that he rejects. *Noesis*, however, is intimately related to the One, which was Plotinus' name for the highest Reality. *Noesis* or *gnosis* is based (from one point of view) on the realization, not of "richness and diversity" on its own level, but of diversity considered as the multiple reflection of Unity. According to Sufi doctrine, the source of the uniqueness of each particular form and moment in the world of manifestation is the Uniqueness of God. Furthermore, the future cannot be rendered *noetic* through mere philosophy, much less political ideology or action. *Gnosis* is not a collective understanding but an individual and trans-individual one. It is the fruit of the individual's labor, in line with Divine grace, to attain self-transcendence and thereby conform his or her soul to the One. Such conformity, however—as Dugin understands—cannot be based on any kind of uniformity, only on the realization, and transcendence, of individual particularity considered as a cosmic reflection of the God's Uniqueness. This realization-and-transcendence must take place—barring the rare exception—within the context of a traditional spiritual collective or *narod*, not on the basis of the individual in his narcissistic isolation, which is nothing but another kind of uniformity. You can't avoid uniformity while *repressing* the individual, however, any more than you can establish social justice while rejecting human rights. And since Dugin is uncomfortable with the idea of the Spirit, rejects the individual as a "heresy," has a magical and therefore counter-Traditional idea of the nature of contemplation, and tends to put the *narod* in the place of God, he is not qualified to speak of the *noetic* dimension in any Traditional sense. Nor can he, to the degree he accepts Heidegger's idea of the fall of the Logos, legitimately speak of the primacy of the *Nous*. Why not? Because the *Nous* is nothing less than the faculty of the Intellect that contemplates the Logos. The Logos is the Word, the vibratory Self-manifesting Radiance of God; the *Nous* is the Eye of the Heart capable of witnessing this Self-manifestation. Dugin cannot grant metaphysical primacy to Chaos and then turn around and invoke the *Nous* as if nothing had happened, precisely because Chaos acts to veil the *Nous*. Chaos is of the Substantial Pole but the *Nous* is of the Essential Pole. From one perspective, the Logos and the *Nous* can be understood as the dynamic and contemplative aspects of the Pole of Essence, in which the formless Source of form, and the trans-formal Power to witness form, are one.

Unfortunately, in this concluding chapter of **The Fourth Political Theory**, the central philosophical fraud perpetrated by Aleksandr Dugin again becomes glaringly apparent, a fraud that inevitably compromises whatever may be positive and helpful in his work—namely, that in view of the fact that his worldview is postmodern in almost every respect—which is proved by his constant references to the postmodern philosopher Gilles Deleuze and his fundamental reliance upon the father of Postmodernism, Martin Heidegger (who also influenced Derrida and Foucault)—his claim to be the leader of an international movement against Postmodernism is an insult to human intelligence. And even though Marty Glass sees postmodernist Jean Baudrillard as one of the "unconscious prophets of the *Kali-yuga*" based on his brilliant portrayal of our existential and perceptual dilemma, a similar insult is offered, in one way or another, by virtually every postmodern "intellectual." Having come to the firm conclusion by now that Dugin has more or less been jerking his readers around all along, I might well feel like a fool for having responded to a mountebank with earnest appeals, to an intellectual trickster with fully-formed and consistent thought, and to a metaphysical nihilist with stern moral admonitions. There is nothing more likely to deplete one's life energy than an honest gesture offered to someone whose *modus operandi* is basically deception; in the words of line 5 of Hexagram 58 if the *I Ching*—the hexagram related to speech—"Sincerity toward disintegrating influences is dangerous." Such danger is alluring, however. The relative lack of positive reality that all evil exhibits will often tempt those who serve positive reality to compromise themselves by "charitably" struggling with evil to compensate for its deficiencies—often with disastrous results. And if all I've accomplished in this book is to refute some of Aleksandr Dugin's ideas, I would be entirely justified in concluding that I had wasted my time, seeing that Dugin himself has done a better job of refuting them I ever could. Thankfully, he has also challenged me to articulate various positive metaphysical insights and to produce a certain amount of hopefully useful social analysis in light of them, partly in the area of social psychology; for me, these achievements—all criticism of Dugin aside—are sufficient justification for this book. As for Dugin's tendency to self-refutation, if the U.S. had no problem with creating and then destroying ISIS so as to destabilize the Mid-East, by the same token Dugin seems to have had little problem with first preaching his own ideas and then thoroughly trashing them, possibly because his real goal—conscious or unconscious—is not so much to express a particular set of ideas as to undermine, pervert and destroy the universe of discourse. This is not to say that his ideas are useless, simply that they are *relatively* useless—aside from his brilliant critique of Liberalism and a few other high points—from the standpoint of truth; as examples of the weaponization of the intellect, clearly they have their function.

But that's not the whole story. Outside of the various valid insights that Dugin has provided, which he has taken pains to embed in various false contexts—the most effective lie being the one that has captured elements of the truth, which are then allowed to speak (up to a point) so as to lure those attracted to truth into intellectual ambush—his true achievement is his unparalleled audacity in positing a synthesis of sociology, anthropology, science, metaphysics, religion, philosophy, technology and political practice, and doing so not as a marginalized "outsider" or "mad genius" but within the established world of Russian academia and with the backing of powerful elements of the Russian state and/or crypto-state. Such a synthesis is something that our era desperately needs, and if he has by and large done a pretty shoddy job of it, that is very often the fate and style of those who break new ground but have little sense of how to cultivate it, or what sort of crops it might be expected to yield under optimal conditions. Suffice it to say that Aleksandr Dugin, due to his wide influence both within Russia and outside it, has validated this kind of wide-ranging synthesis as a legitimate goal for intellectual discourse, and so cleared the way for me to try and outdo him in a field that he himself largely opened up. For this, my thanks. Without Aleksandr Dugin, many of the insights I came to in the process of wrangling with him would never have seen the light; Dugin may be described as the irritating grit that has inspired whatever pearls this book may contain.

Dugin, by and large, has simply collected a vast hoard of intellectual material from all points of the compass and dumped it into the postmodern blender—though if his worldview has any center at all, it is probably Heidegger, who himself was without center. I, on the other hand, have done my best to hierarchicalize and synthesize almost as large an idea-hoard under the guidance of Traditional Metaphysics (which Heidegger specifically rejected), thereby putting every type of knowledge in its proper place. Though Postmodernism claims that such a thing is not possible, I offer this book as proof that it can be done. My synthesis is far from complete, but I believe that my goal and my method are sound.

On Appendix I:
"The Threshold of Sacred Action"

In this Appendix, Dugin provides us with a swift, brilliant and penetrating short-course in the phenomenology of postmodern dehumanization as it applies to politics—or rather, to the impossibility of politics. He concludes that The absolute features of the post-humanity of postmodernity are:

—depoliticisation;
—autonomisation;
—microscopisation;
—sub-and transhumanisation (as a special form of dehumanisation);
—*Dividualisation* (fragmentation).

Precisely. He goes on:

The drama of the last humans clashing with post-humans in a political conflict is at once very heroic, tragic, poetic and . . . hopeless . . . political post-anthropology makes such a position almost impossible. The political soldier in the unique conditions of the corrosive waters of postmodernity is immediately converted into a simulacrum. . . . In an anthropological series of political and anthropological forms, postmodernity installs a vicious link. All the threads that connect the political arena of postmodernity with modernity and deeper into political history are broken.

In other words, when linear time has dissolved, under the dominance of the Substantial Pole, into the temporal Chaos of the End Times—when the Logos falls (in its social manifestation, not its essence)—then *dialectic*, and therefore dialectical conflict between thesis and antithesis as defined rational and/or political positions, is no longer possible. And yet Dugin suggests, though he does not clearly delineate, a way out:

My thesis is reduced to the following affirmation: in the context of political post-anthropology, postmodernity and the post-human (dividual) cannot be opposed to modernity and human (individual). Opposing dualities will not be like the dividual vs. individual and post-human vs. human, but like dividual vs. pseudo-individual and post-human vs. pseudo-human. The anthropological fold (Deleuze) of postmodern anthropology is this: a simulacrum meets with a simulacrum.

Consequently, the opposition must be different. It is not a previous anthropological link that is designed to collide with a post-anthropological segment of an anthropological series, which is located *after* the substituted element (knot), but an entirely different figure. That is, one should speak of the political expression of the Radical Subject.

An alternative to political post-anthropology is also post-anthropology, but different. It is not really the human that meets with the post-human in the political post-anthropology, but a pre-human, the pre-concept of the human. The point of origin that came before the human is parallel to him and will remain after him.

Here we can also touch on the delicate theme of angelomorphosis.

There is a pivotal key hidden in this thesis, one that opens the door to the possibility of integral action beyond the universal falsity and fragmentation of Postmodernism, and heralds the notion of Sacred Activism outlined in *Chapter Seven*. Also hidden in it, unfortunately (or fortunately, insofar as it exposes much of Dugin's game), is nothing less than his definition of himself as *an enemy of humanity*, via his identification of *individual* with *human*, which must be understood in light of his repeated declaration, also appearing in *The Rise of the Fourth Political Theory*, that the notion of the individual is a "heresy." So is he really lamenting the rise of the fragmented "dividual," the cyborgs, the clones, or is he slyly siding with them, at least insofar as he tells us it is impossible to side against them? And is this stealthy knife-in-the-back based on a Satanic will to corrupt the truth and thereby destroy the human form, or does it stem from simple intellectual despair, from his inability to see any *real* way out? This is a difficult question to answer, seeing that the central goal of the Satanic agenda is to make us despair, and in view of the correlative fact that despair is Satanic in itself. Man's extremity may be God's opportunity, but it is also Satan's, who will often appear and offer his services to those who see nowhere else to turn.

Be that as it may, Dugin's view of our dilemma, once we clear it of despair and subversion, does reveal an important truth: that the eschatological conflict, the total commitment to a true ontological position that will save the human form, cannot be fought or assumed by historical man, or psychological man, or sociological man, or class-defined man, or ethnic man, or political man, or post-political man, or post-human man, or any version or modification whatsoever of *self-defined man*. The final battle, the war at the end of history, can only be fought, in Aleksandr Dugin's words, by the Radical Self—though what he may actually mean by this term is anybody's guess—operating on the basis of the "pre-human, the pre-concept of the human, the point of origin that came before the human, is parallel to him, and will remain after him." If we translate the notion of "the pre-human" into "the Human Archetype, Humanity *in divinis*"—in other words, into Humanity as directly emerging from the Radical Self—then we have posited the protagonist of the final conflict between Man and the forces bent on the deconstruction of Man as the Eschatological Savior, the initiator of the *parousia* (see *Chapter Eight*).

In my opinion, Aleksandr Dugin doesn't need to be so obscure and ambiguous at this point, so cagey, hip, and postmodern—unless, that is, his basic intent is to subvert the truth, which certainly remains a possibility. As I see it, he has a real opportunity here to drop all this mental slight-of-hand, because he has reached the threshold of one of the privileged points where the vertical path of Spirit and the horizontal path of history intersect, a point at which it becomes possible for socio-political consciousness to be informed by contemplative insight—though it is by no means easy to recognize this point and even harder to employ it as the basis for practical, integral action. Nonetheless the first real step is now available to him, if he is willing to take it—that step being to translate what he has just said about the "pre-human" and the "Radical Self" into the language of Traditional Metaphysics and Eschatology. As soon as he does this, if he can do it with intellectual insight and sincerity, he will suddenly have at his disposal a vast analytical literature, a sophisticated practical methodology, a primordial Tradition filled with illustrative examples of both effective action and principled non-action, and an immense store of spiritual power that—as soon as he learns to *obey* it—will be at his disposal, precisely to the degree that he has placed himself at its disposal. If he is serious about his allegiance to the Guénonian Traditionalist form of Fundamental Conservatism, let him avail himself of this opportunity. If he does, he will have come to the threshold of Sacred Action, part of the *praxis* of which I have delineated in *Chapter Seven*.

One of the things that makes such a step possible at this point is Dugin's highly illuminating definition of the "political":

> The political is power and political identification (the Self/the Other). Each political form provides a different model of power and such identification.

In other words, each political form is a particular construct of *ego*, all ego being based on identification. The human individual, or collective, identifies with a particular set of things, persons and situations in the outer world, thereby incorporating or *introjecting* these objects into its inner world, the habitual landscape of its consciousness. The individual or collective in question then *projects* various elements of its inner landscape back on the outer world, responding positively to those aspects of the perceived world that receive and reflect projections that support its self-image, and negatively to those aspects receiving and reflecting projections which threaten that image. This unconscious and ongoing process of introjection and projection is what maintains, and constitutes, the individual or collective ego, which can be accurately defined as attachment to a particular structure of Self and Other. And since the ego, as the principle of man's self-definition set up in opposition of God's true knowledge of him, it is also the agent of his self-deconstruction, otherwise known as the Adversary.

This definition of politics in terms of various identifications of Self and Other opens the door to a *praxis* of integral Sacred Action, since deconstruction of the ego is the central goal of contemplative practice. Therefore the entire arsenal of contemplative strategies can be applied precisely at this point, the aim being to shift the field of action from the false war between various alienated, postmodern collective ego-identities based on different constructions of Self and Other, to the true war between the Divine—defined as that which creates and maintains and redeems the integral Human Form because it is entirely *beyond* the ego—and the Satanic, defined as that which comprises *all* the various constructions of Self and Other, all the false identities and identifications, all the *egos*. If all humanly-defined realities, both in society and within the psyche, have now become simulacra of themselves, if no real choices or alternatives between one form of political identification and another, or between one form of false, alienated, quasi-humanity and another, any longer exist, this is due to the extreme old age of the *manvantara*—to the fact that the entire global panorama of social and psychological reality is now teetering on the verge of finally being recognized as *ego* and nothing else, and therefore as *illusion*, though the final outcome of this crisis, this potential purification of perception, is by no means settled. Real wars cannot be fought between phantom armies; unfortunately, in cases where the illusory nature of ego-based pseudo-reality is not recognized, armies of phantoms do indeed possess the power to start real wars between real human beings.

It may nonetheless be true that the lateness of the hour, cyclically speaking, might be the very thing that makes it possible for us to discern and respond to this ultimate dialectical polarity between the Divine and the Satanic which—in the words of the ***Book of Apocalypse*** 25:31–46—is the polarity between the Sheep and the Goats. (This polarity is real in relationship to humanity, since God is the Friend of the human race and Satan its enemy, but it has no reality in terms of the Divine Essence *per se*, given that, in the Presence of God, no other presence appears.)

Martin Lings, in his book ***The Eleventh Hour,*** names as one of the graces available in apocalyptic times what I have called "infused detachment": The very fragmentation and depletion of the various forms of postmodern perception make it easier than ever to simply detach from them, to break identification with them, to let them go—which means: to stop trying to block their *self*-deconstruction. The final deconstruction of the ego is made more possible now than ever before—though it is certainly not guaranteed—by the very volatilization and pulverization of postmodern life; this is the path of the Sheep. Unfortunately for those who have been unable to discern and avail themselves of this possibility, nothing is left to them but to hold on to the dying ego at all cost, via a ravenous obsession to incorporate *all* egos, all identifications, all constructions of Self and Other, thus violently inflaming the inherent contradictions between them; this is the path of the Goats. Contemplative practice teaches us not to engage with thought in the belief that we can make something of it, but simply to witness it, thereby withdrawing our identification with it. And since thought is based on *diairesis*, on *yes* and *no*, on Self and Other—in other words, because it is generated precisely by identification—the withdrawal of identification dissolves it. Likewise, in the socio-political field, to withdraw identification through the same act of witnessing dissolves the various political constructs of Self and Other, thereby making the contemplative activist capable of positing, and acting upon, the Absolute Witness or Radical Self that lies beyond the pairs-of-opposites. This sort of action will, of course, generate antitheses, thus returning the activist to the world of Self and Other. Nonetheless, if he succeeds in maintaining consciousness of the Witness when re-entering the field of polarities and identifications, its contradictions will not entrap him; consequently he will be able to continue posting and acting on the basis of the One Self, and the constellation of angelic Truths it emanates, even in the political dimension.

In the language of Tradition, what is the "pre-human, the pre-concept of the human, the point of origin that came before the human, is parallel to him and will remain after him"? Ultimately, it is God. And within God, as a sub-set of Him that is nonetheless also the whole of Him, it is the Human Archetype in God, the *hypostasis* that constitutes God's primal act of self-contemplation—That which, in Christian terms, is called the Second Person of the Blessed Trinity, the One "without Whom nothing was made that was made" [John 1:3], the One Who said "Behold, I am with you all days, even to the consummation of the *aeon*" [Matthew 28:20]. It is not the sub-order of substantial Chaos we need to turn to but the supra-order of transformal Form. It is really there. It can really be known. It can really be contacted. It can really be submitted to. And if It *is* submitted to, both previous to action and in the midst of action, then It can be used.

Exactly what is the Radical Self that Dugin invokes? Since he has not defined it, I will fill in the blank: the Radical Self is the Human Archetype *in divinis*, and the Absolute Witness from which that Archetype arises. It is the *Imago Dei*— the Eye of the Heart—the God within—the Self that St. Paul indicated when he said "It is not I who live, but Christ lives in me" [Galatians 2:20]—the reality that Muhammad alluded to when he said "He who knows himself knows his Lord"—the Self that the Taoists call the Complete Man and the Muslims *Al-Insan al-Kamil*—the Self that the Jews see manifest in the *Tzaddik*, "the upright (vertical) man", and the Buddhists in the *Bodhisattva*, "he whose essence is Enlightenment"—the Self that the Hindus name the *Atman*, the Absolute Witness. This Self is the One Self of All as it exists beyond the veils of ego, beyond false alternatives, beyond all constructions of Self and Other, beyond identifications. Every doctrine of the Guénonian Traditionalists and their successors fundamentally refers only to this Self, to the forces of illusion that veil It and the consequences of this veiling, to the forces of Truth that unveil It and the fruits of this unveiling in terms of the actualization of the Supreme Identity.

You can't *fight chaos*; you can't *conquer fragmentation*. All you can do, and must do, is to hold, at whatever cost, to Divinely-ordered Form—thereby coming into the field of the Radical Self, the Formless Absolute from which primal Form emerges—and then simply let chaos burn itself out, which it is obviously all-too-eager to accomplish on its own, without any help from you.

This principle is illustrated by the account of the attainment of *Samyak Sambodhi* by Gautama Buddha. Gautama, in deep meditation and on the very threshold of Enlightenment, was confronted and attacked by Mara the Tempter, the personification of all the egos, all the passions, all the identifications. Mara marshalled fierce demonic warriors, led forth seductive celestial maidens, hurled fiery mountains. The Buddha's response, however, was not to go to war with these enemies of Enlightenment with his immense spiritual power, but simply to disappear. There was the Lotus Seat beneath the Bodhi Tree, but there was no Buddha sitting on it. Faced with his inability to come to grips with any opponent, Mara simply *burned himself out*. When Jesus Christ said "resist not evil" [Matthew 5:39] he was recommending the same tactic.

The war against the postmodern destruction of the Human Form is not carried on first by *action* but by *attention*, by what the Taoists call *wu wei*, "doing without doing." *Wu wei* is the basic operative principle of the Chinese and Japanese martial arts, Kung Fu and all the others. Whatever action springs from non-action is integral, intelligent, balanced, powerful, and finished. It leaves no residues. It is not defined by its opponent because it sees no opponent, therefore anyone or anything that opposes it is defeated. If conflicts like "dividual vs. individual" or "post-human vs. human" or "dividual vs. pseudo-individual" or "post-human vs. pseudo-human" cannot be won, as they obviously can't—if no conflict in which the fighter is defined by his opponent can be won, or even initiated—then why won't Dugin, who claims to accept Guénonian Tradition-alism, simply go ahead and avail himself of the totality of Tradition where such dilemmas have no meaning, rather than obliquely alluding to Tradition, effec-tively rejecting it by entertaining many, many concepts that totally contradict it, and then trying (like poor Heidegger did) to re-invent it? Why reinvent the Wheel? Why reinvent the Void? It has already dominated you, so why not sub-mit to It? It has already made itself available to you, so why not use It?

There are three further points where I disagree with Dugin. To begin with, when he says

> The revolt of the elites and the oscillation of the intensity level of conscious-ness of the ruling groups are near zero. A classic example is a drug addict as political strategist,

he makes it appear as if the ruling elites are as disordered and deluded as the masses whose disorder and delusion they have partly engineered. It is true that no-one who deliberately spreads chaos and darkness can be entirely immune to their effects, yet the elites pride themselves on their ability to inhabit a higher level of chaos and darkness than the masses are forced to occupy—those "deplorables" (in Hillary Clinton's deservedly famous phrase), those Bal-kanized "locals." The masses exist in a state of engineered madness; as for the elites, however, there is method in their madness, since their activities are based on the "higher, transcendental" worldview of the psychopath, if not the fully-fledged Luciferian. If we simply define the elites as lunatics and drug addicts, we will *not ask* about their plans, methods and agendas. Is this the kind of mass oblivion that Dugin desires? The impression that since the intelligentsia are just as psychically disordered as the rest of the populace, and consequently that the ruling elites could not really be advancing any kind of concerted global agenda, may simply be based on the misconception, common among well-patronized intellectuals, that they are members in good standing of the ruling elites merely because elements of those elites haves flattered them, socialized with them and funded them, whereas in reality they are little more than bought lackeys, hired brains. Worldly intelligence does not grant membership in the elite class; worldly intelligence can be bought and sold. The only true passkey to the com-pound of the global elites is money.

Secondly, when Dugin says

> A person can choose both the structure of power and his identity

he is dead wrong. We may choose (up to a point) which power structure to identify with, but we certainly can't choose the one we will be forced to deal with. And whatever "identity" we think we can "choose" can only be a simu-lacrum, an illusory ego—not to mention the fact that *adopting an identity* is almost always an unconscious process. An identity, since it illusory, is not something we can choose consciously; when we come to full consciousness, when we are entirely *awake* ("buddha"), the adoption and ownership of identities comes to an end. Nonetheless, one choice *is* possible, and also necessary, in the realm of identity: the choice either to sink into the illusory abyss of the ego, the chasm of identification and self-definition, or to die to the ego entirely, and thereby realize the Supreme Identity.

Third and last, the "angelomorphosis" that Dugin apparently places his hopes in cannot really stand as a goal for human aspiration. Something suggesting an angelic transformation of the human form may perhaps be initiated, in a spiritually lawful way, by a *tajalli*, a Divine Self-revelation and the *hal* or spiritual state inspired by it, or else in a false and potentially demonic way by various types of artificial brain-stimulation, including those produced by psychedelic drugs. Some sort of "angelmorphosis" may be legitimate in a certain sense, if all we are hoping for is a temporary transfiguration of consciousness to help us deal with a moment of crisis, but over the long haul of the Spiritual Path, or the human life, it becomes a serious obstacle. What is necessary is not angelomorphosis but actual *Theosis*; for the meaning and import of that word I refer Aleksandr Dugin to the Fathers and Saints of the Eastern Orthodox Church. Literal angelomorphosis is not ontologically possible; it is possible, however, to achieve Theosis, to become virtually divinized, by the realization of what Dugin calls the Radical Self, and the Hindu Vedanta, the *Atman*—though it is also necessary to emphasize that the empirical self can never reach Theosis, while the Radical Self has never departed from it. If few ever actualize this highest possibility, it is because the degree of humility and self-annihilation required to effect it is much too formidable for most people even to consider.

As for the possibility of interacting with real angels, we need to remember that the word *angelos* means "messenger"; the only angels we can lawfully encounter are those sent by God on specific missions. Any angels we may have the misfortune to meet outside that framework—if angels they are, and not members of various other spiritual or psychic races such as the Fairies or the Jinn—will likely be fallen angels, otherwise known as devils. Through the use of various powerful artificial means it is certainly possible to access the Imaginal Plane and there witness beings who may have the appearance of angels. Such appearances, however, can be deceiving. Nor do encounters even with real angels, if we have succeeded in spying on them through various psychic technologies, have the same import as encounters with the angels sent by God—to say the least! If one receives an invitation to meet with a great man in his home, one's experience will be far different from what lies in store for the one breaks into the same home with criminal intent.

In the surah *The Jinn* [72:8-9], the Holy Qur'an recounts the following:

And (the Jinn who had listened to the Qur'an said): We had sought the heaven but had found it filled with strong warders and meteors.

And we used to sit on places (high) therein to listen. But he who listeneth now findeth flame in wait for him.

The literal meaning of these verses is more-or-less as follows: Before the Qur'an arrived, the Jinn were in the habit of ascending to the higher reaches of the psychic plane, their natural environment, from which they were able to eavesdrop on the councils of the Heavenly Court, of Allah and His Angels—but now that avenue is blocked. The operative principle here is that, in the absence of a fully established Divine Revelation, it is sometimes possible for *psychic* powers of perception (symbolized by the Jinn) to arrive at a certain degree of insight from *Celestial* or *Spiritual* sources, as if by stealth. We can see this principle operating in the case of Emmanuel Swedenborg, whose more-or-less "channeled" inspirations were apparently designed to compensate for the loss of the patristic tradition and the sacramental order in much of the West after the Protestant Reformation. But when such a Revelation is in full force, to reject the direct relationship to God that it offers, and try instead to lay hold of spiritual knowledge through psychic thievery, is punishable by the Wrath of God. That Wrath is symbolized in the Qur'an by meteors, conceived of as the spears and arrows of the Angels by which they drive the Jinn back to their own world. When a functioning Spiritual Path based on a Divine Revelation is available, those who try to circumvent it, to raid the mysteries by illicit means, will necessarily encounter the darker forces of the invisible world, and thereby feel the weight of the Left Hand of God.[4]

On Appendix II: "The Metaphysics of Chaos"

[See Chapter Two, Part One of this book:
"Critique of 'The Metaphysics of Chaos'"]

---

4. Marty Glass provides a view of our collective dilemma that is complementary to and supportive of Dugin's. In my book *Vectors of the Counter-Initiation* [Sophia Perennis, 2012] I characterize his view of the quality of our times as follows: "[as] Marty Glass wrote, in *YUGA: An Anatomy of Our Fate* [Sophia Perennis, 2005]: "We're still human, but we lead inhuman lives"; he gives as the five hallmarks of the *Kali-yuga* "The Reign of Quantity, the Fall into Time, the Mutation into Machinery, the End of Nature and the Prison of Unreality." The progression is irreversible, but ephemeral. It is the vanishing away of falsehood to reveal the Truth, which is what "apocalypse" means. What, if anything, will be left of life on earth, and human life, after this process completes itself we can't know. It has to be enough for us to know that the Truth will indeed come; our adherence to orthodox religion and the Spiritual Path is the one thing capable of ensuring that it *will* be enough.

6

Critique of *The Rise of the Fourth Political Theory*

I N THIS CHAPTER I will not attempt as detailed a deconstruction of *The Rise of the Fourth Political Theory* as I did of *The Fourth Political Theory*, but will concentrate on those elements of the Theory that I haven't already critiqued in *Chapters Three* and *Four*, or on particular passages that require a serious response.

On Chapter One: "Democracy: Sacred or Secular?"

In this chapter, Dugin does his best to invalidate Democracy by branding it as an anachronistic holdover from ancient times, based on a primitive "archaic mysticism of collective ecstasy." Archaicism is seen as negative here, while in *The Fourth Political Theory*, in the section "The Metaphysics of Chaos," it is presented as positive, something to be scoured for elements that might be incorporated into Dugin's system, particularly because it might provide us with examples of the "Chaotic Logos." And certainly Dugin's portrayal of the Russian *narod* is filled with elements of "collective ecstasy" considered as entirely positive. Decision-making in these ancient democracies, says Dugin, was based on an invocation of the gods for the purpose of letting them speak through "the soul of the ethnos" or *narod*, which is here seen as primitive or negative, though elsewhere Dugin presents the Russian *narod* in a positive light as just such a mystical group mind subject to "collective ecstasy." This certainly has every appearance of a self-interested contradiction.

The archaic democracies were primitive and negative, says Dugin, because the individual had not yet emerged from the group mind—yet elsewhere in *The Rise of the Fourth Political Theory* he defines the individual as a "heresy." This is another apparent contradiction.

According to Dugin, who quotes Aristotle as saying that "democracy is pregnant with tyranny," the emergence of the individual from the group mind of the archaic democracies—the "first" individual being the *tyrant*—represented

342

an evolutionary *development*. This is in line with his apology for state terror later in the book, but it contradicts his presentation of the individual as the anthropological aspect of the "absolute evil" of Liberalism. And, without notifying us that he has done so, Dugin *inverts* Plato's doctrine that tyranny succeeds democracy by a process of degeneration, presenting it instead as the result of a process of development and growth.

This mass of contradictions seems a good example of the workings of Dugin's "Chaotic Logos."

Dugin goes on to present 21st-century global democracy as the regime of Antichrist—though as I have already made clear, though I believe that western democracy in its degenerate form of late Postmodern Liberalism has certainly made a major contribution to that regime, it is not the only player; Russia and China have their own contributions to make. Given the fact that we are now under the collective dominance of the Substantial Pole at the end of the *manvantara*, in which all previous phases of the cycle are archived, negative and inverted forms of theocracy, aristocracy, and feudalism, as well as bourgeois democracy and the dictatorship of the proletariat, will also play their parts in the system of Antichrist. The Left in the West—to the degree that it criticizes globalism at all—tends to see it as global Fascism, while the Right pictures it as global Communism. Both are right to a degree, but neither can see the true outlines of that system. René Guénon, who implied that the regime of *al-Dajjal* would be a kind of inverted, oligarchic theocracy or feudalism springing from the ground of degenerate democracy, was closer to the truth.

Dugin concludes by attacking the concept of "human rights" as integral to the degenerate postmodern democracy in which all individual differences are suppressed in order to create the "individual." It is true that "human rights" tend to be defined under Postmodernism as springing from "the right to be anything you want to be," which too often means the so-called right to alter, suppress and deconstruct the human form according to the whims and commands of our psychological complexes. But in view of the fact that these complexes have been partly created, and are universally exploited, by the global elites through advertising, propaganda and social engineering, the concept of "human rights" has entirely inverted since Tom Paine wrote *The Rights of Man*. Paine and the architects of the American and French revolutions already had a distorted idea of what true human rights might entail; nonetheless they were still drawing upon a poorly-understood metaphysical truth. Western Christianity sees the human being as made "in the image and likeness of God," as bearing within him the *Imago Dei*. Thomas Jefferson in the U.S. Declaration of Independence, basing himself partly upon this doctrine, spoke of men as being "endowed by their Creator" with the "unalienable rights" to "life, liberty and the pursuit of happiness." Under Postmodernism, however, the *right to liberty* has become the pseudo-right to libertinism, the *right to the pursuit of happiness* has been degraded to the pursuit of dissipation, and the *right to life* has been spawned the license to manipulate and distort one's biological identity in any conceivable way, as well as to sacrifice all other values for physical survival—a right that is obviously not extended, however, to the unborn. In terms of their metaphysical archetypes, however, the right to *life* is the right and the duty to avail oneself of the Infinite Life of God; the right to *liberty* is the right and the duty to freely will to conform oneself to that Life and consequently to liberate oneself, by the grace of It, from the limitations of sin, *karma* and contingent existence; and the right to *the pursuit of happiness* is the right and duty to take one's delight in God and to delight in the good things of earthly life only in and through God. The Qur'an tells us that the *Amana*, the Trust, belongs to the human form alone. By this Trust, humanity is both the perfect slave of God (*'abd*) and the fully-empowered representative of God (*khalifa*) in terrestrial existence. It is the Trust that gives him his truly *human* rights and therefore constitutes the *human dignity* that democracy ideally exists to protect and foster. The Qur'an also laments that man, after assuming the Trust, has in many ways proved *a tyrant and a fool* [Q. 33:72]; unfortunately the same can be said, up to a degree, of democracy. However, as our last protective wall against the ultimate tyranny of the inverted hierarchy, democracy still has an important role to play.

On Chapter Two:
"Conservatism as Project and Episteme"

"Being is primary, time is secondary" says Dugin. If he found this in Heidegger, then he found something true, as when Plato said that "time is the moving image of Eternity." This principle is universal and perennial. Intentionality, however, as the trans-temporal archetype of time, is not secondary to Being, as I have explained above. God is intrinsically Intentional just as He intrinsically Is, since Intentionality in God is precisely His intention to Be, without which His Being would be demoted to a passive attribute, a mere logically necessary abstraction, not the infinite, overflowing, supremely active, superabundant Being that is God. In other words, God's Intentionality is transcended only when His Being is transcended in the realization of Beyond Being.

Dugin:

> The conservative project is a grasping for the concentrated point of being in the future ... that point ... is already absolutely real for [*the conservative*] here and now ... the significance of the conservative project is that it is secured by being itself.

If so, then good. Whatever is "secured by Being itself" is *shanti*, the Great Peace—not Peace as fixity, but a Peace filled with motion and life. However:

The conservative . . . strives to grab hold of being in a direct and actual existential experience, most often through horror and other special operations of metaphysics.

Or perhaps through horror and other special operations of state terror, or of brainwashing and mind-control, or of a very bad trip on some psychedelic drug. Horror flees Being because it experiences Being as horrible. It flees in panic from the rigor of the breakthrough of Eternity into time—and yet, horribly fascinated, it can't look away; it can't break loose from the tremendous shock of this apocalyptic tearing-of-the-curtain, by which God is apparently revealed as Satan himself, because it encounters this Apocalypse with the ego, not with the spiritual Heart. It is only *compassion* that can look with equanimity on the rigor of the breakthrough of Eternity into time. Where horror shrinks in revulsion, compassion impassively remains; sees; and accepts. "My God, my God, why have You forsaken me?," by virtue of "Father, forgive them for they know not what they do," becomes "Into Thine hands I commend my spirit; it is finished" [Matthew 27:46; Luke 23:42; John 19:20]. The Christian has no right to call horror "a special operation of metaphysics" by which Being is grabbed hold of; the Satanist, however, *must* call it that, since his conception of the nature of Being is horrible. Yet in the next paragraph, Dugin tells the truth, the whole truth and nothing but the truth, demonstrating that the traditional eschatologies of the revealed religions present a comprehensive view of the end of the *manvantara* that no worldview based on secular fears and hopes can match. Can he stay with that truth? Can he declare his loyalty to it? Or is it just one more car in the long train of truths and lies that his books are composed of? Listen:

> In Christian teaching, eschatological pessimism and eschatological optimism co-exist. The orthodox know that in the coming-forth the Anti-Christ will come (come forth); but they also know that he will be defeated by Christ in his glorious and terrible Second Coming . . . the conservative project sees suffering, anxiety, horror, fear and catastrophes ahead. However it also sees triumph, victory, the descent to earth of the Heavenly Jerusalem, the universal revealing of eternity and the abolition of death. The task of the conservative, defending eternity, is to change the coming-forth in favor of the coming-to-be or to fight on the side of the coming-to-be against the coming-forth. The Anti-Christ is the coming-forth, but the Second Coming will be.

Forget *Ereignis*! This is the truth that *Ereignis* is too horrified, too terrified of *love*, to ever witness or accept. The only way to mitigate the horror that arises from the certainty of impending apocalyptic catastrophes in the outer world is to meet and undergo that same Apocalypse in the inner world. In the contemplative *podvig* (ascetical exploit) of the unseen warfare, the soul encounters the coming-forth of Antichrist—the full manifestation of the *ego*—followed, God willing, by the defeat of Antichrist by Christ, by the complete dawning of the Presence of God in which the ego is annihilated. And only a daily experience of this inner apocalypse in constant contemplative practice can overcome the horror of Antichrist; a single shocking instance of the breakthrough of Eternity into time in the inner world—especially when it's produced by trauma or various artificial agents, such as psychedelic drugs—cannot.

Sadly, when comparing passages like the above with earlier and later ones, we can see how the truth is only one of Dugin's many options, something that is apparently useful to him mostly for the purpose of screening his actual beliefs, allowing him to reveal only enough to influence the reader by suggestion.

> The initiation of the conservative project in contemporary Russian society, of course, must not, by any means or any circumstances, flirt with technology. . . .

If so, then what does he mean, in *The Fourth Political Theory*, by "the realization of the technological aspect of the project," i.e., of the Fourth Political Practice? And will he or will he not take down his many websites and retract his suggestion that the computer systems of the United States be hacked?

Next Dugin rightly says that, due to the emphasis in both Communism and Liberalism of becoming over Being, the conservative project in Russia lacks the necessary *episteme* to found itself on a sense of Being as preeminent over becoming. At this point I can only repeat my suggestion that such an episteme be founded on a wide study of Traditional Metaphysics from every conceivable source, since the pre-eminence of Being over becoming is central to that discipline.[1]

Dugin now speaks of a true *humanism*, a non-secular humanism that the conservative project can accept and use—the exact humanism I have presented above according to the Quranic doctrine of Man as the holder of the *Amana*. It is this "*homo maximus*" who is the legitimate subject of *human rights*. And on the basis of this understanding of the Human Form as the central site of the union of Heaven and Earth, Dugin—like Julius Evola—defines Holy Empire as the social macrocosm of the human microcosm. True! And Yet René Guénon, in *The Reign of Quantity and the Signs of the Times*, speaks of a counterfeit Holy Empire ruled by an inverted *chakravartin* ("turner of the wheel," universal king)—the Antichrist—as the only new social possibility left to us in the End Times. How will Dugin deal with this contradiction? Orthodox Christian eschatology foresees no legitimate Holy Empire built by human hands in the latter days, but waits on the coming-to-be of the *parousia* of Jesus Christ to

---

1. By far the most comprehensive single-volume review of these sources is *A Treasury of Traditional Wisdom* by Whitall Perry.

usher in the Messianic Kingdom. And yet that Kingdom will not be an *earthly* empire ruled by Christ, since Orthodoxy sees the "millennium" spoken of in the Book of the Apocalypse as the church age, which is now past; in Orthodoxy, the belief in an earthly millennium is the heresy of *chiliasm*.

Next Dugin praises war as one of the conservative man's greatest loves, much in the spirit of W.B. Yeats when he said, in "Under Ben Bulben":

> You that Mitchel's prayer have heard
> "Send war in our time, O Lord!"
> Know that when all words are said
> And a man is fighting mad,
> Something drops from eyes long blind;
> He completes his partial mind
> For an instant stands at ease,
> Laughs aloud, his heart at peace.

Technological warfare, however, is degraded and dehumanized, devoid of the chivalry and heroism that are dear to the conservative man's heart. If Russian conservatives must studiously avoid flirting with technology in any form, then let them not by any means flirt with technological war! Dugin quotes Nietzsche as advising us to "love war more than peace, and the short peace more than the long!" But the sharpest sweetness of the truly just war is in the knowledge that peace is its final cause; when the medieval knight bore an article of his lady's clothing into battle, it was to remind him of this truth. And it is war—when fulfilling its function of surrounding peace with a cordon of protection, as with the *kshatriya* caste in Hinduism whose *dharma* was to protect the *brahmins*, the sacrosanct contemplatives—which lends its clean, sharp edge to the sweetness of peace, which otherwise would cloy.

Dugin invokes the Greater Jihad, the "unseen warfare" of the Spiritual Path, when he tells us how "uninterrupted war with sin goes to the heart of man." True—until victory is achieved, that is; if the war against sin is conceived of as endless, then no victory is possible, and a war with no possible victory is not worth fighting. *Hesychia*, the Great Peace, should not be taxed to pay for the perennial warfare against the demons; rather, all the energies of that warfare should be bent toward achieving and securing this *hesychia*, the "peace that passeth understanding" [Philippians 4:47]. The destruction of spiritual peace by spiritual war is what is known in Sufism as the *nafs al-lawwama*, "the accusing self," which is seen as blameworthy. Only when the accusing self is transcended, when we "repent of repentance," will the *nafs al-mutma'inna*, the self at peace, be attained. It is true, as Dugin says, that Russia has always fought wars and tends to get fat and lazy in times of peace; this is the perennial dilemma of the *kshatriya* character. And yet any civilization where the *kshatriyas* revolt against the *brahmins* and usurp their place is, according to Guénon, a precursor to the Regime of Antichrist; this is something that Baron Julius Evola never understood. War will always be with us, and the dedication of our lives and deaths to God in war will never disappear as a spiritual possibility. And yet, as Jesus demonstrated on the cross, it is the projection of the inner, unseen Spiritual War into the outer world that produces Rome and its legions, the heroic martyrdom of the zealots, and the despairing suicide of Judas Iscariot. Jesus came to show us the way from the outer war to the inner one, from the lesser jihad to the greater, from the war that violates and murders peace till it becomes nothing but a distant, legendary memory to the war that fights to protect that peace and defend it, until "I come not to bring peace but a sword" [Matthew 10:34] ends in "put up your sword: for he who lives by the sword shall die by the sword" [Matthew 26:52]. The warrior in the Greater Jihad, the *muja-hid al-akbar*, like the martyr in the lesser jihad, also knows how to die by the sword—which is why *dhu'l fiqar*, the sword of Hadhrat 'Ali, had two points. The naked Presence of God is a sharp sword that cuts down all enemies in the army of the *nafs al-ammara*, and opens the Eye of the Heart. In the words of William Blake, from his epic poem **Jerusalem**:

> Rouze up O Young Men of the New Age! Set your foreheads against the ignorant Hirelings! For we have Hirelings in the Camp, the Court, & the University: who would if they could for ever depress Mental & prolong Corporeal War.

Dugin ends this chapter by positing Theology, Ethnosociology and Geopolitics, based upon the threefold nature of man as Spirit, soul and body, as the tripartite *episteme* of the conservative project in Russia, with Theology at the top. This is an interesting schema, and possibly a useful one. But if Theology is supreme, then let Aleksandr Dugin cease violating it, and repent of his violations in the past! Until he is willing to do this, who can believe him?

On Chapter Three: "The West and Its Challenge"

In this chapter Dugin provides an interesting and useful view of the roots of the West and the western idea of democracy; of the rise of the myth and reality of "progress" and secularization in the western world; of the transformation of "progress" into globalization and the positions of the United States and the E.U. in this process; and of Postmodernism as the end of "progress." He demotes modernization from its status as an ongoing historical necessity, presents Russia as a civilization rather than a "European nation," gives a picture of the post-Soviet enlistment of Russia by the West in the move toward globalization and world government and of Vladimir Putin's incomplete and unfinished reversal this trend. In presenting Russia as an independent civilization he outlines his project to push back against Russia's westernization, against its integration as a junior partner, or vassal, in the New World Order. Here we see Dugin as the competent, rational, clear and incisive "secular" scholar of history and geopolitics, largely devoid of mythic motivational homilies, heterodox quasi-religious speculations and dialectical smoke-and-mirrors.

Dugin reveals just how close Russia came to being colonized by the West in the dizzy aftermath of the fall of the Soviet Union. Some telling points:

> In 1989 [*under Gorbachev*] a commission of high-standing representatives of the CFR [*Council on Foreign Relations*] was selected in the Kremlin, with Rockefeller, Kissinger and others at its head. The Socialist camp was destroyed, and in 1991 the USSR fell too ... the structures of the CFR in Russia were entirely legalized in the form of the Council on Foreign and Defense Policy ... while the "young economists" formed the backbone of the Yeltsin government and its ideological nucleus.
>
> Before one's eyes [*in the mid-1990's*], Russia was becoming a colony, with the exogenous, fragmentary intrusion of postmodernism and the gradual loss of sovereignty. The Vice-Speaker of the Duma from "The Union of Right Forces," Irena Khakamada, seriously offered to agree to the international division of labor in a "world government," subject to the conditions of "the transformation of Russia into a nuclear waste depository for more developed countries."

All this, by and large, was not reported on a popular level in the United States, which is why it needs to be corroborated, if possible, from sources other than Dugin. All we heard was Ronald Reagan declaiming, "Mr. Gorbachev, tear down this wall!" All we knew was that the Berlin Wall was down, Communism was a thing of the past, the arms race was over, the Cold War was ended and won, the threat of nuclear war was lifted, and the world finally had a chance for peace. As for Russia, it could now live out its "Silk Stockings" fantasy (that's the 1957 cinematic musical comedy "Silk Stockings" with Fred Astaire and Cyd Charisse, about the humorless female Russian commissar who is charmed by love and Paris until she renounces Communism and Russia), and finally have all those wonderful western consumer goods, free speech, free pornography, rock music and Pussy Riot, and be happy at last. Why should they complain? Dugin shows exactly the trap that Russia fell into on the rebound from the hated oppression of Communism, how much the "Russian (and Eastern European) Spring" was like a slightly softer version of the disastrous "Arab Spring" that followed it. He writes:

> Today one can say with certainty that relations between Russia and the West in the 1990's were catastrophic for Russia, as they were based on the crudest delusions, categorically incorrect calculations, a complete incomprehension of the real state of affairs, and, in the last analysis, a direct betrayal of national interests.

In view of these revelations we can begin to understand that one reason Russia is presently being demonized in the U.S. is to punish it for its attempt to pull out of the deals it cut with the U.S. and the globalists after the fall of the Soviet Union, deals by which it apparently came close to agreeing to assume the status of a colony vis-à-vis the Neo-Colonialism of the New World Order. Russia's attempts to protect its sovereignty are routinely spun as expansionist aggression in the western media, while the many attacks against that sovereignty by the West are downplayed. In saying this, however, I do not mean to minimize the danger of a real Russian expansionism. If the game, as initially defined by the West, unexpectedly turns out not to be parity between nations but winner-take-all, what else can Russia do but play that game for all it's worth? Wouldn't you?

Obviously Russia needs to re-invent itself after its loss of the Cold War and the fall of Communism, and if Russia cannot become a truly democratic nation without ending up as a satellite of the West, then democracy may not be appropriate for Russia—especially when we consider that no "democracy" imposed through stealth and coercion by an outside power is worthy of the name. One of the things that Dugin and the rest of the Russian intelligentsia must attempt to grasp, however, is that while democracy came to Russia as a vector of globalism and western control, democracy in the United States—even as weakened and compromised as it is by massive social engineering programs and the dominance of moneyed interests—is our last line of defense *against* globalism. Russia must understand that the American people are not the beneficiaries of the globalization that the U.S. is attempting, with the help of Britain and the European Union, to impose on the rest of the world. Globalism has destroyed the U.S. manufacturing base; eroded our legal and civil rights—as, for example, when the Supreme Court quotes European Union precedents, even though the American people have not the slightest influence on and makeup and actions of the E.U. leadership; destroyed our middle class, resulting in an immense and historically unprecedented disparity between rich and poor; largely replaced our democratically-elected government by a Deep State cryptocracy, a "shadow government"; and done its best—partly by a policy of nearly unregulated immigration—to turn large sections of U.S. domestic society into the equivalent of a third world nation, a nation of "deplorables," occupied though not inhabited by the globalist elite as if by a foreign army. In other words, Russia and the United States are equally victims of globalization, though to different degrees and in different ways; still, they have more common ground in terms of their victimization than Aleksandr Dugin may suspect.

On Chapter Four: "Carl Schmitt's
Principle of 'Empire' and the Fourth Political Theory"

Imputing guilt by association is admittedly an unreliable approach, but not an entirely meaningless one; I only say this by way of expressing my unavoidable suspicion of Carl Schmitt as a Nazi jurist—revisionist Nazi though he may (or may not) have been.

Suspicion, however, is not discernment, only a common substitute for it. Dugin, in this chapter, following Schmitt, considers the U.S. Monroe Doctrine as defining an ethnopolitical "large space" which ultimately expanded, via the League of Nations after the First World War and NATO after the Second, to become today's U.S.-led globalist universalism. According to Dugin, Schmitt's image of the role and meaning of the German Reich was not the purely racial view held by Hitler and Rosenberg, but rather a sense of "Lebensraum" as the ethnopolitical (though multi-ethnic) "large space"—led by Germany, of course—that is proper to Western Europe. In such a space, all nations would have "equal rights" to pursue their own destinies—as if protection without control were actually possible in the world of *realpolitik*. "The legacy of Carl Schmitt," says Dugin, "has become today an inalienable component of the political and juridical culture of the Western elite," echoing the view of those who see a European Union centered around Germany as having attained, by legal and economic gradualism, what the Nazis failed to achieve via the explosive military expansionism of the Third Reich. Dugin conceives of his projected Eurasian "large space," centered on Russia, as the equivalent of the multi-ethnic Third Reich of Schmitt and the U.S. sphere-of-influence as defined by the Monroe Doctrine. He says:

> Let us notice that other potential "large spaces" and other peoples are all without exception interested in an Eurasianist renaissance starting in Russia. Everybody wins from this, since Eurasianists speak up strongly not for universalism, but for "large spaces," not for imperialism but for "empire," not for "the interests of any one people" but for "the rights of peoples."

"Other peoples are all without exception interested! Everybody wins!" This is a great ad for a great product. I especially like the idea of "empire without imperialism." The only item of information that has not yet been released to the public is how much all this is going to cost.

On Chapter Five: "The Project 'Empire'"

In this chapter Dugin speaks of the possibility of an Empire without an Emperor—undoubtedly to avoid, among other things, the appearance of an appeal to the Romanov restorationists—and defines his idea of Empire as an entity with a strong central authority, which nonetheless allows certain degree of autonomy to various local centers of power, including those based on religion or ethnicity—a model that has been used, in one form or another, by the Byzantine, Ottoman, Austro-Hungarian, Chinese, Mongolian, Iranian, Soviet and Liberal American empires. He presents the self-concept of this last entity, which is "Liberal" in the larger historical sense, though Neo-Conservative within what Dugin defines as a Liberal context, as that of a "Benevolent Empire"—though exactly when, or if, it will finally be able and willing to demonstrate this supposed benevolence is anybody's guess.

He goes on to present the Neo-Leftist plans for global opposition to the Liberal American Empire put forward by Antonio Negri, and by Michael Hardt in his book *Empire*. From Dugin's description these writers would appear to be proposing a *Blade Runner*-like techno-anarchism (a reference to the famous science fiction novel by Philip K. Dick) that the mass of the exploited, using "narcotics, all kinds of perversions, genetic engineering, cloning and other forms of bio-intellectual mutations," should marshal to counter Imperial control. This program is reminiscent in many ways of the lurid futuristic fantasies of the Beat Generation writer William Burroughs, whose ideas have been highly influential within various artistic and political avant-garde circles. The problem with this approach—outside its quintessential evil—is that it envisions the Empire as if it were a control system administered by "straight people" whose ideal is legal and moral order, a system that (as Burroughs maintained) can and should be countered by the use of weaponized chaos. A fundamental misconception is operating here. The Liberal American Empire is not ruled, as it once was, by "Christian Anti-Communists" dedicated to enforcing moral purity, but by global elites who have weaponized chaos and degeneracy far more thoroughly and strategically than any independent techno-anarchist insurgency ever could—as, for example, through the MK-Ultra mind-control program, during which the CIA (according to Peter Levenda in *Sinister Forces: A Grimoire of American Political Witchcraft*) funded the manufacture of millions of doses of LSD, obviously for general distribution throughout U.S. society. So much evidence exists of the sponsorship of social chaos by the powers that be that one is forced to speculate that the idea for the kind of techno-anarchist insurgency that Negri and Hardt propose may represent a covert social engineering program sponsored by the elites themselves in view of creating a controlled opposition—or rather, a controlled collusion. In my system of the Four Archons, who act as the fundamental constituting principles of the regime of Antichrist, an anti-imperial techno-anarchism would represent a collusion between the Chaos Archon and the Selfhood Archon so as to mount a simultaneous rebellion against the compulsive morality of the Fate Archon, through the use of Chaos, and against the Law Archon, through the assertion of

Promethean Selfhood. The futility of this approach is demonstrated by the fact that, according to my system, Chaos inevitably transforms into Fate at one point—just as, under Postmodern Liberalism, moral degeneracy becomes a moral imperative—while Selfhood is transformed into Law, this being the fate of most revolutionary insurgencies after they triumph and become "establishment." Dugin goes on:

> Thus, the category of "empire" becomes the cornerstone of the ideological constructs of the global leftist movement, anti-globalism and alter-globalism. In fact, alter-globalism is the direct consequence of Negri and Hardt's ideas: one must not fight with globalization, but rather use its capitalistic and imperialist forms (existing today) for an anti-capitalist revolutionary war.

As should be obvious, Aleksandr Dugin's Neo-Eurasian movement is, or must become if it is to survive, simply one more brand of alter-globalism.

Next, Dugin lists the various alternatives to the global American empire: the extension of the Yalta-based status quo, founded on the pretense that parity still exists between Russia and the United States as two superpowers, as if the fall of the Soviet Union and the subsequent beginning of the deconstruction of the Russian Empire had never taken place; the dream of a renewed Islamic Caliphate; and the inherently unstable model provided by the European Union. (My critique of the notion of a renewed Caliphate, along with other of Dugin's beliefs and statements regarding Islam, is found in *Chapter Three:* "Vectors of Duginism," section "Dugin and Religion"; in *Chapter Four:* "Critique of *The Fourth Political Theory*, Part I," section "Dugin's Ignorance of Islam"; and in *Chapter Seven:* "Sacred Activism," Part Three: "Sacred Activism, United Front Ecumenism and the Attack on Religion," subsection "Dugin and Jihadism; Dugin and Sufism"). Among the forces within Russia struggling to regain and maintain Russian sovereignty he contrasts those who believe that Russia can simply "take its place in the family of nations" on the basis of parity, and those who hold to the more realistic idea that Russia must become an empire again within the outlines of the old Soviet sphere-of-influence or risk being dismembered. Dugin envisions the possibility a future friendly alliance between the Eurasian Empire and the European Union—a development that the United States would be expected to do all in its power to prevent—and ends by declaring:

> Eurasianism proposes to synthesize all the previous imperial ideas, from Genghis Khan to Moscow as the Third Rome, to raise on this foundation a common denominator: the formula of an empire-building will. History, culture, the Russian language, a common fate, the peculiarities of their labor psychology, and a similar ethical and religious structure unite the peoples of Northern Eurasia. . . .
> Eurasianism as a political philosophy fits more than anything the demands

for the construction of the coming [coming-forth] empire. This is an imperial philosophy, an impressive Russian philosophy, directed toward the future [coming-to-be], though also founded on the firm foundation of the past.

Note that Aleksandr Dugin uses the same term, "coming-forth," to denote the advent of Antichrist.

❧

As for what form a renewed imperial Russia might take, I have little to say about it since it is not in my area of expertise; as an American I must contend with the myth and the reality of the American Empire. In addition, I am an activist at this stage of my life only because of the providential re-appearance of the covenants of the Prophet Muhammad, peace and blessing be upon him. But for what it's worth, I will say that I believe Russia has as much right to defend itself from further dismemberment through the agency of outside forces as the U.S. would have to take the strongest steps against a separatist movement in, say, Montana, armed and funded by The Russian Federation. As for any divine warrant for the establishment and manifest destiny of the United States of America, which many have invoked over our history—whether in more-or-less traditional Christian terms or according to the counter-Christian myth of the Freemasons—I consider this mythical empire of the Spirit to have a kind of metaphorical reality from a certain perspective, but in no way a legitimizing one. At this point in our history, though we are still one nation, we definitely do not appear to be "one nation under God"—though the present militant atheistic movement to expunge this notion from the American psyche is an even worse thing than the struggle to retain it, no matter how hypocritical and self-congratulatory that notion may seem, since if we no longer see ourselves as under God, this is tantamount to an admission that our true gods are the global elite.

On Chapter Six: "Eurasianism (A Political Poem)"

In this chapter Dugin the motivational myth-maker returns, consequently I will only reply to those elements of Dugin's myth that stand out as examples or violations of metaphysical truth and the Primordial Tradition.

Dugin on Love

It was one of the central principles of Soviet Communism that personal, human love is reactionary and bourgeois, that the only truly "progressive" love is love of the class, of the proletariat. Down with Dr. Zhivago! Love of the earth, suitably sanitized, was also allowed, as when San Francisco poet, Kabbalist and "stage Communist," Jack Hirschman, declaimed in one of his poems, "*The earth—the black earth—the Soviet black earth. . . ."* In "Eurasianism (A Political Poem)," Aleksandr Dugin demonstrates that a serious hangover from the Communist period still lingers in the Russian soul:

> [*According to Eurasianism*] the *narod* appears as absolute. [*It is the*] love [*that*] propels the waves of generations that deliver ever more and more offspring, create families, and carry out the continuation of the kin . . . as love, it gives a man everything: his look, his life, his language, his culture. . . . The torrent of ethnosocial love gave us our corporeality. We are only an episode in this ethnosocial body, which precedes us as the collective body of our ancestors. . . . We carry within ourselves the embryos of future Russian corporeality in the same way that the human body, according to the teaching of the Orthodox Elders, carries in itself the embryo of the body of the resurrection. But the fundamental basis of Eurasianist philosophy, the basic element and foundational meaning, is precisely the *narod*.

In other words, Eurasianism is opposed to Christianity; the Absolute, according to Eurasianism, is not God, but *narod*—consequently Jesus Christ, by remaining unmarried and producing no corporeal offspring, betrayed the *narod*, defied the Absolute. *Narod* could have been for Dugin a wonderful understanding of the gift of corporeality given by Adam, through the Theotokos, to Christ, the Second Adam, which allowed for His Incarnation and His redemption of the human essence from sin and death, both within this terrestrial life and in the *aeon* to come. It could have deepened the Christian understanding of Christ's restoration of humanity to a greater, entirely spiritualized corporeality, one that our earthly corporeality is a true though partial expression of, beyond these "garments of skin" that we assumed—out of prideful shame at our created limitations—so as to hide the Divinity within us [cf. Genesis 3:21]. But Dugin has turned *narod* from a blessing given by God and perpetually returning to God into a curse, an idol set up to replace Him and deny Him. In the language of Hinduism, he has rejected *devayana*, the vertical path, the road of the gods, for *pitriyana*, the horizontal path, the road of the ancestors. Only *devayana*, however, can redeem *pitriyana* from the darkness and suffering of endless conditional existence, where everything is always becoming and dying, but nothing can ever *be*. Consequently Aleksandr Dugin can never say, with Jesus Christ, "Before Abraham came to be, I Am" [John 8:58]. And if *narod* is the Absolute then it will necessarily be there for us after we die; if it is not there, if it is only eternal *in time* as the human germplasm, which doesn't apply to us since we are dead now and can no longer contribute to the life of the *narod* or receive life from it, but only from God directly, then it cannot be the Absolute. If, therefore, we believe that *narod* is indeed the Absolute, that it is worthy to take the place of God, then we are simple atheists. In saying "*Narod* is absolute," Aleksandr Dugin is telling Jesus Christ, "I never knew You" [cf. Matthew 7:23]. A *narod* that lives, through faith, more directly *in God* than in the group ego, can be known as the unfolding and flourishing through time of the human race as the privileged mirror of God in the terrestrial world. If, the group ego predominates, however, then the *narod* in question becomes nothing but an ongoing temporal propagation, through original sin, of the Fall of Man.

You cannot make God an afterthought. You cannot say, "God, too, is good, and has His part to play. First we must deal with more pressing matters, but when the time comes, after these matters are finished with, certainly we will get back to Him." God cannot be *part* of our program, our agenda, our worldview. God does not play a *part* because God is the All. Only those who put God first in all things, who cannot love the earth, their lovers, their brothers and sisters or their *narod* unless these good things are loved in God, can be said to really believe in Him. Therefore when Dugin declares that *narod*, not God, is his absolute, he formally and explicitly renounces Eastern Orthodox Christianity. If there is a *staretz* left in Russia with the courage to tell him this to his face, then Aleksandr Dugin has found his spiritual father.

He goes on:

> The world is the energy of love. The ancients taught: "Stones love one another. Flowers love one another." Now very much is said about the eroticism of flowers: scholars even measure the sexual activity of plants. It is understandable that animals and humans love one another. But stones? Yes, even stones have love. Both the life of stones and the erotic tensions of mineral energies represent a gigantic area. They love differently, which is why we cannot understand this exorbitant, transcendental love. Maybe the stone loves some kind of grass, some kind of plant. The love of a stone for a tree— sycamore, cypress—undoubtedly represents some kind of energy not grasped by us, but wonderful and clearly present in world. . . .
>
> The Russian *narod* is open, and our love is open. . . . We love, really love. But this means that, with our act of love, Russian love, we transcend the concrete person. But, you will think—the person! One, another, a third . . . still, the most important thing is love. It is more important than [*the concrete person*]. The most important thing is openness, the gigantic energy of the life of the *narod*.

So when the husband gets drunk, embraces all the girls in the room, and wakes up the next morning in bed with a woman who is not his wife, he had better have a good excuse already composed and practiced—perhaps something like the above paragraph. When he finally gets home to face his angry wife, maybe he could recite this paragraph. Eventually it might even become the standard excuse used by the wayward husbands of the Eurasian Movement, signed and authorized by "Professor Aleksandr Dugin": "All that happened, *lapochka*, was that I became immersed in the torrent of ethnosocial love that gives us our corporeality. As Professor Dugin teaches, any Russian girl is as good as another—as long as she's fertile. We must all make sacrifices (or at least *you* must) for the good of the *narod.*" I'd be extremely interested to learn just how such an excuse would play out on the Russian domestic battlefield.

Dugin's theory of love is actually quite contemporary, so it ought to be fairly easy to sell; his Fourth Erotic Theory would seem to be reducible to the following:

1) Love of *narod*: *allowed, encouraged and quasi-compulsory*
2) Love of the earth: *allowed, encouraged and quasi-compulsory*
3) Love of individual human beings: *second rate at best*
4) Love of God: *never mentioned and assumed prohibited*

Is it possible that Aleksandr Dugin secretly attended a Liberal university in the United States for several years without telling anybody? He would certainly not have learned Love Number 1 in such an institution, but the valuation of the other three "Loves" would have been drummed into his head day and night. This promiscuous "strength through joy" attitude is the height of irresponsibility and crassness. Without the love of *mere individual persons* there is no loyalty in friendship, no faithfulness in marriage, no generation of young people who are privileged to know both their mothers and their fathers . . . a *narod* without filial piety, without strong marriages and friendships, is rotten to the core— take it from a 21st-century American who knows whereof he speaks.

Dugin's section on the love of trees and stones is beautiful and meaningful— but why must people today believe that the erotic vision of the natural world and the love of the Transcendent God are fundamentally opposed? Has no-one read the beautiful nature meditations of the Celtic Christian monks, or the profound meditations by Origen or Maximos the Confessor or Evagrius of Pontus on the natural world as the ensemble of the signs of the Almighty? The Holy Qur'an as well has many verses to the same effect. As St. Paul wrote in Romans 1:20:

> Ever since the world began, [*God's*] invisible attributes, that is to say His everlasting power and deity, have been visible to the eye of reason in the things He has made.

If we do not love the natural world or other people *in God*, we will love them only in appearance, not essence; our erotic energy will flow out to them through glamour and fascination, by the power of a spell like the one cast by vodka or hashish, only for it to be dissipated and lost in the wilderness of the elements—which is another way of saying that it will be devoured by the ego. Since we do not *respect* other people we will not love them in their uniqueness and reality; we will simply be attracted to them by virtue of our own projections. We will not love them as they really are, but only as functions of ourselves, our egos. In the words of the German poet Rainer Maria Rilke, "love . . . consists in this, that two solitudes protect and border and salute each other." Either Aleksandr Dugin has never known this kind of love, or it bit him so hard on at least one occasion that he vowed never to be hurt by it again.

And it is no accident that the denigration of personal, human love is found side-by-side with a stony silence regarding the love of God—because *only in God can we appear as persons*. Outside God, in the glamorized materialism of the Substantial Pole, we are as Aleksandr Dugin presents us: herds of fat, sleek cattle, their hides rippling in the sun, cows with their udders bursting with milk, bulls with the strength of the earth in their horns and loins—and not a single human face among them.

The first stanza of the Middle English lyric "Alisoun" (with notes for the modern reader) is as follows—now listen to the Laws of Love:

> Bitweene Merch and Averil, *in the seasons of*
> When spray biginneth to springe,
> The litel fowl hath hire wil *pleasure*
> On hire leod to singe. *In her language*
> Ich libbe in love-longinge *I live*
> For semlokest of alle thinge. *seemliest, fairest*
> Heo may me blisse bringe: *she*
> Ich am in hire baundoun. *power*
> An hendy hap ich habbe yhent, *A gracious chance I have received*
> Ichoot from hevene it is me sent: *I know*
> From alle wommen my love is lent, *all other/removed*
> And light on Alisoun. *alights*

Note the course, the hierarchy, the dialectic: The *natural eros of the earth* in Spring awakens in the lover a *personal eros* for his beloved Alisoun, which, after it has arrived, is recognized as something springing from the *transpersonal eros* of heaven. By this natural eros become personal and human through the transpersonal power of God, the collective love for "alle wommen" is gathered and concentrated into the quintessential form of Alisoun, who is Love's Central Sun.

This is what is known as True Love: impersonal love becomes personal love under the blessing of transpersonal love. Aleksandr Dugin, however, inverts this "supernaturally natural" process—as he has inverted so many other things— first by denying God, after which personal love, deprived of transpersonal grace, sinks into the impersonality of earth and *narod*, falling from there through the caverns of the elements—those "caves of ice" in Coleridge's poem "Kubla Khan," the realms of promiscuity and dissipation—then going on to lose itself in the material deadness of the unpurified Substantial Pole—that "lifeless ocean" from which "Kubla heard . . . ancestral voices prophesying war"—until it finally makes its contribution to the deep ground-ice of infernal hate.

Personal, human love—True Love—is a gift of the grace that comes to us through the transformal Source of all form, the Essential Pole. This love, due to its exalted lineage, is the point of the greatest concentration of *form* in earthly reality; it is stately; statuesque; *muy formosa*. If we are going to exert ourselves to invent worlds like Eurasia that don't even exist yet, then why not invent a world that has True Love in it?

Eros According to Dugin and Schuon

No two personalities or worldviews are more unalike than those of Aleksandr Dugin and Frithjof Schuon, yet they do have one thing in common: their relegation of love, especially personal love, to a secondary place in their philosophies. Dugin writes on the love of the group, the *narod*, as well as the love of trees for stones, but we hear nothing from him about the love of particular human beings or the love of God—which is not surprising, since Dugin rarely mentions God in any context, though he certainly doesn't mind talking about religion. Schuon, on the other hand, has something to say about God on almost every page of his many books. Yet neither Schuon nor Dugin are entirely comfortable with the idea that God is Love—something they both have in common, up to a point, with the World, the Flesh and the Devil. Love holds an important though usually secondary position in Schuon's philosophy, either as an element of the Way to God or as something that characterizes the love of the spiritual devotee, the *bhakta*, the "passional mystic," whose method is all very well for "that sort of person," but is clearly secondary to the more elevated and complete way of the intellectual sage, the *jñani*, the *arif*, the *gnostic*. Furthermore, like Dugin, Schuon's approach to love on the terrestrial plane includes the love of "Virgin nature"—conceived, in his case, as a support for the contemplation of God, which is entirely legitimate—as well as the love of the "ideal human form," usually the feminine form, though this is not considered as an element of personal love between the sexes so much as an "aesthetic theophany of the Divine"—most often, judging by Schuon's own practice, in a group context. As many have pointed out, a devotion to Love and a will to Power are mortal enemies, which means that if sexuality is not wedded to Love, it will eventually become a concubine to Power—and the first step in divorcing sexuality from Love and turning it over to Power is to render it impersonal and collective rather than personal and individual. Both Dugin and Schuon appear to have taken this step, to one degree or another, Dugin through his attraction to the herd-warmth of the *narod*, Schuon through his exaltation of the aesthetic beauty of the ideal type over the love of the concrete person—this being the dark side of Islamic *eros*, just as maudlin romantic sentimentality is the dark side of Christian *eros*. It is this tendency to reduce human love to sexuality by de-personalizing and collectivizing it that reveals both Dugin and Schuon as devotees of the kind of worldly *eros*—an orientation Guénon was apparently free of—that is entirely in line with the mores of the globalist elites. If Traditionalism has a particular shadow, a characteristic Achilles' heel, this is it.

One of the many differing accounts of the identity and career of the mysterious St. Valentine, who is traditionally celebrated in Europe and America on Valentine's Day, is that he was a priest who performed a clandestine marriage between a Roman soldier (undoubtedly a secret Christian) and his bride, in a time when the soldiers of Rome were not legally allowed to marry, since marriage was seen as compromising their readiness to rape, pillage etc. The prohibition of married soldiers began under Augustus, indicating that a demotion of marriage was central to the ethical orientation of the Roman Empire as opposed to that of the Republic: the soldier was "married" to Rome and was expected to remain faithful "until death do us part." (This leads us to speculate that the traditional Sacrament of Matrimony—which, according to Catholic doctrine, is administered not by the priest, who simply witnesses it, but by the couple themselves—might have been instituted in this form partly to prevent the love between the sexes from being appropriated by the power of the State.) Likewise it is a commonplace of cult psychology and morality that all the women of the group are "married" to the guru, who sometimes rewards his followers for their devotion by licensing an indiscriminate group promiscuity, under the regime of which "irregular" and exclusivist liaisons, such as marriage, are frowned upon, or at least subjected to various degrees of oppression. Hitler, as is well known, remained unmarried until the end of his life to encourage the women of Germany to look on him as their "real" husband; the first step in the destruction of love—as was clearly indicated by the Nazi "Strength through Joy" movement as well as the history of the U.S. counterculture—is to make it "universal." And to the degree that a given society becomes imperialistic—which will necessarily include the exaltation of the military as a higher caste, albeit a caste of slaves—the institution of marriage will likewise be compromised. Empires do not look kindly on loyalty and devotion to objects other than the Empire itself, which is why the strength and independence of the local community, the church, the family etc. must be curtailed. This may explain Rama Coomaraswamy's prediction, in a private conversation with my wife Jenny, that in the future, marriage will be forbidden. Let Aleksandr Dugin vow never to let his projected Eurasian Empire take this road, if he in any way can prevent it: it is the road of the globalist elites.

∾

Dugin and Schuon have one other noteworthy similarity: both tend to "bracket" the world religions as elements of a greater vision or synthesis. For Schuon this greater vision was his "quintessential" or "plenary esoterism" in relation to which he saw the "confessional esoterisms" of the particular religions as secondary; nonetheless he denied he had brought any new Revelation and maintained that each religion, as it were, virtually contains all the religions because the Truth is One. For Dugin, though several of his articles on traditional Eastern Orthodoxy appear on his websites, his greater vision is the Fourth Political Theory—which at one point he calls a "prophetic school"—as well as whatever may be his actual "esoteric" beliefs, the true nature of which might well be indicated by his address to Edom as "Sire," for which see below. According to my own understanding of Traditionalism, on the other hand, one's chosen religion is the royal road to the realization of the Absolute, consequently there is nothing higher than the esoteric dimension of that religion but God Himself.

Dugin's Anthropology: The Individual *vs.* the *Narod*

The three following quotes give the substance of Aleksandr Dugin's anthropology, his conception of the nature of the human form. In his section "The Problem of the 'I,'" he says:

> A person is the embodiment of the *narod* and the earth. In other words, the person by himself does not exist.

And in "The Heresy of the Individual":

> Against our Eurasianist doctrine of man as an ethnic being there stands the noxious Atlanticist heresy about the individual. Atlanticism speaks thus: "That is not a man, not a Russian, but simply Vasya. As he is named, so he is. There is only Vasya, only the individual. Belonging to a race, narod, language has no significance. Today he has this language, tomorrow another; today he lives here; tomorrow, there. But always and in all circumstances he is only an individual . . . his nationality, his culture—these are secondary.

And in "Man is Simply a Conditionality":

> Our concept of man is Eurasian and that man is a conditionality, simply a conditionality. And then he can expand the borders of his "I" to limitlessness. For instance upward in order to say: "I am a soul." Or laterally, in order to affirm: "Three or five people live in me. Here's Vasya, here's Petya, here are two Mashas, maybe someone else, or someone I dragged in here for nothing. . . ." There you have it, a wonderful, broad soul. What a broad life

there will be! What an excellent experience. The broadening of human borders and the notion of "the great man" is called "maximal humanism." A man can broaden even downward and proclaim sadly, "What a pig I am!" and he'll also be right. He has a right also to his swinishness.

The Eurasian concept of man is that he is an embodiment of his *narod* and a temporary phenomenon, a variable value. Today he is "that" and "thus," tomorrow a little "different." The day after tomorrow more "something." But there are constant things: the *narod* and the space; and eternity which lives through us.

Here we are treated to the aimless flailing about of someone desperate to escape the status of an abstract individual monad, imposed to a degree by "Atlanticism," but more fundamentally enforced by the *ego*. According to this theory as to the nature of the human being, no human love is possible. In *The Fourth Political Theory*, Dugin says: "the rejection of the essence of post-modernity...is possible...because it arises from man's free will and his spirit." But if the individual is a "heresy," a mere "conditionality," then the human free will has no field of operation. Those seeking political power, particularly authoritarian power, like to believe that "the People" can "speak with one Voice" because they want to be the ones to give the People their Voice, this being only one step from actually becoming that Voice themselves and silencing all other voices. No collective, however, can really be of a single mind, and to the degree that it approaches this condition it most often does so not by exercising free will but by renouncing it. In some great collective crisis affecting an entire people, their voices and their wills can sometimes approach unity and unanimity through the active sacrifice of free will for the good of the *narod*, though not through the passive abdication of it under state terror; it is in terrible, privileged moments like these that the tremendous outline of the Primordial Man may suddenly become visible, is if in a flash of lightning on a dark night. Under such conditions the only sacrifice to God that can allay the Divine Wrath is that of the ego of the individual. As Christ died alone, so must each one of us. The "individual" that Dugin calls a heresy and a conditionality, however, can never be this kind of pure victim; under a regime of Postmodern Liberalism, such a counterfeit man cannot sacrifice his free will to God because he never effectively possessed it in the first place, due to the fact that Liberalism was only able to create and address itself to the *abstract* individual by repressing, denying and deleting most of what constitutes the *real* individual. He is nothing now but the Liberal/Postmodern simulacrum or puppet of the true man; perhaps he was never anything else. And even though he may feel safe in his self-abandonment because he has nothing real to lose, by the same token he stands face to face with eternal shame because has nothing real to give.

To say "a person is an embodiment of the *narod* and the earth ... the person by himself does not exist" is a Satanic inversion and counterfeit of the esoteric doctrine that the individual is "without self-nature" (Buddhism), that he is a manifestation of one of the Names of God and has no ultimate essence besides God (Sufi Islam), that "it is not I who live but Christ lives in me" [Galatians 2:20] (Christianity). It is both Satanic and impossible because the ultimate essence of one contingent being (man) cannot be another contingent being (earth). From an esoteric standpoint, the Individual is indeed a virtual reality with no independent principle of existence other than God. Yet it is only via the individual state that earthly humanity can transcend itself and be reunited with its Archetype *in divinis*; this is why it is imperative that we recognize, cultivate and defend the dignity of the human person. Proudhon's famous declaration that "property is theft" might be esoterically paraphrased as "the ego is theft," since the ego creates itself by identifying with, and thereby taking possession of, whatever it can appropriate from the things, persons and situations of the inner and outer worlds, which it falsely sees as its "properties," its inherent qualities. It is only through the sacrifice of this ego that we can transcend ourselves—but if an ego never develops, this sacrifice cannot take place. This principle was illustrated by Sri Ramana Maharshi when he stole his brother's college money to buy train fare to Tiruvannamalai, where he went into deep meditation, nearly died from his austerities and remained virtually without personal possessions, other than those donated by the devotees who gradually gathered around him, for the rest of his life. In the process he became perhaps the greatest Indian saint of modern times. He illustrated the birth and death of the ego by stealing from the world and then surrendering his ill-gotten gains to God. Ibrahim ibn Adhem sacrificed the kingship of Balkh to join the Sufis; the magnitude of that sacrifice resulted in great success on the Spiritual Path. If we have amassed no identity that we can sacrifice to God, we cannot advance; this is why solid character-formation should normally precede full commitment to the life of self-transcendence. In the words of Simon Weil, "If we were exposed to the direct radiance of [God's] love without the protection of space, of time and of matter, we should be evaporated like water in the sun; there would not be enough 'I' in us to make it possible to surrender 'I' for love's sake."

The field of human dignity is the individual. The person who enters a monastery dies to his family, to his nation-state, to his *narod*; all these outer identities are peeled away precisely to reveal his true individuality. The one who has found that individuality has a chance to realize that his dignity as an individual is nothing other than the presence of God within him, and that he has found that true individuality only for the purpose of devoting it and sacrificing it to the One who gave it. The family, the nation-state, the *narod* cannot pass through the needle's eye of self-transcendence; only the individual can do that.

"A person is an embodiment of the *narod* and the earth" is what comes of seeing things from the standpoint of the Substantial Pole alone, in ignorance—or rejection—of the Essential Pole. We get our stature, our skin color, our cheek bones, our genetic strengths and weaknesses, our language, our accent, from the *narod*. Likewise we get the water we drink, the air we breathe, the food we eat from the earth. And without the light of the sun, nothing edible would grow, nothing on earth could live. Therefore all these things—the sun, the earth, the air, the water, our ancestors, our fellow human beings, are falsely taken to be our *creators*—our gods. This way of looking at things is nothing but paganism, materialism. You can't be a Christian, or a Muslim, or a follower of any other of the true and God-given religions—or a in any way a Guénonian Traditionalist—and think like that. Certainly all these necessary *materials* of life are provided by the elements and the ancestors. But only God provides the *form* of these things, the unity of them. Only God provides the soul, the essence. And of course it was God who created all the material elements in the first place—created them with a view toward His final creation, which was to be Man. Only God is the Creator, the Creator of the *narod* and everything else. When he created Adam, he created everything that was hidden in the loins of Adam—every individual, every race, every *narod*. And we might also consider at this point the parallels between Dugin's exaltation of the Substantial Pole over the Essential Pole and both Darwinian evolution, where it is erroneously believed that the material cause of more complex life-forms is to be found in simpler life-forms—ultimately in lifeless matter—and Marxist dogma, where the cause of the development of classes and social systems is believed to arise from the material "base" of society, from labor-value and the ownership of the means of production, rather than from the cultural, intellectual, artistic and religious "superstructure." Marx and Engels saw this superstructure as secondary, derived from the base and acting as a mystification of the true causes of social forms which are only to be found in the base. In other words, Dugin's and Heidegger's story of the fall of the Logos has definite affinities with the Marxist demotion of the cultural superstructure in favor of the material base as the prime causal factor for human society.

This is one more manifestation of Dugin's apparent atheism; I say "apparent" because I cannot really know his secret with God. Nonetheless it *appears* to me as if he thinks he believes in God, but in actual fact does not. First let him face his atheism (if atheism it is), overcome it, and then talk to us about religion. Or, alternately, let him face it, realize that he can't overcome it—or that he doesn't want to—and admit that he has nothing to say to us about religion. Otherwise he is like a chess master who thinks his mastery of chess makes him a great astronomer, or a historian who believes his historiography makes him a competent physician. We are now living in the golden age of atheistic religion, the religion born in the Far West, the land where the sun of the Spirit sinks into the darkness of matter. Never have there been more atheists fascinated with religion than today! Even Pope Francis has declared that "God does not exist."[2] If Dugin wants to avoid being branded a crypto-Atlanticist, he had better turn his spiritual gaze away from the West, the land of chaos and materialism, and direct it East towards the Spirit, the source of all Form. Nor should he gaze too long toward the South either, the place where Nature appears as a self-created, closed system, where love of the Earth and the Motherland do not serve God, but instead replace Him. He should be looking instead toward the East, to the point where the Spirit of God dawns to enlighten this terrestrial earth, or else toward the Hyperborean North, "the still point of the turning world," the visible point of Eternity in the created order.

> Thus did We show Abraham the kingdom of the heavens and the earth that he might be of those possessing certainty:
> When the night grew dark upon him he beheld a star. He said: This is my Lord. But when it set, he said: I love not things that set.
> And when he saw the moon uprising, he exclaimed: This is my Lord. But when it set, he said: Unless my Lord guide me, I surely shall become one of the folk who are astray.
> And when he saw the sun uprising, he cried: This is my Lord! This is greater! And when it set he exclaimed: O my people! Lo! I am free from all that ye associate (with Him).
> Lo! I have turned my face toward Him Who created the heavens and the earth, as one by nature upright, and I am not of the idolaters. [Q. 6:75-79]

By this quotation I do not mean to imply that there are no Muslims who worship Narod instead of Allah, none who say: "I speak Arabic, I have a turban (or a baseball cap inscribed with the name of Allah), I have a nose with such-and-such a shape, therefore I must be a Muslim." My brothers and sisters, who make up the Muslim *ummah*, are here to help me turn toward Allah, just as I am here to help them. But if I worship them instead of Him, and myself by means of them, then I am breaking *adab* with Allah, and doing both myself and my brothers and sisters the greatest possible disservice.

As for man being a "conditionality," this tenet—apart from its close resemblance to the Counter-Initiatory teachings of G.I. Gurdjieff—is actually held both by Dugin's "Eurasianism" and by the "Atlanticism" he presents only in order to reject it. "Atlantis" sees the human being as a plastic material capable of being almost infinitely reshaped and remolded by social, psychological and medical/technological forces, by alterative surgery or social engineering or genetic engineering, as a being who is only "conditionally" a man, or a woman,

---

2. http://novusordowatch.org/2014/10/francis-god-does-not-exist/.

or the member of a race, or the inheritor of a particular religion or spiritual Way. Eurasia (according to Dugin) sees the human being as limitlessly "expandable" so as to become a "soul" or a "multiple personality" or a "pig" or whatever else he or she might imagine. Both these conceptions are equally anti-Traditional; they are also very much alike. Western Capitalism used to exalt the "self-made man," by which it of course meant the economic man. As being "self-made" in economic terms became less and less possible to the majority of Americans, the idea of the "self-made man" was progressively transferred to the psychological and spiritual dimensions; this "sublimation of the entrepreneurial spirit" was one of the roots of the New Age movement, leading ultimately to various Promethean pseudo-religions which see the Divine as nothing more than a passive natural resource to be exploited for personal gain, with the help of drugs, de-contextualized yoga, or other spiritual "technologies." And in reality this idea of "self-help" or "self-improvement" had been a kind of secular religion of American capitalist culture for quite a while before the New Age came along. Books like *The Power of Positive Thinking* by Norman Vincent Peale and *How to Win Friends and Influence People* by Dale Carnegie made the equation between changing oneself and changing one's circumstances; the man who was able to improve his personality, overcome his psychological problems and correctly orient his spirit would be more confident and more outgoing, and thus better able to network with potential employers to advance his career, and with his potential customers in order to "move the product." The waning of Tradition and the traditional religious outlook in the United States brought such worldly "spiritualities" to the fore, most of which included an element of unexpressed Calvinism, where the notion of proving oneself a predestined member of the "elect," now translated into economic terms, largely took the place of the Catholic emphasis on repentance and the forgiveness of sins. Consequently Dugin's idea of the "Eurasian" man who, since he is merely a conditionality, can be greatly expanded—either up, down or sideways—owes a lot to the "entrepreneurial spirituality" of American Capitalism, which in turn is founded on a distorted version of the traditional Christian doctrine of free will. Dugin writes as if the pre-eminence of the human form is based on its potential "breadth," its great plasticity. How excellent that we can "decide" to be souls, or explore the many sides of our personality, or roll in the mud with the pigs if we want to! That's real freedom! There is no religion on earth, however, that is foolish enough to teach such a doctrine—certainly not Christianity. Would Aleksandr Dugin, preaching to the Russian army, tell them that their military excellence lies in their freedom to bravely engage the enemy, or else to run away, or to blow their own brains out if they so desired? It's exactly the same with the "unseen warfare," the "greater jihad." The excellence of the spiritual warrior is that he courageously engages the enemy—his ego, his passions, his *nafs*—not that he runs away, or becomes distracted by booze or butterflies or pretty women. The freedom to indulge our passions is slavery; our willing slavery to the Will of God is freedom.

Nor is the human person in any sense a soul *simply because he decides to be.* He is a soul embodied in living flesh because that's how God made him; he himself had no say in the matter—except to agree, in his nothingness, to be created, to respond to God's pre-eternal question, *Am I not your Lord?* by answering *Yea!* [Q. 7:172]. Being a creature of "spiritual body and celestial earth," he was then tasked with realizing his own true nature, of finding the precious jewel hidden under the 70,000 veils of space, time, matter and energy—a task that he can never accomplish by his own power, but only by the Power of God, presuming that he has the willingness and has been given the right guidance to call upon that Power. If, instead, he squanders his spiritual potential by wandering through the endless booths—lavish or cramped, impoverished or palatial—of the vast marketplace of the human psyche, as many of my own generation did, the day may come when he retains neither the remembrance of the Spirit nor enough true intentionality, even if he were to remember It, to turn in Its direction. He will have become everything in potential but nothing much in actuality—nothing but a broken egg, a spilled yolk, a virtual being without sufficient integrity of self to present a true self to God when God demands that he sacrifice of all that he has become, all that he is. Consequently, he will be among the losers. And if he decides instead to follow the pigs, what can I say? Only that there is no choice harder to reverse, harder to even remember making in the first place, than this one. The names of those who have made this choice are no longer spoken or remembered among either angels or men.

We can see in the picture of the "Eurasian" soul painted by Aleksandr Dugin the universal postmodern *fear of Unity.* The good postmodernist believes as unalterable dogma that to be *one* is to be frozen, paralyzed, turned to stone. Only by the grace of disintegration, only in the delirious freedom of Chaos can he be freed from the curse of unity, from the strait-jacket of the human form. He knows this because he has heard the promise of it straight from the horse's mouth, from the polluted Substantial Pole, from the Baba Yagá—whose other name is the Medusa. The delusion here is that the unity of the human form is a *psychic* unity. The psyche, however, is intrinsically multiple since it derives its archetype, its intrinsic nature, from Possible Being. Only the Spirit is unified, because it springs from Necessary Being. To attempt to forcibly construct a psychic unity by psychic means will indeed produce the kind of constriction-of-soul that postmodern man fears, and from which he flees for relief into the embrace of Chaos, since such an attempt can only be made on the basis of self-will enforcing its own idea of things through repression and projection, and any house built on the sand of repression and projection will eventually fall.

Unity is our origin and our destiny, our stability and our freedom, but the only true source of that Unity is the Spirit, because Spirit is a direct manifestation of God, the One—and one of the things contemporary people don't seem to realize is that there is so much more room, so much more *space* in the One than there is in the many. Our soul is called to become one, but it can never do so on the basis of its own contingencies, only by virtue of the gift of God's Unity—God who is One *intrinsically*. We can attain to the degree of unity destined for us only by submission to Him, annihilation in Him, and eternal subsistence in Him.

The notion of limitless plasticity of soul is just another face of self-will, of the "self-made man" of Capitalist theology. Since redemption via the submission of the individual will to the Will of God is no longer considered central to salvation, having been replaced with a literalistic and one-sided doctrine of predestination, the Calvinist will becomes a "free agent" with no point of reference outside itself—and only a self-will whose obedience or lack of obedience to God is an irrelevant consideration could conceive a desire to exploit a supposed limitless plasticity-of-soul. Instead of simply accepting the fact that who we really are—*whoever* we are, and whatever changes we may go through—is nothing more or less than what God knows us to be and has made us to be, postmodern humanity foolishly aspires to endless transformations which will allow us to travel through endless worlds. Unfortunately, whoever cannot rest content with his or her own intrinsic form, and the limitations of it, will not be satisfied with limitless shapeshifting either.

When I worked at the Civic Center Library in Marin County, California, the library hosted a Harry Potter Day for the children, since it appeared at that point that only the wildly successful Harry Potter books by J.K. Rowling were keeping the younger generation interested in reading and literacy. The children (one dressed as Harry) were restless, agitated; some were crying. After they settled down, the hippy clown who was master-of-ceremonies of the event began his spiel, the gist of which was: "You can be anything you want to be!" When I was helping him pack up his props after the gig was over, I told him: "No traditional fairy tale tells children they can be anything they want to be; it tells them that it is their responsibility to be the *one thing* they are destined to be. They must find the magic sword, the golden bird, the water of life. Only that *one thing* will free the abducted princess, or heal the wounded king, or save the kingdom that has become a wasteland. Nothing else, no other 'alternative,' will do." The Harry Potter books are a late-Capitalist mythology, written to train the young to pursue, not human value, but technique. Nothing is particularly *true* in those books; instead, the idea is to learn sorcery—for which read high technology—so you can *make things happen* and get what you want. And the notion that the individual is self-created and self-transforming (even though

Dugin has just finished saying that our actual creator is the *narod*, in relation to which the individual does not even exist, this being one more major contradiction in his worldview) is presented by him as intrinsic to the Eurasian character, the source of its enviable breadth—a Promethean anthropology that is inseparable from the magical worldview, as well as being intrinsic to Atlanticist mythology.

Furthermore, when it is announced that "man is simply a conditionality," it is all-important for us to determine exactly who is announcing it. When a Buddhist teacher says this, he means: "You are taking yourself as an unchanging object instead of an ongoing process; this causes suffering. To the degree that you train yourself to overcome obsessive self-definition and world-definition, and open to what is actually going on in self and world without imposing preconceived ideas, you will come into the field of *shunyata* and *karuna*, of Voidness inseparable from Compassion, which is the ultimate Reality. You will thereby achieve *bodhi*, Enlightenment, the end of suffering." When an advertising executive or social engineer or mind control technician says it, he means: "The consciousness of the public, or the individual, can be limitlessly altered and manipulated to serve our needs, to sell our products, to implant our ideas, because there is no knowledge or understanding or insight or wisdom truly intrinsic to the human being. He effectively has no 'inside'; his 'inner self' is a blank slate upon which we can write anything we want." And when the state official says it, it means: "The human being"—as Aleksandr Dugin has said in more than one place—"has no intrinsic 'rights,' no such thing as 'human dignity,' no spiritual Heart capable of hosting the *Imago Dei*; consequently when the *gulag* becomes hungry, we are free to shovel its belly full with the necessary quantity of human material." William Blake, on the other hand, was of the firm conviction that

> Man Brings All that he has and can have Into the World with him. Man is Born Like a Garden ready Planted & Sown. This World is too poor to produce one Seed. . . . Innate Ideas are in Every Man, Born with him; they are truly Himself. The Man who says that we have No Innate Ideas must be a Fool & Knave. . . .

Lastly, from the Christian point of view—in fact from the point of view of any of the Abrahamic religions—to say "man is a conditionality, the individual does not exist" is to say "man has no soul, nothing that can be redeemed, or damned, or saved at last after posthumous purgation. Therefore when Jesus on the cross said to the Good Thief, "this day you will be with Me in Paradise," he was making a promise he couldn't keep, speaking either as a naïve religious idealist or a compassionate charlatan offering a condemned criminal a moment of illusory terminal solace. Dugin claims to be a Christian, as well as (in some sense) a follower of the Traditionalist School, or at least someone who has been influenced by that School. To be a Traditionalist, however, requires adherence to Christian orthodoxy, or the orthodoxy of another of the God-given religions, therefore no-one who says "man is a conditionality" while professing Christianity can be a Traditionalist, or a Christian either. And if humanity is a mere conditionality, if we are now, according to Dugin, in an era of "post-anthropology," then there is no way that we can stand against the deconstruction of the human form that Dugin says he fears, the transformation of what was once humanity into a mass of industrially-produced bio-technological devices. Only a true metaphysical anthropology, an accurate understanding of the human essence, of *what a human being really is*—either that or the total destruction of human civilization and technology—can prevent this horrendous development. To the degree that Dugin believes that "man is a conditionality," he is on the side of the cyborgs, the chimeras, the clones.

Dugin also has something to say about Eurasianist Anthropology—if it can actually be called an anthropology, which is debatable—in his book *Eurasian Mission*, though here he appears to believe that the *narod* is just as illusory as the individual:

> The individual, the class, and the nation (race) are all artificial constructions of the perverted and nihilistic metaphysics of the Enlightenment. They are forms of inauthentic existence, for they mislead the real Self of being t/here and promote the totalitarian dictatorship of liberalism, one way or another, and of impersonal mechanical power.

No they're not. The nation or race or *narod* is a real, though relative and limited, collective entity with discernible characteristics; the individual is always more real than the race, because in him or her the characteristics of the race, and of the human species as a whole, are synthesized and concentrated. The class is a more-or-less artificial abstraction, susceptible to producing alienated notions of humanity but also useful to give a certain idea of the aspirations, limitations, forms of exploitation, skills, virtues, prejudices, obsessions and characteristic fates of various groups of real people. The individual is always more real than the class, if for no other reason than that he or she is not necessarily bound to one class over the course of a lifetime. The preeminence of the individual as a unique rendition of the universal human archetype is clearly indicated by the fact that only individuals, not races or classes or communities or religions, can become saints. In the words of the Holy Qur'an [5:32], *Whosoever killeth a human being for other than manslaughter or corruption in the earth, it shall be as if he had killed all mankind, and whoso saveth the life of one, it shall be as if he had saved the life of all mankind.* In the words of Jesus, "Whatever ye do unto one of the least of these, my brothers, ye do unto Me" [Matthew 25:40]. The illusion and the evil of individuality are not characteristics of the individual per se, but constitute the myth, idol and heresy of *individualism*, a transgression that the Christians call "the sin of self-love" or *philautia*. Self-love is the idea that society and the earth owe the individual everything while he owes them nothing; any individual who accepts this belief betrays his individuality, thereby becoming less than himself. The true individual, however, is not less than himself but more than himself, more than either what society thinks he is or what he thinks he is—infinitely more. Society—especially Liberal, Capitalist society—thinks of him as an exploitable bundle of low desires and fears. The true individual, however, knows that he is only what God knows him to be—and God knows nothing but God. "Individual" means "indivisible," which is a Name of God: *Al-Ahad*, the One. But the individual in his ego, in his passions, in his fears and desires—the one Dugin calls the "dividual"—is supremely divisible, almost infinitely so. The individual who knows that He is in God's Presence, however, and that God sees him as he really is, is truly individual, truly indivisible, because he or she participates in the Unity of God—not through ego-identification but through self-annihilation. The individual can only become him- or herself in the context of his or her intrinsic Humanity—and, as Dugin seems to understand, this is extremely difficult, if not effectively impossible, if normal elements of the human form, such as ethnicity, culture and gender, are suppressed. Nonetheless, only through self-annihilation in God is the real, authentic Self, Heidegger's dimly-imagined "self of *dasein*," realized.

It is fairly obvious that Aleksandr Dugin's "Eurasianist anthropology" is little more than a polarized reaction against what he sees as the Atlantean ethos, the radical idolatry of the abstract individual. "Atlantis" (at its worst) says: "The 'human being' has no intrinsic form, no intrinsic context. He, she, or it can be an animal, a machine, a being of either sex, or a third sex, or no sex, an entity without family, without religion, without culture, without history, a monad, a particle; an 'atomic individual.'" "Atom" means "indivisible"—but now, of course, the atom has been split, and its fragments further split, apparently *ad infinitum*. And "Eurasia," at its worst, says: "The 'human being' has no individuality, nothing that distinguishes him or her from other human beings of the same *narod*. He or she is, and is limited to, his or her ethnic group, religion, culture, history, and locality. If that human being imagines, or conceives of, or learns of, or invents, or develops, or creates, or receives an inspiration for, *anything* that is not yet in the set of the accepted characteristics or archetypes of the *narod*, let him or her renounce that innovation, that heresy, or be driven from the fold and left to die in the wilderness." But do either of these alternatives lead to the fullness of authentic human being? Of course not. And this dichotomy of extremes is a perfect example of the kind of hopeless choices we are increasingly being offered in these times, everywhere, all over the world. This is the Age of Extremism, when any kind of wholeness is outlawed, when we are all forced to live inside fragments of ourselves—and every fragment is necessarily an "extremist," a part that is struggling violently, and hopelessly, to become the whole. As a race, as a planet, we face apparently insoluble problems, but because we no longer really believe in God as our ancestors did—in both Atlantis *and* Eurasia—we cannot resign ourselves to His Will. Nothing is any more "an act of God," not even the weather. Everything is an act of man, a result either of our enemies' machinations or our own triumphs or screw-ups; this is the consequence of the collective human aspiration to take the weight of the Earth off the shoulders of the Titan Atlas—the one after whom Atlantis was named—and shoulder it ourselves. And since God is no longer in the picture, the words of W. B. Yeats, from his poem "The Second Coming," describe our situation exactly:

> Things fall apart; the centre cannot hold;
> Mere anarchy is loosed upon the world. . . .
> The best lack all conviction, while the worst
> Are full of passionate intensity.

We equate "the Center" with limp moderation, sloth and apathy. The only "life" we can imagine can exist nowhere but at the extremes—which simply means, in the words of T. S. Eliot's poem "The Love Song of J. Alfred Prufrock," that we would rather see the world end with a "bang" than a "whimper." The prime virtue of the Hesychasts of Orthodox Christianity is *apatheia*, dispassion, a profound *centeredness* without which there can be no *love*. That the Greek word *apatheia* has become the English word "apathy" is the perfect sign of the degeneration of our sense of the concrete reality of God. In the words of the *hadith qudsi*, "Heaven and Earth cannot contain Me, but the Heart of My loving slave can contain Me." The Heart is the Center—but we have no Center any more, effectively no Heart, and therefore no God. Consequently—whether in quiet desperation or with unparalleled and merciless violence—we are all virtually insane, except for those of us who know, either consciously or on the basis of a voiceless intuition, how to turn our hearts to the All-Merciful.

Does Aleksandr Dugin know this? Or is he trapped in the *dvandvas*, the "pairs-of-opposites"—the horses of them firmly strapped to his right and left arms and charging in opposite directions? Without the Center, nothing is left but universal war, war rooted in self-division. And in answer to the question that will inevitably arise at one point, the question as to whether or not an intuition of the inner Center could have an outer, socio-political expression, I offer as evidence the Covenants of the Prophet Muhammad, peace and blessings be upon him, with the Christians, the Jews, the Samaritans and the Zoroastrians of his time, which according to the Prophet's testimony, were directly inspired by Allah Himself. *He is the First and the Last, and the Outward and the Inward; and He is Knower of all things* [Q. 57:3].

∾

In his sections "The Ontological Map of the World (Suhrawardi)," "The Well-springs of Western Exile," "The Journey to the Country of the East" and "The Integration of the West unto Eurasia (The Descent into Hell)," Aleksandr Dugin deals with the lore of Sacred Geology, with what might be called "the soul of geopolitics," largely based on the teachings of Shahab al-Din Yahya ibn Habash Suhrawardi (1154–1191), founder of the *Ishraqi* or "Illuminist" School of Persian theosophical mysticism. He has much of value to say about this important subject, which is so rarely dealt with in established intellectual circles. And yet (in my opinion) there are certain implications of the symbolism of East and West that he has not yet arrived at.

When Aleksandr Dugin replaces God as an Absolute with the Earth and the *narod*, he is saying, in effect: "My homeland is my god." I, on the other hand, can only say: "God is my Homeland." To consecrate the forms of our earthly life to God, through the ritual remembrance of our ancestors, pious regard for our national folkways, and love for our native land, is one of the intrinsic poles of human terrestrial existence. The other pole is the inescapable intuition that we are only sojourners here, strangers in a strange land, that this terrestrial world itself is the "Far West" of cosmic existence, that we are all in Suhrawardi's "occidental exile." Eurasia, as a spiritual reality, may indeed stand as the heartland of the spiritual Earth, home to the Var of Yima, the sacred kingdoms of Agartha and Shambhala. If so, then America is the doorway to our lost *celestial* homeland; it is the clime where the dead material husks of things crack and crumble, releasing the shining Seed of the Spirit. When the Hyperborean North descends to Earth, it arrives from the East; when Hyperborea calls its earthly exiles home to Caer Sidi, the Revolving Castle of the polar stars, that call is issued first of all to the West.[3]

The symbolic meanings of East and West are dealt with by the Persian Sufi poet Mahmoud Shabestari (1288–1340), author of the famous *The Secret Rose Garden* (*Gulshan-i Rāz*). Eurasia is Shabestari's city of *Jabolqa*, situated in the Orient of the Essence; Atlantis is his *Jabolsa*, located in the Occident of physical body. "Whatever rises from the Orient of the Essence," says Shabestari, "sets in the Occident of human determination, becoming hidden in the human form." Every human being on earth is a citizen of both cities; if we fail to recognize this dual citizenship, which is intrinsic to us and cannot be renounced, we will turn both Orient and Occident into idols. To worship the Idol of the West is to descend into material disintegration and fragmentation, to petrify and volatil-

---

3. For a luminous presentation of the Imaginal Plane where such sacred kingdoms as Agartha, Shambhala and the Var of Yima exist, see *Iconostasis* by the Eastern Orthodox writer Vladimir Lossky.

ize at the same time, to let our souls be pulverized by the "techno-elves" that "psychonaut" Terrence McKenna saw under the influence of DMT, to be "hyperrealized" by electronic pseudo-experience, to replace the vision of the Celestial Paradise with the lurid glare of virtual reality. It is to be devoured by Leviathan, the Sea-Beast—the fate of all those who *relativize the Absolute*. To worship the Idol of the East is to congeal, to identify the Celestial Paradise with its earthly reflection like Nicholas Roerich did, to trap the Spirit inside a statue of stone, to dynamite the Chinvad Bridge and thereby destroy all hope of return to the Father, to live inside a sacred prison under a petrified sky. It is to be eaten by Behemoth, the Land-Beast—the fate of all those who *absolutize the relative*, as Dugin does in his sections "The Russian Person as an Absolute" and "The Absolute Motherland."[4]

The Gothic architecture of the West, the upward aspiration of the pointed arch, is a sign of God's Transcendence; the Byzantine architecture of the East, its churches designed like mystery-caves where Paradise is brought to earth, is a sign of His Immanence. God is necessarily both, while in no way being *divided* between both. As a consequence of this, the ultimate spiritual principles behind Dugin's Atlantis and Eurasia are intertwined like the Yin and Yang in the Chinese symbol of the *T'ai Chi*. Within Eurasia is a dot of the trans-Atlantean tincture, the point of God's Transcendence. Within Atlantis is a dot of the trans-Eurasian tincture, the point of God's Immanence. One cannot exist without the other; whoever accepts one but rejects the other seeks to destroy terrestrial existence.

∾

[The section of "Eurasia (A Political Poem)" entitled "The Individualization of Supra-Individual Experience," the section "For the Absolute and Against the Relative," and the section "There is No Time," are analyzed in *Chapter Two*, Part Two.]

∾

In his section "The Purple Archangel of Russia," Aleksandr Dugin is again caught in possession of stolen goods, this time with a rare spiritual artifact hid-

---

4. Both Eurasia and Atlantis—in their spiritual essences, not their idolatrous counterfeits—are also reflected in the spiritual heart of America. The classic expression of the first is "This Land is Your Land" by Woody Guthrie; this song is truly our "populist national anthem." It can be heard on You Tube at: https://www.youtube.com/watch?v=Ol0rRdF5L1c. The quintessential expression of the second is the song "I Can't Feel at Home in This World Any More" by the Carter Family, on You Tube at: https://www.youtube.com/watch?v=yE3kW9-tjO8. And perhaps the finest contemporary poem on the relationship between the remembered terrestrial paradise and the hoped-for celestial one is "Occidental Exile" by Seyyed Hossein Nasr; it can be found at: http://desmontes.blogspot.com/2009/09/occidental-exile-by-seyyed-hossein-nasr.html.

den in his saddlebag: the Purple Archangel. This is the archangel who figures in Suhrawardi's *The Recitation of the Purple Archangel.* The Purple (or Crimson) Archangel—*al-'Aql al-Surkh*—is an imaginal manifestation of the Active Intellect (*'Aql*) who appears in order to conduct Suhrawardi to the summit of Mt. Qaf and the attainment of *haqiqa,* the fullness of spiritual Truth. In other words, the Purple Archangel is, precisely, an Iranian *Ishraqi* version of the *Logos,* which Aleksandr Dugin, in "The Metaphysics of Chaos" from *The Fourth Political Theory,* has declared null and void. To him, however, the Purple Archangel is

> The true dawn of Great and Sacred Asia, which is the secret angel, the secret substance of Russia, her historical, spiritual mission spread over every-thing—politics, culture, sociology, our history.

Here Dugin, like the magician he is, attempts to take illegal possession the archetypal essence of Iran (Suhrawardi being the sage who, more than anyone else, made a synthesis between the spiritual universes of Islamic and pre-Islamic, Zoroastrian Persia), doing so as an act of subtle-plane conquest in the *Alam al-Mithal,* the realm of Objective Imagination. The ancient Romans, with similar intent, appropriated the gods of their conquered peoples and installed them in the Pantheon as symbols of imperial domination. If the Purple Archangel is the angel of any earthly clime, he is the Angel of Iran—but much more than this, he is the precise hierophany through which God invested Suhrawardi with the knowledge of the Divine that was destined for him. If God struck Uzzah dead merely for touching the Ark of the Covenant to prevent it from falling [2Samuel 6:1-7; 1Chronicles 13:9-12], what will he strike Aleksandr Dugin with for the attempted abduction of an archangel? This is an act of theft so brazen, so lacking in any normal sense of holy fear, that I don't know what to compare it with. And in addition to being sacrilegious, it is patently absurd. I might just as well claim that Fyodor Dostoyevsky was a great American novelist, or that the real Kremlin is in Pennsylvania somewhere and the one shown in Moscow only a later copy; I have *more right* to do this, in fact—even though I have no right to do this at all—than Dugin has to loot the Purple Archangel of Suhrawardi. Let him be very careful when he is in fishing in foreign waters; he might hook a fish so big that it will pull him under the waves, never to be seen again.

And—as we have already seen—this is not the only place where Dugin betrays his fascination with angels. His eagerness to invoke the angelic coupled with his hesitation to embrace the Divine indicates a desire on his part, common to both Renaissance ceremonial magicians and New Age practitioners, to access the *Alam al-Mithal* or Imaginal Plane from below, through manipulation or artificial stimulation of the psyche, rather than standing in wait until God elects to imaginally manifest Himself from above, possibly by sending one of

His messengers or *angels—angelos*, as we have already seen, being the Greek word for "messenger." Celestial angels are never *accessed* by those who truly venerate them; only when these angels are traveling on specific missions for their Lord are they encountered by human beings. Likewise those angels who allow themselves to be accessed by persons seeking to raid the mysteries for knowledge or power—through the use of psychedelic drugs, for example—are necessarily fallen angels, beings who offer themselves to the magician to be commanded only to hide the fact that their real intent is to command the magician, to make him their slave in both this world and the next.

Inverted Prophesy and the King of Edom

In "Eurasianism (A Political Poem)," Aleksandr Dugin explicitly declares Eurasianism to be a religion, with himself as its prophet—so *goodbye to Christianity*. In the words of Fr. Seraphim Rose, the American Eastern Orthodox priest who was influenced by René Guénon and who followed the great St. John Maximovitch the Wonderworker of Shanghai and San Francisco, "In our time, Satan has walked naked into human history." Dugin says:

> The Eurasian doctrine is in the first place a spiritual doctrine. In a sense it is a prophetic school. It is a point of confluence of great streams of thought, a perfectly self-sufficient doctrine that gives people everything: a meaning of life, energy for creation, and the correct orientation to love.
>
> Eurasianism is thought with the help of the heart; it is the depths of heart-based thinking. Eurasianism is an invitation to the prophetic experience. Let us remember who the biblical prophets were. They strengthened the identity of their *narod*, saying: "Awaken, Israel, awaken *narod*. You've fallen completely; you've completely degenerated; this is not permitted. How long can you give yourself up to your own occupations? Return to your own being."
>
> Do we not, Eurasianists, say the same thing? We call out; "O *narod*; O Russia; O Eurasian peoples, what are you doing? You've turned into such pigs! That is enough. It is time to put an end to the fall. Russia, arise!" We are doing what the prophets did. We are returning the *narod* to our own identity.

What are you going to do with a man who cynically spits on Judaism, Christianity, Islam, Zoroastrianism and a lot more besides by claiming that a political movement, a movement that *postpones God*, can do and be what only the religions intended and revealed by God can do and be? He goes on:

> What else do prophets do? They restore the connection between reason and consequences. "Come to your senses, Edom; come to your senses, Sire; you fell away from the worship of the true God, and therefore God punished you, destroyed your walls, your city. Where is the kingdom of Babylon that stood strong? The kingdom of Babylon is no more. Why? Because they rejected the

one God. In our time, this function corresponds to political analysis, the depths of political science [*politologia*].

Dugin is having fun here at the expense of the unwary. He warns us "prophetically" that the kingdom of Babylon is no more because it rejected God, and then gives us, as an example of the prophetic character of Eurasianism, a "political science" specifically conceived, in largely Heideggerian terms, without God, or which only makes a few passing references to Him, while granting a much greater role and significance to *angels*. But his references to Edom are even more interesting. The kingdom of Edom, descended from Esau as Israel was from Jacob, was the hereditary enemy of the Jews in the Old Testament. Obadiah 1:1–2 says:

> Thus says the Lord God concerning Edom: We have heard a report from the Lord, and a messenger has been sent among the nations: "Rise up! Let us rise against her for battle! Behold I will make you small among the nations; you shall be utterly despised."

In other words, the Bible does not call for Edom to awake, as Dugin suggests, but for Israel to awake and destroy Edom; here again Dugin's obsession with secretly inverting the meanings of spiritual principles—though obviously not as secretly as he had hoped—is clearly in evidence. Edom is also denounced by the prophets Ezekiel [25:12–14] and Joel [3:19–21]. And who might the figure be that Dugin identifies with Edom and addresses as "Sire"? Edom is a kingdom, not a king. In Judaism, Edom is another name for Esau, the earthly, material man, brother and opponent of Jacob who was to become Israel, the Spiritual man; this seems in line with Dugin's rejection of Logos and the Essential Pole in favor of Chaos and the Substantial Pole. But who is the King, who is the Sire, of Edom? In the Rabbinical writings, the guardian angel of Esau and the angelic patron of the kingdom of Edom is Samael, the Angel of Death and Destruction, who is identified with Satan and sometimes called by that name. In *Pirke De-Rabbi Eliezer* from the *Midrash*, dated to the period of the spread of Islam, Samael appears as both Satan and the Serpent in *Genesis*; he bears an obvious similarity to Iblis, the Muslim Satan, since Samael—like Iblis, who is made of fire and proud of it—disapproves of God's creation of Adam from the lowly dust of the earth [cf. Q. 7:11–18].

I can only describe this revelation of Dugin's primary allegiance as an unexpected mercy. I thought I might be going too far in calling Aleksandr Dugin a Satanist, letting my spleen run away with me and hurling unfair personal accusations against someone simply because I disagreed with his ideas. And I also worried that my characterization of his "angels" as *fallen* angels might be going over the line. So it comes as a great personal relief for me to hear him openly invoking his Sire. As Dugin himself says in the same chapter:

This is very important knowledge, but negative knowledge, general demonology, if you prefer. After all, not only Satanists studied the names of demons;
abbots, respectable Catholic theologians, were also interested in this question.

In the face of this unexpected and illuminating revelation—part of the text
for which, quoted above, was drawn from Dugin's section "Spiritual Teaching:
The Call to Repentance"—I now invite Aleksandr Dugin to repent, to renounce
the Angel Samael and make his submission to the true God, whose Mercy is
always available to those who turn to Him. I hope I have been able to do this in
full recognition that the Judgment of God is impartial and cannot be owned or
wielded by any man or angel, and consequently that the invocation of that
Judgment must necessarily fall equally on both accuser and accused, and that it
is a Judgment that will inevitably make those places in my own soul where I
have failed of full submission to Allah extremely hot for me, hopefully hot
enough to force me to release them as quickly as possible. And I also stand
ready to hear and ponder whatever criticisms of me and my position Aleksandr
Dugin or his followers may wish to offer, since I don't believe in shooting from
cover; whoever wants to "count coup" must fully expose himself to the enemy.

Furthermore—all Satanism apart—no "prophet" can prophesy to a *narod* in
the name of that same *narod*. If Isaiah or Ezekiel or Jeremiah, instead of saying:
"Hear, Israel! Thus sayeth the Lord," had opened with "Hear, Israel! Thus sayeth Israel," they might have legitimately been met with puzzlement, if not deri-
sion. The Jews would have been justified in retorting "We already know what *we*
say because we *are* Israel. What we are still in the dark about is what God will
say. If you can't bring us news from God, what sort of prophets are you?" A
prophet who puts his nation in the place of God and prophesies accordingly, to
it but also from it, is teaching that nation collective self-worship, which is both
the sin of Lucifer and the sin of those Jews who, while never forgetting their
"chosenness," have forgotten the God who chose them.

At a stretch it might be possible to admit that Aleksandr Dugin does satisfy
part of the definition of a prophet, though in an entirely inverted manner; he
does indeed tell some uncomfortable truths, and in that sense "speaks truth to
power." But as a Kremlin insider and the apparent protégé of at least one Russian oligarch, he is also speaking truth—or his twisted version of it—*from*
power. And for him to shamelessly proclaim his courageous honesty is, as we
say in the English-speaking world, "a bit much"—especially when we factor in
his Satanic orientation and the many falsehoods he happily publishes, some of
which have been exposed in this book. Furthermore, when Dugin takes Satan
the Rebel, or Samael the Adversary, as the patron of his Eurasianism—possibly
through an inverted Kabbalah of the dark side, the *Sitra Achra*—he necessarily
casts the principalities and powers of Atlanticism as the Angels of God, and

thus as the destined victors. This is ill-conceived to say the least. If he and I agree on anything, it's that Divine sanction is an honor that Atlanticism in no way deserves.

Dugin returns to his Eurasian Absolutism:

> When you see people deny any element of what we are saying . . . know that these are enemies, these are Atlanticists. In a certain sense they know perfectly well what they are doing, whom they are serving, and against whom they are fighting.

"Eurasianism is the Absolute Good and Atlanticism the Absolute Evil." Who can argue with that? If I demonstrate that Dugin has contradicted himself, has betrayed the very values he claims to champion, then I am of course the enemy of Eurasianism—I, but also Aleksandr Dugin. We are brothers in the same enmity, I the open and external enemy, he the secret fifth column; if we work together we will certainly prevail. I am, of course, speaking ironically here. I have made it clear in a number of places that I see some good in Eurasianism, and that I share Dugin's hatred of Atlanticism, as long as this is defined as Liberal globalism and postmodern technocracy, not as the West as a whole. It's simply that I believe in God, and therefore can see no Absolute Good but in Him and no Absolute Evil but in the rebellious ego that denies Him—though "Absolute Evil" is actually an incorrect term, given that only the Good, only God, is truly Absolute, and that evil—as a *privatio boni*, a deficiency in the power of Good under particular limited, relative conditions—can never be Absolute, seeing that the abyss into which it has cast itself is truly bottomless. One of the ways in which the human being learns is through criticism; he learns both by accepting it and by repudiating it. Dugin, however, has made sure that he will never learn anything by this method. Why should he? *He already knows.* From his point of view—or at least according to his stated public position—anyone who criticizes him in the slightest, even constructively, is an agent of Absolute Evil. This of course makes me a cunning agent of Atlanticism, charged with the duty of weakening the Eurasian movement by sowing uncertainty and dissension. And since I have neither the ability nor the inclination to defend myself against this charge, I'll move on to another question.

Eurasian Mind-Control Explained

When it comes to mind-control—which includes both the ability to control and/or break the psyche of the individual and to pull the wool over the eyes of the general public—one of the first requirements is the devaluation of logic and rationality. The doctrine that the Logos is exhausted and that we are now under the reign of Chaos is obviously an ideal metaphysic to further this goal. In line with his organizing agenda, Aleksandr Dugin provides a very clear picture, in the following passage, of the sub-rational configuration-of-soul that is required for the "individual" to fully embrace Eurasianism:

> Truly, Eurasianism turns out to be that moment when you implement the unpleasant command of a leader, exercising your own whim, and when the command corresponds with your whim, your wishes, with the movements of your soul. That is true Eurasianism, when absolute freedom merges into an inseparable synthesis with absolute discipline.

In Christianity the human being is considered to have free will, which is what allows him to follow God's commands willingly, to freely submit his will to God's Will, to say, with Christ, "Not my will but Thine be done" [Luke 22:42]. In Eurasianism, the individual is seen as having no free will, only "whims" or "wishes," largely unconscious impulses. Yet somehow these unconscious impulses are discovered to be right in line with the "unpleasant command" of the leader. In Sufism, the unconscious ego that acts by generating such "whims" in us, rather than conscious decisions and deliberate actions, is known as the *nafs al-ammara b'l su*, "the soul commanding to evil." Sufism, and Islam in general, also recognize the reality and negative spiritual influence of *Shaytan* or Satan. Satan may send delusive glamours to darken our minds or tempt us to "freely" indulge our passions, but he cannot overpower our free will; his only avenue of access to us is the *nafs al-ammara b'l su*. The *nafs* experiences God's commands as the "unpleasant" and unreasonable demands of a Leader who, "ideally," should have no rights over the self-will of our unconscious impulses. After the *nafs* has become purified through spiritual practice, however, it is transformed into the *nafs al-mutma'inna*, the "soul at peace," the soul that submits to God's commands gladly. Eurasianism, however, appeals directly to the unconscious impulses of its devotees in their original unregenerate state; in doing so it does not ask for deliberate, conscious submission on the part of the human individual endowed with free will, but rather bypasses this free will entirely—a much more efficient method. In other words, it operates according to the methods of advertising and other common methods of mind-control. The dupe of the American advertising industry suddenly discovers new desires in him- or herself—desires which miraculously turn out to be in complete accord with the advertised virtues of a product that is actually available! This "miracle" is easily explained, however: the manufacturers of that product, via advertising, have *implanted* the desire for it in the unconscious psyche of the consumer. The axiomatic "absolute freedom of choice" accorded the consumer in a so-called "democratic society" to buy the product in question thus perfectly coincides with the *command* of the manufacturer that he buy it. The understanding of how this process works is elementary to any even half-conscious American, but after 70 years of Communism, based as it was more on relatively obvious ideological training and propaganda, enforced by explicit commands and prohibitions, than on the kind of mass-media hypnosis common in the United States, which is inseparable from the illusion of infinite freedom of choice, perhaps it appears as a kind of miracle to the average Russian—which is something that Aleksandr Dugin may in fact be banking on.

Freedom and discipline can be united in two different and diametrically opposed ways. On the Spiritual Path common to all the world's Divinely-revealed religions, the human person in submission to the Will of God finds a real though negative freedom from the destructive commands of the *nafs al-ammara*, and at the same time realizes a positive freedom in his or her relationship to God conceived of as the Guarantor of the integrity of the human person, if not as that person's truest Self, a Self which he or she shares with all things; as Meister Eckhart put it, "My truest 'I' is God."

The opposite alternative to this state of true freedom is the submission of the human person to the dictatorial whims and passions of the *nafs al-ammara b'l su*, unpleasant from the standpoint of our human integrity but all-too-pleasant to the part of us that wants to "relax," shirk all responsibility, and thereby obtain a spurious and inverted *unity*. This false sense of psychic integrity and wholeness is produced by the careful suppression of the irritating and uncomfortable inner division between the conscious ego that is endeavoring to live according to the spiritual principles of the Logos and the seductive inner Chaos of the passions with their promise of sweet relief—a relief that always ends in mortal anguish. The union of discipline and freedom in God necessarily starts with the recognition and full development of free will, followed by the conscious dedication and renunciation of that will, whereas in the inverted, Satanic dimension, the union of *being-controlled* with *capitulation-to-being-controlled* —a state reminiscent of demonic possession—laughs at free will and does all it can to portray this necessary constituting element of the human person as a foolish and idealistic illusion. It would appear, from Dugin's description in the above passage, that Eurasianism follows this latter method.

Lastly, Dugin's inversion of the central Christian doctrine of free will moving toward loving obedience to God is complemented and completed by his inversion of St. Paul's method of spreading the Gospel by being "all things to all men":

> When approaching workers, [*the Eurasianist*] begins to speak of the workers' movement, of the fact that oligarchs are bastards, etc. [*being careful, of course, not to mention that one of these oligarchs is Dugin's sponsor*]. When he comes to intellectuals, he speaks of the great Russian culture, of Pushkin, of the fact that he erred in certain things, though that is not important. The main thing is that you know how to enter into dialogue and through a momentary situation advance the model of your Eurasianist approach.

This is the union of discipline and impulse from the point of view of the disciplinarian. It is one thing to tell the same Truth in many different languages, like the Apostles did on Pentecost, or like St. Paul in his Epistles, speaking to the Corinthians in Corinthian terms, to the Ephesians in Ephesian terms, to the Romans in Roman terms, etc. But it is quite another to pretend to believe what the Christians believe while subverting Christian doctrine, to pretend to be in sympathy with Islam while wooing the Takfiris who are intent on destroying Islam until nothing is left but the name, to pretend to hate the oligarchs and support trade unionism in Russia while reportedly being bankrolled buy an oligarch and (in *The Rise of the Fourth Political Theory*) counting "big bankers" as part of the Eurasianist movement, to pretend to love Russian literary culture while cranking out book after book like those I am now in the process of deciphering. To virtually *become* the person you wish to influence is a venerable tactic of the "confidence" profession. It is done by inducing the mark to make an unconscious and virtually total identification with you while you continue to view him coldly and "objectively," noting any useful weaknesses, desires, fears or beliefs by which he can be manipulated; a similar technique has become second nature to the manipulative psychiatrist. The follower cannot oppose the leader because the follower *is* the leader; unfortunately for him, the leader is not also the follower—a configuration of psychic energy that might be called "unipolar boundary-loss," similar in many ways to the psychotherapeutic technique of inducing of "transference." The self-discipline of the mind-controller that allows him to appear totally sympathetic, while in reality giving nothing, automatically tempts the target of his control to give too much, thereby hooking him. Here we can see how the correct Eurasian *praxis*, based on the principle that "man is a conditionality," is to *condition* him. But why Dugin would openly admit to Non-Eurasianists that they should not believe the words of Eurasianists is beyond me . . . unless it's an illustration of the principle that if you don't consciously practice honesty it will sink into your shadow and start acting as an unconscious saboteur, or else another example of "revelation of the method."

On Chapter Seven:
"The Structure of Russia's Sociogenesis"

Here Dugin the intelligent, balanced, comprehensive, insightful secular sociologist appears again—that particular Dugin who has no need to constantly contradict himself or infuse his academic *theoria* with some kind of potent theurgical *praxis*, no matter how dark, irrational and inverted it might be, so as to translate his abstract ideas into concrete action. All I can say is, anyone interested in the history and future prospects of Russian should make a thorough study of Dugin's schemas as presented in this chapter. He covers all the discrete phases of Russian history—the Russian Federation being the tenth—from the standpoint of the primacy and constancy of the *narod* vis-à-vis the variability and secondary nature of the state, and presents the persistence of the Russian *narod* and its change and development through time as the true essence of Russia, considered neither as the geography and history of a single racial group nor in terms of a specific form of government or economy, but as a full-fledged Russian Civilization. Much useful social analysis might be built on Dugin's analysis.

On Chapter Eight:
"The Russian Leviathan (State Terror)"

As I have already observed above, we live in the Age of Extremism. Therefore if Liberal "Atlanticist" democracy in Russia is, in Dugin's words, "individualized, relaxed, Westernized, devoid of purpose and meaning, oriented toward one's personal career, comfort and material prosperity," the "Eurasian" contrary to this must be a society that suppresses the individual, remains vigilant, looks to Asia for its models of government, is dominated by a collective purpose, and is willing to sacrifice comfort and prosperity in order to pursue that purpose. Every government must comprise elements of rigor, inflexibility, justice, and authority; the rule of law without the possibility of severe punishment is compromised from the outset. Governments have both the right and the duty to apprehend and punish criminals, defend the nation against foreign attack, and put down armed rebellion. The cause of such rebellion may even be just, but no government can simply accede to being overthrown. However, to define the power of the state as a "divine right" rather than a simple necessity of *realpolitik* is only appropriate in the case of those governments who spring from, and exist in order to defend, Divine revelations—not to mention the fact that if such governments violate the norms of these revelations even while acting in their name, their divine right to govern is withdrawn.

Dugin, in this chapter, does his best to establish the State as a deity—in sharp contrast to his position in Chapter Six, where he characterized the State as

> a very rotten thing . . . it must be aggressive externally and firm, in accordance with necessity, like armor. But internally it is very gentle, in order not to infringe on, not to trouble the process of national spiritual life, erotic life, which constantly and invisibly flows in our *narod*. . . . The state in itself is a detrimental, evil thing; it is too formal, too cold. In this steel, in these machines, in these cruel instruments of torture there is little that is attractive.

Here, however, Dugin says:

> The German historian of religion and theologian Rudolph Otto, describing the phenomenon of the sacred (the holy, *das Heilege*), underscores that this

feeling combines opposite human emotions: admiration, ecstasy, love and horror, trembling, panic. Moreover, all this cannot be separated from joy and delight.

To the extent that the sacralization of power, the state, politics and social institutions exists for a *narod*, this complicated complex of strong emotions extends to them too. We cannot separate the fear factor as something isolated. Horror before the sacralized political echelon is not separable from love and reverence: consequently, this phenomenon is rather complicated, and to study it correctly, it is necessary to preliminarily describe the structure of the sacred.

Undoubtedly, in Russian history political power and the state were most often taken as something sacred, although it different periods this sacrality has a different nature. Thus, fear before the ruling authority was most often a complicated complex of veneration, love and reverence. . . .

It is true that God necessarily inspires both love and fear, but it emphatically *not* true that whatever inspires both love and fear is God; if Rudolph Otto believed this, then he was (I'm sorry to say) an idiot, and a dangerous one at that. We may also feel love-and-fear for evil, delusion, murder, addiction, suicide, atrocity; some of the most effective brainwashing techniques work by alternating pain (fear) with relief ("love"). When Dostoyevsky stood before the firing squad, about to be executed for sedition, and the courier arrived at the last second with a pardon from the Czar, that's when he became a "believer"— before spending four years in a Siberian prison. Perhaps the Russian state had saved him from a worse fate, that of becoming one of the twisted nihilistic revolutionaries he described in *The Possessed*, or perhaps it simply ground him under the heel of blind power. Be that as it may, he expressed the higher possibilities of repentance in *Crime and Punishment*, where Raskolnikov, though broken down by the insidious pressure of police inspector Porfiry Petrovich (who was likely the original model for the American TV detective "Colombo"), was only truly saved through the love of Sonya—who, when he confessed to her that he had committed murder, responded with: "*What have you done to yourself?*" To give to a mere human government the love and awe that we owe to God alone is the height of idolatry; whoever asks us to do this is working to turn that government from one that might or might not rule with the blessing of God, and lie under His protection, into a pagan idol, a Moloch—a comparison that Dugin himself uses to characterize the "Russian Leviathan." When the armies of Islam conquered the Persian Empire, they announced: "We have come to teach you to worship God, not men."

Fully understanding that what I criticize here may simply be a bad translation from the Russian (or the German), I will define the word "horror" as denoting a terror that is polluted with feelings of revulsion and disgust. Terror in the presence of the Divine Wrath is an element of piety; horror at the dark aspects of life coupled with the sense that they represent a cruel, ghoulish, meaningless distortion of life's real meaning is impious when the darkness is seen as coming from God, but entirely appropriate when it is seen as the work of the Devil. A terror of God is the beginning of wisdom; a *horror* of God is a deluded and blasphemous transformation of God into Satan. We have a right and a duty to be terrified at God's rigor, but we have no right to be revolted or disgusted by Him.

One of the spiritual states or stations enumerated by the Sufis is Awe (*Haybat*). In my book *Day and Night on the Sufi Path* I had this to say about the state of Awe, considered both from the standpoint of the Heart, which accepts Awe because it sees it as coming from Allah, and of the *nafs*—the partly-unconscious ego—that flees from Awe because it sees it as cruel and meaningless:

> Awe from the standpoint of the Heart is rapture in the face of God's Majesty, trembling on the brink of Annihilation. In the state of Awe, God is too tremendous a Reality to draw near to, and at the same time too powerful a Force to escape or hide from; in the face of the Divine Majesty, the sense of separate self-existence becomes unbearable, and begs to be released. Awe from the standpoint of the Nafs is the slanderous accusation that God is a cruel tyrant, a lie that results in a freezing or petrification of the affections, coupled with a headlong flight into despair and self-destruction.... The Nafs may also produce in you the blasphemous tendency to play the tyrant yourself, to appoint yourself the representative of God's Majesty in the foolish belief that you will then not be subject to his Wrath because you are the agent of it. There are plenty self-appointed servants of the Wrath of God, however, who will end up as close companions of that Wrath for all eternity—unless God relent. All Wrath is from Allah, but this certainly does not mean that all who are wrathful are true servants of Allah! According to Ibn al-'Arabi, to extend Mercy is simultaneously to receive it; likewise to extend Wrath, without God's express command, is to be equally subject to Wrath. God does not first punish or reward us in recompense for our actions, but by means of them.

The Nafs does its best to turn Awe into anger, and then offers us lust as a way of appeasing that anger, thus corrupting Awe and Intimacy at the same time. Awe may indicate that the one experiencing it is brought near to Allah while still in a state of transgression and idolatry; the traveler's closeness to the Majestic purges his Heart of its impurities, until *Al-Jalal* gives way to *Al-Jamal*, Awe to Intimacy. Conversely, Intimacy may be seen as Allah's seductiveness, his drawing of the traveler, by means of the unveiling of His Beauty, inexorably toward His Majesty, so that *Al-Jamal* gives way to *Al-Jalal*, conducting the *faqir* to a state of nearness that would have been impossible to him to approach or endure if Allah had unveiled His Majesty at the outset. But in any case, both Awe and Intimacy only arrive after God has become entirely real to the *faqir*—real and inescapable; thus the finished and established sense of the Presence of God may be seen as the synthesis of the Majesty of God and the Beauty of God. Awesome Majesty is a Beauty too great for us to encompass—and Beauty itself, however merciful, however welcoming, has its own awesomeness; it is the first sign of the swift arrival of death, the herald of Annihilation. But just as "My Mercy has precedence over My Wrath" [Bukhari], so, in the experience of His faithful servants, His Beauty has precedence over His Majesty. To the lover of Allah, the Majesty of Allah is no less beautiful than His Beauty, and the very Awe of Him the deepest Intimacy conceivable.

Awe is the shocking realization that the Fires of Jahannam [Hell] are also the Fires of Allah, that the Presence of God is relentless, inescapable, and that the unrepentant Nafs can no way stand in the face of it. The Presence of Allah is awesome, tremendous, devastating. How can you face it—especially since you can't turn away from it? Maybe the shocks of life, the shocks of the Heart and the soul and the body, are really the shocks of God. Why does man make war? Maybe because war is the poor man's mysticism, because most of us are not close enough to Allah to feel His tremendousness in the *Batin* [the Inner] without first creating tremendous stress in the *Zahir* [the Outer]. As Hazrat Ali said, "Paradise is beneath the shadow of the swords." But how can we withstand the tremendous Presence of Allah if we are not yet ripe for Annihilation? Only through Absence. Awe heralds Absence; Absence heralds Annihilation; Annihilation is the essence and gateway of Subsistence. *There is no refuge from God but in Him* is a way of saying that there is no refuge from Awe except in Absence. And while you are Absent, all that's left you is being pounded—both out of shape and into it—on the anvil of Allah.

Awe according to the Heart is to be transfixed and motionless in witnessing the Victory of Allah, His triumph over all things, His abasement of all that would presume to stand against Him. The King has stormed the city of the Heart, breached its walls, broken its gate and subdued the Nafs with the sword of His Power. In the state of Awe, the terror of the Nafs and rapture of the Heart are identical: there is not the slightest shadow of separation between them.

> When You unveiled Your tremendous
>   Majesty
> And I knew there was no escape,
> I went and lay down on Your anvil
> Under the hammers of Your remembrance.
> What I had made of myself, You unmade
> With the blows of Your speech,
> The relentless pounding of Your moments
> That mark the course of time.
>
> When You unveiled the fires of Your
>   Absolute Justice
> Against which there is no appeal,

> I crept into the forge and lay down
> Under the bellows of Your remembrance.
> Your Face gave light
> Till I reached white heat.
>
> What refuge from the hammer, except on
>   the anvil?
> What refuge from the fire
> Except in the forge itself?
> What does it matter if I become a cup or
> a blade, a stirrup or the head of an axe,
>   If I bear the stamp of the Master?

Awe according to the Nafs is delight in the presence of anger considered to be your legitimate heritage and intrinsic power—a delight that, when you come to realize that to embrace anger is to become the victim of it, is transformed into a tremendous horror and despair before Allah falsely conceived of as a merciless tyrant, a torturer, King of the *Shayatin* and the Chief of them; its fruits are panic, cowardice and headlong flight into destruction. In the absence of Love, of *Mahabbah*, the Nafs is willing to endure even this so as to hold on to the sense of its own existence apart from God; instead of dying before it is made to die, it tries to kill itself, over and over again, precisely in order to take total possession of itself and so *avoid death*. In the words of Ali ibn Abi Talib, "Anger is a raging fire. Whoever can subdue his anger puts out the fire; whoever cannot gets burnt himself." And as for those who fail to put out this fire, "It is reported—but Allah knows best—that the Prophet Muhammad—may peace be upon him—said, 'He who commits suicide by throttling himself shall keep on throttling himself in the Hell Fire forever and he who commits suicide by stabbing himself shall keep on stabbing himself in the Hell-Fire forever . . . [and] whoever commits suicide with a piece of iron [*or a bomb*] will be punished with the same piece of iron [*or bomb*] in the Hell Fire'" [Related in the *Sahih Bukhari* on the authority of Abu Hurayra].

Taslim [submission] in the state of Awe is simply not to flee the awesome Presence of Allah through pursuit of passion, distraction or oblivion, but to gaze in nakedness upon naked destruction, enduring blow after blow and continuing on until you know the ecstasy hidden inside pain and witness the Beauty hidden inside Majesty—witness it and are ravished by it, to the limit of endurance and beyond. This *Taslim* has the power to free you from all anger, to release whatever anger was in you so that it returns to the Wrath of God. All anger belongs to Allah, none belongs to you; whatever anger you thought of as yours was really His all along. By identifying with it you became subject to it and were forced to suffer the consequences of it; but now you are free from it. The Wrath of Allah, once you recognize its presence and under-stand its true nature, has the power to pull all the anger right out of you, returning it to the only One with both the right and the power to satisfy it.

Nothing in this world, including states and governments, deserves either our truest Love or our truest Awe. These belong to God, arrive only from God, and return only to God. As Allah Himself says in the *hadith qudsi*: "Who seeks Me, finds Me; who finds Me, knows Me; who knows Me, loves Me; who loves Me, I love him; whomever I love, I kill; whomever I kill, I Myself am his blood price." Those who truly know God know Him through both His Mercy and His Wrath—but they also know that, in the words of the *hadith qudsi*, "My Mercy has precedence over My Wrath," the necessary correlative to which is the understanding that His Wrath is the servant of His Mercy. The one who has lost God, however, can never know the root of either true Mercy or true Wrath, true love or true fear, and will consequently be tempted to give his love-and-fear to an unworthy object; in Dugin's case, this temptation appears to include an attraction to the earthly government of the well-known "oriental despot." Should I denounce this? Lament it? Cynically accept and applaud it? What exactly do I expect from this world? Something new and unheard of, a sudden idealistic convulsion at this late date, at this darkest point of human history? Should I at least point out that, as a sometime apologist for Satanic evil, Dugin has no right to employ the doctrines and categories of religion? From my present point of view, none of this is either appropriate or necessary, seeing that the best response has already been given by Jesus Christ: "There needs be evil, but woe to him through whom evil comes" [Luke 17:1]—a warning that also entirely applies to "Atlantean" America. And though Jesus said it best, the words of the solitary American poet of the wild California coast, Robinson Jeffers, are not out of place here:

Be Angry at the Sun (1941)

That public men publish falsehoods
Is nothing new. That America must accept
Like the historical republics corruption and empire
Has been known for years.

Be angry at the sun for setting
If these things anger you. Watch the wheel slope and turn,
They are all bound on the wheel, these people, those warriors,
This republic, Europe, Asia.

Observe them gesticulating,
Observe them going down. The gang serves lies, the passionate
Man plays his part; the cold passion for truth
Hunts in no pack.

You are not Catullus, you know,
To lampoon these crude sketches of Caesar. You are far

From Dante's feet, but even farther from his dirty
Political hatreds.

Let boys want pleasure, and men
Struggle for power, and women perhaps for fame,
And the servile to serve a Leader and the dupes to be duped.
Yours is not theirs.

Religion and metaphysics have always been appropriated to serve the ends of worldly power; this is what the Gospel [Matthew 24:15; Mark 13:14] calls "the Abomination of Desolation standing in the Holy Place." And if the perversion of religion has a long and distinguished history, so do the terrible and eternal consequences of such perversion for all who attempt it. For the state to take the place of God, either overtly or covertly, for the despot to claim the rights of the Deity as the Pharaoh did, is nothing new; for the representatives of true religion to denounce the worldly usurpers of religion is nothing new either.

In the traditional view, which I accept, this world is not the realm of destiny, it is the realm of choice—the choice between God and the ego, between submission to Truth and submission to concupiscence and self-will. Therefore evil is woven into its very fabric. If evil were eliminated, the world as we know it, and as God has willed it, would cease to exist—which means that, as an intrinsic consequence of the nature of existence, this world could not go on without the ministrations of damned souls, in high places and low, souls with great scope for the performance of evil as well as those other souls whose narrow compass allows them little more than the passive acquiescence to evil. Hell is a choice, and since this world is a world of choice, the road to Hell must remain open.

Yet the Good is always there. God is always pronouncing His Name at the invisible heart of the world, while evil only occupies the visible periphery. He sent Jesus, who said: "My kingdom is not of this world." He sent Muhammad, who said: "The world is given into my hands." Islam sees the true Christian way as only possible in a monastic context; in any case, for Christianity to have survived so as to still be barely recognizable after two thousand years, the works and days of souls who were ultimately damned, side-by-side with the witness of the saints, were necessary elements. Evil ultimately serves the Good, while still remaining evil, but Good can never serve evil and still remain the Good. Muhammad established social justice, care for the poor, justice and chivalry in war, and the command offered to all hearts that they turn and remember God—offered, but not enforced. If he had not done so, Islam would not still be discernible in this world after fourteen-hundred years. Nonetheless, *By the declining day! Lo, mankind is in the way of loss* [Q. 103:1-2]. The Good is established in time—and then time begins its work. Constantine makes the church of Christ an offer it can't refuse; the Khajirites assassinate Ali; Yazid martyrs

Hussain; the Borgia popes turn the Vatican into a whorehouse; Da'esh presents us with the Prophet Muhammad as a psychopathic killer and Allah as Shaytan. Every role must be played, every Name of God, from *Al-Rahman*, the All-Merciful, to *Al-Darr*, the Punisher, *Al-Khafid*, the Abaser, and *Al-Muntaqim*, the Avenger, must find its field of operation—otherwise, how could we choose? In the words of Frithjof Schuon, we are "condemned to freedom"—which is to say, God is not going to deny to any of us our inalienable right to be damned. The Choice bears down on us. The *Saifullah*, the sword of God, draws its line in the sand, between the sheep and the goats. To pray that all evil be removed from earthly existence is to ask that choice be withdrawn, and this is not the reason that man was given the Trust. Therefore, as far as making my own little answer to Caesar is concerned, let the **Book of Apocalypse** [22:11] speak for me in this matter: "Let the filthy be filthy still."

Next, Dugin introduces the biblical theme of the two beasts, Leviathan and Behemoth.

In the **Book of Job**, after the Lord appears and answers Job out of the whirlwind, the Lord shows him Leviathan the sea-beast and Behemoth the land-beast. These are elemental powers that humanity is helpless to control; only the Lord Himself can subdue them, and make the treasures they contain available to the human race for the next *aeon*. In the Apocalypse they appear as Gog and Magog, and also as Babylon, who is Leviathan, and the Beast, who is Behemoth, and is further identified with Antichrist. Babylon is pictured as a luxurious and decadent mercantile empire, ruled by the Whore; this Dugin associates—quite profoundly and brilliantly so—with the Atlanticist Collective. And the Beast or Behemoth, in Dugin's mythology, is the Russian/Eurasianist Collective. Leviathan, in an eschatological context, represents the terminal dominance of the Substantial Pole, the Negative Feminine Principle, as the end of the *manvantara* approaches, while Behemoth or the Beast is the negative Masculine Principle, the inverted hierarchy, the counterfeit "restoration" of the Essential Pole within the matrix of the decadent, polluted, unpurified Substantial Pole. This inverted hierarchy and the false "Holy Empire" it projects are the central elements in René Guénon's picture of the regime of Antichrist from **The Reign of Quantity and the Signs of the Times**. They are like Dante's Satan, frozen up to his chest in Cocytus, the lake of ice in which all the souls of the most deeply damned are imprisoned, paralyzed in every conceivable contorted posture, as if petrified in the midst of convulsion—the perfect image of a *frozen Chaos*. Satan here is the archetype of the inverted hierarchy, Cocytus of the Substantial Pole at the end of the *aeon*, not yet purified in the fires of Apocalypse, which purification will restore to it the mirror-like ability to receive, from the Essential Pole, the formal imprint of the *aeon* to come.

The clear teaching relating to the figures of Whore and Beast, Gog and

Magog in the book of Apocalypse, the spiritual imperative they manifest, is the divine command *not to become involved with them*, but rather flee them until the eschatological Christ, the Word of God, the rider on the White Horse, arrives to deal with them. "Come out of her, my people" . . . [etc.] says Chapter 18, speaking of Babylon, whereas Chapter 13 warns us not to receive the Mark of the Beast on the forehead (the Intellect) or the right hand (the Will). The Mark of Eurasia that Dugin tells us, in "Eurasia (A Political Poem)," that the Eurasianist will carry on his forehead, immediately suggests the Mark of the Beast, particularly since Dugin identifies Eurasia with Behemoth. In other words, it would appear that Aleksandr Dugin has made the great mistake of allying himself with Behemoth in order to overcome Leviathan/Babylon, whereas the true *Christian* way is to renounce and escape both Leviathan and Behemoth, Gog and Magog, to transcend the pairs-of-opposites manifesting at the end of the *aeon* as every kind of false alternative, with a view to finding and joining the Remnant made up of those waiting on the *parousia*, ready either to join the army of the Rider on the White Horse, or else "flee into the wilderness" of holy contemplation, until God has done His work. Nor has Dugin's declared allegiance to Behemoth in any way freed him from Leviathan, any more than Satan is freed from Cocytus by the power of his own self-will, since the "metaphysical Chaos" that Dugin takes as his first principle, and which manifests as Cocytus in Dante's *Inferno*, *is* Leviathan.

Without an *esoteric* understanding of Behemoth and Leviathan it is impossible to come to an accurate view of them as forces operating on the field of society and history. Leviathan in the Bible is pictured as a sea-serpent; the name means "coiled." Likewise, according to the lore of the human subtle nervous-system in the Hindu yoga tradition, the "serpent-power" that lies at the root- or *muladhara-chakra* at the base of the spine—which is, precisely, the Substantial Pole in the human microcosm—is the *kundalini*, a word that also means "coiled." The *kundalini* is thus analogous in some ways to the *nafs* in Sufi spiritual anthropology. Both the *kundalini* and the *nafs* are seen as the principle of passion and obscuration—that is, until the *kundalini*, in response to the descent of Divine Grace, awakens and ascends through the successively higher *chakras* of the subtle nervous system, at the end of which course of development it is united with the *sahasrara* or "thousand-petalled lotus" at the crown of the skull, the microcosmic Essential Pole. Likewise the *nafs* goes through a series of transformations on the Sufi path until it no longer acts as a veil hiding the face of Allah but instead becomes the full theophany of Allah, at the station known as *Ma'rifa an-Nafs*. This sublimation of the passions is pictured in both the *Book of Kings* and the *Surah an-Naml* (the Ant) of the Qur'an as the journey of the polytheistic Queen of Sheba from her kingdom in the South (the Substantial Pole) to the kingdom of Solomon in the North (the Essential Pole), at which point the Queen renounces her polytheism, accepts monotheism and marries the King.

In terms of a metaphysically-based spiritual psychology, Leviathan is *concupiscence based on unconscious impulse* and Behemoth is *Promethean self-will*— passive decadence (remembering that the words "passion" and "passivity" are related) and active Luciferian rebellion—the Whore and the Beast precisely. Someone who has not overcome concupiscence in his own soul, or gone a long way toward overcoming it, can never combat Leviathan in the outer world, just anyone who turns to Behemoth, to Luciferian self-will, in the foolish belief that by doing so he can gain the power to conquer Leviathan, to dominate both the world and himself, will instead find himself imprisoned in her, and petrified by her, in the very act of his apparent "conquest." Simply stated, the person who thinks that hard-ass self-will and lazy concupiscence are real *alternatives* is deeply deluded. They merely pose as alternatives to hoodwink those who can't see Being as hierarchical, but can only think—or rather, mentally react— according to the horizontal and mutually-contradictory categories provided by the Darkness of This World. One moment of *real* thought will make it obvious that Behemoth and Leviathan create each other, that they are partners in the same game, that game being the deconstruction of the human form.

This is neither the Muslim nor the Christian way. Instead of courting the Nietzschean *Übermensch* or the Evolian warrior-initiate, the true Christian understands the meaning of "our strength is perfected in weakness" [2 Corinthians 12:9] and "whoever tries to keep his life will lose it, but whoever loses his life, for My sake, will find it" [Mark 8:35; Matthew 16:25; Luke 9:24]. He follows Jesus, not Apollonius of Tyana. He does not treat Christianity as simply one more piece on his geopolitical chessboard to be moved however he will; he is not so foolish as to think that he can dominate the Apocalypse and turn it to his own ends. Instead, he fixes the Eye of his Heart on the fullness of time, and waits on the Second Coming, which is both yet to arrive and arriving even now. Likewise the true Muslim does not dream of effecting a worldly restoration of the Caliphate by political intrigue and military force, only to find himself under the thumb of the mad dogs of ISIS. He waits on the rise of the Mahdi, and the descent of the Prophet Jesus to slay *al-Dajjal*, the Antichrist, yet to arrive and yet presently arriving. The true Christian and the true Muslim do not try to seize power with their shrunken human fists that can hold only a grain of it; instead, they put themselves in the way of *real* power, Almighty power—and they certainly do not arrogate to themselves either the ability or the right to say what the power of the Almighty will be used for. He has His own ideas about that.

In addition to taking Leviathan as the spiritual principle of Atlantis and Behemoth as the contrary spiritual principle of Eurasia, Dugin also identifies

Behemoth with the Russian *narod* and Leviathan with the protective, outer shell of the *narod*, i.e., the Russian State (or any other state), the political superstructure of a nation as distinguished from its the cultural core. He takes his notion of Leviathan as the type of the modern, secular state, especially the imperialistic state, from the title of Thomas Hobbes' famous treatise on statecraft, *Leviathan*—a work that William Blake brilliantly critiqued and satirized in his engraving entitled "The spiritual form of Nelson guiding Leviathan, in whose wreathings are infolded the Nations of the Earth." (If Aleksandr Dugin wants to get his hands on the perfect visual representation of Atlanticism to use as a target for his spells, let him by all means secure a good reproduction of this engraving.) Dugin explains how Hobbes—who, incidentally, was an important influence on Cultural Marxist Walter Benjamin—presents the secular state as the Machiavellian principle of Fear that is necessary to keep the human race in line, based on his view that *homo homini lupus est*, "man is wolf to man," which is closely related to the Calvinist doctrine of the "total depravity" of man in the absence of the "irresistible grace" that God is free to arbitrarily give or withhold. Dugin sees the terror imposed by the pragmatic Leviathan-state as desacralized, while asserting that the mysterious terror manifested by the *narod* has a sacred dimension. He makes a serious error, however, when he claims that the "man is wolf to man" principle is "shared on the whole by the majority of liberals." I disagree. Liberalism's essential rationale for championing the freedom of the individual, opposing an established church, and legitimizing all individual actions that do not directly and obviously harm other individuals—including virtually every form of "consensual" sex—are originally based on the notion that man is essentially good, that "left to himself," free of the distortions to his soul produced by a sense of guilt arbitrarily imposed by religion, he will "naturally" pursue a rational and compassionate course, without the help of "grace" of any kind. American psychologist William James expressed this view in *The Varieties of the Religious Experience* [1902], when he wrote: "The advance of liberalism, so-called, in Christianity, during the past fifty years, may fairly be called a victory of healthy-mindedness within the church over the morbidness with which the old hell-fire theology was more harmoniously related." The belief that (to coin a phrase) "man is lamb to man"—at least in his original essence, unconditioned by the artificial strictures of society—was the fundamental principle behind the Human Potential Movement, the "Spiritual Revolution" of the hippies, and the New Age Movement in the second half of the 20th century in the U.S. And though Sigmund Freud took a generally darker view of the human soul than spiritual optimists like William James, Norman Vincent Peale and Dale Carnegie, as well as highly influential liberal psychologists such as Abraham Maslow, Carl Rogers and Fritz Perls, he nonetheless believed that socially-imposed guilt was more destructive to his "polymorphously perverse" human individual than that individual's own perversity. Likewise when Aleister Crowley declared that "Do what thou wilt shall be the whole of the Law," he was directly profiting from the dominance of the Liberal ethos, though he took his "Liberalism" in a far different and more sinister direction than the "healthy-minded" William James could ever have imagined. It is only now, in Liberalism's postmodern old age, that the impetus to impose "compulsory immorality" through various forms of social engineering and legal coercion has pushed aside the old principle of "classical Liberalism" according to which the human individual has the inalienable right "to do whatever he wants in his private life." This principle has fallen into increasing disrepute—though it is still put forward (dishonestly) as a justification for compulsory immorality so as to falsely portray this engineered concupiscence as free individual choice—largely because the advent of cyberspace has more-or-less destroyed the "private life."

Dugin goes on to analyze the four major challenges that call for the application of state terror: ideological dissent, "separatist" rebellion, conspiracies directed toward staging a coup, and theft and other economic crimes. (For some reason Dugin sees this fourth category more in terms of bureaucratic bribery and corruption than the wholesale plundering of the Russian economy by the oligarchs—probably because he still has to be careful to keep at least one of those oligarchs happy.) It is against these challenges that the Russian Leviathan has a right to move—except for the fact that this Leviathan is now relatively weak and domesticated; if this weakness continues, says Dugin, the Russian *narod* is in grave danger of losing the protection provided by the stern element of state terror and of dissolving under the combined blows of external attack and its own irresponsible self-fascination. Dugin's depiction of the spirit of the Russian *narod* is poetic, evocative and well worth repeating:

> the Russian *narod* in its soul is as freedom-loving as can be, unruly, absolutely not inclined to discipline, proud, contemplative (if you wish: lazy, sacredly lazy), suffering no higher authority over itself, fascinated by its own mysteriousness, aflame with spiritual beauty, pierced through with a black light, sprouting from the Russian soil, hidden in seclusion from lunar rays and unbending like spring from sea to sea, from ocean to ocean by its whim, easily, carefree, fatefully, and festively. This is a *narod* of wind and fire, with the scent of windrow and the piercing sidereal downfall of dark blue nights, a *narod* carrying God in its womb, gentle, like bread and milk, resilient, like the muscular, magical river fish cleansed by sweet waters.

Is this manipulative flattery or genuine love? In the urgency and the heat of wooing it is often very hard to tell the difference; the fractional distillation and separation of the elements that were once confused in the state of fascination comes much, much later. All I can say is, if the Russian *narod* rejects God because it suffers no higher authority over itself, it will eventually be captured by a different authority, and if it really carries God in its womb then it had better give birth to Him soon, or—as far as Russia in the present *aeon* is concerned—He will be stillborn. And *contemplation is not laziness*; as one contemporary Buddhist teacher put it, "meditation is manual labor."

Dugin names two avenues now open to the Russian *narod* to protect itself from dissolution and regain its former potency: a revival of the *oprichnina* or traditional apparatus of police-state repression, the Russian Leviathan, or else an ill-defined resurgence of the collective sense of the sacrality of the *narod* itself, of the spirit of the land-beast Behemoth, coupled with forms of terror proper to the sacred Russian *narod* alone.

In any case, terror is an effective tool not just for controlling populations, or followers, but also for manipulating readers. To directly threaten harm is nowhere near as effective as to casually mention such things as "horror and other special operations of metaphysics" in a seemingly-irrelevant context and then pass on to something else; unconscious fear is a much more effective tool of control than conscious fear. If you simultaneously present the mind-control subject with something terrifying and something reassuring, for no apparent purpose and in no discernible common context, he or she will unconsciously gravitate toward the pleasant impression and away from the unpleasant one. This will implant the terrifying possibility as a suggestion in the subject's unconscious, and establish the seductive possibility as an unconscious identification. Repeated arbitrary contradiction, such as Dugin employs, also strikes terror—the terror of the destruction of the human mind.

On Chapter Nine: "Questioning Modernization"

In this chapter, Alexandr Dugin asks one of the big questions: Can we have technical modernization without more and more cultural modernization, for which read "degeneracy"? And can we separate what is intrinsically evil from what is simply dangerous, and the dangerous from what is useful to humanity *as* humanity, within technology itself? As Dugin says, when modernism and "progress" end, postmodern fragmentation begins, along with the cumulative archiving of the fragments so as to produce a fragmented culture; and Postmodernism must inevitably end in posthumanism.

This chapter might have been Dugin's great short manifesto of the Traditional, sacred worldview. He says:

> modernization destroys man's moral foundations. It destroys the concept of man.... In traditional society, man was thought of as God's slave. Today people would say that this is savagery, because man is not a slave. He is free. But he was called God's slave because he was free from everything else. He was a slave only to God....

Within the confines of this freedom, man could choose: should he be a slave of God and master of everything else, of passion and sin, or should he be a slave of sin, the devil's slave, a slave of momentary passions, but remain free from God? This is a moral choice. In traditional society, it was thought that it is right to be God's slave and wrong to be a slave to passion. In the era of modernization, especially in the era of the Enlightenment, it was decided to change this morality. Man is now understood unambiguously as free from God, but not from passion, not from sin, not from the devil. Thus he took the first step to modernization.

As stated, this is impossible for me to disagree with. Slavehood to God is the essence and ideal of Islam, and perfect slavehood, even to the point of self-annihilation, is the essence and ideal of Sufism. Yet the perceptive reader must withhold his or her agreement until the glaring contradictions between what Aleksandr Dugin says here what he says in so many other places are confronted and explained. Does someone who perverts Christian doctrine, denies the Christic Logos in the name of a subhuman Chaos, messes around with Satanic mythologies, calls Edom his "Sire," inverts every spiritual principle he encounters, tells us that our relationship to the Spirit must be "delayed" until we plumb the roots of the Abyss, names magic as his political praxis and explicitly calls on the Russian people to worship Narod instead of God—does such a person have the right to set down the words quoted above? The words may be right, even profoundly right, but Aleksandr Dugin has no right to pronounce them. If he wants to gain that right, let him reject—explicitly, and in print—his quasi-satanic jugglery, his appeals to magic, his implicit atheism, his invocation of angels with no mention of God, and his direct violations of Orthodox Christian doctrine. Maybe his Satanism is only "art" or "sport" to him—no matter, it still absolutely disqualifies him from presenting himself as a slave of God. And in point of fact, he has not so presented himself, but has repeatedly—and sometimes explicitly—appeared in the guise of a magician. If he refuses to renounce his magic, whether "sporting" or deadly serious—and those with insight into "the mystery of iniquity" will understand that a lack of seriousness in no way protects us from evil, but very often opens the door to it—then no spiritually intelligent human being will believe a word he says.

It is heartbreaking that someone who makes no secret of his virtual rejection of God could compose a passage like the one quoted above. Perhaps it does represent a real desire in him to remember God, to recover the Traditional sense of the sacred. But a pious belief in the Almighty cannot simply be layered on over the top of an ongoing and many-sided rejection of Him. If God is to occupy the City of the Heart, our allegiance to other-than-God must entirely vacate the premises. And even if Dugin's invocation of humanity's Traditional slavehood to God does represent a fond hope on his part—fond, but obviously also ephemeral—the actual effect of his telling of this truth is simply to hide a bigger lie, thereby serving the lie and corrupting the truth. In Dante's *Inferno*, the principle that the most powerful delusions are produced by truths that have been abducted by the Lie and forced to serve it is represented by the monstrous figure of Geryon, a creature with the face of an honest man, the torso of a warm and sympathetic animal, the lower parts of a cold serpent, and the tail of a scorpion—Geryon, the Spirit of Fraud.

On Chapter Ten:
"Interests and Values After Tskhinvali"

In this concluding chapter of *The Rise of the Fourth Political Theory*, Aleksandr Dugin once again makes it clear that western values are not universal, that China, Dar al-Islam and Russia have different values, which they have a "quasi-absolute" right to defend within their own civilizations. He therefore asserts Russia's right to its own civilizational values, along with its right to protect the perimeters of Greater Russia from subversion and military attack from the West—in the former Yugoslavia, in Georgia, in the Ukraine and the Crimea, and elsewhere. I gladly accede to Russia both of these rights. Dugin goes on to say that, after the 2008 Battle of Tskhinvali, the capital of South Ossetia, in the Russo-Georgian War, the legitimacy of "westernization" in Russia is dead—a reality that was sharply punctuated by the Trump Administration's bombing of Muhammad Assad's Syria in April of 2018, as the present chapter of this book was being composed. This act of reckless aggression took place in the context of a growing U.S. demonization of Russia on all fronts, despite—or perhaps because of—her indispensable aid in the task of terminating ISIS. I will end my critique of *The Rise of the Fourth Political Theory* at this point, because to continue—unless God has mercy on humanity (a mercy that, as always, is undeserved)—it will take us too far into the field of events that are still unfolding.

ॐ

Appendix One, "Aleksandr Dugin on Martin Heidegger," has already been critiqued in *Chapter Three* of this book, "Vectors of Duginism"—and Appendix Two, since it is in the form of a table, is too abbreviated for me to address.

7

Principles of Sacred Activism

NOW THAT the reader has had a chance to assimilate the greater part of my critique of the Fourth Political Theory, it is time for me to shift from *theoria* to *praxis*. Social critics are often asked, "What alternative do you propose to the evils you see? What is your solution to the problems you've named?"—so I need to make clear before we go any further that I am not one of those who believe that every problem has a solution simply because it can be clearly defined. Plenty of situations—more all the time, actually—fall under the category of "you're damned if you do and you're damned if you don't."

In this chapter I will nonetheless posit a life-path that I've named—following the lead of Andrew Harvey—"sacred activism," which can be defined as: "action in the world, based on Divine guidance, through the mediation of prayer."

Sacred Activism is not a technique; it is a call. I am not foolish enough to believe that consciously submitting strategic questions to God could easily find a place in political activism and organizing as they are carried on today—but I *am* foolish enough to hope that this call will be heard by more than just a handful of impractical idealists.

Sacred activism, in itself, does not matter. It does not matter whether a call to act comes or does not come. And if it does come, it does not matter whether the action is "successful" or "unsuccessful" in worldly terms. It is not necessary to take the reins of action; all that is required is to submit one's own will to God's Will. It is not necessary to take the warrior's oath, but only to remember God's Presence; constancy in this remembering is warfare enough. What does matter is the one condition that makes sacred action possible: *virginity of soul.*

PART ONE:
SACRED ACTIVISM, TRADITIONAL METAPHYSICS,
AND THE COVENANTS OF THE PROPHET

Aleksandr Dugin and I seem to agree that in a post-Fascist, post-Communist, and soon-to-be-post-Liberal world it has become unexpectedly possible, even necessary, to draw on traditional eschatology and metaphysics to provide paradigms comprehensive enough and deep enough to begin to make sense of the titanic forces that have been unleashed in the 21st century, the place of humanity in this new and terrible arena, and the correct human response to the rigors of the times. Dugin, however, sees metaphysics not as a spiritual science that has everything to do with the eternal destiny of the soul, but primarily as a hoard of powerfully motivating ideas, many of which are capable of being exploited ideologically and politically by those with the insight and the audacity to attempt it. In view of this I have felt duty-bound to present my own views as to how metaphysics might relate to political action, not in the context of ideology, however, but in the context of prayer.

Dugin's "Fourth Political Theory"—whether we see it as an actual theory or as no more than a method of conjuring up a global pro-Russian and anti-Liberal coalition under the cover of various *ad hoc* pseudo-theories—has as its fundamental praxis the work of political organizing; therefore it necessarily seeks numbers. Sacred Activism, on the other hand, starts with the individual. Its *ideal* context is that of an intact spiritual tradition based on a Divine revelation—presuming that such a context can still be found—and the community of believers in that particular sacred form. Within such a context, however, the act of prayer is paramount—individual prayer supported by communal prayer and liturgy, by ritual and sacrament, but reducible in the last analysis to the solitary soul alone with God. The individual, however, is not the recipient or inheritor or *telos* of the spiritual power that grows out of deep prayer and meditation, or the one with the right to wield it and the freedom to determine how it is to be used. God alone is both the Source and the Destination of that power, the ultimate Purpose of it, and the only One with the right to use it. If we dare to invoke it, it is because that Power has first invoked us, demanded our full submission, and received it.

It will sound strange to many ears when I call for prayer and meditation as central elements in the kind of social activism that is proper to the eschatological times we live in, to these Latter Days of the *manvantara*, days of the *fitan*, the Tribulation. Why would I mention such things, open this particular can of worms, seeing that counterfeit forms of prayer and meditation have produced so much lunacy and fanaticism and wasted effort over the past two or three generations? Why would I bet on such an uncertain prospect? And what's in it for me? I am recruiting for no religion (except unavoidably—in other words, by example), offering initiation into no spiritual circle, selling no classes or lessons in any yogic or meditative practice; I am not presenting myself as a spiritual guide or a "life-coach" or a personal trainer; I am not someone who claims to know you better than you know yourself because "I used to be like you." I am simply stating that if we have no way of putting ourselves in effective contact with the Source-of-all-things-transcending-all-things, with a Reality that lies beyond society and history and conditions, then we will find no way of working to change society, history and conditions without being totally controlled—body mind and soul—by society, history and conditions. It's as simple as that. If Liberalism and Communism and Fascism, along with every other conceivable ideology that we might draw upon to confront the titanic horror of our times, have proved woefully insufficient to satisfy our primary spiritual needs, and thereby save us from existential despair, what can be expected from a heterogeneous grab-bag of *ad hoc*, random fragments of these exhausted worldviews such as Dugin proposes in the form of his Fourth Political Theory? As I see it, we have no recourse but to jettison our own failed agendas and turn our spiritual attention back to the Always So, the Source of all things, so as to make ourselves ready to intuit *His* agenda, and then act upon it. And this can only be reliably accomplished, with certain unpredictable exceptions, within the context of Tradition in Guénon's sense of the word, which is primarily expressed in our age through the major world religions: Judaism, Christianity, Islam, Hinduism and Buddhism. The language I have been using would seem not to be applicable to Buddhism as a "non-theistic" religion; yet Buddhism also recognizes a Supreme Principle—Nirvana, the Buddha Nature, the Adi-Buddha, the Dharmakaya—and to the degree that Buddhist realization is pictured as a union of Wisdom and Compassion, it certainly might result in enlightened action in the world for those who are called to it, especially since one of the pillars of Buddhism is *sila*, morality, which of course must include social morality.

This chapter, "Principles of Sacred Activism," might be seen as my most direct answer to Aleksandr Dugin's *The Fourth Political Theory*—except for the fact that it is not itself a political theory. Dugin has thrown together a set of theories comprising some rather scattered and contradictory notions of the nature of human society and historical dynamics, hoping to use them as motivations and contexts for political action, the primary goal of such action being to destroy Liberalism and to break the global hegemony of "Atlantean" USA. In my opinion, though his writings may be of help in enlisting various conservative, or traditional, or Anarchist, or Neo-Pagan, or "Alt Right" groups and movements in this crusade—as well as certain extreme Left groups that by their very extremism have elements in common with the extreme Right—he provides no actual political theory capable of truly encompassing them by discerning in them a common form or spirit. This deliberate deficiency is, of course, part and parcel of the postmodernist rejection of any "overarching paradigm" as tyrannous, hegemonic and "unipolar"—a rejection which is inseparable from the rejection of God considered as the Unity of Truth. And given that Dugin has formulated no unified theory, he can propose no integral *praxis*.

"Principles of Sacred Activism," on the other hand, posits a unified *theoria* based on Traditional Metaphysics, one which inevitably manifests as a *praxis* organically intrinsic to the metaphysical worldview and the active and contemplative spiritual practices common to the great Divine Revelations. And while such Activism can certainly operate in the political arena, it is not, nor can it ever be, a political theory and method capable of guiding and motivating a mass movement—therefore to consider Sacred Activism as an "alternative" or an "answer" to the Fourth Political Theory is *asymmetrical* to say the least; the two operate by entirely different methods in entirely different contexts with entirely different goals. What I can assert with absolute certainty, however, is that Sacred Activism has everything to do with Traditional Metaphysics, and the Fourth Political Theory next to nothing.

As we have already pointed out, Sacred Activism differs radically from the Fourth Political Theory in that it is directed only to individuals—specifically, to qualified individuals: those who have both dedicated their wills to God and are specifically called by God to actively serve His Will in this world. Such individuals, while they may certainly participate in social movements as either leaders or followers, are ultimately responsible—as we all are, if we only knew—to God alone.

This, of course, is a dangerous saying in the postmodern world. It immediately invokes the image of the imbalanced lunatic who believes he is channeling world-transforming philosophies from space aliens or spirit entities, or the criminal madman who is compelled to commit atrocities by the promptings of an "inner voice." And certainly the paranoid or fanatical or truly Satanic counterfeits of Sacred Activism are much more in evidence in today's world than the reality they mimic. At this point we would do well to remember Jalaluddin Rumi's saying, "counterfeit gold is only in circulation because true gold exists"; we should also recall truly heroic examples of Sacred Activism such figures as Amir 'Abd al-Qādir al-Jazā'irī and Mohandas K. Gandhi, clear examples of leaders whose activism was entirely permeated and informed by religious faith and spiritual power.

Principles of Sacred Activism is written in the form of an exposition of spiritual principles, the laws of Spirit-in-action. From another point-of-view, however, it is simply the story of the advent, growth and development of the Covenants Initiative as I have experienced it, told not as a historical narrative but in entirely "principial" terms. It is my belief that the success of the Initiative—which, outside of the labor of the publisher, editors and printers, and various intermittent and informal alliances we have made with journalists and other activists, is basically the work of two individuals—can only be explained by the fact that God willed it. It is a part of the virtue of faith to remain open to this possibility, while remembering that God's Will can be expressed in innumerable different ways in our lives, that no human being is exempt from that

Will, and consequently that to receive a command from Him is in no way a badge of status, spiritual or otherwise, but rather a serious duty that must not be ignored. "To whom much is given, from him much will be required" [Luke 12:48].

While true spiritually-based social action, even militant action, can certainly be carried on within a Christian framework, it will always be secondary to the interior life of prayer and contemplation, and the grace of the sacraments. After all, Jesus Christ (peace and blessings be upon him) said, "My kingdom is not of this world." Unlike Christ, however, the Prophet Muhammad (peace and blessings be upon him) was sent not only as a mystical sage and a moral teacher, but also as a husband, a father, a business man, a diplomat, a judge, an administrator and a military leader. Consequently Sacred Activism within a Muslim context is less subject to internal contradictions than a hybrid spiritual/political theory like Liberation Theology is within a Christian context. On the other hand, the integration into the religion of Islam of the perennial human necessity for militant action becomes a great danger when the essential spirituality of the religion, including the "organized mysticism" of the Sufi orders, becomes weakened. The vast damage done by an "Islamicist" militancy when it cuts itself loose from the "just war" doctrine and rules of warfare to be found in the traditional *shari'ah*—not the latter-day perversion of the *shari'ah* promulgated by the Wahhabi/Salafis—is now obvious to all. The continuing evidence of support for certain Islamicist elements by the United States and other outside powers must also be taken into consideration, in light of which it should be painfully clear that it is next to impossible for Islam to wage any kind of just war against western neo-colonialism when terrorist armies, fighting in the name of Islam, are willing to accept funds and arms from the West. By the same token, the "turn the other cheek" doctrine of Christianity, which represents the height of spiritual heroism when the faith is strong, is in danger of becoming a culpable form of cowardice in the face of political, moral and spiritual evil when the faith loses force. It's as if Christianity, in its decadence, is vulnerable to infection by the Dark Feminine principle—something that is certainly visible, for example, in the Catholic pedophilia scandal—whereas when Islam degenerates it tends to manifest the Dark Masculine principle in the form of terroristic brutality—which is certainly not to say that Christians can never be terrorists! And just as Christianity continues to abandon its virility in the face of internal decay, militant secularism and the Islamicist threat—though we must remember here that many more Muslims than Christians have died at the hands of terrorist groups such as the so-called Islamic State—so the compromised manhood of Islam, which has also been weakened by both external attack and internal decay, becomes even more vicious and perverted under the influence of Christian weakness and apostasy—a weakness that tempts militant

Islam, or rather *something that is no longer Islam* as soon as it succumbs to this temptation, to every kind of excess. Thus effeteness and barbarism create each other. Regarding the suicidal passivity of degenerate Liberal Christianity, it should be remembered at this point that, according to traditional Catholic moral theology, to "give scandal" and thus become "an occasion of sin" for other people is sinful in itself. Given that cowards are a standing temptation to bullies, anyone who will not defend him- or herself, assuming the capacity to do so, from invasion or unjust oppression bears part of the guilt of the oppressor—not to mention the fact those who won't defend themselves will certainly not be willing or able to defend anybody else. Likewise no Muslim should ever forget the following two *hadith* of the Prophet:

> Someone who unjustly kills a *dhimmi* [*member of an accepted religious minority within Islam, including Christians and Jews*] cannot get a whiff of Heaven. [Sahih Bukhari, *Jizya*, 5]

> Whoever oppresses a *dhimmi* or loads a work that is over his strength or takes something away from him by force, I am his foe on the Day of Judgment. [Abu Dawud, *Kharaj*, 31–33]

The Covenants of the Prophet, which have left a clear historical and textual trail that traces back to their original composition by the Prophet Muhammad himself, peace and blessings be upon him, are precisely in line with *hadith* like this. As soon as Dr. John Andrew Morrow began to make these documents known to the Muslim world—which had begun to forget their existence, or at least their continuing significance—Muslims from all walks of life, including many prominent scholars, began to join our movement and make it their own. Less than a year after the publication of *The Covenants of the Prophet Muhammad with the Christians of the World*, Dr. Morrow was denouncing ISIS before the House of Lords in London. And, from one point of view at least, our movement was powerfully confirmed in 2016 by the Marrakesh Declaration, issued by the leaders of many Muslim nations after a convention in Marrakesh, Morocco, which renewed the traditional protections granted to non-Muslim religious minorities within Muslim nations, based on the Prophet's Constitution of Medina. We were told by officials of the Islamic Society of North America that our work with the Covenants Initiative was one of the inspirations for that Declaration. In 2016, in response to an appeal from Bishop Francis Y. Kalabat, Eparch of the Chaldean Catholic Church (of Iraq) now in exile in Detroit, Michigan, the Covenants Initiative launched a project called the Genocide Initiative, which was a call to "all political players" to declare the actions of ISIS war crimes and genocide; it took the form of a petition posted on Change.org. The Genocide Initiative formed part of the push that led to the unanimous passage of the (unbinding) Fortenberry resolution in the House of Representatives, in March of 2016, affirming our position on ISIS; soon afterwards, Obama's Secretary of State John Kerry felt it necessary to make a public statement to the same effect: that the actions of ISIS constitute genocide. And one more powerful sign of our success of our movement appeared in May of 2017. When ISIS burned St. Mary's Cathedral in Mindanao, the Philippines, the Governor of the Autonomous Region in Muslim Mindanao immediately invoked the Covenants of the Prophet to prove that this action of ISIS was "un-Islamic"; we have every reason to believe this declaration grew in large part out of our efforts since 2013. We didn't expect any of this or feel ourselves competent to create it; yet it happened. So we are led to ask, and we also invite the reader to ask, what else God might have in store.

Sacred Activism is one of the many ways God's Will can manifest in the lives of those who love Him. It is certainly not necessary to the spiritual life, consequently there is no way I can "recommend" it. If it is part of God's Will for you, then He will eventually present you with it. If not, then you should not have to live in the shadow of it—though it would still probably be a good idea if the faithful of the Traditional religions could get some notion of what it entails, since a time may come when militant action under God's guidance will become a spiritual if not a physical necessity for many more people than today. The main thing to remember, in my opinion, is that the spiritual life requires two things if we want to live out the fullness of it: a connection to one of the Divine revelations or wisdom-traditions—or else a sincere effort to make this connection, since circumstances may make such an affiliation difficult in particular instances—and a degree of insight into God's specific Will for *you*, along with a total willingness to obey that Will as it unfolds. This is what the Hindus call *swadharma*, one's individual spiritual destiny: "Better to perform your own duty, however poorly," they say, "than the duty of someone else, no matter how well." And even more fundamental than insight into God's Will for you is the willingness to follow it, not only after it appears but especially *before* it appears. Submission does not grow out of insight; insight grows out of submission. If God does not see in you a willingness to obey Him, why should He give you further insight into His Will?

This "metaphysical history" should not necessarily be taken as a model for other people's movements and projects, only as a picture of what God can do when we human beings realize that we can do nothing without Him. As the Noble Qur'an informs us, *Every day doth some new work employ Him* [Q.55:29].

PART TWO:
PRINCIPLES OF SACRED ACTIVISM

for Andrew Harvey

The Presence is the meeting-place of the hearts of initiates: They take refuge in it and dwell therein. Then, when they descend to the heaven of obligation and the earth of varied fortune, they do so with authority, stability and profundity of certitude. For they have not descended to obligations through improper conduct or forgetfulness, nor to fortune through passion and pleasure; but instead they have entered therein by God and for God and from God and to God.

My God, you have commanded me to return to created things, so return me to them with the raiment of lights and the garment of inner vision, so that I might return from them to You just as I entered You from them, with my innermost being protected from looking at them and my fervor raised above dependence on them. "Truly, over everything You are the Omnipotent."

—Ibn 'Ata'illah, *Kitab al-Hikam*

We live in an age that is profoundly suspicious of any "meta-theory" or "over-arching paradigm" claiming to explain reality as a whole. Religion is taken as no more than the product of ideological indoctrination operating within a particular sector of the world's population, an indoctrination which pretends to have in view the salvation of the soul but whose real goal is cultural, social or political power. The science of astrophysics may still be seeking (in Stephen Hawking's phrase) a "theory of everything," but in the socio-historical sphere we no longer subscribe to any theory of universal application such that we might base our actions upon it—unless we include the theories produced by the degeneration of religious doctrine into political ideology, which are nothing more or less than the terminal convulsions of this or that dying faith. Communism, Fascism, Liberal Democracy have "have been tried, and failed"; consequently our strategies for social or political action have either devolved into an endless series of *ad hoc* tactical reactions to the challenge of increasingly chaotic events, or else coalesced into the nearly-universal application—largely covert—of social engineering in service to the global elites. Neither of these styles of action, however, are based on any worldview that embraces both a sense of essential principles, either ethical or metaphysical, and the methods by which such principles may be discerned and applied. The ultimate effect of this state of affairs is universal social and moral destruction, a "transvaluation of all values" as Nietzsche called it, that in its rage to deconstruct all certainties leaves only one set of principles untouched: those of Traditional Metaphysics. How this Metaphysics can function as the basis of principled action, and also throw the clear light of transcendental objectivity on the social conditions of our time, is the subject of this section.

What is Sacred Activism?

Although Sacred Activism can be described in a number of ways, its most general definition might be: "action under the authority of the Sacred to advance and defend the expression of Sacred in this world." This, of course, begs the question: "what is the Sacred"?

The Sacred is the expression in this world of the Supreme Principle of things, whether this Principle is conceived of in personal or impersonal terms. This expression takes three main forms: Virgin Nature, the Human Form, and the Divine Revelations of God (or however the Supreme Principle may be envisioned) to humanity. Whatever damages, distorts or obscures any of these three central manifestations of the Supreme Principle violates the Sacred, and in so doing cries out for Sacred Action to redress these violations and re-establish, insofar as is possible in this age of darkness, the balance of things which allows the Sacred to appear in this world, and be recognized as the underlying principle that keeps this world in existence. And the central reality, virtue and power that underlies and gives life to the Sacred is Love—the indissoluble solidarity of God with His Creation, the indissoluble brotherhood and sisterhood of all those who recognize the Supreme Principle and follow it, necessarily including those others who recognize It only half-consciously because they are uninformed as to Its true nature and have no name for It, but who nonetheless remain faithful to It as the principle of their own integrity.

Any social action, individual or collective, that is consciously carried on in defense of the Sacred, or any particular aspect of it, falls under the definition of Sacred Action; therefore any individual who supports such a cause is, to some degree, a sacred activist. I say "to some degree" because not every person involved in Sacred Action is necessarily obeying God's Will *directly* in their work, constantly seeking Divine Guidance in all circumstances, because in many cases that Will is mediated, with a greater or lesser degree of accuracy, through the agenda and leadership of the group. But a deeper degree of Sacred Action than group allegiance in a sacred cause is also possible, one that applies only to individuals because only individuals can directly and intentionally submit to the Will of God. A sacred activist who submits to that Will may become a leader, or remain a follower, or act as a free agent. If he or she leads, that leadership will be based directly on God's leadership; if he or she follows, that allegiance will be an expression of that person's allegiance to God. A sacred activist may act alone, or in the context of a group, or in an equal alliance with other activists who have put the Will of God first in their lives. In such an alliance, leadership will appear as a collegiate function that passes from one ally to another as the Spirit moves; to the degree that the leadership of God is mutually recognized, all will immediately follow the one upon whom that Spirit lights most directly during a given phase of things, with absolutely no attachment to the identity of either "leader" or "follower." This ideal, of course, will rarely be attained, but it's important to keep it before our eyes, since it represents the true state of things in the spiritual order.

The Metaphysical Basis for Sacred Activism

God is Absolute, Infinite and Perfect. As Personal God and Sovereign of the Universe He is Pure Being—and in His unknowable Essence He is beyond even Being. Even to assert that "God Is" is to place Him in the duality of Being vs. Non-Being, and His Absolute Unity—so Absolute that it is not even describable as "Oneness," since the number "one" implies all the other numbers—will not admit of such duality. On this level, Transcendent to the point where it cannot even be called a level, God is not impersonal but Transpersonal—which is to say that the Personhood of God is transcended only when Being itself is transcended. In His Secret Essence He is One without a second, non-dual, formless, absolute, inaccessible, in communion with none but Himself, and that by virtue of a communion that absolutely transcends any union of two terms; He *is* His Knowledge of Himself and His Knowledge of Himself is *He*, without the barest hint of either division or unification. He is the immediate, eternal, and perfect Actualization of His Infinite Potential, in such a way that the terms "Actualization" and "Potential" have no effective meaning.

Consequently, within the secret depths of His own Nature—Unique, Incomparable, Aloof, Impermeable, Inaccessible—He is totally devoid of any intention, beyond all agendas, the Giver of no Law, the Author of no Plan. On the level of His Pure Being and Personhood, however, He is the Universal Reservoir of every intention, every agenda, every law, every plan. In relation to persons, human and otherwise, He necessarily shows His Personal Face, revealing It to be the one Source of all personhood, just as in relation to the impersonal forces of Nature He shows His impersonal Face, revealing It to be the one Source of all natural law affecting the matrix of matter, energy, space and time. His Personal Face is higher and more essentially real and more synthetically unified than His Impersonal Face, while His Transpersonal Face, His Faceless Face, is higher than both His Personal and Impersonal faces, and acts as the Absolute Guarantee that His Personal aspect is in no way limited by the limits of persons, and that His Impersonal aspect in no way limited by the limits of insentient matter and involuntary force.

Since He is the One Reservoir of all intentions, laws, plans and agendas by virtue of the Personal Face He unveils to all persons seeking the Source of their own personhood, He shows a different intention, a different law, a different plan, a different agenda—that is to say, a different spiritual destiny—to each unique individual He has created out of His own universal Uniqueness. Each is formed upon a different one of His Infinite Names, and is called by Him through that Name and no other, just as He Himself is called by each of His unique creations according to the one Name upon which they are woven, and no other. Nonetheless, when that Name gives way for a particular unique individual to the Thing Named, then all the Names of God are intelligible to and available to be invoked by that individual. And God also has His Names which are shared by all individuals of a single class, just as all human beings share, and are created out of, the Name "Humanity."

And though Mercy and Justice do not apply in the slightest degree to God in His Absolute Unknowable Essence, in relation to His Universal Manifestation, to which He necessarily shows the Face of His Absolute Personhood (since only sentient beings are conscious of this Manifestation), God is both All-Merciful and All-Just. Furthermore, His Mercy has eternal precedence over His Justice, which is why His Justice must necessarily be the servant of His Mercy. Consequently the Will of God, for the world of earthly humanity, must be Perfect Justice and Perfect Mercy, since Mercy allows and blesses all things, while Justice disciplines and sets limits to all things, such that no thing will be able assert itself to the point where it violates Mercy without eventually tasting Justice.

Since all the individual potentials within God long to be realized, His Mercy dictates that He create them. On the other hand, since no individual created thing has either the power or the right to stand eternally next to God as if it were a second God, His Justice dictates that all things be destroyed in their imperfect createdness and returned to their perfect Uncreatedness in Him.

Because: If manifestation were not imperfect and subject to imbalances, it could never appear; if it did appear in its Absolute Perfection it would necessarily be God, Who transcends all formal appearance. God, however, never appears purely in His own Essence; he does so only by virtue of His manifestation, which is ontologically subordinate to Him. But to assure that created things, beset by the imbalances that have drawn them into outward manifestation, never remain eternally fixed in their various imperfections, God has endowed the mortal things among them, such as rocks or animals or stars or material human bodies, with a set term bounded by annihilation, and the immortal things among them, such as angels and human souls, with a free will, allowing them to choose either to return voluntarily to the Face of Mercy and Divine Perfection by virtue of spiritual annihilation, or else to seek out the Face of Wrathful Justice—which acts always to restore the Divine Perfection—by virtue of the worship of their own self-will.

Consequently, it is possible—for those called to this possibility because they were created under the sign of the Name of God from which it emanates—to embrace the way of Sacred Activism. Nonetheless, one might be led to wonder how the Will of God could be perfectly obeyed by even one human being in this world, unleashed into this world in all its Absoluteness, without annihilating all suffering and all injustice in a single stroke. If God's Mercy has precedence over His Justice, why does it not immediately swallow up all the distorted and the evil things that cry for Justice, returning them, by means of Divine Mercy, to the Perfection of God? The answer is, because of *Time*. Without Time, no thing could be manifested in the sort of matrix where God's Absoluteness doesn't immediately swallow up His total potential manifestation before it could ever be manifested, consequent to which there would be no world. In Time all things meet Justice, and all justified things meet Mercy, and all things subject to Mercy return to the Absolute Face of God. But not now, says Time, and not yet. Therefore the work of manifesting God's Mercy in this world of suffering through His Justice, and of serving and promoting the swallowing up of all things subject to His Justice in the Ocean of His Mercy, is possible, sanctioned, justified, of real practical use, and found to be actually functioning. One aspect of this function, or one name for it, is Sacred Activism.

> Why do they complain to Me of the changes of fortune brought about by Time? I *am* Time.
>
> —*hadith qudsi*

The Three Principles of Sacred Activism

Metaphysical realization produces three things. The first is sobriety and detachment; the second is a supreme objectivity which allows us to see things as they are—two qualities which are indispensable if we are to actively engage with the truly apocalyptic conditions the world now faces, at least without darkening our minds, corrupting our wills, and breaking our hearts. And the third principle, the final flower of the virtues of sobriety, detachment and metaphysical objectivity, is the unbreakable certainty that only God is the Doer. The Sacred activist plans and works as strategically as possible, as if transforming the situation he or she is called on to deal with were the sole purpose of his or her action. Yet the works of such an activist are not primarily strategic, but rather liturgical; they are performed as acts of worship and sacrifice to God. The quest for strategic perfection, though we must be untiring in our pursuit of it, is not ultimately to be taken as an end in itself, but rather as a way of preparing a worthy sacrifice, of comporting ourselves honorably in the face of the truly inhuman stresses that have now become inescapable to humanity as the present cycle of manifestation draws to a close. We will certainly not win every battle, nor can an overall triumph on the field of history really be expected in a war whose final armistice will be the end of time. Nonetheless there are certain profound spiritual values that cannot be forged at any other point in the cycle, given that their emergence is based on the confrontation between our fully dedicated humanity and the ultimate betrayal of the human form now confronting us in every field. These values are the monuments that will endure beyond time; the actions we perform, for good or ill, at this ultimate hour of human history, will remain engraved on the matrix of Eternity.

One: Detachment

In order to reach metaphysical understanding, the attention must be centered on the Absolute, or on the particular cosmic reflection of the Absolute that is closest to the prospective sacred activist's present level of consciousness. And for this orientation of attention to become constant, various distractions must be met and dealt with. These distractions are the passions; the work of overcoming these passions can also, with equal accuracy, be described as the development of the virtues. The essence of this spiritual labor is the willing cooperation with the Grace of God through obedience to His commandments; the pre-existence of the metaphysical Reality that the prospective sacred activist aspires to realize, whether or not he or she is presently conscious of it, is the essence of this Grace.

Every passion pays court to a particular idol, or can be described as an idol in itself. An "idol" may be defined as a limited reality that we have put in the place of God's Reality, a limited intent or agenda that has replaced God's Will in our lives. Thus the development of the virtues may be defined as the progressive overthrow of the idols that have collected within the sanctuary of the Heart. The Spiritual Heart is the doorway through which we can contemplate God and through which He witnesses us; when it is cluttered with various idols, our vision of Him is distorted, and His vision of us obscured. In a larger sense God is never truly ignorant of us, since He is omniscient; yet the particular sort of Grace-filled attention he pays to those who have fixed their attention on Him with faith and devotion is effectively blocked when idols fill the Heart. The overthrow of these idols and the development of the moral and spiritual virtues are two ways of talking about the same thing.

To the degree that the idols of the Heart are deconstructed, and the virtues take their place, the budding sacred activist may be said to have achieved Detachment. Speaking in the spiritual sense, the "world" we perceive ourselves as living in, and that we pay court to, is composed of all the idols that still occupy the Heart—idols which are drawn in turn from the set of passions and attachments that the world provides. The passions, in aggregate, may be called the "ego"; the world the ego perceives is based on the passions it is composed of.

And as the ego projects the world, so the world "charters" and validates that ego. This world so to speak "taxes" the many egos it is composed of in order to maintain its illusory existence. Thus the illusion of the ego and the illusion of the world are two sides of the same coin.

While we remain attached to various idols we must dance to their tune. The World, which certainly embraces the Principalities and Powers of advertising, propaganda, social engineering and economic and political oppression, as well as every other conceivable obsession or addiction or worldly ambition, still has control of us as long as any attachment remains unbroken, as long as any idol still occupies the Kaaba of the Heart. And while the world exercises this kind of control over us, we can do nothing to improve conditions or help our fellow human beings in any fundamental way. If we approach social activism while still in servitude to idols we will inevitably be drawn to forms of "service" that ultimately do more harm than good, and to forms of "opposition to the establishment" that only go to build the power of that establishment, or rather of the hidden Principalities and Powers that secretly command it; some of these forms are in fact provided by these Principalities and Powers themselves, in the guise of various "licensed obsessions" or "controlled oppositions," in order to do just that. There is no way we can change the world while we remain slaves to the world.

Most people, even those who are thoroughly educated, widely informed and highly skilled in the ways of the world, have certain places in their souls where, try as they might, they can't see things as they are, because if they ever did their whole worldview upon which they have based their lives would collapse. But the Sacred Activist has liquidated his or her investments in such fatally protective illusions. Such a person has broken attachment to any agendas other than those of God Himself. He or she does not serve the idols of class, or race, or gender, or nation, or political party, or social movement, or religion, or his or her own cherished plans, but is a slave to nothing but God's Command in this moment. Thus the sacred activist is liberated from the chains of the world, and consequently free to represent the presence God's Will within the world, either through spiritually-based action, or through withdrawal from the world when action, under this or that particular circumstance, would be contrary to that Will.

Two: Objectivity

As soon as we identify with something, claiming it as part of our self-concept, we can no longer see it as it is; it is not love that is blind, but identification. Only those who have broken their identification with the world can see what is really going on in it; thus the fruit of spiritual Detachment is metaphysical Objectivity.

Every idol occupying the spiritual Heart becomes an element in the habitual worldview of the person harboring that idol; its passions and illusions are accepted uncritically as part of the intrinsic nature of things. But the sacred activist who has cast the idols out of his or her spiritual Heart has become conscious of the specific idols this world is composed of and exactly how they operate, thereby allowing him or her to develop flexibility of action coupled with acute strategic insight. Each time an idol is removed from the Heart the corresponding idol is unmasked in the world, until certainty is reached that a Power infinitely greater than those idols is the true Author of all events.

The one who has succeeded in conquering the passions, in casting out the idols, in overcoming attachment to the various aspects of the darkness of this world, has reached a station of emotional Sobriety and willing Submission to God, the necessary consequence of which is metaphysical Objectivity. Because the eternal metaphysical Principles underlying all manifestation, the Names and Qualities of God, have been unveiled to the sacred activist, he or she can contemplate the world of manifestation produced by these Principles from the standpoint of God's own Objectivity, or a certain degree of it. Free from the dominance of the passions and the stranglehold of fear and desire, the activist has gained the power to see things as they are. Consequently the initiatives and plans of action conceived by the sacred activist are morally and strategically sound because they are in line with the Will of God—with the nature of things.

There are many stations on the way to this total objectivity, many battles still to be fought against the passions and the illusions they impose; as each higher station is reached, a higher, more comprehensive, more accurate picture of the laws that govern all manifestation is unfolded. Some of these "laws" and "principles" and "paradigms" will be so compelling that the prospective sacred activist may be in danger of making new idols out of them, of transforming them into new passions—which will, of course, ultimately turn out to be nothing but unfamiliar faces of the same old idols, the same old passions. Some of these conceptions may be quite useful under certain strategic conditions, but none of them can be applied to *all* conditions, nor is there any conception, no matter how profound it may be or how useful it may have proved in the past, that will not ultimately be superseded by something greater, as we come more fully into the Absolute Objectivity of God. Therefore the sacred activist, when he or she, by God's Grace, receives a new strategic paradigm from the higher spiritual worlds, must always remember to say, "but God knows best," and be ready to follow God's Will in the present spiritual moment, even if sweeps away his most cherished conceptions, and takes him in an entirely new and unexpected direction. *We* are bound by God's Word—but He is not.

Three: Only God is the Doer
Metaphysical objectivity progressively opens onto the realization that *only God*

is the Doer; this is the central principle of Sacred Activism. The process of this opening is more-or-less as follows:

Once we have come into the field of the Names of God, it is impressed upon us that the play of these Names is the origin not only of all the events that happen in the universe, but also of all the intentions that are conceived within us. And when the Face of God is unveiled, we immediately understand that we exist not as our own ideas of ourselves, but solely as God Himself sees us, that His vision of us is the very source of our existence, our one true identity. Furthermore, we understand that His conception of us is the origin of everything that has previously appeared to us as "our own actions," as well as of all the events presently transpiring, or having already transpired, or still yet to transpire, in the entire universe. *We* do not act; it is He who acts within us, and around us. His actions pass through the world, and through our inmost souls, like clouds crossing an empty sky.

And yet, paradoxically, even in the face of the universality of God's actions, such that no event, no matter how vast or how minute, is ever outside the field of them, the human will is still free. We are not simply God's puppets; we are either his fully active and responsible servants, by virtue of our willingness to be receptive to His Will, or else the passive rejecters of that Will, a choice which will eventually result in every conceivable active rebellion and transgression. So the essence of Sacred Activism as a spiritual practice is to purify our intent and fully assume every legitimately delegated responsibility to the point where our individual will, in *active submission*, is totally swallowed up in the Will of God.

Any student of the Far Eastern martial arts will understand how, after the practitioner has trained with complete dedication and fully established his or her skill-set, the point comes where the Tao—the immanent Will of God in the Chinese tradition—takes over his or her entire body and mind, and carries on the fight from beyond the conscious intent of the fighter. Real musicians will understand that the same is true of their music; true calligraphers will recognize how the same progression from imitative practice to "second nature" happens in terms of their own art; the same realization is arrived at by the master of any of the arts, including writing. Metaphysical realization draws the will deeper and deeper into submission to Allah, until it is finally understood that no one is doing anything or willing anything but HE—a realization the Sufis call "annihilation in the (Divine) Acts." This annihilation of the individual will in God's Will, perfectly expressed in the words of Jesus, "not my will but Thine be done" [Luke 22:42], was exemplified in the life of the Prophet Muhammad by the incident at the battle of Badr when he took up a handful of pebbles and threw them at the enemy, after which the tide of battle turned in favor of the Muslims; this event is commented on in surah 8, verse 17 of the Qur'an: *It was not you who threw when you threw, but Allah threw.*

In my book *Day and Night on the Sufi Path* [Angelico Press, 2015], I wrote the following about the doctrine that only God is the Doer; as will be apparent, this book was written specifically for Muslims, and is consequently limited to the terms and concepts of Islam:

> Throughout this book we have emphasized, based on the verse *You cannot will unless Allah wills* [Q. 76:30], that only Allah is the Doer, and that all things we possess, and all that we are, are gifts from Him. And one of the greatest of these gifts is *effort. . . . You cannot will unless Allah wills* does not mean that you should make no effort; it means that effort neither begins nor ends with you: it is a gift of Allah, and returns only and inevitably to Him. It is our responsibility to accept this gift with gratitude, not reject it out of a sense of false humility and helplessness that is really nothing but laziness, cowardice, ingratitude and despair. It is said that we should perform every one of our actions for Allah, and dedicate it to Him. But what exactly does this mean? If we do not grasp the reality of effort, such dedication will amount to no more than a formal courtesy—better than nothing, certainly, but nowhere near as effective as a true and concrete understanding of what action is, and Who is acting. In reality, to dedicate every action *to* Allah is to see every action as coming *from* Allah—the formal support for this vision being the *basmalah. . . .* If the first breath we draw when we wake up in the morning is drawn in His Name, if we recognize it as an echo of the *nafas al-Rahman*, the Breath of the Merciful by which He has created us and through which He holds us in existence, second by second, then we may (insha'Allah) continue to draw our life, our intent, and our guidance from Him alone—He Who is *Al-Hayy* (the Living), *Al-Muqtadir* (the All-Determiner) and *Al-Hadi* (the Guide)—throughout the Day and into the Night. And if we see Him as the Source of our actions, then those actions will become not self-assertions but offerings; as soon as we perform them they will pass out of our hands, and return to the Source that sent them.

Elsewhere in the same book I commented on the qualities, strengths, dangers and limitations of Sacred Activism:

> We may see final victory, insha'Allah, in the Greater Jihad on the field of the Inner, but we will likely never see such victory on the field of the Lesser Jihad to establish peace, justice and true religion in the Outer world of society and history, except in the most limited and temporary of terms—unless Allah wills otherwise. Islamic eschatology declares that a restoration of peace and justice must take place before the coming of the Hour, when the Mahdi arises and Jesus the Messiah returns to slay the Antichrist, but whether this is to be manifest in the Outer or take place only in the Inner, is known only to Allah. Nonetheless, before the final Event, we are faced with the inevitable limitations of the human power to enact Good and proclaim Truth within *al-Dunya* (the Darkness of This World) coupled with the fact that Allah acts within His own time and for His own purposes. Furthermore, whatever

strictly limited power Allah may grant us to do good works in the Outer World can only be based on our victories—or rather *God's victories over us*—in the Inner World; a call to perform a work in the Outer is only a valid expression of the Will of Allah, and can only remain in touch with and submitted to that Will, if it also supports our work in the Inner, if it is in fact something now required of us if we are to take the next concrete step on the Spiritual Path. An attraction to the Lesser Jihad in a given instance may be no more than a temptation emanating from the *Nafs al-ammara b'l su*, the "Self Commanding to Evil" (i.e., the passions), to pervert or abandon the Greater Jihad. But it may also be a grace given us by Allah to help us heal and purify an Innerness that has degenerated into self-involvement and stagnation under the influence of that same "Commanding Self." Unfulfilled duties in the Outer act to block our progress in the Inner, but a faithful completion of such active duties—as well as a conscious renunciation of action when circumstances have revealed that further advance along a particular line has become impossible to us, or at least impossible without incurring spiritual damage and opening to spiritual darkness—is sometimes the very thing that, by the power of Allah, can turn our hearts more deeply toward the Inner, free of the clutter of conflicting impulses and stagnant self-will. Certainly any militant action in the world makes the one performing it vulnerable to the sin of pride, but such action may also be seen as a battle *against* pride, in both one's enemy and oneself. If the Lesser Jihad to humble the pride of the oppressor is not accompanied by an inner, Greater Jihad to humble the pride of the *fata* or *javanmard* himself, the one upon whom has been laid the duty of heroic spiritual action in the world, then *al-Dunya* has conquered him before he begins—not to mention the fact that all militant action in either the Inner or the Outer Jihad is inseparable from the experience of abasement and defeat: no warrior can encounter only victories. [NOTE: *Fata* and *javanmard* are the Arabic and Persian synonyms for the English word *knight*; all three words mean "young man," with the connotation of "young hero."] In terms of the Inner Jihad, this abasement, if the *fata* is capable of fully accepting it as God's Will, is precisely the sign of victory—of God's victory over *him*, which is the only triumph he seeks. And in terms of the Outer Jihad, the *élan* of struggle both inflames and chastens the will, since it pushes the *fata* on to the point where action is no longer possible, and defeat inevitable. While he is acting within the Will of Allah, he is victorious; as soon as he departs from that Will, either because his submission to Allah wavers or because he has unconsciously transgressed the limits of the action which Allah has ordained, he is defeated; in terms of the Greater Jihad, this defeat, if accepted in the right spirit, is his best chance for victory. By the same token, the victories he sees in the Outer are in no way his, but precisely the victories of Allah: *It was not you who threw when you threw, but Allah threw* [Q. 8:17]. It is necessary for the *fata* to gain the power to discern the objective limits of the effective outer manifestation of this Truth in any given instance, the boundary of the Command of Allah, beyond which lies nothing but the outer darkness; and this is not always easy, because action produces its own momentum. Such momentum often feels like power, but it is really nothing but the blind will of the situation, which is inseparable from self-will of the person entangled with it, seeing that *al-Dunya* and *al-Nafs al-ammara b'l su* are two sides of the same coin. The one blinded by action has fallen into self-will through unconscious identification with the outer situation he confronts, and consequently has lost his ability to discern the Will of Allah. Action in submission to that Will is aware of its own inherent boundaries; action outside that Will is not. May Allah grant us the unerring light to tell the one from the other.

> I was sleeping safe in my scabbard—
> Then God drew me like a sword.
> I awoke to war: to victory and defeat.
> The clean design woven in air by this
>   flashing of blades
> Was drawn from the lettering
> Of the Mother of the Book,
> Written down before first breath
>   was drawn on earth,
> Or the earthen floor laid to receive
> The prints of beasts and men.
> The pounding of feet in battle
> Writes the pre-eternal script of the stars
> On the Guarded Tablet,
> And all these forms of bodies
> Transfigured in their moment of struggle
> Have long since gone to their rest
> In Garden or Fire.
> *It was not you who threw when you threw,*
> *But God threw;*
> And the outcome, and the agon,
> And all the exquisite uncertainty—
> To human eyes—of the hour of contest—
> *He* enacted, and *He* knew.

The perfection of the knowledge that only God is the Doer is the understanding that everything is already done. The echoes of God's actions appear as the events of this world, but His true actions happen in Eternity.

Contemplation and Action

Saint Thomas Aquinas maintained that the contemplative life is higher than the active one, while the life that combines contemplation and action is the highest of all. This should not be taken to mean, however, that a life *divided* between contemplation and action is the ideal. The life of contemplative activism is only pre-eminent when action is the expression—the overflow, as it were—of contemplation itself. Contemplation is the most active pursuit possible to the human being, since it demands the realization of God as Pure Act; no kind or degree of merely human "activism" can equal it. And yet, as any true practitioner of the Far Eastern martial arts will tell you, contemplation-in-action is also possible, at least to those who are called to that life. The basis of such contemplation-in-action is what the Taoists call "doing without doing," or *wu wei,* the Chinese term for the activity of the Tao: the Will of God immanent in conditions.

Those who are working toward the kind of synthesis of contemplation and action in which contemplation always remains paramount will most likely experience an alternation of emphasis between contemplation and action, the Inner and the Outer. The inner world, the realm of contemplation, is the place where all manifestation of the Names of God has its beginning; the end-point of this manifestation is the outer world of material and social conditions. As the Catholic writer Charles Péguy put it, "everything begins in mysticism and ends in politics." After this limit is reached, the last remaining phase is the return of all manifestation to the place where it began, in the Night of the Unseen, the place where the One Who is manifested by all things abides alone. In God, the synthesis between Inner and Outer is complete and perfect; in the words of the Qur'an, *He is the First and the Last, and the Outward and the Inward* [Q. 57:3]. However, in the case of the human being striving to become conformed to God, this synthesis will necessarily be incomplete; therefore an alternation of attention between Inner and Outer will likely be experienced. While navigating the currents of this alternation, the sacred activist must strive to remember God as the perfect union of Inner and Outer, understanding that what is unfinished in him or her is already perfect in God, and consequently that the ongoing submission to That One, rather than some self-willed mental balancing-act designed to rope action and contemplation together in some form or another, is the royal road to the eventual union of action and contemplation in earthly human life. In the beginning phase, contemplation veils action and action veils contemplation. In the intermediate phase, contemplation veils action, but action does not veil contemplation. In the final phase, neither does action veil contemplation nor contemplation action; the One Acting is witnessed as God alone.

To Accept or Reject Destiny

But if God is the Doer, then must not destiny be fixed, since He has full knowledge of what He has ordained and what He will do in what, from our point of view, is the "future"? How, then, can there be such a thing as Sacred Activism, which has as its goal the transformation of conditions? If God is the only Doer, then conditions are what they are by His will—so wouldn't any action on our part to change them necessarily constitute a rebellion against what God has ordained?

This a very naïve way of viewing the question of destiny, though it is actually quite common among believers who accept the omnipotence of God but not their own responsibility to actively cooperate with it. Such people view submission to God as a kind of hopeless resignation, which they nonetheless hope will be compensated for by a future reward. According to this conception, those who passively suffer human life on earth will be rewarded by the right to enjoy eternity in an equally passive paradise. People holding beliefs like this are easy prey for political and religious leaders who are eaten up with self-will, and who have no compunction against presenting their own agendas as the Will of God. To mechanically conform to behavioral and ritual norms without any real active engagement with them is good training for a similar conformity to the dictates of authoritarian despots, who will sometimes present their dupes with opportunities for intense (and intensely destructive) activity, thus giving them the illusion that they have at last thrown off their passivity and suddenly become courageous, godly and powerful over night.

If God wills conditions to be what they are, then he also wills the human desire to change and improve them; consequently if one hears a real call to Sacred Action, but refuses it because all action against the status quo is falsely defined as rebellion against God, then this very refusal is just such a rebellion. But doesn't God's rank as the Only Doer imply that He also wills the actions of evil men, wills every rebellion against Him, even wills our own self-will? This is certainly true in one sense, seeing that nothing can depart from the universal and sovereign Will of God. Included in that Will, however, is His will that the human will be free. Whatever choice we make falls under, is formed upon, and is ultimately empowered by, one of His infinite Names. If we choose to obey the norms He has laid down, as well as His Command issued to us directly, then we come under the Names of Mercy; if we transgress those norms, refuse that Command, and worship self-will in their place, then we come under the Names of Rigor. Both outcomes are entirely lawful, entirely in line with God's intentions. Human life in this terrestrial world is not the place of final reward and punishment, but the realm specifically designed by the All-Merciful for the exercise of human free will, the place of testing in the face of warring alternatives. God knows "beforehand" all the choices we will make, but this in no way limits our freedom—since, as the Christian philosopher Boethius explained it, to watch someone do something is not to make him do it. God may command us to perform a particular action, but we remain free to accept or reject that command. If we accept it, this indicates that we are destined by God for felicity;

if we reject it, then He has destined us for torment. Yet the choice between destinies remains ours, paradoxical as this may sound. God resides in Eternity, and Eternity underlies the moments of our lives rather than simply coming before or after them; therefore God's eternal knowledge of my actions does not negate my free will, nor does it mechanically predetermine my daily choices in passing time, since it can with equal validity be seen as the final sum of them. Our free actions in time are the expression of our eternal character in the mind of God, just as that eternal character is the essence and outcome of those free actions—which is to say, we are free to be ourselves. Does anything less truly deserve the name of "freedom"?

In terms of Sacred Activism, God's decree commanding a particular action can be freely accepted because it is in no way an alien compulsion, but rather an expression of the true character of the one receiving it. On the other hand, every action has its limits. It may be our destiny to change conditions according to God's Will, but there is also a destiny in conditions that limits the manner and the degree to which they can be changed; this is also God's Will. As Allah says in the Holy Qur'an, *I will show them My signs on the horizons and in themselves, until they know that it is the truth. Is it not enough for you that I am Witness over all things?* [Q. 41:53] If it is an error to identify the "will of events" with the Will of God, it is also an error to strictly identify our impulse to change events with that Will. The result of the first is hopeless resignation; the result of the second is titanic arrogance. God shows us His Signs and expresses His Will both on the horizons of the outer world and within our own souls—but if we concentrate upon and choose to follow one set of these signs to the exclusion of the other, then we are idolaters; we are in *de facto* rebellion against God, and are consequently laboring under the Names of Rigor rather than the Names of Mercy. Furthermore, a clear command from God that we perform a certain action is no guarantee that the action will "succeed" according to our human conception of things. Success and failure, victory and defeat, are equally willed by God, so that we can learn modesty and gratitude in victory and faithful resignation in defeat. God does not will, nor could He will, to transform this world of polarities and contradictions into a second God by decreeing the total success of every wish or plan conceived by every one of His believers. Victory proves His Generosity and His Mercy; defeat proves His Sovereignty and His Majesty—not to mention the fact that the "victories" proposed by This World are really defeats, and that many of the defeats dealt by This World are actually secret victories. Ultimately there is no true defeat except rebellion against God, nor any real victory except grateful submission to Him, in both victory and defeat.

This World

Al-Dunya, This World, is a collective conception of material conditions based on the beliefs, intentions and agendas of those who recognize nothing beyond material reality and its psychic echoes. And since everyone is a slave to his or her own conception of reality, with no hope of rebelling against it until that conception changes—or even any way of imagining what such a rebellion might look like—This World is a great and tyrannical power that controls our every thought, feeling and intention, until we awaken to the Reality that lies beyond it.

In the case of profane action, the field of activity is the World. Reward is expected, and punishment feared, only from the World. In the case of Sacred Action, though the field of activity is still the World, reward and punishment are expected from God alone, and consequently welcomed; this is what it means to be "in the World but not of it." Punishment is seen as correction, perfection of strategy or purification of intent; reward is accepted only in the form of advancement on the Spiritual Path. The watchword of *karma-yoga* (the way of action) from the **Bhagavad-Gita** is: "Act, but dedicate the fruits of action to Me." The dedication of the fruits of action to God is the method by which worldly reward is transformed into spiritual reward—and spiritual reward is seen not in terms of a future paradise or even a present consolation, but strictly as a progressive unveiling of the Face of God. Present consolation, the merit by which we deserve a future paradise, and even worldly rewards on the material plane are not to be rejected, since to reject God's gifts is to reject God. They are, however, to be immediately re-dedicated to Him, so as to advance the work of Sacred Action.

The Question of Magic

One of the more common illusions confronted by those who feel called to perform social service or action from a spiritual standpoint is the temptation of magic, which is based on a false metaphysic. Those attracted to the metaphysical view of reality but repelled by "organized religion" and "limited" theistic beliefs will often consider the doctrine of a Personal God Who knows, acts, and expresses various intentions in relationship to humanity to be no more than a primitive superstition, more-or-less represented in their minds by the image of "an old man with a white beard in the sky." They view an "anthropomorphic" God as a naïve, invented concept, a false deity created in the image of humanity; the traditional notion that the human person is actually a "theomorphic" being, created in the image of God, largely escapes them. But as soon as God in His personal aspect is denied, and the Deity consequently deprived of all ability to conceive and initiate action, as well as any awareness of earthly humanity, of our needs, deeds, dilemmas and intentions, then God is necessarily reduced to something on the order of an automatically-operating natural force or a vast yet passive reservoir of cosmic energy—a reservoir that is available to be tapped by the "adept" who is capable of understanding the impersonal laws by which It functions. When God is conceived of as passive, then the active pole must be assumed by the human self-will. Consequently, instead of submitting to the Will of God and working to serve His plan in the world, the magical activist believes that he or she can tap the infinite energy of God to empower the humanly-devised agenda of his or her party, or class, or social movement, or clandestine elite, or individual self, and is entirely justified in doing so.

The metaphysical contradiction of such an approach, apart from the wrong concept of the Deity on which it is based, is as follows: The Infinite Power of God can only be accessed by those who have succeeded in totally sacrificing self-will, along with the limited and passion-based agendas that self-will always pursues, including the various collective allegiances that mask that will and provide it with much of its field of operation; a limited agenda can no more command an unlimited Power than the ocean can be contained in a teacup. The sacred activist will of course often be called upon to serve a particular group or movement, but there is a vast distance between serving something by the Will of God and worshipping it in the place of God. And since the human will is free by God's design, He will always allow that will to make the choice of refusing to submit to His greater Will—at which point the flow of Infinite Power through the human form necessarily drops to zero. Those who do not resist the current of a river but allow it to carry them have availed themselves of the entire power of that current; those who resist the current by choosing a different direction of travel than the current has willed have embraced only weakness and exhaustion.

The ones who fail, as they must, to tap God's power for their own purposes, or have never actually made this attempt because their sense of God's reality is deficient or delusional, may be attracted to the literal practice of magic. The fundamental fallacy of the magical worldview is that human intent can affect conditions on subtle planes of reality without being affected by them—but as the Peter O'Toole character of Lawrence of Arabia remarked in the film of the same name, (to repeat a line already quoted above) "you can do anything you want, but you can't want anything you want." This is a truth we often forget, since those dominated and deluded by self-will routinely see themselves as totally self-determined. Once you realize that each higher and subtler plane of being is causal in relation to the plains below it—that (for example) a treatment to the etheric or subtle-energy body will sometimes cure a condition in the physical body, or that a dream on the psychic or imaginal plane can function as a "seed" for a later event on the physical plane—you may get the idea that the "control panel" for physical reality is now available to you, to operate however you will. This erroneous belief ignores the fact that a person who acts upon the etheric plane is simultaneously being acted upon through the psychic plane, and that the would-be manipulator of the psychic plane has received his or her ability to affect imaginal reality, along with the specific parameters and limits to that ability that are destined for him, from the angelic plane or the plane of Spirit—and this is true in all cases, whether or not the person in question is conscious of it; there is no true "Archimedean point" outside God Himself. The decree governing every action and determining every event comes ultimately from Him; our will is completely free only when confronted by the choice either to cooperate with that decree, thus unfolding all the potentials hidden within it, or else to resist it, thereby cutting ourselves off from the flow of creative energy. And those who choose to resist it through a belief in magical action may encounter a further danger: the delusion that the phenomena sometimes apparently produced by magic are being controlled by them, whereas they are actually being controlling by those phenomena, and the invisible powers behind them. If God is the only Creator, then the manifestations following upon magical action must represent a reality that is less effective, less imbued with vital energy, fundamentally less real than the eternal Act by which God maintains the cosmos, which we can fully participate in by submitting to it—and the *glamour* attending those magical events exists precisely to hide this fact. To allow one's vital energy and sense of reality to be depleted, in the deluded belief that they are actually being enhanced, is the just punishment suffered by all who turn against the One Source of Life and Truth: not just the out-and-out magicians, but also every technologist or politician or social engineer or social activist who hopes to manipulate Reality without first obeying It.

The established certainty that only God is the Doer breaks all attachment to magic, as well as to "the will of events" and the effects of one's past actions; it overcomes both self-will and fatalism. The challenge of events must be met, the consequences of one's past actions must be dealt with, but neither of these tasks should be allowed to become one's master. To obey outer events or the momentum of one's own actions in the place of God is to depart from the way of Sacred Activism. The sacred activist always sees God as the First Cause superseding all others, not in the past but in this very moment; thus the work of dealing with unfolding events or the consequences of past actions is always carried on under God's direction, by His Power, and as an act of worship dedicated to Him alone.

The Paradigm of War

The most extreme and rigorous form of action is war; consequently the principles of Sacred Activism stand out most clearly in the context of *holy* war—by which I emphatically do *not* mean any war that uses religion as a pretext. In the Muslim universe, the Lesser Jihad is war, by word or deed, against the enemies of truth and justice in the outer world; the Greater Jihad is the war against the inner enemy who attacks the spiritual Heart. Both wars are commanded by God, but both are to be carried on only within strict limits of chivalry and justice; unbridled ruthlessness against the outer enemy, or against oneself, can in no way serve the cause of Reality. In the Hindu universe the central manual of Sacred Activism—also known is *karma-yoga*—is the **Bhagavad-Gita**, whose setting is the great war between the Pandavas and the Kauravas on the battlefield of Kurukshetra, as recounted in the epic poem the **Mahabharata**. Krishna, the charioteer of the Pandava archer-hero Arjuna, who advises him to put his doubts to rest and take up the fight, is God Himself. Even Gandhi, whose battle-tactic was *satyagraha* or "truth-force" (non-violent resistance), went to war against an enemy: namely, the will to place one's personal safety and survival above obedience to the Divine mandate. And as for the Christian universe, Jesus Christ declared: "I come not to bring peace, but a sword."

Sacred Activism, conceived of as holy war, encounters two enemies and requires two sacrifices. When entering the field of battle, the enemy to be overcome, and sacrificed, is Fear. When leaving the field of battle, when returning from War to Peace, the enemy to be overcome, and sacrificed, is Anger. (In Gandhi's case, these two enemies were encountered and dealt with as one, in line with his personal view of the **Mahabharata** that "Kurukshetra is in the heart of man.") The laws of spiritual motion are analogous to those of physical momentum; in both cases the "G-force," the force of resistance, appears at two specific points: acceleration and deceleration. In many ancient cultures, both tribal and national, the warrior undergoes a ritual of dedication to death before entering battle, and a ritual of purification from the residues of death when returning to life in human society. And the best warrior knows how to sacrifice anger not only after the war is ended, but in the very heat of battle. Once when 'Ali ibn Abi Talib overtook an enemy he had been long pursuing and drew his sword Dhulfiqar to finish him off, the man spit in his face—at which point 'Ali sheathed his sword, turned and walked away. He had experienced a momentary fit of rage, and it was his firm practice never to kill in anger. "Dhulfiqar" means "two-pointed." It was a real historical sword; nonetheless its two points or blades undoubtedly also symbolize the Lesser and Greater Jihads, and the fact that no Outer jihad that does not serve the Inner one, the cause of self-transcendence, is any jihad at all.

Both fear and anger are aspects of self-will. Fear is the refusal of God's command; anger is the assertion of one's own will in the place of God's command. Thus the inner enemy in Sacred Activism considered as the Greater Jihad is self-will and nothing else. Self-will blocks submission to God; it also distorts strategic insight, since it replaces the true vision of what is, based on the Divine Objectivity, with a false one based on what we hope will happen, and what we fear might happen.

It is necessary to return from war to peace in order to reach the certainty that peace is greater than war, closer to the real nature of things, closer to the truth of God, and so come to the realization that peace is present in the face of war itself as its ultimate matrix. In the words of Morihei Ueshiba, the founder of the martial art of Aikido: "A warrior is always engaged in a life-and-death struggle for Peace." Any war that does not have peace as its final goal is not worth fighting; conflict for the sake of conflict is the worst addiction and the worst blindness.

Peace in itself is a great power; it is not simply the apparent absence of conflict after a military triumph, or ease and security in every-day civilian life. It is a higher energy-state than war—so high that when it encounters an energy-state that is lower than war—ignorance, stagnation, silent oppression and despair—the result is conflict. (In terms of the Hindu Samkya philosophy, peace is the *satwa-guna*, war the *raja-guna*, and stagnation and oppression the *tamo-guna*, these being the three modes of *Prakriti* or Universal Substance.) The Arabic word for peace, *salaam*, also denotes flawlessness, perfection. It is the perfection that the eye of Love alone can see, beyond all fractures, distortions, and veils. Peace is how God sees the universe when He gazes into its deepest essence, and witnesses only Himself.

The Unseen Warfare

An agenda which has as its goal the destruction of the human form can have no human author. The loss of our civic and human rights, environmental degradation, widespread starvation and malnutrition, the outbreak of new diseases, transhumanism and transgenderism (whose victims deserve our compassion, not our hate), universal surveillance, the impoverishment and political subjugation of great masses of humanity, the failure of states, the growth of drug cartels and terrorist networks, outbreaks of meaningless violence, the collective engineering of human consciousness and belief, the mechanization of reproduction by which the human person is degraded to the level of an industrial product, the destruction of the heritage of millennia of human culture, the perversion and deconstruction of our religious traditions, and the myriad other assaults on our essential humanity that we confront today, including unjust war itself—which together make up not so much a set of problems to be solved as a long-predicted season in human time—are Satanic in conception, in practice, and in ultimate conclusion, often overtly so; this is the present makeup of the *Dunya*, the Darkness of This World. No human being, regardless of how rich, how powerful or how evil he or she may be—no billionaire, transnational corporate head, spymaster or occult financial wizard—no master of propaganda, mind control and social engineering—no mad scientist or Luciferian hierophant or general of secret armies, can benefit from the transformation of this earth into a living Hell; the only conceivable beneficiary of such abominations could be Hell itself. Unfortunately, however, for the denizens of that sorry kingdom, Hell is a destination no benefit can ever reach. So the whole thing, the whole titanic effort, to which so many have sacrificed their last hope for human happiness, is only loss, loss and nothing else. There is *no victory,* no payoff, nothing but the descent into infernal despair—horrible, yes, but from another point of view simply pathetic, and therefore worth no more than a passing nod, soon to be followed by a decent forgetfulness of things not worth remembering. Human consciousness is designed to contemplate the Truth, from which it draws its life, not to exhaust itself in trying to make sense out of lies and illusions, or in struggling to redeem those who, in embracing falsehood, have willingly agreed to their own damnation. In the words of Jesus, "let the dead bury their dead" [Matthew 8:22]; in the words of the Holy Qur'an, *All is perishing except His Face* [Q. 28:88].

In terms of Sacred Activism, given the fact that the globalist agenda that must be combated is demonic both in its original conception and in its final outcome, the activist will encounter demonic enemies as well as human ones. These spiritual adversaries will always be there, whether or not they or their actions are apparent at any given time. In view of this, some traditional form of protection against demonic influence should be part of the arsenal of every sacred activist: the last two surahs of the Qur'an and the invocation *audu-bilahi min ash-shaytan al-rajim* for Muslims, holy water or the St. Michael prayer for Christians, other forms for those following other traditions. But in order to use these forms effectively, one must possess some degree of "discernment of spirits," or be in the process of developing it. The invisible world is teeming with denizens of all kinds, including demons, angels, good fairies, helpful jinn, mischievous elementals, the various sub-personal psychic residues that we know as ghosts . . . the list goes on. Therefore the discernment of spirits must take two forms: discrimination between good and evil influences, and discrimination between Spiritual and psychic entities. The rule is that we should ask for protection only from God Himself, or from angelic beings resident on the Spiritual plane and acting in His name. Benevolent beings inhabiting the psychic plane—helpful fairies, the faithful Muslim jinn, etc.—should not be invoked; their help must be accepted if they are acting under the direction of Divine or angelic influences, but if they are, their actions will likely not be apparent; any fairy or jinn who *calls attention to itself,* whatever its intentions may appear to be, should immediately be banished. As for angels, their help and influence should be welcomed—but they must never be invoked as if they were independent powers. The word "angel" means "messenger"—messenger of God. Angels bring no messages and impart no wisdom of their own, but act directly under the command of the Almighty; this is why we do not pray to angels as if they were gods, though we may pray to God that He send His angels to help us, if such is His will. God alone should be invoked; God alone should be obeyed; God alone should be thanked. [NOTE: These rules are generally applicable within the context of the great revealed religions and wisdom traditions. When it comes to shamanism, however, other rules apply in some instances, norms and techniques which I have neither the inclination nor the right to evaluate. Be that as it may, all those called to serve humanity with guidance and power from the Unseen World are part of the extended brotherhood and sisterhood of Sacred Activism. In the words of the Holy Qur'an: *And each one hath a goal toward which he turneth; so vie with one another in good works. Wheresoever ye may be, Allah will bring you all together. Lo! Allah is Able to do all things* [Q. 2:148].]

This warfare against the demons should not be *dramatized*, nor should the activist fall into an excessive attraction to the paranormal simply because the prosaic fact of demonic influence is recognized. Fighting demons does not make you special, any more than keeping your toilet clean to avoid spreading disease makes you a hero. The prophylactic and curative actions we must take in the face of the demonic, which is virtually universal in the world today, are simply forms of normal spiritual hygiene that every sacred activist should know and practice. And it should never be forgotten that the beginning and end of all warfare against the demonic is the pacification, renunciation and transcendence of human self-will. Without self-will and the ego it generates, which provide the demons with a point of entry, they would have no power.

In regard to this it is crucial to remember that we should never fight the demons using our own strength, any more than we should *argue* with them using our own intelligence. The first opens us to the temptation to magic, the second to that of heterodoxy and spiritual delusion. Often our unseen adversaries will try to pick a fight with us so as to tempt us to rely on our own power, knowing that we will discover in the process that we are helpless against them, and thus hopefully descend into despair. In the face of demonic attack we must invoke God's help and turn the battle over to Him as swiftly and completely as possible. Without Him we can do nothing—and if our encounter with demonic forces teaches us this truth, and then they have been soundly defeated.

The Importance of Weakness

Many people are attracted to the notion of spiritual warfare and/or Sacred Activism because they want to feel powerful; the idea of confronting the massed legions of Hell and its earthly agents on the field of battle with Divine power and favor backing you up is a pretty dramatic proposition. At this point it would be good to remember the words of St. Paul, "our strength is perfected in weakness" [2 Corinthians 12:9]; this is also the basic principle behind the Muslim fast in Ramadan. The *feeling* of power is not power; it is nothing but the appropriation of the power of God by the human ego. Such an appropriation only sabotages and undermines the power that God has given us to fulfill His commands; its final outcome is not power, but weakness—not a humble weakness that is willingly accepted as a trial sent by God, in the knowledge that might and power belong to Him alone, but a despairing and terminal weakness that arrives only when our last remaining freedom to submit to God's Will has been sabotaged by arrogance and delusion.

The weakness in which our strength is perfected, since it is based on the *willing* submission to God, is the exact opposite of the spiritual bankruptcy produced by self-will. And no person who does not recognize his or her intrinsic poverty as a door that opens directly upon the Divine wealth and generosity— as the *only* door opening in that direction—will be able to submit to Him; consequently he or she will be driven onward by the demon of self-will until both that self-will, and that person's potential for genuine submission to the Will of God, are exhausted. But when the intrinsic weakness and poverty of the human condition are no longer opposed, but recognized and accepted, then we have come into the real Presence of God; consequently the Power of God will begin to flow into the receptive vessel of our human weakness. Only the Heart that is empty of self-will can be filled with God's Will.

The Path of Least Resistance

But the question remains: How do we know the Will of God in actual strategic terms, given that His commands as addressed to the conscious mind are rarely explicit when it comes to the timing and conduct of specific actions? One key to understanding the Divine mandate is: "Follow the path of least resistance." The path of the greatest resistance is an expression of self-will, that of least resistance the manifestation of God's Will. As Lao Tzu put it in the *Tao Te Ching*— the Tao being essentially the Will of God immanent in conditions—"yield and overcome." This, however, is a dangerous saying, one that is highly susceptible to self-serving misinterpretation. If we approach "yield and overcome" on the level of a shallow understanding of the forces of life, it becomes synonymous with "give up the fight"; cowardice, too, may be defined as "the path of least resistance." Only when we have penetrated below the visible surface of the flow of events and plumbed the depths of their hidden power and meaning can we say we have truly encountered the Tao, the concrete presence of "only God is the Doer," and entered the dimension where following the path of least resistance is the essence of strategic wisdom. It will do no good to take only a moral imperative from the Almighty without the accompanying power to realize it. If we attempt this we will find ourselves beating our heads against a stone wall in God's name, hoping that the suffering we are experiencing and the damage we are doing ourselves in His cause will be enough to move Him to help us. Instead of this kind of self-willed "obedience," we need to find the place where "what wants to happen" and "what God wants to happen" are one and the same, where the deep potentials in the situation we confront begin to reveal themselves as the living *potencies* of God's secret action. Only after we have intuited these potencies, and united ourselves with them, will the true "path of least resistance" open before us.

Balance

Ours is a time when many are searching for, and attempting to rely upon, things designed to *replace* human life rather than enhance it. One's job, one's religion, one's cause are often seen not so much as contributing to the quality and substance of life as providing substitutes for it. The same, of course, can also be said of sports, drug and alcohol addiction, computer games, and innumerable other postmodern distractions. The choice for many people seems to have come down to addiction to frivolous entertainment vs. commitment to some violent obsession. Things like home, family, social standing within the community etc., which "came naturally" to almost everyone in our parents' or grandparents' generations, are now increasingly difficult to scrape together, obtainable only by some rare and extravagant tour-de-force—or simply to be despaired of, especially by the younger generation now facing economic hard times and wide-spread cultural breakdown. How many of us will soon be driving cheap, single-seat automobiles and sleeping in pods? How long will it be before the refugee camp—if not the prison—becomes the new standard model for human society? A smart-phone, a café and a bunk somewhere now define the borders of life outside the workplace for an increasing number of young people in the western nations. And this state of affairs is inseparable from the meta-agenda of those global elites who are moving to destroy the last vestiges of the Sacred on earth. If faith in God is relegated to "the scrap-heap of history," any human life worthy of the name will eventually follow, since the Human Form is the central reflection of God in this world.

Sacred Activism must never be allowed to become one more item on the long list of substitutes for life available in these latter days. For us to do our best to become complete human beings, whose lives are expressions of good will, breadth of sympathy and clarity of intellect, is a duty laid upon us by our Creator; no matter how difficult it may be to achieve this under present worldly conditions, we must make the effort. Without intelligence, we will not know how to carry on Sacred Action; without love, we will have no idea of why such Action is important. And when action is performed without the intelligence and the love necessary to make it a balanced expression of the human mandate, it will depart from the certainty that only God is the Doer, and descend into a state of self-willed obsession and violence.

Even Gandhi was not immune to this tendency. On one occasion he tried to impose his own dietary restrictions, which he had vowed before God to faithfully observe, upon his young son who was seriously ill, forgetting in his political leader's obsession that no one can make a vow for another. His son needed goat's milk and was in danger of death without it, but Gandhi refused to allow it—until his wife Kasturbai put her foot down: her son got the goat's milk, and ultimately survived. Here we have a good example of the well-known tunnel-vision of the activist, or politician, or scientist. The sacred activist is working in the service of human life, therefore he or she must never sacrifice human life in the cause of Sacred Activism. If God calls someone to take a dangerous stand that results in that person's death, this is the privilege of martyrdom—but if the Sacred Activist throws away his or her life, or the lives of family, friends and colleagues, in the name of a cause, this is self-centered idiocy and cruelty masquerading as compassion and service. The Sacred Activist sacrifices his ego on the altar of God, not his health or his friendships or the peace of contemplation on the altar of his ego. Mother Theresa was known the world over for self-sacrificing compassionate service to the poor and the dying—but when the bell rang for prayer, she would stop whatever she was doing, leave the bedside of whoever she was ministering to, and answer that call. All her compassion for the suffering, all her power to relieve that suffering, came to her only because she always put God first.

The Four Levels of Sacred Action

Only God is the Doer; let us grant that much. It certainly seems, however—at least on most occasions—that we are the ones doing the work, reaping the benefits, and taking the blows. If our ability to remain consciously in the Presence of God were perfect, the question of the perfection or imperfection of our own actions would never arise, since we, along with our every act and every intention to act, would subsist, purified of all traces of self-reference, in Him; when God takes the field of battle He needs no ally and meets no enemy—because only God is.

But the ability to seek, find and withstand the constant Presence of God does not develop over night; in terms of the Way of Action, there are (let us say) four steps to it: the Moral, the Elect, the Submissive, and the Annihilated. On the Moral level, we devote ourselves to obedience to those of God's commands which apply to our organization or movement, our whole spiritual community, and/or to every human being who hopes to fulfill the responsibilities of the Human Trust. On the Elect level, I make myself available to the *particular* commands of God directed to me alone, and (God willing) I receive them; they pass into my hands and I proceed to enact them, guided and empowered by the *angel* of each act. On the level of Submission, I perceive these commanded actions not as undertaken by me in obedience to God, but as performed by God Himself, with myself as the passive witness. On the level of Annihilation, even this act of witnessing is dissolved; God acts alone, on His own terms, as witnessed only by Himself.

On the Moral level we strive for constancy in obedience to the laws God has laid down, but we do not expect to hear His Voice speaking to us directly; on the level of Annihilation, neither striving nor constancy nor obedience nor Divine Audition make their appearance. On the levels of Election and Submission, however, we see ourselves as acting within the felt Presence of God; this is the central field of Sacred Activism. But assuming that our consciousness of God's Presence is imperfect and intermittent (and this is a fair assumption), our active submission to His Will when He places in our hands an act to perform, commanding and empowering us to perform it, will appear as a cycle, which can be described in eight stages:

The Eightfold Cycle of Action

First Stage: The Announcement

To begin with, our desire that God choose us to perform a specific work by His command and under His guidance must be evaluated. From one point of view, the Almighty is under no obligation to send us on a special mission, nor do we have any right to demand that He do so; from another, each human being has a particular role that God wants him or her to fulfill, but in most cases that role will not be made consciously explicit, other than through the general command—on the Moral level—to fulfill the spiritual and material duties of one's "station in life" (to use the Catholic phrase), in line with the unique character according to which each of us has been created, with all its inherent strengths, weaknesses, and ways of meeting life. These obligations certainly provide all the opportunities a person needs to reach the station of perfect Submission to God.

The Spiritual Path may be imagined as a ladder, the rungs of which are the ever-higher stations that are reached as the traveler draws nearer to God. But spiritual stations, unlike worldly ones, have the unique *holographic* property that allows one station to embrace all the others; thus perfection in the single station in which God has placed us, in the present moment of spiritual time, is sufficient to complete the whole course. And while the progressive "stations" (*maqamat*) of the Spiritual Path, in the Sufi sense, are certainly not equivalent to the various social "stations" in life, nonetheless there are certain analogies. In Dante's **Paradiso**, the souls of the blessed are *ranged in ranks* [cf. Q. 37] stretching from the lowest rank within the sphere of the Moon, up through the spheres of the higher planets and the fixed stars to the Primum Mobile and the Empyrean; these ranks are Dante's image of the stations of the Spiritual Path such as are rendered in various ways by many Sufi writers, as well as by Christian Fathers such as St. John Climacus. Yet those in the lower ranks do not yearn to rise any higher nor do they envy those who are placed above them; they know that their true relationship to God can come only through the perfection of their one spiritual destiny. In relative terms this destiny may be high or low; in Absolute terms it incomparable. Consequently the strict hierarchy of Heaven, in Dante's vision, is compensated for by a fundamental equality, a "communion of the saints" that allows any soul to visit any sphere. Transposed to the terrestrial plane, the same principle applies. A perfect blacksmith, or farmer, or father, has complete spiritual pre-eminence over an imperfect knight, or priest, or ruler, or philosopher. Nor does imperfection in a particular station in life necessarily mean that God is calling us to a different one; like the Hindus say, "better to perform one's own duty, no matter how poorly, than the duty of another, no matter how well." Likewise, in terms of the Spiritual Path, we are not called on to strain with our spiritual aspiration and imagination to "reach" ever higher stations, but rather to work to perfect the station at which God has presently placed us, as if there were no other. The Almighty will certainly not judge us worthy of higher tasks if we fail to complete the task at hand.

If, however, we do hear a call to a particular action that seems to transcend our present station in life, whether that action is more-or-less explicit in our minds or exists only as a nameless longing, we must first determine where this call is actually coming from: from human society, from our individual psyche, from the demonic realms, or from God.

Contemporary society presents us with many ideals of service, a number of which are actually satanic, since they represent radical departures from the Sacred and violations of the human form. Even some causes which are more or less in line with the Sacred will end by paying tribute to the World because they have been co-opted by the World. The sacred activist must be beyond the influence of worldly threats, promises and agendas—or at least consciously working toward this kind of freedom—in order to even begin to understand what God may require of him. Nonetheless his field of operation is earthly existence; how can he operate within a social or political context if he is totally detached from the social world? The answer is: through compassion. When the Gospel of John tells us that "God so loved the world, that he gave his only begotten Son, that whosoever believeth in him should not perish, but have everlasting life" [John 3:16], the writer is not saying that God loved the Darkness of This World and the Principalities and Powers that rule it, but that he loved the souls struggling under the oppression by those Powers. To be in the world but not of it, to love the living beings who make up this world but not the system of pseudo-reality that imprisons them, requires detachment—and the highest form of detachment is compassion.

The unconscious ego may mimic the call to Sacred Activism on the basis of at least three motives: the hunger for self-esteem, the desire for self-knowledge, and the quest for a stronger faith in God. Those whose self-esteem is low may be attracted to heroic enterprises that will give them a better opinion of themselves. Those who fear they are ignorant of their own strengths, weaknesses and motives may search for difficult tasks that they hope will bring these things to light. And those whose faith in God is weak may seek dramatic and convincing manifestations of the Divine Will so as to strengthen that faith. These motives are normal, legitimate, even admirable for those whose basic principle of living is self-determination—but once the truth that only God is the Doer is recognized and accepted, they are out of place. And any one of these motives may open one to the whole range of transgressions that self-worship and the hunger for power so often result in—particularly pride, desire for notoriety, greed, anger and lust. Any these passions, particularly if they remain unconscious, may counterfeit the call to Sacred Activism, thus providing the one ruled by them with wider opportunities to live them out.

This picture is complicated, however, by the fact that God Himself may call us to overcome low self-esteem, to reach greater self-knowledge, and to deepen our faith in Him. The desire to seek self-aggrandizement may simply be the ego's mis-interpretation and perversion of a true command from God to overcome an inner self-hatred and despair. The quest for self-knowledge is a good thing if it is initiated by God in order to bring a particular human soul closer to Him, according to the *hadith* "he who knows himself knows his Lord"— although any self-willed attempt by the ego to understand and explore itself can only be futile and destructive. And God is always calling us to a deeper faith in Him, though the ego may invert this call by replacing the faith and trust in God necessary to undertake a difficult task with an insolent demand that God produce a particular desired outcome, for which we will then presume to reward *Him* by demonstrating greater devotion to Him—as if our own acts of worship could somehow bribe the Almighty. In view of these dangers, any intuition that God may be calling us to a particular action in His service should immediately be met with prayers that He protect us from the temptations of pride and cowardice and delusion and self-will; that whatever self-worship or self-hatred may infect our souls be transmuted into self-respect; and that we always remain open to the Divine Commands hidden in any deepening of faith or expansion of self-knowledge, in the spirit of "not my will but Thine be done" [Luke 22: 42].

When it comes to the action of demons to counterfeit, attack or pervert Sacred Activism, St. Maximos the Confessor has this to say:

> The demons of pride, self-esteem, desire for popularity, and hypocrisy, never act by trying to dampen the ardor of the virtuous man. Instead, they cunningly reproach him for his shortcomings where the virtues are concerned, and suggest that he intensify his efforts, encouraging him in his struggle. They do this in order to entice him to give his full attention to them; in this way they make him lose a proper balance and moderation, and lead him imperceptibly to a destination other than the one to which he thought he was going.... A person pursuing the spiritual way is perhaps quicker to recognize the other demons [*the one who inflame the passions and tempt to obvious sins*], and so he more easily escapes the harm that they do; but in the case of the demons that appear to co-operate with the progress of virtue and pretend they want to help in building a temple to the Lord, surely no intellect is so sublime as to recognize them without the assistance of the active and living Logos, who pervades all things and pierces "even to the dividing asunder of soul and spirit" [Hebrews 4:12]—who discerns, in other words, which acts or conceptual images pertain to the soul, that is, are natural forms or expressions of virtue, and which are spiritual, are supranatural and characteristic of God, but bestowed on nature by grace [from the *Philokalia*].

The demons who go to war against the one dedicated to Sacred Action have many possible avenues of attack. They will do their best to turn Detachment into cruel and cold-hearted aloofness, Objectivity into a mass of fixed ideas which blot out compassion and human relatedness, and the knowledge that only God is the Doer into either paralysis or a titanic arrogance that knows no limit. They will inflame the passions, especially fear, anger, greed and lust (usually by presenting them as virtues) so as to destroy the work of the activist, and then do their best to plunge him or her into guilt and despair in the face of this devastation, thereby hiding the truth that only God is the Doer, and that Divine help is always available. They will work to replace the activist's trust in God with the suggestion that he or she should struggle to attain perfection on the basis of individual self-will—and then, when the futility of this attempt becomes apparent, either accuse their victim of unfaithfulness to God (the unfaithfulness they have only an instant ago suggested that he adopt) or else claim that God has abandoned him. And they will do their best to transform submission to metaphysical principles into spiritual pride, transferring the activist's obedience from God to the "spiritual" ego that supposedly acts in the name of God, and finally to Satan himself as the transpersonal archetype of all ego and all pride. In the words of St. Augustine, "All the other vices attach themselves to evil, that it may be done; only pride attaches itself to good, that it may perish."

The demons will also work to replace true ideals well worth serving because they are in line with God's Will with delusive counterfeits, presenting all sorts of unnatural and subhuman possibilities as the height of spiritual realization, the ultimate goal of human "evolution." Last but not least, they will falsify the relationship between the sacred activist and God, inserting a hidden self-will even into his or her acts of petition or praise or thanksgiving, thereby transforming prayer itself into a subtle magic; these two final avenues of attack together constitute the "Luciferian" imposture. How right St. Maximos is when he tells us that only the Logos, the immanent Divinity, can expose the activities of those demons who seem to serve wisdom and virtue, and defend us from their attacks; the idea that we might stand a chance against the great fallen Cherubim and Seraphim on the basis of our own feeble intellect and limited personal power is itself a demonic delusion.

How, then, can one discern a Divine call? Does it have any particular marks by which it can be clearly recognized? Only faith can truly answer this question; nonetheless a few indications may be in order. A call that comes from God will probably not arrive via some uncanny or paranormal channel. For example, if you hear a voice, audibly or silently, claiming to be the voice of God and issuing a command, your first response should be to take refuge in God from that voice, and pray to be protected from spiritual deception. If you do this and the call is true, the shape of it will slowly become clear; if deceptive, it will be exposed as false by some telltale sign such as absurdity, grandiosity of style, or temptation to foolish or sinful actions. Conversely a true call will most likely appear in one of two ways. Often it will seem to manifest at all points at once, through both inner indications (intuitions, dreams, etc.) and outer signs, signs that are most commonly provided by the various human beings that God sends our way, whether or not they recognize themselves as carrying significant messages; as the Qur'an says, *I will show them My signs on the horizons and in themselves, until they know that it is the truth* [Q. 41:53]. In other instances, a true call will appear simply as an established fact, a foregone conclusion. Nonetheless, dramatic or shocking manifestations, like the appearance of Christ to St. Paul on the road to Damascus, can't be entirely ruled out. Suffice it to say that if you are not familiar with prayer or with the notion that submission to the Will of God is the basis of the spiritual life, Sacred Activism is not for you. Even a contemplative method such as the Theravada Buddhist *vipassana*, based on bare attention to whatever is going on, here and now, in *body, feelings, mind* (fundamental mind-set) and *mind-contents* (words and images), is a form of submission to God, even though in this case the Absolute Principle is not conceived of in personal terms. To be aware of *what is* without fleeing from it, rebelling against it or struggling to change it is, precisely, to *submit* to it as a direct manifestation of Reality—and Reality is another name for God.

Second Stage: Acceptance of the Trust

Once a command from God has become clear to us, the next step is to *accept* it. To accept with the will what has been revealed to the Intellect always entails a struggle, the outcome of which is by no means a foregone conclusion. Many times when a duty or a concrete opportunity arrives we will reject it, even if we have prayed for it as fervently and sincerely as we know how. This is a sign that the imaginal fields of endless possibility are more beautiful to us than a single concrete reality. But the truth is, the one reality is more beautiful than the million possibilities, because it is the direct reflection of God, the Absolute Truth, the Only Being. This is the First Crisis in the cycle of Sacred Action, the crisis of Fear—fear of the injuries one might suffer on the path of action, but also the simple fear of responsibility and the limitations that go with it, of the loss of the ease and lyrical beauty we experienced in the paradise before the birth of the Command. (William Blake, in his *Book of Thel*, tells the story of the failure of a soul at the point of the First Crisis, and its consequent refusal of the Trust.)

The spiritual Intellect, also known as the *Nous* or the Eye of the Heart, contemplates the Always So—not simply the eternal metaphysical Principles, but the actions of God in their eternal aspect. From the standpoint of the Intellect these actions are seen both as inevitable and as already complete, given that the Intellect contemplates only Necessary Being, and within the context of Necessary Being all possibilities are realized. This is one of the meanings of the well-known saying of Jesus, "With God all things are possible" [Matthew 19:26].

The will, however—though submission to God as the Always So anchors it in Eternity—operates in the dimension of time; it moves from concept to realization, from "potency" to "act." What in Eternity is *necessary*, what *must* be because it is already accomplished, in time is only *possible*, only something that *might* be; therefore *might*—power—is required for any possibility to be realized. No one but God possesses such power or has the right to wield it.

To submit to the reception of a concept larger than one can conceive, of a mandate that is completely beyond one's own power to enact, requires suffering. The mouse gives birth to the elephant, and one's entire self-concept and world-concept are shattered in the process. It's not simply that things formerly undreamed of have now become possible, that Potency has been transformed into Act, but that the heretofore Impossible is suddenly revealed as the Necessary. Clearly no one but God can accomplish this.

The suffering that accompanies the reception of a Divine command is an expression of the sacrifice of identifications. Our attachment to who we think we are and what we think the world is must die so that Divine Power can take their place. This crisis of receptivity to God's mandate is dramatized in the *Bhagavad-Gita* as Arjuna's initial unwillingness to fight. He sees many of his own relatives in the ranks of the enemy, the Kauravas, and doubts whether the cause of his own clan, the Pandavas, is sufficiently superior to justify the slaughter to come, in which both sides will suffer grievous losses. To this understandable reluctance we may add—at least in our own cases—the uncertainty at the outset of any conflict as to what the outcome will be, and the fear that one's initial trust in Divine guidance will be lost somewhere in the fog of war, to be replaced by cruelty, brutalization and blind self-will. But if one's charioteer is God Himself, if one has placed the reins of his life in the hands of the Almighty, such misgivings are out of place. Arjuna's reluctance to fight is not based on cowardice or the fear of death, but on a genuine, and entirely honorable, moral uncertainty; if he had not been a man of honor at the outset, he would never have met God. As it is, all his scruples are dispelled by his Divine charioteer—Krishna—in two ways. On the human level, Krishna simply reminds him of his dharma as a *kshatriya* of the warrior caste, and tells him: "Do your duty." But since Arjuna is called to fight in response to a Divine command, Krishna opens to him the dimension from which all such commands originate: he unveils his own Universal Form, blazing like a million suns, composed of the shapes of all things, held in the embrace of a single incandescent Form that absolutely transcends them. From this higher standpoint the battle is a foregone conclusion. In eternity it has already taken place; all who are destined to die in it have already passed on, already been devoured by God, the Devourer of all things. It is simply Arjuna's duty not to resist this truth, but to willingly play his part within it. His misgivings are swept away, and he fights. And if we hope to respond—like Arjuna—to a Divine Command that will ruthlessly take us beyond ourselves, we too must see our actions as already accomplished, and ourselves as already annihilated in the abyss of God, to Whom the entire universe is negligible—essentially snuffed out—no more than a speck of dust swirled in the current of the Divine Wind. If we are capable, with God's help, of seeing things like this, then our response will be, in the words of the Virgin Mary, "be it done unto me according to Thy Word" [Luke 1:38]. If we can make this sacrifice, accepting beforehand all the unknown consequences of the task that confronts us only because it is God's Will, then we will have reached Certainty—and Certainty is Peace. As the Irish poet W.B. Yeats put it, in his poem "Under Ben Bulben," some of which we have already quoted above:

> Know that when all words are said
> And a man is fighting mad,
> Something drops from eyes long blind;

He completes his partial mind
For an instant stands at ease,
Laughs aloud, his heart at peace.
Even the wisest man grows tense
With some sort of violence
Before he can accomplish fate,
Know his work, or choose his mate.

I would only add that to be "fighting mad" in the cause of God does not include hatred of or desire to harm any human being; it is a righteous anger against whatever damages or falsifies the Divine Presence in this world. Among the examples of this Presence may be included the *innocent*, those who are so often exploited, oppressed or victimized by the violent and the powerful. The Love of the Presence in all its manifestations is the root of righteous anger, the justification for it, the criterion that prevents it from getting out of bounds, and the Divine Power that stands behind it.

Third Stage: The Command Begins to Flow

As soon as the First Crisis is past and the Command accepted, power from God begins to shine into the heart and mind and will of the sacred activist. This power, given that it is based on the precise shape of the Command it exists to serve, is inseparable from objective strategic insight; thus it immediately overflows into the situation the activist is called on to work with, throwing light on opportunities for practical action and suggesting viable strategies for making use of them. At this point it is possible to formulate real plans, but since the situation is fluid these plans do not become fixed imperatives. We do not become attached to them as idols, as if they were ends in themselves; rather, we serve God's ongoing Will as it unfolds in the present moment. Yet our obedience to this Will, though it is spontaneous and without resistance, is not impulsive, but rather conscious and deliberate. The time in which it unfolds is not the closed and contracted present moment of passion and reactivity, but the temporal reflection of the Eternal Present, in which the "now" of present time, soberly contemplated, is the clear, central point that defines an open field, filled with past actualities we can learn from and future potentials we can work to realize.

In Aristotelian/Thomistic terms, this is the stage at which *form* and *matter* unite. The more clearly the form of the Command is discerned in relation to its outer field of activity, the greater the availability of the material and human resources necessary to actualize it. These two, the form and the matter, the plan and the resources, arrive together, as needed, over the duration of the Command. In a passage of the Qur'an that I never tire of repeating because it can be applied in so many contexts, *I will show them My signs on the horizons and in their own souls until they are satisfied that this is the Truth. Is it not enough for you, that I am Witness over all things?* [Q. 41:53]. Obviously the form and the matter of the Command will not arrive all at once, but the sense that *the whole thing is already there,* like the figure of the statue yet to be carved that Michelangelo tells us is already hidden in the stone, will be clear enough to let us wait, in faith, for God to act in His own time. As St. Paul put it, "Faith is the substance of things hoped for, the evidence of things not seen" [Hebrews 11:1].

Fourth Stage: Enacting the Command

This is the stage where God places the responsibility for fulfillment of His Command squarely in our own hands. We take firm hold of it and assume full responsibility for it. We don't just say "God is the Doer, so let Him take care of it"; we clearly realize that if we don't do it, nobody will. In the field of Sacred Activism the commands of God are not simply general admonitions, but specific directives issued at specific times to specific individuals; what God has commanded you to do no one else can take responsibility for, nor will it ever be accomplished without you. (Maybe the best literary dramatization of this truth appears in C.S. Lewis' "science fiction" novel **Perelandra.**) Here personal responsibility is obedience, while a false image of God as the only Doer, with ourselves as nothing but His passive puppets, is disobedience. We understand that it is our duty to evaluate our own actions in light of the Command we have received, to do our best to correct any departures from it, to make up for any deficiencies in our commitment to it, and to complete any unfinished tasks which might have been assigned by it. At this point, in addition to praying for guidance, we must also pray for energy, strength and courage.

We must remember, however, that to demand constant reassurances from God before fulfilling the duties He has already laid upon us is a sign of immaturity and imperfect submission, just as to continue to drive ahead in a particular direction when God is sending us sign after sign, both *on the horizons and in ourselves,* indicating that He wants us to change direction, or simply to slow down or stop for a while, is a sign of arrogance and obsession. And, unfortunately, both Divine reassurance and Divine prohibition can be counterfeited by one's unconscious ego, as well as by demonic forces. This is why it is absolutely necessary to possess both a sufficient degree of self-knowledge, along with some level of discernment of spirits, before entering into the levels of Election and Submission which are proper to the cycle of Sacred Action, and to constantly petition God for guidance while operating within it—even (or especially) at the Fourth Stage where personal responsibility is paramount. By the same token, however, we must not let our petitions degenerate into the demand that every twist and turn of the path always be made explicit to us, as if God were some kind of transcendental GPS system. If we have true faith and true submission, we will also have the certainty that Divine Guidance is always there, whether or not we are presently conscious of it. In the words of the poet and astronomer Omar Khayyam:

> Up from earth's center through the seventh gate
> I rose, and on the throne of Saturn sate
> And many a knot unraveled on the road
> But not the master-knot of human fate.
>
> There was a veil through which I might not see
> There was a door to which I found no key
> Some little talk of "me" and "thee" awhile there was
> Then no more talk of thee and me.
>
> Then to the rolling Heaven itself I cried
> What lamp had destiny to guide
> Her little children, stumbling in the dark?
> "A blind understanding," Heaven replied.

Fifth Stage: Recognition of God as the Doer in the Midst of Action

Before our will is fully in line with God's Will, it will appear as if there were two wills, ours and His, and that the lesser one (ours) is called on to submit to the Greater. That things should appear this way is a strict metaphysical necessity, given that the human will is free. But to the degree that this submission becomes complete, the truth that there is only one Will, the Divine Will, is revealed. When the Qur'an says *You cannot will unless Allah wills* [Q. 76:30], this does not mean that God, conceived of as an external force, controls all our actions; it means that whatever we intend or perform necessarily happens as a direct expression of His Will and His Action—in Beauty or in Majesty, in Mercy or in Wrath—from which nothing in His universe can ever depart. If our actions are in line with His wish, then He wills reward; if they are opposed to His wish, then He wills punishment. If God has elected to reward us, then His Command and our obedience to that Command will be inseparable and simultaneous; if he has decreed punishment, then His Command and our resistance to it will be equally simultaneous—necessarily so, because the freedom of the human will is a reflection of the freedom of God Himself; from what other store could that freedom possibly be drawn? This realization that God is the only Doer, not simply as a theoretical postulate but in the context of my own concrete actions, fully owned and enacted in obedience to His Command, along with all the burden of them, places those actions entirely within the flow of Divine Action, my effort within His Effortlessness, my suffering within His Peace, my struggle and *agon* within His Almighty Power: *It was not you who threw when you threw, but Allah threw* [Q. 8:17]. If we are fully willing to carry the task, with no shirking and no excuses, then God will carry us.

Sixth Stage: Discerning the Limit of the Command

The Command to Sacred Action dictates to the activist; it also dictates to the world. Its purpose is to manifest in the world something of God and the metaphysical order, to turn those aspects of the world that fall within its mandate toward God and place them in His service—even if the world is largely not aware that this is being done—and consequently to elevate the world (albeit locally, temporarily and imperfectly) to a higher spiritual station. Shaykh Al-'Arabi al-Darqawi says:

> By God, if we were to leave the world, in the end it would seek us out and find us, as we have sought after it and been unable to find it; it would run after us and come to meet us, as we have run after it and failed to meet it; it would weep over us and we would need to console it, as we have wept for it without finding consolation in it; it would yearn for us and need us, as we have yearned for it when it had no need of us, and so forth. God is our Warrant for what we say. It is said that the world comes, despite itself, to him who is sincere in his asceticism, and that if a cap falls from heaven it will fall on the head of him who does not wish for it.

If, however, we find ourselves seeking the world and running after it, expecting consolation from it, yearning for it etc.—if, instead of us elevating the world, the world drags us down—then either God's command to us has reached limit of its manifestation, while we have failed to discern or observe that limit, or else we have deviated from His Command and betrayed it.

Some say "the end justifies the means"; others maintain that false or evil means can never produce a true or sacred end; the author of this book holds with the latter perspective. Applying pressure, exercising cunning, wooing the reluctant—power in its various guises—all have their place in Sacred Activism. But when applying pressure becomes oppression, when cunning becomes lying, when wooing becomes seduction, when Divine Power becomes self-will, then we have switched masters; we are no longer servants of God but slaves to the *Dunya*.

If we take the *Dunya* as our master, we will become angry or despondent if things do not always go our way. We will beat our heads against wall after wall. We will start to ask "what's in it for me?" We will discover that some of our well-intentioned interventions have actually made things worse rather than better. If we are courted by the rich and powerful of this world, we will respond to that courtship. We will misinterpret various attempts by the ruling elites to co-opt and neutralize us as signs that our influence is growing, if not as indications that we ourselves have been admitted into those elites. We will become susceptible to flattery. We will take God's Command as a sign of our justification and a license to do as we will, but we will forget to submit each new decision to His judgment. We will mis-read the bribes offered by the *Dunya* as God's rewards for our faithful service. Certainly God can send us help through material conditions, and allies who are powerful in worldly terms can be very useful—but only a powerful Divine Command that is still fully in force, and that we consciously recognize, can prevent such obvious benefits from turning into liabilities.

If we are able to resist these temptations and remain in the center of the Divine Will, we may find that our mandate from God appears to be drawing to a close in objective terms. The world's capacity to absorb the Command we have been serving has reached its limit. Doors that opened at a touch now resist much greater pressure. Opportunities for effective action arrive in fewer and fewer numbers. This may simply represent a pause in the flow of Sacred Action for the purpose of rest, re-evaluation and renewal, or it may be God's way of saving us from walking into a minefield, some hidden danger that will later come to light. But it may also be a sign that the present cycle of action is drawing to a close.

Here is where the Command may take the form of: "Don't seek to acquire new territory, but consolidate what you have." If your mandate includes the founding of an ongoing organization, then your duties will begin to include organizational development, fundraising, administration etc. Things will settle onto a more even keel. The Moral level of action will begin to take over from the levels of Election and Submission. The form that God has willed to bring into the world will have found its place in the world, and will continue to spread a beneficent influence.

On the other hand, if your mandate does not include the administration of a particular territory, then it is time to let the responsibility for such administration naturally pass into other hands. Of course something will be lost in the process; the virtues of preservation and stable administration do not exhibit the power and numinosity of the earlier campaigns, when it seemed as if the heavens opened every day. Nonetheless, this is as it should be.

If we have been commanded to open a particular territory but not to administer it, then it is time to turn the fruits of our spiritual labor over to those commanded to preserve and guard it—recognizing that, in doing so, we are dedicating this labor to God in the clearest and most concrete of terms. We need to be certain, however, that we are really called to do this, that we aren't simply shirking our responsibility to God because we resist His assignment to us of more prosaic duties. But if it becomes clear that the torch has been passed, then we need to resign, with grace and humility, and bless the coming generation. And to the degree that the Command now passing has taken us out into the world, the Command now arriving may carry us an equal distance into the inner world. Once the prophet Muhammad (peace and blessings upon him), after returning with his warriors from battle, said to them: "Now we return from the Lesser Jihad to the Greater Jihad." "What is the Greater Jihad, O

Prophet?" they asked him. "The war against the soul," he answered. "The soul" here refers to the lower self, the ego; the renunciation of the identity of Holy Warrior before the eyes of the world, and the eyes of our brothers and sisters in Sacred Action, is one of the greatest and most effective sacrifices the sacred activist can make; it is nothing less than the Key to the Heart. Here is where the merit gained in the outer struggle can be turned to the cause of the inner one. This ego, the reality that the Sufis call the *nafs al-ammara b'l su*, "the soul commanding to evil," is the seed and root of the *Dunya*. We will never be able to win the war against evil on the field of the Outer, at least in any stable and ongoing way; "politics is the art of the ephemeral." But on the field of the Inner, with the help of God, that war can be won. The sun sets in the West but rises in the East; consequently the Inner takes precedence.

Seventh Stage: Releasing the Residues of Action

This is the point where the expansion that began at Stage Three starts to contract, and where the scattering of energy and multiplication of attention accompanying that expansion begin to be gathered together again, re-centered, recollected. This requires a degree of suffering. In the midst of action and at the height of battle, God's Will and mine were one. But now, as the Command recedes and the manifestation of God's Power in the world, in terms of the particular Command I have received, begins to move into its twilight, my will appears again as a separate factor, one that is seen to be dissipated through identification with many things, persons and situations, and one that, insofar as it resists letting go of these identifications—the hopes, the plans, the self-congratulations, the regrets—is revealed to be in a state of self-will. Each time an identification with a particular thing, person or situation in the outer material world, or a particular self-image in the inner psychic one, is released, an element of that self-will is deconstructed, and our submission to God goes one step deeper. The many projections we had made upon various conditions we had been working with are progressively taken back, and our true human self reconstituted and unveiled, in the understanding that we are not defined by what we do, but rather by who we are in the sight of God. Identification with action is traded for repose in being. And as the projections are withdrawn into the Spiritual Heart, the residues of action are released. These residues are the spent ashes of self-will, the blind momentum of actions whose impulse has gone beyond their original reason for being and the bounds of the Command that gave them birth. Since nothing is destined to come of these fading impulses, the best thing is simply to let them fade. This, however, cannot be completed without making a conscious sacrifice of them to God, and renouncing all claim to them. The point at which this sacrifice presents itself as the next necessary step is the Second Crisis, the crisis of Anger. How wonderful it was, how seemingly effortless, to swim in the center of the deep stream of God's Will, fully backed up—and most of all, fully *justified*—by His Knowledge and His Power. To be asked to give all this up (as if it hadn't already largely withdrawn on its own), to be forced to renounce all our cherished privileges, will confront us like nothing else with whatever remains in our soul of the passion and sin of anger. As Divine Power withdraws, self-will imperceptibly takes its place—and there is nothing weaker than self-will. Therefore if we hope to avoid the maddening frustration of beating our heads bloody against the stone wall of God's Will, we had better renounce self-will as soon and as completely as possible: "not my will but Thine be done" [Luke 22:42]. And the best hour at which to begin this process of renunciation is at the hour of victory. It is hard to discern, due to the exaltation of the moment, the exact point where the wave crests and begins to subside; after all, who wants to be a "wet blanket" by pointing out that such exaltation cannot last? However, as is symbolically expressed in certain traditional forms of execution, including the Crucifixion of Christ, noon is the hour of death. (Christ's "victory" was Palm Sunday; He did not renounce it at that point, but lived out the full consequences of it, because it was His mission to suffer and die for the sins of the human race.) To fail to discern the first signs of decline and decay is to make oneself vulnerable to them farther down the line, whereas if we anticipate them and withdraw in time, many of their consequences can be avoided. When a victorious Roman general was voted a triumph by the Senate, allowing him to parade himself, his heroic troops, his plundered booty and his captured slaves before cheering crowds, preceded by the high-born maidens of Rome scattering petals of roses, standing next to him in his triumphal chariot was a slave, who whispered to him: "Remember, glory is fleeting; death comes to all."

The Taoists were wiser. In the words of Lao Tzu:

> Weapons are instruments of fear; they are not a
>   wise man's tools.
> He uses them only when he has no choice.
> Peace and quiet are dear to his heart,
> And victory no cause for rejoicing.
> If you rejoice in victory, then you delight in killing;
> If you delight in killing, you cannot fulfill yourself.
> On happy occasions precedence is given to the left,
> On sad occasions to the right.
> In the army the general stands on the left,
> The commander-in-chief on the right.
> This means that war is conducted like a funeral.
> When many people are being killed,
> They should be mourned in heartfelt sorrow.
> That is why a victory must be observed like a funeral.

The moment of triumph is the time when it is hardest to remember that only God is the Doer; therefore it is the most crucial time, and the best time. Much good will come from renunciation of self-will and self-satisfaction at the moment of victory. To triumph is to demand from the world what only God can give; to renounce triumph is to be granted a secret mercy from the hand of the Friend.

The renunciation of triumph helps us see the need to release the residues of action on deeper and deeper levels. If the Lesser Jihad must serve the Greater one on pain of being no jihad at all, then the task laid by God on the sacred activist must serve the needs of his or her soul as well as those of the worldly situation the activist is commanded to engage with. Consequently the release of the residues of a given action will likely also catalyze the release of certain deeply-buried residues of past actions. Sometimes a person will understand that he is in debt to God, and that this debt is so great that he will never be able to pay it, even through the labor and sacrifice of a lifetime. In such cases, God in His Mercy may "hire" the one owing that debt for the purpose of letting him "work it off." This is how a work of Sacred Activism, God willing, may allow the activist to release the burden of past transgressions, omissions and delusions. A prophet, a bodhisattva, a fully-enlightened being may come into this world as a total expression of God's Mercy, but most of us are born in a state of debt, called by the Hindus and Buddhists "karma," by the Christians "original sin," and by the Muslims "forgetfulness." Consequently our life here is designed by the Creator to provide us with opportunities to satisfy that debt. God has created us purely out of Mercy; this is why we owe Him what might be called *the debt of our existence*, which we can only pay back by offering ourselves to Him unreservedly, to dispose of as He wills.

However, in order to truly release to God one's attachments to self-will and the residues of past actions, it is first necessary to *find* them—to dig down through layer upon layer of reactivity and forgetfulness and distraction until you reach the exact point where you are holding on, and see precisely what you are holding on to. Until that point is reached, the common admonishment to "just let it go" has little meaning. I imagine a cartoon (maybe somebody can draw it) where a bear has hold of a man's leg; sitting next to them in a chair is the Freud-like figure of a psychiatrist with a notebook, who intones: "Let the bear go . . . it's time to let go . . . let it go now. . . ."—to which the other man replies, "Sure, Doctor—*but tell that to the bear.*" Until we reach the real place where we are holding on, until we become fully aware of our actual *intent* to hold on, which until now had been largely unconscious, our intent to submit to God's Will, no matter how sincere it may be, remains merely secondary and has little immediate effect. An abstract, blanket intent to follow the Will of God may be better than nothing, but nothing much of a substantive nature will be accomplished until one's *will to rebel against that Will* has been found, and confronted, and renounced. There is nothing we can effectively sacrifice as a *substitute* for the ego; we must sacrifice the ego itself—and to do this, we need to find out where our ego actually lives, name our true idols, discern and admit what we are really attached to. Spiritual literature and pop psychology alike present us with many myths and legends of what the sacrifice of attachments might look like; consequently it is all too easy to make a theatrical sacrifice so as to avoid going through with the real one, sacrificing money when what we are really attached to is fame, sacrificing fame when what we are really attached to is self-involved isolation, sacrificing romantic attraction when what we are really attached to is power. Religious cultures who practiced blood sacrifice always selected the most perfect victim for the rite; when this practice degenerated, when animal sacrifice began to be seen as an easy way to get rid of the runt of the litter while still appearing pious, that culture was on its way out. Likewise in those archaic civilizations that allowed human sacrifice, the practice of offering living human beings to the Divine Order began as *self*-sacrifice. Later the sacrificial dispensation devolved into the sacrifice of a pure victim chosen by the priests—a victim who nonetheless considered his election a great privilege. The next step on the downward path involved the sacrifice of an acceptable victim, albeit against his will. And the final degeneration arrived when human sacrifice became no more than a convenient method for disposing of prisoners of war, unwanted infants, criminals and riff-raff; this often resulted, as with the Aztecs, in quantity taking the place of quality. But self-sacrifice remained the invisible origin and archetype of the whole rite—and the essence of self-sacrifice is not sacrifice of the body, but sacrifice of the *ego*. Our ego, our cherished self-will, is the one thing we most fear to let go of, so much so that we will sometimes sacrifice our lives in hopes of holding on to it. But—as ought to be perfectly obvious—to throw our lives away because we fear to confront our essential rebellion against God is the most foolish and destructive act imaginable.

The release of the residues of past action can be understood according to the metaphors of the overcoming of addiction, and of psychic or physical purification. *After* the central attachments produced by the cycle of action now coming to a close have been discovered and consciously sacrificed on the level of the *Spirit*, various techniques for the detoxification of the *psyche* and the *body* may prove useful. If the sacred activist has found certain methods such as fasting or retreat or reiki or the sweat lodge useful in the past, now would be a good time to use them—but only *after* the fundamental sacrifice to God has been made: the sacrifice of self-will.

Eighth Stage: Receptivity to the Next Announcement

As soon as one cycle ends, another begins, though there will generally be an "interregnum" between them, a period of latency, rest, and secret germination. The succeeding cycle may manifest as a renewal and re-authorization of the last one, or it may appear as something entirely different. One cycle may manifest in the Outer, another in the Inner. One may be of collective import, another entirely personal. One may take the form of contemplation in the context of action, another of action in the context of contemplation. At this point we must be careful to avoid the common temptation to expect or ask God for more of the same, forgetting that the All-Merciful never repeats Himself; in the words of the Qur'an, *Every day doth some new work employ Him* [Q. 55:29]. If we succumb to this temptation it is a sign of ego identification with the previous cycle, indicating that our release of the residues of the actions of that cycle is not yet complete. As William Blake put it, "More! More! is the cry of a mistaken soul; less than All can never satisfy man." Suffice it to say that we cannot become still enough to be receptive to the announcement of God's next Command to us, or silent enough to hear His "still, small voice," if we are still making demands. All that is over now. No dramatic Command from God may ever come again—and that in itself is a Command: a Command to patience, simplicity, resignation, and contentment. In the *I Ching*, the hexagram relating to this stage, the one indicating the beginning and end of all action, is number 52, "Keeping Still," whose image is the mountain. The judgment attached to that Hexagram is as follows:

> Keeping his back still
> So that he no longer feels his body,
> He goes into his courtyard
> And does not see his people.
> No blame.

The "courtyard," here, is a symbol of the Spiritual Heart.

To Conclude

Sacred Activism is one of the several ways provided by God for fully confronting life in these Latter Days. It is not the only way. The activist must guard against developing the ego of the proud warrior who scorns the cowardly civilians, forgetting in the process that those "civilians" are his or her main responsibility—because the essential work of Sacred Activism is: to defend the *humanity* of the human race. In the words of the surah *An-Nas*, the last surah of the Qur'an:

In the name of Allah, the Beneficent, the Merciful.
Say: I seek refuge in the Lord of mankind,
The King of mankind,
The God of mankind,
From the evil of the sneaking whisperer,
Who whispereth in the hearts of mankind,
Of the jinn and of mankind.

This surah directs us to turn to the specifically *human* face of God, the site of the Archetype of Man *in divinis*, so as to resist the darkest temptation of the end times: the temptation to renounce the Human Form.

∽

The schematic presentation of Sacred Activism in this section has all the strengths and all the weaknesses of most schematic presentations. *Schemata* can be very useful in throwing light on certain forms of truth which otherwise might appear random or chaotic, but they should never be taken literally or applied mechanically. The Thing Itself is always more subtle, more unpredictable, and more stunningly appropriate than words can catch. Sacred Activism is not a *technique*; how could it be, if God is the only Doer? It is a possibility that is available only to those who have dedicated their lives to the path of self-transcendence.

This begs the questions: "What is self-transcendence? How is it accomplished?" Self-transcendence can be defined as a condition in which one no longer takes oneself as a possession, no longer reserves the right to dispose of oneself however one wishes, because one's attention is fixed upon the Creator, not the creature, upon the Essence, not the form. As for how self-transcendence is to be accomplished, the safest and most conservative answer is: through finding and devoting oneself to the inner Essence of any of the world's great religions, otherwise known as the Spiritual Path. But since this resource may not be available to everyone, it is also necessary to give a more open-ended answer: that self-transcendence is the pursuit of, and devotion of oneself to, the highest Reality—however that Reality may be conceived—as long as it is understood that such transcendence cannot be achieved through any course of *self-directed self-development*, since transcendence-of-self is the Way as well as the Goal; nor through the pursuit of psychic powers; nor by means of any "religion" where "getting what you want and avoiding what you fear" are the primary goals. Anyone who knows for certain that he or she has achieved at least a degree of self-transcendence may consider the way of Sacred Activism; those who have not had better leave it alone. I am fully aware that not everyone will be able to take or understand this kind of advice, and consequently that what I have written may result in a number of melodramas that will at least be valuable as object lessons to outside observers. To propose Sacred Activism in times as dark as these is an extremely radical and dicey proposition; it is part and parcel of the mass revelation of esoteric doctrine that characterizes the Latter Days—a revelation sent to a world that, except for certain brilliant and providential exceptions, can in no way assimilate it, and which will therefore be judged by it.

As for a fitting motto and battle-cry for Sacred Activism, a number of stirring phrases come to mind. In my opinion, however, the best and most suitable of all might simply be: *Stay Human*. Until death overtakes us, and the final fruits of our labors are harvested God's sight, that's the work.

PART THREE:
SACRED ACTIVISM, UNITED FRONT ECUMENISM, AND THE ATTACK ON RELIGION

Had not God repelled some people by the might of others, the monasteries, churches, synagogues, and mosques in which God's praise is celebrated daily, would have been utterly demolished. God will certainly help those who help His cause. . . . [Q.22:40–41]

Traditionalist Ecumenism

Integral Traditionalism, springing from René Guénon and Ananda Kentish Coomaraswamy and passing, in the Anglo-Swiss-American line, to Frithjof Schuon, Martin Lings, Titus Burckhardt, Marco Pallis, Whitall Perry, Charles LeGai Eaton, Seyyed Hossein Nasr and others, has never defined Traditionalist doctrine as something translatable into political ideology. The Traditionalist School as I have known it generally preaches withdrawal from the world, and the a-political and world-renouncing aspects of Traditionalism are certainly in line with the contemplative traditions of all the world religions, and the metaphysical doctrines that inform and support them.[1] If Traditionalism is "against the modern world" (as the title of Mark Sedgwick's book on the Traditionalist School implies) it is primarily because—at least theoretically—it is against the *world* per se, in precisely the sense Jesus intended when he said, "my kingdom is not of this world" [John 18:36].

On the other hand, now that the names "Guénon" and "Traditionalism" have

---

1. Zachary Markwith, however, in his article "The Politics of the Maryamiyya Sufi Order: Between Quietism and Collusion" (paper presented at the Transnational Sufism in Contemporary Societies Conference, Venice, November 10, 2017) details the many liaisons between several Traditionalist figures—notably Martin Lings, Seyyed Hossein Nasr and Nasr's immediate circle—and various Muslim potentates, as well as such notable members of the elites as past-CIA-director Richard Helms, Henry Kissinger, and—Aleksandr Dugin.

begun to gain wider currency in various political movements of the extreme Right, most particularly Aleksandr Dugin's "Neo-Eurasianism"—that is, in movements that are opposed to nearly everything René Guénon stood for— then Integral Traditionalism must respond. But is it enough to simply demonstrate, in a few well-chosen words, why Aleksandr Dugin is not a Traditionalist, as Anton Shekhovtsov and Andreas Umland have done in their important article "Is Aleksandr Dugin a Traditionalist? 'Neo-Eurasianism' and Perennial Philosophy"? Is it enough merely to disown him, to disclaim him, to rise above him?[2] We Integral Traditionalists have opted to take refuge in the *batin*, the Inner, and leave the *zahir*, the Outer, to those who (we believe) will never understand us, and who therefore, in our rather self-involved view, are not worthy to associate with us. But what if those "others," worthy or not, begin raiding our storehouses and burning our crops? In my considered opinion, the incursions of such poachers and cattle rustlers call for a much more vigorous response. Therefore I have posed the question: "Is there such a thing as a legitimate, outward, socio-political expression of Integral Traditionalism and its central doctrine, the Transcendent Unity of Religions? If the organizations and movements of those Traditionalists who claim to base their political ideologies in part on the writings of René Guénon—Conservative Revolution; the European New Right; those who identify with Julius Evola's Warrior-Initiation; certain schools of political Neo-Paganism; and Aleksandr Dugin's Neo-Eurasianism—do not truly represent Guénon's and Coomaraswamy's and Schuon's doctrines in the world of action, then what would?"

Most of my colleagues in the Traditionalist School in the English-speaking world have long resigned themselves to social marginalization, willingly accepted their apparent duty to keep the lamp of Traditional Metaphysics burning, even though they might have to hide it under a bushel basket to prevent it from being snuffed out by the Darkness of This World. That some version of Traditionalist doctrine, which we had considered to be essentially a-political, could suddenly rise to prominence in the United States, Russia and elsewhere in terms of various political ideologies, has come as a real shock to many of us. Our surprise can partly be explained by the de-emphasis of Julius Evola in our branch of Traditionalism, since Evola has been the main road for many toward a political application, legitimate or otherwise, of Guénon's ideas. Suffice it to say that, after my last period of peace activism in the 1980s, I had sincerely believed that my activist days were over, since I saw every campaign to promote

---

2. A more comprehensive critique of Dugin's philosophy, by "Malic´," appeared in 2015 on the Kali Tribune website, "Against the Gnostics: Anti-Traditional and Anti-Christian Core of Alexander Dugin's 4th Political Theory": http://en.kalitribune.com/against-the-gnostics-anti-traditional-and-anti-christian-core-of-alexander-dugins-4th-political-theory/.

peace and social justice that was visible on my radar screen as shot through with terminal contradictions, and therefore likely to do more harm than good. All this changed, however, in 2013, when *The Covenants of the Prophet Muhammad with the Christians of the World* and the Covenants Initiative came into my life. I immediately saw this development as heralding the very outer, socio-political expression of the Transcendent Unity of Religions that I had been searching for, one that was not based on an illegitimate diversion of Guénonian metaphysics in the direction of political ideology such as Baron Julius Evola had initiated, but rather on an intrinsic solidarity of the God-given faiths in the face of a secular world that is dedicated to co-opting and/or destroying them.

United Front Ecumenism

In my book *The System of Antichrist* I posited a "United Front Ecumenism" as an alternative to the "promiscuous Liberal ecumenism" that erodes fundamental doctrinal differences in the name of overcoming "divisiveness," subtly promotes syncretism, and consequently works toward the creation of a One-World Religion:

> The doctrines of the Traditionalist School ... demonstrate that the great revealed religions of the world—Hinduism, Buddhism, Judaism, Christianity, and Islam—have more intrinsic affinity with each other, infinitely more, than any one of them has with Neo-Paganism or the New Age—certain more or less ironic social trends notwithstanding. A liberal ecumenism which ignores or compromises doctrine is only destructive to the cause of religion. A united front ecumenism, which would work toward a common understanding among the revealed religions of the spiritual, cultural and intellectual forces which menace all of them—not least of which are Postmodernism, globalism, militant ethnic and religious separatism, Neo-Pagan and New Age doctrines—and do so without empty fraternization or limp doctrinal compromise, is a much more fruitful possibility. Such an inter-religious understanding would include not merely a respect for theological differences but a mutual will to accentuate doctrinal particularities: let the Jews be more Jewish, the Christians more Christian, the Hindus more Hindu, the Buddhists more Buddhist, the Muslims more Muslim, in the realization that the One Truth can be approached only through the particular forms of Divine revelation, not through whatever lowest ethical or doctrinal common denominator all the religions might be able to agree upon—and whatever quasi-political "oversight committee" might emerge, via the United Religions Initiative or some similar attempt, in the name of it. The basis of such an understanding would be the principle that Frithjof Schuon called The Transcendent Unity of Religions, according to which the paths represented by the

various orthodox revelations can finally meet only on the plane of the Transcendent, only in God Himself.

This doctrine, unfortunately, is highly susceptible to misinterpretation, that being one of its eschatological features: it must be announced, and it must—at least by some—be misinterpreted.... According to Schuon ... the fact that more than one religion is necessary in this manifest world is also an esoteric truth, which is why he characterizes the various Divine revelations as "relatively Absolute." In *Christianity/Islam: Essays in Esoteric Ecumenism*, he says:

> Every religion by definition wants to be the best, and "must want" to be the best, as a whole and also as regards its constitutive elements; this is only natural, so to speak, or rather "supernaturally natural" ... religious oppositions cannot but be, not only because forms exclude one another ... but because, in the case of religions, each form vehicles an element of absoluteness that constitutes the justification for its existence; now the absolute does not tolerate otherness nor, with all the more reason, plurality.... To say form is to say exclusion of possibilities, whence the necessity for those excluded to become realized in other forms.... (p. 151)

The primary purpose of a united front ecumenism would be to oppose *both* globalist syncretism and militant ethnic/religious separatism, not necessarily in any high-profile way—unless God wills otherwise, and who is to say He won't?—in order to help the traditional religions purify their doctrines from the influence of them. Little can perhaps be done to reverse the degeneration of religion on a collective level, but it is still possible, and certainly worthwhile, to more clearly define the real parting of the ways between the Transcendent Unity of Religions and a globalist syncretism which is emphatically not an expression of the unity-in-multiplicity of God's self-revelation, but the mere ape of it—a counterfeit contrived in the cleverness of the human mind attempting to operate beyond the bounds of that revelation, in the darkness outside.

In addition, in *Vectors of the Counter-Initiation* I characterized the established Interfaith Movement as being in many ways a counterfeit version of United Front Ecumenism and the Transcendent Unity of Religions; in doing so, I asserted three things:

1) The global elites are committed to moving the world toward one or another form or degree of "global governance."

2) The Interfaith Movement represents an important element in the push for global governance as envisioned by the elites, or at least by many influential individuals and institutions among them.

3) Through the Interfaith Movement and other venues, the global elites support ever-increasing secular control of the world religions; some elements at

least loosely associated with these elites are concurrently doing "research and development" with a view to establishing a single, unified One World Religion.

I also warned in that book against the "globalist agenda . . . the ultimate goal of [*which*] in the religious sphere appears to be the federation of the traditional religions under a non-religious authority." Assuming that Aleksandr Dugin has read my books—which is a fair assumption, since as far as I know I am the only Traditionalist writer in the English-speaking world who has seriously tried to apply René Guénon's "dialectic of apocalypse" to contemporary social analysis, though Martin Lings did much of the groundwork in his book *The Eleventh Hour*—I may have influenced him to come up with his own brand of "United Front Ecumenism," though it is equally possible that he simply drew his own conclusions from Guénon's writings—conclusions which are in some ways quite similar to my own, in other ways radically different.

In *Eurasian Mission* Dugin says:

> There are secularized cultures, but at the core of all of them, the spirit of Tradition remains, religious or otherwise. By defending the multiplicity, plurality and polycentrism of cultures, we are making an appeal to the principles of their essences, which we can only find in the spiritual traditions. But we try to link this attitude to the necessity for social justice and the freedom of differing societies in the hope for better political regimes. The idea is to join the spirit of Tradition with the desire for social justice.

I agree with this completely—especially since we have now entered an age when the national and global elites—as the Second Vatican Council made clear—have definitively withdrawn their sponsorship (though not their attempt to control) from Traditional religion and transformed it to anti-Traditional "progressive" religion, as well as to the crypto-modernism of the reactionary "fundamentalists." However, Dugin goes on to say:

> And we don't want to oppose [*Tradition to social justice*] because that is the main strategy of hegemonic power: to divide Left and Right, to divide cultures, to divide ethnic groups, East and West, Muslims and Christians. We invite Right and Left to unite, and not to oppose traditionalism and spirituality [*to*] social justice and social dynamism. So we are not on the Right or on the Left. We are against liberal postmodernity. Our idea is to join all the fronts and not let them divide us. When we stay divided, they can rule us safely. If we are united, their rule will immediately end. That is our global strategy. And when we try to join the spiritual tradition with social justice, there is an immediate panic among liberals. They fear this very much. . . .
>
> What we are against will unite us, while what we are for divides us. Therefore, we should emphasise what we oppose. The common enemy unites us, while the positive values each of us are defending actually divide us. There-

fore, we must create strategic alliances to overthrow the present order of things, of which the core could be described as human rights, anti-hierarchy, and political correctness—everything that is the face of the Beast, the anti-Christ or, in other terms, *Kali-yuga*.

These passages from *Eurasian Mission* bear an uncomfortable resemblance to those, quoted above, on the United Front Ecumenism that I proposed in *The System of Antichrist*, at least insofar as they are applicable specifically to the religions and not to the secular political spectrum. They appear similar, and yet there is a fundamental difference between them that might not be immediately apparent. In my conception, the religions are "united by a common enemy" only insofar as the hatred of this enemy for all the revealed religions testifies to their Transcendent Unity. I emphatically do not agree that "the positive values that each of us are defending actually divide us"; if that were the case, the many religions would not be able to testify, from their differing perspectives, to the One Reality. Certain elements of those differing perspectives are providentially irreducible; were it not for this, the multiplicity of religions necessary for the full Self-Revelation of God in human history would not be supportable, or would never have appeared. But beyond these necessarily irreducible elements, the religions have much in common both doctrinally and morally. Dugin, however, posits an intrinsic enmity between the religions that, in the absence of a common enemy that could bring them together into an alliance of convenience, would necessary result—if and when that enemy were defeated—in total war between them, a war of mutual annihilation. In reality, however, the religions are not united by what they are against except insofar as the attacks of their common enemy testify to their Transcendent Unity. That enemy has risen against them out of hatred for their common Essence—an Essence that, though it transcends any possibility of explicit doctrinal unification in the realm of theology, unites them metaphysically, not by what they are against but by what they *are*, this being the several primary Self-revelations of God to man. The Covenants of the Prophet Muhammad are eloquent testimony to this principle. That Aleksandr Dugin, one of whose characteristic philosophical practices is to invert whatever fundamental religious or metaphysical principles he can get his hands on, has taken the trouble to invert the Transcendent Unity of Religions, is powerful testimony to the truth of that doctrine.

Furthermore, YOU CAN'T "OVERTHROW" THE *KALI-YUGA*, any more than you can prevent the sun from setting by holding it at gunpoint. To believe this is to contradict René Guénon, the Hindu *Puranas*, and every other traditional eschatology. What can be done is to form a Traditionalist Remnant oriented to the *parousia*, as will be explained in the next chapter.

Dugin and Jihadism; Dugin and Sufism

The passage from *Eurasian Mission* quoted above continues in an ominous direction:

> the main strategy of hegemonic power [*is*] to divide Left and Right, to divide cultures, to divide ethnic groups, East and West, Muslims and Christians. We invite Right and Left to unite, and not to oppose traditionalism and spirituality, social justice and social dynamism. So we are not on the Right or on the Left. We are against liberal postmodernity. Our idea is to join all the fronts, and not let them divide us.... Jihadis are universalists.... We don't like any universalists, but there are universalists [*i.e., the western Liberal hegemony*] who attack us today and win, and there are also non-conformist universalists who are fighting against the hegemony of the Western, liberal universalists, and therefore they are tactical friends for the time being.... I don't like Salafists. It would be much better to align with traditionalist Sufis, for example. But I prefer working with the Salafists against the common enemy than to waste energy in fighting against them while ignoring the greater threat....

Here is where Dugin and I abruptly part company, on a number of fronts. On the first front, he lumps the world's religions together with all sorts of secular, pseudo-religious and anti-religious forces—including the jihadis, who for the most part are phony Muslims who massacre both Christians and their fellow Muslims indiscriminately, and who—judging from their actions, which speak much more loudly than their words—mortally hate the Prophet Muhammad, peace and blessings be upon him, and reject the norms of the Holy Qur'an, not to mention the fact that their ranks are filled with mercenaries from the four corners of the earth, and the further fact that they are willing to take arms, funds and logistical if not strategic direction from the Western nations, especially the United States, in the proxy war of the West against Russia and Iran, just as they have been doing ever since the British supported the Wahhabi insurgency against the Ottoman Empire before World War I. In the quoted passages, published in 2014, Dugin is obviously bidding, in the name of Russia, against the U.S. for control of the Salafists in Syria and Iraq (and possibly also trying to turn the Chechen rebels against the U.S. instead of Russia, if such a thing were possible). He is also sending out trial balloons to see if he can catch any Sufis in his net, which may mean that he may also be bidding against the CIA, possibly in the name of the Russian intelligence forces, for the allegiance of the Sufi orders, seeing that a clandestine spy-war has been going on for some time Central Asia—in Uzbekistan, for example—between Russian intelligence and the CIA, in which certain Sufi groups figure prominently, most particularly the Naqshbandi Order, whose membership numbers in the tens of millions.[3] One would have thought that no Sufi would be caught dead having any dealings with Aleksandr Dugin, a man who, at least as of 2014 (if not 2017), expressed his willingness to fight alongside the Salafi Jihadists, seeing that the Salafi/Takfiris universally consider the Sufis to be heretics and have been massacring them for generations. Nonetheless, worldly power—or at least worldly recognition—remains a powerful temptation. And it should be obvious that for Dugin to say "It would be better to align with the Sufis; nonetheless I am willing to work with the Salafis if necessary" is for him, in effect, to *threaten* to align with the Salafis, to whom the blood of any Sufi is considered *halal*, unless the Sufis get in line. My policy towards such implied threats is based on my belief that, while self-justification may be a sin in the world of *tasawwuf*, self-defense is not.

The attempt to bring the Islamicist Jihadists into the Neo-Eurasian Movement—that is, to place them under the control of Russia—has been part of Dugin's agenda for some time. In the English version of *The Fourth Political Theory*, published in 2012, Dugin says:

> The most recognised form at present [*for the rejection of globalization*] is the Islamist world vision, which aspires toward the utopia of an individual state based upon a strict interpretation of Islamic law, or else a Universal Caliphate which will bring the entire world under Islamic rule. This project is as much opposed to the American-led transitional [*transitional to globalism*] architecture as it is to the existing status quo of modern nation-states. Osama bin Laden's Al-Qaeda remains symbolic and archetypal of such ideas, and the attacks which brought down the towers of the World Trade Centre in New York on 9/11, and which are supposed to have "changed the world," are proof of the importance of such networks.

Here is where we must decide whether this passage represents abysmal ignorance or crass misrepresentation of the truth. I vote for the latter. In August of 2012, a Defense Intelligence Agency document was obtained by the investigative group Judicial Watch, through a lawsuit pursuant to the Freedom of Information Act, which makes it clear that the creation of a Salafist State in Syria along the lines of ISIS is exactly what the powers supporting the anti-Assad opposition wanted. Below is Section 8, paragraph C of that document, probably the most relevant passage:

> If the situation unravels there is the possibility of establishing a declared or undeclared Salafist principality in eastern Syria (Hasaka and Der Zor), and this is exactly what the supporting powers to the opposition want, in order to

---

3. See "Sufi Muslim Council a Karimov/CIA Front" by Craig Murray, former British ambassador to Uzbekistan, at https://www.craigmurray.org.uk/archives/2009/03/sufi_muslim_cou/.

isolate the Syrian regime, which is considered the strategic depth of Shia expansion (Iraq and Iran).[4]

This "principality" is obviously what went on to become the so-called Islamic State. The story of U.S. support for the creation of ISIS is told by Seumas Milne in his June 2015 article in the *Guardian*, "Now the truth emerges: how the U.S. fuelled the rise of ISIS In Syria and Iraq."[5] My colleague Dr. John Andrew Morrow was denouncing ISIS at the House of Lords in London in the summer of 2013, after their Satanic nature had become abundantly clear based on their own "public relations" campaign. Dugin probably could not have foreseen the rise of ISIS in 2009 when *The Fourth Political Theory* first appeared— though the so-called "Arab Spring" began soon after, in December of 2010—but by 2012 when the English version was published it should have been obvious to those knowledgeable in international affairs that the U.S. was backing Islamicist terrorism. It was also common knowledge by that time that the U.S. had armed and organized al-Qaeda to fight the *Russian* invasion of Afghanistan (1979–1989). Also available was over a decade of mounting evidence that both the United States and Israel had a hand in the attack on the Twin Towers on September 11, 2001, in order to justify the massive U.S. intervention in the Mid-East that followed in short order, obviously according to plans that were already in place. Maybe Dugin was just a little slow, not quite paying attention, dreaming of his Hyperborean Eurasia with his head in the clouds; maybe Russian intelligence had been asleep at the wheel for 30 years. Or, as is much more likely, maybe Russia was still placing bids against the United States for the services of the Wahhabi/Salafi terrorists as of 2012. Perhaps some are still naïve enough to believe that ISIS and al-Qaeda broke free from U.S. control at one point, switched sides and suddenly became "opposed to the American-led transitional architecture" in the name of Islam. This version of events ignores a number of realities: 1) that the destabilization of the Mid-East brought about by ISIS, al-Qaeda and the battle against them by the U.S. led coalition perfectly serves the process of globalization by preventing the growth of strong national entities in the region, reducing it to an outlaw area of failed states that require ongoing outside intervention to keep them contained; 2) that in November of 2017, the U.S. granted safe-conduct to ISIS fighters out of Raqqa in Syria just as the city was about to fall—these privileged personages undoubtedly representing the leadership, the elite mercenaries on the U.S. payroll, not the expendable

---

4. The entire text is available at http://www.judicialwatch.org/wp-content/uploads/2015/05/Pg.-291-Pgs.-287-293-JW-v-DOD-and-State-14-812-DOD-Release-2015-04-10-final-version11.pdf.

5. https://www.theguardian.com/commentisfree/2015/jun/03/us-isis-syria-iraq?CMP=share_btn_fb.

lower tier cannon fodder made up of gullible true believers;[6] this means either that Donald Trump had been turned from his initial intention to destroy ISIS, or that he was never firm in that intention to begin with, or that he is not in effective control of all aspects of the military and this outcome simply represents the best "deal" be could make; 3) that it is a firm principle in American foreign policy that the U.S. always betrays its puppets—we call it "the Noriega Syndrome." In view of these facts it is extremely interesting that Aleksandr Dugin and the leadership of the United States are unanimous in propagating the lie that the Islamicist Jihadists are dedicated fighters for Dar al-Islam against the West, instead of what they really are: a fifth column of mercenaries and traitors largely organized by the West to destroy Islam in its ancient heartlands. This unanimity of propaganda between Dugin and the U.S. military and State Department suggests—though it does not prove—a covert strategic collusion on the highest levels, possibly global in scope. However, *Eurasian Mission* and *The Fourth Political Theory* were published before the game-changing Grozny Declaration appeared. In August 2016, at a conference in Chechnya sponsored by Russia, a group *fatwa* was issued by a number of Grand Muftis, including the Grand Shaykh of al-Azhar, the highest authority in Sunni Islam, explicitly declaring the "Salafi-takfirists, Daesh (so-called 'Islamic State')" and similar outfits to be "not Muslim." The Declaration was accompanied by a *fatwa* to the same effect from the Russian Council of Muftis.[7] Given this development, Aleksandr Dugin may find himself forced to recant his willingness to work with the Salafi/Takfiris. As of 2017, however, his position had not changed. In *The Rise of the Fourth Political Theory* he says:

> In the confrontation between the U.S. and "Al-Qaeda," however strange and disproportionate such a duel of the leading world state with extraterritorial "international terrorism" may seem, we are dealing with a clash of equally great ideological projects.... The declaration by Islamic radicals that their major adversary is the U.S. is sufficient proof that we are dealing with a serious and important project: the project of an alternative world empire.

Perhaps Aleksandr Dugin still hopes to lure the Takfiri Jihadists away from the circle of U.S. influence by portraying himself and his Russian backers as stupid enough to take them at their word. The image of an enemy that one wishes to damage and exploit inexplicably leaving himself open by demonstrating an astounding degree of foolishness is a temptation very difficult to resist. But whether it is a case of Russia and America bidding against each other for the services of the Takfiris, or the Takfiris playing Russia and America off against

6. https://www.cbsnews.com/news/report-us-allowed-isis-fighters-escape-raqqa-sdf-deal/.

7. The full text of the Grozny Declaration appears at: http://chechnyaconference.org/material/chechnya-conference-statement-english.pdf.

each other, or both, whatever "empire" the likes of al-Qaeda or ISIS might some day be able to come up with, no matter how unlikely such an outcome may be, would by no stretch of the imagination be "Islamic."

However, as we have seen, Dugin says he would rather align himself with the Sufis. In **Eurasian Mission**, he presents Sufism, due in part to its "folk" aspects as well as to its expression as many independent *ṭarīqas*, as a representative of "diversity," the principle supposedly behind Eurasianism, rather than the "universalism" of the Atlantean Globalists. He says:

> the Arab world, stretching from Muslim North Africa to the countries of the Maghreb and the Middle East . . . falls within the historical boundaries of the Ottoman Empire. These territories must be integrated into one geopolitical structure. . . . The fact that these territories are under the domination of Islamic traditions may be an additional factor in integration. There are some forms of Islamic radicalism—those that pretend to be universal—that oppose the basic Eurasian principles of cultural diversity and a system of autonomies. . . . Thus, the main Eurasian allies in the Arab world who adhere to Islam and also respect local traditions are the Sufi ṭarīqas, Shi'ites, and those ethnic groups in the region who promulgate spiritual and cultural diversity.

So apparent the plan is to resurrect the ghost of the Ottoman Empire with its autonomous regions, its ethnic/religious *millets*, not necessarily or entirely in the name of Islam but nonetheless "integrated into one geopolitical structure." This *regional universalism*, however, is precisely the main agenda of the "Islamic radicalism" that Dugin (intermittently) rejects, apparently opting instead for the "diversity" represented by, among other sectors, the Sufi *tariqas*. But if this Neo-Ottoman Region—which also bears a certain structural resemblance to the Soviet Union—is to be peopled by a "system of autonomies" based on "cultural diversity," where is that principle of *integration* going to come from? Where else but from Russia? The Eurasian Hegemony is consequently envisioned as a unity that is *imposed* (or as Dugin might be more likely to spin it, *allowed*) by an outside force.

Here we need to take a closer look at the notions of "universalism" and "diversity." As a resident of the Atlantean Hegemony, I can vouch for the fact that one of the pillars of our brand of cultural universalism is, precisely, *pluralism*. The Postmodern Liberalism of us Atlanticists is, as Dugin repeatedly and correctly emphasizes, a galling homogeneity and universalism imposed by the United States and its allies on the rest of the world, as well as on its own native populations. Yet the dominant ideology, the *illusory self-image* of this universalism is one of pluralism, of the "celebration of diversity." This leads us to ask whether the "cultural diversity" preached by the Eurasianists might simply be the false outer projection of an *alternative universalism*. I, for one, believe that it is.

Diversity, after all, can only be recognized *as* diversity from a relatively universalist, cosmopolitan point of view that has sufficient scope to discern it and name it. No traditional, indigenous racial or religious group ever promulgates *diversity*; Dugin's connection with the Russian Orthodox Old Believers ought at least to have taught him that much. Ethnic/religious groups can learn to live together in the same communities as good neighbors given a sufficiently stable civic framework that orders them, contains them and does so without excessive interference in their day-to-day activities, though this is usually not possible without a rigorous authoritarianism standing in the background but always ready to intervene when necessary; this was more-or-less true, at least during certain periods, of the Christians and Muslims of Eastern Europe under the Austro-Hungarian Empire, the Russian Empire, and especially the Ottoman Empire. But such close-knit ethnic/religious communities never promulgate diversity; they are too culturally introverted to think in those terms. If, however, the imperial power begins to waver, due either to internal decay or external pressure, many of these groups will wake up to the possibility of "self-determination" and begin to dream of establishing, not diversity, but their own sacred uniqueness, on a much wider scale. Be that as it may, cultural diversity coupled with limited autonomy cannot be maintained without a central power waiting in the wings. Dugin's Eurasianism may or may not be able to make a more fruitful union between diversity and autonomy than Atlanticism has been able to do, one less vulnerable to imposed cultural homogeneity, but in neither case is diversity possible without a corresponding universalism. And I am confident that Aleksandr Dugin is very clear on this point, though he does not choose to admit it.

Diversity and universalism are the cultural reflections of the metaphysical principle of the Many and the One. *Because* God, the Absolute, is *Al-Ahad*, the One, He necessarily expresses Himself as the Many, like the Sun reflected in many dew-drops. This is His Universality, as designated by His Name *Al-Wasi'*, the Vast. If the Many were capable of existing apart from the One, the One would not be the One, since it would be relative to the Many and therefore only one among the Many. On the other hand, every reflection of the Sun is unique—as if it were, in its own terms at least, the only reflection; likewise, each of us experiences himself as "the only *me*"; this is what Frithjof Schuon calls "the enigma of diversified subjectivity." Because God is the Unique, *Al-Wahid*, every entity or location in space or moment in time is also unique; this is Leibniz's (and Guénon's) doctrine of "non co-possibles." Each separate reflection of the Sun manifests the uniqueness of the Sun. The Many is the Relative; the One is the Absolute. If the One is taken to exclude and negate the Relative, its necessary manifestation, then both the Absolute and the Relative disappear; in that case there is no universe, because the Absolute has no way to manifest. Likewise if the Relative is seen as capable of existing without the Absolute, then both the Relative and the Absolute likewise disappear; in that case as well there is no universe, because the Relative has no Principle, no Source of Being, and consequently cannot exist.

In terms of the cultural reflection of this principle, every universalism must express itself as a diversity, and every diversity must, from another point of view, imply or constitute a universalism; this is perfectly represented by Dugin's symbol of Eurasia: eight arrows pointing in eight different directions from a common center. In terms of the future imperial society he envisions, Dugin claims to be for the many (diversity) and against the One (universalism), an orientation he expresses in quasi-metaphysical terms by naming Chaos rather than Logos as his central principle. In *The Rise of the Fourth Political Theory*, however—in another of his great self-contradictions—he declares his "general principle" to be "We are the supporters of the Absolute, and we are against the relative"—*Dugin against Dugin* once again. This principle, when transposed into social terms, becomes one more telling indication of the Absolute Eurasia, the Absolute Russia behind the relativity and diversity of the projected Eurasian Empire's semi-autonomous but in no way independent satellites.

It is a highly interesting fact that both Aleksandr Dugin and the Western Globalists see some sort of politicized Sufism as an alternative to the Jihadists, as witness Dugin's overtures to the Sufi shaykh and Guénoniste, Imran Hosein. From the Western point-of-view, the matter is put succinctly in an article entitled "State-sponsored Sufism" by Ali Eteraz which appeared in June of 2009 on the website of the Council for Foreign Relations; the author, though he appears to disagree with the policy of the western powers to groom Sufism as the spearhead of anti-Islamicist "moderate" Islam, nonetheless treats this policy as common knowledge. Here is his summary of the article:

> *Why are U.S. think tanks pushing for state-sponsored Islam in Pakistan?*

> Once certain ideas go mainstream, it often takes a pretty big flop to disprove them. The United States was supposed to be hailed as the liberator of Iraq, just as it was going to be easy to turn Afghanistan into a democracy. Well now, according to commentators from the BBC to the *Economist* to the *Boston Globe*, Sufism, being defined as Islam's moderate or mystical side, is apparently just the thing we need to deal with violent Muslim extremists. Sufis are the best allies to the West, these authors say; support them, and countries as diverse as Pakistan and Somalia could turn around.

> The Sufi theory has a lot of variations, but at its core, it's pretty simple: Violent Muslim extremism, rather than having material and political bases, is caused by certain belligerent readings of Islam usually associated with Salafism, a movement that attempts to resurrect the Islam of the prophet Mohammed's time, and Wahhabism, a similarly conservative branch. If Muslims can be indoctrinated with another, softer, interpretation of Islam, then the militants, insurgents, and guerrilla fighters will melt away. [http://www.cfr.org/publication/19959/fp.html]

This highly-informative perspective nonetheless ignores the possibility that, under certain circumstances, individual Sufi *tariqas*—already well-organized, disciplined, used to clandestine existence and fanatically loyal to their shaykhs—might be recruited by the western globalists as paramilitary forces, as has apparently happened on at least one occasion in Iraq in the struggle against the Salafi Jihadists, and is likely also going on in Central Asia, especially in the case of the Naqshbandis. This alone is enough to explain Dugin's overtures to the Sufis. As for the view of Sufism held by the globalist-influenced western Interfaith Movement, *tasawwuf* is routinely portrayed as a kind of peaceful, tolerant *universalism*, which is in most cases better represented by de-Islamicized "New Age" pseudo-Sufism, or the "soft Sufism" of people like Fetullah Gülen, than by the more traditional forms of *tasawwuf*.

Furthermore, if "the globalization of the elites leads to the balkanization of the masses," then the "diversity" of Sufism, as well as of various ethnic and religious separatist groups, ought to be fertile ground for the extension of globalist influence, whether Russian or American, seeing that strong, unified nations are the major barrier to globalization. In metaphysical terms this is the Satanic or ego-based counterfeit of the principle of the One and the Many, of the reality that God, the Absolute One, necessarily expresses Himself in terms of the Many, and embraces the Many as the multiple manifestation of His Unity. Here, however, the imposed pseudo-absolute of Monopolar Globalism ruthlessly fragments religions and civilizations and nations, making them "many" so as to more easily sweep them up into its totalitarian hegemony. God, Necessary Being, the One, mercifully expresses Himself—in His Name *Al-Rahman*, the All-Merciful—as Creation, Possible Being, the Many, so that—in His Name *Al-Rahim*, the Compassionate—He may progressively gather that Many back to the embrace of His Unity. The Antichrist, on the other hand, shatters and pulverizes all integral essences, whether cultural, psychological, spiritual or biological, so he can ship the debris of them back to his furnaces where they can be melted down to forge the earthly image of Lucifer, in direct defiance of God. "I lay before you death and life ... therefore choose life" [Deuteronomy 30:19].

The Transcendent Unity of Religions and United Front Ecumenism

As for our second basic disagreement, Dugin's notion of the relationship between particularism and universalism is the direct opposite of mine. Dugin sees religious pluralism, which he supports, as strictly opposed to religious universalism, which he hates, though he is still willing to ally with universalism as long as it expresses a relative particularity or "non-conformity" vis-à-vis the Western Liberal Hegemony. In other words, he does not see Truth as One, which is another way of saying that he doesn't believe in God. He believes in religion, of course; never in human history have more pseudo-believers, crypto-atheists or openly declared atheists been attracted to religion than are flocking to it today; according to some estimates, 30% of Russian Orthodox "believers" identify today as atheists, and of course Pope Francis has stated in an interview that "God does not exist."[8] It is clear that Dugin's own "universalism," since he does not believe in the Unity of Truth, is nothing more or less than the universalism of power: "Our idea is to join all the fronts." And the source and goal of this power-play is the Eurasianist Hegemony, which in terms of present time is nothing more or less than a fancy name for Russia. I, on the other hand, consider universalism to be the guarantee that each particular religious form will remain open to Transcendence since it prevents the Living God from degenerating into some tribal deity, while the providential and God-given particularity and uniqueness of each of the faiths guarantees that they will not be amalgamated into some worldly union *against* Transcendence such as Dugin is trying to create—a false union which would be nothing less than a worldly counterfeit of the Unity of God. Simply stated, I believe in the Transcendent Unity of Religions—which I take to be a *truth*—whereas Dugin believes in the worldly, power-based unity of religions, and of everything else, against the Atlanticist Hegemony, and the truth be damned.

As for our third point of divergence, the main goal of United Front Ecumenism as I envision it would be to protect the independence and authority of the religions against outside control—either overt or clandestine—by any secular power, whereas the control of the religions by the secular power of the Russian State, both directly and via some sort of "Religious International," seems to be what Dugin is after. Consequently United Front Ecumenism, embracing Sacred Activism as its central *praxis*, might legitimately be seen as a challenge, on certain levels, to Dugin's Fourth Political Theory—as long as it is clearly understood that United Front Ecumenism as I envision it does not claim the right to appropriate religion so as to serve the interests of any imperialist-hegemonic or national or ethnic collective or movement. It is rather envisioned as a stance of resistance on the part of the traditional religions themselves to control by any form of national authority or globalist hegemony, whether Western, Russian, Chinese or entirely trans-national, that threatens to attack their doctrinal integrity or curtail their catechetical freedom.

---

8. http://novusordowatch.org/2014/10/francis-god-does-not-exist/. In 2015 I contacted the Apostolic (Papal) Nuncio to the United States, Archbishop Carlo Maria Viganò, in the name of the Covenants Initiative, suggesting to him that he appeal to Pope Francis to remove the text of the Vatican Radio interview containing "God does not exist" from the Vatican website, since it would give ISIS and other Takfiri terrorists further cause to massacre Christians. Nothing was done, and the damning statement remained until 2018.

My vision of a United Front Ecumenism—which I conceived of, in entirely abstract and conjectural terms, in 2001—was unexpectedly and powerfully confirmed, 12 years later, by Dr. Morrow's publication of *The Covenants of the Prophet Muhammad with the Christians of the World* in 2013, an almost inconceivable development given the thick darkness of the times. The appearance of the Covenants of the Prophet at the eleventh hour has all the marks of a prophetic sign—but a sign of what? Is Integral Traditionalism finally "coming into its own" to the point where it is capable of generating a legitimate social *praxis* to reflect its essential *theoria*? Or has the Darkness of This World at last found a way to co-opt and neutralize it? Time will tell—if, that is, we know how to read time because we are awake to the Reality that lies beyond its borders.

Meanwhile, however, we need to understand that if there ever was a moment when the world's religions must stand together against common enemies, it is now. The forces of militant secularism, false magical/psychic religion and fundamentalist extremism are attacking *all* the God-given religions. The time is therefore ripe for a United Front Ecumenism that recognizes this threat and begins the serious work of developing strategies to counter it.

Unexpectedly, Guénon's categories from *The Reign of Quantity and the Signs of the Times* have proved highly useful for analyzing the emerging globalist hegemony—a fact that has hardly been grasped and only marginally exploited by either Julius Evola or Aleksandr Dugin, who—especially in the case of Dugin—have done little more than pry certain elements of Guénon's analysis from their proper settings so as to apply them, on a more-or-less *ad hoc* basis, to his own agendas. The emerging relevance of René Guénon's *eschatological* social analysis is partly due to the fact that, at least since the Iranian Revolution, religion has begun to have a greater influence on social change and social conflict than (perhaps) at any time since the Reformation. One face of global hegemony is the direct atheist/secularist attack on religious faith; this would correspond to Guénon's "Anti-Tradition." The false magical or psychic religion of the New Age, its predecessors and successors, which includes both populist and elitist sectors, fits Guénon's definition of "Pseudo-Tradition." And the Luciferianism of the higher eschelons of the global elites expresses the very essence of his categories of "Counter-Tradition" and "Counter-Initiation."

The globalist master plan to wipe the traditional religions off the face of the earth is based on two main strategies. The first is to weaken the faiths by infiltrating them with Pseudo-Traditional doctrines and practices, many of which are based on the idea that all the religions are naturally "evolving" toward one universalist meta-religion which will incorporate the "best" of each in the process of supplanting all of them—a meta-religion of which the globalist elites themselves would constitute the priesthood. The long-term Freemasonic attack against Roman Catholicism is perhaps the clearest and most successful example of this strategy. (Parenthetically, the greatest contradiction—and irony—in Guénon's doctrines is his hope that Masonry could be used to re-introduce a true esoteric spirituality into the Western world; he never seems to have realized that the Freemasonic lodges almost perfectly satisfy his own definition of Counter-Initiatic organizations.) And even if the goal of a One-World Religion, or a federation of all the world's religions under a single secular authority, is never in fact established, nonetheless the push for it will have so weakened the traditional religions that they will no longer be able to stand in any effective way against the globalist hegemony.

One of the tools employed by the global elites in their attack on the traditional religions is the established Interfaith Movement, which is heavily subsidized and directed by national governments, including the U.S. State Department, as well as various globalist foundations and think-tanks. This criticism certainly does not apply to all Interfaith organizations, nonetheless the globalist influence remains a dangerous factor which is not often recognized for what it is in the Interfaith world. The globalist-influenced Interfaith Movement subtly pressures the religions to soft-pedal any "divisive" doctrines in the name of "tolerance" and "unity," thus weakening their intellectual structure and making them more vulnerable to Pseudo-Traditional incursions. The Traditionalist doctrine of the Transcendent Unity of Religions is strictly opposed to this sort of promiscuous Liberal ecumenism since it takes the differences between the faiths as providential and sees their unity not as a desirable worldly possibility but as a Transcendent reality; the paths of the various faith finally come together only in God. Likewise the Covenants Initiative does not require any degree of doctrinal unanimity between Islam and Christianity outside the belief in One God or Supreme Principle, necessarily supplemented by the understanding that any traditional religion that affirms this belief will find itself a target of the globalist elites.[9]

The second strategy, conceived and directed by these same elites, is to subsidize various radical fundamentalist movements within the traditional religions—movements which, ironically, have often grown up as blind, narrowminded and ill-conceived reactions *against* globalism: a perfect example of the

---

9. In addition to its effect of homogenizing and diluting orthodox religious doctrines, the established Interfaith Movement has also become a vector that allows "philanthropy" from Saudi Arabia and other crypto-Jihadist Muslim sources to infiltrate the Liberal Christian seminaries of the United States—many of which are now being transformed into Interfaith seminaries without most Christians being aware of it—thereby providing an ideal cover for continued covert support for ISIS, al-Qaeda and other unrepentant Jihadists guilty of the mass murder of both Christians and Muslims in Syria, Iraq and elsewhere; this is the point where the two prongs of the globalist pincers-movement against the traditional religions, namely false interfaith unity and engineered interreligious conflict, meet. Instead of the old-style Wahhabi-influenced mosques of the West where militant fanatics railed against everything Western—an approach that has become too hot to handle since

venerable technique of the "controlled opposition." The radical fundamental-ists—who are actually another form of Anti-Tradition, religious rather than atheistic—are useful to the elites because they tend to oppose and attack both the traditional forms of the religious tradition out of which they have devel-oped, seeing it as degenerate and heretical compared with the supposed "origi-nal purity" of the faith, and all the other religions as well, defining them as false, Satanic counterfeits of the One True Religion. This allows the elites to turn various hired religious or pseudo-religious terrorist organizations—ISIS is a prime example—against both the religion they profess to follow and every other traditional faith they can get their hands on, thereby helping them evolve, or rather devolve, beyond Anti-Tradition to Counter-Initiation. This is why I believe that the meta-strategy of the globalists in supporting Islamic terrorism is to neutralize ALL the religions. After all, why should an elite cadre of oli-garchs backed by global finance who aspire to world domination sit back and do nothing when the beliefs and aspirations and moral standards of *billions* of people are determined by "outmoded" religious institutions that those oli-garchs do not control? And if anyone still doubts that both "religious tolerance" and mutually-destructive interreligious war could be subsidized by the same people at the same time for the same purpose, I can report from personal expe-rience that, during the Obama administration, the Christian/Muslim Dialogue in my home town Lexington, Kentucky was hosting speakers from Homeland Security, the Federal Attorney's Office, the State Department and the FBI, at the very same time that this administration, via the CIA and other entities, was subsidizing and directing the Arab Spring and the growth of ISIS.

Be that as it may, the emerging globalist hegemony, whether it is ultimately headed by the United States or Russia or China or some other center of power (remembering that Pope Francis recently sold the Chinese Catholics down the river by colluding with the Chinese Communist government to establish a state-

---

9/11, as well as being of limited use now that social media has replaced the Saudi-funded mosque as the main medium for Jihadist recruitment in the U.S.—the new tactic features crypto-Jihadists mak-ing generous donations to shore up faltering Liberal seminaries, which are faced with funding short-falls due to the shrinkage of the old-line Protestant denominations, thereby essentially hiring Liberal Christians as allies in the struggle against Islamophobia (though generally not Christophobia) in North America. This effort, while worthy in itself, has also unfortunately lent itself to degrees of gull-ibility (on the part of the Liberal Christians) and hypocrisy (on the part of the crypto-Jihadist Mus-lims) rarely matched in the annals of human history. As a litmus test for the sincerity of such partnerships, I suggest that the broad dissemination of the stories of the many heroic actions taken by ordinary Muslims around the world to defend Christians from ISIS and other enemies, often at the risk of their lives, be proposed as the most powerful and effective way of combating Islamopho-bia. If certain "philanthropic" Muslims do not seem to immediately *warm* to this idea, Christians and their true Muslim friends should note this as indicating the possible presence of a hidden agenda. Links to 43 such stories may be found at: https://charles-upton.com/2018/10/16/muslims-defending-christians-around-the-world/. *They plot, but Allah also plots; and Allah is the best of plotters.* [Q. 8:30] controlled pseudo-Catholic church), and whether or not it finally takes the form of a One-World Religion or incorporates such a religion as one of its "ministries," perfectly fits the prophesy of René Guénon, in *The Reign of Quantity and the Signs of the Times*, that the Counter-Tradition will ultimately express itself in terms of a visible organization that would be "the counterpart, but by the same token the counterfeit, of a traditional conception such as that of the 'Holy Empire'"—a regime controlled by an "inverted hierarchy" which would be nothing less than the kingdom of Antichrist, the one-eyed being that Muslims call *al-Dajjal*, "the Deceiver."

Nonetheless, we must not let the spectre of Antichrist paralyze us. Given the ominous nature of the times, we may inadvertently find ourselves "awaiting" the Antichrist rather than standing in wait for the Mahdi and the eschatological Jesus, seeing that nearly all visible signs seem to point to the advent of *al-Dajjal*, whereas the signs of Christ's Second Coming are increasingly contracted and obscured. On the other hand, one of the central signs of the *parousia* is nothing less than the rise of the Deceiver; the unwitting herald of Christ is, precisely, Antichrist. Therefore Sacred Activism, from one point of view, could be defined as the practice of parting the veil of Antichrist to reveal the eternal presence of the eschatological Messiah standing behind him—though this definition equally applies to *any* legitimate spiritual practice, whatever form it may take and whatever particular Revelation may serve as its field of operation—seeing that, in terms of the human microcosm, the archetype of Antichrist is the *ego*, and the ego is the veil that hides the Presence of God in the Spiritual Heart.

One Possible Project For United Front Ecumenism

As for what United Front Ecumenism might look like as a concrete *praxis*, I envision two main thrusts:

(1) *Research*

A think-tank should be organized to scope out and exhaustively research the whole spectrum of attacks upon, and subversion of, the various religions, particularly the traditional religions, in today's world, including its roots in the "tradition" of anti-religious ideologies springing from Communism, Fabian Socialism, Freemasonry, secular humanism, scientism, heretical Christianity, heterodox Judaism, Takfirism, Luciferianism, Neo-Paganism, Darwinism, Freudianism, behaviorism, occultism, etc. Such research would go a long way towards answering the more comprehensive question, "who are the globalist elites?" These attacks on religion include but are not necessarily limited to:

Government suppression and/or control
Infiltration by spies and/or change agents

Doctrinal subversion
Attempts to federate the religions under a single secular authority
Attempts to formulate the theology of a One-World Religion
Overt or covert attempts to create inter-religious conflict
Sponsorship of extremist or terrorist groups in the name of a particular
    religion or as directed against a particular religion
Attacks by atheist organizations, or Satanist groups, or any "alternative reli-
gion," whether new of or long standing, opposed to the traditional   faiths
Fraudulent scholarship
Anti-religious propaganda in academia, entertainment and the arts

Perpetrators of such attacks, who should be named and exposed, might include:

Governments
Corporations
Foundations
Think-tanks
Universities
Intelligence agencies
Law enforcement agencies
Militaries
Secret societies
Political parties or movements
Covert funding sources
International governing bodies
Obsessed individuals
Psychologists and physicians researching or applying various forms of mind-
    control
Professional writers, artists or film producers
Bloggers and podcast or You Tube producers
Social engineers
Organized atheists
LBGTQ activists
Organized Satanists
Transhumanists

Specific methods of attack include, but are not be limited to:

Disinformation
Slander of groups or individuals
Threats
Acts of vandalism or property destruction
Murder or assault
Anti-religious laws or rulings
Hacking
Subliminal suggestion targeting either individuals or populations

Overt anti-religious propaganda
Censorship, including book banning or exclusion from social media,
    Facebook, YouTube, Wikipedia etc.
Economic attacks via boycotts, exorbitant fees, tax audits etc.
Unfair legal or regulatory rulings
Covert surveillance

Finally, areas of expertise that could be drawn upon to conduct this research
might include, but not necessarily be limited to:

Historians and sociologists of religion
Theologians
Anthropologists and social psychologists
The law enforcement profession
The diplomatic profession
The legal profession
Private investigators
Media experts
Publishers
Experts and researchers on propaganda, social engineering and mind control
Information technologists
Film, art and literary critics
Freelance investigative reporters and researchers
Religious defense organizations, anti-defamation leagues etc.

The above three lists map the attack on religion and a possible response to it
from a more-or-less North American perspective; other regions would require
different maps. Given sufficient funding from sources that can be determined,
with reasonable certainty, to be part of the solution rather than part of the
problem, the initial planning phase for such research could begin now.

(2) *Alliances for Mutual Defense*

These would be harder to organize given mutual distrust between the religions,
either of long standing or as produced or exacerbated by contemporary propaganda, *agents provocateurs*, etc. The common practice on the part of the religions of relating to each other, or the world, only on the basis of missionary
activity or apologetics, or else via an Interfaith Movement where no potentially
inflammatory issues are raised and everything is sacrificed so as to present an
image of friendship and solidarity with nothing much backing it up, and with
little effect on conditions "on the ground," would also be a difficult hurdle to
clear. However, a list should at least be made of the various organizations for
religious defense—excluding militias—that already exist in the U.S. and elsewhere. Whether representatives of such groups would agree to sit down in the
same room together is far from certain, however. In addition, conservative
Christians would be much more heavily represented in many groups than Lib-

eral Christians, who often (rather short-sightedly in my opinion) see little need for defense. And an exclusive reliance on the established Muslim leadership in North America, given that some leaders have made common cause with Liberal Christians and various extreme-Left groups, might skew Islamic representation away from the more traditional Muslim majority. In addition, there is always the possibility that extreme Rightist groups or Islamicist networks might be exercising covert influence on some of the organizations that we would initially approach in hopes of forming a coalition to pursue United Front Ecumenism.

It would be a powerful witness if Christians and Muslims could agree to support each other, both directly and in the media, whenever a mosque or church is attacked by vandals or a law limiting freedom of religion is proposed, perhaps under the auspices of an organization like the Shoulder-to-Shoulder Campaign (http://www.shouldertoshouldercampaign.org/). It may be, however, that only after the research element of United Front Ecumenism has done its work will the religions begin to wake up to the fact that they face a common enemy and should therefore consider making alliances for mutual defense.

United Front Ecumenism in the Context of the End Times

In conclusion, we must never forget that the ever-present shadow of the Transcendent Unity of Religions, with United Front Ecumenism as one of its legitimate outward expressions, is the System of Antichrist, which will likely appear on certain levels as a parody of such ecumenism; therefore we must take care that United Front Ecumenism doesn't end by re-introducing the notion of a One-World Religion through the back door. As I have already pointed out, any alliance of the religions against their common enemies must not be based on doctrinal agreement as a necessary pre-requisite, nor should it push for such agreement. Nonetheless, the very fact that globalist forces exist who desire the destruction of all the faiths should be enough to demonstrate to those faiths that they have much in common. The fact is that the traditional religions do in fact already constitute—on many levels, though certainly not on all—a "Unanimous Tradition"; and it may naturally become easier, after a rigorous period of companionship-in-arms, to begin to recognize this truth. The essence of the Transcendent Unity of Religions is certainly not a push for doctrinal unification, though a certain amount of "comparative religion" or "esoteric ecumenism" might naturally begin to grow up in the trenches. The essence of doctrine of the Transcendent Unity of Religions is simply the recognition that God, or whatever the Supreme Principle of existence may be called, is One— necessarily so, seeing that the "gods" of the various faiths are not separate deities but rather differing perspectives. Such Divinely-authorized perspectives on the nature of God cannot, however, be reduced to a collective belief or a common subjectivity, given that each Revelation, since it is an unveiling of an Objective Reality, necessarily has an objective aspect that transcends the collective consciousness of its believers. If this were not the case, *no* religion could claim that its own conception of the Supreme Principle was any more than a reflection of the group mentality without any objective referent, a *belief* in God with no real God there to believe in; this would represent the triumph of the postmodern worldview and the final deconstruction of religion. But just as the true distance of a star may be determined by parallax, by sighting it from two or more points on the earth's orbit around the sun, so the multiple conceptions of God that Ibn al-'Arabi called "the gods created in belief" in fact testify to the Unity of the True God, who in His Absolute Essence is beyond conception entirely. Only if we turn to God as He is in Himself, not simply to our imperfect images of Him, will we find the power to stand fast in our struggle against those global forces whose agenda includes gaining control over the traditional religions, denaturing them, or wiping them from the face of the earth.

In the contemporary world, established religious institutions who want to survive *as* institutions are increasingly being drawn, or pressured, to seek patronage from some powerful geopolitical entity, either Gog or Magog, either Behemoth (Dugin's "Eurasia") or Leviathan (Dugin's "Atlantis")—though whether this patronage will help or hinder their survival as Divine revelations is far from certain. One of the clearest examples of this is the stance of the Roman Catholic Church, which has apparently offered itself as something like "the chaplaincy of the New World Order." Instead of preserving the remnants of Christian Empire, Benedict XVI, in his encyclical *Caritas in Veritate*, called for a "true world political authority," a secular One-World Government. As René Guénon predicted in *The Reign of Quantity and the Signs of the Times*, the regime of Antichrist will take the form of "an organization that would be like the counterpart, but by the same token also the counterfeit, of a traditional conception such as that of the 'Holy Empire,' and some such organization must become the expression of the 'counter-tradition' in the social order. . . ." (As the reader will probably notice I have already quoted this passage more than once, since I consider it to be of crucial importance, especially in view of Aleksandr Dugin's "Project Empire.") The call for a "world political authority" becomes even more explicit in "Towards Reforming the International Financial and Monetary Systems in the Context of Global Public Authority," a paper produced by the Pontifical Council for Justice and Peace in October of 2011, during Benedict's tenure, which contains the following passage:

> one can see an emerging requirement for a body that will carry out the functions of a kind of "central world bank" that regulates the flow and system of monetary exchanges similar to the national central banks . . . [*the stages in the creation of this bank*] ought to be conceived of as some of the first steps in

view of a public Authority with universal jurisdiction. . . . In a world on its way to rapid globalization, the reference to a world Authority becomes the only horizon compatible with the new realities of our time and the needs of humankind. However, it should not be forgotten that this development, given wounded human nature, will not come about without anguish and suffering. Through the account of the Tower of Babel [Genesis 11:1-9], the Bible warns us how the "diversity" of peoples can turn into a vehicle for selfishness.

A universal world authority brought about through anguish and suffering, where diversity is in effect outlawed—a true imposed unification—is what the Novus Ordo Catholic Church is openly calling for in this document. Here the failure of the Tower of Babel is used as an image of *the evils of diversity*, symbolized by "the confusion of tongues." What these *aggiornamento* Catholics conveniently forget is that the Tower in Genesis was the emblem of Nimrod's Promethean opposition to God, and that the confusion of tongues that prevented it from being finished was ordained by God Himself.

From one point of view, the struggle over the question of worldly patronage is simply the perennial predicament of any religion that attempts to maintain its existence in the context of an empire it has not been totally identified with from the beginning, or within one it is no longer totally identified with, or a in the face of a new empire that is extending its influence. The dilemma facing the religions in the 21st century, however, is more complex and more ambiguous. The ideologies, empires and imperialist nation-states of the modern and postmodern eras—Nazism, certain aspects of Communism, the sometimes-covert and sometimes-overt control exercised over the religions by the New World Order of the Western globalists, as well as Aleksandr Dugin's projected Neo-Eurasian Empire—all exhibit certain "religious" features, as if they were something like beta-versions or trial runs for the System of Antichrist. A false "worldly religion" with imperialist aspirations—like the regime of Nimrod in the Book of Genesis, who attempted to build the Tower of Babel to reach heaven, and whom Guénon, in *Traditional Forms and Cosmic Cycles*, identifies with the revolt of the *kshatriya* or warrior caste against the *brahmin* or priestly caste—can be known by the fact that it presents itself as a quasi-spiritual absolutism-of-this-world, a unity-without-Transcendence, and thus as either a cunning counterfeit, or an open, defiant usurpation, of the Unity of God.

Those in the western world, usually Evangelical Protestants, who envision Christian eschatology as unfolding in contemporary history will often—like Aleksandr Dugin—identify the New World Order quite literally with the System of Antichrist; this may be one of the origins of the Russophilia of some conservative Christians. However, as I observed in *The System of Antichrist* in 2001,

> The One World Government shows many signs of being the predicted regime of Antichrist. But as I have already pointed out, it's not quite that simple,

since the "tribal" forces reacting against globalism are ultimately part of the same system. According to one of many possible scenarios, the satanic forces operating at the end of the Aeon would be quite capable of establishing a One World Government only to set the stage for the emergence of Antichrist as the great leader of a world revolution *against* this government, which, if it triumphed, would be the *real* One World Government.[10]

I hastened to add that I was not prognosticating, only giving one possible scenario as an example of the ambiguities and contradictions of the Latter Days. But whether or not we feel justified in seeing Aleksandr Dugin, the organizer of what he calls the Global Revolutionary Alliance, as one possible rendition of this "great leader," both the rise of an "inverted hierarchy" out of the universal leveling of the regime of the Substantial Pole that Guénon predicted in *The Reign of Quantity* (which might well have been suggested to him by the rise of Nazism in reaction to Communism), and the emergence of the Beast to annihilate Babylon the Great in the *Book of Apocalypse*, appear to be referring to the same development. An inverted hierarchy is nothing less than an attempt to supplant the Hierarchy of Being established by God with a hierarchy of mere human power. In traditional hierarchically-ordered societies, social hierarchy is designed to mirror ontological hierarchy—though the danger always exists of the growth of a social hierarchy that doesn't mirror but rather counterfeits the Hierarchy of Being, and is thus transformed into a Counter-Initiatory tyranny, a development symbolized in both *Exodus* and the Holy Qur'an by the Pharaoh of Egypt. This was often the fate of the ancient hieratic civilizations in their degeneracy, which is why God established the lineage of the Abrahamic prophets to free His people from petrified hieratic regimes like Egypt and Babylon, from Empires based on the *kshatriya* revolt such as Rome or Assyria, and from later empires that exhibited certain counterfeit-hieratic elements in their old age, notably Persia and Byzantium. Therefore no empire of the Latter Days with hieratic pretensions, such as Dugin's Neo-Eurasian Hegemony might well become if it were to succumb to the Counter-Initiatory temptation, could in any way protect and support the Divine Revelations; it could only counterfeit

---

10. A development like this would represent an attempt to co-opt the energy, insight, effort and sacrifice of all anti-globalist forces worldwide. It would be nothing less than a move to transform, on the global level, virtually every movement of organized dissent into a controlled opposition under the covert direction of the oligarchs. Will this turn out to be an accurate description of certain aspects of Aleksandr Dugin's Neo-Eurasian movement? Is Dugin an agent hired by the oligarchs to mount a global movement against the oligarchs under the control of the oligarchs in order to permanently cement the hegemony of the oligarchs? This will remain a very difficult question to answer for the foreseeable future. The reason I pose it, thereby expanding "conspiratorial paranoia" to its ultimate limit, is simply to emphasize that the global elites, despite the spiritual narrowness of their outlook, definitely know how to *think big* in worldly terms.

them, enslave them, or liquidate them. Vladimir Putin's protection of the traditional religions within the Russian State and his support of traditional morality are certainly hopeful signs; nonetheless the danger of a "repressive tolerance" resulting in a denaturing of the traditional faiths with the heavy hand of "protection," whether deliberate or inadvertent, is always present. After all, the present Patriarch of Moscow, Kiril, was once a member of the KGB.

Dante Alighieri, author of the great *Divine Comedy*, also faced the dilemma of achieving a balance between spiritual authority (the Papacy) and temporal power (the Holy Roman Empire) in 14th-century Italy. Of the three parties involved in this controversy, the Ghibellines wanted an Emperor to whom the Pope would be subordinate; the Black Guelphs wanted the Pope himself to be a kind of universal monarch, to whom all kings and emperors would be subject; the White Guelphs wanted a Pope largely independent of the Emperor, and an Emperor strong enough to rule the Christian Empire in such a way that the Pope would not be drawn away from his spiritual function and forced to meddle in politics. If I had lived in the 14th century I would probably been a White Guelph, while Aleksandr Dugin might well have been a Ghibelline. (Both Dugin and Schuon seem to believe, for some reason, that Dante was a Ghibelline. He wasn't. He was a White Guelph.) The Ghibellines manifested Guénon's "revolt of the *kshatriyas*," while the Black Guelphs exhibited elements of his closely-related "Counter-Tradition"—not the overt domination of spiritual authority by temporal power such as the Ghibellines wanted to impose, but the transformation of spiritual authority itself into a temporal power with false spiritual pretensions. The White Guelphs, on the other hand, supported the notion of a relative separation of Church and State, something like the one established by the First Amendment to the U.S. Constitution.

The fact remains, however, that any religion that rejects patronage or control by one worldly power or another, in this time of the clash of titans, of Gog and Magog, must consciously prepare itself to become a Remnant, and thereby fix its eyes on the Second Coming of Christ, the birth of the Messiah, the advent of the Kalki Avatara, the appearance of Saoshyant, the dawning of Maitreya, or the rise of the Mahdi and the descent of the Prophet Jesus to slay *al-Dajjal*—and no Remnant has any kingdom in the world of geopolitics. Thus the prime sociopolitical role of United Front Ecumenism would be to preserve and defend the traditional religions out on the marches, on the borderlands between their respective spiritual Centers and the encroaching temporal power that threatens to smother them, until such time as a true Remnant or Remnants can be constituted by legitimate spiritual authority—whether or not this can still be identified by then with visible institutional authority—emanating from those Centers. This is perhaps all that we have either the ability or the right to project as a viable goal for United Front Ecumenism; the rest is in God's hands.

8

Parousia and
the Laws of Apocalypse

IT IS COMMONLY BELIEVED today that anyone who openly admits that our times are apocalyptic, and who therefore advises the human race to face this fact and tap the spiritual potentials hidden within it, must actually *want* the world to end. To the secularist, the end of this world, of this *manvantara* or cycle-of-manifestation, can only be a meaningless tragedy. Likewise those fanatics whose belief in God and the celestial order is distorted by an unconscious worldliness will believe that it is somehow their duty to bring in the apocalypse themselves, to engineer the fulfillment of the End Times, thereby forcing God's hand and initiating their own particular apocalyptic scenario; they want to ensure that the Messiah, the eschatological Christ, the Mahdi will dutifully appear according to their own timetable. People like this believe that they are faithful believers, whereas they actually closer to the person described by the existentialist philosopher Albert Camus in his book *The Rebel*, the one who sees suicide as the great act of "self-determination," the idea being that even though we cannot create ourselves, we can still seize the reins of our own destiny by destroying ourselves. The traditional Christian response to the End Times is quite otherwise: "Ye know neither the day nor the hour wherein the Son of man cometh" [Matthew 25:13]. Likewise the Jewish Kabbalists, after the disaster of the false Messiah Shabatai Zevi, as well as the attempt by some of their practitioners to invoke the Messiah's advent through certain arcane rites, made it a firm rule that no-one was to "press for the end": omega and alpha, End and Beginning, are in God's hands. In the words of the Qur'an, *If Allah were to take mankind to task for their wrong-doing, he would not leave a single living creature on earth, but He reprieveth them to an appointed term, and when their term cometh they cannot put it off an hour nor yet advance it* [16:61].

In eschatological times such as ours, the center of spiritual orientation gradually shifts from the merciful advent of the religion-founding prophet or savior or avatar to the *parousia*, his rigorous and majestic "second coming"—without, however, his first advent being eclipsed or superseded.

474

This growing orientation toward the *parousia* manifests itself, among believers, in terms of three different attitudes, only one of which is fertile. The first is *promethean theurgy*, the attempt to actively invoke the Messiah, to command His presence. The second is a *pseudo-pious passivity* that does not actually engage with the *parousia*, but simply waits for the Messiah—or claims to wait for Him—without really expecting Him. The third is an *active and vigilant receptivity* that consciously works to purify the individual soul of self-will—while doing what it can to purify the collective soul at the same time—so as to make it a fit vessel for the full manifestation of God's Will. This third attitude is the orientation of the Remnant—the only one that capable of bearing fruit. (The Catholic visionary Anne Catherine Emmerich saw the Virgin Mary as the final flower, among the Jewish Essenes, of the work of generations of holy women—the ones known as "handmaidens of the Lord" who fulfilled the role of Temple seamstresses—to perfect their self-effacement and receptivity to God so that one of them would at last be chosen, in "the fullness of time," to give birth to the Messiah. In our own times, this remains the proper attitude and practice for the Remnant—those who await his Second Coming.)

The Apocalypse, the Second Coming of Christ, the rise of the Mahdi, the return of the Prophet Jesus, the advent of the Kalki Avatara, the dawning of Maitreya Buddha—how are we to understand these prophesies without transforming them into simple-minded theatrical productions, imaginary pictures of anticipated developments we take so narrowly and literally that we may miss or discount many of the actual events that herald them, or even fulfill them, merely because they do not exactly match our pre-conceived scenarios? Suffice it to say that all lines—socio-historical, financial, psychological, ethical, technological, ecological and spiritual—point to a rapidly-approaching moment of finality for this planet. Seen from the materialistic point of view that Aleksandr Dugin tends to adopt without fully understanding that he has done so—the perspective of the not-yet-fully-purified Pole of Substance, littered with the residues of the past—these happenings herald nothing beyond a tragic and meaningless dissolution. But from the spiritual point of view, from the perspective of the Essential Pole, they point to a new Advent, the arrival of the activating Divine Word of the next *manvantara*. Both poles incarnate certain aspects of reality, but the Pole of Essence holds eternal precedence over the Pole of Substance—except at the final and original moment when Substance has become perfectly Virginal, when it is finally purified from the last traces and residues of the superseded form of the *aeon* just now ending, and so has become the perfect Mirror of the entire Form and Word of God for the *aeon* just now beginning. Speaking in cosmic rather than transcendental terms, it is only in this timeless and eternal Moment of theophany that Form and Matter, Essence and Substance, Shiva and Shakti are seamlessly united. And given that this eternal

Moment can fully break through only when the entire formal structure of the cycle-of-manifestation dissolves and returns to its trans-temporal Archetype—not when *history reverses* but when *time ends*—what could possibly be more foolish than to believe that mere human will, individual or collective, could somehow profit by, or even influence the outcome of, the Will of God at its moment of ultimate triumph on the terrestrial plane?

And if it is difficult to talk about the Apocalypse without generating projections and illusions, that goes double for the Antichrist. The challenge in making sense of the prophesies relating to the Beast—the Muslim *al-Dajjal*, "the Deceiver"—is, first, to avoid the kind of frivolity and paranoia that generates all sorts of delusions and projections on the order of: "Henry Kissinger is the Antichrist; Bill Gates is the Antichrist; Barack Obama—or no, wait, Donald Trump—is the Antichrist," etc., etc. (Arnold Schwartzenegger, in the 1999 motion picture "End of Days," plays a character who battles Satan to prevent the birth of the Antichrist, with the result that some people today believe that Arnold Schwartzenegger *is* the Antichrist.) Once this rudimentary level of literalistic fantasy and superstition is pacified, the next challenge is to demonstrate how this figure—or this regime—is dialectically and logically necessary, given certain metaphysical premises. The premises themselves, being of a spiritual nature, will not be acceptable to those with a modernist or secular humanist worldview, but for those willing to take them as axiomatic, a fairly logical picture of the unfolding of the End Times will emerge, according to which the rise of Antichrist constitutes a necessary phase in the dialectic of Apocalypse. We must face the fact that, in Aleksandr Dugin's myth, metaphysics and eschatology have emerged as prominent elements in the ideology of a major political thinker and organizer in the "western world," possibly for the first time since Dante. Consequently no researcher who is working on the basis of a secular humanist worldview can evaluate Dugin in terms of his first principles, since such a critic must immediately dismiss these principles as "all that religious, occult sort of nonsense." Likewise it will seem outlandish and irrational to any secular ideologue for me to ask whether or not Dugin is thinking and acting according to the principles of the Antichrist. It was Aleksandr Dugin himself, however, who opened the door to the introduction of the figure of Antichrist into political discourse by using that name to describe Liberalism, "Atlanticism," and the United States of America. And since he names the Traditionalism of René Guénon, Julius Evola and others as one of the main pillars of his Neo-Eurasianist ideology—Guénon who gave us a metaphysically-based dialectic of Antichrist in *The Reign of Quantity and the Signs of the Times*—we cannot assume that Dugin's use of the term "Antichrist" is a mere rhetorical flourish.

Lastly, who or what is the Messiah? Some traditions see him as a man among men, some as a sheet of lightning shining from east to west, some—mysteriously—as both. But however the Messiah manifests, He will be the Alpha and Omega for this *aeon*. We cannot relate to Him by thinking we can move Him like a piece on our geopolitical chessboard, or by believing we can date His advent, or compel that advent through arcane invocations like some deviated Kabbalists have done, or delay or ward off that advent like King Herod thought he could, or profit from it in worldly terms like some Evangelical Christians seem to believe; whoever attempts any of these courses of action will end by mistaking the Antichrist for the Messiah and worshipping the Deceiver instead. The Messiah is the eternally-creative Logos, the Always So; His presence is unveiled as soon as the structure of lies and illusions and self-willed power-plays the human race has created to deny the existence of God falls of its own dead weight. The Messiah must come because Truth must triumph over false-hood, given that falsehood has no intrinsic reality, while Truth *is* Reality. *And say: Truth hath come and falsehood hath vanished away. Lo! falsehood is ever bound to vanish.* [Q. 17:81]

The Apocalypse of Tradition *vs.* The Apocalypse of Dugin

Anton Shekhovtsov, in "The Palingenetic Thrust of Russian Neo-Eurasianism: Ideas of Rebirth in Aleksandr Dugin's Worldview," presents some troubling apocalyptic imagery produced by the "occultist" Aleksandr Dugin in essays he wrote on the black magician Aleister Crowley and the painter Sergey Kury-okhin:

> If the "integral Traditionalist" philosophy is distorted and manipulated by Dugin, the teachings of Crowley are used in a more curious manner. While claiming to be an Orthodox Christian (an Old Believer), Dugin approvingly refers to the legacy of the British occultist, who once proclaimed himself "To Mega Therion" (*Greek*, the Great Beast) and is considered one of the most important authors of modern Satanism. This oddity, however, does not mean indiscriminateness on the part of Dugin. On the contrary, the consis-tency of his agenda clicks into place if the reason behind his references to Crowley's doctrine is revealed. Dugin wrote two essays on Crowley and tried to explain why "the Great Beast's" ideas are significant to the builders of the "New Eurasian Order." In these essays, Crowley was presented as a "conserva-tive revolutionary" who promoted ideas of renewal of the modern world:

>> [*Between the aeons of Osiris and Horus*], there is a special period, "the tem-pest of equinoxes." This is the epoch of the triumph of chaos, anarchy, revo-lutions, wars, and catastrophes. These waves of horror are necessary to wash away the remnants of the old order and clear the space for the new one. According to Crowley's doctrine, "the tempest of equinoxes" is a positive moment, which should be celebrated, expedited, and used by all the votaries of "the aeon of Horus." This is why Crowley himself supported all the "sub-

versive" trends in politics—Communism, Nazism, anarchism and extreme liberation nationalism (especially the Irish one). [Dugin, "Chelovek s sokolinym klyuvom" (note 58), p. 173]. . . .

In an essay on the late Russian musical genius Sergey Kuryokhin, Dugin wrote:

> The new aeon will be cruel and paradoxical. The age of a crowned child, an acquisition of runes, and a cosmic rampage of the Superhuman. "Slaves shall serve and suffer." The renewal of archaic sacredness, the newest and, at the same time, the oldest synthetic super-art is an important moment of the eschatological drama, of "the tempest of equinoxes." In his *Book of the Law*, Crowley argued that only those who know the value of number 418 can proceed into the new aeon . . . [418 masok sub'ekta (esse o Sergee Kuryokhine)," in Aleksandr Dugin, *Russkaya veshch. Ocherki natsional'noy filosofii* (Moscow: Arktogeya-tsentr, 2001), vol. 2, p. 193.]

The usual, more-or-less sane response to such views is something on the order of: "These are the rantings of an unbalanced madman; if he ever comes to a position of real power in Russia—as he may have already—the world has much to fear." I certainly wouldn't disagree with this assessment, and I would also add: "Enough of this childishness. Humanity and the earth have already suffered enough from this or that brand of armed immaturity. Perhaps such pseudo-mystical rabble-rousing might have found some place, in *practical* terms, before the development of nuclear weapons and intercontinental ballistic missiles; today it is simply irresponsible, since we all now know that a total thermonuclear war between the Atlantic and Eurasian collectives would spell the end of human life, and most other life, on earth." Nonetheless it may be that Dugin has grown past his admiration for Crowley and his surrealistic and Counter-Traditional view of the Apocalypse; if so, I retract my criticism.

It is also possible, however, to see such lurid imagery as simply the product of an imperfect understanding of the laws of Apocalypse, based on a picture of the transition from one *manvantara* to the next as seen from the standpoint of the Substantial Pole alone, ignoring the role of the Essential Pole and the breakthrough of Eternity into time. If our horizon is limited to this material world, yet we somehow intuit that the end of "this" world is not the end of everything, all we can do is fill the void in our metaphysical understanding of the doctrines of Eternity and cyclical time with all sorts of dragons, witches and goblins— and then, in the midst of our terrified ignorance, do our best to anesthetize ourselves against the things we fear by trying to take a kind of fiendish delight in them so we won't become the cringing victims of them. This is not a viable strategy from any point of view.

The attempt to envision the transition from one *aeon* to the next without any reference to the Essential Pole most often results in the erroneous belief that "order spontaneously arises out of chaos." Those who are blind to Eternal order, and the descent of order from Eternity into time, must either despair, or else make the fatal error of believing that, since chaos is the source of order, to create chaos must somehow be a way of invoking order. This is as foolish and destructive as believing that, since "you have to hit rock bottom before you can be helped," the best way to overcome alcoholism is to drink more alcohol, or that the most effective method of curing opioid addiction is to ingest more opiates.

Let's take the fall of the Roman Empire as an illustrative example of a minor Apocalypse. Somebody "on the ground," with little perspective, little historical sense and a severely truncated worldview, might—if he lived much longer than the normal human lifespan—come to believe that order automatically comes out of chaos. First the Barbarians invade. Then the Empire breaks up. Next a Dark Age of warring tribes and private armies makes life a living Hell. Security is nowhere to be found. Starvation and disease are rampant. But then, little by little, things take a turn for the better. Population that had been declining begins to recover. Settled life starts to come back. Infrastructure is repaired. Food supplies improve. Peace becomes more than just an exhausted lull between raids and battles. Civic order returns. And in some ways the new society is better than the old one, especially for some of the lower classes. The people have hope again. So our observer may conclude that order comes out of chaos, and that chaos is useful to break down an old, oppressive order and introduce a new one.

What this more-or-less plausible view of history ignores is the *true name of the order* that, to our poorly-educated observer, appears to have sprung from chaos by the agency of chaos. The name of that order is: Christ. At the height of the Roman Empire's power and apparent stability, a child was born in Bethlehem of Judaea, sent by God to be the founding Avatar of the age that was to succeed Rome. He attained adulthood, taught, performed miracles, was arrested by the authorities, was executed by crucifixion. Then he rose from the dead, gave his disciples his final teachings, and ascended into Heaven. As the result of his life, death and resurrection a new religious movement sprang up— a Church that, after growing largely in secret for 300 years, was sufficiently organized, ready and hopeful for the future to act as the seed of a new age when the Roman Empire had passed away. The Essential Pole (the Father) emanates the new principle of order (the Son) who provides a new design for human life, a design perfectly incarnated in his own Person. If the Essential Pole had not acted, there would have been nothing to take the place of Rome when it descended into chaos; the unity of Europe might have died then and there. But our peasant on the ground—if, that is, he were not a Christian—would have known nothing of this. The reality of Eternity, of Divine Providence, of the Form-giving Mercy of the Essential Pole would have meant nothing to him. And if that peasant were somehow able, at one point in his long life, to become a philosopher, possibly he could have made his living as some kind of Stoic, but never as a Platonist, never as a Christian, since—like the narrow-minded materialist he was—he would have had to construct his worldview based on what Blake called "the ratio of the perishing vegetable memory." If you can't see Heaven, you can't really see Earth; if you don't know God, you have no real way of understanding Man.

So if we want to understand the specific errors in Dugin's eschatology rather than just being revolted by it, we will need to come to a clearer idea of what "Apocalypse" means in Traditional metaphysical terms, as well as (for all its apparent chaos) the specific principles it obeys. And no metaphysical writer can be of greater help to us in this than René Guénon, especially in his prophetic masterpiece *The Reign of Quantity and the Signs of the Times.*

The term "Tradition," for René Guénon, refers to the "horizontal" transmission of the essential knowledge of the Divine and cosmic orders of being, of God in His relationship to His creation, from the prehistoric origins of humanity to the present day. This transmission is maintained and renewed by a series of Divine Revelations arriving "vertically" from Eternity—as, on another level, each moment of time is renewed, seeing that time draws its life and motion from the Eternity in which it is embedded. Tradition is therefore a manifestation of the Logos—in intellective terms, the knowledge of Being; in existential terms, the Divine Power that brings Being into existence in space and time—both "the true Light which lighteth every man that cometh into the world" [John 1:9] and "the Word . . . without [*whom*] was not anything made that was made" [John 1:1–3], seeing that "in Him was life, and the life was the light of men [John 1:4]." Therefore the separation between the intellective and existential aspects of the Logos, by people like Martin Heidegger and Aleksandr Dugin—the separation of Light from Life—is not warranted. Light without Life is darkness; Life without Light is death.

One of the many brilliant lines in Dugin's *The Fourth Political Theory* is: "Modernism has killed eternity and postmodernism is killing time." Modernism kills Eternity by devaluing it, rejecting it, ignoring it; this is what Guénon called "Anti-Tradition." Postmodernism kills time by deconstructing it according to the method of *reductio ad absurdum*; this is the initial "achievement" of Guénon's Counter-Tradition, which must deconstruct time so it can set up a counterfeit eternity. And the effects of Anti-Tradition and Counter-Tradition are also evident, interestingly enough, in the degeneration of the Roman Catholic and Eastern Orthodox churches respectively. As my wife Jenny says: "Modernism destroyed Catholicism; Postmodernism will destroy Orthodoxy."

As the *manvantara* descends towards its consummation, the "cosmic environment" solidifies, becoming increasingly opaque to the creative and illuminating light of God; this solidification also affects the human soul. Celestial realities become less plausible; faith weakens; materialism takes over. This opacity can never be complete, however, because if it were, existence would be annihilated to the point where it could no longer be renewed, consequently the cyclical cosmic manifestation of the Absolute would cease, which is impossible. This is the phase of "Anti-Tradition," during which social imperatives are derived from a shrunken, secularized, materialistic vision of things.

At one point, however, the solidification of the cosmic environment results in a condition of "brittleness." Cracks begin to appear in the "great wall" separating the material world from the subtler planes of being, the nearest and most accessible of which is the psychic plane. Initially these cracks appear in the "downward" direction; consequently the world is invaded by "infra-psychic" forces, including demonic entities. This is the phase where "Pseudo-Tradition" and "Counter-Tradition" begin to take over from "Anti-Tradition." Pseudo-Tradition is false religion based on fantasy; Counter-Tradition is religion as practiced by various "change agents" who have sufficient knowledge of the laws of the psychic plane to construct a plausible yet inverted counterfeit of true religion for the purpose of destroying it. These are the conscious Luciferians, the *awliya al-Shaytan*. Under Pseudo-Tradition, social imperatives are derived from the delusions of the human mind, uninformed by either spiritual or material reality. Under Counter-Tradition they are the consciously-designed agendas rising up from of the infernal regions.

Pseudo-Tradition and Counter-Tradition have been virtual since the beginning of the *manvantara*, but until recently they have had little room to expand due to the dominance of Tradition. In the final phases of the *Kali-yuga*, however, their day finally arrives; Pseudo-Tradition and Counter-Tradition supplant Anti-Tradition. The 19th century was in many ways the age of Anti-Tradition, of triumphant materialism, yet it also saw the widespread outer manifestation of Pseudo-Tradition—Spiritualism, Theosophy, psychic research, etc.—the soil in which the seeds of Counter-Tradition were beginning to sprout.

As the incursion of infra-psychic and demonic forces intensifies, the wizards of the Counter-Tradition begin to use them—and be used by them—to destroy true religion, to hide and ultimately liquidate Tradition, thereby working to found the regime of Antichrist. This is the phase we are in now.

Simultaneously, however, preparations have been ongoing to discern, and thereby open, a new "crack," or aperture, or door in the cosmic environment, this time in the "upward" direction. An intuition of the Transcendent begins to become possible again; the way to spiritual elevation is cleared. But since the world is now fully infected with materialism and Satanism, this upper way becomes much harder to locate than it was in the past. At the same time, the world, through a synthesis of petrification and fragmentation, of paralysis and chaos, has become incapable of receiving the Spirit on a collective level, either because it is resistant to Spirit based on Anti-Tradition; or because, in its pulverized "infra-psychic" condition, it can provide no stable material foundation for it; or because demonic forces now act to repel the Spirit directly via the Counter-Tradition, the final result being that, at the moment when the Spirit fully breaks through again into terrestrial existence, the cycle-of-manifestation is dissolved because it is no longer capable of receiving that Spirit. This is why Christ in His second coming does not redeem the world, but judges it. This dissolution of the cycle purifies and unveils the Substantial Pole, the *prima materia*, which can now once again mirror the Spirit and receive its imprint, the form-giving design emanating from the Essential Pole, thus allowing it to act as the seed for the cycle-of-manifestation to come.

This "crack" in the upward direction is the door of the *parousia*, the site of the arrival of the Eschatological Christ—in Hindu terms, the last Avatara of Vishnu—who will conclude this *manvantara* and usher in the next. Other religions recognize this same terminal Judge and Savior by other names. The agents of the *parousia*, who work to "prepare the way of the Lord" through repentance and self-transcendence, are the Elect or the Remnant; these constitute the direct counterforce to the agents of the Antichrist.

According to one way of looking at it, the *parousia* is a discrete event that must occur during the terminal phase of the cycle. In another sense, however, the *parousia* is ongoing. The Eternal Christ—the power that the Muslims call the *Nafas al-Rahman*, the Breath of the Merciful—has always been returning, has always been descending out of Eternity into time, both to create the world and to destroy it. To the degree that the Substantial Pole, the substratum of cosmic existence, is receptive to the eternal advent of the Logos from the Essential Pole, that Logos appears as the Creator. To the degree that it is not, that Logos functions as the Destroyer. Insofar as the cosmic environment is opaque to the Light of God, the Divine Light shatters it. Insofar as it is open to the Light of God, that Light fertilizes it. And because the Elect or the Remnant have been working to open the "upper door" in the cosmic environment to the *parousia* by opening the analogous door within their own souls, "for the sake of the Elect, those days will be shortened" [Matthew 24:22].

The Necessary Correspondence Between the Renewal of the Macrocosm and the Redemption of the Microcosm

As we have already explained, at the beginning of the *manvantara* the Substantial Pole, like a mirror, is receptive to the formative Light of the Essential Pole, the Logos, which imprints the Form of the *aeon* now beginning upon the subtle material substratum or Substance destined to give birth to it in space and time; the spirit of God moves upon the face of the waters [Genesis 1:2].

As the *manvantara* progresses, however, the Substantial Pole—the cosmic environment which, in terms of the human microcosm, is the collective and individual psyche—becomes overwritten and obscured with the impressions of past temporal experience, thus interrupting, to a greater or lesser degree, the *aeon*'s continuing receptivity to the eternal Form that creates and maintains it. Consequently the cosmic environment progressively degenerates.

However, since the Substantial Pole is not yet entirely obscured, it will still experience periodic breakthroughs of creative and regenerative Form from the Essential Pole in the form of avatars, prophets, and the new religious dispensations they bring. These dispensations are not really innovations but rather renewals or redresses of the *manvantara* by virtue of their power to unveil once more—at least to some degree—the original constituting Form that created it and continues to maintain it. The Holy Qur'an makes this clear when it says: *He hath revealed unto thee (Muhammad) the Scripture with truth, confirming that which was (revealed) before it, even as He revealed the Torah and the Gospel aforetime, for a guidance to mankind....* [Q. 3:3–4]. This is why Islam is called *al-Din al-Fitrah*, the religion of the Primordial Human Form. These renewals are effected by the power of Eternal Form to cleanse the mirror of the Substantial Pole from the psychic residues of past experience so that it may once again reflect the light of the Logos, the Essential Pole. Because the Virgin Mary, the Theotokos, could say "my soul doth magnify the Lord . . . be it done unto me according to Thy Word" [Luke 1:38], Jesus Christ could say, "behold, I make all things new" [Apocalypse 28:5].

The time arrives, however, when the collective renewal of the human receptivity to God is no longer possible on a large scale, consequently no more religious dispensations (except various imperfect or counterfeit ones such as that of the Baha'i) will arrive. Islam was the last divine Revelation, and consequently inaugurated the last religious dispensation for this cycle. After this there will be no more prophets per se—though as the Prophet Muhammad says in a *hadith*: "The *arifun* (gnostics, knowers) of my community are like the prophets of the Sons of Israel." This is why the Sufis consider the saints, the *awliyya*, to be "the heirs of the Prophet." After this point, the only renewals possible will come through the saints, even though these "revivals" are miniscule—at least on the outer, collective level—when compared with the great spiritual renewals brought by the prophets and avatars. Nor can these smaller revivals be based on any new private *revelations* received by the saints themselves—though Divine *inspirations* will still arrive—since they are constrained to operate within the framework of a particular revelation or dispensation already established by God—for the Hindus, the *shruti* or revealed scriptures and the *smriti* or inspired commentaries; for the Jews, the Torah; for the Christians, Christ and His Sacraments; for the Muslims, the Holy Qur'an and the Prophet Muhammad. If they reject these orthodox frameworks they are recruited by the Counter-Initiation; they cease to be the *awliyya al-Rahman*, the saints of God, and become the *awliyya al-Shaytan*, the saints of Satan.

To say that all the renewals that come after the final Revelation—that of the Qur'an to the Prophet Muhammad—and before the inauguration of the "new heaven and the new earth" by the advent of the Avatara who will initiate the next *manvantara*, will be effected by the saints is to say that they will be based on *sanctification and repentance*. And the goal of sanctification and repentance is, precisely, to become *virginal*, to polish the Mirror of the Heart so that it may once again reflect the countenance of God.

The Mirror of the Heart is polished by human activity operating under spiritual Guidance—activity that is initiated by, works directly in line with, and is finally swallowed up in, the Grace of God. The Mirror of the Heart must be purified of two things which are really one thing: of vices and of errors, of passions and of delusions. There is no sin or passion that is not based, somewhere, on a false notion of the laws of existence and the nature of God; likewise there is no error or heresy or delusion that does not in part maintain its existence by offering itself to us as a justification for some sin or passion that we would rather not let go of. As the Substantial Pole of the macrocosm is polluted by the psychic residues of the earlier phases of the *manvantara*, so the Mirror of the Heart, the Substantial Pole of the microcosm, is obscured by what the Hindus call the *sanskaras* and the Buddhists the *klesas*, the psychic residues of past experience, the most stubborn and obdurate of which are the imprints of the passions. A "passion" can be defined as an addiction to a particular type of experience that we continually seek to repeat, or cannot help repeating, because we are attached to it. Lust and greed and pride and anger are obviously passions according to this definition, but so are fear and sorrow and revulsion and nostalgia. As the person pursuing sainthood works to cut through, dissolve and eliminate these errors and passions and the psychic residues that maintain them—a process so rigorous that the Eastern Orthodox Christians call it the "unseen warfare" and the Muslims the "greater jihad"—this results in a *metanoia* in the human microcosm that is strictly analogous to Apocalypse in the macrocosm. The "old heaven and the old earth"—the set of distorted ideas that affect us and the various destructive passions and chaotic forms of life based on them—pass away. At the same time, the "new heaven and the new earth"—the Eternal Metaphysical Principles and the well-ordered forms of life that make up their earthly projections—descend out of heaven from God, according to a saying of Blake's that I never tire or repeating: "When an individual rejects Error and embraces Truth, a Final Judgement passes on that individual."

This *metanoia* of the microcosm can also be understood in alchemical terms. In the sacred art of alchemy, the *metanoia* in the human microcosm is presented in existential rather than intellective terms, not as a renewal of mind but as a transformation of the psychophysical substance. The alchemical *magnum opus* resulting in the fabrication of the "philosopher's stone"—the Substantial Pole newly imprinted with, and informed by, spiritual Form emanating from the Essential Pole—can be understood as passing through three distinct stages: *melanosis* or "blackening," *leucosis* or "whitening," and *iosis* or "reddening." In terms of the science of repentance, *melanosis* is sin—or rather the *conviction* of sin, the humbling and deconstruction of personal pride and self-will; *leucosis* is purification, the polishing of the Mirror of the Heart; and *iosis* is the full reception of the Grace of Sanctification. Analogously, in terms of the sacramental art of icon-writing, *melanosis* is the imperfect conception of the particular spiritual truth that the icon is designed to redeem, an imperfection which the artist must confront and repent of before his work can begin; *leucosis* is the preparation of the *gesso*, the white surface coating the wooden panel, symbolizing the return to virginity of the Substantial Pole, the removal of the veils concealing the potentiality of spiritual conception; and *iosis* is the application of the pigments, the actual painting, symbolizing the Form-giving action of the Essential Pole, the spiritual conception itself.

In terms of René Guénon's doctrine of the *manvantara* and the traditional stages of the alchemical process, Aleksandr Dugin's image of the Apocalypse appears to be largely limited to the perspective of the Substantial Pole alone, and within that severe limitation, to the phase of *melanosis*. Such errors are quite common. The prospect of the end of the macrocosm, or at least the *known* macrocosm, if it is not understood according to clear spiritual principles, will commonly produce all kinds of delusional projections based on ignorance, fear, horror, confusion, guilt, and any number of other infernal fascinations. *Apocalypse* means, precisely, "Revelation," the full revelation of God to humanity, unhampered by the illusions of the world, the passions of the flesh, and the lies of the Devil. But this notion is often so poorly understood that we hear things like, "we must somehow prevent the apocalypse or we are all doomed!", whereas it is the very *lack* of apocalypse, of the collective sense of the Presence of God, that constitutes the doom we are already immersed in. Apocalypse, in its quintessence, is not punishment and destruction, but liberation and redemption. Nonetheless, apocalypse requires purification, and the purgatorial fires that lead to the discovery of sin and the repentance from it, especially when these fires break out on the collective level, are more than rigorous enough to explain the "apocalyptic" imagery of our collective paranoia.

René Guénon, possibly to avoid inflaming the more lurid projections that his analysis of the Apocalypse and Antichrist might be expected to evoke, spoke in sober, almost mathematical terms: time will accelerate, progressively dissolving space, until a point of "singularity" is reached at which time will end and space suddenly reassert itself, this being the beginning of the Golden Age of the new *manvantara*. And certainly many New Age teachers have spoken and acted as if a kind if "earthly rapture" were possible that might deliver the Elect to the Golden Age of the next cycle without the necessity of the cataclysmic passing-away of the old heaven and the old earth, or even the inconvenience of personal death. At least Aleksandr Dugin doesn't fall into this particular delusion! Nonetheless his various images of Apocalypse, grim as they are, seem entirely devoid of any sense of purification, repentance, or the breakthrough of Eternity into time. In other words, the main truth missing in Dugin's conception of the end of the present age is: that the purpose of Apocalypse is, precisely, *to restore the virginity of the human soul*—though we must admit that this is not much of a rallying-cry when one's actual purpose is to recruit young postmodern extremists itching for battle and to resurrect and expand the Russian Empire.

Furthermore, Dugin radically misrepresents Guénon's eschatology by assigning the quality of Time at the end of the present *manvantara*, and the quality of Space at the beginning of the new one, to two contemporary *spacial* realities—Atlantis and Eurasia. In **Eurasian Mission** he says: "The history of Russia is . . . the vanguard of the spatial system (East) that is opposed to the "temporal" one (West)." He is implying here that the Atlanticists of the West will be devoured by Guénon's ever-accelerating Time while the Eurasian heartland of the East will be the Space that, according to Guénon, is destined to be "reinstated" when time and the West are no more. Atlantis, the West, and Time are a house founded on sand, but Eurasia, the East, and Space will inherit the earth. This is pure magical thinking, nothing but a deluded attempt to simplistically and literally apply eschatological categories to contemporary history and politics. Atlantis and Eurasia as geopolitical entities may or may not be *distant reflections* of the cosmological principles behind Time and Space; nonetheless the acceleration of Time toward dissolution and the sudden reinstatement of Space as the new *manvantara* is inaugurated must affect the entire terrestrial environment, including its subtle dimensions; Apocalypse and the end of the *manvantara* can in no way be limited to the Western Hemisphere! Eurasia is not Shambhala. Dugin's rejection of the myth of progress, and his own myth of the reversibility of time, appear to be an attempt to let the volatile Atlantean lemmings jump from their cliffs and drown while the solid bears of Eurasia stand fast and watch them die—and on *some level* there may actually be some truth in this notion. Even this late in the *Kali-yuga*, if an entire society were to truly embrace Tradition and thereby orient itself to the Always So, it might conceivably develop a partial immunity to the dissolutionary effects of a "progress" now revealed to be nothing better than mass suicide. Nonetheless, the true field where the rejection of Time and progress, and the return of Space and Tradition, can be realized *before* the end of the *manvantara*—the archetype of this whole possibility—is the field of contemplation. Only in contemplation can the Always So, Necessary Being, the unchanging Truth of God, be fully actualized, leaving Possible Being, the realm of contingencies, the ever-changing world of appearances—the veil of *Maya* that the illusion of self-will makes us believe we can analyze, predict and control—speeding ever more swiftly towards its end. When the Presence of God dawns, the presence of other-than-God does not just evaporate—it is revealed as never having existed in the first place. *Truth hath come and falsehood hath vanished away. Lo! falsehood is ever bound to vanish* [Q. 17–81].

Guénon's Dialectic of the Antichrist *vs.* Dugin's Inversion of It

The following account of the nature and destiny of the Antichrist is based largely on Guénon's *The Reign of Quantity and the Signs of the Times.* Nonetheless, since I have brought out certain implications of Guénon's exposition that he himself did not emphasize, as well as adding a couple of elements of my own, we need to begin this section by distinguishing my doctrines from his.

Guénon teaches that Substantial Pole will become dominant at the end of the *manvantara,* and that Substance, of which the "matter" of physics is merely one aspect, is characterized by quantity and number rather than quality. He speaks of the death of traditions as the *manvantara* moves towards its end, and of the "harvesting" by sorcerers of the psychic residues of these traditions for magical purposes. Lastly, he says that "the Antichrist must be as near as it is possible to be to 'disintegration' . . . [*he must be one who realizes*] confusion in 'chaos' as against fusion in principial Unity," and characterizes the Counter-Tradition that Antichrist will be the ultimate expression of as "a heap of residues, 'galvanized' . . . by an 'infernal' will." My contribution to Guénon's eschatology has been to "connect the dots," a bit more explicitly than he did, at two specific points: first, by characterizing the Substantial Pole as the "archive" of all the psychic residues released by the withdrawal of spiritual Form over the course of the *manvantara,* and secondly by explicitly identifying the Antichrist as the "Great Wizard" who completes the tasks of the lesser wizards by taking possession of the totality of these residues. All of this, however, is clearly implied in Guénon's exposition. What Guénon did not do, however, is make the connection that I have made between the etiology and fall of Antichrist in the macrocosm and the crisis of ego-transcendence in the microcosm. Furthermore, he apparently failed to understand, or at least did not choose to clarify, that the fall of Antichrist and the Counter-Tradition coincides with the purification of the Substantial Pole from the psychic residues of the *manvantara* just ending, allowing her to function as the virginal Mirror of the Essential Pole for the *manvantara* just beginning. Nor did he see the purification of the macrocosmic

Substantial Pole as strictly analogous to the purification of the Spiritual Heart. That said, René Guénon's doctrine of the rise of Antichrist—with my elucidations and additions—is roughly as follows:

When a spiritual form descends into earthly manifestation, it will magnetize to itself whatever psychic material it needs to form a soul or subtle body in this world. Human spirits, as they incarnate, attract the psychic residues of past human lifetimes from the "psychic gene pool"; this process of *metempsychosis* accounts for the "memories of past lives" that some erroneously take as evidence for literal reincarnation. Likewise when a Divine Revelation enters the terrestrial plane, it attracts to itself, from older religions, cultures and philosophies, whatever material it needs to form the psychophysical vehicle that allows it to take its place in time and history. By the same token, when a human being dies and the spirit of the deceased returns to the celestial world, he or she will leave behind not only a physical corpse but also a *psychic* corpse—except in the case of the saints, that is, whose souls or psyches have been "saved" during life by being perfectly conformed to their indwelling spirits, and who consequently generate no ghosts. Furthermore, if human beings can leave psychic residues behind on their departure, so can religions, nations, ethnic groups, esoteric schools, human groupings of any kind. These group psychic corpses, these thought-forms or *egregores* of human collectives that have dissolved because their informing spiritual archetypes have departed, can be quite toxic.

According to Guénon, certain wizards or sorcerers are in the habit of trapping and appropriating such individual and collective psychic residues in order to use them for magical purposes—like the Voodoo practitioners who invoke Baron Samedi, *loa* of the graveyards, an entity who is identified with the planet Saturn, the principle of contraction and materialization, whose alchemical metal is Lead. And, in point of fact, this is precisely what any *ego* will do: it will identify with and attempt to manipulate all the psychic residues it can get its hands on so as to increase its ghostly substance and widen the scope of its power.

And if wizards, whose god is their own ego, operate by amassing psychic residues, by recruiting ghosts, then it stands to reason that the Great Wizard known as Antichrist, who is the collective ego of the human race, will do everything in his power to collect into one place all the psychic residues of the earth, including the various residue-hoards scraped together by all the little wizards, so he can place his *mark* upon them. The dominance of the Substantial Pole and the withering-away of the Essential Pole at the end of the *manvantara*—the disappearance of spiritual *form* and the resulting aggregation of relatively formless *matter*—make this kind of psychic imperialism relatively easy to accomplish.

On the other hand, those who are traveling a real Spiritual Path, whose goal is self-transcendence and self-annihilation, understand that the essence of any true esoteric and/or contemplative spirituality is to deconstruct identifications rather than collecting them, to release attachments, to dissolve and eliminate all the psychic residues that obscure and tarnish the Mirror of the Heart, in the understanding that when the ego can no longer find anything to identify with, it dies. These are the Elect, the Remnant.

The followers of Antichrist, and the Antichrist himself, operate on the opposite principle. They *collect* all the identifications, attachments and psychic residues they can find so as to build the biggest ego possible, an ego that will be so massive that no one will be able to "buy and sell," to trade in ego-material— that is, in *identifications*—without being taxed by it, one that will loom so large that *no one will be able to identify with anything at all* without in some way worshipping it [cf. Apocalypse 13:16–17]. This is what it means to bear the Mark of the Beast.[1]

The distinction between collection of identifications and the release of them is the precise point where the path of the Remnant and the path of the Antichrist diverge—where the Sheep and the Goats go their separate ways. And, as should be crystal clear by now, the agenda and political organizing method of Aleksandr Dugin, his way of attracting all the "residues" released by the decay of Postmodern Liberalism, as well as those of any suppressed religion, culture, ethnic group, contemplative order or esoteric school he can get his hands on, no matter how incompatible and mutually-contradictory they may be—and this by means of *inducing identification* on their part with the all-inclusive everything/nothing of Neo-Eurasianism—follows not the way of the Remnant but the way of the Antichrist. Not only that, but his organizing method actually seems to have incorporated certain elements of the dialectic of the rise of the Beast from Guénon's *Reign of Quantity and the Signs of the Times.*

As a number of people have already pointed out, Dugin is not a Guénonian Traditionalist because his politically-oriented Traditionalism was strongly influenced by Julius Evola who departed from Guénon's doctrines in important ways, and because Dugin himself went even further afield than Evola. But now we can begin to see that Dugin also returned to Guénon in a sense—or never left him—not because he follows Guénon in any basic way but because he has apparently learned how to use an inverted form of *The Reign of Quantity and the Signs of the Times* as a political organizing manual for apocalyptic times. Is he doing this consciously or unconsciously? No-one but God knows for sure; however, it may be that his strategy goes something like this:

---

1. In J.R.R. Tolkien's *The Lord of the Rings*, the struggle of the Hobbit Frodo is not to take the Ring of Power and wield it as a wizard might, but rather to relinquish it according to "not my will but Thine be done" [Luke 22:42]. The chthonic, volcanic fires of Mordor in which the Ring is destroyed are thus the eschatological fires of the Substantial Pole at the crisis of its alchemical purification—the fires of the Goddess Kali.

If everything is coming under the universal leveling power of the Substantial Pole, then why not use that power? How? First, by coming up with a brilliant, apocalyptic social critique of Postmodern Liberalism, so as to attract everybody and every system of ideas that also rejects Liberalism; secondly, by using the universal leveling-and-dissolving power of the Substantial Pole, the power of Chaos— in other words, the power of Postmodern Liberalism itself—both to incite insoluble conflicts in places like the U.S. and the E.U., and to invalidate and break down whatever ideologies may support the "Atlanticists." Use Chaos to accelerate the dissolution of the Atlanticist Hegemony and then sweep as many fragments as possible into the Eurasian camp—initially by promising equality, autonomy, freedom, celebration of diversity: "Let a thousand flowers bloom; let a hundred schools of thought contend."

It is not hard to see how this method is entirely in line with Guénon's picture of the wizard who "harvests" the psychic residues of the dead, as well as of dead or dying religions, civilizations and belief-systems, in order to collect more *materia* for his spells. Maybe this is why Dugin can say, "what we are divides us, what we are against unites us," seeing that all the antipathies and distinctions that characterize the living are abandoned when they meet death, the "great equalizer". This certainly sounds like a recipe for disaster in social terms, since when "what we are against" is defeated, when the enemy of my enemy is no longer my friend because my enemy is gone, then the whole uneasy coalition must dissolve into total conflict—UNLESS those cultural, psychic and ideological residues are now so exhausted, so effectively dead, that they can be mixed, melted down and frozen together to build the Eurasian juggernaut. And the next phase? The next phase is Guénon's "inverted hierarchy." Just as Weimar begged for Hitler, so an exhausted, chaotic, leveled-out Liberalism begs for hierarchy, authority, order. Consequently the very lack of center in Dugin's mass of psycho-cultural residues automatically invokes its opposite: the One Monolithic Center, in which diversity is not "celebrated" but used instead to create a system that is fragmented and petrified at the same time, like the Lake of Cocytus in the 9th circle of Hell in Dante's *Inferno*, holding the contorted frozen forms of all the most deeply damned—a condition that would make any sort of rebellion against the new status quo supremely difficult. Here we can see how Dugin may actually be *using* Guénon's profound dialectic of the End Times to defeat the exhausted West and put Eurasia on top. Unfortunately for all of us, this dialectic is Guénon's picture of the rise of the regime of Antichrist—a prophesy that Dugin appears to be taking seriously precisely by doing all he can to fulfill it. I am not saying that Aleksandr Dugin literally *is* the Antichrist— which, as I have stated above, is a rather *gauche* accusation, besides being very difficult to prove. I am simply pointing out that Dugin is following his method. Who the ultimate Antichrist of this *manvantara* will be cannot yet be discerned, seeing that there are so many contenders for the title. Dugin could sincerely aspire to become the Antichrist (as Crowley apparently did), spend a lifetime struggling to achieve that goal, and still fall short of it; history is littered with disappointed aspirants to the name of *al-Dajjal* who ultimately had to reconcile themselves to being remembered only as the fomenters of various "local" evils. And Dugin certainly remains free to change his goals and methods at any time.

It might well be the case, however, that not all of the plan I have outlined above is entirely conscious and explicit, even to Aleksandr Dugin. As we survey the dark agendas of the Latter Days, we are struck by the realization that many of these End Time schemes—the Postmodern Liberal campaign to destroy gender, for example, or the transhumanist program—exhibit a weird synthesis of immense cunning and immense stupidity. The methods by which such plans are formulated and carried out show an astounding degree of what might be called *transhuman* intelligence—and yet, if they were actually put in place, *no single human being on earth would benefit.* And this description certainly applies to an apocalyptic war between the Eurasian and the Atlanticist collectives. This transhuman synthesis of cunning and stupidity, in my considered opinion, is a sure sign of the *infernal* origin of the ideas and plans in question. In the angelology of Dionysius the Areopagite, the *Cherubim*, who appear as vast celestial wheels, their rims studded with eyes, are the second highest order of angels, secondly only to the Seraphim. It is in the Cherubim that the possibility first appears of a Knowledge that is not entirely identified with and swallowed up in Love, as is the case with the Seraphim. Therefore, in my own "mythology"— undoubtedly influenced by *The Screwtape Letters* of C.S. Lewis—I have imagined the infernal agendas of the End Times as "working papers" produced by demonic beings—specifically, by the great *fallen Cherubim.* If we were able to hack into the Devil's computer system and recover the text of one of these papers—one that might well have been subliminally suggested to Aleksandr Dugin as the basis of some (certainly not all) of his Fourth Political Theory—it might read something like this:

At the end of the manvantara, *which is where we are now, the Substantial Pole becomes dominant; the reign of Chaos, of formless quantity, dissolves the last vestiges of form, of Logos. Therefore—since Liberalism IS Chaos—let's use the power of Chaos against itself in order to dissolve the Liberal Atlanticist Hegemony that's based on it, after which we will sweep up all the psychic and cultural residues of that Hegemony into the Eurasianist orbit. Let us simultaneously invoke Chaos (without naming it) as the destructive power of the universally-hated Liberalism that levels all hierarchy and destroys all essential distinctions—doing this so as to mobilize all available hierarchical/essentialist forces in a global revolution against Liberalism—and at the same time present Chaos, on a more explicit level, as the self-determination and free self-expression that all the distinctive cultures, all the social and ethnic and religious essences, will enjoy under the sheltering protection of the Eurasianist Hegemony—not in order to allow them any real freedom, however, but only to break down whatever remains in them of true hierarchy and true essence, doing so by the same power of universal Chaos that is now dominant in the cosmic environment. This will allow us to use the passive and exhausted residues of their own proper essences as bricks to build Nimrod's Tower, the final inverted hierarchy of the Last Empire. Let us make them hate and fear Chaos as Liberal tyranny, and simultaneously long for it as multi-polarity and self-determination, thus setting up an unconscious contradiction that will paralyze them, stun them into submission. Furthermore, and in much the same way, let us use Hierarchy against Hierarchy in the name of Chaos. Let us use their love of Hierarchy, of Logos, of Essence, of their own particular, traditional and beloved renditions of the Great Chain of Being, to induce them to surrender the last vestiges of Hierarchy, of Logos, of Essence—since, as our great sage Heidegger has announced, the reign of Form and Essence is over, the regime of Logos is dead. And if they love Hierarchy because they hate Liberalism and Chaos, and at the same time love Chaos (or at least can no longer resist the attraction of it) because Hierarchy and Logos are dead—then what else could possibly result from this mass of contradictions but the inverted hierarchy, which the Enemy's great prophet, René Guénon, has declared to be the destined shape of the Last Empire of the* manvantara—*the Empire that is us.*

The end product of this development, as we have already pointed out, would be a frozen Chaos. Chaos, however, cannot remain frozen forever; it is inherently unstable. As Guénon says in **The Reign of Quantity and the Signs of the Times**, "Antichrist must be as near as it is possible to be to 'disintegration.'" Nimrod, the architect of the Tower of Babel, had every reason to believe that his great construct would last for a thousand years, because Nimrod was a *great hunter*—a hunter and killer of old and dying religions, a butcher and scavenger of their spilled and scattered psychic residues. Nonetheless God halted the construction of Nimrod's Tower by introducing a *confusion of tongues*—and that is precisely what any heterogeneous collection of psychic residues actually is, such a collection as the Beast believes he can found his Empire upon: a *babel of tongues*, a formless confusion, whose inevitable fate is not enforced unification into some One-World Religion or Universal Empire, as Nimrod undoubtedly imagined, but mere fragmentation, chaos and dissolution. Thus Nimrod was both a type and precursor of the Antichrist and sign of his destiny.

Furthermore, in view of the fact that nothing can oppose God in fact, even though many things may oppose Him in intent, the Antichrist will ultimately aid the Remnant in their work of purification. The very power of the Beast to magnetize to himself all the residues and dead husks of the *manvantara* can actually help the Remnant to let go of them. Furthermore, the insight of the Elect into the truly infernal nature of *al-Dajjal* will bring home to them, in the most rigorous and undeniable terms, how these residues are in no way treasures to be hoarded, but rather toxic waste to be eliminated.

And when the Antichrist falls, when his massive hoard of psychic residues, in line with the purification of the Substantial Pole in the fires of Apocalypse, is reduced to pure *potentia* at the end of the *aeon*, the transfigured and eternalized Remnant, in obedience to the new constituting Form now emanating from the Essential Pole, will function as the seeds and prototypes of the *aeon* to come, and the purified Substantial Pole as the ground in which they germinate and sprout. According to our usual ways of thinking it is hard to imagine how this might be; nonetheless, according to the Kalachakra Tantra of Vajrayana Buddhism, when this world ends and is re-created, the enlightened ones of the final days, saved up from the former cycle of manifestation, will be the stars in the sky. Likewise Daniel 12:3, speaking of the end of days, says: "They that be wise shall shine as the brightness of the firmament, and they that turn many to righteousness as the stars forever and ever."

Dugin pictures his Fourth Political Theory as the appropriate political practice for the end of the present world-age, when time reverses and the Logos is dissolved in Chaos. In *The Fourth Political Theory* he says:

> The Fourth Political Theory is the amalgamation of a common project and arises from a common impulse to everything that was discarded, toppled, and humiliated during the course of constructing "the society of the spectacle" (constructing postmodernity). "The stone that the builders rejected has become the cornerstone." The philosopher Alexander Sekatsky rightly pointed out the significance of "marginalia" in the formation of a new philosophical age, suggesting the term "metaphysics of debris" as a metaphor.

In terms of traditional eschatology, this passage can be interpreted in two ways. On the one hand, it suggests the possibility of an alliance of the various Remnants of the oppressed but still-living spiritual traditions for mutual defense against the Antichrist. On the other hand, it looks suspiciously like the Antichrist's plan for collecting the dead psychic residues of the *manvantara* to build his kingdom since, from one point of view, everything that has been rejected since the beginning of the cycle might be considered part of what has been "discarded, toppled, and humiliated" to create the present postmodern world—an impression that is only intensified by Dugin's equation of Christ, "the stone that the builders rejected," with *debris*. Nothing living, however, can be built from the dead husks of the past. When a tree fruits and sheds its leaves, the idea is to collect the *seeds*; the dead leaves are good for nothing but to be mulched or burned. We don't need a metaphysic of debris, but a metaphysic of seeds.

Overcoming the Fear of Death

I have said that the Antichrist is the collective ego of the human race; exactly what does this imply?

The ego, facing death, is afraid; this is true of both physical death and psycho-spiritual death. But the ego's fear of psycho-spiritual death, of the contemplative death, of death in God, is greater than its fear of physical death, since psycho-spiritual death must be faced in full consciousness. The ego fearing death, unable to face its end, will try every conceivable ploy to flee, hide, distract itself, or else defy, rebel, claim immortality for itself. It does this through a process of identification. And the ego's last ploy to escape or conquer its fear of death is to attempt to *become* death, since—it reasons—the sum of all fears would have nothing to fear from any lesser terror. (The obsession to impersonate death so as to deny our fear of death is clearly discernible in contemporary clothing and tattoo styles, where symbols of decay and mortality—flaming skulls, etc.—are increasingly common.)

The human race, facing the end of the world, is afraid. In the face of this fear, the human collective—like the individual ego—will also flee, hide, distract itself, defy, rebel, even try to become immortal; the transhumanist "immortality" as computerized information is an eloquent sign of this fear. It will do so by confusing itself with every thing, person, situation, or collective entity it can in any way identify with—a process that is ultimately indistinguishable from collecting and taking possession of the psychic residues of forms of life that have passed away—just as all things, or the ghosts of all things, are archived in cyberspace—in view of the fact that the ego "kills" anything that it identifies with; it can take possession of nothing that truly lives, only of the psychic residues of things, the "ghosts of the dead." Consequently the last strategy of the collective ego of humanity to overcome its fear of death, its terror of the end of the world, is to *become Antichrist.*

This terminal phase of the ego is clearly elucidated in the following symbolic legend, from Vajrayana Buddhism, of the advent of the bodhisattva Yamantaka, who appears as something like a thousand-armed black Minotaur, and whose names means "Destroyer of Death":

A tantric yogi is told by his guru that if he meditates for the next 50 years, he will achieve Enlightenment.

The yogi meditates in a cave for 49 years, 11 months and 29 days, until he is interrupted by two thieves who break in with a stolen bull.

After beheading the bull in front of the hermit, they ignore his requests to be spared for a few hours longer, and behead him as well.

In his near-enlightened fury, the yogi is transformed into Yama, the God of Death. He takes the bull's head and joins it to his body, then kills the two thieves and drinks their blood from cups made from their skulls.

His rage unabated, Yama decides to kill everyone in Tibet.

The people of Tibet, fearing for their lives, pray to Manjusri, the bodhisattva of wisdom, who takes up their cause. He transforms himself into Yamantaka, similar in form to Yama but ten times more powerful and horrific, and goes to war against him.

In their battle, everywhere Yama turns he sees infinite versions of himself, as manifested by Yamantaka. Manjusri-as-Yamantaka defeats Yama, transforming him into a protector of Buddhism.

The two thieves represent the yogi's fear, at the final moment, of the psycho-spiritual death that leads to Enlightenment; their theft of the bull represents the ego's greed for possessions, its need to identify with the things of the world so as to maintain its identity; the thieves are two instead of one because the ego, though it longs to be unified, is always divided, seeing that identification *is* division, intrinsically: if "I am *that*," then I am always divided between myself and *that.*

Just as Manjusri, manifesting as Yamantaka, defeats Yama, so the Eschatological Christ in wrathful mode, the Rider on the White Horse in Apocalypse 19:11—the Prophet Jesus in Muslim eschatology—defeats the Antichrist. And the door through which the Eschatological Christ, the Mahdi, Maitreya Buddha, the Kalki Avatara arrives, at the end of the *aeon*, is *virginity-of-soul*, the self-transcendence and self-annihilation of the Elect: "And for the sake of the Elect, those days will be shortened" [Matthew 24:22]. Whoever cannot embrace spiritual death when the final moment arrives is recruited into the army of Antichrist; whoever can embrace it joins the army of the Prophet Jesus, the army of God. And when God takes the field, He encounters no opposition, He meets no enemy: because only God is.

Sacred Activism in the Context of Apocalypse

Sacred Activism is fundamentally the practice of invoking the merciful, form-giving power of the Essential Pole—of intuiting, grounding and acting upon the impending second advent of the Logos in its new, eschatological context. It is the practice of apocalypse, the work of taking the *eschaton* as guide. It is accomplished by restoring the virginity of the soul, by purifying the Mirror of the Heart. It is certainly not, however, the "immanentizing of the eschaton" as it is usually understood—a "pressing for the end" of the kind that was finally forbidden by the Jewish Kabbalists. What the phrase "immanentizing of the eschaton" actually refers to is the *literalization* of the eschaton, the attempt to force the hand of God and cause Him enact our own chosen and literalized version of the apocalyptic scenario. Certainly the sacred activist *recognizes* the immanence of the eschaton, understanding it both as a necessary element in the quality of our time and as an Eternal reality that is present in any time. But he or she never under any circumstances literalizes the eschaton by trying to "make it happen," recognizing that "ye know not the day nor the hour" [Matthew 25:13], that End and Beginning are strictly in God's hands. Consequently the restoration of the soul's virginity is not primarily for the purpose of receiving new strategic imperatives from God and then enacting them in this world—though that is certainly one of its possible effects—since it is just as likely, if not more so, that God will tell us: "You have seen the Abomination of Desolation standing in the Holy Place, so it's time to head for the hills" [Matthew 24:15]. In human terms, the renewal of the virginity of the human soul is not the *means* but the *end*—and what God chooses to make out of the final end of all human striving is entirely up to Him.

In any case the Sacred Activist, before he or she undertakes to act, must first have cleared his or her own soul—at least up to as point—of the polluted *materia secunda* as it exists under the regime of the Substantial Pole at the end of the *aeon*, of the mass of impurities made up of the impressions of personal experience, the collective psychic residues of the past phases of the *manvantara*, and the darker residues of various infra-psychic or demonic incursions, in order to provide the Word of God a place to be born within the Spiritual Heart. The *active receptivity* to the Will of God practiced by the sacred activist is thus an *anticipation of the parousia*, a rehearsal for the Second Coming; it is the work of "prepare ye the Way of the Lord; make His paths straight" [Mark 1:3]. As the activist progressively learns to receive, discern and enact God's Commands on the individual level, he or she is simultaneously preparing a place for the advent of the Eschatological Messiah on the collective level, widening the Upper Gateway through which he will appear—always remembering, of course, that Sacred Activism itself is not necessary to widen that Gateway; the only necessary thing is virginity of soul. Antichrist, on the other hand—as we have already pointed out—collects together all the psychic residues of the *aeon* so as to form his Counter-Tradition and Counter-Initiation, thereby making himself as opaque to the Light of God as is humanly (or sub-humanly) possible. He would, if he could, close and lock the Upper Gate again—*if he could find it*, that is—thereby blocking the advent of the Eschatological Messiah in the same way that King Herod, earlier in the cycle, attempted to murder the Redeeming Messiah before he could complete his mission, since he knows that the appearance of the Last Avatara will spell his end. And just as Herod failed, Antichrist will fail too.

At the end of the *manvantara* the metaphysical Principles are again unveiled due to the "thinning" of the cosmic environment, the weakening of the wall between this world and the next. However, given the dominance of the Substantial Pole, they are unveiled primarily as residues, as *memories*. These memories nonetheless give the impression, to the uninitiated and the counter-initiated, of being the esoteric Keys to the ultimate understanding and *manipulation* of Reality—that is, of God. The Antichrist believes he can work God like a puppet and make Him dance to his tune, since he sees the Divine, in line with his unpurified Substantial Pole perspective, as little more than a passive resource that is available to be tapped by whoever possesses the skill and the audacity to attempt it. The sacred activist, on the other hand, does not believe that he holds title to the Principles of Reality, nor does he have any separate agenda of his own, outside of God's as-yet-unknown Will, that he might employ these Principles to establish and enforce. For the sacred activist, the metaphysical principles are unveiled not as memories in the embrace of the Substantial Pole but as Eternal realities of the Essential Pole, "archangelic" realities emanating directly from God. He does not attempt to manipulate them because he is not foolish enough to think that he owns them. He serves them instead, because he sees them as the immediate manifestations, on the Celestial or Intelligible Plane, of the Divine Reality, and consequently knows beyond any shadow of a doubt that they own him. Therefore his struggle is not to flee or survive or control the Apocalypse, but to *willingly allow it*. And lest the reader begin to fantasize about the nature of the sacred activist in quasi-mythic terms, we can clarify and de-mystify him simply by saying that he knows how to pray. The laws of Sacred Activism are nothing other than the laws of prayer, which can ultimately be reduced to a single intent: that of laying all one's petitions at the feet of the Throne of God in the spirit of "not my will but Thine be done" [Luke 22:42].

Joining the Remnant is certainly not easy. This is not due to any prideful exclusivism on their part, however, but only because the conviction of sin and the radical purification from it are humbling, and because quintessential aloneness—sometimes in individual isolation, sometimes in the midst of crowds—is a difficult fate. Yet it has its rewards, since that aloneness eventually opens onto the Communion of the Saints. When the Prophet Elijah was living in the wilderness as God had directed, hiding himself from the evil King Ahab whom he had denounced, he was fed by ravens, bread and meat in the morning and bread and meat in the evening [see 1 Kings 17]. The ravens are the dark wisdom of God, the mystery of *Al-Jalal*, the Divine Rigor, within which is hidden *Al-Rahim*, the Divine Compassion. Furthermore—if the truth be known—it is impossible to join the Remnant on one's own initiative, any more that it is possible to initiate oneself so as to travel the Spiritual Path. You have to be entirely willing to volunteer; nonetheless God still has to draft you. *His* is your obedience to Him; *His* is your love for *Him*; *His* is your knowledge of Him. To be willing to be moved, to be swayed this way and that by the hard blows of His Mercy, "like a corpse in the hands of a Washer of the Dead," is all that is required for the practice of Apocalypse, as well as for the simple conduct of human life on earth. "Heaven and earth will pass away, but My Word will not pass away" [Matthew 24:35].[2]

Unexpectedly, A Large Area of Agreement

It is burdensome and depressing to feel compelled, in the name of one's own idea of Truth, to browbeat a person who lives at a distance and cannot immediately defend himself. To always know better than someone else can darken one's mind; to always be more virtuous than someone else can drain one's virtue. How sad it is to have nothing good to say about somebody, to have no respect for anyone but oneself! There is no quicker or surer way to lose whatever self-respect one has been able to hold on to, in the swift, crackling, electric current of demonic energies that is the postmodern world. Therefore it is with both relief and delight that I reproduce a passage from *Eurasian Mission* that I can not only whole-heartedly support, but am frankly jealous that I didn't write myself. A miracle! A true man stands forth from the darkness of the human mind. Listen to this:

> We should strongly oppose any kind of confrontation between religions: Muslims against Christians, Jews against Muslims, Muslims against Hindus, and so on. These interconfessional wars and hatreds work for the cause of the kingdom of Antichrist, which tries to divide all the traditional religions in order to impose its own pseudo-religion, the eschatological parody. We need to unite the Right, the Left, and the traditional religions in a common struggle against the common enemy. . . .

True but for the last sentence, which is nearly half-true, though it still treats the religions not as Divine Revelations whose authority transcends all others, but as social "sectors" or "constituencies." But now:

> Earlier wars were fought between ethnic groups, or between religions, or between empires, or between national states. In the twentieth century, wars were fought between ideological blocs. Today a new era of warfare has come, where the protagonist is always the global oligarchy, carrying out its plans, either with the direct use of American forces and NATO troops, or by organizing local conflicts in such a way that its scenario is consistent with the interests of this elite, albeit indirectly. In some cases, conflicts, wars, and unrest are provoked with the participation of many groups, none of which

2. Required reading for all who aspire to be sacred activists in the time of apocalypse is Leo Schaya's seminal essay "The Eliatic Functon," *Studies in Comparative Religion* vol. 13 nos. 1 and 2 (Middlesex, England: Perennial Books Ltd., 1979), pp. 31–40.

represent the interests of the global oligarchy directly; then we are dealing with a situation of controlled chaos, the design and aim of which American strategists first developed in the 1980s. In other cases, the global oligarchy stands simultaneously on both sides of the two warring parties, manipulating them to its advantage. A correct analysis of modern war is thus reduced to defining the algorithm of this behavior and singling out the tactical and strategic goals of the global oligarchy and the American state in each particular case. This sort of analytics requires a new methodology derived from a revolutionary and global consciousness. . . .

The global oligarchy maliciously incites one group against another to distract both from what should be their primary struggle. That's why only those groups (large ones, as carriers of particular world religions, and small ones, as independent associations of citizens on a common platform) should be allowed to join the ranks of the Global Revolutionary Alliance that are clearly aware of the fact that in any local and regional confrontations, the main enemy is usually hidden. It is the global oligarchy. To defeat it, if necessary, they must unite even with their worst enemies (on the local level), if they are also oriented against this oligarchy. Those who challenge this principle play into the hands of the global oligarchy and can be blamed as accomplices. . . . The future must be based on the principle of solidarity and on societies as organic, holistic units. Each culture will come to enshrine its values within a particular spiritual and religious form. This form will be different in each, but they all have something in common: there can be no such thing as genuine cultures, religions, and states, which consider materialism, money, physical comfort, mechanical efficiency and vegetative pleasure to be their highest values. Matter alone can never reproduce its own form—it is formless. But such an absolutely materialistic civilization is being built on a global scale by the global oligarchy, which is exploiting the basest, most tangible incentives and the most primitive impulses of the human being. At the very bottom of the soul sleep shameful, semi-animalistic, semi-demoniac energies which are drawn toward the material world in order to merge with organic, physical beings. These sluggish energies, which are resistant to fire, light, concentration, and elevation, are the very backbone of the machinations being exploited by the global system. It cultivates these things, flattering those who gallivant. This bottom of the soul, or the voice of materialism, ruins any cultural form, any ideal, and any norm, regardless of whatever it is. . . .

This is the way societies lose their future. Every culture opposes these basest appetites and energies of spiritual entropy and decay, but does so in its own way and sets a waymark for its norms, ideas, and spirit. Despite the fact that the lineaments and configurations of these forms and ideals are different, they all have one thing in common—in fact this commonality exists anywhere *we are talking about form, not substance; about the idea, and not about physicality; and about norms and exerting effort, but not about dissipation, entertainment, and debauchery.* Therefore, the vision of the future for which all the elements of the Global Revolutionary Alliance fight against the global oligarchy, in all their diversity, is a common one.

True and true! This is my analysis precisely—and the global alliance that Dugin calls for here clearly goes *beyond* the notion of "what we are divides us" to a true common spirituality and humanity. It is crucial for Dugin to understand, however, that "Form," "Idea" and "Norm" are, precisely, LOGOS—not in the limited mental sense of "logic" but in the larger spiritual sense which includes the mental sense but is not limited to it, or by it. Therefore to "postpone such notions as the dimension of spirit and the divine," as he advises in **The Fourth Political Theory**, as well as to adopt Chaos as a metaphysic, to seek "ontic roots" rather than "ontological heights", is to work directly *against* "fire, light, concentration, and elevation," to fall into the grip of those very "shameful, semi-animalistic, semi-demoniac energies" that sleep at the bottom of the soul, and thereby to give aid and comfort to the global oligarchy—that oligarchy whose principle is, precisely, not Form, but Substance, not Logos but Chaos; a "man of substance" is a man of *money*. In the above passage Dugin shows himself to be fully aware of the of the evils of Chaos as the principle of global oligarchy, of the demonic aspect of the Substantial Pole, yet he can see no way to invoke the one Power that can free us from the dark side of Substance, the power of *Logos renewed*. In his paean "The Knights Templars of the Proletariat," he says:

> [*The*] evil demon of substance has taken hostage delicate and frail Life, the Sun Maiden. It is . . . form stolen by a harsh usurper—matter. It can be saved only by [*a*] heroic deed, a stubborn, terrifying, relentless war against the ground ice of reality.

Wrong! Self-will can never free Form from the grasp of Substance because the effect of self-will is, precisely, to transmute Form *into* Substance. Self-will is the Counter-Alchemy, the inverted *goeteia* that transforms Gold into Lead. Only the purification of Substance, only virginity-of-soul can receive the new and merciful Form that can raise the Sun Maiden from the permafrost, take her by the hand and lead her into the Land Behind the North Wind, the kingdom of *Sol Invictus*, the Sun Unconquered. And, yes, it takes Fire to purify Substance from the dead archive of the *aeon*, from the residues of shattered Form and disintegrated Logos—not the stubborn ice of self-will, but the fire of the Holy Spirit. Dugin stares into what he *calls* Chaos, and sees there a mysterious All-Nothing seething with unknown possibilities. *Is this the Chaos of the murmuring psychic residues of the polluted Substantial Pole, the precise energy that the global oligarchs draw upon to spread the subliminal suggestions and infernal temptations that they hope to impose upon the rest of us—not only by material operations but also by psychic influences, seeing that there are working Satanists among them (and we sincerely hope Dugin will not end by becoming of their number)—only to discover, to their dismay, that they themselves are fatally infected by it? Or is it the Silent Thunder of the Logos, the as-yet-unknown but always-pressing-to-be-known Will of God? When we undertake to step beyond the known truth and the logic of it, it is absolutely crucial that we learn how to separate these two forces, that we be willing to do the work and make the sacrifice necessary to distinguish between them—because we can rest assured that both principles, infernally confused, will be present and operating.* ONCE WE HAVE SEEN THE DIFFERENCE BETWEEN THEM, WE MUST CHOOSE THE ONE AND REJECT THE OTHER. WE CAN'T HAVE IT BOTH WAYS. AS SOON AS THIS CHOICE HAS ARRIVED, WE MUST DECLARE OUR ALLEGIANCE TO THE LIGHT OR BE MARKED AS COLLABORATORS WITH THE DARKNESS.

How is this choice to be made? Each true and God-given religion tells us precisely how. My religion says, "Surrender your life to Allah, and thereby recognize the *fitrah*, the Primordial Human Essence, and assume the *Amana*, the Perennial Human Trust." The religion Dugin claims to follow says: "Love the Lord your God with your whole heart and your whole soul and your whole mind and your whole strength, and your neighbor as yourself; not my will but Thine be done" [Matthew 22:37–40; Luke 22:42].

My own contribution to the search for Norm and Form and Idea is *Chapter Seven* of this book. Norm and Form and Idea do not come only from the ancestors, from the *narod*; if they did they would be little more than "the dead hand of Tradition." They also come from God—*first* from God—directly, vertically, and in this very moment. Tradition is preserved, and enlivened, and carried forward, in horizontal terms, by the Word of God that is always descending, in vertical terms. That Word, that Logos, *is* Norm and Form and Idea, coming down not to bury Tradition but to provide it with the next living breath, and the next, and the next. We know, and it is our sacred duty to remember, the Forms that God has sent and blessed and authorized and laid down as law for us. What we do not know is what He will say next, in the next breath, the next instant. We know that He comes not to destroy Form [cf. Matthew 5:17], but what He will do to fulfill Form is totally inconceivable—until, that is, it knocks at the door of the spiritual Heart, demanding to be conceived. Satan threatens and promises, murmurs and suggests, but the Silence of God is louder than all his whispering. If we can tell them apart, then we are called into His Presence and given our marching orders. If we can't tell them apart, then we are nothing but the mouthers of dead names, men and women filled with the muttering debris of human language which once was living human intent, disintegrated hosts to infernal psychic residues that not even death has been able to silence.

But "the Rulers of the Darkness of This World" [Ephesians 6:12] are not only "the most primitive impulses ... shameful, semi-animalistic, semi-demoniac energies which are drawn toward the material world in order to merge with organic, physical beings ... sluggish energies which are resistant to fire, light, concentration, and elevation," seeing that we also have to contend with "spiritual wickedness in high places" [Ephesians 6:12]—not only with heavy, sluggish, *Satanic* energies but also with lightning-swift *Luciferian* energies that move at the speed of thought—energies which are, precisely, *powers of angelic darkness*, forces that are entirely capable of impersonating and counterfeiting "fire, light, concentration, and elevation" in precisely the same way that the Devil is able to transform himself into an angel of light [cf 2Corinthians 11:14].

If Aleksandr Dugin is willing to learn how to submit all his strategic imperatives to God, not just once but over and over again, at every turn, not only hoping that they will be confirmed or refined or added to, but also entirely willing that they be revised or censored or thrown on the trash-heap if such is His Will—if he not only opens himself to God's mysterious, unpredictable and ongoing Will for him, wide enough so he can clearly hear what it is telling him, but also stands ready to *obey* that Will, immediately and without protest—to obey it unquestioningly, even before he knows what it is, even while he is still asking questions—then, God willing, he will be liberated both from the heavy grasp of Satanic materialism and from the lightning-fast suggestions and misdirections of the fallen angels who are host to the Luciferian intellect. Word and Norm and Form and Idea will descend upon him; *parousia* will begin within him; the Logos will be reborn; the Essential Pole will unveil itself again in his spiritual Center. What else is the monastery for, the cell, the skete, the oratory, the Holy Mountain, but to make the Heart available to this descent?

If he is not willing, however, then he may well find himself in the camp of Antichrist, along with many of the rest of us who thought that we could "lead our own lives" as self-initiated, self-determined free agents. (Aleksandr Dugin rejects the concept of "the individual," yet it appears that he has lived his life in the most individual terms imaginable; perhaps, like any self-worshipper, he simply wants to be the *only* individual.) And it would be a crying shame if Dugin's ability to provide a deep, clear, comprehensive, sane, humanly respectful and spiritually sound picture of our present dilemma, as he has done here and in a number of other places, were only one of his many skills, a mere technique of convenience. The Truth is never more deeply hidden than when it is presented, in postmodern garb, as merely one of innumerable "alternative views." If Truth is veiled and guarded she retains her aura of sanctity and power, even under great oppression; if she is relativized in the name of "the celebration of diversity," if she is released from her prison and allowed to walk the streets with the other girls, then she is devalued, cheapened, prostituted. Truth is never more deeply hidden than when it is used to lend plausibility and respectability to lies and illusions. When God Himself appears as Truth, however, when He is unveiled in His Name of *Al-Haqq*, He will *single out* His earthly reflection, throw a cordon of angelic guardians around it, and hammer down the city of the Lie. He will also purify me—in whatever world I may then reside—from the arrogance of virtue and the stupidity of intelligence. And if it is certain that some day He *will* come—then why not today? Why not now?

Appendix One:
Templar Resonances

by Charles Upton and Dr. John Andrew Morrow

Some of the text of this Appendix has already been quoted above. However, since Aleksandr Dugin has attempted to add the history and myth of the Knights Templar to his list of the identifications available to those who would follow him, most notably in his book **Templars of the Proletariat** *(2015), and in view of the fact that the metaphysical function of the Templars was of great importance to René Guénon, I have decided to include at greater length the research on the Poor Fellow-Soldiers of Christ and of the Temple of Solomon produced by Dr. John Andrew Morrow and myself in the context of the Covenants Initiative. A true knowledge of the Knights Templar and their spiritual significance provides a valuable historical perspective on the Transcendent Unity of Religions; consequently the name "Templar" must not be allowed to degenerate into a cheap political slogan. "Templar Resonances" was originally published in* Knights Templar *magazine, June & July issues, 2017.*

D R. JOHN ANDREW MORROW, in the course of his ongoing researches on the covenants of Prophet Muhammad with the Christians of his time, and other Peoples of the Book, has made a number of intriguing discoveries. The bulk of this research appears in his seminal book *The Covenants of the Prophet Muhammad with the Christians of the World* as well as the two-volume anthology edited by him and entitled *Islam and the People of the Book: Critical Studies of the Covenants of the Prophet*. This much-needed scholarship has gone a long way toward resurrecting the Prophetic Covenants from obscurity, throwing light on the just and equitable norms the Prophet laid down governing how Muslims were to treat Peoples of the Book and other religious minorities within the growing Islamic State, and establishing the covenants, treaties and letters of Muhammad, side-by-side with Qur'an and *ahadith*, as a third foundational source for the Islamic tradition. It has also struck a new chord in interfaith relations, one which is not dependent upon the norms of secular Liberalism, but springs directly from the Abrahamic tradition itself. As such, it has begun to define a true exoteric expression and context for the relatively esoteric doctrine of the Transcendent Unity of Religions. In light of this it is strikingly appropriate that, in the course of his studies, Dr. Morrow seems to have inadvertently come across material which throws a new light on the origins and doctrines of the Knights Templar, whom René Guénon saw as early expositors of the Transcendent Unity of Religions and guardians of the Primordial Tradition. The historical data brought to light by Dr. Morrow also resonates with some of my own more metaphysical, symbolic and mythopoetic speculations on the Templars and other matters; some of these can be found in my books *Findings: in Metaphysic, Path and Lore* [Sophia Perennis, 2010], and *Vectors of the Counter-Initiation* [Sophia Perennis, 2012]. Excerpts appear below.

ﾠ

ᖇ

**From "The Covenant of the Prophet Muhammad with the
Armenian Christians of Jerusalem" by Dr. John Andrew Morrow,
included in *Islam and the People of the Book: Critical Studies of
the Covenants of the Prophet*, Cambridge Scholars, 2017**

The text of *Covenant of the Prophet Muhammad with the Armenian Christians of Jerusalem* [*as Dr. Morrow reproduces it in* Islam and the People of the Book] derives from R.P. Paylaguian's *Histoire ecclésiastique arménienne* (pp. 79–80) which was rendered into French by Albert Khazinedjian in *Des serviteurs fidèles, Les enfants de l'Arménie au service de l'État turc* (p.16), as well as the translation provided by Bernard Falque de Bezaure. According to the latter, this *firmān* was issued in Madīnah; it was written down by Zayd ibn Thābit (d. 660) and was later copied by 'Umar and 'Alī. Falque de Bezaure describes the background of this Covenant as follows:

> Muḥammad receives Jewish and Christian ambassadors in the guest-house of Ramlah bint al-ḥārith in the neighborhood of Najdariyyah. It is the year known as *am al-wufūd*, namely, the year of ambassadors during which delegations were received by Muḥammad. It is Bilāl, the black muezzin, who guides the ambassadors ... one of whom is Abraham, the Armenian abbot from the Monastery of St. James in Jerusalem and the Monastery of Zion, who is the ambassador of the Katholikos of Armenia, who resides in the oldest abbey in the world, Etchmiadzin, founded in 285 on the foothills of Mount Ararat, on the site where Gregory the Illuminator received a revelation from God by means of an illumination that was identical to the one that Saint Paul had received on the road to Damascus. ... Muḥammad asked him a question: "In Jerusalem there is a (monotheistic) Christian sect that worships Sirius, the dog-star; what does that dog and that star symbolize?" Abraham answered: "The star symbolizes the illumination that Saint Gregory the Illuminator received on Mount Ararat. This night star has 16 rays; the one of

Dikpala represents the Vanatur of Mount Ararat[1] ... both the morning and evening stars have 8 rays... [*like the Christmas Star that overshadows the Virgin and Child in Eastern Orthodox iconography—C.U.*] Together, they symbolize the manifestation of God by means of illumination. The dog... represents the ṭarīqah which signifies a Spiritual Path; it is the guide of those who submit to God ... revealed by the evening star" (Apocalypse of John, pointed out by Jean-Charles Pichon in *Les Sectes des temps anciens*). Muḥammad was pleased to see that Abraham submitted to God in his monastery in Jerusalem. (in Arabic, the word *Muslim* literally means "to submit to God"). "Submission to God is my tradition," responded the Prophet.[2]

Comment by Charles Upton

Although the Semites, both Jew and Arab, tend to despise dogs and regard them as unclean—the appearance of a dog as guardian of the Companions of the Cave in the *Surah of the Cave* notwithstanding—the dog occupies an honored position in Zoroastrianism as "the friend of Man." Consequently the dog as symbol of the *ṭarīqah* or Spiritual Path suggests the possibility of a Persian influence (see *Dogs from a Sufi Point of View* by Dr. Javad Nurbakhsh, Khaniqahi Nimatullahi Publications, 1992). "Canine esoterism" could have formed part of the doctrine of the Nazirite Brotherhood,[3] who sometimes worked as shepherds. The Talmud mentions a certain "Nazirite shepherd," and the prophet Amos, who was himself a shepherd, laments the persecution and degeneracy of the Brotherhood. In the words of the Prophet Muhammad, "there has never

---

1. The meaning of the phrase "the one of Dikpala represents the Vanatur of Mount Ararat" is unclear. The Dikpala are the gods of the eight directions in Hinduism; such groups of gods are common in many religions. Vanatur is the chief god in the ancient pre-Christian Armenian religion; the name, which literally means "Lord of (Lake) Van," is used as an epithet for Aramazd, who is essentially identical to the Zoroastrian Ahura Mazda. Perhaps the symbolism of the 8-pointed star derives from the Armenian version of the Dikpala, with Ararat, the seat of Vanatur, representing the Ninth point, the Center.

2. The tradition in question was related by Virgil Gheorghiu in his book, *La Vie de Mahomet*, which was translated from Romanian into French by Livia Lamoure (1962: 416–17; 1989: 304–5). The reference mentions that this event took place in the 9th year of the *hijrah* and is also referenced by Maqrizī (1363–1442) and Muḥammad Ḥamīdullāh (1908–2002).

3. The Nazirites, who are mentioned in Numbers 6:1–21, are thought to have pre-dated Moses. The Nazirite vow forbade wine-drinking and cutting the hair, and could be taken on either a temporary or a lifetime basis. Samuel, Samson and John the Baptist were Nazirites. Jesus made various pronouncements that, according to some, identified him as a Nazirite [cf. Mark 14:22–25 and Luke 22:15-18]. That he was criticized as a "winebibber" [cf. Matthew 11:19] is puzzling, since drinking wine was no sin for Jews in general, but it would have made sense if by drinking wine he had broken his Nazirite vow. (Wine drinking in itself, however, did not terminate the vow.) Nazirites were forbidden to approach corpses, but perhaps Jesus fulfilled this taboo in his own unique way: by bringing the corpses back to life. When a temporary Nazirite reached the end of his vow he was required to sacrifice a ewe, a lamb and a ram. At the expiration of his own vow—which was his life—did Jesus, the Lamb of God, fulfill this ritual duty by sacrificing—himself?

been a prophet but that he was a shepherd." And if the Nazirites were shepherds, they must have employed dogs. Some, such as the Christian visionary Anne Catherine Emmerich, present evidence that the shepherds who were present at the birth of Christ were in spiritual contact with the Zoroastrian Magi;[4] the same connection has been claimed for the Essenes. Those "shepherds who watched their flocks by night" in the narrative of Christ's nativity in the Gospel of Luke were most likely Nazirites; to "watch one's flock by night" is to act as spiritual guide for an esoteric school. Dogs, too, keep watch by night and carry on mysterious discourses in the darkness in an unknown language; they also howl in veneration of the Moon, emblem of the Prophet Muhammad. The notion of the dog as guardian of the mysteries can be traced back to the Egyptian god Anubis, who conducted the souls of the dead—the sheep who made up his flock, insofar as he was originally a sheep-dog—to the other world. (That Anubis, the jackal-god, was originally a sheep-dog is not impossible; the shepherds of the Balkans used to interbreed their sheep-dogs with jackals.) Speaking in esoteric terms, this is precisely the function of the *ṭarīqah*, the Spiritual Path: to conduct those who have "died before they die" to the world beyond time. That the mystics of Islam are named *Sufis* ("wool-clad"), and that Jesus Christ (who is depicted with the long hair of a Nazirite) called himself "the Good Shepherd," are part and parcel of the same constellation of symbols. Furthermore, the word for "dog" in Arabic is *kalb*, while the word for "spiritual Heart" is *qalb*. Is the Cave guarded by the Dog in the *Surah of the Cave* actually that point of ultimate spiritual depth within the human being that the Hindus call "the Cave of the Heart"?

As for the "worship" of a star, I am indebted to Gautier Pierozak[5] for informing me that Louis Charbonneau-Lassay, author of the celebrated *Bestiary of Christ*, had access to archives from the 16th century that were loaned to him by representatives of a secret Catholic group named *l'Estoile Internelle*, the Inner Star, and which contained lore relating to the Holy Grail, among other themes. Items of this lore later appeared in René Guénon's *Symbols of Sacred Science*, most likely thanks to his extensive correspondence with Charbonneau-Lassay, in the course of which he elucidated many of the symbols that the author of the *Bestiary* had compiled. The Grail, of course, has a legendary association with the Knights Templar. Charbonneau-Lassay also collected material on the Templars from other sources—and, as is well known, Guénon believed that the Knights Templar had made contact with representatives of the Supreme Center of the Primordial Tradition during their occupation of the Holy Land. Be that

---

4. See Anne Catherine Emmerich, *The Life of Christ and Biblical Revelations*, TAN Books edition, volume 2, p. 270.

5. See https://fr.ulule.com/gauthierpierozak/.

as it may, the notion of the star as a symbol of inner illumination, whether or not it can be proved to bear any special relation to Templar doctrine and practice, is directly in line with both the New Testament and the Holy Qur'an. 2 Peter 1:19 says:

> So we have the prophetic word made more sure,
> to which you do well to pay attention as to a lamp shining in a
>   dark place,
> until the day dawns, and the Morning Star arises in your hearts.

Cf. also the *Surah at-Tariq* ("The Night-Visitor"), the first four verses of which are:

> By the heaven and the Morning Star—
> Ah, what will tell thee what the Morning Star is?
> The piercing Star!
> No human soul but hath a guardian over it.

The *Surah al-Najm* ("The Star"), on the other hand, begins as follows:

> By the Star when it setteth,
> Your comrade [*Muhammad*] erreth not, nor is deceived;
> Nor doth he speak of (his own) desire.

"The Star when it setteth" indicates the Evening Star, which, according to the Armenian Abbot Abraham, reveals—or, let us say, heralds—Sirius, the Dog Star of the full night, who represents the *ṭarīqah*, the Spiritual Path; likewise verse 49 of the *Surah al-Najm* reads:

> And that He it is Who is the Lord of Sirius.

The Morning Star would seem to symbolize the light of God as it comes into this world, both as Revelation and in the form of new-born human souls, each with its angelic guardian. Consequently the Evening Star would represent initiation into the Spiritual Path as the response of the human soul to the light of Revelation, its transcendence of the created world and its return, together with all things, to its point-of-origin in Allah. *Al-Najm* is the surah which describes the advent of the Angel Gabriel, or Jibrail, to bring the revelation of the Holy Qur'an; Allah is assuring the Prophet that his vision of Jibrail is truth, not deception, because Muhammad is on the *ṭarīqah*, the Path of return to God. Sirius would then be the Illumination or *Ma'rifa* which is the final fruit of that Path, the eternal Knowledge of God which synthesizes Revelation and Realization because it is beyond birth and death, beyond the two worlds.

෴

Comment by Dr. Morrow

Falque de Bezaure's account of the transmission of the Covenants of the Prophet is ground-breaking. He relates that:

> These firmāns would become *aḥadīth* in the Muslim corpus known as the Sunnah and would later be transcribed in the houses of wisdom in Baghdād and Damascus. They later passed into the hands of the Umayyad, 'Abbāsid, and Fāṭimid Caliphs. . . . These are also the documents that were given, in the eleventh century, by Michael, monophysite bishop and patriarch of Antioch, to the dynasty of Armenian kings, the Rupenids, and to Mleh, the Master of the Templars of Armenia, in particular, at the same moment that the 'Alawī-Hashashīn-Nusayrī documents entered the chain of Armanus in Sicily. These [*latter*] documents concern the mysteries of illumination of the ancient Christian and Jewish prophets as well as Muḥammad. They represent the foundations and the basis of the secret spiritual meditations that were given by Hugues de Payens, the ordained priest of the Saint Sepulcher [*the Church of the Holy Sepulcher*], to the thirty-one proto-Templars cited in the Armenian chronicles of the aforementioned Michael the Syrian. [*This would certainly seem to corroborate Guénon's belief that the Templars received esoteric initiation in the Holy Land from the keepers of the Primordial Tradition.—C.U.*] According to Migne, this was the secret of the meditations of the Jesuits.[6]

In both the *Covenants of the Prophet Muḥammad with the Christians of the World* and this current book, *Islam and the People of the Book: Critical Studies on the Covenants of the Prophet*, attempts have been made to explain the mode of transmission of the Muḥammadan Covenants. The theory proposed by Bernard Falque de Bezaure certainly makes a great deal of sense. Founded by Caliph Hārūn al-Rashīd (r. 786–809), the *Bayt al-ḥikmah* brought together leading Muslim and non-Muslim scholars from all around the known world, including many of Christian background. They translated ancient books into Arabic. They preserved Arabic and Islamic sources. Within a century and a half, the House of Wisdom had grown into the largest repository of books in the world.

Bernard Falque de Bezaure theorizes that the Covenants of the Prophet Muḥammad all found their way to the *Bayt al-ḥikmah* where multiple copies were made by scribes. These, in turn, were sent to a series of Caliphs who, in turn, included them in their own library collections. Other copies were certainly provided to other Muslim authorities, administrators, and judges. Copies of the Covenants of the Prophet were probably provided to libraries

---

6. See manuscript n• 37 of the Bibliothèque de Nîmes, and *Milites Templi* by Bernard Falque de Bezaure, chapter "Hugues le Pêcheur."

throughout the Muslim world. The *Bayt al-ḥikmah* of Baghdād and Damascus would have been focal points in the geographic dissemination of the Muḥammadan Covenants. With the destruction of the House of Wisdom following the Mongol Siege of Baghdād in 1258 many if not most of the original copies of the letters, Covenants, and treaties of the Prophet Muḥammad were destroyed, leaving only copies in circulation. It was, after all, in the *Bayt al-ḥikmah* or one of its branches that the original copy of the Covenant of the Prophet Muḥammad with the Christians of Najrān was brought to light in 878. This lends credence to the claim that the House of Wisdom was the repository of many original writings of Muḥammad ibn ʿAbd Allāh, the man known to the world as the Messenger of Allāh.

As if this were not enough of an accomplishment, Bernard Falque de Bezaure advances another astonishing and audacious theory; namely, that the secrets granted, and jealously guarded, protected, and transmitted by the Knights Templar and other secretive Christian societies, consisted of the Covenants of the Prophet Muḥammad. Since the Dome of the Rock contains some of the most ancient examples of early Arabic and Islamic writing, it is also likely that the complex contained precious documents from the dawn of Islām, including, apparently, copies of the Muḥammadan Covenants. Many have theorized that the Knights Templars were actually converts to Shīʿite Islām. Their veneration of a holy woman, who was supposedly not the Virgin Mary, allegedly alludes to Fāṭimah al-Zahrāʾ. The symbolism of fourteen pillars, two of which are identical, is found in their architecture, and is said to symbolize the fourteen infallibles, Muḥammad, Fāṭimah, and the Twelve Imāms from the Progeny of the Prophet.

If this theory is correct, and not some New Age nonsense founded in fantasy as opposed to fact, some Crusaders may have come to the Holy Land as Christian conquerors and, after coming across the Covenants of the Prophet at the Dome of the Rock, were so moved by the protections that the Prophet granted Christians that they embraced Islām, wishing to imitate such a just and righteous man. The Knights Templar would thus have become the Keepers of the Covenants of the Prophet, committed to protecting the true teachings of the Messenger of Allāh until the end of ages. Seeing how far Muslims had departed from the path of the Prophet, and how certain rulers had systematically attempted to suppress and corrupt the *sunnah*, they assumed the responsibility of protecting the Covenants of the Prophet from Muslims themselves. When word of their initiation ceremonies reached King Philip IV of France (1268–1314), he set out to eradicate the Templars on the grounds that they were worshippers of Baphomet, a corruption of Mahomet or Muḥammad. Whether or not one accepts any or all of this interpretation has no bearing on [*the question of the validity of*] the Covenant of the Prophet Muḥammad with the Armenian Christians of Jerusalem. It simply opens an entirely novel line of enquiry.

Comment by Charles Upton

The Arabic root TRQ, upon which the Arabic word *ṭarīqah* is based, refracts itself into various words meaning *path; road; spiritual Way; one who knocks* (as a metaphor for *night visitor*), and *path or orbit for the passage of stars or other heavenly bodies* (who are also "night visitors"). Jesus (speaking in Aramaic, closely allied to Arabic) called himself "the *Way*," and said: "Behold, I stand at the door and *knock*." And in Luke, Chapter 11, he tells the parable of the man, a night visitor, who knocks on his friend's door at midnight asking for bread to feed his guest, and says "*knock* and it shall be opened unto you."

Also highly interesting is the fact that stars are commonly associated with angels, even with angelic armies; Luke 2:13 refers to the angels as "the Host (Army) of Heaven." Did the Templars think of themselves as earthly reflections or representatives of this Angelic Army, charged by God with the secret governance of the world?

ॐ

Charles Upton, from *Findings: in Metaphysic, Path and Lore*

One day, as I was reading the *Surah of the Cave* in the Rodwell translation of the Noble Qur'an, the answer to the riddle posed therein—i.e., the exact number of the Youths known as the Companions of the Cave—came to me. And after a short internet search, I was fortunately able (to my great relief) to confirm to my own satisfaction what at first had been no more than an intuition. Here is the pertinent passage according to Rodwell, Q.18:8–26 [Pickthall, 18:9–28; Muhammad Asad and Yusuf Ali, 18: 9–27]:

> Hast thou reflected that the Inmates of the Cave and of al-Rakim were one of Our wondrous signs?
>
> When the youths betook them to the cave they said, "O our Lord! grant us mercy from before Thee, and order for us our affair aright."
>
> Then struck We upon their ears with deafness in the cave for many a year:
>
> Then We awaked them that We might know which of the two parties could best reckon the space of their abiding.
>
> We will relate to thee their tale with truth. They were youths who had believed in their Lord, and in guidance had We increased them;
>
> And We had made them stout of heart, when they stood up and said, "Our Lord is Lord of the Heavens and of the Earth: we will call on no other god than Him; for in that case we had said a thing outrageous.
>
> These our people have taken other gods beside Him, though they bring no clear proof for them; but, who is more iniquitous than he who forgeth a lie of God?
>
> So when you shall have separated you from them and from that which they

worship beside God, then betake you to the Cave: Your Lord will unfold His mercy to you, and will order your affairs for you for the best."

And thou mightest have seen the sun when it arose, pass on the right of their cave, and when it set, leave them on the left, while they were in its spacious chamber. This is one of the signs of God. Guided indeed is he whom God guideth; but for him whom He misleadeth, thou shalt by no means find a patron, director.

And thou wouldst have deemed them awake, though they were sleeping: and We turned them to the right and to the left. And in the entry lay their dog with paws outstretched. Hadst thou come suddenly upon them, thou wouldst surely have turned thy back on them in flight, and have been filled with fear at them.

So We awaked them that they might question one another. Said one of them, "How long have you tarried here?" They said, "we have tarried a day or part of a day." They said, "Your Lord knoweth best how long you have tarried: Send now one of you with this your coin into the city, and let him mark who therein hath purest food, and from him let him bring you a supply: and let him be courteous, and not discover you to anyone.

For they, if they find you out, will stone you or turn you back to their faith, and in that case it will fare ill with you forever."

And thus made We their adventure known to their fellow citizens, that they might learn that the promise of God is true, and that as to "the Hour" there is no doubt of its coming. When they disputed among themselves concerning what had befallen them, some said, "Build a building over them; their Lord knoweth best about them." Those who prevailed in the matter said, "A place of worship will we surely raise over them."

Some say, "They were three; their dog the fourth:" others say, "Five; their dog the sixth," guessing at the secret: others say "Seven; and their dog the eighth." Say: My Lord best knoweth the number: none, save a few, shall know them.

Therefore be clear in thy discussions about them, and ask not any Christian concerning them.

Say not thou of a thing, "I will surely do it tomorrow;" without, "If God will." And when thou has forgotten, call thy Lord to mind; and say, "Haply my Lord will guide me, that I may come near to the truth of this story with correctness."

And they tarried in their cave 300 years, and 9 years over.

Say: God best knoweth how long they tarried: With Him are the secrets of the Heavens and of the Earth: Look thou and hearken unto Him alone. Man hath no guardian but Him, and none may bear part in His judgments:—

And publish what hath been revealed to thee of the Book of thy Lord—none may change His words,—and thou shalt find no refuge beside Him.

Rodwell's translation of part of his verse 22, *and ask not any Christian concerning them*, appears to be an extrapolation based on the fact that the legend of the Seven Sleepers of Ephesus, with whom the Companions of the Cave are often identified, was current in the Christian world, and remains so today, where they are identified as Christian martyrs. They are part of the Roman martyrology; there is even an Eastern Orthodox icon depicting them. Other translators, however, either leave those whom Muslims are not to question about the number of the Companions unidentified, or identify them with the Pagans, or never define such a group at all. Following Rodwell's translation, however—or his extrapolation—we can further conjecture that the number of the Companions was not seven, since any Muslim who asked the Christians their number would likely have been answered "seven," in line with the Seven Sleepers story. And the Qur'an even more explicitly denies that the number is either three or five, since these are defined as mere "guesses."

According to the inner voice I heard, their number is "Nine," with their Dog (presumably) being the Tenth. What evidence might be brought forward in support of this intuition? And (assuming that Nine is the right answer and that I was not subject to deception) what might the Nine Companions and their Dog symbolize in terms of the more arcane levels of meaning enfolded by the Noble Qur'an? The Book itself tells us to *be clear in your discussions of them* (Rodwell), or *contend not concerning them except with an outward contending* (Pickthall), or *do not argue about them other than by way of an obvious argument* (Muhammad Asad), or *enter not, therefore, into controversies concerning them, except on a matter that is clear* (Yusuf Ali). We are being told, in other words, that the answer to this riddle is something clear and explicit, not a vague ethical sentiment or mystical reverie. And this, if the truth be known, is the way with all good riddles: they carefully avoid abstraction; their answers are always clear and concrete. Likewise, in performing exegesis of sacred scripture, the best practice is always to first clarify the literal meaning as much as possible; only then will the concrete symbols appear that can support a more *batini ta'wil*, a more esoteric hermeneutic.

In quest of such clarity, I did a short internet search, and found a *Wikipedia* article on the legend of the Seven Sleepers, where it was asserted—incorrectly— that the Qur'an explains the 300 + 9 years that the Sleepers occupied their cave as representing the 9-year discrepancy between 300 solar years and the same length of time computed in lunar years, since during their long sleep the calendar had been changed from solar to lunar. The unnamed writer of the article undoubtedly drew upon a second writer, also unnamed, who saw in the number 300 + 9 in the *Surah of the Cave* the discrepancy between solar and lunar calendars; it is to this second writer that I am *absolutely* indebted for the confirmation of my original intuition. And so, calculating as *clearly, explicitly* and *outwardly* as I can—since I was unwilling to leave an assertion by an unknown source uncorroborated—I can now confidently state, given that a solar year is approximately

365.24 days, and a lunar year, approximately 354.38 days, that over 300 solar years the discrepancy between lunar and solar time amounts to approximately 9 (lunar) years. The Youths in the Cave symbolize these Nine years, with their Dog—the *Tenth*—representing the *remainder* of .0077886 years—in the *decimal* system, that is, based on the number ten. The Dog waiting quietly at the mouth of the Cave over the long centuries, with his two paws outstretched, also immediately suggests the posture of the Sphinx, patroness of riddles—and the Egyptian solar calendar, or the calendar they used to keep a time closest to solar time, with a discrepancy of only 12 minutes per year from true solar time, was calculated based on the rising of Sirius, the Dog Star.

∾

Comment by Charles Upton

Since the same period of time calculated in days and hours amounts to both 300 solar years and 309.0077886 lunar years, the number Nine (plus .0077886) represents the union of Sun and Moon. In Islamic symbolism this indicates the end of the present world or cycle-of-manifestation; in the science of Alchemy it symbolizes the union of Soul and Spirit, which in esoteric terms comes to the same thing, since the Soul perfectly conformed to the Spirit has transcended the cycles of time. Nine is also the traditional number of the original brotherhood of the Knights Templar, which (as I once speculated) might have been intended to suggest the Nine Choirs of Angels in the system of St. Dionysius the Areopagite. Dionysian angelology was adopted in slightly altered form by St. Bernard of Clairvaux, who sponsored the Templars and gave them their rule. Nine is also the symbolic number of Beatrice in Dante's **La Vita Nuova**; met her when she was nine years old, "courted" her for nine years, etc. A number of scholars, including René Guénon, Julius Evola, Dante Gabriel Rosetti, Luigi Valli, Eugene Aroux, Mircea Eliade, Alfonso Ricolfi, Arthur Schult, Henry Corbin and William Anderson, have asserted that Dante was an initiate of an esoteric spiritual order known as the Fede Santa ("Holy Faith") or Fedeli d'Amore, the "Faithful of Love," who have been described as a Third (lay) Order of the Templars—and he, as the Templars were supposed to have done, venerated "a holy woman who was not the Virgin Mary"—Beatrice herself.

Furthermore, Miguel Asín y Palacios, in his 1919 book **La Escatologia Musulmana en la Divina Comedia**, demonstrated that Dante derived much of his lore from popular Islamic accounts of Muhammad's *miraj* or Ascension to Heaven, as well as from the works of the Shaykh al-Akbar, the "Greatest (Sufi) Shaykh," Ibn al-'Arabi. Therefore we are justified in speculating that the story of the Nine Original Templars might have been a symbolic fable patterned upon the Companions of the Cave from the Qur'an—particularly since *thirty-one* as the actual number of the first Templars (according to Michael the Syrian) has more historical evidence backing it up—and also that Dante's veneration of Beatrice could have been derived from a Christian/Courtly Love imitation, as practiced by the Fedeli d'Amore, of the Shi'ite veneration of Fātimah.

∾

Charles Upton, from *Vectors of the Counter-Initiation,* with deletions and additions

Some scholars speculate that Freemasonry has its origin in various esoteric contacts made by the Templars in the Holy Land. Craft guilds, such as masonry, tended to take on some of the characteristics of esoteric secret societies in both Islam and Christianity, as they indeed did in classical antiquity. They were considered to have been founded by a certain saint or prophet with a legendary association with the craft in question, and they possessed "trade secrets" that were often given a symbolic/esoteric interpretation; outside of masonry, the craft where such tendencies are most clearly evident is that of alchemy. And it is often asserted that some Templars, after the suppression of the Order, took refuge with the Freemasons. It stands to reason that the Dome of the Rock and the al-Aqsa Masjid on the Temple Mount [*where the Templars had their headquarters in the Holy Land*] would have been repaired and maintained by such a guild of masons, seeing that the maintenance of a holy site, the third holiest in Islam, was unlikely to have been simply "outsourced" to the lowest bidder. The gothic arch, which appeared in France in the 12th century, could well have been based upon the pointed arch used in Islamic architecture, the first appearance of which was as part of the al-Aqsa Masjid;[7] the Knights Templar also constructed octagonal churches reminiscent of the Dome of the Rock. And given that the Templars occupied al-Aqsa, they certainly could have had dealings with a guild of sacred masons charged with the maintenance of the site, whose techniques would most likely have been interpreted symbolically, and thus quasi-esoterically; they did in fact make renovations to this building,[8] as well as retaining as slaves all captured Muslim craftsmen, whom they employed in many capacities.[9] Such a guild might have presented itself to the Templars as one group of "spirituals" to another who shared with them a veneration for the same sacred site, and have been eminently capable of fascinating them with tales of the history and symbolism of the Dome of the Rock and the Temple Mount, possibly in hopes of mitigating their hatred of Islam and moderating their depredations

7. http://www.muslimheritage.com/article/pointed-arch.

8. http://erenow.com/postclassical/the-real-history-behind-the-templars/13.html.

9. See John J. Robinson, *Dungeon, Fire and Sword: The Knights Templar in the Crusades*, 1991, pp. 347–48.

in the Holy Land. The Knights Templar in turn could have established and maintained an alliance with such an order of esoteric stonemasons, some of whom might have accompanied them to the west. The Knights, who built castles in Palestine and churches In Europe, employed many stonemasons; and since they apparently incorporated certain design features that were taken from Islamic architecture, the construction techniques if not the technicians themselves would have entered the west through their patronage. Such techniques would likely have been given symbolic interpretations by the Muslim craft guilds who used them, and this lore could certainly have passed to the Templars. As Peter Levenda points out, "if the architectural innovations came from the Middle East, then it stands to reason that someone had to train the local European craftsmen in these techniques and designs. These would have been men who served in some capacity in the Crusades, either as masons and carpenters hired by the military orders to build fortifications or as members of the orders themselves" [Peter Levenda, *The Secret Temple*, p. 66]. And who would the Templars have been more likely to hire to repair the al-Aqsa Masjid than the local craftsmen charged with maintaining it? It is possible, then, that Freemasonry grew out of something like a Sufi *tariqah*—perhaps, as some have speculated, *al-Banna*, "the Builders," reputedly founded by the great Sufi Dhu'l Nun Misri, who is said to have incorporated ancient Egyptian lore into the Sufi tradition. This or some similar initiatory order would have been entirely orthodox within the context of Islam, but would have inevitably deviated into heterodoxy if it attempted to become, under the Templar influence, a kind of "esoteric Christianity." This would explain the highly ambiguous nature of western Freemasonry, its uneasy blend of quasi-esoteric universalism with a subversive, anti-clerical hatred of the Catholic Church, at least in certain jurisdictions and at certain historical periods. (This enmity was certainly reciprocated, especially under Popes like Pius X.) A derivation of Freemasonry from Islamic esoterism may never be provable; it is none-the less highly interesting, in view of some of our speculations above, that Ibn al-'Arabi's book on Dhu'l Nun is entitled *Al-Kawkab al-durri: fi manaqib Dhi-l Nun al-Misri*—in English, *The Brilliant Star: On the Spiritual Virtues of Dhu-l-Nun the Egyptian*.

At one point the Templars entered into a military alliance with the Hashishim—who, as Shi'a, were also opposed to Saladin, a Sunni; and it is entirely possible that the Shi'a saw the conquest of the Holy Land by the "Franks" as a chance to throw off the Sunni yoke. The Hashishim, like the Templars, were a brotherhood of "sacred warriors" with grades of initiation; this could have led certain Shi'a scholars or theosophers in Jerusalem to make overtures to the Templars, especially after their hunger for spiritual and esoteric lore, now that they had reached the archetypal Holy City of Jerusalem, became better known.

Jerusalem, specifically the Temple Mount, was the first *qibla* or direction-of-prayer in Islam before the *qibla* was transferred to the Kaaba; this fact could have led Muslims to read the Apocalypse, with its prophesy of the descent of a *cube-shaped* Heavenly Jerusalem [cf. Apocalypse 21:16], as predicting the later pre-eminence of Islam, and esoteric Muslims to see the Kaaba itself as a kind of three-dimensional hermeneutic of Temple lore in terms of sacred geometry (see Henry Corbin, *Temple and Contemplation*). And the Templars might well have been open to this kind of esoteric/symbolic lore. Medieval Christians generally saw Muslims either as Pagans or as a heretical Jewish sect; the high regard in which Muslims held Jesus could have come to the Templars as an intriguing shock, and led them to enquire further.

∾

Comment by Charles Upton

Regarding Falque de Bezaure's theory that the Templars converted to Shi'a Islam, I think it more probable that they would simply have adopted certain doctrines and symbols from the Shi'a—as well as from other groups they could have made contact with in Palestine, such as the Sufis and the "Johannite Christians"—rather than converting *in toto*. Instead of seeing Islam as an *alternative* to Christianity, the notion that the Saracens, in line with the Holy Qur'an, venerated Jesus and the Virgin Mary, would more likely have expanded their conception of Judeo-Christianity to include Islam as an integral part of the larger "Abrahamic Tradition." If this was in fact the case, they would have faced the dilemma that all who accept the Transcendent Unity of Religions will inevitably encounter: the need to determine exactly where to draw the line between a heterodox, exoteric syncretism and a truly esoteric universalism whose fundamental doctrine is: "The Truth is One because God is One."

Appendix Two:
The Soul of Aleksandr Dugin, the Soul of Russia

I CAN THINK WITH MY HEART and I can think with my brain, but I can also think with my liver. If I couldn't think with my liver, I could never have begun to understand either Aleksandr Dugin or the Russian soul. And since Dugin, in *Eurasian Mission*, has described the U.S. as "a community of deeply individualistic mystics"—a very interesting half-truth that applies to certain aspects of the American character, though obviously not to such manifestations as the Superbowl or the World Series—I thought I would reply by defining the Russian character in equally simplistic terms.

One way of understanding of the soul of Russia might go something like this: Old Man Karamazov had three sons. The first, the youngest, was Alyosha, the pure monk. The second was Ivan, the ironic, nihilistic, self-contradicting intellectual, the one who met the Devil and went mad. The third, the eldest, was Miyta, the drunken soldier, the reckless libertine, the genuine party animal. (According to esoteric anthropology, Mitya would symbolize the passions, the soul-commanding-to-evil—*al-nafs al-ammara bi'l su*, Ivan the intellect—*al-'aql*—and Alyosha the Heart—*al-Qalb*.) When Old Man Karamazov was murdered, suspicion fell, of course, on Mitya, who had already spent more nights in jail than anyone could remember. But after Mitya had been tried and convicted, Aloysha agreed with the family's plan to spring him from prison, because he *knew* that Mitya was innocent, and because "blessed are the merciful, for they shall obtain mercy."

According to his widow, Fyodor Dostoevsky had planned to compose a sequel to *The Brothers Karamazov*, but died before he could begin work on it—so what would undoubtedly have been the great revelation of the Russian soul became, instead, a riddle. The riddle was: "Who killed Old Man Karamazov?"

The answer is: "Alyosha killed him"—Alyosha the innocent, Alyosha the pure monk. He killed him because his father had foully insulted Alyosha's holy *staretz*, Father Zosima. But the real reason he killed him was that Father Zosima had terminated Alyosha's stay at the monastery and sent him out into the world, and whoever goes out into the world must sin, and be forgiven, and suffer for his sin, and be purified. Alyosha had to take upon himself the sins of the world like Christ did, and also thereby the sins of Russia. And—according to the dark logic of the novel, though certainly not in the view of orthodox Christian doctrine—the only way he could do that, since he had no sins of his own, was to shoulder the burden of the sins and the guilt of his father, Fyodor Karamazov, precisely by killing him.[1] So the foul and ugly old man—an apt symbol of libertinism, or of today's Liberalism insofar as he was the offshoot of a decadent ruling class—was done away with, and justice was done. But if with guilt comes justice, it is also true that with justice comes guilt; this is what is known as "the curse of the law." Justice must be done, the law must be satisfied, guilt must be expiated and incurred, but—and this should never be forgotten—only Mercy, not battling the "absolute evil" or the reversal of time or keeping all your options open, can lift the curse; if there is nothing but justice, then there is no justice! And once we have invoked Christ by invoking Christianity—Christ Who, for the Christian, is the only one who can forgive and expiate the burden of sin we have taken on, in the act of being born—it's obviously too late to forget the Kingship of Mercy, forget it so thoroughly that we never even mention it, because everything is now being done in the Holy Presence. But if we are foolish enough, or hopeless enough, to reject Mercy in the very presence of Mercy—then what hope?

As for the soul of Aleksandr Dugin, what can I say? I cannot know his secret with God, nor his deepest intent, nor God's decision regarding him. Nonetheless, it *appears* to me that he has laid hands on the Sacred in both its Christian and its Islamic forms, as well as on the sacred science of metaphysics, with the intent of perverting them for personal and political ends—something that does not bode well for the destiny of his immortal soul. And since he has been outrageous enough to declare that war between the United States and Russia is inevitable, that *Carthago delenda est*—"Carthage (Atlantis; the USA) must be destroyed"—I feel that he has granted me license to propose something even more outrageous than that. Therefore, since he has issued a call to repentance to the Russian people in *The Rise of the Fourth Political Theory*, I now call upon Aleksandr Dugin himself to repent, before he does himself and the world irreparable damage. If one is guilty, repentance is the cure; if one is not guilty, still, repentance is good practice if we want to maintain our ongoing spiritual health; as the famous woman Sufi, Rabi'a al-Awadiyya, said to a young man who told her that he had never sinned, "Alas, my son, thine existence is a sin

---

1. Although Smerdyakov, the degenerate half-brother, "confesses" his murder of Fyodor Karamazov to Ivan while blaming him for inspiring it, he does this only to drag Ivan's elevated idea of eliminating his father via a principled, quasi-political "assassination" down through the dirt of Smerdyakov's own depraved soul, thereby effectively satirizing any notion of an *idealistic* evil.

wherewith no other sin may be compared." There is great intelligence and great courage in Aleksandr Dugin, possibly even a streak of the prophetic character, and he is not entirely lacking in love either. He would make a fine catch for the Devil, and in any case we don't want to see anyone spend a quasi-eternity rolling in hellfire. In America we sometimes say of our enemies, "I'll see you rot in Hell" or "Revenge is sweet." But the truth is, revenge is not sweet, or at least never sweet enough. It always leaves a bitter taste in the mouth. And since I can find in myself no desire to see Aleksandr Dugin damned, he must not—in any fundamental, personal sense—be my enemy, only (for present purposes) my adversary. In any case, if a person really does lie under the Wrath of God, whoever appoints himself an agent of Divine retribution against that person makes himself just as much a target of that Wrath as the sinner he condemns. So I say to Aleksandr Dugin, "Do yourself a favor: repent, accept the forgiveness of God, and do His work." All of us are much closer to death, to the moment of truth, than it is possible for us to imagine—and no matter how firmly one may be implanted and imbedded and grafted in to one's *narod* in *this* life, still, each of us must die alone. So I pray that he accepts the good that God has in store for him, and that he doesn't waste the great gift of life the Almighty has given him by spending his time contriving ever more successful ways of spreading power-motivated ambiguities and justifications for imperialist war. If the world is ending, is this a good time to thicken the chain that holds us to Earth? Let him do some good for himself, accept God's healing, and become a true man for once—because, as long as he remains "he," he will not be given a second chance. And if I am wrong in my worries about the state of his soul, which I certainly could be, then let him ignore all my judgments and criticisms, insofar as they apply to him personally, and take only my best wishes.

However, even more fundamental than repentance, in my opinion, is our duty to play the role that God has assigned us; this single intent carries all that He has in store for us of His Bounty and His Generosity, of His Chastisement and His Purification. If we "repent" in such a way that we separate ourselves from our God-written destiny, such repentance is barren, and that destiny will find us in any case; it will find us *unprepared*. Every role is necessary to the drama, and should be played to the hilt—otherwise, what on earth are we doing here? Each role is a mask, and God is behind every one of them. He is the Writer (*Al-Khaliq*), the Producer (*Al-Mubdi*), the Director (*Al-Musawwir*), along with every Player—and, in His Name *Al-Shahid*, the Universal Witness, He is the entire Audience too. The great Indian saint Sri Ramakrishna, devotee of the Goddess Kāli, recognized this truly formidable aspect of Universal *Maya*—which, while never negating morality, goes far beyond it. When a questioner asked Ramakrishna why there is evil in the universe, his answer was: "To thicken the plot!" Likewise Ibn al-'Arabi, the Shaykh al-Akbar, the "greatest (Sufi) shaykh," taught that everything that actually happens, good or evil, does so according to God's Will. In addition to that Will, however, God also has a Wish. He wishes that all beings be saved, that all beings be happy, but He knows that not every one of them will respond to that Wish. Therefore He Wills that every being receive a destiny that matches its own pre-eternal design. This design does not simply pre-determine a being's choices, however, since—according to the mysterious, reciprocal relationship between Eternity and Time—it is both the source of those choices and the final sum of them; this is undoubtedly what Frithjof Schuon meant when he wrote that we are "condemned to freedom." But Jesus undoubtedly said it best, in words both compact and conclusive: "There needs be evil, but woe to him through whom evil comes [Matthew 18:7]."

Astaghfirullah

Astaghfirullah

Astaghfirullah

To reject Mercy in the very presence of Mercy . . . but the truth is, Mercy is *not* present to Aleksandr Dugin. In his invocation "Knights Templars of the Proletariat," Dugin cries:

> For many centuries and eons, the Titans are waging a struggle against entropy of the Universe. Working class. Workers' brotherhood. Workers' Order. . . . After swallowing Dionysus, following long eons, they have been saturated with his flesh. That is why they regard with such reverence the holy intoxication of the resurrected Bacchus. . . . But sooner or later he [*the Proletarian*] will look up and . . . deliver his last blow. With a crowbar against the deathly dull eye-socket of the computer, at the glowing window of a bank, at the twisted face of an overseer. The proletarian will Awaken. Rebel. Murder. His mission in history is not finished. Demiurge still breathes. The Soul of the World still weeps. Her tears raise a dismal howl in the black consciousness of the Creator. . . . It is the sounding of Angelic Trumpets. They—smiths of Tartar—once again yearn for their proletarian Revolution. Real Revolution. Final Revolution.[2]

There is obviously no mercy here, for either the avengers or their victims. No mercy, because Heaven is never taken by storm; according to the Prophetic Books of William Blake, Orc the rebel, in revolution against Urizen, who (in his fallen state) is the tyrant of the alienated, abstract Logos, finally *becomes* Urizen,

---

2. Note how the "Eucharist" here becomes the body and blood of Dionysus, not of Christ. Note also how Dugin writes almost as "the Wovoka of Communism."

and so still lies under his oppression. This is the unalterable decree of the Kalachakra, the Black Wheel of Time. The Titans, the Asuras, the Jötun, fighting and dying and coming back to life again throughout all eternity, lay siege to Heaven, sacrifice and strive to win it, but they can never enter it. They can never come into the City of Light because as soon as they do, the City that they longed for immediately becomes the City of Hades. Everything the Titans, the Asuras, the Jötun touch is transformed into the land of the shades, the iron walls of the same familiar prison—because that is their nature. Self-will cannot enter Heaven; it can only build its own characteristic Hell. Whoever struggles to plunder a freely-given gift rejects it, drives it back it its Source. Gold turns to lead at his touch. Form can never, by the power of self-will, fight free from the leaden grasp of Substance; Substance can only be purified of dead Form so as to receive new and living Form: "Be it done unto me according to Thy Word" [Luke 1:38].

Those Titans who welcomed the Gods *became* the Gods, like Thor among the Aesir. Those who struggled against the Gods to keep hold on their primordial treasure lost it forever in the bottomless chasm of dead matter. Dugin surveys the people of Russia, and sees them only as the dead—as dead souls, defeated soldiers, buried under the geological strata of aeons of hatred, despair and betrayed hope. And his compassion for them is buried just as deep, under that same hatred, that same despair. So if Aleksandr Dugin calls for a Third World War as he sometimes appears to do, it is for only one reason: because when the world ends, the dead rise.

But those who have died in self-will, which is self-contradiction, are not liberated by that resurrection; they are sealed instead inside tombs of ice until the galaxies have fled from one another in terror, and eternal night descends upon the universe: that is the law.[3] It takes courage to die and courage to live, but the

---

3. Every materialistic cosmology based on a logical interpretation of accurate measurements according to a particular set of assumptions will reflect an element of metaphysical truth. Any theory that does not take metaphysics into account, however, is necessarily partial, and is therefore destined to be displaced by another partial theory reflecting a different element of, or perspective on, the metaphysical order. And only the complete perspective of metaphysics itself has the power to discern the metaphors and symbols of metaphysical truth hidden in this or that physical theory. The "law" referred to here is based on the *myth* of the Big Bang—the legend that recounts how the universe of space, time, matter and energy began as a single point and has been expanding ever since, its rate of expansion continually increasing. According to this myth, when every particle in the universe is flying apart from every other at the speed of light, the universe will cease to exist—just as, according to René Guénon's doctrine, the present cycle of manifestation will end when ever-accelerating time first annihilates space, then becomes space. The flight of the galaxies from one another after the Big Bang also suggests Husserl's doctrine that the origin of time is the *panic* of conditional existence in the face of Eternity. Titanic self-will can never conquer Heaven precisely because it was born as, and continues to manifest the quality of, a headlong flight from God [cf. Q. 33:72].

greatest courage of all is demanded by only one thing: the ordeal of Mercy, the passage from "My God, my God, why hast Thou forsaken Me?" [Matthew 27:46] to "Into thine hands I commend My Spirit: it is finished" [Luke 23:42; John 19:20]. When Christ harrowed Hell, what took three days from the standpoint of the dead, in His Eternal Essence all happened in the split second between those two cries. Mercy pierces all the armor, tears off all the masks; whoever can submit to Mercy has conquered every enemy.

Can you face Mercy, Aleksandr Dugin? Can I? Do either of us have the stomach for it?

We will both learn the answer to that question, seeing that there is no way to avoid it. *It is a fearful thing to fall into the hands of the Living God* [Hebrews 10:31].

Made in the USA
Middletown, DE
23 August 2022

72004461R00319